Economics

Contents

Frank • *Microeconomics and Behavior, Sixth Edition*

Begg–Fischer–Dornbusch • *Economics, 8th Edition*

1

THINKING LIKE AN ECONOMIST

Much of microeconomics entails the study of how people choose under conditions of scarcity. Hearing this description for the first time, many people react by saying that the subject is of little real relevance to most citizens of developed countries, for whom, after all, material scarcity is largely a thing of the past.

This reaction, however, takes too narrow a view of scarcity. Even when material resources are abundant, other important resources are always in short supply. At his death, Aristotle Onassis was worth several billion dollars. He had more money than he could possibly spend and used it for such things as finely crafted whale ivory footrests for the barstools on his yacht. And yet, in an important sense, he confronted the problem of scarcity much more than most of us will ever have to. Onassis was the victim of *myasthenia gravis*, a debilitating and progressive neurological disease. For him, the scarcity that mattered was not money but time, energy, and the physical skill needed to carry out ordinary activities.

Time is a scarce resource for everyone, not just the terminally ill. In deciding which movies to see, for example, it is time, not the price of admission, that constrains most of us. With only a few free nights available each month, seeing one movie means not being able to see another, or not being able to have dinner with friends.

Time and money are not the only important scarce resources. Consider the economic choice you confront when a friend brings you along as his guest to a buffet brunch. It is an all-you-can-eat affair, and you must decide how to fill your plate. Even if you are not rich, money would be no object, since you can eat as much as you want for free. Nor is time an obstacle, since you have all afternoon

4   CHAPTER 1   THINKING LIKE AN ECONOMIST

*"Oh, it's great here, all right, but I sort of feel uncomfortable
in a place with no budget at all."*

and would rather spend it in the company of your friend than be anywhere else. The important scarce resource here is the capacity of your stomach. A smorgasbord of your favorite foods lies before you, and you must decide which to eat and in what quantities. Eating another waffle necessarily means having less room for more scrambled eggs. The fact that no money changes hands here does not make your choice any less an economic one.

Every choice involves important elements of scarcity. Sometimes the most relevant scarcity will involve money, but in many of our most pressing decisions it will not. Coping with scarcity in one form or another is the essence of the human condition. Indeed, were it not for the problem of scarcity, life would be stripped of much of its intensity. For someone with an infinite lifetime and limitless material resources, hardly a single decision would ever matter.

In this chapter we examine some basic principles of microeconomic theory and see how an economist might apply them to a wide variety of choices involving scarcity. Later chapters more formally develop the theory. For now, our only goal is to get an intuitive feel for that distinctive mindset known as "thinking like an economist." And the best way to do that is to work through a series of problems familiar from actual experience.

THE COST-BENEFIT APPROACH TO DECISIONS

Many of the choices economists study can be posed in the form of the following question:

Should I do activity x?

For the choice confronting a moviegoer, "... do activity x?" might be, for example, "... see *Casablanca* tonight?" For the person attending the buffet brunch, it might be ". . . eat another waffle?" Economists answer such questions by comparing the costs and benefits of doing the activity in question. The decision rule we use is disarmingly simple. If $C(x)$ denotes the costs of doing x and $B(x)$ denotes the benefits, it is:

If $B(x) > C(x)$, do x; otherwise don't.

To apply this rule, we need some way to define and measure costs and benefits. Monetary values are a useful common denominator for this purpose, even when the activity has nothing directly to do with money. We define $B(x)$ as the maximum dollar amount you would be willing to pay to do x. Often $B(x)$ will be a hypothetical magnitude, the amount of money you would be willing to pay if you had to, even though no money will actually change hands. $C(x)$, in turn, is the value of all the resources you must give up in order to do x. Here too $C(x)$ need not involve an explicit transfer of money to anyone.

For most decisions, at least some of the benefits or costs will not be readily available in monetary terms. To see how we proceed in such cases, consider the following simple decision.

Should I turn down my stereo?

EXAMPLE 1.1

You have settled into a comfortable chair and are listening to your stereo when you realize that the next two tracks on the album are ones you dislike. If you had a programmable compact disc player, you would have programmed it not to play them. But you don't, and so you must decide whether to get up and turn the music down or to stay put and wait it out.

The benefit of turning it down is not having the songs you don't like blare away at you. The cost, in turn, is the inconvenience of getting out of your chair. If you are extremely comfortable and the music is only mildly annoying, you will probably stay put. But if you haven't been settled for long or if the music is really bothersome, you are more likely to get up.

Even for simple decisions like this one, it is possible to translate the relevant costs and benefits into a monetary framework. Consider first the cost of getting out of your chair. If someone offered you 1 cent to get up out of a comfortable chair and there were no reason other than the penny to do it, would you take the offer? If you are like most people, you would not. But if someone offered you $1000, you would be on your feet in an instant. Somewhere between 1 cent and $1000 lies your **reservation price**, the minimum amount it would take to get you out of the chair.

To see where the threshold lies, imagine a mental auction with yourself in which you keep boosting the offer by small increments from 1 cent until you reach the point at which it is barely worthwhile to get up. Where this point occurs will obviously depend on circumstance. If you are rich, it will tend to be higher than if you are poor, because a given amount of money will seem less important; if you feel energetic, it will be lower than if you feel tired; and so on. For the sake of discussion, suppose your reservation price for getting out of the chair turns out to be $1. You can conduct a similar mental auction to determine the maximum sum you would be willing to pay someone to turn the music down. This reservation price measures the benefits of turning the music down; let us suppose it turns out to be 75 cents.

reservation price of activity x the price at which a person would be indifferent between doing x and not doing x.

In terms of our formal decision rule, we then have $x =$ "turn my stereo down," with $B(x) = \$0.75 < C(x) = \$1$, which means that you should remain in your chair. Listening to the next two songs will be unpleasant, but less so than getting up would be. A reversal of these cost and benefit figures would imply a decision to get up and turn the music down. If $B(x)$ and $C(x)$ happened to be equal, you would be indifferent between the two alternatives.

THE ROLE OF ECONOMIC THEORY

The idea that anyone might actually calculate the costs and benefits of turning down a stereo may sound a little strange, not to say absurd. Economists have come under heavy criticism for making unrealistic assumptions about how people behave, and outsiders are quick to wonder what purpose is served by the image of a person trying to decide how much he would pay to avoid getting up out of his chair.

There are two responses to this criticism. The first is that economists don't assume that people make explicit calculations of this sort at all. Rather, many economists argue, we can make useful predictions if we assume that people act *as if* they made such calculations. This view is forcefully expressed by Nobel laureate Milton Friedman, who illustrates his point by looking at the techniques expert pool players use.[1] He argues that the shots they choose, and the specific ways they attempt to make them, can be predicted extremely well by someone who assumes that the players take careful account of all the relevant laws of Newtonian physics. Of course, very few expert pool players have had formal training in physics, and hardly any can recite such laws as "the angle of incidence equals the angle of reflection." Nor are they likely to know the definitions of "elastic collisions" and "angular momentum." Even so, Friedman argues, they would never have become expert players in the first place *unless* they played as dictated by the laws of physics. Our theory of pool player behavior assumes, unrealistically, that pool players know the laws of physics. Friedman urges us to judge this theory not by how accurate its central assumption is but by how well it predicts behavior. And on this score, it performs very well indeed.

Like pool players, the rest of us must also develop skills for coping with our environments. Many economists, Friedman among them, believe that useful insights into our behavior can be gained by assuming that we act as if governed by the rules of rational decision making. He feels that by trial and error we eventually absorb these rules, just as pool players absorb the laws of physics.

A second response to the charge that economists make unrealistic assumptions is to concede that actual behavior does often differ from the predictions of economic models. Thus, as economist Richard Thaler puts it, we often behave more like novice than expert pool players—ignoring bank shots and having no idea about putting the proper spin on the cue ball to position it for the next shot. We will see considerable evidence in support of this second view.

But even where economic models fail on descriptive grounds, they often provide very useful guidance for making better decisions. That is, even if they don't always predict how we *do* behave, they may often give useful insights into how to achieve our goals more efficiently. If novice pool players have not yet

---

[1]Milton Friedman, "The Methodology of Positive Economics," *Essays in Positive Economics*, Chicago: University of Chicago Press, 1953.

internalized the relevant physical laws, they may nonetheless consult those laws for guidance about how to improve. Economic models often play an analogous role with respect to ordinary consumer and business decisions. Indeed, this role alone provides a compelling reason for learning economics.

COMMON PITFALLS IN DECISION MAKING

Some economists are embarrassed if an outsider points out that much of what they do boils down to an application of the principle that we should perform an action if and only if its benefits exceed its costs. That just doesn't sound like enough to keep a person with a Ph.D. busy all day! There is more to it, however, than meets the eye. People who study economics quickly discover that measuring costs and benefits is a tricky business. Indeed, it is as much an art as a science. Some costs seem almost deliberately hidden from view. Others may seem relevant but, on a closer look, turn out not to be.

Economics teaches us how to identify the costs and benefits that really matter. An important goal of this book is to teach you to become a better decision maker. A good place for us to start is to examine the kinds of decisions that many people make incorrectly, some common pitfalls in decision making. The principles economists use are simple and commonsensical, but they are ones that many people ignore in everyday life.

Pitfall 1. Ignoring Implicit Costs

One pitfall is to overlook costs that are not explicit. If doing activity x means not being able to do activity y, then the value to you of doing y (had you done it) is an *opportunity cost* of doing x. Many people make bad decisions because they tend to ignore the value of such forgone opportunities. This insight suggests that it will almost always be instructive to translate questions such as "Should I do x?" into ones such as "Should I do x or y?" In the latter question, y is simply the most highly valued alternative to doing x. The following example helps drive this important point home.

Should I go skiing today or work as a research assistant?   EXAMPLE 1.2

There is a ski area near your campus, and you often go skiing there. From your experience you would confidently judge that a day on the slopes is worth $60 to you. The charge for the day is $40 (which includes bus fare, lift ticket, and equipment). However, this is not the only cost of going skiing. You must also take into account the value of the most attractive alternative you will forgo by heading for the slopes. Suppose that if you don't go skiing, you will work at your new job as a research assistant for one of your professors. The job pays $45 per day, and as a matter of fact you like it just well enough that you would be willing to do it for free. The question you face is, "Should I go skiing or work as a research assistant?"

Here the cost of skiing is not just the explicit cost of the ski package ($40) but also the opportunity cost of the lost earnings ($45). The total costs are therefore $85, which exceeds the benefits of $60. Since $C(x) > B(x)$, you should stay on campus and work for your professor. Someone who ignored the opportunity cost of the forgone earnings would decide incorrectly to go skiing.

8

CHAPTER 1   THINKING LIKE AN ECONOMIST

You might have wondered why in Example 1.2 we brought in your feelings about the research job. The fact that you liked it just well enough to have been willing to do it for free is another way of saying there were no psychic costs associated with doing it. This is important because it means that by not doing the job you would not have been escaping something unpleasant. Of course, not all jobs fall into this category. Suppose instead that your job is to scrape plates in the dining hall for the same pay, $45/day, and that the job is so unpleasant that you would be unwilling to do it for less than $30/day. Assuming your manager at the dining hall permits you to take a day off whenever you want, let us now reconsider your decision about whether to go skiing.

EXAMPLE 1.3

Should I go skiing today or scrape plates?

There are two equivalent ways of looking at this decision. One is to say that one benefit of going skiing is not having to scrape plates. Since you would never be willing to scrape plates for less than $30/day, avoiding that task is worth that amount to you. Going skiing thus carries with it the indirect benefit of not scraping plates. When we add that indirect benefit to the $60 direct benefit of the skiing, we get $B(x) = \$90$. In this view of the problem, $C(x)$ is the same as before, namely, the $40 ski charge plus the $45 opportunity cost of the lost earnings, or $85. So now $B(x) > C(x)$, which means you should go skiing.

Alternatively, we could have viewed the unpleasantness of the plate-scraping job as an offset against its salary. By this approach, we would subtract the $30/day of unpleasantness of the job from its $45/day earnings and say that the opportunity cost of not working in the dining hall is only $15/day. Then $C(x) = \$40 + \$15 = \$55 < B(x) = \$60$, and again the conclusion is that you should go skiing.

It makes no difference in which of these two ways you handle the valuation of the unpleasantness of scraping plates. It is critically important, however, that you do it either one way or the other. Don't count it twice!

Example 1.3 makes clear that there is a reciprocal relationship between costs and benefits. Not incurring a cost is the same as getting a benefit. By the same token, not getting a benefit is the same as incurring a cost.

Obvious as this sounds, it is often overlooked. Consider, for example, the case of a foreign graduate student who got his degree some years ago and was about to return to his home country. The trade regulations of his nation permitted people returning from abroad to bring back a new automobile without having to pay the normal 50 percent tariff. The student's father-in-law asked him to bring him back a new $10,000 Chevrolet and sent him a check for exactly that amount. This put the student in a quandary. He had been planning to bring back a Chevrolet and sell it in his home country. Because, as noted, new cars normally face a 50 percent import tax, such a car would sell at a dealership there for $15,000. The student estimated that he could easily sell it privately for $14,000, which would net him a $4000 gain. Thus the opportunity cost of giving the car to his father-in-law for $10,000 was going to be $4000! Not getting this big benefit was a big cost. In the end, it was one the student elected to bear because he valued keeping peace in the family even more. Even from a strictly economic point of view, the best decision is not always the one that leaves you with the most money in your pocket.

Should I work first or go to college first?

EXAMPLE 1.4

The costs of going to college are not limited to tuition, fees, housing, food, books, supplies, and the like. They also include the opportunity cost of the earnings forgone while studying. The amount you earn increases with the amount of experience you have. The more experience you have, the larger the earnings you must forgo to attend college. This opportunity cost of attending college is therefore lowest when you are right out of high school.

On the benefit side, one big gain of a college education is that it leads to sharply higher earnings. The sooner you go to college, the longer you will be able to take advantage of this bene-

Why do most students start college right after finishing high school?

fit. Another benefit is the pleasantness of going to college as opposed to working. In general, the kinds of jobs people hold tend to be less unpleasant (or more pleasant) the more education and experience they have. By going to college right away, you thus avoid having to work at the least pleasant jobs. For most people, then, it makes sense to go to college first and work afterward. Certainly it makes more sense to attend college at age 20 than at age 50.

A common exception to this general rule involves people who are too immature right out of high school to reap the benefits of college work. For them, it will often be sensible to work for a year or two and then go to college.

The college example is a perfect illustration of Friedman's argument about how to evaluate a theory. No one would pretend that high school seniors make their decisions about when to attend college on the basis of sophisticated calculations involving opportunity costs. On the contrary, most students go to college right out of high school simply because that is what most of their peers do. It is the thing to do.

But this begs the question of how it got to *be* the thing to do. Customs such as going to college right out of high school do not originate out of thin air. A host of different societies have had centuries to experiment with this issue. If there were a significantly better way of arranging the learning and working periods of life, some society ought to have long since discovered it. Our current custom has probably survived because it is so efficient. People may not make explicit calculations about the opportunity cost of forgone earnings, but they often behave *as if* they do.[2]

As simple as the opportunity cost concept is, it is one of the most important in microeconomics. The art in applying the concept correctly lies in being able to recognize the most valuable alternative that is sacrificed by the pursuit of a given activity.

---

[2]This does not mean that all customs necessarily promote efficiency. For example, circumstances may have changed in such a way that a custom that promoted efficiency in the past no longer does so. In time, such a custom might change. Yet many habits and customs, once firmly entrenched, are very slow to change.

Pitfall 2. Failing to Ignore Sunk Costs

An opportunity cost may not seem to be a relevant cost when in reality it is. On the other hand, sometimes an expenditure may seem to be a relevant cost when in reality it is not. Such is often the case with *sunk costs*, costs that are beyond recovery at the moment a decision is made. Unlike opportunity costs, these costs *should be* ignored. Not ignoring them is a second pitfall in decision making. The principle of ignoring sunk costs emerges clearly in the following example.

EXAMPLE 1.5

Should I drive to Boston or take the bus?

You are planning a 250-mile trip to Boston. Except for the cost, you are completely indifferent between driving and taking the bus. Bus fare is $100. You don't know how much it would cost to drive your car, so you call Hertz for an estimate. The Hertz representative tells you that for your make of car the costs of a typical 10,000-mile driving year are as follows:

Suppose you calculate that these costs come to $0.50/mile and use this figure to compute that the 250-mile trip will cost you $125 by car. And since this is more than the $100 bus fare, you decide to take the bus.

Insurance	$1000
Interest	2000
Fuel & oil	1000
Maintenance	1000
Total	$5000

If you decide in this fashion, you commit the error of counting sunk costs. Your insurance and interest payments do not vary with the number of miles you drive each year. Both are sunk costs and will be the same whether or not you drive to Boston. Of the costs listed, fuel and oil and maintenance are the only ones that vary with miles driven. These come to $2000 for each 10,000 miles you drive, or $0.20/mile. At $0.20/mile, it costs you only $50 to drive to Boston, and since this is much less than the bus fare, you should drive.

In Example 1.5, note the role of the assumption that, costs aside, you are indifferent between the two modes of transport. This lets us say that the only comparison that matters is the actual cost of the two modes. If you had preferred one mode to the other, however, we would also have had to weigh that preference. For example, if you were willing to pay $60 to avoid the hassle of driving, the real cost of driving would be $110, not $50, and you should take the bus.

Exercises such as the one below are sprinkled throughout the text to help you make sure that you understand important analytical concepts. You will master microeconomics more effectively if you do these exercises as you go along.

EXERCISE 1.1

How, if at all, would your answer to the question in Example 1.5 be different if the worth of avoiding the hassle of driving is $20 and you average one $28 traffic ticket for every 200 miles you drive?

Frank: Microeconomics
an/ Behavior, Sixth E/ition

I. Intro/uction

1. Thinking Like an
Economist

© The McGraw–Hill
Companies, 2005

9

As a check, the answers to the in-chapter exercises are at the end of each chapter. Naturally, the exercises will be much more useful if you work through them before consulting the answers.

The pizza experiment.

EXAMPLE 1.6

A local pizza parlor offers an all-you-can-eat lunch for $3. You pay at the door, and then the waiter brings you as many slices of pizza as you like. A former colleague performed this experiment: He had an assistant serve as the waiter for one group of tables.[3] The "waiter" selected half the tables at random and gave everyone at those tables a $3 refund before taking orders. Diners at the remaining half of his tables got no refund. He then kept careful count of the number of slices of pizza each diner ate. What difference, if any, do you predict in the amounts eaten by these two groups?

Diners in each group confront the question "Should I eat another slice of pizza?" Here, the activity x consists of eating one more slice. For both groups, $C(x)$ is exactly zero: Even members of the group that did not get a refund can get as many additional slices as they want at no extra charge. Because the refund group was chosen at random, there is no reason to suppose that its members like pizza any more or less than the others. For everyone, the decision rule says keep eating until there is no longer any extra pleasure in eating another slice. Thus, $B(x)$ should be the same for each group, and people from both groups should keep eating until $B(x)$ falls to zero.

By this reasoning, the two groups should eat the same amount of pizza, on the average. The $3 admission fee is a sunk cost and should have no influence on the amount of pizza one eats. *In fact, however, the group that did not get the refund consumed substantially more pizza.*

Although our cost-benefit decision rule fails the test of prediction in this experiment, its message for the rational decision maker stands unchallenged. The two groups logically *should* have behaved the same. The only difference between them, after all, is that patrons in the refund group have lifetime incomes that are $3 higher than the others'. Surely no one believes that such a trivial difference should have any effect on pizza consumption. Members of the no-refund group seemed to want to make sure they "got their money's worth." In all likelihood, however, this motive merely led them to overeat.[4]

What's wrong with being motivated to "get your money's worth"? Absolutely nothing, as long as the force of this motive operates *before* you

---

[3]See Richard Thaler, "Toward a Positive Theory of Consumer Choice," *Journal of Economic Behavior and Organization* 1, 1980.

[4]An alternative to the "get-your-money's-worth" explanation is that $3 is a significant fraction of the amount of cash many diners have available to spend *in the short run*. Thus members of the refund group might have held back in order to save room for the dessert they could now afford to buy. To test this alternative explanation, the experimenter could give members of the no-refund group a $3 cash gift earlier in the day and then see if the amount of pizza consumed by the two groups still differed.

CHAPTER 1 THINKING LIKE AN ECONOMIST

enter into transactions. Thus it makes perfectly good sense to be led by this motive to choose one restaurant over an otherwise identical competitor that happens to cost more. Once the price of your lunch has been determined, however, the get-your-money's-worth motive should be abandoned. The satisfaction you get from eating another slice of pizza should then depend only on how hungry you are and on how much you like pizza, not on how much you paid for the privilege of eating all you can eat. Yet people often seem not to behave in this fashion. The difficulty may be that we are not creatures of complete flexibility. Perhaps motives that make sense in one context are not easily abandoned in another.

EXERCISE 1.2

Jim wins a ticket from a radio station to see a jazz band perform at an outdoor concert. Mike has paid $18 for a ticket to the same concert. On the evening of the concert there is a tremendous thunderstorm. If Jim and Mike have the same tastes, which of them will be more likely to attend the concert, assuming that each decides whether to attend the concert on the basis of a standard benefit–cost comparison?

Pitfall 3. Measuring Costs and Benefits as Proportions Rather than Absolute Dollar Amounts

When a boy asks his mother "Are we almost there yet?" how will she answer if they are ten miles from their destination? Without some knowledge of the context of their journey, we cannot say. If they are near the end of a 300-mile journey, her answer will almost surely be yes. But if they have just left on a 12-mile journey, she will undoubtedly answer no.

Contextual clues are important for a variety of ordinary judgments. Thinking about distance as a percentage of the total amount to be traveled is natural and informative. Many also find it natural to think in percentage terms when comparing costs and benefits. But as the following pair of simple examples illustrates, this tendency often causes trouble.

EXAMPLE 1.7a

Should you drive to WalMart to save $10 on a $20 clock radio?

You are about to buy a clock radio at the nearby campus store for $20 when a friend tells you that the very same radio is on sale at WalMart for only $10. If WalMart is a 15-minute drive away, where would you buy the radio?

EXAMPLE 1.7b

Should you drive downtown to save $10 on a $1000 television set?

You are about to buy a new television set at the nearby campus store for $1010 when a friend tells you that the very same set is on sale at WalMart for only $1000. If WalMart is a 15-minute drive away, where would you buy the television?

There is no uniquely correct answer to either of these questions, both of which ask whether the benefit of driving to WalMart is worth the cost. Most people say that the trip would definitely be worth making in the case of the clock radio, but definitely not worth making in the case of the television set. When pressed to explain why, they explain that driving yields a 50-percent savings on the clock radio, but less than a 1-percent savings on the television.

These percentages, however, are irrelevant. In each case the benefit of driving down to WalMart is exactly the $10 savings from the lower purchase price. What is the cost of driving to WalMart? Some people might be willing to make the drive for as little as $5, while others might not be willing to do it for less than $50. But whatever the number, it should be the same in both cases. And that means that your answers to the questions just posed should be the same. For example, if you would be willing to make the drive for, say, $8, then you should buy both the clock radio and the television at WalMart. But if your reservation price for making the drive is, say, $12, then you should buy both appliances at the nearby campus store.

When using the cost-benefit test, you should express costs and benefits in absolute dollar terms. Comparing percentages is not a fruitful way to think about decisions like these.

EXERCISE 1.3

You are holding a discount coupon that will entitle you to a fare reduction on one of the two trips you are scheduled to take during the coming month. You can either get $100 off the normal $200 airfare to New York City, or you can get $120 off the normal $2400 airfare to New Delhi. On which trip should you use your coupon?

Pitfall 4. Failure To Understand the Average-Marginal Distinction

So far we have looked at decisions about whether to perform a given action. Often, however, the choice we face is not whether to perform the action but rather the extent to which it should be performed. But even in this more complex case, we can still apply the cost–benefit principle by reformulating the question. Instead of asking "Should I do activity x?," we repeatedly pose the question "Should I increase the level by which I am currently engaging in activity x?"

To answer this question, we must focus on the benefit and cost of an *additional* unit of activity. The cost of an additional unit of activity is called the **marginal cost** of the activity, and the benefit of an additional unit is called its **marginal benefit.**

The cost–benefit rule tells us to keep increasing the level of an activity as long as its marginal benefit exceeds its marginal cost. But as the following example illustrates, people often fail to apply this rule correctly.

marginal cost the increase in total cost that results from carrying out one additional unit of an activity.

marginal benefit the increase in total benefit that results from carrying out one additional unit of an activity.

Should Tom launch another boat?   EXAMPLE 1.8

Tom manages a small fishing fleet of three boats. His current daily costs of operations, including boat rentals and fishermen's wages, are $300, or an average of $100 per boat launched. His daily total revenue, or benefit, from the sale of fish is currently $600, or an average of $200 per boat launched. Tom decides that since his costs per boat are less than his revenues per boat, he should launch another boat. Is this a sound decision?

average cost the average cost of undertaking *n* units of an activity is the total cost of the activity divided by *n*.

average benefit the average benefit of undertaking *n* units of an activity is the total benefit of the activity divided by *n*.

To answer this question, we must compare the marginal cost of launching a boat with the marginal benefit of launching a boat. The information given, however, tell us only the **average cost** and **average benefit** of launching a boat—which are, respectively, one-third of the total cost of three boats and one-third of the total revenue from three boats. Knowing the average benefit and average cost per boat launched does not enable us to decide whether launching another boat makes economic sense. For although the average benefit of the three boats launched thus far *might* be the same as the marginal benefit of launching another boat, it might also be either higher or lower. The same statement holds true regarding average and marginal costs.

To illustrate the nature of the problem, suppose that marginal cost of launching a boat and crew is constant at $100 per boat per day. Then Tom should launch a fourth boat only if doing so will add at least $100 in daily revenue from his total fish catch. The mere fact that the current average revenue is $200 per boat simply doesn't tell us what the marginal benefit of launching the fourth boat will be.

Suppose, for example, that the relationship between the number of boats launched and the daily total revenue from the catch is as described in Table 1.1. With three boats per day, the average benefit per boat would then be $200, just as indicated above. If Tom launched a fourth boat, the *average* daily revenue would fall to $160 per boat, which is still more than the assumed marginal cost of $100. Note, however, that in the second column the total revenue from four boats is only $40 per day more than the total revenue from three boats. That means that the marginal revenue from launching the fourth boat is only $40. And since that is less than its marginal cost ($100), launching the fourth boat makes no sense.

TABLE 1.1
How Total Cost Varies with the Number of Boats Launched

Number of boats	Daily total benefit ($)	Daily average benefit ($/boat)
0	0	0
1	300	300
2	480	240
3	600	200
4	640	160

The following example illustrates how to apply the cost-benefit principle correctly in this case.

EXAMPLE 1.9

How many boats should Tom launch?

The marginal cost of launching a boat and crew is again constant at $100 each day. If total daily revenue from the catch again varies with the number of boats launched as shown in Table 1.1, how many boats should Tom launch?

Tom should keep launching boats as long as the marginal benefit of doing so is at least as great as the marginal cost. With marginal cost constant at $100 per launch, Tom should thus keep launching boats as long as the marginal benefit is at least $100.

Applying the definition of marginal benefit to the total benefit entries in the second column of Table 1.1 yields the marginal benefit values in the third column of Table 1.2. (Because marginal benefit is the change in total benefit that results when we change the number of boats by one, we place each marginal cost entry midway between the rows showing the corresponding total benefit entries.) For example, the marginal benefit of increasing the number of boats from one to two is $180, the difference between the $480 total revenue that results with two boats and the $300 that results with one.

TABLE 1.2
How Marginal Benefit Varies with the Number of Boats Launched

Number of boats	Daily total benefit ($)	Daily marginal benefit ($/boat)
0	0	
		300
1	300	
		180
2	480	
		120
3	600	
		40
4	640	

Comparing the $100 marginal cost per boat with the marginal benefit entries in the third column of Table 1.2, we see that the first three launches satisfy the cost-benefit test, but the fourth does not. Tom should thus launch three boats.

EXERCISE 1.4

If the marginal cost of launching each boat had not been $100 but $150, how many boats should Tom have launched?

The cost-benefit principle tells us that *marginal* costs and benefits—measures that correspond to the *increment* of an activity under consideration—are the relevant ones for choosing the level at which to pursue the activity. Yet many people compare the *average* cost and benefit of the activity when making such decisions. As Example 1.8 should have made clear, however, increasing the level of an activity may not be justified, even though its average benefit at the current level is significantly greater than its average cost.

USING MARGINAL BENEFIT AND MARGINAL COST GRAPHICALLY

The examples just discussed entail decisions about an activity that could take place only on specific levels—no boats, one boat, two boats, and so on. The levels of many other activities, however, can vary continuously. One can buy gasoline, for example, in any quantity one wishes. For activities that are continuously variable, it is often convenient to display the comparison of marginal benefit and marginal cost graphically.

FIGURE 1.1
The Optimal Quantity of Conversation.
The optimal amount of conversation is the quantity for which the marginal benefit of conversation is just equal to its marginal cost.

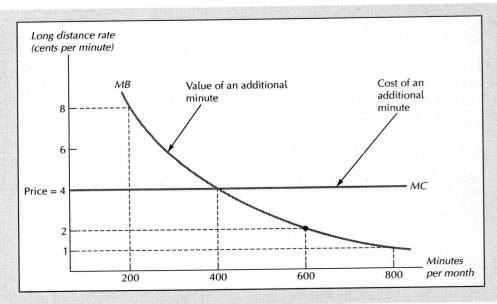

| EXAMPLE 1.10 | **How much should Susan talk to Hal each month?** |

Susan has a telephone plan for which the charge is 4 cents per minute for a long-distance call to her boyfriend Hal. (Fractional minutes are billed at the same rate, so a 30-second call would cost her 2 cents.) The value to Susan, measured in terms of her willingness to pay, of an additional minute of conversation with Hal is as shown on curve *MB* in Figure 1.1. How many minutes should she spend on the phone with Hal each month?

The downward slope of curve MB reflects the fact that the value of an additional minute of conversation declines with the total amount of conversation that has occurred thus far. (As we will see in Chapter 3, it is a common pattern that the more someone has of a good, the less value he assigns to having additional units of it.) Curve *MC* in the diagram measures the cost of each additional minute, assumed to be constant at $0.04. The optimal quantity of conversation is the quantity for which these two curves cross—namely, 400 minutes per month. If Susan speaks with Hal for less than that amount, the marginal benefit from adding another minute would exceed the marginal cost, so she should talk longer. But if they speak for more than 400 minutes per month, the amount she would save by speaking less would exceed the benefit she would sacrifice, which means they should speak less.

| EXERCISE 1.5 | |

If her marginal benefit curve is again as given in Figure 1.1, how many minutes should Susan speak with Hal each month if the long-distance rate falls to 2 cents per minute?

THE INVISIBLE HAND

One of the most important insights of economic analysis is that the individual pursuit of self-interest is often not only *consistent* with broader social objectives, but actually even *required* by them. Wholly unaware of the effects of their actions, self-interested consumers often act as if driven by what Adam Smith called an *invisible hand* to produce the greatest social good. (Smith's Invisible Hand will receive much more detailed attention in Chapter 16.) In perhaps the most widely quoted passage from *The Wealth of Nations*, Smith wrote:

> It is not from the benevolence of the butcher, the brewer, or the baker that we expect our dinner, but from their regard of their own interest. We address ourselves not to their humanity, but to their self-love, and never talk to them of our necessities, but of their advantage.

Smith observed that competition among sellers fostered attempts to develop better products and cheaper ways of producing them. Those who succeeded first in those attempts enjoyed higher profits than their rivals, but only temporarily. As others copied the new products and methods, their offerings put inevitable downward pressure on prices. Smith's insight, in a nutshell, was that although sellers were seeking only to promote their own advantage, the ultimate beneficiaries were consumers.

Modern economists sometimes lose sight of the fact that Smith did not believe that *only* selfish motives are important. In his earlier treatise, *The Theory of Moral Sentiments*, for example, he wrote movingly about the compassion we feel for others:

> How selfish soever man may be supposed, there are evidently some principles in his nature, which interest him in the fortune of others, and render their happiness necessary to him, though he derives nothing from it, except the pleasure of seeing it. Of this kind is pity or compassion, the emotion which we feel for the misery of others, when we either see it, or are made to conceive it in a very lively manner. That we often derive sorrow from the sorrow of others, is a matter of fact too obvious to require any instances to prove it; for this sentiment, like all the other original passions of human nature, is by no means confined to the virtuous and humane, though they perhaps may feel it with the most exquisite sensibility. The greatest ruffian, the most hardened violator of the laws of society, is not altogether without it.

Smith was well aware, moreover, that the outcome of unbridled pursuit of self-interest is sometimes far from socially benign. As the following example illustrates, the invisible hand mechanism breaks down when important costs or benefits accrue to people other than the decision makers themselves.

Should I burn my leaves or haul them into the woods?   **EXAMPLE 1.11**

Suppose the cost of hauling the leaves is $20 and the cost to the homeowner of burning them is only $1. If the homeowner cares only about costs that accrue directly to herself, she will burn her leaves. The difficulty is that burning leaves entails an important **external cost**, which means a cost borne by people who are not directly involved in the decision. This external cost is the damage done by the smoke from the fire. That cost accrues not to the homeowner who makes the decision about burning the leaves but to the people

external cost of an activity a cost that falls on people who are not directly involved in the activity.

18   CHAPTER 1   THINKING LIKE AN ECONOMIST

who live downwind. Suppose the smoke damage amounts to $25. The good of the community then requires that the leaves be hauled, not burned. From the perspective of the self-interested homeowner, however, it seems best to burn them.[5]

External costs and benefits are often the underlying reason for laws that limit individual discretion. (External costs and benefits will be our focus in Chapter 17.) Most communities, for example, now have laws prohibiting the burning of leaves within city limits. Such laws may be viewed as a way of making the costs and benefits seen by individuals more nearly resemble the costs and benefits experienced by the community as a whole. With a law against burning leaves in effect, the potential leaf burner weighs the penalty of breaking the law against the cost of hauling the leaves. Most people conclude it is cheaper to haul them.

WOULD PARENTS WANT THEIR DAUGHTER OR SON TO MARRY *HOMO ECONOMICUS*?

Many economists and other behavioral scientists remain skeptical about the importance of duty and other unselfish motives. They feel that the larger material payoffs associated with selfish behavior so strongly dominate other motives that, as a first approximation, we may safely ignore nonegoistic motives.

With this view in mind, the stereotypical decision maker in the self-interest model is often given the label *Homo economicus*, or "economic man." *Homo economicus* does not experience the sorts of sentiments that motivate people to vote, or to return lost wallets to their owners with the cash intact. On the contrary, personal material costs and benefits are the only things he cares about. He does not contribute voluntarily to private charities or public television stations, keeps promises only when it pays to do so, and if the pollution laws are not carefully enforced, disconnects the catalytic converter on his car to save on fuel. And so on.

Obviously, many people do not fit the me-first caricature of the self-interest model. They donate bone marrow to strangers with leukemia. They endure great trouble and expense to see justice done, even when it will not undo the original injury. At great risk to themselves, they pull people from burning buildings and jump into icy rivers to rescue people who are about to drown. Soldiers throw their bodies atop live grenades to save their comrades.

This is not to say that selfish motives are unimportant. They obviously account for a great deal. When a detective investigates a murder, for example, her first question is, "Who stood to benefit from the victim's death?" When an economist studies a government regulation, he wants to know whose incomes it enhances. When a senator proposes a new spending project, the political scientist tries to discover which of his constituents will be its primary beneficiaries.

Our goal in much of this text is to understand the kinds of behaviors to which selfish motives give rise in specific situations. But throughout this process, it is critical to remember that the self-interest model is not intended as a prescription for how to conduct your own affairs. On the contrary, we will see in later chapters that *Homo economicus* is woefully ill suited to the demands of social existence as we

---

[5]Of course, if the homeowner interacts frequently with the people downwind, self-interest may still dictate hauling the leaves, to preserve goodwill for future interactions. But where the people downwind are anonymous strangers, this motive will operate with much less force.

know it. Each of us probably knows people who more or less fit the *Homo economicus* caricature. And our first priority, most of the time, is to steer clear of them.

The irony here is that to be a purely self-interested person carries with it a degree of social isolation that is not only bad for the soul but also harmful to the pocketbook. To succeed in life, even in purely material terms, people must be able to work together, to form alliances and relationships of trust. But what sensible person would be willing to trust *Homo economicus*? Later chapters present specific examples of how unselfish motives confer material rewards on the people who hold them. For the present, however, bear in mind that the self-interest model is intended only to capture one part of human behavior, albeit an important one.

THE ECONOMIC NATURALIST

Studying biology enables people to observe and marvel at many details of life that would otherwise escape them. For the naturalist, a walk in a quiet woods becomes an adventure. In much the same way, studying microeconomics enables someone to become an "economic naturalist," a person who sees the mundane details of ordinary existence in a sharp new light. Each feature of the manmade landscape is no longer an amorphous mass but the result of an implicit cost-benefit calculation. Following are some examples of economic naturalism.

Why is airline food so bad?

Everyone complains about airline food. Indeed, if any serious restaurant dared to serve such food, it would go bankrupt in short order. Our complaints seem to take for granted that airline meals should be just as good as the ones we eat in restaurants. But why should they? The cost-benefit perspective makes clear that airlines should increase the quality of their meals if and only if the benefits would outweigh the costs of doing so. The benefits of better food are probably well measured by what passengers would be willing to pay for it, in the form of higher ticket prices. If a restaurant-quality meal could be had for, say, a mere $5 increase in costs, most people would probably be delighted to pay it. The difficulty, however, is that it would be much more costly than that to prepare significantly better meals at 39,000 feet in a tiny galley with virtually no time. It could be done, of course. An airline could remove 20 seats from the plane, install a modern, well-equipped kitchen, hire extra staff, spend more on ingredients, and so on. But these extra costs would be more like $50 per passenger than $5. For all our complaints about the low quality of airline food, few of us would be willing to bear this extra burden. The sad result is that airline food is destined to remain unpalatable because the costs of making it better outweigh the benefits.

ECONOMIC NATURALIST 1.1

Many of us respond warmly to the maxim "Anything worth doing is worth doing well." After all, it encourages a certain pride of workmanship that is often sadly lacking. Economic Naturalist 1.1 makes clear, however, that if the maxim is interpreted literally, it does not make any sense. It is completely unmindful of the need to weigh costs against benefits. To do something well means to devote time, effort, and expense to it. But time, effort, and expense are scarce. To devote them to one activity makes them unavailable for another. Increasing the quality of one of the things we do thus necessarily means to reduce the quality of others—yet another application of the concept of opportunity cost. Every intelligent decision must be mindful of this trade-off.

Everything we see in life is the result of some such compromise. For Justine Henin-Hardenne to play tennis as well as she does means that she cannot become a concert pianist. And yet this obviously does not mean that she shouldn't spend any time playing the piano. It just means that she should hold herself to a lower standard there than in the tennis arena.

ECONOMIC NATURALIST 1.2

Why do manual transmissions have five forward speeds, automatics only four?

The more forward speeds a car's transmission has, the better its fuel economy will be. The additional gears act like the "overdrive" of cars of the 1940s, conserving fuel by allowing cars to cruise at highway speeds at lower engine speeds. Most cars in current production offer five forward speeds on their manual transmissions, only three or four on their automatics. Since fuel economy is obviously a good thing, why limit the number of speeds on automatics?

The reason is that fuel economy is not our only objective. We also want to keep the price of the car within limits. Automatic transmissions are more complex than manual ones, and the cost of adding an extra speed is accordingly much greater in automatics. The benefits of adding an extra speed, by contrast, are the same in both cases. If carmakers follow the rule "Add an extra speed if its benefit outweigh its cost," then automatics will have fewer speeds than manuals.

The reasoning in Economic Naturalist 1.2 also helps make clear why many manual transmissions now have five forward speeds when 50 years ago most had only three (and many automatic transmissions only two). The benefit of adding an extra speed, again, is that it increases fuel economy. The value of this benefit, in dollar terms, thus depends directly on the price of fuel. The price of gasoline relative to other goods is much higher than it was 50 years ago, which helps explain why transmissions have more speeds than they used to.

ECONOMIC NATURALIST 1.3

Why did paper towels replace hot-air hand dryers in public restrooms in the 1970s?

In the 1950s and 1960s, paper towel dispensers were replaced by electric hot-air hand dryers in many public restrooms. More recently, however, it is the hot-air dryers themselves that are being replaced by paper towel dispensers. The explanation for these movements naturally has to do with the costs and benefits of the different methods of drying hands. The hot-air dryers made their original appearance on the heels of a steady decline in the price of electricity. When power became cheap, as it did in the 1950s and 1960s, electric dryers became less expensive to operate and maintain than the traditional paper towel dispensers. With the Arab oil embargoes of the 1970s, however, the price of energy rose dramatically, making paper towels once again the hand-drying method of choice.

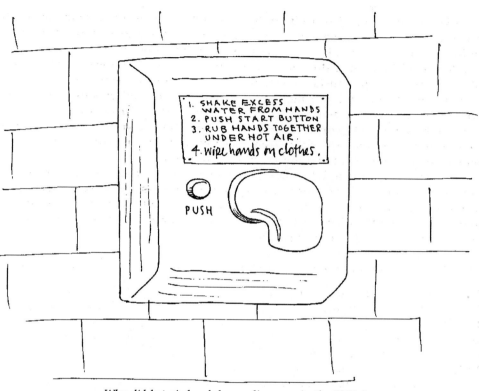

Why did hot-air hand dryers disappear in the 1970s?

Some economic naturalists may also find it amusing to speculate about why the paper towel dispensers of today are so different from the earlier ones. Most current designs feature a continuous hand crank. The paper inside is on a roll; and the longer you turn the crank, the longer the sheet of paper towel you get. Older designs also had a roll of paper inside, but you had to pull the paper out by hand. Most of the older models would also release only a limited amount of paper with each pull. To get more, you had to reset the release mechanism by pushing a button on the front of the dispenser.

The advantage of the older design, from the establishment's point of view, was that it induced people to use less paper. Indeed, if your hands were wet enough, it was difficult to get any paper at all because, when you pulled, the wet paper would simply tear away in your hands.

But if establishments saved on paper with the old design, why have they switched to the new one? The answer is that saving on paper is not their only objective. They also want satisfied customers. Incomes are higher now than they were 40 years ago, and customers are willing to pay more for a more convenient way of drying their hands. The current design may use a little more paper, but it is so much less frustrating that customers seem happy to pay more for their meals or their gasoline in order to cover the extra costs.

Some people may respond that the old design, infuriating though it was, was better because of its paper-saving property. These people feel that it is wrong to waste paper and that we ought to be willing to tolerate plenty of inconvenience to avoid doing so. The same people also often lament the thousands of trees that must be cut down in order to print each Sunday's *New York Times.* But trees are a renewable resource, which means there is no reason to treat them differently from any other scarce but renewable resource. When the demand for paper is high, we cut down more trees, to be sure. But the market also provides a strong incentive to plant new ones. The irony here is that the more paper we use, the more trees we have. If every metropolitan newspaper were to cease publication tomorrow, we would ultimately have *fewer* acres of forest, not more.

This is not to say, however, that private markets always provide the correct incentives to conserve important resources. In the Pacific Northwest, for example, logging companies are currently cutting down the few remaining stands of virgin redwoods to supply contractors with timber to build homes. Many of these trees are more than 2000 years old, a national treasure we can never hope to replace. To the logging companies, however, they are worth more as lumber than as monuments to the past.

Many of us so dislike the idea of these trees being cut down that we would gladly make a donation to someone who could prevent it. And yet it is probably impractical for the lumber companies to realize the true value we place on these trees. It wouldn't work, for example, to wall off their land and charge admission to see them. The invisible hand breaks down when the incentives in private markets do not lead us to protect nonreproducible resources that society wants to see preserved. In such cases, it is the responsibility of government to protect them. But where reproducible resources are concerned, we do not confront the same difficulty.

POSITIVE QUESTIONS AND NORMATIVE QUESTIONS

normative question
a question about what policies or institutional arrangements lead to the best outcomes.

positive question
a question about the consequences of specific policies or institutional arrangements.

Whether the remaining stands of virgin redwoods ought to be protected is in the end a **normative question**—a question involving our values. A normative question is a question about what *ought* to be or *should* be. By itself, economic analysis cannot answer such questions. A society that reveres nature and antiquity may well decide the fate of the redwoods differently from one that holds other values, even though members of both societies are in complete agreement about all the relevant economic facts and theories. Economic analysis is on firmer ground when it comes to answering **positive questions**—questions about what the consequences of specific policies or institutional arrangements will be. If we ban the cutting of virgin redwoods, what will happen to the price of lumber? What substitute building materials are likely to be developed, and at what cost? How will employment in the logging and housing industries be affected? These are all positive economic questions, and the answers to them are clearly relevant to our thinking about the underlying normative question.

MICROECONOMICS AND MACROECONOMICS

Our focus in this chapter is on issues confronting the individual decision maker. As we proceed, we'll also consider economic models of groups of individuals—for example, the group of all buyers or all sellers in a market. The study of individual choices and the study of group behavior in individual markets both come under the rubric of microeconomics. Macroeconomics, by contrast, is the study of broader aggregations of markets. For example, it tries to explain the national unemployment rate, the overall price level, and the total value of national output.

Economists are much better at predicting and explaining what goes on in individual markets than what happens in the economy as a whole. When prominent economists disagree in the press or on television, the subject is much more likely to be one from macroeconomics than from microeconomics. But even though economists are still not very good at answering macroeconomic questions, there is no denying the importance of macroeconomic analysis. After all, recessions and inflation disrupt the lives of millions of people.

Modern economists increasingly believe that the key to progress in macroeconomics lies in more careful analysis of the individual markets that make up broader aggregates. As a result, the distinction between micro and macro has become less clear in recent years. The graduate training of all economists, micro and macro alike, is increasingly focused on microeconomic analysis.

SUMMARY

- Microeconomics entails the study of choice under scarcity. Scarcity is ever present, even when material resources are abundant. There are always important limitations on time, energy, and the other things we need to pursue our goals.

- Much of the economist's task is to try to answer questions of the form "Should I do activity x?" The approach to answering them is disarmingly simple. It is to do x if and only if its costs are smaller than its benefits. Not incurring a cost is the same as getting a benefit.

- We saw that the cost-benefit model sometimes fails to predict how people behave when confronted with everyday choices. The art of cost-benefit analysis lies in being able to specify and measure the relevant costs and benefits, a skill that many decision makers conspicuously lack. Some costs, such as sunk costs, will often seem relevant but turn out not to be. Others, such as implicit costs, are sometimes ignored, even though they are of central importance. Benefits too are often difficult to conceptualize and measure. Experience has taught that becoming aware of the most common pitfalls helps most people become better decision makers.

- When the question is not whether to perform an activity but rather at what level to perform it, marginal analysis draws our attention to the importance of marginal benefits and marginal costs. We should increase the level of an activity whenever its marginal benefit exceeds its marginal cost.

- The principles of rational choice are by no means limited to formal markets for goods and services. Indeed, some form of implicit or explicit cost-benefit calculation lies behind almost every human action, object, and behavior. Knowledge of the underlying principles casts our world in a sharp new light, not always flattering, but ever a source of stimulating insight.

QUESTIONS FOR REVIEW

1. What is the opportunity cost of your reading a novel this evening?

2. Your roommate is thinking of dropping out of school this semester. If his tuition payment for this semester is non-refundable, should he take that payment into account when making his decision?

3. Give three examples of activities that are accompanied by external costs or benefits.

4. Why is the opportunity cost of attending college higher for a 50-year-old than for a 20-year-old?

5. Why should sunk costs be irrelevant for current decisions?

6. How can the cost-benefit model be useful for studying the behavior of people who do not think explicitly in terms of costs and benefits?

24   CHAPTER 1   THINKING LIKE AN ECONOMIST

PROBLEMS

1. Jamal has a very flexible summer job. He works every day but is allowed to take a day off anytime he wants. His friend Don suggests they take off work on Tuesday and go to the amusement park. The admission charge for the amusement park is $15 per person, and it will cost them $5 each for gasoline and parking. Jamal loves amusement parks and a day at the park is worth $45 to him. However, Jamal also enjoys his job so much that he would actually be willing to pay $10 per day to do it.
    a. If Jamal earns $10 if he works, should he go to the amusement park?
    b. If Jamal earns $15 . . . ?
    c. If Jamal earns $20 . . . ?

2. Tom is a mushroom farmer. He invests all his spare cash in additional mushrooms, which grow on otherwise useless land behind his barn. The mushrooms double in size during their first year, after which time they are harvested and sold at a constant price per pound. Tom's friend Dick asks Tom for a loan of $200, which he promises to repay after 1 year. How much interest will Dick have to pay Tom in order for Tom to be no worse off than if he had not made the loan?

3. The meal plan at University A lets students eat as much as they like for a fixed fee of $500 per semester. The average student there eats 250 lb of food per semester. University B charges students $500 for a book of meal tickets that entitles the student to eat 250 lb of food per semester. If the student eats more than 250 lb, he or she pays extra; if the student eats less, he or she gets a refund. If students are rational, at which university will average food consumption be higher?

4. You are planning a 1000-mile trip to Florida. Except for the matter of cost, you are completely indifferent between driving and taking the bus. Bus fare is $260. The costs of operating your car during a typical 10,000-mile driving year are as follows:

Insurance	$1000
Interest	2000
Fuel & oil	1200
Tires	200
License & registration	50
Maintenance	1100
Total	$5550

Should you drive or take the bus?

5. Al and Jane have rented a banquet hall to host a party in celebration of their wedding anniversary. Fifty people have already accepted their invitation. The caterers will charge $5 per person for food and $2 per person for drinks. The band will cost $300 for the evening, and the hall costs $200. Now Al and Jane are considering inviting 10 more people. By how much will these extra guests increase the cost of their party?

6. You loan a friend $1000, and at the end of 1 year she writes you a check for $1000 to pay off this loan. If the annual interest-rate on your savings account is 6 percent, what was your opportunity cost of making this loan?

7. Bill and Joe live in Ithaca, New York. At 2 PM, Bill goes to the local Ticketmaster outlet and buys a $30 ticket to a basketball game to be played that night in Syracuse (50 miles north). Joe plans to attend the same game, but doesn't purchase his ticket in advance because he knows from experience that it is always possible to buy just as good a seat at the arena. At 4 PM, a heavy, unexpected snowstorm begins, making the prospect of the drive to Syracuse much less attractive than before. If both Bill and Joe have the same tastes and are rational, is one of them more likely to attend the game than the other? If so, say who and explain why. If not, explain why not.

8. Two types of radar weather-detection devices are available for commercial passenger aircraft: the "state-of-the-art" machine and another that is significantly less costly, but also less effective. The Federal Aviation Administration (FAA) has hired you for advice on whether all passenger planes should be required to use the state-of-the-art machine. After careful study, your recommendation is to require the more expensive machine only in passenger aircraft with more than 200 seats. How would you justify such a recommendation to an FAA member who complains that all passengers, irrespective of the number of seats in the aircraft in which they happen to find themselves, have a right to the best weather-detecting radar currently available?

9. A group has chartered a bus to New York City. The driver costs $100, the bus costs $500, and tolls will cost $75. The driver's fee is nonrefundable, but the bus may be canceled a week in advance at a charge of only $50. At $18 per ticket, how many people must buy tickets so that the trip need not be canceled?

10. Residents of your city are charged a fixed weekly fee of $6 for refuse collection. They are allowed to put out as many cans as they wish. The average household disposes of three cans per week in this way.

    Now, suppose that your city changes to a "tag" system. Each can of refuse to be collected must have a tag affixed to it. The tags cost $2 each.

    What effect do you think the introduction of the tag system will have on the total quantity of trash collected in your city?

11. Suppose that random access memory (RAM) can be added to your computer at a cost of $2.50 per megabyte. Suppose also that the value to you, measured in terms of your willingness to pay, of an additional megabyte of memory is $200 for the first megabyte, and then falls by one-half for each additional megabyte. Draw a graph of marginal cost and marginal benefit. How many megabytes of memory should you purchase?

12. Suppose in Problem 11 the cost of RAM falls to $1.25 per megabyte. How many megabytes of memory should you purchase now? Suppose additionally that your benefit for an additional megabyte of memory rises to $400 for the first megabyte, also falling by one-half for each additional megabyte. How many megabytes of memory should you purchase now, with both the lower price and the larger benefit?

*13. Dana has purchased a $40 ticket to a rock concert. On the day of the concert she is invited to a welcome-home party for a friend returning from abroad. She cannot attend both the concert and the party. If she had known about the party before buying the ticket, she would have chosen the party over the concert. *True or false:* It follows that if she is rational, she will go to the party anyway. Explain.

*14. Yesterday you were unexpectedly given a free ticket to a Dave Matthews concert scheduled for April 1. The market price of this ticket is $75, but the most you could sell it for is only $50. Today you discover that Ani DiFranco will be giving a concert that same evening. Tickets for the Ani DiFranco concert are still available at $75. Had you known before receiving your Dave Matthews ticket yesterday that Ani DiFranco would be coming, you definitely would have bought a ticket to see her, not Dave Matthews. *True or false:* From what we are told of your preferences, it follows that if you are a rational utility maximizer, you should attend the Ani DiFranco concert. Explain.

*15. Mr. Smith recently faced a choice between being (*a*) an economics professor, which pays $60,000/yr, or (*b*) a safari leader, which pays $50,000/yr. After careful deliberation, Smith took the safari job, but it was a close call. "For a dollar more," he said, "I'd have gone the other way."

    Now Smith's brother-in-law approaches him with a business proposition. The terms are as follows:

    * Smith must resign his safari job to work full-time in his brother-in-law's business.
    * Smith must give his brother-in-law an interest-free loan of $100,000, which will be repaid in full if and when Smith leaves the business. (Smith currently has much more than $100,000 in the bank.)

* The business will pay Smith a salary of $70,000/yr. He will receive no other payment from the business.

The interest rate is 10 percent per year. Apart from salary considerations, Smith feels that working in the business would be just as enjoyable as being an economics professor. For simplicity, assume there is no uncertainty regarding either Smith's salary in the proposed business or the security of his monetary investment in it. Should Smith join his brother-in-law and, if so, how small would Smith's salary from the business have to be to make it NOT worthwhile for him to join? If not, how large would Smith's salary from the business have to be to make it worthwhile for him to join?

*16. You have just purchased a new Ford Taurus for $20,000, but the most you could get for it if you sold it privately is $15,000. Now you learn that Toyota is offering its Camry, which normally sells for $25,000, at a special sale price of $20,000. If you had known before buying the Taurus that you could buy a Camry at the same price, you would have definitely chosen the Camry. *True or false:* From what we are told of your preferences, it follows that if you are a rational utility maximizer, you should definitely not sell the Taurus and buy the Camry. Explain.

ANSWERS TO IN-CHAPTER EXERCISES

1.1. Someone who gets a $28 traffic ticket every 200 miles driven will pay $35 in fines, on the average, for every 250 miles driven. Adding that figure to the $20 hassle cost of driving, and then adding the $50 fuel, oil, and maintenance cost, we have $105. This is more than the $100 bus fare, which means taking the bus is best.

1.2. The $18 Mike paid for his ticket is a sunk cost at the moment he must decide whether to attend the concert. For both Jim and Mike, therefore, the costs and benefits should be the same. If the benefit of seeing the concert outweighs the cost of sitting in the rain, they should go. Otherwise they should stay home.

1.3. You should use your coupon for the New Delhi trip, because it is more valuable to save $120 than to save $100

1.4. Two boats. Referring to Table 1.2, note that if marginal cost is $150, it now pays to launch the second boat (marginal benefit = $180) but not the third.

1.5. At 2 cents per minute, Susan should talk for 600 minutes per month.

*Problems marked with an asterisk (*) are more difficult.

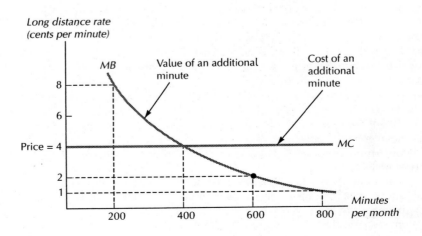

CHAPTER

2

SUPPLY AND DEMAND

In 1979 I was working for the federal government and living in Washington, D.C. Outside my apartment window stood a gas station. With 16 pumps, it was larger than most, but otherwise typical of the modern urban self-serve station.

In April of that year, a major oil supply interruption occurred in the Mideast, which sent gasoline prices skyrocketing. To keep prices from rising still further, the Carter administration implemented a complex system of fuel allocations and price controls. One result of this program was that in many urban markets substantially less gasoline was available than motorists wanted to buy at the regulated prices. At the gas station outside my apartment window, this showed up as a line of cars that stretched for several blocks.

Quarrels over position in such queues were common during the summer of 1979, and many motorists got into fistfights and shouting matches with one another. One motorist was shot and killed for butting into line. Tensions continued until the gasoline lines dwindled with the passing of the heavy-travel months.

The government's system of price controls and allocations tried to accomplish a task that we usually relegate to private market forces. The Washington experience was typical of similar interventions in other times and places. It is the rule, not the exception, for these programs to produce confusion and conflict. Of course, the unfettered market can itself produce outcomes we do not like. But rarely does it fail to allocate available supplies in a smooth, efficient manner.

28   CHAPTER 2   SUPPLY AND DEMAND

Doonesbury copyright 1975 G. B. Trudeau. Reprinted with permission of Universal Press Syndicate. All rights reserved.

CHAPTER PREVIEW

In this chapter we will explore why markets function so smoothly most of the time and why attempts at direct allocation are so often problematic. The early part of the chapter will look at basic supply and demand analysis. First, we'll review the usual descriptive features of supply and demand analysis covered in the introductory course. Next, we'll see that, for given attributes of buyers and sellers, the unregulated competitive market yields the best attainable outcome, in the sense that any other combination of price and quantity would be worse for at least some buyers or sellers.

We'll also see that despite this attractive feature, market outcomes often do not command society's approval. Concern for the well-being of the poor has motivated the governments of every Western society to intervene in a variety of ways—for instance, by adopting laws that peg prices above or below their equilibrium levels. Such laws, we will see, almost always generate harmful, if unintended, consequences.

We will also see that a generally more efficient solution to the problems of the poor is to boost their incomes directly. The law of supply and demand cannot be repealed by the legislature. But legislatures can alter the underlying forces that govern the shape and position of supply and demand schedules.

Finally, we will explore supply and demand analysis as a useful device for understanding how taxes affect equilibrium prices and quantities. In particular, it helps dispel the myth that a tax is paid primarily by the party on whom it is directly levied; rather, the burden of a tax falls most heavily on whichever side of the market is least able to avoid it

SUPPLY AND DEMAND CURVES

Our basic tool for analyzing market outcomes is supply and demand analysis, already familiar to most of you from your introductory course. Let us begin with the following working definition of a market.

Definition: A market consists of the buyers and sellers of a good or service.

Some markets are confined to a single specific time and location. For example, all the participating buyers and sellers (or at least their designated representatives) gather together in the same place for an antiques auction. Other markets span vast geographic territory, and most participants in them never meet or even see one another. The New York Stock Exchange is such a market. The Internet provides access to markets of this type for many goods.

Sometimes the choice of market definition will depend on the bias of the observer. In antitrust cases, for example, current policy prohibits mergers between companies whose combined share of the market would exceed a given threshold. Accordingly, government prosecutors who oppose a merger will often try to define markets as narrowly as possible, thereby making the combined market share as large as possible. The merging companies, by contrast, tend to view their markets in much broader terms, which naturally makes their combined market share smaller. The Stouffer's Corporation, when it wanted to merge with Nestlé, told the court that both firms were in the business of selling "frozen dinners." The Justice Department argued to the same court that the two companies were in the business of selling "high-priced ethnic entrees." In general, as in this particular instance, the best market definition will depend on the purpose at hand.

Over the years, economists have increasingly recognized that even subtle product differences matter a great deal to some consumers, and the trend in analysis has been toward ever narrower definitions of goods and markets. Two otherwise identical products are often classified as separate if they differ only with respect to the times or places they are available. An umbrella on a sunny day, for example, is in this sense a very different product from an umbrella during a downpour. And the markets for these two products behave very differently indeed. (My editor tells me that low-quality umbrellas in Manhattan sell for $10 on rainy days, only $5 on sunny days.)

To make our discussion concrete, let us consider the workings of a specific market—say, the one for $1\frac{1}{2}$-pound lobsters in Hyannis, Massachusetts, on July 20, 2006. For this market, the task of analysis is to explain both the price of lobsters and the quantity traded. To do this, we begin with the basic *demand curve*, a simple mathematical relationship that tells how many lobsters buyers wish to purchase at various possible prices (holding all else constant). The curve *DD* depicted in Figure 2.1, for example, tells us that 4000 lobsters will be demanded at a price of $4 each, 1000 at a price of $10, and so on.

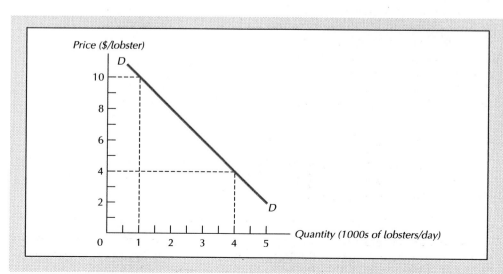

FIGURE 2.1
The Demand Curve for Lobsters in Hyannis Mass., July 20, 2006
The demand curve tells the quantities buyers will wish to purchase at various prices. Its key property is its downward slope; when price falls, the quantity demanded increases. This property is called the law of demand.

CHAPTER 2 SUPPLY AND DEMAND

If a visitor from Mars were told only that lobsters sell for $4 each, he would have no way of knowing whether they were cheap or expensive. In 1900, a $4 lobster would have been out of reach of all but the wealthiest consumers. In 2006, by contrast, lobsters would have been considered an incredible bargain at that price. Unless otherwise stated, the price on the vertical axis of the demand curve diagram will refer to the **real price** of the good, which means its price relative to the prices of all other goods and services. Thus, the prices on the vertical axis of Figure 2.1 represent lobster prices on July 20, 2006, and the context within which those prices are interpreted by buyers is the set of prices of all other goods on that same date.

real price of a product its price relative to the prices of other goods and services.

The discussion above describes the demand curve as a schedule telling how much of a product consumers wish to purchase at various prices. This is called the *horizontal interpretation* of the demand curve. Under this interpretation, we start with price on the vertical axis and read the corresponding quantity demanded on the horizontal axis. For instance, at a price of $10 per lobster, the demand curve in Figure 2.1 tells us that the quantity demanded will be 1000 lobsters per day.

A second interpretation of the demand curve is to start with quantity on the horizontal axis and then read the marginal buyer's reservation price on the vertical axis. Thus when the quantity of lobsters sold is 4000 per day, the demand curve in Figure 2.1 tells us that the marginal buyer's reservation price is $4 per lobster. This second way of reading the demand curve is called the *vertical interpretation*.

The demand curve shown in Figure 2.1 happens to be linear, but demand curves in general need not be. The key property assumed of them is that they are downward sloping: the quantity demanded rises as the price of the product falls. This property is often called the **law of demand.** Although we will see in Chapter 4 that it is theoretically possible for a demand curve to be upward sloping, such exceptions are virtually never encountered in practice. To be sure, the negative slope of the demand curve accords in every way with our intuitions about how people respond to rising prices.

law of demand the empirical observation that when the price of a product falls, people demand larger quantities of it.

As we will see in more detail in Chapter 4, there are normally two independent reasons for the quantity demanded to fall when price rises. One is that many people will switch to a close substitute. Thus, when lobster gets more expensive, some consumers may switch to crab, others to meat or poultry. A second reason people buy less when the price rises is that they are not *able* to buy as much as before. Incomes, after all, go only so far. When the price of a product goes up, it is not possible to buy as much as before unless we at the same time purchase less of something else.

The demand curve for a good is a summary of the various cost-benefit calculations that buyers make with respect to the good, as we will see in greater detail in the next chapter. The question each person faces is, "Should I buy the product?" (and usually, "If so, how much of it?"). The cost side of the calculation is simply the price of the product (and implicitly, the other goods or services that could be bought with the same money). The benefit side is the satisfaction provided by the product. The negative slope of the demand schedule tells us that the cost-benefit criterion will be met for fewer and fewer potential buyers as the price of the product rises.

On the seller's side of the market, the corresponding analytical tool is the supply schedule. A hypothetical schedule for our lobster market is shown as line *SS* in Figure 2.2. Again, the linear form of this particular schedule is not a

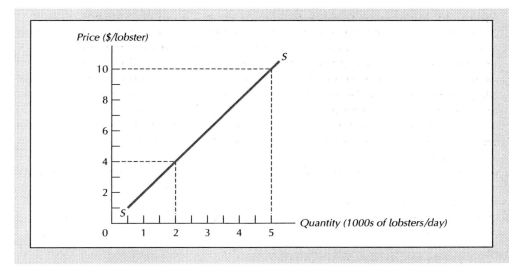

FIGURE 2.2
A Supply Schedule for Lobsters in Hyannis, Mass., July 20, 2006
The upward slope of the supply schedule reflects the fact that costs tend to rise when producers expand production in the short run.

characteristic feature of supply schedules generally. What these schedules do tend to have in common is their upward slope: The quantity supplied rises as the price of a product rises. This property can be called the **law of supply**. For a supplier to be willing to sell a product, its price must cover the marginal cost of producing or acquiring it. As we will see in detail in Chapter 9, the cost of producing additional units often tends to rise as more units are produced, especially in the short run. When this is the case, increased production is profitable only at higher prices.

law of supply the empirical observation that when the price of a product rises, firms offer more of it for sale.

In our lobster market, the reasons for this are clear. Suppliers harvest the lobsters closest to shore first, and then work their way farther offshore as they try to enlarge their catch. The more lobsters they try to harvest, the farther they have to go, and hence the more it costs.

Another factor contributing to the upward slope of the supply curve is substitution on the part of fishermen. As the price of lobsters increases, more producers switch to lobsters, rather than continue to fish for, say, cod.

Like demand curves, supply curves can be interpreted either horizontally or vertically. Under the horizontal interpretation, we begin with a price, then go over to the supply curve to read the quantity that sellers wish to sell at that price on the horizontal axis. For instance, at a price of $4 per lobster, sellers in Figure 2.2 wish to sell 2000 lobsters per day.

Under the vertical interpretation, we begin with a quantity, then go up to the supply curve to read the corresponding marginal cost on the vertical axis. For example, if sellers in Figure 2.2 are currently supplying 5000 lobsters per day, the opportunity cost of the last lobster supplied by the marginal seller would be $10. In other words, the supply curve tells us that the marginal cost of delivering the 5000th lobster is $10. If someone could deliver a 5001st lobster for less than $10, she would have had an incentive to do so, in which case the quantity of lobster supplied at a price of $10 would not have been 5000 per day to begin with. By similar reasoning, when the quantity of lobster supplied is 2000 per day, the marginal cost of delivering another lobster must be $4.

An alternative way of describing the supply schedule is to call it the set of price-quantity pairs for which suppliers are satisfied. The term "satisfied" has a technical meaning here, which is that any point on the supply schedule represents the quantity that suppliers want to sell, *given the price they face*. They would obviously be happy to get even higher prices for their offerings. But for any given price, suppliers would consider themselves worse off if forced to sell either more or less than the corresponding quantity on the supply schedule. If, for example, the price of lobsters in Figure 2.2 were $4, suppliers would not be satisfied selling either more or fewer than 2000 lobsters a day.

The demand schedule may be given a parallel description. It is the set of price-quantity pairs for which buyers are satisfied in precisely the same sense. At any given price, they would consider themselves worse off if forced to purchase either more or less than the corresponding quantity on the demand schedule.

EQUILIBRIUM QUANTITY AND PRICE

With both the supply and demand schedules in hand, we can describe the *equilibrium quantity and price* of lobsters. It is the price-quantity pair at which both buyers and sellers are satisfied. Put another way, it is the price-quantity pair at which the supply and demand schedules intersect. Figure 2.3 depicts the equilibrium in our lobster market, at which a total of 3000 lobsters is traded at a price of $6 each.

If we were at any price-quantity pair other than the one in Figure 2.3, either buyers or sellers, or both, would be dissatisfied in the sense described above. If the price happened for some reason to lie above the $6 equilibrium level, sellers would tend to be the ones who are frustrated. At a price of $8, for example, buyers would purchase only 2000 lobsters, whereas sellers would offer 4000. (See Figure 2.4.) Buyers would be satisfied at a price of $8, but sellers would not. A situation in which price exceeds its equilibrium value is called one of **excess supply,** or *surplus*. At $8, there is an excess supply of 2000 lobsters.

excess supply   the amount by which quantity supplied exceeds quantity demanded.

If, by contrast, the price happened to lie below the equilibrium price of $6, then buyers would be the ones dissatisfied. At a price of $4, for example, they would want to purchase 4000 lobsters, whereas suppliers would be willing to sell only 2000. A situation in which price lies below its equilibrium value is

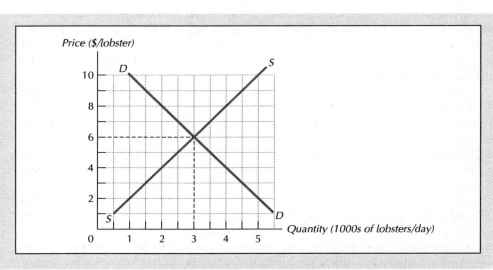

FIGURE 2.3
Equilibrium in the Lobster Market
The intersection of the supply and demand curves represents the price-quantity pair at which all participants in the market are "satisfied": Buyers are buying the amount they want to buy at that price, and sellers are selling the amount they want to sell.

ADJUSTMENT TO EQUILIBRIUM   33

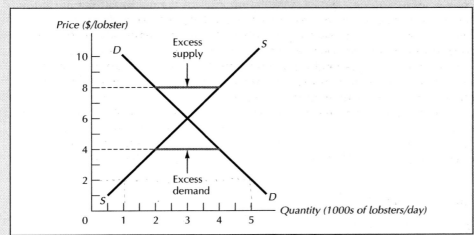

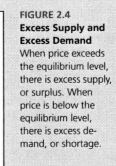

FIGURE 2.4
Excess Supply and Excess Demand
When price exceeds the equilibrium level, there is excess supply, or surplus. When price is below the equilibrium level, there is excess de-mand, or shortage.

referred to as one of **excess demand,** or *shortage.* At a price of $4 in this lobster market, there is an excess demand of 2000 lobsters. At the market equilibrium price of $6, both excess demand and excess supply are exactly zero.

> **excess demand** the amount by which quantity demanded exceeds quantity supplied.

EXERCISE 2.1

At a price of $2 in this hypothetical lobster market, how much excess demand for lobsters will there be? How much excess supply will there be at a price of $10?

ADJUSTMENT TO EQUILIBRIUM

When price differs from the equilibrium price, trading in the marketplace will be constrained—by the behavior of buyers if the price lies above equilibrium, by the behavior of sellers if below. At any price other than the equilibrium price, one side or the other of the market is dissatisfied. At prices above equilibrium, for example, sellers are not selling as much as they want to. The impulse of a dissatisfied seller is to reduce the price. In the seafood business, after all, the rule of thumb is "sell it or smell it." At a price of $8 each, 2000 lobsters are being sold, but another 2000 go unclaimed. Each seller reasons, correctly, that if he were to cut his price slightly, while other sellers remained at $8, he could move all his unsold lobsters. Buyers will abandon sellers who charge $8 in favor of those who charge only $7.95. But then the deserted sellers themselves have a motive for cutting price. And if all sellers cut price to $7.95, each will again have a large quantity of unsold lobsters. Downward pressure on price will persist as long as there remain any dissatisfied sellers—that is, until price falls to its equilibrium value.

When price is below $6, buyers are dissatisfied. Under these conditions, sellers will realize that they can increase their prices and still sell as much as they wish to. This upward pressure on price will persist until price reaches its equilibrium value. Put another way, consumers will start bidding against each other in the hope of seeing their demands satisfied.

34   CHAPTER 2   SUPPLY AND DEMAND

An extraordinary feature of this equilibrating process is that no one consciously plans or directs it. The actual steps that consumers and producers must take to move toward equilibrium are often indescribably complex. Suppliers looking to expand their operations, for example, must choose from a bewilderingly large menu of equipment options. Buyers, for their part, face literally millions of choices about how to spend their money. And yet the adjustment toward equilibrium results more or less automatically from the natural reactions of self-interested individuals facing either surpluses or shortages.

SOME WELFARE PROPERTIES OF EQUILIBRIUM

Given the attributes—tastes, abilities, knowledge, incomes, and so on—of buyers and sellers, the equilibrium outcome has some attractive properties. Specifically, we can say that no reallocation can improve some people's position without harming the position of at least some others. *If price and quantity take anything other than their equilibrium values, however, it will always be possible to reallocate so as to make at least some people better off without harming others.*

Sticking with the lobster example, suppose that the price is $4 and that suppliers therefore offer only 2000 lobsters. As indicated in Figure 2.5, the vertical interpretation of the demand curve tells us that when only 2000 lobsters are available, buyers are willing to pay $8 apiece for them. Similarly, the vertical interpretation of the supply curve tells us that when 2000 lobsters a day are supplied, the marginal cost of delivering another lobster is only $4. When the value to the buyer of the last lobster caught ($8) is higher than the cost of harvesting it ($4), there is room to cut a deal.

Suppose, for example, a dissatisfied buyer were to offer a supplier $5 for a lobster. The supplier would gladly sell an additional lobster at this price (since, at 2000 lobsters, additional lobsters cost only $4 each to harvest). This transaction would improve the buyer's position by $3 (the difference between the $8 value he attaches to the lobster and the $5 he paid for it). It would also improve the seller's position by $1 (the difference between the $5 she got and the $4 cost of

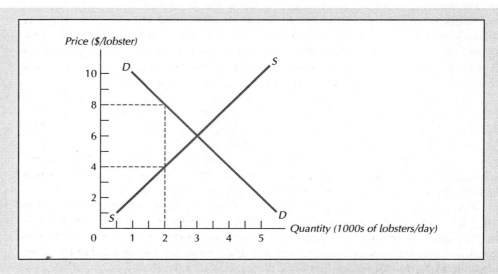

FIGURE 2.5
An Opportunity for Improvement in the Lobster Market
When the quantity traded in the market is below (or above) the equilibrium quantity, it is always possible to reallocate resources in such a way that some people are made better off without harming others. Here, a dissatisfied buyer can pay a seller $5 for an additional lobster, thus making both parties better off.

Frank: Microeconomics
an/ Behavior, Sixth E/ition

I. Intro/uction

2. Supply an/ Deman/

© The McGraw–Hill
Companies, 2005

33

harvesting the extra lobster). No one suffers any harm from this transaction (except the extra lobster!), and the two participants reap a total of $4 additional benefit from it ($3 for the buyer, $1 for the seller). A similar argument can be made concerning any price that is below the equilibrium value. For any such price, it will always be possible to make some people better off without hurting others.

What if the price had been higher than the equilibrium price to begin with? Suppose that price is $8 and that trading is therefore limited by buyers' demands for 2000 lobsters. (Again, see Figure 2.5.) Now a dissatisfied seller can propose a transaction that will make both the seller and some buyers better off. Suppose, for example, a seller offers an additional lobster for sale for $7. Since buyers value additional lobsters at $8, whoever buys it will be better off by $1. And since lobsters cost only $4 to harvest, the seller will be better off by $3. Again, no one is injured by this transaction, and again the two parties gain a total of $4.

Thus, no matter whether price starts out above or below its equilibrium value, it will always be possible to put together a transaction that benefits all participants. We'll examine the welfare properties of the market system in much greater detail in Chapter 16. But for now, we may observe that the equilibrium price and quantity constitute the best outcome attainable, given the initial attributes and endowments of buyers and sellers.

FREE MARKETS AND THE POOR

The fact that market equilibrium outcomes are efficient in the sense just described does not mean that they are necessarily desirable in any absolute sense. All markets may be in perfect equilibrium, for example, and yet many people may lack sufficient incomes to purchase even the bare necessities of life. The claim that market equilibrium is efficient does not challenge the notion that it is difficult, often even painful, to be poor. Efficiency says merely that, *given the low incomes of the poor,* free exchange enables them to do the best they can. One can hold this view and yet still believe it desirable to provide public assistance to people who are unable to earn adequate incomes in the marketplace.

Concern for the well-being of the poor motivates most societies to try to alter market outcomes, as in the gasoline price control example mentioned earlier. The difficulty, as in that example, is that many of our direct interventions in markets produce unintended and often harmful consequences. Indeed, some of them clearly do much more harm than good. As we will see, a more thorough understanding of the workings of the market mechanism would prevent many of the most costly consequences of our current approach.

Denied boarding compensation.   EXAMPLE 2.1

What are the efficiency and distributional implications of handling excess demand for seats on overbooked flights through a first-come, first-served policy as opposed to an auction mechanism?

It has always been a common practice for commercial airlines to issue more reservations than there are seats on a flight. Because many reservation holders fail to show up for their flights, this practice seldom causes difficulty. Occasionally, however, 160 passengers will show up for a flight on which there are only, say, 150 seats. Before the late 1970s, airlines dealt with overbooked flights by boarding passengers on a first-come, first-served basis.

Why is an auction a better way to allocate seats on an over-booked flight than first-come, first-served?

The difficulty with this solution is that it gives insufficient weight to the interests of passengers with pressing needs who may be a bit late to arrive at their final destinations on time. With this problem clearly in mind, the Civil Aeronautics Board (CAB), the government agency that used to regulate the commercial aviation industry, proposed a simple regulation. When too many people showed up for a flight, the airline would be required to call for volunteers to abandon their seats in return for either a cash payment or an in-kind payment, such as a free air ticket. The airline would be required to keep increasing its offer until it got enough volunteers.

The advantage of the CAB proposal was that it would allow passengers to decide for themselves how pressing their schedules were. People with important meetings could simply refuse to volunteer. Others with time on their hands could agree to wait a few hours, often in return for several hundred dollars or a free trip to Hawaii. By comparison with the first-come, first-served solution, the CAB proposal promised a better outcome for all passengers.

Or at any rate, so it seemed. A consumer-action group immediately objected to the CAB's proposal on the grounds that it was unfair to low-income passengers. The group's complaint was that the auction method of soliciting volunteers would almost always result in the poorest ticket holders being the ones to wait for the next flight.

Now, a poor person will surely be more likely to find a cash payment a compelling reason to volunteer. But by the act of volunteering, a person says that the cash payment is *worth* the wait. It is one thing to say that the world would be a better place if poor people had higher incomes and were not tempted by their poverty to give up their seats on airplanes. But the consumer group was not proposing to give the poor higher incomes. Rather, it wanted to see the industry stick with the system that bumped passengers from overbooked flights irrespective of the value they attached to remaining on board.

It is hard to see how poor people would feel their interests well served by a consumer-action group that prevented them from earning extra cash by volunteering to wait for the next flight. And in the end, the CAB adopted its denied-boarding-compensation proposal, to the benefit of air travelers at all income levels.

Many critics of the market system complain that it is unfair to ration goods and services by asking how much people are willing to pay for them. This criterion, they point out, gives short shrift to the interests of the poor. But as Example 2.1 clearly illustrates, serious contradictions are inherent in alternative schemes of allocation. Consider again our hypothetical lobster market. Suppose we are concerned that the equilibrium price of $6 will exclude many deserving poor persons from ever being able to know the pleasure of a lobster dinner. And suppose that, with this in mind, we adopt a system that periodically gives free lobsters to the poor. Wouldn't such a system represent a clear improvement in the eyes of any person who feels compassion for the poor?

Frank: Microeconomics
an/ Behavior, Sixth E/ition

I. Intro/uction

2. Supply an/ Deman/

© The McGraw–Hill
Companies, 2005

35

The answer, as in Example 2.1, is that for the same cost we can do even better. When a poor person, or indeed even a rich person, does not buy lobster because the price is too high, she is saying, in effect, that she would prefer to spend her money on other things. If we gave such a person a lobster, what would she want to do with it? In an ideal world, she would immediately sell it to someone willing to pay the $6 equilibrium price for it. We know there will be such persons because some of the lobsters that would have been bought for $6 were instead given to the poor. The poor person's sale of the lobster to one of these people will bring about a clear improvement for both parties—for the buyer, or else he would not have bought it, and for the seller because the lobster is worth less than $6 to her.

The practical difficulty, as we will see in detail in later chapters, is that it would take time and effort for our hypothetical poor person to find a buyer for the lobster. In the end, she would probably eat it herself. True enough, she might enjoy her lobster dinner. But by her own reckoning, she would have enjoyed the $6 even more.

The structure of the problem is much the same in the gasoline price controls example. The controls were implemented in the sincere belief that they were needed to protect the poor from the economic burden of sharply higher gasoline prices. Their effect, however, was to induce a host of behaviors that helped neither the rich nor the poor.

Despite statements to the contrary by critics of the market system, people are highly responsive to energy prices when they make decisions about how to spend their incomes. If gasoline costs $3.00/gal, for example, many people will form car pools or purchase fuel-efficient cars, even though they would do neither of these things if gasoline prices were only $1.50/gal. Whether a long trip is considered worth taking will also clearly depend on the price of gasoline.

Whether or not fuel is in unusually short supply, it is in everyone's interest—rich or poor—to restrict its uses to the ones people value most. But the costs of a policy that does not do this are particularly high when fuel is scarce. Selling gasoline for less than the equilibrium price is just such a policy. It encourages people to use gasoline in wasteful ways.

Rent Controls

It has been said that the surest way to destroy a city, short of dropping a nuclear bomb on it, is to pass a rent control law. Such laws, like so many others, are motivated by an honest concern for the well-being of low-income citizens. But their economic consequences are no less damaging for being unintended.

Basic supply and demand analysis is again all we need to see clearly the nature of the difficulties. Figure 2.6 depicts the supply and demand schedules for a hypothetical urban apartment market. The equilibrium rent in this market would be $600/month, and at this level there would be 60,000 apartments rented. The

Why are rent-controlled apartments less well maintained than unregulated units?

FIGURE 2.6
Rent Controls
With the rent control level set at $400 a month, there is an excess demand of 40,000 apartments a month.

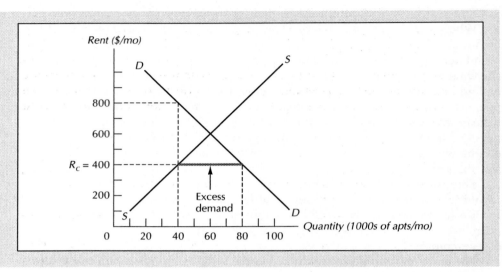

price ceiling   level above which the price of a good is not permitted by law to rise.

city council, however, has passed a law that holds rents at $R_c = \$400$/month, or $200 below the market-clearing value. R_c in this example constitutes a **price ceiling** for rents, a level beyond which rents are not permitted to rise. At $400/month, buyers would like to rent 80,000 apartments, but suppliers are willing to offer only 40,000. There is an excess demand of 40,000 units. And if the rent control level remains fixed at $400/month, excess demand will tend to grow over time as population grows and inflation reduces the value of money.

In an unregulated market, the immediate response to such a high level of excess demand would be for rents to rise sharply. But here the law prevents them from rising above R_c. Yet there are other ways the pressures of excess demand can make themselves felt. One is for owners to spend less on maintaining the quality of their rental units. After all, if there are two renters knocking at the door of each vacant apartment, a landlord has considerable room to maneuver. Clogged drains, peeling paint, broken thermostats, and the like are not apt to receive prompt attention when rents are set well below market-clearing levels.

Nor are these the most serious difficulties. With an offering of only 40,000 apartments per month, we see in Figure 2.6 that renters would be willing to pay as much as $800/month for an apartment (again, the vertical interpretation of the demand curve). This pressure almost always finds ways, legal or illegal, of expressing itself. In New York City, for example, it is not uncommon to see "finder's fees" or "key deposits" as high as several thousand dollars. Owners who cannot charge a market-clearing rent for an apartment also have the option of converting it to a condominium or co-op, which enables them to sell their asset for a price much closer to its true economic value.

Even when rent-controlled apartment owners do not hike their prices in these various ways, serious misallocations result. A widow steadfastly remains in her seven-room apartment even after her children have left home because it is much cheaper than alternative dwellings not covered by rent control. It would be much better for all concerned if she relinquished that space to a larger family. But under rent controls, she has no economic incentive to do so.

> **Suppose the rent control is lowered (strengthened) to $200/month. What is the excess demand, and how does it compare with the excess demand when rents were limited (more loosely) to $400/month?**
>
> At $200/month, buyers would like to rent 100,000 apartments, but suppliers are willing to offer only 20,000. Thus there is an excess demand of 80,000 units. The excess demand is greater than the excess demand of 40,000 units at the $400/month rent control.

EXAMPLE 2.2

EXERCISE 2.2

In the market for apartments described in Figure 2.6, what would happen if the rent control level were set at $625/mo?

In response to the kinds of problems described above, some rent-control programs have been modified to allow landlords to raise rents when a tenant moves out of an apartment. Such changes reduce, but do not eliminate, misallocations. And they may even create new problems. For example, a landlord who knows that a tenant's departure would permit a rent increase may take any available lawful steps to make the tenant's life unpleasant if he remains.

There are much more effective ways to help poor people than to give them cheap gasoline, rent-controlled apartments, or free lobsters. One would be to give them additional income and let them decide for themselves how to spend it. Chapter 18 examines some of the practical difficulties involved in transferring additional purchasing power into the hands of the poor. In brief, the most pressing problem is that it is hard to target cash to the genuinely needy without attracting others who could fend for themselves. But as we will see, economic reasoning also suggests practical ways to overcome this difficulty. There are no simple or easy solutions. But given the enormous losses caused by policies that keep prices below their equilibrium levels, these issues surely deserve our most serious attention.

PRICE SUPPORTS

The rent control example considered a case in which the government imposed a price ceiling to prevent the price from rising to its equilibrium level. For many agricultural products, the government's policy has been to impose not price controls but *price supports*, or **price floors,** whose effect is to keep prices above their equilibrium levels. By contrast to the price ceiling case, which required merely the announcement of a level beyond which prices were not permitted to rise, price supports require the government to become an active buyer in the market.

price floor a minimum price for a good, established by law, and supported by government's offer to buy the good at that price.

Figure 2.7, for example, depicts a price support level of P_s in the market for soybeans. Because P_s is above the equilibrium price, there is an excess supply of 200,000 tons/yr. To maintain the price at $P_s = \$400/\text{ton}$, the government must purchase 200,000 tons/yr of soybeans. Otherwise farmers would face powerful incentives to cut their prices.

An important purpose of farm price supports is to ensure prices sufficiently high to provide adequate incomes for farm families. In practice, however, the

FIGURE 2.7
A Price Support in the Soybean Market
For a price support to have any impact, it must be set above the market-clearing price. Its effect is to create excess supply, which the government then purchases.

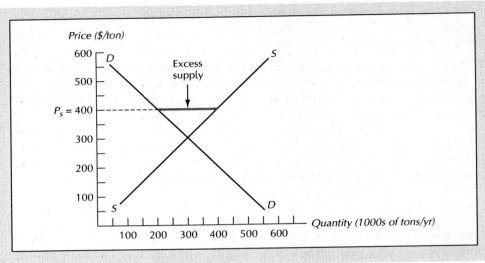

supports have proved an extremely costly and inefficient instrument for that task. One problem is the disposition of the surplus bought by the government each year. To produce this surplus requires valuable labor, capital, fertilizer, and other inputs. Yet often the surplus is simply left to decay in government storage bins. Another difficulty is that much of the surplus is produced by large corporate farms, whose owners are in no need of support. For every extra dollar that price supports put into the hands of a needy family farmer, several more go into the coffers of prosperous agribusinesses. Price supports also raise the food bills of all families, and often even raise prices for goods that are not directly supported. (See Example 2.3 later in this chapter.) If society wants to subsidize small family farms, there are much more efficient and direct means of doing so than with agricultural price supports.

THE RATIONING AND ALLOCATIVE FUNCTIONS OF PRICES

Prices serve two important and distinct functions. First, they ration existing supplies of goods. Scarcity is the universal feature of economic life. People want more of virtually everything than could be supplied at a price of zero. Equilibrium prices serve to curtail these excessive claims by rationing scarce supplies to the users who place the highest value on them. This is the **rationing function of price**. It is a short-run function, in the sense that its focus is the distribution of output that already exists.

The second function of price is that of a signal to direct productive resources among the different sectors of the economy. In industries in which there is excess demand, firms are able to charge more than they need to cover their costs of production. The resulting profits act as a carrot that lures additional resources into these industries. The other side of this coin is that losses act as the stick that drives resources out of those industries in which there is excess supply. This is the so-called **allocative function of price**, the driving force behind Adam Smith's invisible hand. It is a long-run function in the sense that its focus is to induce resources to migrate from industries with excess supply to those with excess demand.

rationing function of price the process whereby price directs existing supplies of a product to the users who value it most highly.

allocative function of price the process whereby price acts as a signal that guides resources away from the production of goods whose prices lie below cost toward the production of goods whose prices exceed cost.

Rent controls subvert both critical functions of the price mechanism. The rationing function is undercut by the alternative mechanisms that distribute housing with little regard to the value people place on it. The underlying needs of renters are relegated to secondary status. Both luck and the people you happen to know are often decisive. Artificially low rents undercut the allocative function of price by sending a false signal to investors about the need for additional housing. With rent controls in effect, apartment builders earn less than they could by investing their money in other industries. And it is hardly surprising, therefore, that many of them do precisely that. The cruel irony is that the pressing need in many communities with rent controls is for more low-income housing units, not fewer—which is precisely what the market would produce on its own if the poor were given more money.

DETERMINANTS OF SUPPLY AND DEMAND

Supply and demand analysis is useful not only for the normative insight it offers into questions of public policy but also for a rich variety of descriptive purposes. Most important, it helps us to predict how equilibrium prices and quantities will respond to changes in market forces. Because supply and demand curves intersect to determine equilibrium prices and quantities, anything that shifts these curves will tend to alter equilibrium values in a predictable way. In the next several chapters, we investigate in detail the forces that determine the shape and position of market demand curves. For the moment, let's discuss a few whose roles are intuitively clear.

Determinants of Demand

Incomes   It is obvious that income will influence the amount of most goods and services people will purchase at any given price. For most goods, the quantity demanded at any price will rise with income. Goods that have this property are called *normal goods*. So-called *inferior goods* (such as ground beef with high fat content) are the exception to this general pattern. For such goods, the quantity demanded at any price will fall with income. The idea is that consumers abandon these goods in favor of higher-quality substitutes (such as leaner grades of meat in the ground beef case) as soon as they can afford to.

Tastes   Not all people share the same tastes. Nor do tastes always remain fixed over time. In Western societies, culture instills a taste for sitting on padded furniture, whereas in many Eastern societies, people are conditioned to favor sitting cross-legged on the floor. The demand for armchairs thus tends to be larger in the West than in the East. By the same token, the demand for skirts with hemlines above the knee tends to vary sharply from one decade to another.

Prices of Substitutes and Complements   Bacon and eggs play a complementary role in the diets of some people. For such people, a sharp increase in the price of bacon would lead not only to a reduction in the quantity of bacon demanded but also to a reduction in the demand for eggs. Such goods are considered *complements:* An increase in the price of one good decreases demand for the other good. In the case of close *substitutes,* such as coffee and tea, an increase in the price of one will tend to increase the demand for the other.

42　　　　　CHAPTER 2　SUPPLY AND DEMAND

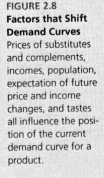

FIGURE 2.8
Factors that Shift Demand Curves
Prices of substitutes and complements, incomes, population, expectation of future price and income changes, and tastes all influence the position of the current demand curve for a product.

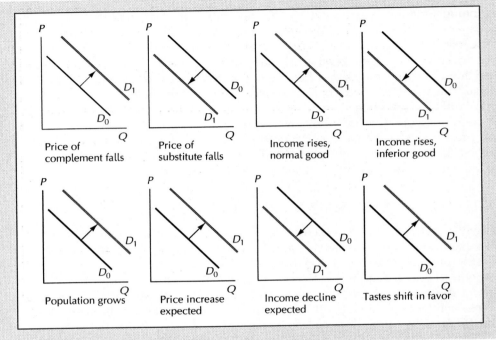

Expectations

People's expectations about future income and price levels also affect their current purchase decisions. For example, someone who expects sharply higher income in the future is likely to spend more today than an otherwise identical person who expects a much smaller income in the future. (After all, with a higher expected income, the need to save for the future diminishes.) Similarly, people will often accelerate their current purchases of goods whose prices are expected to rise sharply in the months to come.

Population

In general, the larger a market, the more a good or service at any given price will be purchased. Thus, in cities with growing populations, the demand for housing increases from year to year, whereas it tends to fall in cities with declining populations.

Figure 2.8 graphically displays some factors that shift demand curves. We will revisit these factors in more detail in Chapters 4 and 10.

Determinants of Supply

Technology

The amount suppliers are willing to offer at any price depends first and foremost on their costs of production. These costs, in turn, are closely linked to technology. For instance, the discovery of a more efficient lobster trap will reduce the cost of harvesting lobsters, which results in a rightward shift in the supply schedule.

Factor Prices

Another important determinant of a supplier's costs is the payment it must make to its factors of production: labor, capital, and so on. If the

DETERMINANTS OF SUPPLY AND DEMAND   43

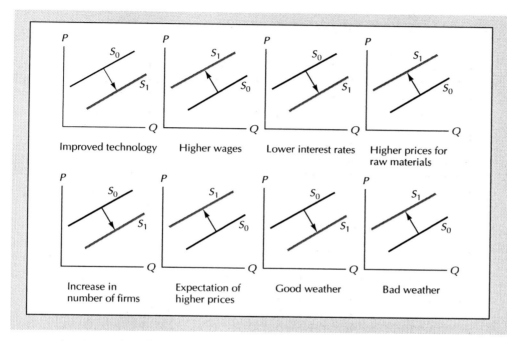

FIGURE 2.9
Factors that Shift Supply Schedules
Technology, input prices, the number of firms, expectations about future prices, and the weather all affect the position of the supply schedule for a given product.

price of lobster boats rises, or if the wage paid to lobstermen goes up, the supply schedule for lobsters will shift to the left.

The Number of Suppliers   The more firms there are that can supply any product, the greater will be the quantity supplied of that product at any given price. The supply schedule of personal computers has shifted sharply to the right as more and more companies have begun producing them.

Expectations   Suppliers too will take expected changes in prices into account in their current production decisions. For example, if ranchers expect beef prices to rise sharply in the future because of an epidemic affecting young cattle, they are likely to withhold current supplies of mature livestock to take advantage of the higher future prices.[1]

Weather   For some products, particularly agricultural ones, nature has a great deal to say about the placement of the supply schedule. In years of drought, for example, the supply schedule for many foodstuffs will be shifted sharply to the left.

Figure 2.9 shows the effects of some factors that shift supply schedules.

Neither of the preceding lists of supply and demand shifters is meant to be exhaustive.

---

[1]Note that supply is the quantity offered for sale at various prices, not necessarily current production (when suppliers are able to store inventory). Hence, the ranchers reduce sales of cattle in the current period, since they can sell them in a later period when prices are higher.

Changes in Demand versus Changes in the Quantity Demanded

When economists use the expression *change in demand*, they mean a shift in the entire demand curve. Thus, when the average income level of buyers changes, the demand curve shifts—there is a change in demand. When we say *change in the quantity demanded*, we mean a movement along the demand curve. When the price of a good falls, for example, the result is an increase in the quantity demanded, not an increase in demand.

Analogous interpretations attach to the expressions *change in supply* and *change in the quantity supplied*. These terminological distinctions are important for clear communication both in classroom discussion and on exams. And if the experience of previous generations of students is any guide, it requires effort to keep them straight.

PREDICTING AND EXPLAINING CHANGES IN PRICE AND QUANTITY

To predict or explain changes in equilibrium prices and quantities, we must be able to predict or account for the shifts in the relevant supply and/or demand schedules. When supply and demand curves have the conventional slopes, the following propositions about equilibrium prices and quantities will hold:

- An increase in demand will lead to an increase in both the equilibrium price and quantity.
- A decrease in demand will lead to a decrease in both the equilibrium price and quantity.
- An increase in supply will lead to a decrease in the equilibrium price and an increase in the equilibrium quantity.
- A decrease in supply will lead to an increase in the equilibrium price and a decrease in the equilibrium quantity.

These simple propositions permit us to answer a variety of questions.

ECONOMIC NATURALIST 2.1

Why do the prices of some goods, like apples, go down during the months of heaviest consumption while others, like beachfront cottages, go up?

The answer is that the seasonal consumption increase is the result of a supply increase in the case of apples, a demand increase in the case of cottages. As shown in Figure 2.10, these shifts produce the observed seasonal relationships between equilibrium prices and quantities. (The subscripts *w* and *s* in Figure 2.10 are used to denote winter and summer values, respectively.) When demand increases (as for cottages), the increase in the equilibrium quantity occurs concurrently with an increase in the equilibrium price. When supply increases (as for apples), the increase in the equilibrium quantity occurs concurrently with a decrease in the equilibrium price.

EXERCISE 2.3

What will happen to the equilibrium price and quantity in the fresh seafood market if each of the following events occurs: (1) a scientific report is issued saying that fish contains mercury, which is toxic to humans, and (2) the price of diesel fuel (used to operate fishing boats) falls significantly?

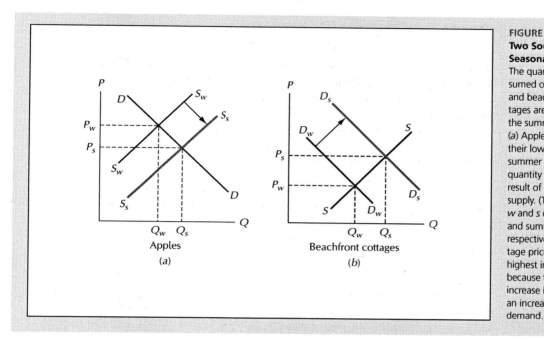

FIGURE 2.10
Two Sources of Seasonal Variation
The quantities consumed of both apples and beachfront cottages are highest in the summer months. (a) Apple prices are at their lowest during the summer because the quantity increase is the result of increased supply. (The subscripts w and s denote winter and summer values, respectively.) (b) Cottage prices are at their highest in summer because the quantity increase is the result of an increase in demand.

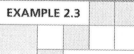

If soybeans are one of the ingredients in cattle feed, how does a price support program in the soybean market affect the equilibrium price and quantity of beef?

EXAMPLE 2.3

The price support program raises the price of cattle feed, which causes a leftward shift in the supply schedule for beef. (See Figure 2.11.) This, in turn, results in an increase in the equilibrium price and a reduction in the equilibrium quantity of beef.

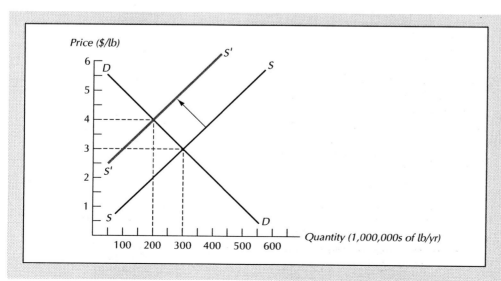

FIGURE 2.11
The Effect of Soybean Price Supports on the Equilibrium Price and Quantity of Beef
By raising the price of soybeans, an input used in beef production, the price supports produce a leftward shift in the supply curve of beef. The result is an increase in the equilibrium price and a reduction in the equilibrium quantity.

46   CHAPTER 2   SUPPLY AND DEMAND

THE ALGEBRA OF SUPPLY AND DEMAND

The examples thus far have focused on a geometric approach to market equilibrium. This approach is fine for illustrating the basic principles of the theory. But for actually computing numerical values, it usually is more convenient to find equilibrium prices and quantities algebraically. Suppose, for example, the supply schedule for a product is given by

$$P = 2 + 3Q^s, \tag{2.1}$$

and its demand schedule is given by

$$P = 10 - Q^d, \tag{2.2}$$

where P is the product price and Q^s and Q^d stand for the quantity supplied and the quantity demanded, respectively. In equilibrium, we know that $Q^s = Q^d$. Denoting this common value as Q^*, we may then equate the right-hand sides of Equations 2.1 and 2.2 and solve:

$$2 + 3Q^* = 10 - Q^*, \tag{2.3}$$

which gives $Q^* = 2$. Substituting $Q^* = 2$ back into either the supply or demand equation gives the equilibrium price, $P^* = 8$.

Needless to say, we could have graphed Equations 2.1 and 2.2 to arrive at precisely the same solution (see Figure 2.12). The advantage of the algebraic approach is that it is much less painstaking than having to produce accurate drawings of the supply and demand schedules.

EXERCISE 2.4

Find the equilibrium price and quantity in a market whose supply and demand curves are given by $P = 4Q^s$ and $P = 12 - 2Q^d$, respectively.

FIGURE 2.12
Graphs of Equations 2.1 and 2.2
The algebraic and geometric approaches lead to exactly the same equilibrium prices and quantities. The advantage of the algebraic approach is that exact numerical solutions can be achieved more easily. The geometric approach is useful because it gives a more intuitively clear description of the supply and demand curves.

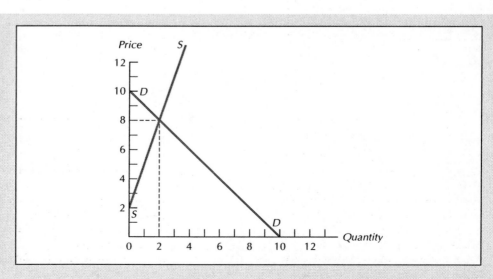

SUMMARY

* The supply curve is generally an upward-sloping line that tells what quantity sellers will offer at any given price. The demand curve is a downward-sloping line that tells what quantity buyers will demand at any given price. In an unregulated market, the equilibrium price and quantity are determined by the intersection of these two curves.

* If price is above its equilibrium, there will be dissatisfied sellers, or excess supply. This condition motivates sellers to cut their prices. By contrast, when prices are below equilibrium, there will be dissatisfied buyers, or excess demand. This condition motivates sellers to charge higher prices. The only stable outcome is the one in which excess demand and excess supply are exactly zero.

* Given the attributes of buyers and sellers, the equilibrium price and quantity represent the best attainable outcome, in the sense that any other price-quantity pair would be worse for at least some buyers or sellers.

* The fact that market outcomes are efficient in this sense does not mean they necessarily command society's approval. On the contrary, we often lament the fact that many buyers enter the market with so little income. Concern for the well-being of the poor has motivated the governments of almost every society to intervene in a variety of ways to alter the outcomes of market forces.

* Sometimes these interventions take the form of laws that peg prices above or below their equilibrium levels. Such laws often generate harmful, if unintended, consequences. Programs such as rent control, for example, interfere with both the rationing and allocative functions of the price mechanism.

They lead to black marketeering and a rapid deterioration of the stock of rental housing. By the same token, price support laws in agriculture tend to enrich large corporate farms while doing little to ease the plight of the small family farm. In almost every instance, it is possible to design an alternative intervention that is better in every respect.

* If the difficulty is that the poor have too little money, the solution is to discover ways of boosting their incomes directly. Legislatures cannot repeal the law of supply and demand. But legislatures do have the capacity to alter the underlying forces that govern the shape and position of supply and demand schedules.

* Supply and demand analysis is the economist's basic tool for predicting how equilibrium prices and quantities will change in response to changes in market forces. Four simple propositions guide this task: (1) an increase in demand will lead to an increase in both the equilibrium price and quantity; (2) a decrease in demand will lead to a decrease in both the equilibrium price and quantity; (3) an increase in supply will lead to a decrease in the equilibrium price and an increase in the equilibrium quantity; and (4) a decrease in supply will lead to an increase in the equilibrium price and a decrease in the equilibrium quantity.

* Incomes, tastes, the prices of substitutes and complements, expectations, and population are among the factors that shift demand schedules. Supply schedules, in turn, are governed by such factors as technology, input prices, the number of suppliers, expectations, and, for agricultural products, the weather.

QUESTIONS FOR REVIEW

1. What is the difference between "scarcity" and "shortage"?

2. What would the supply curve look like for a good that is not scarce? Assuming the good is useful, what would its demand curve look like? Explain why a positive price for a commodity implies that it is scarce.

3. Give two examples of actions taken by the administration of your college or university whose effect is to prevent specific markets from reaching equilibrium.

What evidence of excess supply or excess demand can you cite in these examples?

4. What is the difference between "a reduction in supply" and "a reduction in the quantity supplied"?

5. Identify each of the following as (1) a change in demand or (2) a change in the quantity demanded.
   a. Grape consumption falls because of a consumer boycott.
   b. Grape consumption falls because of a tax on grape producers.

c.   Grape consumption rises because of a good harvest.

d.   Grape consumption rises because of a change in tastes.

6.   When there is excess supply, why is any single seller able to sell all she wants to by offering only a small reduction below the current market price?

7.   Give an example of a market in which the allocative function of price is not very important.

8.   Suppose you are a government official and need to collect revenue by taxing a product. For political reasons, you want the burden of the tax to fall mostly on consumers, not firms (who have been substantial contributors to your campaign fund). What should you look for when picking a product to tax?

9.   Which would a poor person be more likely to accept and why?

a.   A $50,000 Mercedes (immediate resale value = $30,000)

b. $35,000 cash

PROBLEMS

1.   Assume that tea and lemons are complements and that coffee and tea are substitutes.
a.   How, if at all, will the imposition of an effective ceiling price on tea affect the price of lemons? Explain.
b.   How, if at all, will the imposition of an effective ceiling price on tea affect the price of coffee? Explain.

2.   The market for digital video disks (DVDs) has supply and demand curves given by $P' = 2Q^s$ and $P = 42 - Q^d$, respectively.
a.   How many units will be traded at a price of $35? At a price of $14? Which participants will be dissatisfied at these prices?
b.   What quantity of DVDs at what price will be sold in equilibrium?
c.   What is the total revenue from DVD sales?

3.   Hardware and software for computers are complements. Discuss the effects on the equilibrium price and quantity
a.   In the software market, when the price of computer hardware falls.
b.   In the hardware market, when the price of computer software rises.

4.   Suppose a newly released study shows that battery-powered toys harm a child's development and recommends that parents adjust their purchasing behavior accordingly. Use diagrams to show the effect on price and quantity in each of the following markets:
a.   The market for battery-powered toys.
b.   The market for D batteries.
c.   The market for yo-yos (which do not require batteries).

5.   Using diagrams, show what changes in price and quantity would be expected in the following markets under the scenarios given:
a.   *Crude oil:* As petroleum reserves decrease, it becomes more difficult to find and recover crude oil.
b.   *Air travel:* Worries about air safety cause travelers to shy away from air travel.
c.   *Rail travel:* Worries about air safety cause travelers to shy away from air travel.
d.   *Hotel rooms in Hawaii:* Worries about air safety cause travelers to shy away from air travel.
e.   *Milk:* A genetically engineered hormone enables large milk producers to cut production costs.

6.   For each scenario in Problem 5, state whether the effect is a change in demand or just a change in quantity demanded.

7. Suppose demand for seats at football games is $P = 1900 - (1/50)Q$ and supply is fixed at $Q = 90{,}000$ seats.
   a. Find the equilibrium price and quantity of seats for a football game (using algebra and a graph).
   b. Suppose the government prohibits tickets scalping (selling tickets above their face value), and the face value of tickets is \$50 (this policy places a price ceiling at \$50). How many consumers will be dissatisfied (how large is excess demand)?
   c. Suppose the next game is a major rivalry, and so demand jumps to $P = 2100 - (1/50)Q$. How many consumers will be dissatisfied for the big game?
   d. How do the distortions of this price ceiling differ from the more typical case of upward-sloping supply?

8. The demand for apartments is $P = 1200 - Q$ while the supply is $P = Q$ units. The government imposes rent control at $P = \$300/\text{month}$. Suppose demand grows in the market to $P = 1400 - Q$.
   a. How is excess demand affected by the growth in demand for apartments?
   b. At what price would the government have to set the rent control to keep excess demand at the same level as prior to the growth in demand?

9. Suppose demand is $P = 600 - Q$ and supply is $P = Q$ in the soybean market, where Q is tons of soybeans per year. The government sets a price support at $P = \$500/\text{ton}$ and purchases any excess supply at this price. In response, as a long-run adjustment, farmers switch their crops from corn to soybeans, expanding supply to $P = (1/2)Q$.
   a. How does excess supply with the larger supply compare to excess supply prior to the farmers switching crops?
   b. How much more does the government have to spend to buy up the excess supply?

10. How would the equilibrium price and quantity change in the market depicted below if the marginal cost of every producer were to increase by \$2/pound? (Hint: Recall the vertical interpretation of the supply curve discussed in Chapter 1.)

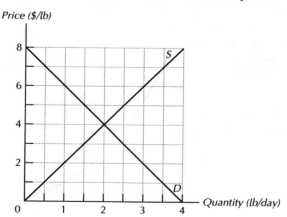

ANSWERS TO IN-CHAPTER EXERCISES

2.1. At a price of \$2/lobster, the quantity demanded is 5000 lobsters/day and the quantity supplied is 1000 lobsters/day, making excess demand equal to 4000 lobsters/day. At a price of \$10/lobster, excess supply is 4000 lobsters/day.

2.2. A rent control level set above the equilibrium price has no effect. The rent will settle at its equilibrium value of \$600/mo.

50   CHAPTER 2   SUPPLY AND DEMAND

2.3. The fall in the price of diesel fuel shifts the supply curve to the right. The report on mercury shifts the demand curve to the left. As shown in the following diagrams, the equilibrium price will go down (both panels) but the equilibrium quantity may go either up (panel *b*) or down (panel *a*).

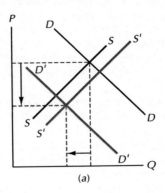 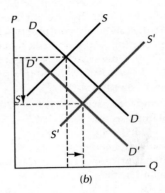

(a)   (b)

2.4. $4Q^* = 12 - 2Q^*$, which yields $Q^* = 2$ and $P^* = 4Q^* = 8$.

APPENDIX

2

HOW DO TAXES AFFECT EQUILIBRIUM PRICES AND QUANTITIES?

Supply and demand analysis is also a useful tool for analyzing the effects of various taxes. In this section we consider a constant tax per unit of output. How will the equilibrium price and quantity of a product be affected if a tax of $T = 10$ is levied on each unit sold by the producer? There are two equivalent ways to approach this question. The first is to suppose that the tax is levied on the seller. In Figure A.2.1, the line SS denotes the original supply schedule. At a price of $P_0 = 25$, sellers were willing to supply Q_0 units of output. When a tax $T = 10$ is levied on sellers, the market price would have to be $P_0 + 10 = 35$ for them to get the same net payment that they used to receive when the price was $P_0 = 25$. At a price of 35, then, suppliers will offer the same amount of output they used to offer at a price of 25. The resulting after-tax supply schedule is the original supply schedule shifted upward by $T = 10$.

In Figure A.2.2, DD represents the demand curve facing the sellers who have been taxed $T = 10$ per unit of output. The effect of the tax is to cause the equilibrium quantity to fall from Q^* to Q_1^*. The price paid by the buyer rises from P^* to P_1^*; and the price, net of the tax, received by the seller falls to $P_1^* - 10$.

Note in Figure A.2.2 that even though the seller pays a tax of T on each product purchased, the total amount the seller receives per unit lies less than T below the old equilibrium price. Note also that even though the tax is collected from the seller, its effect is to increase the price paid by buyers. The burden of the tax is thus divided between the buyer and the seller.

Algebraically, the seller's share of the tax, denoted t_s, is the reduction in the price the seller receives, divided by the tax:

$$t_s = \frac{P^* - (P_1^* - T)}{T}. \tag{A.2.1}$$

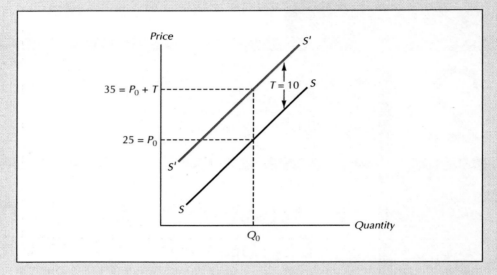

FIGURE A.2.1
A Tax of $T = 10$ Levied on the Seller Shifts the Supply Schedule Upward by T Units
The original supply schedule tells us what price suppliers must charge in order to cover their costs at any given level of output. From the seller's perspective, a tax of $T = 10$ units is the same as a unit-cost increase of 10 units. The new supply curve thus lies 10 units above the old one.

Similarily, the buyer's share of the tax, t_b, is the increase in price (including tax) divided by the tax:

$$t_b = \frac{P_1^* - P^*}{T}.$$ (A.2.2)

EXERCISE A.2.1

Verify that $t_s + t_b = 1$.

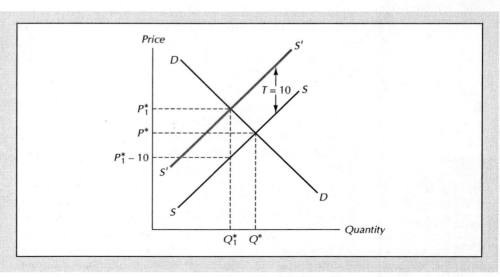

FIGURE A.2.2
Equilibrium Prices and Quantities When a Tax of $T = 10$ Is Levied on the Seller
The tax causes a reduction in equilibrium quantity from Q^* to Q_1^*. The new price paid by the buyer rises from P^* to P_1^*. The new price received by the seller falls from P^* to $P_1^* - 10$.

HOW DO TAXES AFFECT EQUILIBRIUM PRICES AND QUANTITIES?   53

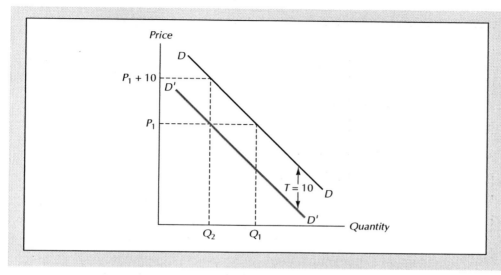

FIGURE A.2.3
The Effect of a Tax of $T = 10$ Levied on the Buyer
Before the tax, buyers would buy Q_1 units at a price of P_1. After the tax, a price of P_1 becomes $P_1 + 10$, which means buyers will buy only Q_2. The effect of the tax is to shift the demand curve downward by 10 units.

In general, t_b and t_s depend on the shapes of the supply and demand schedules. If, for example, supply is highly unresponsive to changes in price, t_b will be close to zero, t_s close to 1. Conversely, if demand is highly unresponsive to price, t_b will be close to 1, t_s close to zero. These claims amount to a statement that a tax tends to fall most heavily on the side of the market that can least escape it. If buyers have no substitute products to which they are prepared to turn, the lion's share of the tax will be passed on to them by suppliers. But if suppliers have no alternative other than to go on supplying a product, most of the burden of a tax will fall on them. As long as the supply curve is positively sloped and the demand curve is negatively sloped, however, both t_s and t_b will be positive.

The second way of analyzing the effect of a tax of $T = 10$ per unit of output is to imagine that the tax is collected directly from the buyer and to analyze how that would affect the demand curve for the product. In Figure A.2.3, the demand curve before the imposition of the tax is denoted by the line DD. At a price of P_1, buyers would demand a quantity of Q_1. After the imposition of the tax, the total amount that buyers have to pay if the product price is P_1 will be $P_1 + 10$. Accordingly, the quantity they demand falls from Q_1 to Q_2. In like fashion, we can reckon the quantity demanded at any other price after imposition of the tax. The resulting after-tax demand curve will be the line $D'D'$ in Figure A.2.3. It is simply the original demand curve translated downward by 10 units.

If line SS in Figure A.2.4 denotes the supply schedule for this market, we can easily trace out the effects of the tax on the equilibrium price and quantity. The equilibrium quantity falls from Q^* to Q_2^*, and the equilibrium pretax price falls from P^* to P_2^*. The total price paid by the buyer after imposition of the tax rises to $P_2^* + 10$.

Is the effect of a tax on the seller any different from the effect of a tax levied on the buyer? Not at all. To illustrate, suppose the supply and demand curves for a market are given by $P = Q^s$ and $P = 10 - Q^d$, respectively, and consider first the effect of a tax of 2 per unit of output imposed on the seller. Figure A.2.5a shows the original supply and demand curves and the new after-tax supply curve, $S'S'$. The original equilibrium price and quantity are both equal to 5. The

54

APPENDIX 2   HOW DO TAXES AFFECT EQUILIBRIUM PRICES AND QUANTITIES?

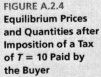

FIGURE A.2.4
Equilibrium Prices and Quantities after Imposition of a Tax of $T = 10$ Paid by the Buyer
The tax causes a reduction in equilibrium quantity from Q^* to Q_2^*. The new price paid by the buyer rises from P^* to $P_2^* + 10$. The new price received by the seller falls from P^* to P_2^*.

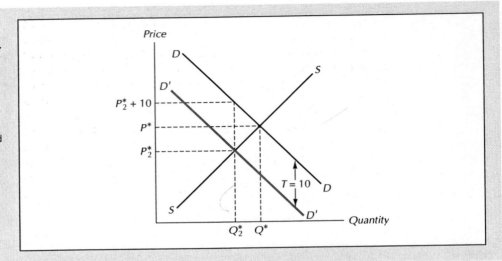

new equilibrium price to the buyer (inclusive of tax) and quantity are 6 and 4, respectively. The price received by sellers, net of the tax, is 4.

Now, consider a tax of 2 per unit of output imposed on the buyers. Figure A.2.5b shows the original supply and demand curves and the new after-tax demand curve, $D'D'$. Note that the effects on price and quantity are exactly the same as in the case of the tax levied on sellers shown in panel a.

EXERCISE A.2.2

Consider a market whose supply and demand curves are given by $P = 4Q^s$ and $P = 12 - 2Q^d$, respectively. How will the equilibrium price and quantity in this market be affected if a tax of 6 per unit of output is imposed on sellers? If the same tax is imposed on buyers?

FIGURE A.2.5
A Tax on the Buyer Leads to the Same Outcome as a Tax on the Seller
The price received by sellers (net of the tax), the price paid by buyers (including tax), and the equilibrium quantity will all be the same when the tax is collected from sellers (panel a) as when it is collected from buyers (panel b).

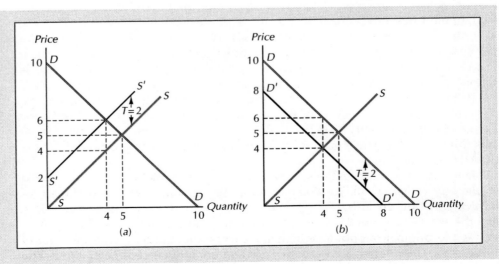

When tax revenues must be raised, many political leaders find it expedient to propose a sales tax on corporations because "they can best afford to pay it." But careful analysis of the effects of a sales tax shows that its burden will be the same whether it is imposed on buyers or sellers. The *legal incidence of the tax* (whether it is imposed on buyers or on sellers) has no effect on the *economic incidence* of the tax (the respective shares of the tax burden borne by buyers and sellers). Economically speaking, the entity from which the tax is actually collected is thus a matter of complete indifference.

A word of caution: When we say that the economic burden of the tax does not depend on the party from whom the tax is directly collected, this does not mean that buyers and sellers always share the burden of taxes equally. Their respective shares may, as noted, be highly unequal. The independence of legal incidence and economic incidence simply means that the burden will be shared in the same way no matter where the tax is placed.

EXERCISE A.2.3

True or false? The steeper the demand curve for a good relative to the supply curve for that good, the greater the proportion of a tax on that good that will fall on buyers. Explain.

PR♀BLEMS

1. The government, fearful that a titanium shortage could jeopardize national security, imposes a tax of $2/oz on the retail price of this rare metal. It collects the tax from titanium sellers. The original supply and demand schedules for titanium are as shown in the diagram. Show, in the same diagram, how the short-run equilibrium price and quantity of titanium will be affected by the tax. Label all important points clearly.

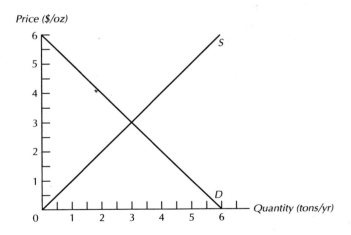

2. In the market for titanium described in Problem 1 (with no tax), suppose that a price floor of $4/oz results in sales of only 2 tons/yr (with no tax). Describe a transaction that will make some buyers and sellers better off without harming others.

3. Suppose the titanium market in Problem 1, with a tax of $2/oz, experiences growth in the demand for titanium because of new-found medical uses. The new demand

curve is $P = 8 - Q$. Find the change in government tax revenue due to the heightened demand for titanium.

4. Suppose instead the titanium market in Problem 2, with no tax but a price floor at \$4/oz, suffers a reduction in supply because of dwindling titanium reserves. The new supply curve is $P = 2 + Q$. How does excess supply change due to the reduction in supply? Is the price floor still binding (does it cause price to rise from its equilibrium level)?

5. Suppose state government levies a tax of \$9 on each DVD sold, collected from sellers.
   a.   What quantity of DVDs will be sold in equilibrium?
   b.   What price do buyers pay?
   c.   How much do buyers now spend in total?
   d.   How much money goes to the government?
   e.   Show the above results graphically.

6. For the tax described in Problem 5,
   a.   What fraction of the tax does the seller bear?
   b.   What fraction of the tax does the buyer bear?

7. President Reagan negotiated a "voluntary" import quota on Japanese cars sold in the United States in the early 1980s. Some of his advisers had recommended that he impose a higher import tax (tariff) instead. Assuming the tariff was in the form of a constant tax T per Japanese car sold in the United States and that T was chosen to produce the same quantity reduction as the quota, how will the prices paid for Japanese cars by U.S. consumers compare under the two policies?

8. Many studies on rats and mice have established that charred meat grilled over hot coals causes cancer. Since the government cannot easily regulate home cooking methods, an alternative method has been proposed to discourage the consumption of barbecued meat. The proposal is to place a 100 percent tax at the retail level on charcoal briquets. Suppose the daily demand for charcoal was $P = 120 - 2Q$ and the supply was $P = 30 + Q$, where P is in dollars and Q is the number of 20-lb bags of charcoal sold weekly.
   a.   What is the before- and after-tax price of charcoal?
   b.   What is the before- and after-tax quantity of charcoal?
   c.   How is the tax divided among sellers and buyers?

9. Supply is $P = 4Q$, while demand is $P = 20$, where P is price in dollars and Q is units of output per week.
   a.   Find the equilibrium price and quantity (using both algebra and a graph).
   b.   If sellers must pay a tax of $T = \$4$/unit, what happens to the quantity exchanged, the price buyers pay, and the price sellers receive (net of the tax)?
   c.   How is the burden of the tax distributed across buyers and sellers and why?

10. Repeat Problem 9, but instead suppose the buyer pays the tax, demand is $P = 28 - Q$, and supply is $P = 20$.

ANSWERS TO APPENDIX EXERCISES

A.2.1 $t_s + t_b = [(P^* - P_1^* + T) + (P_1^* - P^*)]/T = T/T = 1.$

A.2.2   The original price and quantity are given by $P^* = 8$ and $Q^* = 2$, respectively. The supply curve with the tax is given by $P = 6 + 4Q^s$. Letting P' and Q' denote the new equilibrium values of price and quantity, we now have $6 + 4Q' = 12 - 2Q'$, which yields $Q' = 1$, $P' = 10$, where P' is the price paid by buyers. $P' - 6 = 4$ is the price received by sellers. Alternatively, the demand curve with a tax of 6 levied on buyers is given by $P = 6 - 2Q^d$, and we have $4Q' = 6' - 2Q'$, which again yields $Q' = 1$. $P'' = 4$, where P'' is the price received by sellers. $P'' + T = P'' + 6 = 10$ is the price paid by buyers.

A.2.3   True.

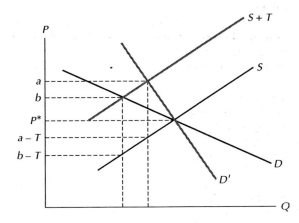

Buyer's share for tax with $D' = (a - P^*)/T$
Buyer's share for tax with $D = (b - P^*)/T$

CHAPTER

3

RATIONAL CONSUMER CHOICE

You have just cashed your monthly allowance check and are on your way to the local music store to buy an Eric Clapton CD you've been wanting. The price of the disc is $10. In scenario 1 you lose $10 on your way to the store. In scenario 2 you buy the disc and then trip and fall on your way out of the store; the disc shatters as it hits the sidewalk. Try to imagine your frame of mind in each scenario.

a. Would you proceed to buy the disc in scenario 1?
b. Would you return to buy the disc in scenario 2?

These questions[1] were recently put to a large class of undergraduates who had never taken an economics course. In response to the first question, 54 percent answered yes, saying they would buy the disc after losing the $10 bill. But only 32 percent answered yes to the second question—68 percent said they would *not* buy the disc after having broken the first one. There is, of course, no "correct" answer to either question. The events described will have more of an impact, for example, on a poor consumer than on a rich one. Yet a moment's reflection reveals that your behavior in one scenario logically should be exactly the same as in the other. After all, in both scenarios, the only economically relevant change is that you now have $10 less to spend than before. This might well mean that you will want to give up having the disc; or it could mean saving less or giving up some other good or service that you would have bought instead. But your choice should not be affected by the particular way you happened to become $10 poorer. In both scenarios, the cost of the disc is $10, and the benefits you will

---

[1]These questions are patterned after similar questions posed by decision theorists Daniel Kahneman and Amos Tversky (see Chapter 8).

62   CHAPTER 3   RATIONAL CONSUMER CHOICE

receive from listening to it are also the same. You should either buy the disc in both scenarios or not buy it in both scenarios. And yet, as noted, many people said they would behave differently in the two scenarios.

CHAPTER PREVIEW

Our task in this chapter is to set forth the economist's basic model for answering questions such as the ones posed above. This model is known as the theory of *rational consumer choice*. It underlies all individual purchase decisions, which in turn add up to the demand curves we worked with in the preceding chapter.

Rational choice theory begins with the assumption that consumers enter the marketplace with well-defined preferences. Taking prices as given, their task is to allocate their incomes to best serve these preferences. Two steps are required to carry out this task. Step 1 is to describe the various combinations of goods the consumer is *able* to buy. We will see that these combinations depend on both her income level and the prices of the goods. Step 2 then is to select from among the feasible combinations the particular one that she *prefers* to all others. Analysis of step 2 requires some means of describing her preferences, in particular, a summary of her ranking of the desirability of all feasible combinations. Formal development of these two elements of the theory will occupy our attention throughout this chapter. Because the first element—describing the set of possibilities—is much less abstract than the second, let us begin with it.

THE OPPORTUNITY SET OR BUDGET CONSTRAINT

bundle a particular combination of two or more goods.

For simplicity, we start by considering a world with only two goods,[2] shelter and food. A **bundle** of goods is the term used to describe a particular combination of shelter, measured in square yards per week, and food, measured in pounds per week. Thus, in Figure 3.1, one bundle (bundle *A*) might consist of 5 sq yd/wk of shelter and 7 lb/wk of food, while another (bundle *B*) consists of 3 sq yd/wk of shelter and 8 lb/wk of food. For brevity's sake, we may use the notation (5, 7) to denote bundle *A* and the notation (3, 8) to denote bundle *B*. More generally,

FIGURE 3.1
Two Bundles of Goods
A bundle is a specific combination of goods. Bundle *A* has 5 units of shelter and 7 units of food. Bundle *B* has 3 units of shelter and 8 units of food.

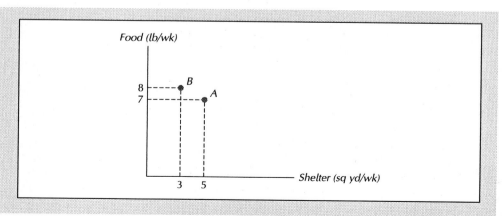

---

[2]As economists use the term, a "good" may refer to either a product or a service.

(S_0, F_0) will denote the bundle with S_0 sq yd/wk of shelter and F_0 lb/wk of food. By convention, the first number of the pair in any bundle represents the good measured along the horizontal axis.

Note that the units on both axes are *flows,* which means physical quantities per unit of time—pounds per week, square yards per week. Consumption is always measured as a flow. It is important to keep track of the time dimension because without it there would be no way to evaluate whether a given quantity of consumption was large or small. (Suppose all you know is that your food consumption is 4 lb. If that's how much you eat each day, it's a lot. But if that's all you eat in a month, you're not likely to survive for long.)[3]

Suppose the consumer's income is $M = \$100/\text{wk}$, all of which she spends on some combination of food and shelter. (Note that income is also a flow.) Suppose further that the prices of shelter and food are $P_S = \$5/\text{sq yd}$ and $P_F = \$10/\text{lb}$, respectively. If the consumer spent all her income on shelter, she could buy $M/P_S = (\$100/\text{wk}) \div (\$5/\text{sq yd}) = 20$ sq yd/wk. That is, she could buy the bundle consisting of 20 sq yd/wk of shelter and 0 lb/wk of food, denoted (20, 0). Alternatively, suppose the consumer spent all her income on food. She would then get the bundle consisting of $M/P_F = (\$100/\text{wk}) \div (\$10/\text{lb})$, which is 10 lb/wk of food and 0 sq yd/wk of shelter, denoted (0, 10).

In the preceding discussion, note that the units in which consumption goods are measured are themselves subject to the standard rules of arithmetic. For example, when we simplify the expression on the right-hand side of the equation $M/P_S = (\$100/\text{wk}) \div (\$5/\text{sq yd})$, we are essentially dividing one fraction by another, so we follow the standard rule of inverting the fraction in the denominator and multiplying it by the fraction in the numerator: $(\text{sq yd}/\$5) \times (\$100/\text{wk}) = (\$100 \times \text{sq yd})/(\$5 \times \text{wk})$. After dividing both the numerator and denominator of the fraction on the right hand side of this last equation by \$5, we have 20 sq yd/wk, which is the maximum amount of shelter the consumer can buy with an income of \$100/wk. Similarly, $M/P_F = (\$100/\text{wk}) \div (\$10/\text{lb})$, simplifies to 10 lb/wk, the maximum amount of food the consumer can purchase with an income of \$100/wk.

In Figure 3.2 these polar cases are labeled K and L, respectively. The consumer is also able to purchase any other bundle that lies along the straight line that joins points K and L. [Verify, for example, that the bundle (12, 4) lies on this same line.] This line is called the **budget constraint** and is labeled B in the diagram.

Recall the maxim from high school algebra that the slope of a straight line is its "rise" over its "run" (the change in its vertical position divided by the corresponding change in its horizontal position). Here, note that the slope of the budget constraint is its vertical intercept (the rise) divided by its horizontal intercept (the corresponding run): $-(10\text{ lb/wk})/(20\text{ sq yd/wk}) = -\frac{1}{2}\text{ lb/sq yd}$. (Note again how the units obey the standard rules of arithmetic.) The minus sign signifies that the budget line falls as it moves to the right—that it has a negative slope. More generally, if M denotes the consumer's weekly income, and P_S and P_F denote the prices of shelter and food, respectively, the horizontal and vertical intercepts will be given by (M/P_S) and (M/P_F), respectively. Thus the general formula for the slope of the budget constraint is given by $-(M/P_F)/$

budget constraint the set of all bundles that exactly exhaust the consumer's income at given prices. Also called the *budget line.*

---

[3]The flow aspect of consumption also helps us alleviate any concern about goods not being divisible. If you consume 1.5 lb/mo; then you consume 18 lb/yr, which is a whole number.

64   CHAPTER 3   RATIONAL CONSUMER CHOICE

FIGURE 3.2
The Budget Constraint, or Budget Line
Line *B* describes the set of all bundles the consumer can purchase for given values of income and prices. Its slope is the negative of the price of shelter divided by the price of food. In absolute value, this slope is the opportunity cost of an additional unit of shelter—the number of units of food that must be sacrificed in order to purchase one additional unit of shelter at market prices.

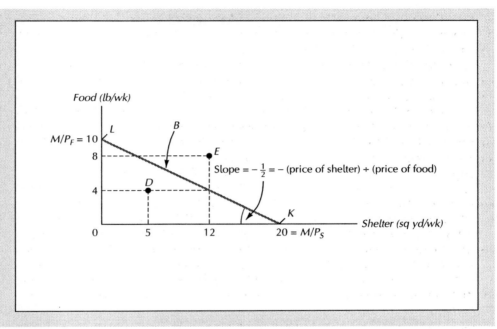

affordable set   bundles on or below the budget constraint; bundles for which the required expenditure at given prices is less than or equal to the income available.

$(M/P_S) = -P_S/P_F$, which is simply the negative of the price ratio of the two goods. Given their respective prices, it is the rate at which food can be exchanged for shelter. Thus, in Figure 3.2, 1 lb of food can be exchanged for 2 sq yd of shelter. In the language of opportunity cost from Chapter 1, we would say that the opportunity cost of an additional square yard of shelter is $P_S/P_F = \frac{1}{2}$ lb of food.

In addition to being able to buy any of the bundles along her budget constraint, the consumer is also able to purchase any bundle that lies within the *budget triangle* bounded by it and the two axes. *D* is one such bundle in Figure 3.2. Bundle *D* costs \$65/wk, which is well below the consumer's income of \$100/wk. The bundles on or within the budget triangle are also referred to as the *feasible set,* or **affordable set.** Bundles like *E* that lie outside the budget triangle are said to be *infeasible,* or *unaffordable.* At a cost of \$140/wk, *E* is simply beyond the consumer's reach.

If *S* and *F* denote the quantities of shelter and food, respectively, the budget constraint must satisfy the following equation:

$$P_S S + P_F F = M, \tag{3.1}$$

which says simply that the consumer's weekly expenditure on shelter ($P_S S$) plus her weekly expenditure on food ($P_F F$) must add up to her weekly income (M). To express the budget constraint in the manner conventionally used to represent the formula for a straight line, we solve Equation 3.1 for *F* in terms of *S*, which yields

$$F = \frac{M}{P_F} - \frac{P_S}{P_F} S \tag{3.2}$$

Equation 3.2 is another way of seeing that the vertical intercept of the budget constraint is given by M/P_F and its slope by $-(P_S/P_F)$. The equation for the budget constraint in Figure 3.2 is $F = 10 - \frac{1}{2} S$.

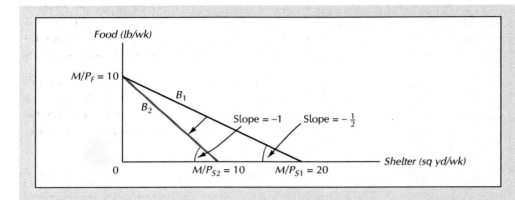

FIGURE 3.3
The Effect of a Rise in the Price of Shelter
When shelter goes up in price, the vertical intercept of the budget constraint remains the same. The original budget constraint rotates inward about this intercept.

Budget Shifts Due to Price or Income Changes

Price Changes   The slope and position of the budget constraint are fully determined by the consumer's income and the prices of the respective goods. Change any one of these factors and we have a new budget constraint. Figure 3.3 shows the effect of an increase in the price of shelter from $P_{S1} = \$5/\text{sq yd}$ to $P_{S2} = \$10$. Since both weekly income and the price of food are unchanged, the vertical intercept of the consumer's budget constraint stays the same. The rise in the price of shelter rotates the budget constraint inward about this intercept, as shown in the diagram.

Note in Figure 3.3 that even though the price of food has not changed, the new budget constraint, B_2, curtails not only the amount of shelter the consumer can buy but also the amount of food.[4]

EXERCISE 3.1

Show the effect on the budget constraint B_1 in Figure 3.3 of a fall in the price of shelter from $5/sq yd to $4/sq yd.

In Exercise 3.1, you saw that a fall in the price of shelter again leaves the vertical intercept of the budget constraint unchanged. This time the budget constraint rotates outward. Note also in Exercise 3.1 that although the price of food remains unchanged, the new budget constraint enables the consumer to buy bundles that contain not only more shelter but also more food than she could afford on the original budget constraint.

EXERCISE 3.2

Show the effect on the budget constraint B_1 in Figure 3.3 of a rise in the price of food from $10/lb to $20/lb.

---

[4]The single exception to this statement involves the vertical intercept (0, 10), which lies on both the original and the new budget constraints.

66   CHAPTER 3   RATIONAL CONSUMER CHOICE

Exercise 3.2 demonstrates that when the price of food changes, the budget constraint rotates about its horizontal intercept. Note also that even though income and the price of shelter remain the same, the new budget constraint curtails not only the amount of food the consumer can buy but also the amount of shelter.

When we change the price of only one good, we necessarily change the slope of the budget constraint, $-P_S/P_F$. The same is true if we change both prices by different proportions. But as Exercise 3.3 will illustrate, changing both prices by exactly the same proportion gives rise to a new budget constraint with the same slope as before.

EXERCISE 3.3

Show the effect on the budget constraint B_3 in Figure 3.3 of a rise in the price of food from $10/lb to $20/lb and a rise in the price of shelter from $5/sq yd to $10/sq yd.

Note from Exercise 3.3 that the effect of doubling the prices of both food and shelter is to shift the budget constraint inward and parallel to the original budget constraint. The important lesson of this exercise is that the slope of a budget constraint tells us only about *relative prices*, nothing about how high prices are in absolute terms. When the prices of food and shelter change in the same proportion, the opportunity cost of shelter in terms of food remains the same as before.

Income Changes   The effect of a change in income is much like the effect of an equal proportional change in all prices. Suppose, for example, that our hypothetical consumer's income is cut by half, from $100/wk to $50/wk. The horizontal intercept of the consumer's budget constraint then falls from 20 sq yd/wk to 10 sq yd/wk, and the vertical intercept falls from 10 lb/wk to 5 lb/wk, as shown in Figure 3.4. Thus the new budget, B_2, is parallel to the old, B_1, each with a slope of $-\frac{1}{2}$. In terms of its effect on what the consumer can buy, cutting income by one-half is thus no different from doubling each price. Precisely the same budget constraint results from both changes.

FIGURE 3.4
The Effect of Cutting Income by Half
Both horizontal and vertical intercepts fall by half. The new budget constraint has the same slope as the old but is closer to the origin.

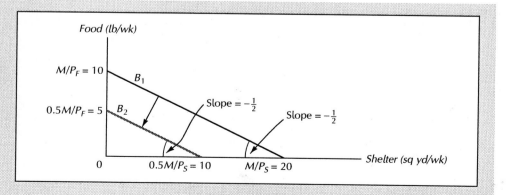

EXERCISE 3.4

Show the effect on the budget constraint B_1 in Figure 3.4 of an increase in income from \$100/wk to \$120/wk.

Exercise 3.4 illustrates that an increase in income shifts the budget constraint parallel outward. As in the case of an income reduction, the slope of the budget constraint remains the same.

Budgets Involving More Than Two Goods

The examples discussed so far have all been ones in which the consumer is faced with the opportunity to buy only two different goods. Needless to say, not many consumers face such narrow options. In its most general form, the consumer budgeting problem can be posed as a choice between not two but N different goods, where N can be an indefinitely large number. With only two goods ($N = 2$), the budget constraint is a straight line, as we just saw. With three goods ($N = 3$), it is a plane. When we have more than three goods, the budget constraint becomes what mathematicians call a *hyperplane,* or *multidimensional plane.* The only real difficulty is in representing this multidimensional case geometrically. We are just not very good at visualizing surfaces that have more than three dimensions.

The nineteenth-century economist Alfred Marshall proposed a disarmingly simple solution to this problem. It is to view the consumer's choice as being one between a particular good—call it X—and an amalgam of other goods, denoted Y. This amalgam is generally called the **composite good.** By convention, the units of the composite good are defined so that its price is \$1 per unit. This convention enables us to think of the composite good as the amount of income the consumer has left over after buying the good X. Equivalently, it is the amount of money the consumer spends on goods other than X. For the moment, all the examples we consider will be ones in which consumers spend all their incomes. In Chapter 5 we will use the rational choice model to analyze the decision to save.

To illustrate how the composite good concept is used, suppose the consumer has an income level of \$$M$/wk, and the price of X is given by P_X. The consumer's budget constraint may then be represented as a straight line in the X, Y plane, as shown in Figure 3.5. Because the price of a unit of the composite

composite good in a choice between a good X and numerous other goods, the amount of money the consumer spends on those other goods.

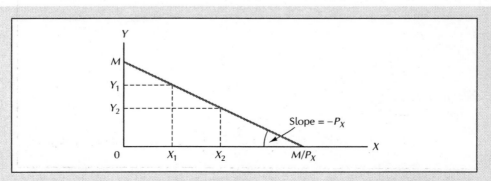

FIGURE 3.5
The Budget Constraint with the Composite Good
The vertical axis measures the amount of money spent each month on all goods other than X.

68   CHAPTER 3   RATIONAL CONSUMER CHOICE

good is taken to be $1, if the consumer devotes none of his income to X, he will be able to buy M units of the composite good. All this means is that he will have M available to spend on other goods if he buys no X. Alternatively, if he spends all his income on X, he will be able to purchase the bundle $(M/P_X, 0)$. Since the price of Y is assumed to be 1/unit, the slope of the budget constraint is simply $-P_X$.

As before, the budget constraint summarizes the various combinations of bundles that exhaust the consumer's income. Thus, the consumer can have X_1 units of X and Y_1 units of the composite good in Figure 3.5, or X_2 and Y_2, or any other combination that lies on the budget constraint.

Kinked Budget Constraints

The budget constraints we have seen so far have all been straight lines. When relative prices are constant, the opportunity cost of one good in terms of any other is the same, no matter what bundle of goods we already have. But sometimes the budget constraints we encounter in practice are kinked lines. By way of illustration, consider the following example of quantity discounts.

EXAMPLE 3.1

The Gigawatt Power Company charges $0.10 per kilowatt-hour (kWh) for the first 1000 kWh of power purchased by a residential customer each month, but only $0.05/kWh for all additional kWh. For a residential customer with a monthly income of $400, graph the budget constraint for electric power and the composite good.

If the consumer buys no electric power at all, he will have $400/mo available for the purchase of other goods. Thus the vertical intercept of his budget constraint is the point (0, 400). As shown in Figure 3.6, for each of the first 1000 kWh he buys, he must give up $0.10, which means that the slope of his budget constraint starts out at $-\frac{1}{10}$. Then at 1000 kWh/mo, the price falls to $0.05/kWh, which means that the slope of his budget constraint from that point rightward is only $-\frac{1}{20}$.

FIGURE 3.6
A Quantity Discount Gives Rise to a Nonlinear Budget Constraint
Once electric power consumption reaches 1000 kWh/mo, the opportunity cost of additional power falls from $0.10/kWh to $0.05/kWh.

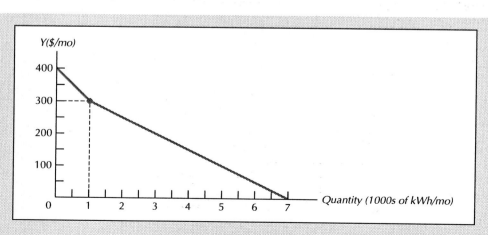

Note that along the budget constraint shown in Figure 3.6, the opportunity cost of electricity depends on how much electricity the consumer has already purchased. Consider a consumer who now uses 1020 kWh each month and is trying to decide whether to leave his front porch light on all night, which would result in an additional consumption of 20 kWh/mo. Leaving his light on will cost him an extra \$1/mo. Had his usual consumption level been only 980 kWh/mo, however, the cost of leaving the front porch light on would have been \$2/mo. On the basis of this difference in the opportunity cost of additional electricity, we can predict that people who already use a lot of electricity (more than 1000 kWh/mo) should be more likely than others to leave their porch lights burning at night.

EXERCISE 3.5

Suppose instead Amperage Electric Power charged \$0.05/kWh for the first 1000 kWh of power purchased by a residential consumer each month, but \$0.10/kWh each for all additional kilowatt-hours. For a residential consumer with a monthly income of \$400, graph the budget constraint for electric power and the composite good. What if the rate jumps to \$0.10/kWh for *all* kilowatt-hours if power consumption in a month exceeds 1000 kWh (where the higher rate applies to all, not just the additional, kilowatt-hours)?

If the Budget Constraint Is the Same, the Decision Should Be the Same

Even without knowing anything about the consumer's preferences, we can use budgetary information to make certain inferences about how a rational consumer will behave. Suppose, for example, that the consumer's tastes do not change over time and that he is confronted with exactly the same budget constraint in each of two different situations. If he is rational, he should make exactly the same choice in both cases. After all, if the budget constraint is the same as before, the consumer has exactly the same menu of possible bundles available as before; and since we have no reason to believe that his ranking of the desirability of these bundles has changed, the most desirable of the bundles originally available will again be the most desirable available bundle. As the following example makes clear, however, it may not always be immediately apparent that the budget constraints are in fact the same.

EXAMPLE 3.2

On one occasion, Gowdy fills his car's tank with gasoline on the evening before his departure on a fishing trip. He awakens to discover that a thief has siphoned out all but 1 gallon from his 21-gallon tank. On another occasion, he plans to stop for gas on his way out the next morning before he goes fishing. He awakens to discover that he has lost \$40 from his wallet. If gasoline sells for \$2/gal and the round-trip will consume 5 gallons, how, if at all, should Gowdy's decision about whether to take the fishing trip differ in the two cases? (Assume that, monetary costs aside, the inconvenience of having to refill his tank is negligible.)

Suppose Gowdy's income is M/mo. Before his loss, his budget constraint is line B_1 in Figure 3.7. In both instances described, his budget constraint at the moment he discovers his loss will shift inward to B_2. If he does not take the trip, he will have $M - \$40$ available to spend on other goods in both cases. And if he does take the trip, he will have to purchase the required gasoline at \$2/gal in both cases. No matter what the source of the loss, the remaining opportunities are exactly the same. If Gowdy's budget is tight, he may decide to cancel his trip. Otherwise, he may go despite the loss. But because his budget constraint and tastes are the same in the lost-cash case as in the stolen-gas case, it would not be rational for him to take the trip in one instance but not in the other.

Note that the situation described in Example 3.2 has the same structure as the one described in the broken-disc example with which we began this chapter. It too is one in which the decision should be the same in both instances because the budget constraint and preferences are the same in each.

Although the rational choice model makes clear that the decisions *should* be the same if the budget constraints and preferences are the same, people sometimes choose differently. The difficulty is often that the way the different situations are described sometimes causes people to overlook the essential similarities between them. For instance, in Example 3.2, many people erroneously conclude that the cost of taking the trip is higher in the stolen-gas case than in the lost-money case, and so they are less likely to take the trip in the former instance. Similarly, many people were less inclined to buy the disc after having broken the first one than after having lost \$10 because they thought, incorrectly, that the disc would cost more under the broken-disc scenario. As we have seen, however, the amount that will be saved by not buying the disc, or by not taking the trip, is exactly the same under each scenario.

To recapitulate briefly, the budget constraint or budget line summarizes the combinations of bundles that the consumer is able to buy. Its position is determined jointly by income and prices. From the set of feasible bundles, the consumer's task is to pick the particular one she likes best. To identify this bundle, we need some means of summarizing the consumer's preferences over all possible bundles she might consume. We now turn to this task.

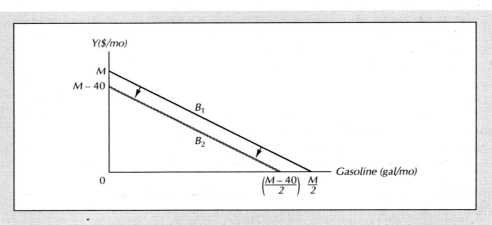

FIGURE 3.7
Budget Constraints Following Theft of Gasoline, Loss of Cash
A theft of \$40 worth of gasoline has exactly the same effect on the budget constraint as the loss of \$40 in cash. The bundle chosen should therefore be the same, irrespective of the source of the loss.

CONSUMER PREFERENCES

For simplicity, let us again begin by considering a world with only two goods: shelter and food. A **preference ordering** is a scheme that enables the consumer to rank different bundles of goods in terms of their desirability, or order of preference. Consider two bundles, *A* and *B*. For concreteness, suppose that *A* contains 4 sq yd/wk of shelter and 2 lb/wk of food, while *B* has 3 sq yd/wk of shelter and 3 lb/wk of food. Knowing nothing about a consumer's preferences, we can say nothing about which of these bundles he will prefer. *A* has more shelter but less food than *B*. Someone who spends a lot of time at home would probably choose *A*, while someone with a rapid metabolism might be more likely to choose *B*.

> **preference ordering** a scheme whereby the consumer ranks all possible consumption bundles in order of preference.

In general, we assume that for any two such bundles, the consumer is able to make one of three possible statements: (1) *A* is preferred to *B*, (2) *B* is preferred to *A*, or (3) *A* and *B* are equally attractive. The preference ordering enables the consumer to rank different bundles but not to make more precise quantitative statements about their relative desirability. Thus, the consumer might be able to say that he prefers *A* to *B* but not that *A* provides twice as much satisfaction as *B*.

Preference orderings often differ widely among consumers. One person will like Rachmaninoff, another the Red Hot Chili Peppers. Despite these differences, however, most preference orderings share several important features. More specifically, economists generally assume four simple properties of preference orderings. These properties allow us to construct the concise analytical representation of preferences we need for the budget allocation problem.

1. Completeness   A preference ordering is *complete* if it enables the consumer to rank all possible combinations of goods and services. Taken literally, the completeness assumption is virtually always false, for there are many goods we know too little about to be able to evaluate decisively. It is nonetheless a useful simplifying assumption for the analysis of choices among bundles of goods with which consumers are familiar. Its real intent is to rule out instances like the one portrayed in the fable of Buridan's ass. The hungry animal was unable to choose between two bales of hay in front of him and starved to death as a result.

2. More-Is-Better   The more-is-better property of preference orderings means simply that, other things equal, more of a good is preferred to less. We can, of course, think of examples of more of something making us worse off rather than better (as with someone who has overeaten). But these examples usually contemplate some sort of practical difficulty, such as having a self-control problem or being unable to store a good for future use. As long as people can freely dispose of goods they don't want, having more of something can't make them worse off.

As an example of the application of the more-is-better assumption, consider two bundles: *A*, which has 12 sq yd/wk of shelter and 10 lb/wk of food, and *B*, which has 12 sq yd/wk of shelter and 11 lb/wk of food. The assumption tells us that *B* is preferred to *A*, because it has more food and no less shelter.

3. Transitivity   If you like steak better than hamburger, and you like hamburger better than hot dogs, then you are probably someone who likes steak better than hot dogs. To say that a consumer's preference ordering is *transitive* means that, for any three bundles *A*, *B*, and *C*, if he prefers *A* to *B* and prefers *B* to *C*, then he always prefers *A* to *C*. For example, suppose *A* is (4, 2), *B* is (3, 3), and *C* is (2, 4). If you prefer (4, 2) over (3, 3) and you prefer (3, 3) over (2, 4), then you must prefer (4, 2) over (2, 4). The preference relationship is thus assumed to be like the relationship used to compare heights of people. If O'Neal is taller than Horry and Horry is taller than Bryant, we know that O'Neal must be taller than Bryant.

Not all comparative relationships are transitive. The relationship "half sibling," for example, is not. I have a half sister who, in turn, has three half sisters of her own. But her half sisters are not my half sisters. A similar nontransitivity is shown by the relationship "defeats in football." Some seasons, Ohio State defeats Michigan, and Michigan defeats Michigan State, but that doesn't tell us that Ohio State will necessarily defeat Michigan State.

Transitivity is a simple consistency property and applies as well to the relation "equally attractive as" and to any combination of it and the "preferred to" relation. For example, if *A* is equally attractive as *B* and *B* is equally attractive as *C*, it follows that *A* is equally attractive as *C*. Similarly, if *A* is preferred to *B* and *B* is equally attractive as *C*, it follows that *A* is preferred to *C*.

The transitivity assumption can be justified as eliminating the potential for a "money pump" problem. To illustrate, suppose you prefer *A* to *B* and *B* to *C*, but now suppose you actually prefer *C* over *A*, so that your preferences are intransitive. If you start with *C*, you would trade *C* for *B*, trade *B* for *A*, and then trade *A* for *C*. This cycle could continue forever. If in each stage you were charged a tiny fee for the trade, you would spend all your money on trading and make the other trader very rich. Clearly, preferences that permit you to be drained of all your money are problematic.

As reasonable as the transitivity property sounds, we will see examples in later chapters of behavior that seems inconsistent with it. But it is an accurate description of preferences in most instances, and unless otherwise stated, we will adopt it throughout as a working assumption.

4. Convexity   Mixtures of goods are preferable to extremes. If you are indifferent between two bundles *A* and *B*, your preferences are convex if you prefer a bundle that contains half of *A* and half of *B* (or any other mixture) to either of the original bundles. For example, suppose you are indifferent between *A* = (4, 0) and *B* = (0, 4). If your preferences are convex, you will prefer the bundle (2, 2) to each of the more extreme bundles. This property conveys the sense that we like balance in our mix of consumption goods.

Indifference Curves

Let us consider some implications of these assumptions about preference orderings. Most important, they enable us to generate a graphical description of the consumer's preferences. To see how, consider first the bundle *A* in Figure 3.8, which has 12 sq yd/wk of shelter and 10 lb/wk of food. The more-is-better assumption tells us that all bundles to the northeast of *A* are preferred to *A*, and that *A*, in turn, is preferred to all those to the southwest of *A*. Thus, the more-is-better assumption tells us that *Z*, which has 28 sq yd/wk of shelter and 12 lb/wk of food, is preferred to *A* and that *A*, in turn, is preferred to *W*, which has only 6 sq yd/wk of shelter and 4 lb/wk of food.

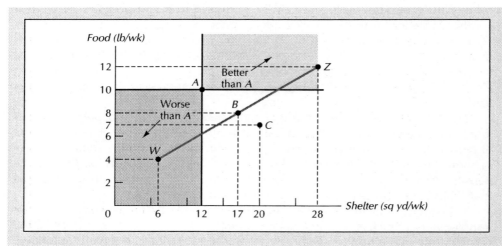

FIGURE 3.8
Generating Equally Preferred Bundles
Z is preferred to A because it has more of each good than A has. For the same reason, A is preferred to W. It follows that on the line joining W and Z there must be a bundle B that is equally attractive as A. In similar fashion, we can find a bundle C that is equally attractive as B.

Now consider the set of bundles that lie along the line joining W and Z. Because Z is preferred to A and A is preferred to W, it follows that as we move from Z to W we must encounter a bundle that is equally attractive as A. (The intuition behind this claim is the same as the intuition that tells us that if we climb on any continuous path on a mountainside from one point at 1000 feet above sea level to another at 2000 feet, we must pass through every intermediate altitude along the way.) Let B denote the bundle that is equally attractive as A, and suppose it contains 17 sq yd/wk of shelter and 8 lb/wk of food. (The exact amounts of each good in B will of course depend on the specific consumer whose preferences we are talking about.) The more-is-better assumption also tells us that there will be only one such bundle on the straight line between W and Z. Points on that line to the northeast of B are all better than B; those to the southwest of B are all worse.

In precisely the same fashion, we can find another point—call it C—that is equally attractive as B. C is shown as the bundle (20, 7), where the specific quantities in C again depend on the preferences of the consumer under consideration. By the transitivity assumption, we know that C is also equally attractive as A (since C is equally attractive as B, which is equally attractive as A).

We can repeat this process as often as we like, and the end result will be an **indifference curve,** a set of bundles all of which are equally attractive as the original bundle A, and hence also equally attractive as one another. This set is shown as the curve labeled I in Figure 3.9. It is called an indifference curve because the consumer is indifferent among all the bundles that lie along it.

An indifference curve also permits us to compare the satisfaction implicit in bundles that lie along it with those that lie either above or below it. It permits us, for example, to compare bundle C (20, 7) to bundle K (23, 4), which has less food and more shelter than C has. We know that C is equally attractive as D (25, 6) because both bundles lie along the same indifference curve. D, in turn, is preferred to K because of the more-is-better assumption: It has 2 sq yd/wk more shelter and 2 lb/wk more food than K has. Transitivity, finally, tells us that since C is equally attractive as D and D is preferred to K, C must be preferred to K.

indifference curve a set of bundles among which the consumer is indifferent.

74   CHAPTER 3   RATIONAL CONSUMER CHOICE

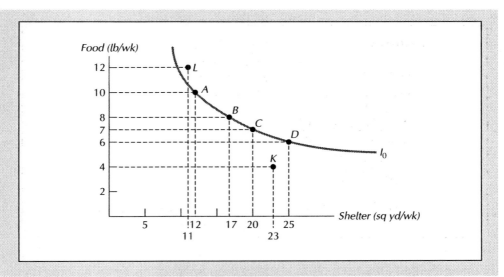

FIGURE 3.9
An Indifference Curve
An indifference curve is a set of bundles that the consumer considers equally attractive. Any bundle, such as *L*, that lies above an indifference curve is preferred to any bundle on the indifference curve. Any bundle on the indifference curve, in turn, is preferred to any bundle, such as *K*, that lies below the indifference curve.

indifference map   a representative sample of the set of a consumer's indifference curves, used as a graphical summary of her preference ordering.

By analogous reasoning, we can say that bundle *L* is preferred to *A*. *In general, bundles that lie above an indifference curve are all preferred to the bundles that lie on it. Similarly, bundles that lie an indifference curve are all preferred to those that lie below it.*

The completeness property of preferences implies that there is an indifference curve that passes through every possible bundle. That being so, we can represent a consumer's preferences with an **indifference map,** an example of which is shown in Figure 3.10. This indifference map shows just four of the infinitely many indifference curves that, taken together, yield a complete description of the consumer's preferences.

The numbers $I_1, \ldots, I_4$ in Figure 3.10 are index values used to denote the order of preference that corresponds to the respective indifference curves. Any index numbers would do equally well provided they satisfied the property $I_1 < I_2 < I_3 < I_4$. In representing the consumer's preferences, what really counts is the *ranking* of the indifference curves, not the particular numerical values we assign to them.[5]

The four properties of preference orderings imply four important properties of indifference curves and indifference maps:

1. Indifference curves are ubiquitous. Any bundle has an indifference curve passing through it. This property is assured by the completeness property of preferences.

2. Indifference curves are downward-sloping. An upward-sloping indifference curve would violate the more-is-better property by saying a bundle with more of both goods is equivalent to a bundle with less of both.

3. Indifference curves (from the same indifference map) cannot cross. To see why, suppose that two indifference curves did, in fact, cross as in Figure 3.11. The following statements would then have to be true:

---
[5]For a more complete discussion of this issue, see pp. 96–98 of the appendix to this chapter.

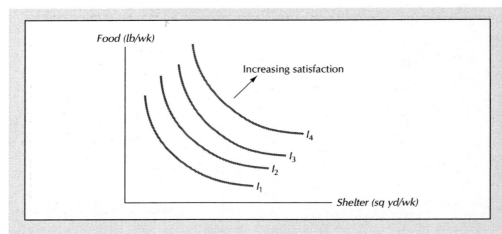

FIGURE 3.10
Part of an Indifference Map
The entire set of a consumer's indifference curves is called the consumer's indifference map. Bundles on any indifference curve are less preferred than bundles on a higher indifference curve, and more preferred than bundles on a lower indifference curve.

E is equally attractive as D (because they each lie on the same indifference curve).

D is equally attractive as F (because they each lie on the same indifference curve).

E is equally attractive as F (by the transitivity assumption).

But we also know that

F is preferred to E (because more is better).

Because it is not possible for the statements E *is equally attractive as F* and *F is preferred to E* to be true simultaneously, the assumption that two indifference curves cross thus implies a contradiction. The conclusion is that the original proposition must be true, namely, two indifference curves cannot cross.

4. Indifference curves become less steep as we move downward and to the right along them. As discussed below, this property is implied by the convexity property of preferences.

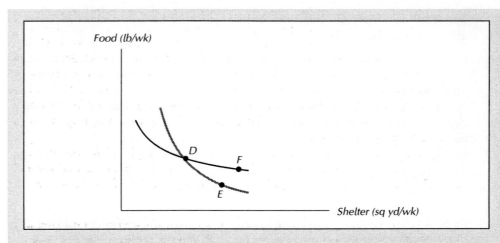

FIGURE 3.11
Why Two Indifference Curves Do Not Cross
If indifference curves were to cross, they would have to violate at least one of the assumed properties of preference orderings.

76   CHAPTER 3 RATIONAL CONSUMER CHOICE

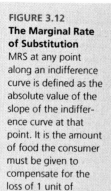

FIGURE 3.12
The Marginal Rate of Substitution
MRS at any point along an indifference curve is defined as the absolute value of the slope of the indifference curve at that point. It is the amount of food the consumer must be given to compensate for the loss of 1 unit of shelter.

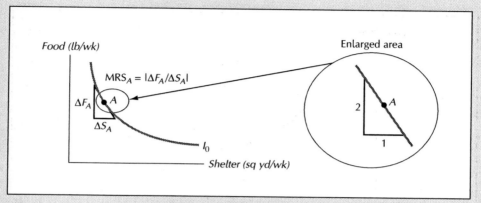

Trade-Offs between Goods

An important property of a consumer's preferences is the rate at which he is willing to exchange, or "trade off," one good for another. This rate is represented at any point on an indifference curve by the **marginal rate of substitution (MRS)**, which is defined as the absolute value of the slope of the indifference curve at that point. In the left panel of Figure 3.12, for example, the marginal rate of substitution at point A is given by the absolute value of the slope of the tangent to the indifference curve at A, which is the ratio $\triangle F_A / \triangle S_A$.[6] (The notation $\triangle F_A$ means "small change in food from the amount at point A.") If we take $\triangle F_A$ units of food away from the consumer at point A, we have to give him $\triangle S_A$ additional units of shelter to make him just as well off as before. The right panel of the figure shows an enlargement of the region surrounding bundle A. If the marginal rate of substitution at A is 2, this means that the consumer must be given 2 lb/wk of food to make up for the loss of 1 sq yd/wk of shelter.

Whereas the slope of the budget constraint tells us the rate at which we can substitute food for shelter without changing total expenditure, the MRS tells us the rate at which we can substitute food for shelter without changing total satisfaction. Put another way, the slope of the budget constraint is the marginal cost of shelter in terms of food, and the MRS is the marginal benefit of shelter in terms of food.

The convexity property of preferences tells us that along any indifference curve, the more a consumer has of one good, the more she must be given of that good before she will be willing to give up a unit of the other good. Stated differently, MRS declines as we move downward to the right along an indifference curve. Indifference curves with diminishing rates of marginal substitution are thus convex—or bowed outward—when viewed from the origin. The indifference curves shown in Figures 3.9, 3.10, and 3.12 all have this property, as does the curve shown in Figure 3.13.

In Figure 3.13, note that at bundle A food is relatively plentiful and the consumer would be willing to sacrifice 3 lb/wk of it in order to obtain an additional square yard of shelter. Her MRS at A is 3. At C, the quantities of food and shelter

marginal rate of substitution (MRS) at any point on an indifference curve, the rate at which the consumer is willing to exchange the good measured along the vertical axis for the good measured along the horizontal axis; equal to the absolute value of the slope of the indifference curve.

---

[6]More formally, the indifference curve may be expressed as a function $Y = Y(X)$ and the MRS at point A is defined as the absolute value of the derivative of the indifference curve at that point: $MRS = |dY(X)/dX|$.

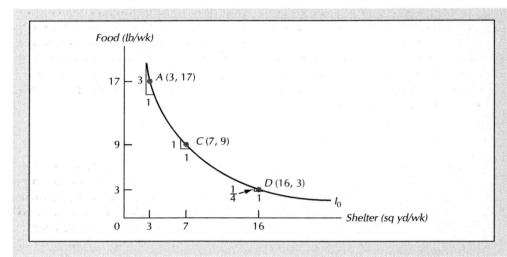

FIGURE 3.13
Diminishing Marginal Rate of Substitution
The more food the consumer has, the more she is willing to give up to obtain an additional unit of shelter. The marginal rates of substitution at bundles A, C, and D are 3, 1, and 1/4, respectively.

are more balanced, and there she would be willing to give up only 1 lb/wk to obtain an additional square yard of shelter. Her MRS at C is 1. Finally, note that food is relatively scarce at D, and there she would be willing to give up only $\frac{1}{4}$ lb/wk of food to obtain an additional unit of shelter. Her MRS at D is $\frac{1}{4}$.

Intuitively, diminishing MRS means that consumers like variety. We are usually willing to give up goods we already have a lot of to obtain more of those goods we now have only a little of.

Using Indifference Curves to Describe Preferences

To get a feel for how indifference maps describe a consumer's preferences, let us see how indifference maps can be used to portray differences in preferences between two consumers. Suppose, for example, that both Tex and Mohan like potatoes but that Mohan likes rice much more than Tex does. This difference in

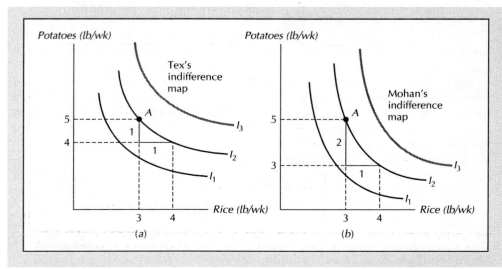

FIGURE 3.14
People with Different Tastes
Relatively speaking, Tex is a potato lover; Mohan, a rice lover. This difference shows up in the fact that at any given bundle Tex's marginal rate of substitution of potatoes for rice is smaller than Mohan's.

78   CHAPTER 3 RATIONAL CONSUMER CHOICE

their tastes is captured by the differing slopes of their indifference curves in Figure 3.14. Note in Figure 3.14*a*, which shows Tex's indifference map, that Tex would be willing to exchange 1 lb of potatoes for 1 lb of rice at bundle *A*. But at the corresponding bundle in Figure 3.14*b*, which shows Mohan's indifference map, we see that Mohan would trade 2 lb of potatoes for 1 lb of rice. Their difference in preferences shows up clearly in this difference in their marginal rates of substitution of potatoes for rice.

THE BEST FEASIBLE BUNDLE

best affordable bundle the most preferred bundle of those that are affordable.

We now have all the tools we need to determine how the consumer should allocate his income between two goods. The indifference map tells us how the various bundles are ranked in order of preference. The budget constraint, in turn, tells us which bundles are affordable. The consumer's task is to put the two together and to choose the most preferred or **best affordable bundle.** (Recall from Chapter 1 that we need not suppose that consumers think explicitly about budget constraints and indifference maps when deciding what to buy. It is sufficient to assume that people make decisions *as if* they were thinking in these terms, just as expert pool players choose between shots as if they knew all the relevant laws of Newtonian physics.)

For the sake of concreteness, let us again consider the choice between food and shelter that confronts a consumer with an income of $M = \$100/\text{wk}$ facing prices of $P_F = \$10/\text{lb}$ and $P_S = \$5/\text{sq yd}$. Figure 3.15 shows this consumer's budget constraint and part of his indifference map. Of the five labeled bundles—*A, D, E, F,* and *G*—in the diagram, *G* is the most preferred because it lies on the highest indifference curve. *G*, however, is not affordable, nor is any other bundle that lies beyond the budget constraint. The more-is-better assumption implies that the best affordable bundle must lie *on* the budget constraint, not inside it. (Any bundle inside the budget constraint would be less preferred than one just slightly to the northeast, which would also be affordable.)

Where exactly is the best affordable bundle located along the budget constraint? We know that it cannot be on an indifference curve that lies partly inside the budget constraint. On the indifference curve I_1, for example, the only points that are even candidates for the best affordable bundle are the two that lie on

FIGURE 3.15
The Best Affordable Bundle
The best the consumer can do is to choose the bundle on the budget constraint that lies on the highest attainable indifference curve. Here, that is bundle *F*, which lies at a tangency between the indifference curve and the budget constraint.

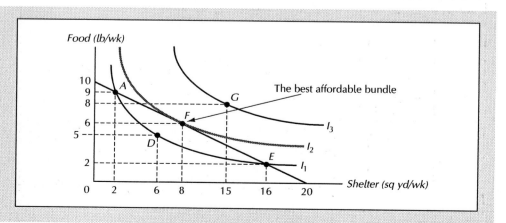

the budget constraint, namely, A and E. But A cannot be the best affordable bundle because it is equally attractive as D, which in turn is less desirable than F by the more-is-better assumption. So by transitivity, A is less desirable than F. For the same reason, E cannot be the best affordable bundle.

Since the best affordable bundle cannot lie on an indifference curve that lies partly inside the budget constraint, and since it must lie on the budget constraint itself, we know it has to lie on an indifference curve that intersects the budget constraint only once. In Figure 3.15, that indifference curve is the one labeled I_2, and the best affordable bundle is F, which lies at the point of tangency between I_2 and the budget constraint. With an income of \$100/wk and facing prices of \$5/ sq yd for shelter and \$10/lb for food, the best this consumer can do is to buy 6 lb/wk of food and 8 sq yd/wk of shelter.

The choice of bundle F makes perfect sense on intuitive grounds. The consumer's goal, after all, is to reach the highest indifference curve he can, given his budget constraint. His strategy is to keep moving to higher and higher indifference curves until he reaches the highest one that is still affordable. For indifference maps for which a tangency point exists, as in Figure 3.15, the best bundle will always lie at the point of tangency.

In Figure 3.15, note that the marginal rate of substitution at F is exactly the same as the absolute value of the slope of the budget constraint. This will always be so when the best affordable bundle occurs at a point of tangency. The condition that must be satisfied in such cases is therefore

$$MRS = \frac{P_S}{P_F} \qquad (3.3)$$

The right-hand side of Equation 3.3 represents the opportunity cost of shelter in terms of food. Thus, with $P_S = \$5/\text{sq yd}$ and $P_F = \$10/\text{lb}$, the opportunity cost of an additional square yard of shelter is $\frac{1}{2}$ lb of food. The left-hand side of Equation 3.3 is $|\triangle F/\triangle S|$, the absolute value of the slope of the indifference curve at the point of tangency. It is the amount of additional food the consumer must be given in order to compensate him fully for the loss of 1 sq yd of shelter. In the language of cost-benefit analysis discussed in Chapter 1, the slope of the budget constraint represents the opportunity cost of shelter in terms of food, while the slope of the indifference curve represents the benefits of consuming shelter as compared with consuming food. Since the slope of the budget constraint is $-\frac{1}{2}$ in this example, the tangency condition tells us that $\frac{1}{2}$ lb of food would be required to compensate for the benefits given up with the loss of 1 sq yd of shelter.

If the consumer were at some bundle on the budget line for which the two slopes are not the same, then it would always be possible for him to purchase a better bundle. To see why, suppose he were at a point where the slope of the indifference curve (in absolute value) is less than the slope of the budget constraint (also in absolute value), as at point E in Figure 3.15. Suppose, for instance, that the MRS at E is only $\frac{1}{4}$. This tells us that the consumer can be compensated for the loss of 1 sq yd of shelter by being given an additional $\frac{1}{4}$ lb of food. But the slope of the budget constraint tells us that by giving up 1 sq yd of shelter, he can purchase an additional $\frac{1}{2}$ lb of food. Since this is $\frac{1}{4}$ lb more than he needs to remain equally satisfied, he will clearly be better off if he purchases more food and less shelter than at point E. The opportunity cost of an additional pound of food is less than the benefit it confers.

EXERCISE 3.6

Suppose that the marginal rate of substitution at point *A* in Figure 3.15 is 1.0. Show that this means the consumer will be better off if he purchases less food and more shelter than at *A*.

Corner Solutions

The best affordable bundle need not always occur at a point of tangency. In some cases, there may simply *be* no point of tangency—the MRS may be everywhere greater, or less, than the slope of the budget constraint. In this case we get a **corner solution,** like the one shown in Figure 3.16, where M, P_F, and P_S are again given by \$100/wk, \$10/lb and \$5/sq yd, respectively. The best affordable bundle is the one labeled *A*, and it lies at the upper end of the budget constraint. At *A* the MRS is less than the absolute value of the slope of the budget constraint. For the sake of illustration, suppose the MRS at $A = 0.25$, which means that this consumer would be willing to give up 0.25 lb of food to get an additional square yard of shelter. But at market prices the opportunity cost of an additional square yard of shelter is 0.5 lb of food. He increases his satisfaction by continuing to give up shelter for more food until it is no longer possible to do so. Even though this consumer regards shelter as a desirable commodity, the best he can do is to spend all his income on food. Market prices are such that he would have to give up too much food to make the purchase of even a single unit of shelter worthwhile.

The indifference map in Figure 3.16 satisfies the property of diminishing marginal rate of substitution—moving to the right along any indifference curve, the slope becomes smaller in absolute terms. But because the slopes of the indifference curves start out smaller than the slope of the budget constraint here, the two never reach equality.

Indifference curves that are not strongly convex are characteristic of goods that are easily substituted for one another. Corner solutions are more likely to occur for such goods, and indeed are almost certain to occur when goods are perfect substitutes. (See Example 3.3.) For such goods, the MRS does not diminish at all; rather, it is everywhere the same. With perfect substitutes, indifference

FIGURE 3.16
A Corner Solution
When the MRS of food for shelter is always less than the slope of the budget constraint, the best the consumer can do is to spend all his income on food.

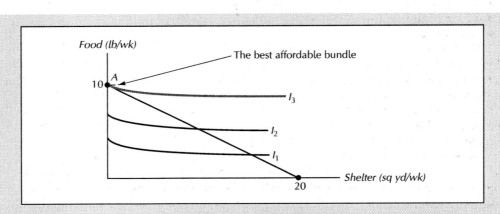

curves are straight lines. If they happen to be steeper than the budget constraint, we get a corner solution on the horizontal axis; if less steep, we get a corner solution on the vertical axis.

Consider the case of Mattingly, a caffeinated-cola drinker. He spends all his soft drink budget on Coca-Cola and Jolt cola and cares only about the total caffeine content of what he drinks. If Jolt has twice the caffeine of Coke, and if Jolt costs $1/pint and Coke costs $0.75/pint, how will Mattingly spend his soft drink budget of $15/wk?

EXAMPLE 3.3

For Mattingly, Jolt and Coke are *perfect substitutes*, which means that his indifference curves will not have the usual convex shape but will instead be linear. The top line in Figure 3.17 is the set of all possible Coke-Jolt combinations that provide the same satisfaction as the bundle consisting of 0 pints of Jolt per day and 30 pints of Coke per day. Since each pint of Jolt has twice the caffeine of a pint of Coke, all bundles along this line contain precisely the same amount of caffeine. The next red line down is the indifference curve for bundles equivalent to bundle (0, 20); and the third red line down is the indifference curve corresponding to (0, 10). Along each of these indifference curves, the marginal rate of substitution of Coke for Jolt is always $\frac{2}{1}$, that is, 2 pints of Coke for every pint of Jolt.

In the same diagram, Mattingly's budget constraint is shown as line B. The slope of his indifference curves is −2; of his budget constraint, $-\frac{4}{3}$. The best affordable bundle is the one labeled A, a corner solution in which he spends all his budget on Jolt. This makes intuitive sense in the light of Mattingly's peculiar preferences: he cares only about total caffeine content, and at the given prices, Jolt provides more caffeine per dollar than Coke does. If the Jolt-Coke price ratio, P_J/P_C had been $\frac{3}{1}$ (or any other amount greater than $\frac{2}{1}$), Mattingly would have spent all his income on Coke. That is, we would again have had a corner solution, only this time on the vertical axis. Only if the price ratio had been exactly $\frac{2}{1}$ might we have seen Mattingly spend part of his income on each good. In that case, any combination of Coke and Jolt on his budget constraint would have served him equally well.

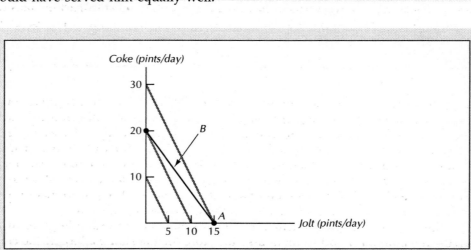

FIGURE 3.17
Equilibrium with Perfect Substitutes
Here, the MRS of Coke for Jolt is 2 at every point. Whenever the price ratio P_J/P_C is less than 2, a corner solution results in which the consumer buys only Jolt. On the budget constraint B, the consumer does best to buy bundle A.

Most of the time we will deal with problems that have not corner but *interior solutions*—that is, with problems where the best affordable bundle will lie at a point of tangency. An interior solution, again, is one where the MRS is exactly the same as the slope of the budget constraint.

EXERCISE 3.7

Suppose Albert always uses exactly two pats of butter on each piece of toast. If toast costs $0.10/slice and butter costs $0.20/pat, find Albert's best affordable bundle if he has $12/mo to spend on toast and butter. Suppose Albert starts to watch his cholesterol and therefore alters his preference to using exactly one pat of butter on each piece of toast. How much toast and butter would Albert then consume each month?

Indifference Curves When There Are More Than Two Goods

In the examples discussed so far, the consumer cares about only two goods. Where there are more than two, we can construct indifference curves by using the same device we used earlier to represent multigood budget constraints. We simply view the consumer's choice as being one between a particular good X and an amalgam of other goods Y, which is again called the composite good. As before, the composite good is the amount of income the consumer has left over after buying the good X.

In the multigood case, we may thus continue to represent the consumer's preferences with an indifference map in the XY plane. Here, the indifference curve tells not the rate at which the consumer will exchange some particular good Y for a good X, but the rate at which he will exchange the composite good for X. Just as in the two-good case, equilibrium occurs when the consumer reaches the highest indifference curve attainable on his budget constraint.

AN APPLICATION OF THE RATIONAL CHOICE MODEL

As the following example makes clear, the composite good construct enables us to deal with more general questions than we could in the simple two-good case.

EXAMPLE 3.4

Is it better to give poor people cash or food stamps?

One objective of the food stamp program is to alleviate hunger among poor people. Under the terms of the program, people whose incomes fall below a certain level are eligible to receive a specified quantity of food stamps. For example, a person with an income of $400/mo might be eligible for $100/mo worth of stamps. These stamps can then be used to buy $100/mo worth of food. Any food he buys in excess of $100/mo he must pay for in cash. Stamps cannot be used to purchase cigarettes, alcohol, and various other items. The government gives food retailers cash for the stamps they accept in exchange for food.

The cost to the government for the consumer in the example given was $100—the amount it had to reimburse the store for the stamps. Would the consumer have been better off had he instead been given $100 directly in cash?

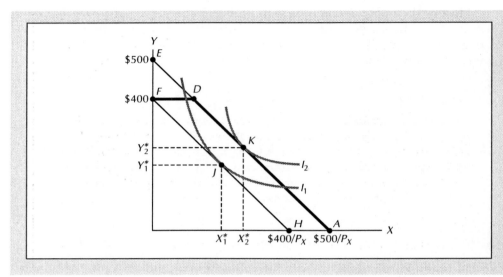

FIGURE 3.18
Food Stamp Program vs. Cash Grant Program
By comparison with the budget constraint under a cash grant (*AE*), the budget constraint under food stamps (*ADF*) limits the amount that can be spent on nonfood goods. But for the consumer whose indifference map is shown, the equilibrium bundles are the same under both programs.

We can try to answer this question by investigating which alternative would get him to a higher indifference curve. Suppose Y denotes the composite good and X denotes food. If the consumer's income is \$400/mo and P_X is the price of food, his initial equilibrium is the bundle J in Figure 3.18. The effect of the food stamp program is to increase the total amount of food he can buy each month from \$400/P_X to \$500/P_X. In terms of the *maximum* amount of food he can buy, the food stamp program is thus exactly the same as a cash grant of \$100.

Where the two alternatives differ is in terms of the maximum amounts of other goods he can buy. With a cash grant of \$100, he has a total monthly income of \$500, and this is, of course, the maximum amount of nonfood goods (the composite good) he can buy. His budget constraint in this case is thus the line labeled AE in Figure 3.18.

With the food stamp program, by contrast, the consumer is not able to buy \$500/mo of nonfood goods because his \$100 in food stamps can be used only for food. The maximum amount of nonfood goods he can purchase is \$400. In Figure 3.18, his budget constraint under the food stamp program is labeled ADF. For values of Y less than \$400, it is thus exactly the same as his budget constraint under the cash grant program. For values of Y larger than \$400, however, his budget constraint under the food stamp program is completely flat.

Note that the consumer whose indifference curves are shown in Figure 3.18 buys exactly the same bundle, namely, bundle K, under both programs. The effect of the food stamp program here is precisely the same as the effect of the cash grant. In general, this will be true whenever the consumer with a cash grant would have spent more on food anyway than the amount of food stamps he would have received under the food stamp program.

Figure 3.19 depicts a consumer for whom this is *not* the case. With a cash grant, he would choose the bundle L, which would put him on a higher indifference curve than he could attain under the food stamp program, which would lead him to buy bundle D. Note that bundle D contains exactly \$100 worth of food, the amount of food stamps he received. Bundle L, by contrast, contains less than \$100 worth of food. Here, the effect of the food stamp program is to cause

84   CHAPTER 3 RATIONAL CONSUMER CHOICE

FIGURE 3.19
Where Food Stamps and Cash Grants Yield Different Outcomes
For the consumer whose indifference map is shown, a cash grant would be preferred to food stamps, which force him to devote more to food than he would choose to spend on his own.

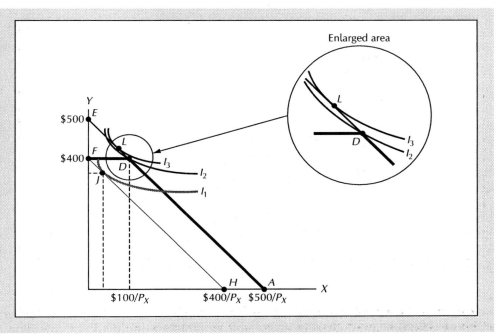

the recipient to spend more on food than he would have if he had instead been given cash.

The face value of the food stamps most participants receive is smaller than what they would spend on food. For these people, the food stamp program leads, as noted, to exactly the same behavior as a pure cash grant program.

The analysis in Example 3.4 raises the question of why Congress did not just give poor people cash grants in the first place. The ostensible reason is that Congress wanted to help poor people buy food, not luxury items or even cigarettes and alcohol. And yet if most participants would have spent at least as much on food as they received in stamps, not being able to use stamps to buy other things is a meaningless restriction. For instance, if someone would have spent $150 on food anyway, getting $100 in food stamps simply lets him take some of the money he would have spent on food and spend it instead on whatever else he chooses.

On purely economic grounds, there is thus a strong case for replacing the food stamp program with a much simpler program of cash grants to the poor. At the very least, this would eliminate the cumbersome step of requiring grocers to redeem their stamps for cash.

As a political matter, however, it is easy to see why Congress might have set things up the way it did. Many of the taxpayers who sponsor antipoverty programs would be distressed to see their tax dollars used to buy illicit substances. If the food stamp program prevents even a tiny minority of participants from spending more on such goods, it spares many political difficulties.

Example 3.4 calls our attention to a problem that applies not just to the food stamp program but to all other forms of in-kind transfers as well: Although the two forms of transfer are sometimes equivalent, gifts in cash seem clearly superior on those occasions when they differ.

Why do people often give gifts in kind instead of cash?

ECONOMIC NATURALIST 3.1

Occasionally someone receives a gift that is exactly what he would have purchased for himself had he been given an equivalent amount of money. But we are all far too familiar with gifts that miss the mark. Who has never been given an article of clothing that he was embarrassed to wear? The logic of the economic choice model seems to state unequivocally that we could avoid the problem of useless gifts if we followed the simple expedient of giving cash. And yet virtually every society continues to engage in ritualized gift giving.

The fact that this custom has persisted should not be taken as evidence that people are stupid. Rather, it suggests that there may be something about gift giving that the rational choice model fails to capture. One purpose of giving a gift is to express affection for the recipient. A thoughtfully chosen gift accomplishes this in a way that a gift of cash cannot. Or it may be that some people have difficulty indulging themselves with even small luxuries and would feel compelled to spend cash gifts on purely practical items. For these people, a gift provides a way of enjoying a small luxury without having to feel guilty about it.[7] This interpretation is supported by the observation that we rarely give purely practical gifts like plain cotton underwear or laundry detergent.

Whatever the real reasons people may have for giving in kind rather than in cash, it seems safe to assume that we do not do it because it never occurred to us to give cash. On the contrary, occasionally we do give cash gifts, especially to young relatives with low incomes. But even though there are advantages to gifts in cash, people seem clearly reluctant to abandon the practice of giving in kind.

"Sweetheart, perhaps we shouldn't exchange gifts this year."

The Appendix to this chapter develops the utility function approach to the consumer budgeting problem. Topics covered include cardinal versus ordinal utility, algebraic construction of indifference curves, and the use of calculus to maximize utility.

---

[7]For a discussion of this interpretation, see R. Thaler, "Mental Accounting and Consumer Choice," *Marketing Science*, 4, Summer 1985.

SUMMARY

- Our task in this chapter was to set forth the basic model of rational consumer choice. In all its variants, this model retains certain common features; in particular, it takes consumers' preferences as given and assumes they will try to satisfy them in the most efficient way possible.

- The first step in solving the budgeting problem is to identify the set of bundles of goods that the consumer is able to buy. The consumer is assumed to have an income level given in advance and to face fixed prices. Prices and income together define the consumer's budget constraint, which, in the simple two-good case, is a downward-sloping line whose slope, in absolute value, is the ratio of the two prices. It is the set of all possible bundles that the consumer might purchase if he spends his entire income.

- The second step in solving the consumer budgeting problem is to summarize the consumer's preferences. Here, we begin with a preference ordering by which the consumer is able to rank all possible bundles of goods. This ranking scheme is assumed to be complete and transitive and to exhibit the more-is-better property. Preference orderings that satisfy these restrictions give rise to indifference maps, or collections of indifference curves, each of which represents combinations of bundles among which the consumer is indifferent. Preference orderings are also assumed to exhibit a diminishing marginal rate of substitution, which means that, along any indifference curve, the more of a good a consumer has, the more he must be given to induce him to part with a unit of some other good. The diminishing MRS property is what accounts for the characteristic convex shape of indifference curves.

- The budget constraint tells us what combinations of goods the consumer can afford to buy. To summarize the consumer's preferences over various bundles, we use an indifference map. The best affordable bundle occurs at a point of tangency between an indifference curve and the budget constraint. At that point, the marginal rate of substitution is exactly equal to the rate at which the goods can be exchanged for one another at market prices.

QUESTIONS FOR REVIEW

1. If the prices of all products are rising at 20 percent per year and your employer gives you a 20 percent salary increase, are you better off, worse off, or equally well off in comparison with your situation a year ago?

2. *True or false:* If you know the slope of the budget constraint (for two goods), you know the prices of the two goods. Explain.

:3. *True or false:* The downward slope of indifference curves is a consequence of the diminishing marginal rate of substitution.

4. Construct an example of a preference ordering over Coke, Diet Coke, and Diet Pepsi that violates the transitivity assumption.

5. Explain in your own words how the slope of an indifference curve provides information about how much a consumer likes one good relative to another.

6. Explain why a consumer will often buy one bundle of goods even though he prefers another.

7. Why are corner solutions especially likely in the case of perfect substitutes?

8. *True or false:* If the indifference curve map is concave to the origin, then the optimal commodity basket must occur at a corner equilibrium, except possibly when there are quantity discounts.

9. If Ralph were given $10, he would spend none of it on tuna fish. But when asked, he claims to be indifferent between receiving $10 worth of tuna fish and a $10 bill. How could this be?

PROBLEMS

1. The Acme Seed Company charges $2/lb for the first 10 lb you buy of marigold seeds each week and $1/lb for every pound you buy thereafter. If your income is $100/wk, draw your budget constraint for the composite good and marigold seeds.

2. Same as Problem 1, except now the price for every pound after 10 lb/wk is $4/lb.

3. Smith likes cashews better than almonds and likes almonds better than walnuts. He likes pecans equally well as macadamia nuts and prefers macadamia nuts to almonds. Assuming his preferences are transitive, which does he prefer:
   a. Pecans or walnuts?
   b. Macadamia nuts or cashews?

4. Originally P_X is $120 and P_Y is $80. *True or false:* If P_X increases by $18 and P_Y increases by $12, the new budget line will be shifted inward and parallel to the old budget line. Explain.

5. Martha has $150 of disposable income to spend each week and cannot borrow money. She buys Malted Milk Balls and the composite good. Suppose that Malted Milk Balls cost $2.50 per bag and the composite good costs $1 per unit.
   a. Sketch Martha's budget constraint.
   b. What is the opportunity cost, in terms of bags of Malted Milk Balls, of an additional unit of the composite good?

6. In Problem 5, suppose that in an inflationary period the cost of the composite good increases to $1.50 per unit, but the cost of Malted Milk Balls remains the same.
   a. Sketch the new budget constraint.
   b. What is the opportunity cost of an additional unit of the composite good?

7. In Problem 6, suppose that Martha demands a pay raise to fight the inflation. Her boss submits and raises her salary so that her disposable income is now $225/wk.
   a. Sketch the new budget constraint.
   b. What is the opportunity cost of an additional unit of the composite good?

8. Picabo, an aggressive skier, spends her entire income on skis and bindings. She wears out one pair of skis for every pair of bindings she wears out.
   a. Graph Picabo's indifference curves for skis and bindings.
   b. Now draw her indifference curves on the assumption that she is such an aggressive skier that she wears out two pairs of skis for every pair of bindings she wears out.

9. Suppose Picabo in Problem 8 has $3600 in income to spend on skis and bindings each year. Find Picabo's best affordable bundle of skis and bindings under both of the preferences described in the previous problem. Skis are $480/pr and bindings are $240/pr.

10. For Alexi, coffee and tea are perfect substitutes: One cup of coffee is equivalent to one cup of tea. Suppose Alexi has $90/mo to spend on these beverages, and coffee costs $0.90/cup while tea costs $1.20/cup. Find Alexi's best affordable bundle of tea and coffee. How much could the price of a cup of coffee rise without harming her standard of living?

11. Eve likes apples but doesn't care about pears. If apples and pears are the only two goods available, draw her indifference curves.

12. Koop likes food but dislikes cigarette smoke. The more food he has, the more he would be willing to give up to achieve a given reduction in cigarette smoke. If food and cigarette smoke are the only two goods, draw Koop's indifference curves.

13. If you were president of a conservation organization, which rate structure would you prefer the Gigawatt Power Company to use: the one described in Example 3.1, or one in which all power sold for $0.08/kWh? (Assume that each rate structure would exactly cover the company's costs.)

14. Paula, a former actress, spends all her income attending plays and movies and likes plays exactly three times as much as she likes movies.
   a. Draw her indifference map.
   b. Paula earns $120/wk. If play tickets cost $12 each and movie tickets cost $4 each, show her budget line and highest attainable indifference curve. How many plays will she see?
   c. If play tickets are $12, movie tickets $5, how many plays will she attend?

88   CHAPTER 3   RATIONAL CONSUMER CHOICE

15. For each of the following, sketch:
   a. A typical person's indifference curves between garbage and the composite good.
   b. Indifference curves for the same two commodities for Oscar the Grouch on *Sesame Street*, who loves garbage and has no use for the composite good.

16. Boris budgets $9/wk for his morning coffee with milk. He likes it only if it is pre-pared with 4 parts coffee, 1 part milk. Coffee costs $1/oz, milk $0.50/oz. How much coffee and how much milk will Boris buy per week? How will your answers change if the price of coffee rises to $3.25/oz? Show your answers graphically.

· 17. The federal government wants to support education but must not support religion. To this end, it gives the University of Notre Dame $2 million with the stipulation that this money be used for secular purposes only. The accompanying graph shows Notre Dame's pre-federal-gift budget constraint and best attainable indifference curve over secular and nonsecular expenditures. How would the university's welfare differ if the gift came without the secular-use restriction?

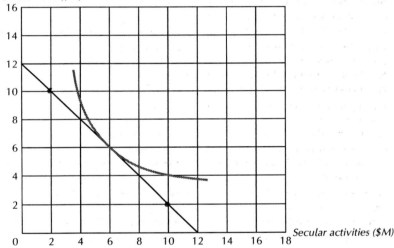

18. Continental Long Distance Telephone Service offers an optional package for in-state calling whereby each month the subscriber gets the first 50 min of in-state calls free, the next 100 min at $0.25/min, and any additional time at the normal rate of $0.50/min. Draw the budget constraint for in-state phone calls and the composite good for a subscriber with an income of $400/mo.

19. For the Continental Long Distance subscriber in Problem 18, what is the opportunity cost of making an additional 20 min of calls if he currently makes
   a. 40 min of calls each month?
   b. 140 min of calls each month?

20. You have the option of renting a car on a daily basis for $40/day or on a weekly basis for $200/wk. Draw your budget constraint for a budget of $360/trip.
   a. Find your best affordable bundle if your travel preferences are such that you require exactly $140 worth of other goods for each day of rental car con-sumption.
   b. Alternatively, suppose you view a day of rental car consumption as a perfect substitute for $35 worth of other goods.

21. Howard said that he was exactly indifferent between consuming four slices of pizza and one beer versus consuming three slices of pizza and two beers. He also said that he prefers a bundle consisting of one slice of pizza and three beers to either of the

first two bundles. Do Howard's preferences exhibit diminishing marginal rates of substitution?

22. Your local telephone company has offered you a choice between the following billing plans:

Plan A: Pay $0.05 per call.

Plan B: Pay an initial $2/wk, which allows you up to 30 calls per week at no charge. Any calls over 30/wk cost $0.05 per call.

If your income is $12/wk and the composite good costs $1, graph your budget constraints for the composite good and calls under the two plans.

*23. At your school's fund-raising picnic, you pay for soft drinks not with cash but with tickets purchased in advance—one ticket per bottle of soft drink. Tickets are available in sets of three types:

Small: $3 for 3 tickets
Medium: $4 for 5 tickets
Large: $5 for 8 tickets

If the total amount you have to spend is $12 and fractional sets of tickets cannot be bought, graph your budget constraint for soft drinks and the composite good.

*24. Consider two Italian restaurants located in identical towns 200 miles apart. The restaurants are identical in every respect but their tipping policies. At one, there is a flat $15 service charge, but no other tips are accepted. At the other, a 15 percent tip is added to the bill. The average food bill at the first restaurant, exclusive of the service charge, is $100. How, if at all, do you expect the amount of food eaten in the two restaurants to differ?

*25. Mr. R. Plane, retired college administrator, consumes only grapes and the composite good $Y(P_Y = \$1)$. His income consists of $10,000/yr from social security, plus the proceeds from whatever he sells of the 2000 bushels of grapes he harvests annually from his vineyard. Last year, grapes sold for $2/bushel, and Plane consumed all 2000 bushels of his grapes in addition to 10,000 units of Y. This year the price of grapes is $3/bushel, while P_Y remains $1. If his indifference curves have the conventional shape, will this year's consumption of grapes be greater than, smaller than, or the same as last year's? Will this year's consumption of Y be greater than, smaller than, or the same as last year's? Explain.

ANSWERS TO IN-CHAPTER EXERCISES

3.1. *Food (lb/wk)*

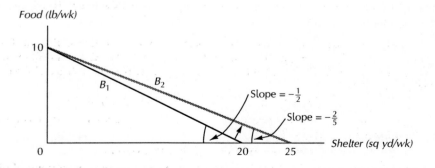

---

*Problems marked with an asterisk (*) are more difficult.

90   CHAPTER 3   RATIONAL CONSUMER CHOICE

3.2. *Food (lb/wk)*

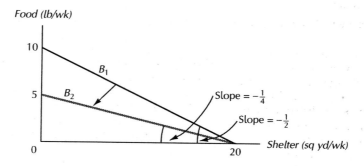

3.3. *Food (lb/wk)*

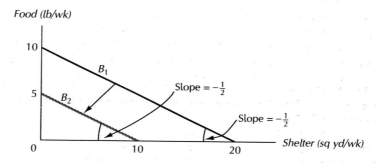

3.4. *Food (lb/wk)*

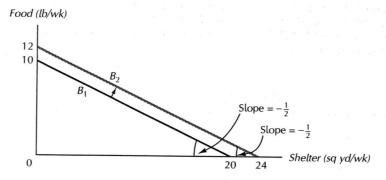

3.5. The budget constraint for a residential consumer with Amperage Electric Power would be kinked outward, as the initial rate for the first 1000 kWh/mo is lower. For power consumption X up to 1000 kWh/mo, the budget constraint has a slope of the lower rate $0.05/kWh.

$$Y = 400 - 0.05X \qquad 0 \le X \le 1000 \text{ kWh/mo}$$

For power consumption X above 1000 kWh/mo, the budget constraint has a slope of the higher rate $0.10/kWh.

$$Y = 450 - 0.10X \qquad X > 1000 \text{ kWh/mo}$$

The kink occurs when $X = 1000$ kWh/mo, where the level of consumption of other goods is $Y = 400 - 0.05X = 400 - 50 = 350$, or equivalently, $Y = 450 - 0.10X = 450 - 100 = 350$. If the rate were instead $0.10/kWh for all kWh that exceeded 1000 kWh/mo, then the budget constraint for $X > 1000$ kWh/mo would be

$$Y = 400 - 0.10X \quad X > 1000 \text{ kWh/mo}$$

and would have a discrete jump from $Y = 350$ to $Y = 300$ at $X = 1000$ kWh/mo.

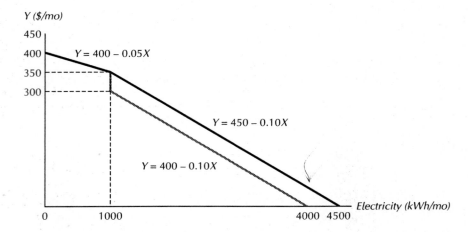

3.6. At bundle A, the consumer is willing to give up 1 lb of food to get an additional square yard of shelter. But at the market prices it is necessary to give up only $\frac{1}{2}$ lb of food to buy an additional square yard of shelter. It follows that the consumer will be better off than at bundle A if he buys 1 lb less of food and 2 sq yd more of shelter.

3.7. Albert's budget constraint is $T = 120 - 2B$. Albert's initial preferences are for two pats of butter for every slice of toast $B = 2T$. Substituting this equation into his budget constraint yields $T = 120 - 4T$, or $5T = 120$, which solves for $T = 24$ slices of toast, and thus $B = 48$ pats of butter each month. Albert's new preferences are for one pat of butter for every slice of toast $B = T$. Substituting this equation into his budget constraint yields $T = 120 - 2T$, or $3T = 120$, which solves for $T = 40$ slices of toast, and thus $B = 40$ pats of butter each month. Not only has Albert cut the fat, but he is consuming more fiber too!

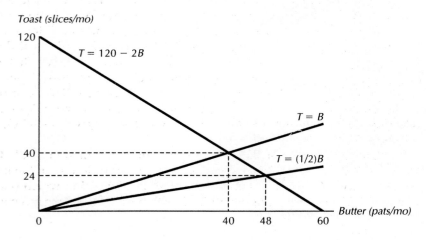

APPENDIX

3

THE UTILITY FUNCTION APPROACH TO THE CONSUMER BUDGETING PROBLEM

THE UTILITY FUNCTION APPROACH TO CONSUMER CHOICE

Finding the highest attainable indifference curve on a budget constraint is just one way that economists have analyzed the consumer choice problem. For many applications, a second approach is also useful. In this approach we represent the consumer's preferences not with an indifference map but with a *utility function* (a formula that yields a number representing the satisfaction provided by a bundle of goods).

A utility function is simply a formula that, for each possible bundle of goods, yields a number that represents the amount of satisfaction provided by that bundle. Suppose, for example, that Tom consumes only food and shelter and that his utility function is given by $U(F, S) = FS$, where F denotes the number of pounds of food, S the number of square yards of shelter he consumes per week, and U his satisfaction, measured in "utils" per week.[1] If $F = 4$ lb/wk and $S = 3$ sq yd/wk, Tom will receive 12 utils/wk of utility, just as he would if he consumed 3 lb/wk of food and 4 sq yd/wk of shelter. By contrast, if he consumed 8 lb/wk of food and 6 sq yd/wk of shelter, he would receive 48 utils/wk.

The utility function is analogous to an indifference map in that both provide a complete description of the consumer's preference ordering. In the indifference curve framework, we can rank any two bundles by seeing which one lies on a higher indifference curve. In the utility-function framework, we can compare any

---

[1]The term "utils" represents an arbitrary unit. As we will see, what is important for consumer choice is not the actual number of utils various bundles provide, but the rankings of the bundles based on their associated utilities.

two bundles by seeing which one yields a greater number of utils. Indeed, as the following example illustrates, it is straightforward to use the utility function to construct an indifference map.

If Tom's utility function is given by $U(F, S) = FS$ graph the indifference curves that correspond to 1, 2, 3, and 4 utils, respectively.

In the language of utility functions, an indifference curve is all combinations of F and S that yield the same level of utility—the same number of utils. Suppose we look at the indifference curve that corresponds to 1 unit of utility—that is, the combinations of bundles for which $FS = 1$. Solving this equation for S, we have

$$S = \frac{1}{F},$$ (A.3.1)

which is the indifference curve labeled $U = 1$ in Figure A.3.1. The indifference curve that corresponds to 2 units of utility is generated by solving $FS = 2$ to get $S = 2/F$, and it is shown by the curve labeled $U = 2$ in Figure A.3.1. In similar fashion, we generate the indifference curves to $U = 3$ and $U = 4$, which are correspondingly labeled in the diagram. More generally, we get the indifference curve corresponding to a utility level of U_0 by solving $FS = U_0$ to get $S = U_0/F$.

In the indifference curve framework, the best attainable bundle is the bundle on the budget constraint that lies on the highest indifference curve. Analogously, the best attainable bundle in the utility-function framework is the bundle on the budget constraint that provides the highest level of utility. In the indifference curve framework, the best attainable bundle occurs at a point of tangency between an indifference curve and the budget constraint. At the optimal bundle, the slope of the indifference curve, or MRS, equals the slope of the budget constraint. Suppose food and shelter are again our two goods, and P_F and P_S are their respective prices. If $\Delta S/\Delta F$ denotes the slope of the highest

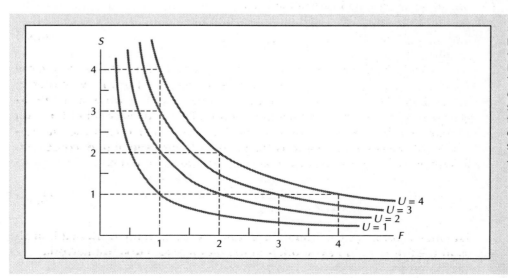

FIGURE A.3.1
Indifference Curves for the Utility Function $U = FS$
To get the indifference curve that corresponds to all bundles that yield a utility level of U_0, set $FS = U_0$ and solve for S to get $S = U_0/F$.

FIGURE A.3.2
Utility Along an Indifference Curve Remains Constant
In moving from K to L, the loss in utility from having less shelter, $MU_s \Delta S$, is exactly offset by the gain in utility from having more food, $MU_F \Delta F$.

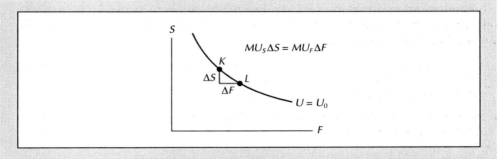

attainable indifference curve at the optimal bundle, the tangency condition says that $\Delta S / \Delta F = P_F / P_S$. What is the analogous condition in the utility-function framework?

To answer this question, we must introduce the concept of *marginal utility* (the marginal utility of a good is the rate at which total utility changes with consumption of the good) which is the rate at which total utility changes as the quantities of food and shelter change. More specifically, let MU_F denote the number of additional utils we get for each additional unit of food and MU_S denote the number of additional utils we get for each additional unit of shelter. In Figure A.3.2, note that bundle K has ΔF fewer units of food and ΔS more units of shelter than bundle L. Thus, if we move from bundle K to bundle L, we gain $MU_F \Delta F$ utils from having more food, but we lose $MU_S \Delta S$ utils from having less shelter.

Because K and L both lie on the same indifference curve, we know that both bundles provide the same level of utility. Thus the utility we lose from having less shelter must be exactly offset by the utility we gain from having more food. This tells us that

$$MU_F \Delta F = MU_S \Delta S. \tag{A.3.2}$$

Cross-multiplying terms in Equation A.3.2 gives

$$\frac{MU_F}{MU_S} = \frac{\Delta S}{\Delta F}. \tag{A.3.3}$$

Suppose that the optimal bundle lies between K and L, which are very close together, so that ΔF and ΔS are both very small. As K and L move closer to the optimal bundle, the ratio $\Delta S / \Delta F$ becomes equal to the slope of the indifference curve at that bundle, which Equation A.3.3 tells us is equal to the ratio of the marginal utilities of the two goods. And since the slope of the indifference curve at the optimal bundle is the same as that of the budget constraint, the following condition must also hold for the optimal bundle:

$$\frac{MU_F}{MU_S} = \frac{P_F}{P_S}. \tag{A.3.4}$$

Equation A.3.4 is the condition in the utility-function framework that is analogous to the MRS $= P_F / P_S$ condition in the indifference curve framework.

THE UTILITY FUNCTION APPROACH TO CONSUMER CHOICE   95

If we cross-multiply terms in Equation A.3.4, we get an equivalent condition that has a very straightforward intuitive interpretation:

$$\frac{MU_F}{P_F} = \frac{MU_S}{P_S}. \tag{A.3.5}$$

In words, Equation A.3.5 tells us that the ratio of marginal utility to price must be the same for all goods at the optimal bundle. The following examples illustrate why this condition must be satisfied if the consumer has allocated his budget optimally.

Suppose that the marginal utility of the last dollar John spends on food is greater than the marginal utility of the last dollar he spends on shelter. For example, suppose the prices of food and shelter are \$1/lb and \$2/sq yd, respectively, and that the corresponding marginal utilities are 6 and 4. Show that John cannot possibly be maximizing his utility.

EXAMPLE A.3.2

If John bought 1 sq yd/wk less shelter, he would save \$2/wk and would lose 4 utils. But this would enable him to buy 2 lb/wk more food, which would add 12 utils, for a net gain of 8 utils.

Abstracting from the special case of corner solutions, a necessary condition for optimal budget allocation is that the last dollar spent on each commodity yield the same increment in utility.

Mary has a weekly allowance of \$10, all of which she spends on newspapers (N) and magazines (M), whose respective prices are \$1 and \$2. Her utility from these purchases is given by U(N) + V(M). If the values of U(N) and V(M) are as shown in the table, is Mary a utility maximizer if she buys 4 magazines and 2 newspapers each week? If not, how should she reallocate her allowance?

EXAMPLE A.3.3

N	U(N)	M	V(M)
0	0	0	0
1	12	1	20
2	20	2	32
3	26	3	40
4	30	4	44
5	32	5	46

For Mary to be a utility maximizer, extra utility per dollar must be the same for both the last newspaper and the last magazine she purchased. But since the second newspaper provided 8 additional utils per dollar spent, which is four times the 2 utils per dollar she got from the fourth magazine (4 extra utils at a cost of \$2), Mary is not a utility maximizer.

To see clearly how she should reallocate her purchases, let us rewrite the table to include the relevant information on marginal utilities. From this table, we see that there are several bundles for which $MU(N)/P_N = MU(M)/P_M$—namely, 3 newspapers and 2 magazines; or 4 newspapers and 3 magazines; or

96   CHAPTER 3 APPENDIX   THE UTILITY FUNCTION APPROACH TO THE CONSUMER BUDGETING PROBLEM

N	U(N)	MU(N)	MU(N)/PN	M	U(M)	MU(M)	MU(M)/PM
0	0			0	0		
		12	12			20	10
1	12			1	20		
		8	8			12	6
2	20			2	32		
		6	6			8	4
3	26			3	40		
		4	4			4	2
4	30			4	44		
		2	2			2	1
5	32			5	46		

5 newspapers and 4 magazines. The last of these bundles yields the highest total utility but costs $13, and is hence beyond Mary's budget constraint. The first, which costs only $7, is affordable, but so is the second, which costs exactly $10 and yields higher total utility than the first. With 4 newspapers and 3 magazines, Mary gets 4 utils per dollar from her last purchase in each category. Her total utility is 70 utils, which is 6 more than she got from the original bundle.

In Example A.3.3, note that if all Mary's utility values were doubled, or cut by half, she would still do best to buy 4 newspapers and 3 magazines each week. This illustrates the claim that consumer choice depends not on the absolute number of utils associated with different bundles, but instead on the ordinal ranking of the utility levels associated with different bundles. If we double all the utils associated with various bundles, or cut them by half, the ordinal ranking of the bundles will be preserved, and thus the optimal bundle will remain the same. This will also be true if we take the logarithm of the utility function, the square root of it, or add 5 to it, or transform it in any other way that preserves the ordinal ranking of different bundles.

CARDINAL VERSUS ORDINAL UTILITY

In our discussion about how to represent consumer preferences, we assumed that people are able to rank each possible bundle in order of preference. This is called the *ordinal utility* approach to the consumer budgeting problem. It does not require that people be able to make quantitative statements about how much they like various bundles. Thus it assumes that a consumer will always be able to say whether he prefers A to B, but that he may not be able to make such statements as "A is 6.43 times as good as B."

In the nineteenth century, economists commonly assumed that people could make such statements. Today we call theirs the *cardinal utility* approach to the consumer choice problem. In the two-good case, it assumes that the satisfaction provided by any bundle can be assigned a numerical, or cardinal, value by a utility function of the form

$$U = U(X, Y). \qquad (A.3.6)$$

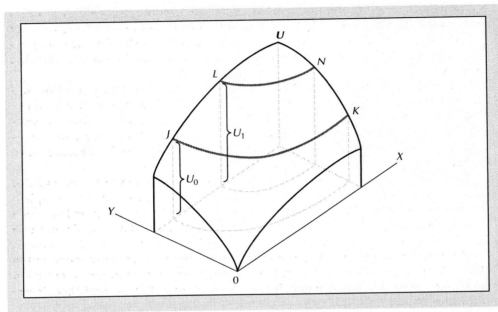

FIGURE A.3.3
A Three-Dimensional Utility Surface

In three dimensions, the graph of such a utility function will look something like the one shown in Figure A.3.3. It resembles a mountain, but because of the more-is-better assumption, it is a mountain without a summit. The value on the U axis measures the height of the mountain, which continues to increase the more we have of X or Y.

Suppose in Figure A.3.3 we were to fix utility at some constant amount, say, U_0. That is, suppose we cut the utility mountain with a plane parallel to the XY plane, U_0 units above it. The line labeled JK in Figure A.3.3 represents the intersection of that plane and the surface of the utility mountain. All the bundles of goods that lie on JK provide a utility level of U_0. If we then project the line JK downward onto the XY plane, we have what amounts to the U_0 indifference curve, shown in Figure A.3.4.

Suppose we then intersect the utility mountain with another plane, this time U_1 units above the XY plane. In Figure A.3.3, this second plane intersects the

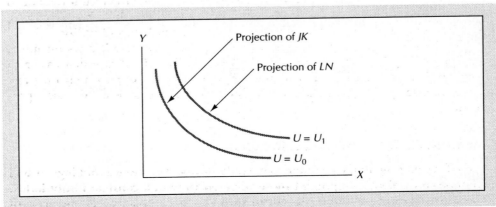

FIGURE A.3.4
Indifference Curves as Projections

98   CHAPTER 3 APPENDIX   THE UTILITY FUNCTION APPROACH TO THE CONSUMER BUDGETING PROBLEM

utility mountain along the line labeled LN. It represents the set of all bundles that confer the utility level U_1. Projecting LN down onto the XY plane, we thus get the indifference curve labeled U_1 in Figure A.3.3. In like fashion, we can generate an entire indifference map corresponding to the cardinal utility function $U(X, Y)$.

Thus we see that it is possible to start with any cardinal utility function and end up with a unique indifference map. *But it is not possible to go in the other direction!* That is, it is not possible to start with an indifference map and work backward to a unique cardinal utility function. The reason is that there will always be infinitely many such utility functions that give rise to precisely the same indifference map.

To see why, just imagine that we took the utility function in Equation A.3.4 and doubled it, so that utility is now given by $V = 2U(X, Y)$. When we graph V as a function of X and Y, the shape of the resulting utility mountain will be much the same as before. The difference will be that the altitude at any X, Y point will be twice what it was before. If we pass a plane $2U_0$ units above the XY plane, it would intersect the new utility mountain in precisely the same manner as the plane U_0 units high did originally. If we then project the resulting intersection down onto the XY plane, it will coincide perfectly with the original U_0 indifference curve.

All we do when we multiply (divide, add to, or subtract from) a cardinal utility function is to relabel the indifference curves to which it gives rise. Indeed, we can make an even more general statement: If $U(X, Y)$ is any cardinal utility function and if V is any increasing function, then $U = U(X, Y)$ and $V = V[U(X, Y)]$ will give rise to precisely the same indifference maps. The special property of an increasing function is that it preserves the rank ordering of the values of the original function. That is, if $U(X_1, Y_1) > U(X_2, Y_2)$, the fact that V is an increasing function assures that $V[U(X_1, Y_1)]$ will be greater than $V[U(X_2, Y_2)]$. And as long as that requirement is met, the two functions will give rise to exactly the same indifference curves.

The concept of the indifference map was first discussed by Francis Edgeworth, who derived it from a cardinal utility function in the manner described above. It took the combined insights of Vilfredo Pareto, Irving Fisher, and John Hicks to establish that Edgeworth's apparatus was not uniquely dependent on a supporting cardinal utility function. As we have seen, the only aspect of a consumer's preferences that matters in the standard budget allocation problem is the shape and location of his indifference curves. Consumer choice turns out to be completely independent of the labels we assign to these indifference curves, provided only that higher curves correspond to higher levels of utility.

Modern economists prefer the ordinal approach because it rests on much weaker assumptions than the cardinal approach. That is, it is much easier to imagine that people can rank different bundles than to suppose that they can make precise quantitative statements about how much satisfaction each provides.

GENERATING INDIFFERENCE CURVES ALGEBRAICALLY

Even if we assume that consumers have only ordinal preference rankings, it will often be convenient to represent those preferences with a cardinal utility index. The advantage is that this procedure provides a compact algebraic way of

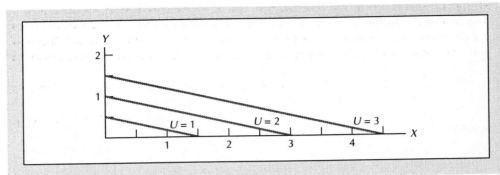

FIGURE A.3.5
Indifference Curves for the Utility Function $U(X, Y) = (\frac{2}{3})X + 2Y$
The indifference curve that corresponds to all bundles yielding a utility level of U_0 is given by $Y = (U_0/2) - (\frac{1}{3})X$.

summarizing all the information that is implicit in the graphical representation of preferences, as we saw in Example A.3.1.

Consider another illustration, this time with a utility function that generates straight-line indifference curves: $U(X, Y) = (\frac{2}{3})X + 2Y$. The bundles of X and Y that yield a utility level of U_0 are again found by solving $U(X, Y) = U_0$ for Y. This time we get $Y = (U_0/2) - (\frac{1}{3})X$. The indifference curves corresponding to $U = 1, U = 2$, and $U = 3$ are shown in Figure A.3.5. Note that they are all linear, which tells us that this particular utility function describes a preference ordering in which X and Y are perfect substitutes.

Using Calculus to Maximize Utility

Students who have had calculus are able to solve the consumer's budget allocation problem without direct recourse to the geometry of indifference maps. Let $U(X, Y)$ be the consumer's utility function; and suppose M, P_X, and P_Y denote income, the price of X, and the price of Y, respectively. Formally, the consumer's allocation problem can be stated as follows:

$$\text{Maximize } U(X, Y) \text{ subject } P_X X + P_Y Y = M. \qquad (A.3.7)$$
$$X, Y$$

The appearance of the terms X and Y below the "maximize" expression indicates that these are the variables whose values the consumer must choose. The price and income values in the budget constraint are given in advance.

The Method of Lagrangian Multipliers

As noted earlier, the function $U(X, Y)$ itself has no maximum; it simply keeps on increasing with increases in X or Y. The maximization problem defined in Equation A.3.8 is called a *constrained maximization problem*, which means we want to find the values of X and Y that produce the highest value of U *subject to the constraint that the consumer spend only as much as his income*. We will examine two different approaches to this problem.

One way of making sure that the budget constraint is satisfied is to use the so-called method of *Lagrangian multipliers*. In this method, we begin by transforming the constrained maximization problem in Equation A.3.7 into the following unconstrained maximization problem:

$$\text{Maximize } \pounds = U(X, Y) - \lambda(P_X X + P_Y Y - M). \qquad (A.3.8)$$
$$X, Y, \lambda$$

The term A is called a Lagrangian multiplier, and its role is to assure that the budget constraint is satisfied. (How it does this will become clear in a moment.) The first-order conditions for a maximum of £ are obtained by taking the first partial derivatives of £ with respect to X, Y, and λ and setting them equal to zero:

$$\frac{\partial £}{\partial X} = \frac{\partial U}{\partial X} - \lambda P_X = 0, \tag{A.3.9}$$

$$\frac{\partial £}{\partial X} = \frac{\partial U}{\partial X} - \lambda P_Y = 0, \tag{A.3.10}$$

and

$$\frac{\partial £}{\partial \lambda} = M - P_X X - P_Y Y = 0. \tag{A.3.11}$$

The next step is to solve Equations A.3.9–A.3.11 for X, Y, and λ. The solutions for X and Y are the only ones we really care about here. The role of the equilibrium value of λ is to guarantee that the budget constraint is satisfied. Note in Equation A.3.11 that setting the first partial derivative of £ with respect to λ equal to zero guarantees this result.

Specific solutions for the utility-maximizing values of X and Y require a specific functional form for the utility function. We will work through an illustrative example in a moment. But first note that an interesting characteristic of the optimal X and Y values can be obtained by dividing Equation A.3.9 by Equation A.3.10 to get

$$\frac{\partial U/\partial X}{\partial U/\partial Y} = \frac{\lambda P_X}{\lambda P_Y} = \frac{P_X}{P_Y} \tag{A.3.12}$$

Equation A.3.12 is the utility function analog to Equation 3.3 from the text, which says that the optimal values of X and Y must satisfy MRS = P_X/P_Y. The terms $\partial U/\partial X$ and $\partial U/\partial Y$ from Equation A.3.12 are called the *marginal utility of* X and the *marginal utility of* Y, respectively. In words, the marginal utility of a good is the extra utility obtained per additional unit of the good consumed. Equation A.3.12 tells us that the ratio of these marginal utilities is simply the marginal rate of substitution of Y for X.

If we rearrange Equation A.3.12 in the form

$$\frac{\partial U/\partial X}{P_X} = \frac{\partial U/\partial Y}{P_Y} \tag{A.3.13}$$

another interesting property of the optimal values of X and Y emerges. In words, the left-hand side of Equation A.3.13 may be interpreted as the extra utility gained from the last dollar spent on X. Similarly, the right-hand side of the equation is the extra utility gained from the last dollar spent on Y. It is easy to see intuitively why, for the optimal values of X and Y, the extra utility gained from the last dollar spent on each must be the same. Suppose, to the contrary, that the extra utility gained from the last dollar spent on Y exceeded the extra utility from the last dollar spent on X. The consumer could then spend a dollar less on X and a dollar more on Y and end up with more utility than he had under the original allocation. The conclusion is that the original allocation could not have been optimal. Only when the extra utility gained from the last dollar

$$U(X, Y) - \lambda(XP_X + YP_Y - M)$$

GENERATING INDIFFERENCE CURVES ALGEBRAICALLY

spent on each good is the same will it not be possible to carry out a similar utility-augmenting reallocation.

An Example To illustrate the Lagrangian method, suppose that $U(X, Y) = XY$ and that $M = 40$, $P_X = 4$, and $P_Y = 2$. Our constrained maximization problem would then be written as

$$\text{Maximize } \pounds = XY - \lambda(4X + 2Y - 40) \qquad \text{(A.3.14)}$$
$$X, Y, \lambda$$

The first-order conditions for a maximum of $\pounds$ are given by

$$\frac{\partial \pounds}{\partial X} = \frac{\partial(XY)}{\partial X} - 4\lambda = Y - 4\lambda = 0, \qquad \text{(A.3.15)}$$

$$\frac{\partial \pounds}{\partial Y} = \frac{\partial(XY)}{\partial Y} - 2\lambda = X - 2\lambda = 0, \qquad \text{(A.3.16)}$$

and

$$\frac{\partial \pounds}{\partial \lambda} = 40 - 4X - 2 = 0. \qquad \text{(A.3.17)}$$

Dividing Equation A.3.15 by Equation A.3.16 and solving for Y, we get $Y = 2X$; substituting this result into Equation A.3.17 and solving for X, we get $X = 5$, which in turn yields $Y = 2X = 10$. Thus (5, 10) is the utility-maximizing bundle.[2]

An Alternative Method

There is an alternative way of making sure that the budget constraint is satisfied, one that involves less cumbersome notation than the Lagrangian approach. In this alternative method, we simply solve the budget constraint for Y in terms of X and substitute the result wherever Y appears in the utility function. Utility then becomes a function of X alone, and we can *maximize* it by taking its first derivative with respect to X and equating that to zero.[3] The value of X that solves that equation is the optimal value of X, which can then be substituted back into the budget constraint to find the optimal value of Y. See Figure A.3.6.

To illustrate, again suppose that $U(X, Y) = XY$, with $M = 40$, $P_X = 4$, and $P_Y = 2$. The budget constraint is then $4X + 2Y = 40$, which solves for $Y = 20 - 2X$. Substituting this expression back into the utility function, we have $U(XY) = X(20 - 2X) = 20X - 2X^2$. Taking the first derivative of U with respect to X and equating the result to zero, we have

$$\frac{dU}{dX} = 20 - 4X = 0. \qquad \text{(A.3.18)}$$

which solves for $X = 5$. Plugging this value of X back into the budget constraint, we discover that the optimal value of Y is 10. So the optimal bundle is again (5, 10), just as we found using the Lagrangian approach. For these optimal values of X and Y, the consumer will obtain $(5)(10) = 50$ units of utility.

---

[2]Assuming that the second-order conditions for a local maximum are also met.

[3]Here, the second-order condition for a local maximum is that $d^2U/dX^2 < O$.

102   CHAPTER 3 APPENDIX   THE UTILITY FUNCTION APPROACH TO THE CONSUMER BUDGETING PROBLEM

FIGURE A.3.6
The Optimal Bundle when $U = XY$, $P_x = 4$, $P_y = 2$, and $M = 40$

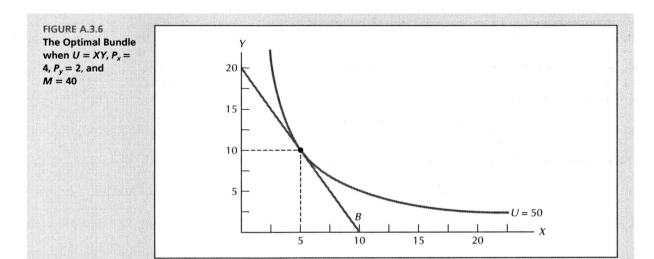

Both algebraic approaches to the budget allocation problem yield precisely the same result as the graphical approach described in the text. Note in Figure A.3.6 that the $U = 50$ indifference curve is tangent to the budget constraint at the bundle (5, 10).

A Simplifying Technique

Suppose our constrained maximization problem is of the general form

$$\text{Maximize } U(X, Y) \text{ subject to } P_X X + P_Y Y = M. \qquad \text{(A.3.19)}$$
$$X, Y$$

If (X^*, Y^*) is the optimum bundle for this maximization problem, then we know it will also be the optimum bundle for the utility function $V[U(X, Y)]$, where V is any increasing function.[4] This property often enables us to transform a computationally difficult maximization problem into a simple one. By way of illustration, consider the following example:

$$\text{Maximize } X^{1/3} Y^{2/3} \text{ subject to } 4X + 2Y = 24. \qquad \text{(A.3.20)}$$
$$X, Y$$

First note what happens when we proceed with the untransformed utility function given in Equation A.3.20. Solving the budget constraint for $Y = 12 - 2X$ and substituting back into the utility function, we have $U = X^{1/3}(12 - 2X)^{2/3}$. Calculating dU/dX is a bit tedious in this case, but if we carry out each step carefully we get the following first-order condition:

$$\frac{dU}{dX} = \left(\tfrac{1}{3}\right)X^{-2/3}(12 - 2X)^{2/3} + X^{1/3}\left(\tfrac{2}{3}\right)(12 - 2X)^{-1/3}(-2) = 0, \qquad \text{(A.3.21)}$$

which, after a little more tedious rearrangement, solves for $X = 2$. And from the budget constraint we then get $Y = 8$.

---

[4]Again, an increasing function is one for which $V(X_1) > V(X_2)$ whenever $X_1 > X_2$.

Now suppose we transform the utility function by taking its logarithm:

$$V = \ln[U(X, Y)] = \ln(X^{1/3}Y^{2/3}) = (\tfrac{1}{3})\ln X + (\tfrac{2}{3})\ln Y. \qquad \text{(A.3.22)}$$

Since the logarithm is an increasing function, when we maximize V subject to the budget constraint, we will get the same answer we got using U. The advantage of the logarithmic transformation here is that the derivative of V is much easier to calculate than the derivative of U. Again, solving the budget constraint for $Y = 12 - 2X$ and substituting the result into V, we have $V = (\tfrac{1}{3})\ln X + (\tfrac{2}{3})\ln (12 - 2X)$. This time the first-order condition follows almost without effort:

$$\frac{dV}{dX} = \frac{\tfrac{1}{3}}{X} - \frac{2(\tfrac{2}{3})}{12 - 2X} = 0, \qquad \text{(A.3.23)}$$

which solves easily for $X = 2$. Plugging $X = 2$ back into the budget constraint, we again get $Y = 8$.

The best transformation to make will naturally depend on the particular utility function you start with. The logarithmic transformation greatly simplified matters in the example above, but will not necessarily be helpful for other forms of U.

PROBLEMS

1. Tom spends all his $100 weekly income on two goods, X and Y. His utility function is given by $U(X, Y) = XY$. If $P_X = 4$ and $P_Y = 10$, how much of each good should he buy?

2. Same as Problem 1, except now Tom's utility function is given by $U(X, Y) = X^{1/2}Y^{1/2}$.

3. Note the relationship between your answers in Problems 1 and 2. What accounts for this relationship?

4. Sue consumes only two goods, food and clothing. The marginal utility of the last dollar she spends on food is 12, and the marginal utility of the last dollar she spends on clothing is 9. The price of food is $1.20/unit, and the price of clothing is $0.90/unit. Is Sue maximizing her utility?

5. Albert has a weekly allowance of $17, all of which he spends on used CDs (C) and movie rentals (M), whose respective prices are $4 and $3. His utility from these purchases is given by $U(C) + V(M)$. If the values of $U(C)$ and $V(M)$ are as shown in the table, is Albert a utility maximizer if he buys 2 CDs and rents 3 movies each week? If not, how should be reallocate his allowance?

C	U(C)	M	V(M)
0	0	0	0
1	12	1	21
2	20	2	33
3	24	3	39
4	28	4	42

CHAPTER

4

INDIVIDUAL AND MARKET DEMAND

A pound of salt costs 30 cents at the grocery store where I shop. My family and I use the same amount of salt at that price as we would if it instead sold for 5 cents/lb or even $10/lb. I also consume about the same amount of salt now as I did as a graduate student, when my income was less than one-tenth as large as it is today.

Salt is an unusual case. The amounts we buy of many other goods are much more sensitive to prices and incomes. Sometimes, for example, my family and I consider spending a sabbatical year in New York City, where housing prices are more than triple what they are in Ithaca. If we ever do go there, we will probably live in an apartment that is less than one-fourth the size of our current house.

CHAPTER PREVIEW

Viewed within the framework of the rational choice model, my behavior with respect to salt and housing purchases is perfectly intelligible. Our focus in this chapter is to use the tools from Chapter 3 to shed additional light on why, exactly, the responses of various purchase decisions to changes in income and price differ so widely. In Chapter 3, we saw how changes in prices and incomes affect the budget constraint. Here we will see how changes in the budget constraint affect actual purchase decisions. More specifically, we will use the rational choice model to generate an individual consumer's demand curve for a product and employ our model to construct a relationship that summarizes how individual demands vary with income.

We will see how the total effect of a price change can be decomposed into two separate effects: (1) the substitution effect, which denotes the change in the quantity demanded that results because the price change makes substitute goods seem either more or less attractive; and (2) the income effect, which denotes the change in quantity demanded that results from the change in purchasing power caused by the price change.

Next we will show how individual demand curves can be added to yield the demand curve for the market as a whole. A central analytical concept we will develop in this chapter is the price elasticity of demand, a measure of the responsiveness of purchase decisions to small changes in price. We will also consider the income elasticity of demand, a measure of the responsiveness of purchase decisions to small changes in income. And we will see that, for some goods, the distribution of income, not just its average value, is an important determinant of market demand.

A final elasticity concept in this chapter is the cross-price elasticity of demand, which is a measure of the responsiveness of the quantity demanded of one good to small changes in the prices of another good. Cross-price elasticity is the criterion by which pairs of goods are classified as being either substitutes or complements.

These analytical constructs provide a deeper understanding of a variety of market behaviors as well as a stronger foundation for intelligent decision and policy analysis.

THE EFFECTS OF CHANGES IN PRICE

The Price-Consumption Curve

Recall from Chapter 2 that a market demand curve is a relationship that tells how much of a good the market as a whole wants to purchase at various prices. Suppose we want to generate a demand schedule for a good—say, shelter—not for the market as a whole but for only a single consumer. Holding income, preferences, and the prices of all other goods constant, how will a change in the price of shelter affect the amount of shelter the consumer buys? To answer this question, we begin with this consumer's indifference map, plotting shelter on the horizontal axis and the composite good Y on the vertical axis. Suppose the consumer's income is $120/wk, and the price of the composite good is again 1. The vertical intercept of her budget constraint will then be 120. The horizontal intercept will be $120/P_S$, where P_S denotes the price of shelter. Figure 4.1 shows four budget constraints that correspond to four different prices of shelter, namely, $24/sq yd, $12/sq yd, $6/sq yd, and $4/sq yd. The corresponding best affordable bundles contain 2.5, 7, 15, and 20 sq yd/wk of shelter, respectively. If we were to repeat this procedure indefinitely for many prices, the resulting points of tangency would trace out the line labeled PCC in Figure 4.1. This line is called the **price-consumption curve**, or **PCC**.

For the particular consumer whose indifference map is shown in Figure 4.1, note that each time the price of shelter falls, the budget constraint rotates outward, enabling the consumer to purchase not only more shelter but more of the composite good as well. And each time the price of shelter falls, this consumer chooses a bundle that contains more shelter than in the bundle chosen previously. Note, however, that the amount of money spent on the composite good

price-consumption curve (PCC) holding income and the price of Y constant, the PCC for a good X is the set of optimal bundles traced on an indifference map as the price of X varies.

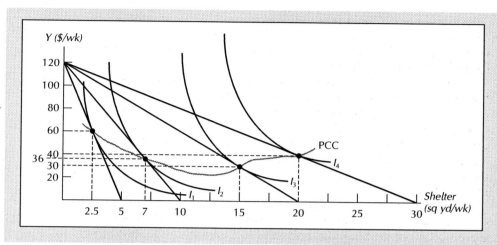

FIGURE 4.1
The Price-Consumption Curve
Holding income and the price of Y fixed, we vary the price of shelter. The set of optimal bundles traced out by the various budget lines is called the price-consumption curve, or PCC.

may either rise or fall when the price of shelter falls. Thus, the amount spent on other goods falls when the price of shelter falls from \$24/sq yd to \$12/sq yd but rises when the price of shelter falls from \$6/sq yd to \$4/sq yd. Below, we will see why this is a relatively common purchase pattern.

The Individual Consumer's Demand Curve

An individual consumer's demand curve is like the market demand curve in that it tells the quantities the consumer will buy at various prices. All the information we need to construct the individual demand curve is contained in the price-consumption curve. The first step in going from the PCC to the individual demand curve is to record the relevant price-quantity combinations from the PCC in Figure 4.1, as in Table 4.1. (Recall from Chapter 3 that the price of shelter along any budget constraint is given by income divided by the horizontal intercept of that budget constraint.)

The next step is to plot the price-quantity pairs from Table 4.1, with the price of shelter on the vertical axis and the quantity of shelter on the horizontal. With sufficiently many price-quantity pairs, we generate the individual's demand curve, shown as the line DD in Figure 4.2. Note carefully that in moving from the PCC to the individual demand curve, we are moving from a graph in which both axes measure quantities to one in which price is plotted against quantity.

Price of shelter (\$/sq yd)	Quantity of shelter demanded (sq yd/wk)
24	2.5
12	7
6	15
4	20

TABLE 4.1
A Demand Schedule
To derive the individual's demand curve for shelter from the PCC in Figure 4.1, begin by recording the quantities of shelter that correspond to the shelter prices on each budget constraint.

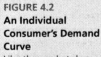

FIGURE 4.2
An Individual Consumer's Demand Curve
Like the market demand curve, the individual demand curve is a relationship that tells how much the consumer wants to purchase at different prices.

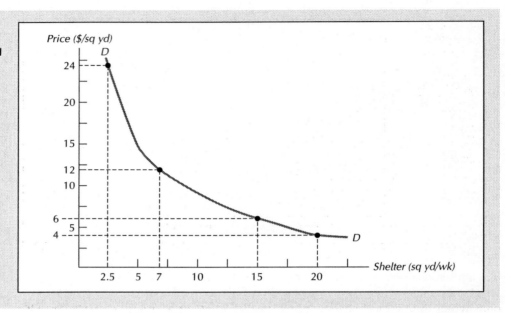

THE EFFECTS OF CHANGES IN INCOME

The Income-Consumption Curve

income-consumption curve (ICC) holding the prices of X and Y constant, the ICC for a good X is the set of optimal bundles traced on an indifference map as income varies.

The PCC and the individual demand schedule are two different ways of summarizing how a consumer's purchase decisions respond to variations in prices. Analogous devices exist to summarize responses to variations in income. The income analog to the PCC is the **income-consumption curve,** or **ICC.** To generate the PCC for shelter, we held preferences, income, and the price of the composite good constant while tracing out the effects of a change in the price of shelter. In the case of the ICC, we hold preferences and relative prices constant and trace out the effects of changes in income.

In Figure 4.3, for example, we hold the price of the composite good constant at 1 and the price of shelter constant at \$10/sq yd and examine what happens when income takes the values \$40/wk, \$60/wk, \$100/wk, and \$120/wk. Recall from Chapter 3 that a change in income shifts the budget constraint parallel to itself. As before, to each budget there corresponds a best affordable bundle. The set of best affordable bundles is denoted as ICC in Figure 4.3. For the consumer whose indifference map is shown, the ICC happens to be a straight line, but this need not always be the case.

The Engel Curve

Engel curve E curve that plots the relationship between the quantity of X consumed and income.

The analog to the individual demand curve in the income domain is the individual **Engel curve.** It takes the quantities of shelter demanded from the ICC and plots them against the corresponding values of income. Table 4.2 shows the income-shelter pairs for the four budget constraints shown in Figure 4.3. If we were to plot indefinitely many income-consumption pairs for the consumer shown in Figure 4.3, we would trace out the line EE shown in Figure 4.4. The

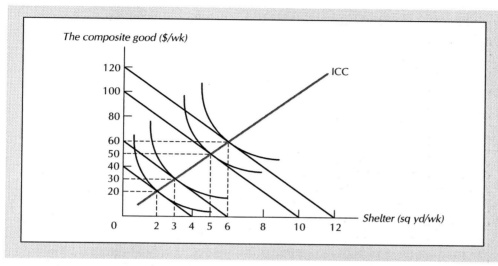

FIGURE 4.3
An Income-Consumption Curve
As income increases, the budget constraint moves outward. Holding preferences and relative prices constant, the ICC traces out how these changes in income affect consumption. It is the set of all tangencies as the budget line moves outward.

Engel curve shown in Figure 4.4 happens to be linear, but Engel curves in general need not be.

Note carefully the distinction between what we measure on the vertical axis of the ICC and what we measure on the vertical axis of the Engel curve. On the vertical axis of the ICC, we measure the amount the consumer spends each week on all goods other than shelter. On the vertical axis of the Engel curve, by contrast, we measure the consumer's total weekly income.

Note also that, as was true with the PCC and individual demand curves, the ICC and Engel curves contain essentially the same information. The advantage of the Engel curve is that it allows us to see at a glance how the quantity demanded varies with income.

Normal and Inferior Goods

Note that the Engel curve in Figure 4.5*a* is upward-sloping, implying that the more income a consumer has, the more tenderloin steak he will buy each week. Most things we buy have this property, which is the defining characteristic of a **normal good.** Goods that do not have this property are called **inferior goods.** For such goods, an increase in income leads to a reduction in the quantity demanded. Figure 4.5*b* is an example of an Engel curve for an inferior good. The more income a person has, the less hamburger he will buy each week.

normal good one whose quantity demanded rises as income rises.

inferior good one whose quantity demanded falls as income rises.

Income ($/wk)	Quantity of shelter demanded (sq yd/wk)
40	2
60	3
100	5
120	6

TABLE 4.2
Income and Quantity of Shelter Demanded

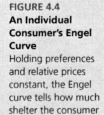

FIGURE 4.4
An Individual Consumer's Engel Curve
Holding preferences and relative prices constant, the Engel curve tells how much shelter the consumer will purchase at various levels of income.

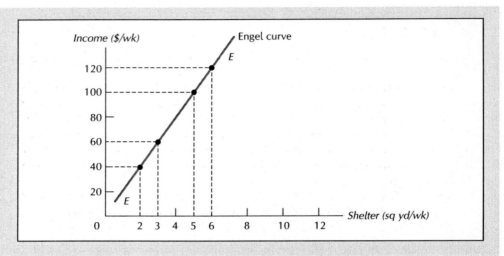

Why would someone buy less of a good following an increase in his income? The prototypical inferior good is one for which there are several strongly preferred, but more expensive, substitutes. Supermarkets, for example, generally carry several different grades of ground beef, ranging from hamburger, which has the highest fat content, to ground sirloin, which has the lowest. A consumer who is trying to restrict the amount of fat in his diet will tend to switch to a leaner grade of meat as soon as he is able to afford it. For such a consumer, hamburger will be an inferior good.

For any consumer who spends all her income, it is a matter of simple arithmetic that not all goods can be inferior. After all, when income rises, it is mathematically impossible to spend less on all goods at once. From this observation, it follows that the more broadly a good is defined, the less likely it is to be inferior. Thus, while hamburger is an inferior good for many consumers, there are

FIGURE 4.5
The Engel Curves for Normal and Inferior Goods
(a) This Engel curve is for a normal good. The quantity demanded increases with income. (b) This Engel curve for hamburger has the negative slope characteristic of inferior goods. As the consumer's income grows, he switches from hamburger to more desirable cuts of meat.

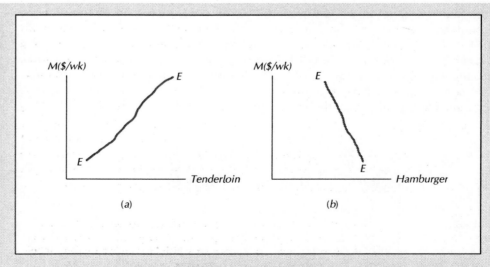

Frank: Microeconomics
an/ Behavior, Sixth E/ition

II. The Theory of Consumer
Behavior

4. In/ivi/ual an/ Market
Deman/

© The McGraw–Hill
Companies, 2005

105

probably very few people for whom the good "meat" is inferior, and fewer still for whom "food" is inferior.[1]

THE INCOME AND SUBSTITUTION EFFECTS OF A PRICE CHANGE

In Chapter 2 we saw that a change in the price of a good affects purchase decisions for two reasons. For concreteness, we will consider the effects of a price increase. (The effects of a price reduction will be in the opposite direction from those of a price increase.) One effect of a price increase is to make close substitutes of the good more attractive than before. For example, when the price of rice increases, wheat becomes more attractive. This is the so-called **substitution effect** of a price increase.

> **substitution effect** that component of the total effect of a price change that results from the associated change in the relative attractiveness of other goods.

The second effect of a price increase is to reduce the consumer's purchasing power. For a normal good, this effect too will reduce the amount purchased. But for an inferior good, the effect is just the opposite. The loss in purchasing power, taken by itself, increases the quantity purchased of an inferior good. The change in the quantity purchased attributable to the change in purchasing power is called the **income effect** of the price change.

> **income effect** that component of the total effect of a price change that results from the associated change in real purchasing power.

The *total effect* of the price increase is the sum of the substitution and income effects. The substitution effect always causes the quantity purchased to move in the opposite direction from the change in price—when price goes up, the quantity demanded goes down; and conversely, when price goes down, the quantity demanded goes up. The direction of the income effect depends on whether the good is normal or inferior. For normal goods, the income effect works in the same direction as the substitution effect—when price goes up [down], the fall [rise] in purchasing power causes the quantity demanded to fall [rise]. For inferior goods, by contrast, the income and substitution effects work against one another.

The substitution and income effects of a price increase can be seen most clearly when they are displayed graphically. Let us begin by depicting the total effect of a price increase. In Figure 4.6, the consumer has an initial income of \$120/wk and the initial price of shelter is \$6/sq yd. This gives rise to the budget constraint labeled B_0, and the optimal bundle on that budget is denoted by A, which contains 10 sq yd/wk of shelter. Now let the price of shelter increase from \$6/sq yd to \$24/sq yd, resulting in the budget labeled B_1. The new optimal bundle is D, which contains 2 sq yd/wk of shelter. The movement from A to D is called the total effect of the price increase. Naturally, the price increase causes the consumer to end up on a lower indifference curve (I_1) than the one he was able to attain on his original budget (I_0).

To decompose the total effect into the income and substitution effects, we begin by asking the following question: How much income would the consumer need to reach his original indifference curve (I_0) after the increase in the price of shelter? Note in Figure 4.7 that the answer is \$240/wk. If the consumer were given a total income of that amount, it would undo the injury caused by the loss in purchasing power resulting from the increase in the price of shelter. The

---

[1]Another useful way to partition the set of consumer goods is between so-called *necessities* and *luxuries*. A good is defined as a luxury for a person if he spends a larger proportion of his income on it when his income rises. A necessity, by contrast, is one for which he spends a smaller proportion of his income when his income rises. (More on this distinction follows.)

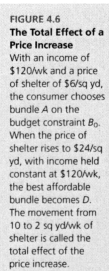

FIGURE 4.6
The Total Effect of a Price Increase
With an income of $120/wk and a price of shelter of $6/sq yd, the consumer chooses bundle A on the budget constraint B_0. When the price of shelter rises to $24/sq yd, with income held constant at $120/wk, the best affordable bundle becomes D. The movement from 10 to 2 sq yd/wk of shelter is called the total effect of the price increase.

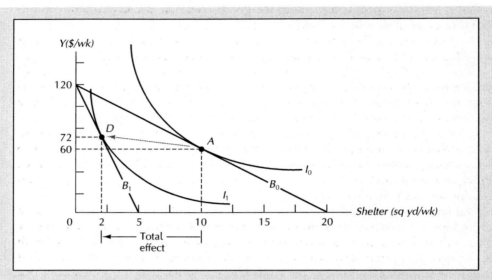

budget constraint labeled B' is purely hypothetical, a device constructed for the purpose at hand. It has the same slope as the new budget constraint (B_1)—namely, -24—and it is just far enough out from the origin to be tangent to the original indifference curve, I_0. With the budget constraint B', the optimal bundle is C, which contains 6 sq yd/wk of shelter. The movement from A to C gives rise

FIGURE 4.7
The Substitution and Income Effects of a Price Change
To get the substitution effect, slide the new budget B_1 outward parallel to itself until it becomes tangent to the original indifference curve, I_0. The movement from A to C gives rise to the substitution effect, the reduction in shelter due solely to the fact that shelter is now more expensive relative to other goods. The movement from C to D gives rise to the income effect. It is the reduction in shelter that results from the loss in purchasing power implicit in the price increase.

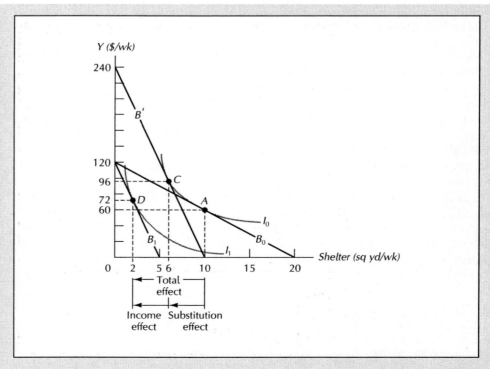

to the substitution effect of the price change—which here involves a reduction of 4 sq yd/wk of shelter and an increase of 36 units/wk of the composite good.

The hypothetical budget constraint B' tells us that even if the consumer had enough income to reach the same indifference curve as before, the increase in the price of shelter would cause him to reduce his consumption of it in favor of other goods and services. *For consumers whose indifference curves have the conventional convex shape, the substitution effect of a price increase will always be to reduce consumption of the good whose price increased.*

The income effect of the price increase stems from the movement from C to D. The particular good shown in Figure 4.7 happens to be a normal good. The hypothetical movement of the consumer's income from \$240/wk to \$120/wk serves to accentuate the reduction of his consumption of shelter, causing it to fall from 6 sq yd/wk to 2 sq yd/wk.

Whereas the income effect reinforces the substitution effect in the case of a normal good, the two effects tend to offset one another in the case of an inferior good. In Figure 4.8, the line B_0 depicts the budget constraint for a consumer with an income of \$24/wk who faces a price of hamburger of \$1/lb. On B_0 the best affordable bundle is A, which contains 12 lb/wk of hamburger. When the price of hamburger rises to \$2/lb, the resulting budget constraint is B_1 and the best affordable bundle is now D, which contains 9 lb/wk of hamburger. The total effect of the price increase is thus to reduce the quantity of hamburger consumed by 3 lb/wk. Budget constraint B' once again is the hypothetical budget constraint that enables the consumer to reach the original indifference curve at the new price ratio. Note in this case that the substitution effect of the price change (the change in hamburger consumption associated with movement from A to C in

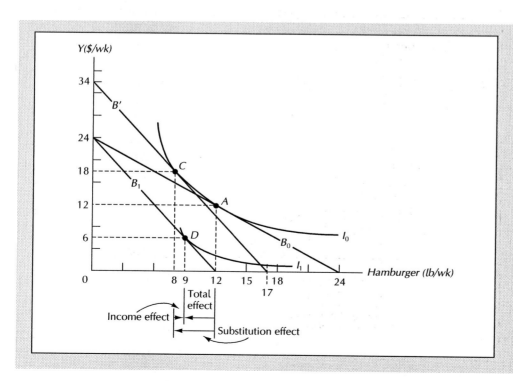

FIGURE 4.8
Income and Substitution Effects for an Inferior Good
By contrast to the case of a normal good, the income effect acts to offset the substitution effect for an inferior good.

Figure 4.8) is to reduce the quantity of hamburger consumed by 4 lb/wk—that is, to reduce it by more than the value of the total effect. The income effect by itself (the change in hamburger consumption associated with the movement from C to D) actually serves to increase hamburger consumption by 1 lb/wk. The income effect thus works in the opposite direction from the substitution effect for an inferior good such as hamburger.

Giffen Goods

Giffen good one for which the quantity demanded rises as its price rises.

A **Giffen good** is one for which the total effect of a price increase is to increase, not reduce, the quantity purchased. Since the substitution effect of a price increase is always to reduce the quantity purchased, the Giffen good must be one whose income effect acts to offset the substitution effect. That is, the Giffen good must be an inferior good—so strongly inferior, in fact, that the income effect is actually larger than the substitution effect.

A much-cited example of a Giffen good was the potato during the Irish potato famine of the nineteenth century. The idea was that potatoes were such a large part of poor people's diets to begin with that an increase in their price had a severe adverse effect on the real value of purchasing power. Having less real income, many families responded by cutting back on meat and other more expensive foods, and buying even more potatoes. (See Figure 4.9.) Or so the story goes.

Modern historians dispute whether the potato ever was really a Giffen good. Whatever the resolution of this dispute, the potato story does illustrate the characteristics that a Giffen good would logically have to possess. First, it would not only have to be inferior, but also have to occupy a large share of the consumer's budget. Otherwise, an increase in its price would not create a significant reduction in real purchasing power. (Doubling the price of keyrings, for example, does not make anyone appreciably poorer.) The second characteristic required of a Giffen good is that it have a relatively small substitution effect, one small enough to be overwhelmed by the income effect.

In practice, it is extremely unlikely that a good will satisfy both properties required of a Giffen good. Most goods, after all, account for only a tiny share of the consumer's total expenditures. Moreover, as noted, the more broadly a good is defined, the less likely it is to be inferior. Finally, inferior goods by their very

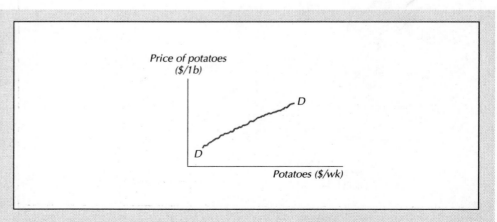

FIGURE 4.9
The Demand Curve for a Giffen Good
If a good is so strongly inferior that the income effect of a price increase dominates the substitution effect, the demand curve for that good will be upward sloping. Giffen goods are a theoretical possibility, but are seldom, if ever, observed in practice.

THE INCOME AND SUBSTITUTION EFFECTS OF A PRICE CHANGE   115

nature tend to be ones for which there are close substitutes. The consumer's tendency to substitute ground sirloin for hamburger, for example, is precisely what makes hamburger tend to be an inferior good.

The Giffen good is an intriguing anomaly, chiefly useful for testing students' understanding of the subtleties of income and substitution effects. Unless otherwise stated, all demand curves used in the remainder of this text will be assumed to have the conventional downward slope.

Income and substitution effects for perfect complements. Suppose skis and bindings are perfect, one-for-one complements and Paula spends all her equipment budget of $1200/yr on these two goods. Skis and bindings each cost $200. What will be the income and substitution effects of an increase in the price of bindings to $400 per pair?

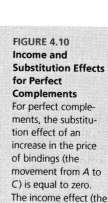

EXAMPLE 4.1

Since our goal here is to examine the effect on two specific goods (skis and bindings), we proceed by devoting one axis to each good and dispense with the composite good. On the original budget constraint, B_0, the optimal bundle is denoted A in Figure 4.10. Paula buys three pairs of skis per year and three pairs of bindings. When the price of bindings rises from $200 per pair to $400 per pair, we get the new budget constraint, B_1, and the resulting optimal bundle D, which contains two pairs of skis per year and two pairs of bindings. An equipment budget of $1800/yr is what the consumer would need at the new price to attain the same indifference curve she did originally (I_0). (To get this figure, slide B_1 out until it hits I_0, then calculate the cost of buying the bundle at the vertical intercept—here, nine pairs of skis per year at $200 per pair.) Note that because perfect complements have right-angled indifference curves, the budget B' results in an optimal bundle C that is exactly the same as the original bundle A. For perfect complements, the substitution effect is zero. So for this case, the total effect of the price increase is exactly the same as the income effect of the price increase.

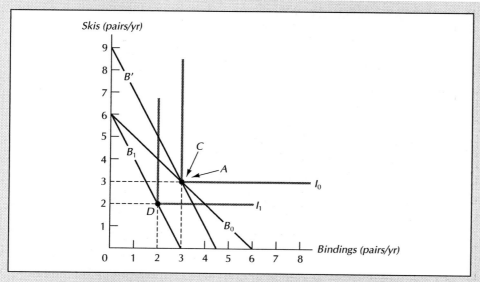

FIGURE 4.10
Income and Substitution Effects for Perfect Complements
For perfect complements, the substitution effect of an increase in the price of bindings (the movement from A to C) is equal to zero. The income effect (the movement from A to D) and the total effect are one and the same.

Example 4.1 tells us that if the price of ski bindings goes up relative to the price of skis, people will not alter the proportion of skis and bindings they purchase. But because the price increase lowers their real purchasing power (that is, because it limits the quantities of both goods that they can buy), they will respond by buying fewer units of ski equipment. The income effect will thus cause them to lower their consumption of both skis and bindings by the same proportion.

EXERCISE 4.1

Repeat Example 4.1 with the assumption that pairs of skis and pairs of bindings are perfect two-for-one complements. (That is, assume that Paula wears out two pairs of skis for every pair of bindings she wears out.)

EXAMPLE 4.2

Income and substitution effects for perfect substitutes. Suppose Pam considers tea and coffee to be perfect one-for-one substitutes and spends her budget of $12/wk on these two beverages. Coffee costs $1/cup, while tea costs $1.20/cup. What will be the income and substitution effects of an increase in the price of coffee to $1.50/cup?

Pam will initially demand 12 cups of coffee per week and no cups of tea (point A in Figure 4.11), since each good contributes equally to her utility but tea is more expensive. When the price of coffee rises, Pam switches to consuming only tea, buying 10 cups of tea per week and no coffee (point D). Pam would need a budget of $14.40/wk to afford 12 cups of tea (point C), which she likes as well as the 12 cups of coffee she originally consumed. The substitution effect is from $(12, 0)$ to $(0, 12)$ and the income effect from $(0, 12)$ to $(0, 10)$, with the total effect from $(12, 0)$ to $(0, 10)$. With perfect substitutes, the substitution effect can be very large: For small price changes (near MRS), consumers may switch from consuming all one good to consuming only the other good.

FIGURE 4.11
Income and Substitution Effects for Perfect Substitutes
For perfect substitutes, the substitution effect of an increase in the price of coffee (the movement from A to C) can be very large.

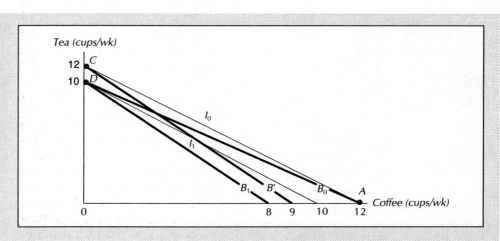

EXERCISE 4.2

Starting from the original price in Example 4.2, what will be the income and substitution effects of an increase in the price of tea to $1.50/cup?

CONSUMER RESPONSIVENESS TO CHANGES IN PRICE

We began this chapter with the observation that for certain goods, such as salt, consumption is highly insensitive to changes in price while for others, such as housing, it is much more sensitive. The principal reason for studying income and substitution effects is that these devices help us understand such differences.

Let us consider first the case of salt. When analyzing substitution and income effects, there are two salient features to note about salt. First, for most consumers, it has no close substitutes. If someone were forbidden to shake salt onto his steak, he might respond by shaking a little extra pepper, or even by squeezing some lemon juice onto it. But for most people, these alternatives would fall considerably short of the real thing. The second prominent feature of salt is that it occupies an almost imperceptibly small share of total expenditures. An extremely heavy user of salt might consume a pound every month. If this person's income were $1200/mo, a doubling of the price of salt—say, from $0.30/lb to $0.60/lb—would increase the share of his budget accounted for by salt from 0.00025 to 0.0005. For all practical purposes, therefore, the income effect of a price increase of salt is negligible.

It is instructive to represent these two properties of salt diagrammatically. In Figure 4.12, the fact that salt has no close substitutes is represented by indifference curves with a nearly right-angled shape. Salt's negligible budget share is captured by the fact that the cusps of these indifference curves occur at extremely small quantities of salt.

Suppose, as in Figure 4.12, the price of salt is originally $0.30/lb, resulting in an equilibrium bundle labeled A in the enlarged region, which contains 1.0002 lb/mo of salt. A price increase to $0.60/lb results in a new equilibrium bundle D with 1 lb/mo of salt. The income and substitution effects are measured in terms of the intermediate bundle C. Geometrically, the income effect is small because the original tangency occurred so near the vertical intercept of the budget constraint. When we are near the pivot point of the budget constraint, even a very large rotation produces only a small movement. The substitution effect, in turn, is small because of the nearly right-angled shape of the indifference curves.

Let us now contrast the salt case with the housing example. The two salient facts about housing are that (1) it accounts for a substantial share of total expenditures (more than 30 percent for many people), and (2) most people have considerable latitude to substitute between housing and other goods. The second assertion may not appear obvious at first glance, but on reflection, its plausibility becomes clear. Indeed, there are many ways to substitute away from housing expenditures. The most obvious is to switch from a larger to a smaller dwelling. Many Manhattanites, for example, can afford to live in apartments larger than the ones they now occupy, yet they prefer to spend what they save in rent on restaurant meals, theater performances, and the like. Another

FIGURE 4.12
Income and Substitution Effects of a Price Increase for Salt
The total effect of a price change will be very small when (1) the original equilibrium bundle lies near the vertical intercept of the budget constraint and (2) the indifference curves have a nearly right-angled shape. The first factor causes the income effect (the reduction in salt consumption associated with the movement from C to D) to be small; the second factor causes the substitution effect (the reduction in salt consumption associated with the movement from A to C) to be small.

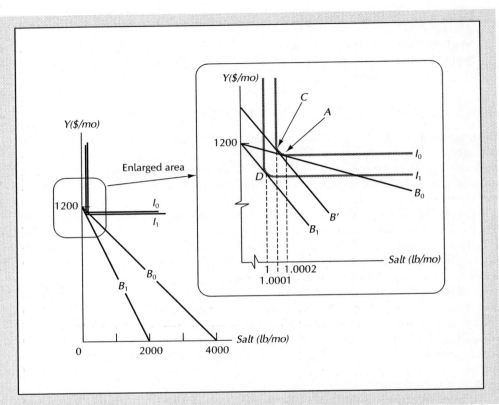

substitution possibility is to consume less conveniently located housing. Someone who works in Manhattan can live near her job and pay extremely high rent; alternatively, she can live in New Jersey or Long Island and pay considerably less. Or she can choose an apartment in a less fashionable neighborhood, or one not quite as close to a convenient subway stop. The point is that there are many different options for housing, and the choice among them will depend strongly on income and relative prices.

In Figure 4.13, the consumer's income is $120/wk and the initial price of shelter is $0.60/sq yd. The resulting budget constraint is labeled B_0, and the best affordable bundle on it is A, which contains 100 sq yd/wk of shelter. An increase in the price of shelter to $2.40/sq yd causes the quantity demanded to fall to 20 sq yd/wk. The smooth convex shape of the indifference curves represents the high degree of substitution possibilities between housing and other goods and accounts for the relatively large substitution effect (the fall in shelter consumption associated with the movement from A to C). Note also that the original equilibrium bundle, A, was a tangency far from the vertical pivot point of the budget constraint. By contrast to the case of salt, here the rotation in the budget constraint caused by the price increase produces a large movement in the location of the relevant segment of the new budget constraint. Accordingly, the income effect for shelter (the fall in shelter consumption associated with the movement

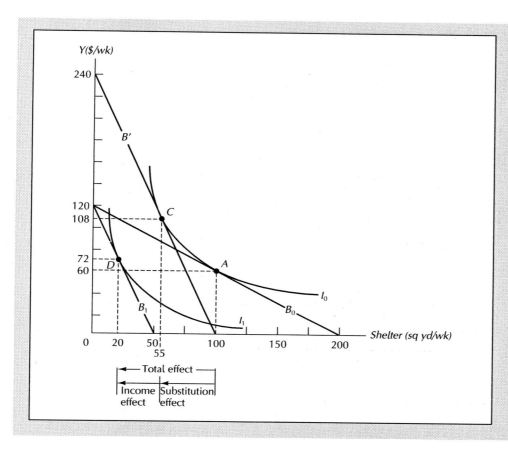

CONSUMER RESPONSIVENESS TO CHANGES IN PRICE   119

FIGURE 4.13
Income and Substitution Effects for a Price-Sensitive Good
Because shelter occupies a large share of the budget, its income effect tends to be large. And because it is practical to substitute away from shelter, the substitution effect also tends to be large. The quantities demanded of goods with both large substitution and large income effects are highly responsive to changes in price.

from C to D) is much larger than in the case of salt. With both a large substitution and a large income effect working together, the total effect of an increase in the price of shelter (the fall in shelter consumption associated with the movement from A to D) is very large.

Deriving individual demand curve for perfect complements. James views car washes and gasoline as perfect complements in a 1-to-10 ratio, requiring one car wash for every 10 gallons of gas. Gas costs $1/gal, and James has $48/mo to spend on gas and car washes. (See Figure 4.14, page 120.) Construct James's demand curve for car washes by considering his quantity demanded of car washes at various prices (such as 2, 6, 14; see Figure 4.15).

EXAMPLE 4.3

James's preferences dictate that his optimal bundle must satisfy $G = 10W$, as his indifference curves are L-shaped. James's budget constraint is $G + P_W W = 48$, or $G = 48 - P_W W$. Substituting $G = 10W$, his budget constraint is $10W + P_W W = 48$,

FIGURE 4.14

A Price Increase for Car Washes

With $48/mo, James buys 4 washes/mo when the price is $2/wash (budget constraint B), 3 washes/mo when the price is $6/wash (budget constraint B'), and 2 washes/mo when the price is $14/wash (budget constraint B").

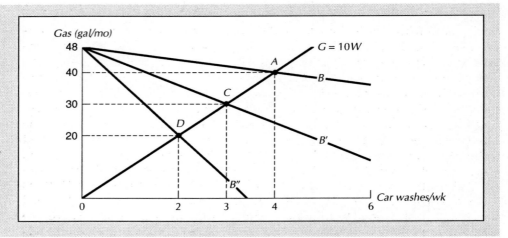

which implies $(10 + P_W)W = 48$. At $P_W = 2$, $W = 4$; at $P_W = 6$, $W = 3$; at $P_W = 14$, $W = 2$, as summarized in Table 4.3.

TABLE 4.3
A Demand Schedule for Car Washes

Price of car wash ($/wash)	Quantity of car washes demanded (washes/mo)
2	4
6	3
14	2
38	1

FIGURE 4.15

James's Demand for Car Washes

The quantity of car washes James demands at various prices forms his demand curve for car washes.

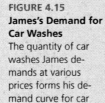

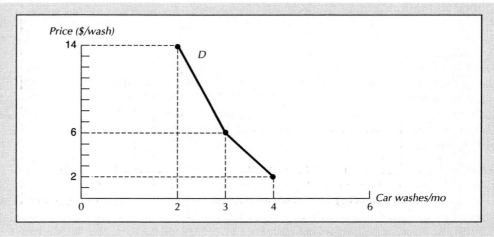

MARKET DEMAND: AGGREGATING INDIVIDUAL DEMAND CURVES

Having seen where individual demand curves come from, we are now in a position to see how individual demand curves may be aggregated to form the market demand curve. For simplicity, let us consider a market for a good—for the sake of concreteness, again shelter—that consists of only two potential consumers. Given the demand curves for each of these consumers, how do we generate the market demand curve for shelter? In Figure 4.16, D_1 and D_2 represent the individual demand curves for consumers 1 and 2, respectively. To get the market demand curve, we begin by calling out a price—say, \$4/sq yd—and adding the quantities demanded by each consumer at that price. This sum, 6 sq yd/wk + 2 sq yd/wk = 8 sq yd/wk, is the total quantity of shelter demanded in the market at the price \$4/sq yd. We then plot the point (4, 8) as one of the quantity-price pairs on the market demand curve D in the right panel of Figure 4.16. To generate additional points on the market demand curve, we simply repeat this process for other prices. Thus, the price \$8/sq yd corresponds to a quantity of 4 + 0 = 4 sq yd/wk on the market demand curve for shelter. Proceeding in like fashion for additional prices, we trace out the entire market demand curve for shelter. Note that for prices above \$8/sq yd, consumer 2 demands no shelter at all, and so the market demand curve for prices above \$8 is identical to the demand curve for consumer 1.

The procedure of announcing a price and adding the individual quantities demanded at that price is called *horizontal summation*. It is carried out the same way whether there are only two consumers in the market or many millions. In both large and small markets, the market demand curve is the horizontal summation of the individual demand curves.

EXERCISE 4.3

Write the individual demand curves for shelter in Figure 4.16 in algebraic form, then add them algebraically to generate the market demand curve for shelter. (*Caution:* Note that the formula for quantity along D_2 is valid only for prices between 0 and 8.)

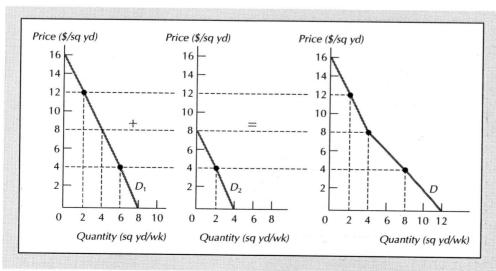

FIGURE 4.16
Generating Market Demand from Individual Demands
The market demand curve (*D* in the right panel) is the horizontal sum of the individual demand curves, D_1 (left panel) and D_2 (center panel).

In Chapter 2 we saw that it is often easier to generate numerical solutions when demand and supply curves are expressed algebraically rather than geometrically. Similarly, it will often be convenient to aggregate individual demand curves algebraically rather than graphically. When using the algebraic approach, a common error is to add individual demand curves vertically instead of horizontally. A simple example makes this danger clear.

<table>
<tr><td>EXAMPLE 4.4</td><td>Smith and Jones are the only consumers in the market for beech saplings in a small town in Vermont. Their demand curves are given by $P = 30 - 2Q_J$ and $P = 30 - 3Q_S$ where Q_J and Q_S are the quantities demanded by Jones and Smith, respectively. What is the market demand curve for beech saplings in their town?</td></tr>
</table>

When we add demand curves horizontally, we are adding quantities, not prices. Thus it is necessary first to solve the individual demand equations for the respective quantities in terms of price. This yields $Q_J = 15 - (P/2)$ for Jones, and $Q_S = 10 - (P/3)$ for Smith. If the quantity demanded in the market is denoted by Q, we have $Q = Q_J + Q_S = 15 - (P/2) + 10 - (P/3) = 25 - (5P/6)$. Solving back for P, we get the equation for the market demand curve: $P = 30 - (6Q/5)$. We can easily verify that this is the correct market demand curve by adding the individual demand curves graphically, as in Figure 4.17.

The common pitfall is to add the demand functions as originally stated and then solve for P in terms of Q. Here, this would yield $P = 30 - (5Q/2)$, which is obviously not the market demand curve we are looking for.

The horizontal summation of individual consumers' demands into market demand has a simple form when the consumers in the market are all identical. Suppose n consumers each have the demand curve $P = a - bQ_i$. To add up the quantities for the n consumers into market demand, we rearrange the consumer demand curve $P = a - bQ_i$ to express quantity alone on one side $Q_i = a/b - (1/b)P$. Then market demand is the sum of the quantities demanded Q_i by each of the n consumers.

$$Q = nQ_i = n\left(\frac{a}{b} - \frac{1}{b}P\right) = \frac{na}{b} - \frac{n}{b}P.$$

FIGURE 4.17
The Market Demand Curve for Beech Saplings
When adding individual demand curves algebraically, be sure to solve for quantity first before adding.

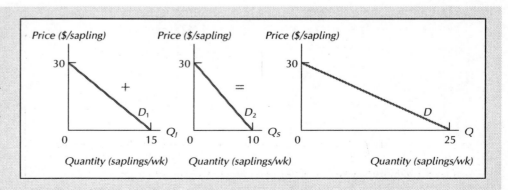

MARKET DEMAND: AGGREGATING INDIVIDUAL DEMAND CURVES   123

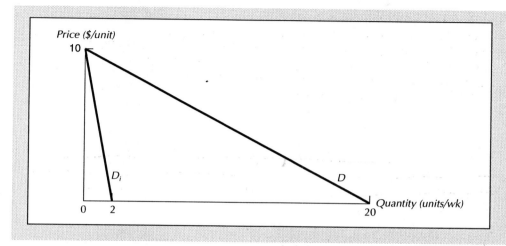

FIGURE 4.18
Market Demand with Identical Consumers
When 10 consumers each have demand curve $P = 10 - 5Q_i$ the market demand curve is the horizontal summation $P = 10 - (\frac{1}{2}) Q$, with the same price intercept and $\frac{1}{10}$ the slope.

We can then rearrange market demand $Q = na/b - n(P/b)$ to get back in the form of price alone on one side $P = a - (b/n) Q$. The intuition is that each one unit demanded by the market is $1/n$ unit for each consumer to demand. These calculations suggest a general rule for constructing the market demand curve when consumers are identical. If we have n individual consumer demand curves $P = a - bQ_i$, then the market demand curve is $P = a - (b/n)Q$.

Suppose a market has 10 consumers, each with demand curve $P = 10 - 5Q_i$, where P is the price in dollars per unit and Q_i is the number of units demanded per week by the ith consumer (Figure 4.18). Find the market demand curve.

EXAMPLE 4.5

First, we need to rearrange the representative consumer demand curve $P = 10 - 5Q_i$ to have quantity alone on one side:

$$Q_i = 2 - \tfrac{1}{5}P.$$

Then we multiply by the number of consumers, $n = 10$:

$$Q = nQ_i = 10Q_i = 10(2 - \tfrac{1}{5}P) = 20 - 2P.$$

Finally, we rearrange the market demand curve $Q = 20 - 2P$ to have price alone on one side, $P = 10 - (\tfrac{1}{2})Q$, to return to the slope-intercept form.

EXERCISE 4.4

Suppose a market has 30 consumers, each with demand curve $P = 120 - 60Q_i$, where P is price in dollars per unit and Q_i is the number of units demanded per week by the ith consumer. Find the market demand curve.

PRICE ELASTICITY OF DEMAND

price elasticity of demand the percentage change in the quantity of a good demanded that results from a 1 percent change in its price.

An analytical tool of central importance is the **price elasticity of demand.** It is a quantitative measure of the responsiveness of purchase decisions to variations in price, and as we will see in both this and later chapters, it is useful for a variety of practical problems. *Price elasticity of demand is defined as the percentage change in the quantity of a good demanded that results from a 1 percent change in price.* For example, if a 1 percent rise in the price of shelter caused a 2 percent reduction in the quantity of shelter demanded, then the price elasticity of demand for shelter would be −2. The price elasticity of demand will always be negative (or zero) because price changes always move in the opposite direction from changes in quantity demanded.

The demand for a good is said to be *elastic* with respect to price if its price elasticity is less than −1. The good shelter mentioned in the preceding paragraph would thus be one for which demand is elastic with respect to price. The demand for a good is *inelastic* with respect to price if its price elasticity is greater than −1 and *unit elastic* with respect to price if its price elasticity is equal to −1. These definitions are portrayed graphically in Figure 4.19.

When interpreting actual demand data, it is often useful to have a more general definition of price elasticity that can accommodate cases in which the observed change in price does not happen to be 1 percent. Let P be the current price of a good and let Q be the quantity demanded at that price. And let ΔQ be the change in the quantity demanded that occurs in response to a very small change in price, ΔP. The price elasticity of demand at the current price and quantity will then be given by

$$\epsilon = \frac{\Delta Q/Q}{\Delta P/P}. \tag{4.1}$$

The numerator on the right side of Equation 4.1 is the proportional change in quantity. The denominator is the proportional change in price. Equation 4.1 is exactly the same as our earlier definition when ΔP happens to be a 1 percent change in current price. The advantage is that the more general definition also works when ΔP is any other small percentage change in current price.

FIGURE 4.19
Three Categories of Price Elasticity
With respect to price, the demand for a good is elastic if its price elasticity is less than −1, inelastic if its price elasticity exceeds −1, and unit elastic if its price elasticity is equal to −1.

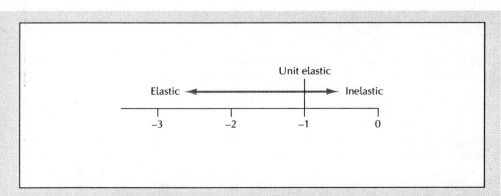

A Geometric Interpretation of Price Elasticity

Another way to interpret Equation 4.1 is to rewrite it as

$$\epsilon = \frac{\Delta Q}{\Delta P}\frac{P}{Q}. \tag{4.2}$$

Equation 4.2 suggests a simple interpretaion in terms of the geometry of the market demand curve. When ΔP is small, the ratio $\Delta P/\Delta Q$ is the slope of the demand curve, which means that the ratio $\Delta Q/\Delta P$ is the reciprocal of that slope. Thus the price elasticity of demand may be interpreted as the product of the ratio of price to quantity and the reciprocal of the slope of the demand curve:[2]

$$\epsilon = \frac{P}{Q}\frac{1}{slope}. \tag{4.3}$$

Equation 4.3 is called the *point-slope method* of calculating price elasticity of demand. By way of illustration, consider the demand curve for shelter shown in Figure 4.20. Because this demand curve is linear, its slope is the same at every point, namely, -2. The reciprocal of this slope is $-\frac{1}{2}$. The price elasticity of demand at point A is therefore given by the ratio of price to quantity at A $\left(\frac{12}{2}\right)$ multiplied by the reciprocal of the slope at A $\left(-\frac{1}{2}\right)$, so we have $\epsilon_A = \left(\frac{12}{2}\right)\left(-\frac{1}{2}\right) = -3$.

When the market demand curve is linear, as in Figure 4.20, several properties of price elasticity quickly become apparent from this interpretation. The first is that the price elasticity is different at every point along the demand curve. More specifically, we know that the slope of a linear demand curve is constant throughout, which means that the reciprocal of its slope is also constant. The ratio of price to quantity, by contrast, takes a different value at every point along

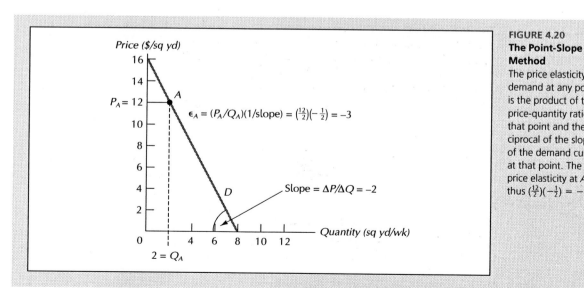

FIGURE 4.20
The Point-Slope Method
The price elasticity of demand at any point is the product of the price-quantity ratio at that point and the reciprocal of the slope of the demand curve at that point. The price elasticity at A is thus $\left(\frac{12}{2}\right)\left(-\frac{1}{2}\right) = -3$.

---

[2]In calculus terms, price elasticity is defined as $\epsilon = (P/Q)[dQ(P)/dP]$.

CHAPTER 4 INDIVIDUAL AND MARKET DEMAND

the demand curve. As we approach the vertical intercept, it approaches infinity. It declines steadily as we move downward along the demand curve, finally reaching a value of zero at the horizontal intercept.

A second property of demand elasticity is that it is never positive. As noted earlier, because the slope of the demand curve is always negative, its reciprocal must also be negative; and because the ratio P/Q is always positve, it follows that the price elasticity of demand—which is the product of these two—must always be a negative number (except at the horizontal intercept of the demand curve, where P/Q, and hence elasticity, is zero). For the sake of convenience, however, economists often ignore the negative sign of price elasticity and refer simply to its absolute value. When a good is said to have a "high" price elasticity of demand, this will always mean that its price elasticity is large in absolute value, indicating that the quantity demanded is highly responsive to changes in price. Similarly, a good whose price elasticity is said to be "low" is one for which the absolute value of elasticity is small, indicating that the quantity demanded is relatively unresponsive to changes in price.

A third property of price elasticity at any point along a straight-line demand curve is that it will be inversely related to the slope of the demand curve. The steeper the demand curve, the less elastic is demand at any point along it. This follows from the fact that the reciprocal of the slope of the demand curve is one of the factors used to compute price elasticity.

EXERCISE 4.5

Use the point-slope method (Equation 4.3) to determine the elasticity of the demand curve $P = 32 - Q$ at the point where $P = 24$.

Two polar cases of demand elasticity are shown in Figure 4.21. In Figure 4.21a, the horizontal demand curve, with its slope of zero, has an infinitely high price elasticity at every point. Such demand curves are often called *perfectly elastic* and, as we will see, are especially important in the study of competitive firm

FIGURE 4.21
Two Important Polar Cases
(a) The price elasticity of the demand curve is equal to $-\infty$ at every point. Such demand curves are said to be perfectly elastic. (b) The price elasticity of the demand curve is equal to 0 at every point. Such demand curves are said to be perfectly inelastic.

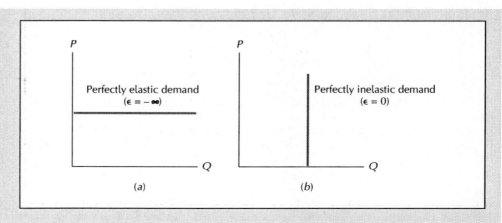

behavior. In Figure 4.21*b*, the vertical demand curve has a price elasticity everywhere equal to zero. Such curves are called *perfectly inelastic*.

As a practical matter, it would be impossible for any demand curve to be perfectly inelastic at all prices. Beyond some sufficiently high price, income effects must curtail consumption of the good. This will be true even for a seemingly essential good with no substitutes, such as surgery for certain malignant tumors. Even so, the demand curve for many such goods and services will be perfectly inelastic over an extremely broad range of prices (recall the salt example discussed earlier in this chapter).

The Unit-Free Property of Elasticity

Another way of measuring responsiveness to changes in price is to use the slope of the demand curve. Other things equal, for example, we know that the quantity demanded of a good with a steep demand curve will be less responsive to changes in price than will one with a less steep demand curve.

Since the slope of a demand curve is much simpler to calculate than its elasticity, it may seem natural to ask, "Why bother with elasticity at all?" One important reason is that the slope of the demand curve is very sensitive to the units we use to measure price and quantity, while elasticity is not. By way of illustration, notice in Figure 4.22*a* that when the price of gasoline is measured in \$/gal, the slope of the demand curve at point C is -0.02. By contrast, in Figure 4.22*b*, where price is measured in \$/oz, the slope at C is -0.00015625. In both cases, however, note that the price elasticity of demand at C is -3. This will be true no matter how we measure price and quantity. And most people find it much more informative to know that a 1 percent cut in price will lead to a 3 percent increase in the quantity demanded than to know that the slope of the demand curve is -0.00015625.

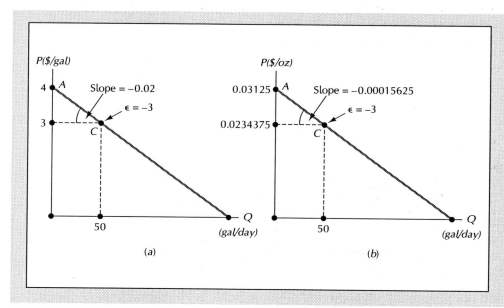

FIGURE 4.22
Elasticity Is Unit-Free
The slope of the demand curve at any point depends on the units in which we measure price and quantity. The slope at point C when we measure the price of gasoline in dollars per gallon (*a*) is much larger than when we measure the price in dollars per ounce (*b*). The price elasticity at any point, by contrast, is completely independent of units of measure.

128   CHAPTER 4 INDIVIDUAL AND MARKET DEMAND

Some Representative Elasticity Estimates

As the entries in Table 4.4 show, the price elasticities of demand for different products often differ substantially. The low elasticity for theater and opera performances probably reflects the fact that buyers in this market have much larger than average incomes, so that income effects of price variations are likely to be small. Income effects for green peas are also likely to be small even for low-income consumers, yet the price elasticity of demand for green peas is more than 14 times larger than for theater and opera performances. The difference is that there are many more close substitutes for green peas than there are for theater and opera performances. Later in this chapter we investigate in greater detail the factors that affect the price elasticity of demand for a product.

Elasticity and Total Expenditure

Suppose you are the administrator in charge of setting tolls for the Golden Gate Bridge, which links San Francisco to Marin County. At the current toll of $3/trip, 100,000 trips per hour are taken across the bridge. If the price elasticity of demand for trips is −2.0, what will happen to the number of trips taken per hour if you raise the toll by 10 percent? With an elasticity of −2.0, a 10 percent increase in price will produce a 20 percent reduction in quantity. Thus the number of trips will fall to 80,000/hr. Total expenditure at the higher toll will be (80,000 trips/hr)($3.30/trip) = $264,000/hr. Note that this is smaller than the total expenditure of $300,000/hr that occurred under the $3 toll.

Now suppose that the price elasticity had been not −2.0 but −0.5. How would the number of trips and total expenditure then be affected by a 10 percent increase in the toll? This time the number of trips will fall by 5 percent to 95,000/hr, which means that total expenditure will rise to (95,000 trips/hr) ($3.30/trip) = $313,500/hr. If your goal as an administrator is to increase the total revenue collected from the bridge toll, you will need to know something about the price elasticity of demand for trips before deciding whether to raise the toll or to lower it.

TABLE 4.4
Price Elasticity Estimates for Selected Products*

Good or service	Price elasticity
Green peas	−2.8
Electricity	−1.2
Beer	−1.19
Movies	−0.87
Air travel (foreign)	−0.77
Shoes	−0.70
Theater, opera	−0.18

*These short-run elasticity estimates are taken from the following sources: H. S. Houthakker and Lester Taylor, *Consumer Demand in the United States: Analyses and Projections,* 2d ed., Cambridge, MA: Harvard University Press, 1970; L. Taylor, "The Demand for Electricity: A Survey," *Bell Journal of Economics,* Spring 1975; K. Elzinga, "The Beer Industry," in Walter Adams (ed.), *The Structure of American Industry,* New York: Macmillan, 1977.

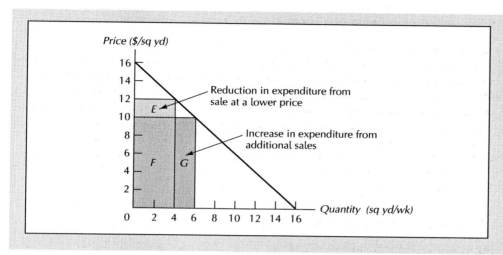

FIGURE 4.23
The Effect on Total Expenditure of a Reduction in Price
When price falls, people spend less on existing units (*E*). But they also buy more units (*G*). Here, *G* is larger than *E*, which means that total expenditure rises.

This example illustrates one of the most important relationships in all of economics, namely, the one between price elasticity and total expenditure. The questions we want to be able to answer are of the form, "If the price of a product changes, how will the total amount spent on the product be affected?" and "Will more be spent on the product if we sell more units at a lower price or fewer units at a higher price?" In Figure 4.23, for example, we might want to know how total expenditures for shelter are affected when the price falls from $12/sq yd to $10/sq yd.

The total expenditure, R, at any quantity-price pair (Q, P) is given by the product

$$R = PQ. \tag{4.4}$$

In Figure 4.23, the total expenditure at the original quantity-price pair is thus ($12/sq yd)(4 sq yd/wk) = $48/wk. Geometrically, it is the sum of the two shaded areas *E* and *F*. Following the price reduction, the new total expenditure is ($10/sq yd)(6 sq yd/wk) = $60/wk, which is the sum of the shaded areas *F* and *G*. These two total expenditures have in common the shaded area *F*. The change in total expenditure is thus the difference in the two shaded areas *E* and *G*. The area *E*, which is ($2/sq yd)(4 sq yd/wk) = $8/wk, may be interpreted as the reduction in expenditure caused by selling the original 4 sq yd/wk at the new, lower price. *G*, in turn, is the increase in expenditure caused by the additional 2 sq yd/wk of sales. This area is given by ($10/sq yd)(2 sq yd/wk) = $20/wk. Whether total expenditure rises or falls thus boils down to whether the gain from additional sales exceeds the loss from lower prices. Here, the gain exceeds the loss by $12, so total expenditure rises by that amount following the price reduction.

If the change in price is small, we can say how total expenditure will move if we know the initial price elasticity of demand. Recall that one way of expressing price elasticity is the percentage change in quantity divided by the corresponding percentage change in price. If the absolute value of that quotient exceeds 1, we know that the percentage change in quantity is larger than the percentage change in price. And when that happens, the increase in expenditure from additional sales will always exceed the reduction from sales of existing units at the lower price. In Figure 4.23, note that the elasticity at the original price of $12 is 3.0, which confirms our earlier observation that the price reduction led to an increase in total expenditure. Suppose, on the contrary, that price elasticity is less than unity. Then the percentage change in quantity will be smaller than the corresponding percentage change in price, and the additional sales will not compensate for the reduction in expenditure from sales at a lower price. Here, a price reduction will lead to a reduction in total expenditure.

EXERCISE 4.6

For the demand curve in Figure 4.23, what is the price elasticity of demand when $P = \$4/$sq yd? What will happen to total expenditure on shelter when price falls from $4/sq yd to $3/sq yd?

The general rule for small price reductions, then, is this: *A price reduction will increase total revenue if and only if the absolute value of the price elasticity of demand is greater than 1.* Parallel reasoning leads to an analogous rule for small price increases: *An increase in price will increase total revenue if and only if the absolute value of the price elasticity is less than 1.* These rules are summarized in the top panel of Figure 4.24, where the point M is the midpoint of the demand curve.

The relationship between elasticity and total expenditure is spelled out in greater detail in the relationship between the top and bottom panels of Figure 4.24. The top panel shows a straight-line demand curve. For each quantity, the bottom

FIGURE 4.24
Demand and Total Expenditure
When demand is elastic, total expenditure changes in the opposite direction from a change in price. When demand is inelastic, total expenditure and price both move in the same direction. At the midpoint of the demand curve (M), total expenditure is at a maximum.

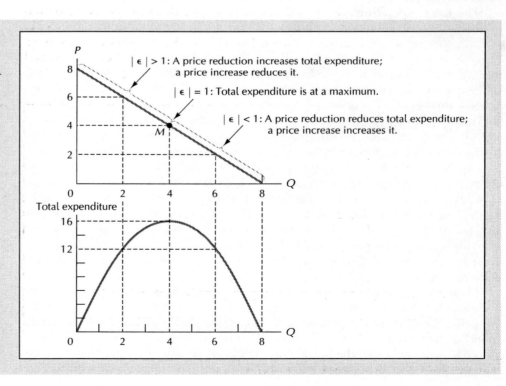

$|\epsilon| > 1$: A price reduction increases total expenditure; a price increase reduces it.

$|\epsilon| = 1$: Total expenditure is at a maximum.

$|\epsilon| < 1$: A price reduction reduces total expenditure; a price increase increases it.

panel shows the corresponding total expenditure. As indicated in the bottom panel, total expenditure starts at zero when Q is zero and increases to its maximum value at the quantity corresponding to the midpoint of the demand curve (point M in the top panel). At that same quantity, price elasticity is unity. Beyond that quantity, total expenditure declines with output, reaching zero at the quantity corresponding to the horizontal intercept of the demand curve.

The market demand curve for bus rides in a small community is given by $P = 100 - (Q/10)$, where P is the fare per ride in cents and Q is the number of rides purchased each day. If the price is 50 cents/ride, how much revenue will the transit system collect each day? What is the price elasticity of demand for bus rides? If the system needs more revenue, should it raise or lower its price? How would your answers have differed if the initial price had been not 50 cents/ride but 75 cents?

EXAMPLE 4.6

Total revenue for the bus system is equal to total expenditure by riders, which is the product PQ. First we solve for Q from the demand curve and get $Q = 1000 - 10P$. When P is 50 cents/ride, Q will be 500 rides/day and the resulting total revenue will be \$250/day. To compute the price elasticity of demand, we can use the formula $\epsilon = (P/Q)(1/\text{slope})$. Here the slope is $-\frac{1}{10}$, so $1/\text{slope} = -10$ (see footnote 3). P/Q takes the value $50/500 = \frac{1}{10}$. Price elasticity is thus the product $(-\frac{1}{10})(10) = -1$. With a price elasticity of unity, total revenue attains its maximum value. If the bus company either raises or lowers its price, it will earn less than it does at the current price.

At a price of 50 cents, the company was operating at the midpoint of its demand curve. If the current price had instead been 75 cents, it would be operating above the midpoint. More precisely, it would be halfway between the midpoint and the vertical intercept (point K in Figure 4.25). Quantity would be only 250 rides/day, and price elasticity would have been -3 (computed, for example, by multiplying the price-quantity ratio at K, $\frac{3}{10}$, by the reciprocal of the demand

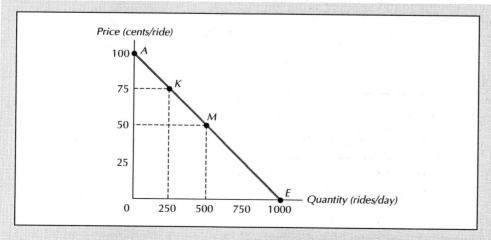

FIGURE 4.25
The Demand for Bus Rides
At a price of 50 cents/ride, the bus company is maximizing its total revenues. At a price of 75 cents/ride, demand is elastic with respect to price, and so the company can increase its total revenues by cutting its price.

---

[3]The slope here is from the formula $P = 100 - (Q/10)$.

curve slope, $-\frac{1}{10}$). Operating at an elastic point on its demand curve, the company could increase total revenue by cutting its price.

Determinants of Price Elasticity of Demand

What factors govern the size of the price elasticity of demand for a product? To answer this question, it is useful to draw first on our earlier discussion of substitution and income effects, which suggests primary roles for the following factors:

- **Substitution possibilities.**   The substitution effect of a price change tends to be small for goods for which there are no close substitutes. Consider, for example, the vaccine against rabies. People who have been bitten by rabid animals have nothing to substitute for this vaccine, and the demand for the vaccine will tend to be highly inelastic. We saw that the same was true for a good such as salt. But consider now the demand for a particular brand of salt, say, Morton's. Despite the advertising claims of salt manufacturers, one brand of salt is a more-or-less perfect substitute for any other. Because the substitution effect between specific brands of salt will be large, a rise in the price of one brand should sharply curtail the quantity of it demanded. In general, the absolute value of price elasticity will rise with the availability of attractive substitutes.

- **Budget share.**   The larger the share of total expenditures accounted for by the product, the more important will be the income effect of a price change. Goods such as salt, rubber bands, cellophane wrap, and a host of others account for such small shares of total expenditures that, for most people, the income effects of a price change are likely to be negligible for these goods. For goods like housing and higher education, by contrast, the income effect of a price increase is likely to be large indeed. In general, the smaller the share of total expenditure accounted for by a good, the less elastic the demand will be.

- **Direction of income effect.**   A factor closely related to the budget share is the direction—positive or negative—of its income effect. While the budget share tells us whether the income effect of a price change is likely to be large or small, the direction of the income effect tells us whether it will offset or reinforce the substitution effect. Thus, a normal good will tend to have a higher price elasticity than an inferior good, other things equal, because the income effect reinforces the substitution effect for a normal good but offsets it for an inferior good.

- **Time.**   Our analysis of individual demand did not focus explicitly on the role of time. But it too has an important effect on people's responses to changes in prices. Consider again the oil price increases of the 1970s. One response of a consumer confronted with a higher price of gasoline is simply to drive less. But many auto trips are part of a larger pattern and cannot be abandoned, or even altered, very quickly. A person cannot simply stop going to work, for example. He can cut down on his daily commute by joining a car pool or by purchasing a house closer to where he works. He can also curtail his gasoline consumption by trading in his current car for one that gets better mileage. But all these steps take time, and as a result, the demand for gasoline will be much more elastic in the long run than in the short run.

THE DEPENDENCE OF MARKET DEMAND ON INCOME   133

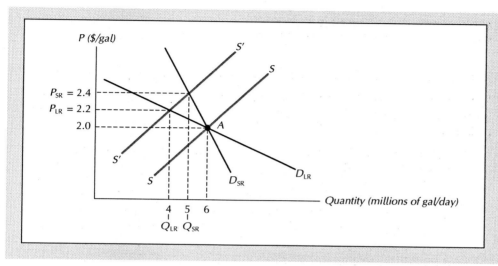

FIGURE 4.26
Price Elasticity Is Greater in the Long Run than in the Short Run
The more time people have, the more easily they can switch to substitute products. The price effects of supply alterations are therefore always more extreme in the short run than in the long run.

The short- and long-run effects of a supply shift in the market for gasoline are contrasted in Figure 4.26. The initial equilibrium at A is disturbed by a supply reduction from S to S'. In the short run, the effect is for price to rise to $P_{SR} = \$2.40/\text{gal}$ and for quantity to fall to $Q_{SR} = 5$ million gal/day. The long-run demand curve is more elastic than the short-run demand curve. As consumers have more time to adjust, therefore, price effects tend to moderate while quantity effects tend to become more pronounced. Thus the new long-run equilibrium in Figure 4.26 occurs at a price of $P_{LR} = \$2.20/\text{gal}$ and a quantity of $Q_{LR} = 4$ million gal/day.

We see an extreme illustration of the difference between short- and long-run price elasticity values in the case of natural gas used in households. The price elasticity for this product is only -0.1 in the short run but a whopping -10.7 in the long run![4] This difference reflects the fact that once a consumer has chosen appliances to heat and cook with, he or she is virtually locked in for the short run. People aren't going to cook their rice for only 10 minutes just because the price of natural gas has gone up. In the long run, however, consumers can and do switch between fuels when there are significant changes in relative prices.

THE DEPENDENCE OF MARKET DEMAND ON INCOME

As we have seen, the quantity of a good demanded by any person depends not only on its price but also on the person's income. Since the market demand curve is the horizontal sum of individual demand curves, it too will naturally be influenced by consumer incomes. In some cases, the effect of income on market demand can be accounted for completely if we know only the average income level in the market. This would be the case, for example, if all consumers in the market were alike in terms of preference and all had the same incomes.

In practice, however, a given level of average income in a market will sometimes give rise to different market demands depending on how income is distributed among persons. A simple example helps make this point clear.

---

[4]H. S. Houthakker and Lester Taylor, *Consumer Demand in the United States: Analyses and Projections*, 2d ed., Cambridge, MA: Harvard University Press, 1970.

134   CHAPTER 4   INDIVIDUAL AND MARKET DEMAND

FIGURE 4.27
The Engel Curve for Food of *A* and *B*
When individual Engel curves take the non-linear form shown, the increase in food consumption that results from a given increase in income will be smaller than the reduction in food consumption that results from an income reduction of the same amount.

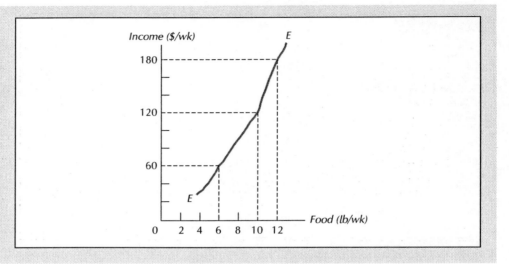

EXAMPLE 4.7

Two consumers, *A* and *B*, are in a market for food. Their tastes are identical, and each has the same initial income level, $120/wk. If their individual Engel curves for food are as given by the locus *EE* in Figure 4.27, how will the market demand curve for food be affected if *A*'s income goes down by 50 percent while *B*'s goes up by 50 percent?

The nonlinear shape of the Engel curve pictured in Figure 4.27 is plausible considering that a consumer can eat only so much food. Beyond some point, increases in income should have no appreciable effect on the amount of food consumed. The implication of this relationship is that *B*'s new income ($180/wk) will produce an increase in his consumption (2 lb/wk) that is smaller than the reduction in *A*'s consumption (4 lb/wk) caused by *A*'s new income ($60/wk).

What does all this say about the corresponding individual and market demand curves for food? Identical incomes and tastes give rise to identical individual demand curves, denoted D_A and D_B in Figure 4.28. Adding D_A and D_B horizontally, we get the initial market demand curve, denoted *D*. The nature of the individual Engel curves tells us that *B*'s increase in demand will be smaller than *A*'s reduction in demand following the shift in income distribution. Thus, when we add the new individual demand curves (D'_A and D'_B), we get a new market demand for food (*D'*) that lies to the left of the original demand curve.

The dependence of market demands on the distribution of income is important to bear in mind when the government considers policies to redistribute income. A policy that redistributes income from rich to poor, for example, is likely to increase demand for goods like food and reduce demand for luxury items, such as jewelry and foreign travel.

Demand in many other markets is relatively insensitive to variations in the distribution of income. In particular, the distribution of income is not likely to

THE DEPENDENCE OF MARKET DEMAND ON INCOME   135

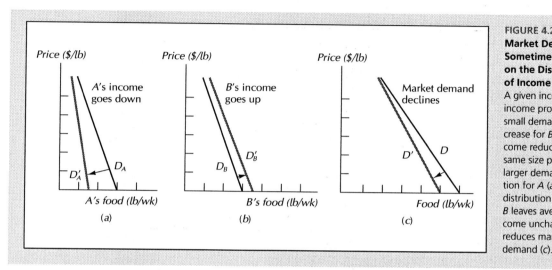

FIGURE 4.28
Market Demand Sometimes Depends on the Distribution of Income
A given increase in income produces a small demand increase for B (b); an income reduction of the same size produces a larger demand reduction for A (a). The redistribution from A to B leaves average income unchanged but reduces market demand (c).

matter much in markets in which individual demands tend to move roughly in proportion to changes in income.

Engel curves at the market level are schedules that relate the quantity demanded to the average income level in the market. The existence of a stable relationship between average income and quantity demanded is by no means certain for any given product because of the distributional complication just discussed. In particular, note that we cannot construct Engel curves at the market level by simply adding individual Engel curves horizontally. Horizontal summation works as a way of generating market demand curves from individual demand curves because all consumers in the market face the same market price for the product. But when incomes differ widely from one consumer to another, it makes no sense to hold income constant and add quantities across consumers.

As a practical matter, however, reasonably stable relationships between various aggregate income measures and quantities demanded in the market may nonetheless exist. Suppose such a relationship exists for the good X and is as pictured by the locus EE in Figure 4.29, where Y denotes the average income level of consumers in the market for X, and Q denotes the quantity of X. This locus is the market analog of the individual Engel curves discussed earlier.

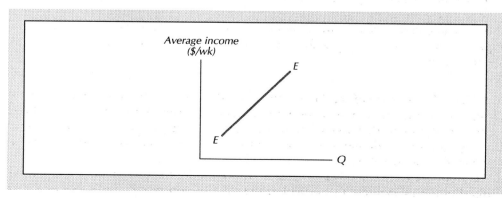

FIGURE 4.29
An Engel Curve at the Market Level
The market Engel curve tells what quantities will be demanded at various average levels of income.

FIGURE 4.30
Engel Curves for Different Types of Goods
(a) The good whose Engel curve is shown has an income elasticity of 1. For such goods, a given proportional change in income will produce the same proportional change in quantity demanded. Thus when average income doubles, from M_0 to $2M_0$, the quantity demanded also doubles, from Q_0 to $2Q_0$. (b) The Engel curves show that consumption increases more than in proportion to income for a luxury and less than in proportion to income for a necessity, and it falls with income for an inferior good.

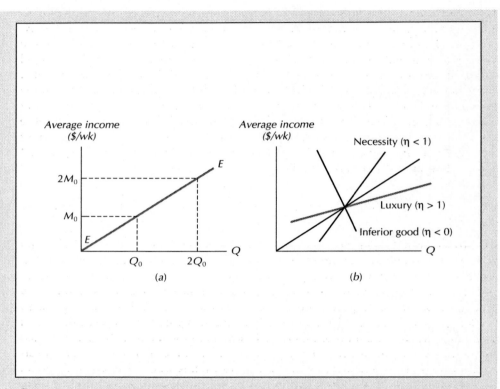

income elasticity of demand   the percentage change in the quantity of a good demanded that results from a 1 percent change in income.

If a good exhibits a stable Engel curve, we may then define its **income elasticity of demand,** a formal measure of the responsiveness of purchase decisions to variations in the average market income. Denoted η, it is given by a formula analogous to the one for price elasticity:[5]

$$\eta = \frac{\Delta Q/Q}{\Delta Y/Y},$$ (4.5)

where Y denotes average market income and ΔY is a small change therein.

Goods such as food, for which a change in income produces a less than proportional change in the quantity demanded at any price, thus have an income elasticity less than 1. Such goods are called *necessities,* and their income elasticities must lie in the interval $0 < \eta < 1$. Food is a commonly cited example. *Luxuries* are those goods for which $\eta > 1$. Common examples are expensive jewelry and foreign travel. Inferior goods are those for which $\eta < 0$. Goods for which $\eta = 1$ will have Engel curves that are straight lines through the origin, as pictured by the locus EE in Figure 4.30a. The market Engel curves for luxuries, necessities, and inferior goods, where these exist and are stable, are pictured in Figure 4.30b.

The income elasticity formula in Equation 4.5 is easier to interpret geometrically if we rewrite it as

$$\eta = \frac{Y}{Q}\frac{\Delta Q}{\Delta Y},$$ (4.6)

---

[5]In calculus terms, the corresponding formula is $\eta = (Y/Q)\,[dQ(Y)/dY]$.

The first factor on the right side of Equation 4.6 is simply the ratio of income to quantity at a point along the Engel curve. It is the slope of the line from the origin (a ray) to that point. The second factor is the reciprocal of the slope of the Engel curve at that point. If the slope of the ray exceeds the slope of the Engel curve, the product of these two factors must be greater than 1 (the luxury case). If the ray is less steep, η will be less than 1 but still positive, provided the slope of the Engel curve is positive (the necessity case). Thus, in distinguishing between the Engel curves for necessities and luxuries, what counts is not the slopes of the Engel curves themselves but how they compare with the slopes of the corresponding rays. Finally, if the slope of the Engel curve is negative, η must be less than zero (the inferior case).[6]

Why has the nature of outdoor cooking appliances changed dramatically in recent decades?

The propane grill I bought during the late 1980s was on a downhill slide for several years. First to go was its ignition button, the crude mechanical spark generator that normally fires up the gas. Lighting the grill suddenly became a delicate operation. I would turn on the gas, wait a few seconds, and then throw a match inside. If I threw it in too soon, it would go out before reaching the burner below. But if I waited too long, it would set off a small explosion. Another problem was that the metal baffle that sat atop the burners had rusted through in the middle. This concentrated an enormous amount of heat over a small area near the center of the cooking surface, but very little elsewhere. I was still able to cook reasonably good chicken and small steaks by quickly rotating pieces in and out of the hot zone. But grilling a big fish filet had become impossible.

My grill's various deficiencies could surely be repaired, but I had no idea by whom. And even if I did, the cost would almost surely exceed the $89.95 I originally paid for it. And so, reluctantly, I found myself in the market for a new one.

I was immediately struck by how profoundly the menu of available choices had changed in the intervening years. I vaguely remember models from the late 1980s that had built-in storage cabinets and shelf extensions on either side. But even with these options, the most you could have spent was a few hundred dollars. There was nothing—absolutely nothing—like today's Viking Professional Grill.

Powered by either natural gas or propane, it comes with an infrared rotisserie that can slowly broil two 20-pound turkeys to perfection as you cook hamburgers for forty guests on its 828-square-inch grilling surface. It has a built-in smoker system that "utilizes its own 5,000-BTU burner and watertight wood chip drawer to season food with rich woodsy flavor." Next to its grilling surface sit two ancillary range-top burners. Unlike the standard burners on your kitchen stove, which generate 7,500 BTUs, these burners generate 15,000 BTUs, a capability that is useful

ECONOMIC NATURALIST 4.1

1989 Sunbeam Grill, $90

---
[6]Note that an inferior good also satisfies the definition of a necessity.

A Well-Equipped Professional grill (Comparable to Viking Professional Grill referenced in text)

Courtesy of Frontgate. Image shown is 48" Frontgate Professional Grill, $3,495.

primarily for the flash-stir-frying of some ethnic cuisines and for bringing large cauldrons of water more quickly to a boil. If you have ever longed to throw together a Szechwan pork dish on your backyard patio, or feared getting off to a late start when you have guests about to arrive and 40 ears of corn left to cook, the Viking has the extra power you may need. The entire unit is constructed of gleaming stainless steel, with enamel and brass accents, and with its fold-out workspaces fully extended, it measures more than seven feet across.

The Frontgate catalog's price of the Viking Professional Grill, not including shipping and handling, is $5,000. Other outdoor cooking appliances are now offered that cost more than ten times that amount. And grills that cost more than $2,000 are by far "the hottest growing sector in the $1.2 billion-a-year industry."[7]

What spawned this dramatic boom in the American outdoor luxury grill market? The short answer is that most of the recent growth in income in the United States occurred among the nation's highest earners. For example, although median after-tax family income grew by only 10 percent between 1979 and 1997, the corresponding growth for the top 1 percent of earners was 157 percent.[8] Still higher up the income ladder, income growth was even more dramatic. Thus CEO's of the largest U.S. corporations, who earned 42 times as much as the average worker in 1980, earned 531 times as much in 2000.[9] Rapid income growth among those with already high incomes spawned increased demand not only for costly outdoor cooking appliances, but for a broad spectrum of other luxury goods as well.

APPLICATION: FORECASTING ECONOMIC TRENDS

If the income elasticity of demand for every good and service were 1, the composition of GNP would be completely stable over time (assuming technology and relative prices remain unchanged). Each year, the proportion of total spending devoted to food, travel, clothing, and indeed to every other consumption category would remain unchanged from the year before.

As the entries in Table 4.5 show, however, the income elasticities of different consumption categories differ markedly. And therein lies one of the most important applications of the income elasticity concept, namely, forecasting the composition of future purchase patterns. Ever since the industrial revolution in the West, real purchasing power per capita has grown at roughly 2 percent per year. Our knowledge of income elasticity differences enables us to predict how consumption patterns in the future will differ from the ones we see today.

---

[7]Gary Strauss, "Upscale Barbeque Grills Spark Hot New Market," *Ithaca Journal*, July 16, 1997: 7A.

[8]http://www.inequality.org/facts_b.html.

[9]*Business Week*, annual executive compensation surveys. See www.inequality.org.

Good or service	Income elasticity
Automobiles	2.46
Furniture	1.48
Restaurant meals	1.40
Water	1.02
Tobacco	0.64
Gasoline and oil	0.48
Electricity	0.20
Margarine	−0.20
Pork products	−0.20
Public transportation	−0.36

TABLE 4.5
Income Elasticities of Demand for Selected Products*

*These estimates come from H. S. Houthakker and Lester Taylor, *Consumer Demand in the United States: Analyses and Projections*, 2d ed., Cambridge, MA: Harvard University Press, 1970; L. Taylor and R. Halvorsen, "Energy Substitution in U.S. Manufacturing," *Review of Economics and Statistics*, November 1977; H. Wold and L. Jureen, *Demand Analysis*, New York: Wiley, 1953.

Thus, a growing share of the consumer's budget will be devoted to goods like restaurant meals and automobiles, whereas ever smaller shares will go to tobacco, fuel, and electricity. And if the elasticity estimates are correct, the absolute amounts spent per person on margarine, pork products, and public transportation will be considerably smaller in the future than they are today.

CROSS-PRICE ELASTICITIES OF DEMAND

The quantity of a good purchased in the market depends not only on its price and consumer incomes but also on the prices of related goods. **Cross-price elasticity of demand** is the percentage change in the quantity demanded of one good caused by a 1 percent change in the price of the other. More generally, for any two goods, X and Z, the cross-price elasticity of demand may be defined as follows:[10]

cross-price elasticity of demand the percentage change in the quantity of one good demanded that results from a 1 percent change in the price of the other good.

$$\epsilon_{XZ} = \frac{\Delta Q_X/Q_X}{\Delta P_Z/P_Z}, \quad \frac{\Delta Q \cdot P_Z}{\Delta P_Z \cdot Q_X} \quad \frac{\Delta Q}{\Delta P_Z} \cdot slope \quad (4.7)$$

where ΔQ_X is a small change in Q_X, the quantity of X, and ΔP_Z is a small change in P_Z, the price of Z. ϵ_{XZ} measures how the quantity demanded of X responds to a small change in the price of Z.

Unlike the elasticity of demand with respect to a good's own price (the *own-price elasticity*), which is never greater than zero, the cross-price elasticity may be either positive or negative. X and Z are defined as *complements* if $\epsilon_{XZ} < 0$. If $\epsilon_{XZ} > 0$, they are *substitutes*. Thus, a rise in the price of ham will reduce not only the quantity of ham demanded, but also, because ham and eggs are complements, the demand for eggs. A rise in the price of coffee, by contrast, will tend to increase the demand for tea. Estimates of the cross-price elasticity of demand for selected pairs of products are shown in Table 4.6.

---

[10]In calculus terms, the corresponding expression is given by $\epsilon_{XZ} = (P_Z/Q_X)(dQ_X/dP_Z)$.

TABLE 4.6
Cross-Price Elasticities for Selected Pairs of Products*

Good or service	Good or service with price change	Cross-price elasticity
Butter	Margarine	+0.81
Margarine	Butter	+0.67
Natural gas	Fuel oil	+0.44
Beef	Pork	+0.28
Electricity	Natural gas	+0.20
Entertainment	Food	−0.72
Cereals	Fresh fish	−0.87

*From H. Wold and L. Jureen, *Demand Analysis*, New York: Wiley, 1953; L. Taylor and R. Halvorsen, "Energy Substitution in U.S. Manufacturing," *Review of Economics and Statistics*, November 1977; E. T. Fujii et al., "An Almost Ideal Demand System for Visitor Expenditures," *Journal of Transport Economics and Policy*, 19, May 1985, 161–171; and A. Deaton, "Estimation of Own- and Cross-Price Elasticities from Household Survey Data," *Journal of Econometrics*, 36, 1987: 7–30.

EXERCISE 4.7

Would the cross-price elasticity of demand be positive or negative for the following pairs of goods: (a) apples and oranges, (b) airline tickets and automobile tires, (c) computer hardware and software, (d) pens and paper, (e) pens and pencils?

SUMMARY

- Our focus in this chapter was on how individual and market demands respond to variations in prices and incomes. To generate a demand curve for an individual consumer for a specific good X, we first trace out the price-consumption curve in the standard indifference curve diagram. The PCC is the line of optimal bundles observed when the price of X varies, with both income and preferences held constant. We then take the relevant price-quantity pairs from the PCC and plot them in a separate diagram to get the individual demand curve.

- The income analog to the PCC is the income-consumption curve, or ICC. It too is constructed using the standard indifference curve diagram. The ICC is the line of optimal bundles traced out when we vary the consumer's income, holding preferences and relative prices constant. The Engel curve is the income analog to the individual demand curve. We generate it by retrieving the relevant income-quantity pairs from the ICC and plotting them in a separate diagram.

- Normal goods are those the consumer buys more of when income increases and inferior goods are those the consumer buys less of as income rises.

- The total effect of a price change can be decomposed into two separate effects: (1) the substitution effect, which denotes the change in the quantity demanded that results because the price change makes substitute goods seem either more or less attractive, and (2) the income effect, which denotes the change in quantity demanded that results from the change in real purchasing power caused by the price change. The substitution effect always moves in the opposite direction from the movement in price: price increases [reductions] always reduce [increase] the quantity demanded. For normal goods, the income effect also moves in the opposite direction from the price change, and thus tends to reinforce the substitution effect. For inferior goods, the income effect moves in the same direction as the price change, and thus tends to undercut the substitution effect.

- The fact that the income and substitution effects move in opposite directions for inferior goods suggests the theoretical possibility of a Giffen good, one for which the total effect of a price increase is to increase the quantity demanded. There have been no documented examples of the existence of Giffen goods, and in this text we adopt the convention that all goods, unless otherwise stated, are demanded in smaller quantities at higher prices.

- Goods for which purchase decisions respond most strongly to price tend to be ones that have large income and substitution effects that work in the same direction. For example, a normal good that occupies a large share of total expenditures and for which there are many direct or indirect substitutes will tend to respond sharply to changes in price. For many consumers, housing is a prime example of such a good. The goods least responsive to price changes will be those that account for very small budget shares and for which substitution possibilities are very limited. For most people, salt has both of these properties.

* There are two equivalent techniques for generating market demand curves from individual demand curves. The first is to display the individual curves graphically and then add them horizontally. The second method is algebraic and proceeds by first solving the individual demand curves for the respective Q values, then adding those values, and finally solving the resulting sum for P.

* A central analytical concept in demand theory is the price elasticity of demand, a measure of the responsiveness of purchase decisions to small changes in price. Formally, it is defined as the percentage change in quantity demanded that is caused by a 1 percent change in price. Goods for which the absolute value of elasticity exceeds 1 are said to be elastic; those for which it is less than 1, inelastic; and those for which it is equal to 1, unit elastic.

* Another important relationship is the one between price elasticity and the effect of a price change on total expenditure. When demand is elastic, a price reduction will increase total expenditure; when inelastic, total expenditure falls when the price goes down. When demand is unit elastic, total expenditure is at a maximum.

* The value of the price elasticity of demand for a good depends largely on four factors: substitutability, budget share, direction of income effect, and time. (1) *Substitutability.* The more easily consumers may switch to other goods, the more elastic demand will be. (2) *Budget share.* Goods that account for a large share of total expenditures will tend to have higher price elasticity. (3) *Direction of income effect.*

Other factors the same, inferior goods will tend to be less elastic with respect to price than are normal goods. (4) *Time.* Habits and existing commitments limit the extent to which consumers can respond to price changes in the short run. Price elasticity of demand will tend to be larger, the more time consumers have to adapt.

* Changes in the average income level in a market will generally shift the market demand curve. The income elasticity of demand for a good X is defined analogously to its price elasticity. It is the percentage change in quantity that results from a 1 percent change in income. Goods whose income elasticity of demand exceeds zero are called normal goods; those for which it is less than zero are called inferior; those for which it exceeds 1 are called luxuries; and those for which it is less than 1 are called necessities. For normal goods, an increase in income will shift market demand to the right; and for inferior goods, an increase in income will shift demand to the left. For some goods, the distribution of income, not just its average value, is an important determinant of market demand.

* The cross-price elasticity of demand is a measure of the responsiveness of the quantity demanded of one good to a small change in the price of another. Formally, it is defined as the percentage change in the quantity demanded of one good that results from a 1 percent change in the price of the other. If the cross-price elasticity of demand for X with respect to the price of Z is positive, X and Z are substitutes; and if negative, they are complements. In remembering the formulas for the various elasticities—own price, cross-price, and income— many people find it helpful to note that each is the percentage change in an effect divided by the percentage change in the associated causal factor.

* The Appendix to this chapter examines additional topics in demand theory, including the constant elasticity demand curve, arc elasticity, and the income-compensated demand curve.

QUESTIONS FOR REVIEW

1. Why does the quantity of salt demanded tend to be unresponsive to changes in its price?

2. Why is the quantity of education demanded in private universities much more responsive than salt is to changes in price?

3. Draw Engel curves for both a normal good and an inferior good.

4. Give two examples of what are, for most students, inferior goods.

5. Can the price-consumption curve for a normal good ever be downward-sloping?

6. To get the market demand curve for a product, why do we add individual demand curves horizontally rather than vertically?

7. Summarize the relationship between price elasticity, changes in price, and changes in total expenditure.

8. Why don't we measure the responsiveness of demand to price changes by the slope of the demand curve instead of using the more complicated expression for elasticity?

9. For a straight-line demand curve, what is the price elasticity at the revenue maximizing point?

10. Do you think a college education at a specific school has a high or low price (tuition) elasticity of demand?

11. How can changes in the distribution of income across consumers affect the market demand for a product?

12. If you expected a long period of declining GNP, what kinds of companies would you choose to invest in?

13. *True or false:* For a budget spent entirely on two goods, an increase in the price of one will necessarily decrease the consumption of both, unless at least one of the goods is inferior. Explain.

14. Mike spends all his income on tennis balls and basketball tickets. His demand curve for tennis balls is elastic. *True or false:* If the price of tennis balls rises, he consumes more tickets. Explain.

15. *True or false:* If each individual in a market has a straight-line demand curve for a good, then the market demand curve for that good must also be a straight line. Explain.

16. Suppose your budget is spent entirely on two goods: bread and butter. If bread is an inferior good, can butter be inferior as well?

PROBLEMS

1. Sam spends $6/wk on orange juice and apple juice. Orange juice costs $2/cup while apple juice costs $1/cup. Sam views 1 cup of orange juice as a perfect substitute for 3 cups of apple juice. Find Sam's optimal consumption bundle of orange juice and apple juice each week. Suppose the price of apple juice rises to $2/cup, while the price of orange juice remains constant. How much additional income would Sam need to afford his original consumption bundle?

2. Bruce has the same income and faces the same prices as Sam in Problem 1, but he views 1 cup of orange juice as a perfect substitute for 1 cup of apple juice. Find Bruce's optimal consumption bundle. How much additional income would Bruce need to be able to afford his original consumption bundle when the price of apple juice doubles?

3. Maureen has the same income and faces the same prices as Sam and Bruce, but Maureen views 1 cup of orange juice and 1 cup of apple juice as perfect complements. Find Maureen's optimal consumption bundle. How much additional income would Maureen need to afford her original consumption bundle when the price of apple juice doubles?

4. The market for lemonade has 10 potential consumers, each having an individual demand curve $P = 101 - 10Q_i$, where P is price in dollars per cup and Q_i is the number of cups demanded per week by the ith consumer. Find the market demand curve using algebra. Draw an individual demand curve and the market demand curve. What is the quantity demanded by each consumer and in the market as a whole when lemonade is priced at $P = \$1/\text{cup}$?

5. a. For the demand curve $P = 60 - 0.5Q$, find the elasticity at $P = 10$.
   b. If the demand curve shifts parallel to the right, what happens to the elasticity at $P = 10$?

6. Consider the demand curve $Q = 100 - 50P$.
   a. Draw the demand curve and indicate which portion of the curve is elastic, which portion is inelastic, and which portion is unit elastic.
   b. Without doing any additional calculation, state at which point of the curve expenditures on the goods are maximized, and then explain the logic behind your answer.

7. Suppose the demand for crossing the Golden Gate Bridge is given by $Q = 10,000 - 1000P$.
   a. If the toll (P) is $3, how much revenue is collected?
   b. What is the price elasticity of demand at this point?
   c. Could the bridge authorities increase their revenues by changing their price?

PROBLEMS   143

    d.   The Red and White Lines, a ferry service that competes with the Golden Gate Bridge, began operating hovercrafts that made commuting by ferry much more convenient. How would this affect the elasticity of demand for trips across the Golden Gate Bridge?

8. Consumer expenditures on safety are thought to have a positive income elasticity. For example, as incomes rise, people tend to buy safer cars (larger cars with side air bags), they are more likely to fly on trips rather than drive, they are more likely to get regular health tests, and they are more likely to get medical care for any health problems the tests reveal. Is safety a luxury or a necessity?

9. Professors Adams and Brown make up the entire demand side of the market for summer research assistants in the economics department. If Adams's demand curve is $P = 50 - 2Q_A$ and Brown's is $P = 50 - Q_B$, where Q_A and Q_B are the hours demanded by Adams and Brown, respectively, what is the market demand for research hours in the economics department?

10. Suppose that at a price of $400, 300 tickets are demanded to fly from Ithaca, New York, to Los Angeles, California. Now the price rises to $600, and 280 tickets are still demanded. Assuming the demand for tickets is linear, find the price elasticities at the quantity-price pairs (300, 400) and (280, 600).

11. The monthly market demand curve for calculators among engineering students is given by $P = 100 - Q$, where P is the price per calculator in dollars and Q is the number of calculators purchased per month. If the price is $30, how much revenue will calculator makers get each month? Find the price elasticity of demand for calculators. What should calculator makers do to increase revenue?

12. What price maximizes total expenditure along the demand curve $P = 27 - Q^2$?

13. A hot dog vendor faces a daily demand curve of $Q = 1800 - 15P$, where P is the price of a hot dog in cents and Q is the number of hot dogs purchased each day.

    a.   If the vendor has been selling 300 hot dogs each day, how much revenue has he been collecting?

    b.   What is the price elasticity of demand for hot dogs?

    c.   The vendor decides that he wants to generate more revenue. Should he raise or lower the price of his hot dogs?

    d.   At what price would he achieve maximum total revenue?

14. Rank the absolute values of the price elasticities of demand at the points A, B, C, D, and E on the following three demand curves.

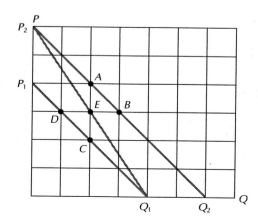

15. Draw the Engel curves for the following goods: food, Hawaiian vacations, cashews, Kmart brand sneakers ($4.99/pr).

144   CHAPTER 4   INDIVIDUAL AND MARKET DEMAND

16. Is the cross-price elasticity of demand positive or negative for the following pairs of items?
    a.   Tennis rackets and tennis balls
    b.   Peanut butter and jelly
    c.   Hot dogs and hamburgers

*17. In 2001, X cost $3 and sold 400 units. That same year, a related good Y cost $10 and sold 200 units. In 2002, X still cost $3 but sold only 300 units, while Y rose in price to $12 and sold only 150 units. Other things the same, and assuming that the demand for X is a linear function of the price of Y, what was the cross-price elasticity of demand for X with respect to Y in 2001?

*18. Smith cannot tell the difference between rice and wheat and spends all her food budget of $24/wk on these foodstuffs. If rice costs $3/lb, draw Smith's price-consumption curve for wheat and the corresponding demand curve.

*19. Repeat the preceding problem on the assumption that rice and wheat are perfect, one-for-one complements.

*20. Suppose your local espresso bar makes the following offer: People who supply their own half-pint carton of milk get to buy a cup of cappuccino for only $1.50 instead of $2.50. Half-pint cartons of milk can be purchased in the adjacent convenience store for $0.50. In the wake of this offer, the quantity of cappuccino sold goes up by 60 percent and the convenience store's total revenue from sales of milk exactly doubles.
    a.   *True or false:* If there is a small, but significant, amount of hassle involved in supplying one's own milk, it follows that absolute value of the price elasticity of demand for cappuccino is 3. Explain.
    b.   *True or false:* It follows that demand for the convenience store's milk is elastic with respect to price. Explain.

ANSWERS TO IN-CHAPTER EXERCISES

4.1. On Paula's original budget, B_0, she consumes at bundle A. On the new budget, B_1, she consumes at bundle D. (To say that D has 1.5 pr of bindings per year means that she consumes 3 pr of bindings every 2 yr.) The substitution effect of the price increase (the movement from A to C) is zero.

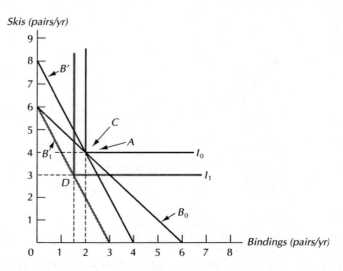

*Problems marked with an asterisk (*) are more difficult.

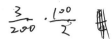

$\dfrac{3}{2.90} \cdot \dfrac{190}{2}$

3

4.2. The income effect, substitution effect, and total effects are all zero because the price change does not alter Pam's optimal consumption bundle.

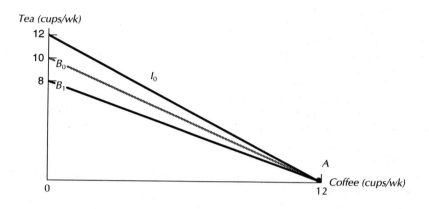

4.3. The formulas for D_1 and D_2 are $P = 16 - 2Q_1$ and $P = 8 - 2Q_2$, respectively. For the region in which $0 \leq P \leq 8$, we have $Q_1 = 8 - (P/2)$ and $Q_2 = 4 - (P/2)$. Adding, we get $Q_1 + Q_2 = Q = 12 - P$, for $0 \leq P \leq 8$. For $8 < P \leq 16$, the market demand curve is the same as D_1, namely, $P = 16 - 2Q$.

4.4. First, we need to rearrange the representative consumer demand curve $P = 120 - 60Q_i$ to have quantity alone on one side:

$$Q_i = 2 - \tfrac{1}{60}P.$$

Then we multiply by the number of consumers, $n = 30$,

$$Q = nQ_i = 30Q_i = 30(2 - \tfrac{1}{60}P) = 60 - \tfrac{1}{2}P.$$

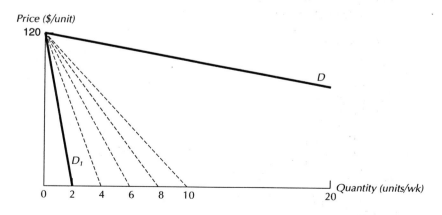

Finally, we rearrange the market demand curve $Q = 60 - \tfrac{1}{2}P$ to have price alone on one side, $P = 120 - 2Q$, to return to the slope-intercept form.

4.5. Since the slope of the demand curve is -1, we have $\epsilon = -P/Q$. At $P = 24$, $Q = 8$, and so $\epsilon = -P/Q = -\tfrac{24}{8} = -3$.

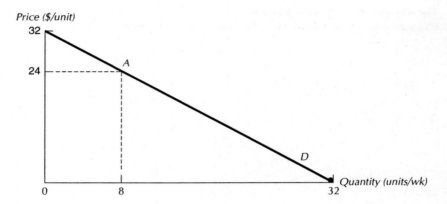

4.6. Elasticity when $P = \$4/$sq yd is $\frac{1}{3}$, so a price reduction will reduce total expenditure. At $P = 4$, total expenditure is $48/wk, which is more than the $39/wk of total expenditure at $P = 3$.

4.7. Substitutes, such as a, b, and e, have positive cross-price elasticity (an increase in price of one good raises quantity demanded of the other good). Complements, such as c and d, have negative cross-price elasticity (an increase in price of one good lowers quantity demanded of the other good).

APPENDIX 4

ADDITIONAL TOPICS IN DEMAND THEORY

THE CONSTANT ELASTICITY DEMAND CURVE

The demand curves discussed so far have been linear demand curves, which, as noted, have the property that price elasticity declines as we move down the demand curve. Not all demand curves have this property, however; on the contrary, there are demand curves for which price elasticity can remain constant or even rise with movements down the demand curve. The *constant elasticity demand curve* is the name given to a demand curve for which elasticity does not vary with price and quantity. Whereas the linear demand curve has the general form $P = a - bQ$, the constant elasticity demand curve is instead written

$$P = \frac{k}{Q^{1/\epsilon}} \qquad (A.4.1)$$

where k and ϵ are positive numbers, specific values of which determine the exact shape and position of the curve.[1] An example with $k = 2$ and $\epsilon = 1$ is pictured in Figure A.4.1.

Let us examine some points on the curve pictured in Figure A.4.1 and verify that they do indeed have the same price elasticity. Consider first the point $P = 2, Q = 1$, and calculate price elasticity as the product of the ratio P/Q and the reciprocal of the slope of the demand curve. To calculate the slope of the demand curve, we need to calculate the ΔQ that occurs in response to a very

---

[1]Using the formal definition of elasticity, it is easy to show that the elasticity at any price-quantity pair along this demand curve is $-\epsilon$:

$$\frac{P}{Q}\frac{dQ(P)}{dP} = \frac{k/Q^{1/\epsilon}}{Q}\frac{1}{(-1/\epsilon)kQ^{-1/\epsilon-1}} = -\epsilon.$$

148   CHAPTER 4 APPENDIX   ADDITIONAL TOPICS IN DEMAND THEORY

FIGURE A.4.1
A Constant Elasticity Demand Curve
Whereas the price elasticity along a linear demand curve declines as quantity increases, it remains the same along a constant elasticity demand curve.

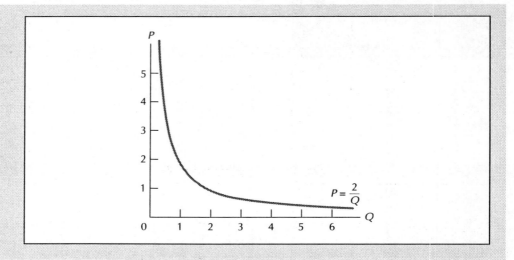

small ΔP near the point (1, 2). Suppose, for example, we use a price change of $+0.001$. If $P = 2.001$, we can solve from the demand curve (that is, from the equation $P = 2/Q$) to get the corresponding $Q = 2/2.001 = 0.9995$. Thus $\Delta Q = 0.9995 - 1 = -0.0005$, and the slope of the demand curve at (1, 2) may be calculated as $\Delta P / \Delta Q$, or $0.001/(-0.0005) = -2$. The reciprocal of the slope is $-\frac{1}{2}$, and so the price elasticity is $2(-\frac{1}{2}) = -1$.

Consider now the point (2, 1). Again using a ΔP of 0.001, we get a new Q of $2/1.001 = 1.998$, or a ΔQ of -0.002. Thus the slope of the demand curve at (2, 1) is $0.001/(-0.002) = -\frac{1}{2}$, and its reciprocal is -2. The price elasticity at (2, 1) is therefore $(\frac{1}{2})(-2)$, or again -1.

EXERCISE A.4.1

Try several other points along the demand curve in Figure A.4.1 and verify that the price elasticity in every instance is equal to −1. [The answer at the end of the chapter uses the points (0.5, 4) and (4, 0.5.)]

The demand curve given by $P = k/Q$ is a special case of the constant elasticity demand curve called the *constant expenditure demand curve.* At every point along such a demand curve, total expenditure is given by the product $PQ = k$, where k is again a positive constant. Thus, unlike the case of the straight-line demand curve, here people spend exactly the same amount when price is high as they do when price is low. Someone who spends her entire allowance on compact discs each month, for example, would have a constant expenditure demand curve for compact discs. The constant k would be equal to the amount of her allowance.

As we move downward along any constant elasticity demand curve ($P = k/Q^{1/\epsilon}$) the fall in the ratio P/Q is exactly counterbalanced by the rise in the reciprocal of the slope. A constant elasticity demand curve with $\epsilon > 1$ has the property that a price cut will always increase total expenditures. For one with $\epsilon < 1$. by contrast, a price cut will always reduce total expenditures.

THE CONSTANT ELASTICITY DEMAND CURVE   149

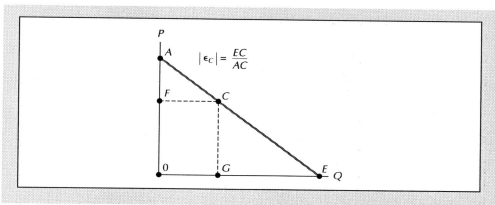

FIGURE A.4.2
The Segment-Ratio Method
The absolute value of price elasticity at any point is the ratio of the two demand curve segments from that point. At point C, the absolute value of the price elasticity of demand is equal to EC/AC.

EXERCISE A.4.2

What happens to total expenditure when price falls from 4 to 3 along the demand curve given by $P = 4/Q^{1/2}$?

Segment-Ratio Method

The price elasticity at a given point along a straight-line demand curve may be given one other useful geometric interpretation. Suppose we divide the demand curve into two segments AC and CE, as shown in Figure A.4.2. The price elasticity of demand (in absolute value) at point C, denoted $|\epsilon_c|$, will then be equal to the ratio of the two segments.[2]

$$|\epsilon_c| = \frac{CE}{AC} \qquad (A.4.2)$$

Equation A.4.2 is called the *segment-ratio* for calculating price elasticity of demand.

Knowing that the price elasticity of demand at any point along a straight-line demand curve is the ratio of two line segments greatly simplifies the task of making quantitative statements about it. Consider the demand curve shown in the top panel of Figure A.4.3. At the midpoint of that demand curve (point M), for example, we can see at a glance that the value of price elasticity is -1. One-fourth of the way down the demand curve (point K in Figure A.4.3), the elasticity is -3; three-fourths of the way down (point L), $-\frac{1}{3}$; and so on. The bottom panel of Figure A.4.3 summarizes the relation between position on a straight-line demand curve and the price elasticity of demand.

---

[2]To see why this is so, we can make use of some simple high school geometry. First, note that the reciprocal of the slope of the demand curve in Figure A.4.2 is the ratio GE/GC and that the ratio of price to quality at point C is GC/FC. Multiplying these two, we get $|\epsilon_c| = (GE/GC)(GC/FC) = GE/FC$. Now note that the triangles AFC and CGE are similar, which means that the ratios of their corresponding sides must be the same. In particular, it means that the ratio GE/FC, which we just saw is equal to the price elasticity of demand at point C, must also be equal to the ratio GE/AC. And this, of course, is just the result we set out to establish.

CHAPTER 4 APPENDIX   ADDITIONAL TOPICS IN DEMAND THEORY

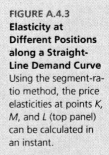

FIGURE A.4.3
Elasticity at Different Positions along a Straight-Line Demand Curve
Using the segment-ratio method, the price elasticities at points K, M, and L (top panel) can be calculated in an instant.

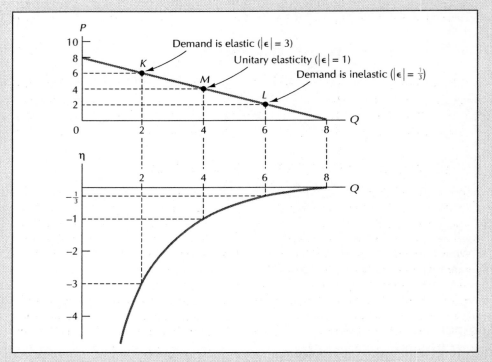

THE CONCEPT OF ARC ELASTICITY

Suppose we start on a hypothetical straight-line demand curve at a point with $P_0 = 10$ and $Q_0 = 100$. Now, let price rise by 10 so that $P_1 = 20$, and suppose the resulting quantity demanded is $Q_1 = 50$. What is the price elasticity of demand for this good? Suppose we try to answer this question using the formula $\epsilon = (\Delta Q / Q)/(\Delta P / P)$. It is clear that $\Delta P = 10$ and $\Delta Q = -50$. But what values do we use for P and Q? If we use the initial values, P_0 and Q_0, we get an elasticity of $(-50/100)/(10/10) = -\frac{1}{2}$. But if we use the new values, P_1 and Q_1, we get an elasticity of $(-50/50)/(10/20) = -2$.

Thus, if we reckon price and quantity changes as proportions of their initial values, we get one answer, but if we compute them as proportions of their new values we get another answer. Neither of these answers is incorrect. The fact that they differ is merely a reflection of the fact that the elasticity of demand differs at every point along a straight-line demand curve.

Strictly speaking, the original question ("What is the price elasticity of demand for this good?") was not well posed. To have elicited a uniquely correct answer, it should have been, "What is the price elasticity of demand at the point (100, 10)?" or, "What is the price elasticity of demand at the point (50, 20)?" Economists have nonetheless developed a convention for answering ambiguous questions like the one originally posed. It is to use the formula for the so-called *arc elasticity of demand*, which is given by

$$\epsilon = \frac{\Delta Q/[(Q_0 + Q_1)/2]}{\Delta P/[(P_0 + P_1)/2]}.$$ (A.4.3)

The arc elasticity approach thus sidesteps the question of which price-quantity pair to use by using averages of the new and old values. The formula reduces to

$$\epsilon = \frac{\Delta Q/(Q_0 + Q_1)}{\Delta P/(P_0 + P_1)} \qquad (A.4.4)$$

and this is the last time you will see it in this text. (The only reason it appears here at all is that questions on standardized tests in economics sometimes refer to it.) Hereafter, all questions having to do with elasticity will be taken up using the measure discussed earlier, which is called *point elasticity*.

THE INCOME-COMPENSATED DEMAND CURVE

The individual demand curves we saw in this chapter take into account both the substitution and income effects of price changes. For many applications, such demand curves will be the relevant tool for predicting people's response to a change in price. Suppose, for example, that gasoline prices rise because of a new OPEC agreement. Such a price increase will have both income and substitution effects, and the individual demand curve described earlier will be the appropriate device for predicting a person's response.

In other situations, however, this demand curve will not be the right tool. During the Carter administration, for example, there was a proposal to tax foreign oil, then cushion the burden of the tax by simultaneously reducing the tax on wage earnings. A tax on oil, taken by itself, would increase the price of oil and produce the corresponding income and substitution effects. But the effect of the simultaneous earnings tax reduction, roughly speaking, would have been to eliminate the income effect of the price increase. The tax comes out of one pocket, but is put right back into the other.

To analyze the effect of such a policy, we must use the **income-compensated demand curve,** which tells the amounts consumers would buy if they were fully compensated for the income effects of changes in price. To generate this curve for an individual, we simply eliminate the income effect from the total effect of price changes. The top panel of Figure A.4.4 shows the income and substitution effects of an increase in the price of shelter from $6/sq yd to $12/sq yd for a consumer whose weekly income is $120. The ordinary demand curve for shelter for the individual pictured here would associate $6 with 10 sq yd/wk and $12 with 6 sq yd/wk. The income-compensated demand curve is always constructed relative to a fixed reference point, the current price. Thus like the ordinary demand curve, it too associates 10 sq yd/wk with the price $6. But with the price $12 it associates not 6 sq yd/wk but 7 sq yd/wk, which is the amount of shelter the consumer would have bought at $12/sq yd if he had been given enough income to remain on the original indifference curve, I_0.

The individual whose responses are described in Figure A.4.4 happens to regard shelter as a normal good, one for which the quantity demanded increases as income rises. For normal goods, the income-compensated demand curve will necessarily be steeper than the ordinary demand curve. In the case of an inferior good, however, the ordinary demand curve will always be the steeper of the two. The relationship between the two demand curves for an inferior good is as pictured in Figure A.4.5.

In applications, the distinction between ordinary and income-compensated demand curves turns out to be particularly important for questions of tax policy.

income-compensated demand curve   demand curve that tells how much consumers would buy at each price if they were fully compensated for the income effects of price changes.

FIGURE A.4.4
Ordinary vs. Income-Compensated Demand Curves for a Normal Good
The ordinary demand curve plots the substitution and income effects of a price change. The income-compensated demand curve plots only the substitution effect. For a normal good, the income-compensated demand curve will always be steeper than the ordinary demand curve.

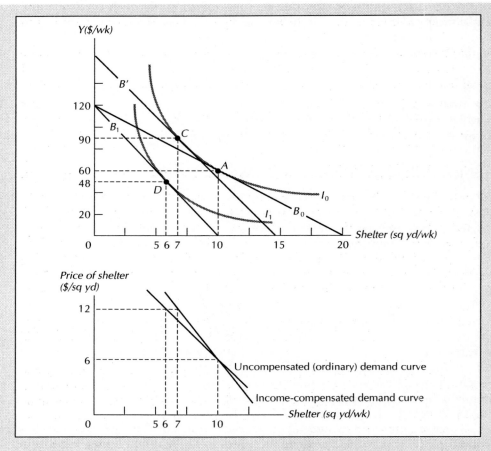

FIGURE A.4.5
Ordinary vs. Income-Compensated Demand Curves for an Inferior Good
The income effect offsets the substitution effect for an inferior good. The income-compensated demand curve, which omits the income effect, is therefore less steep than the ordinary demand curve in the case of an inferior good.

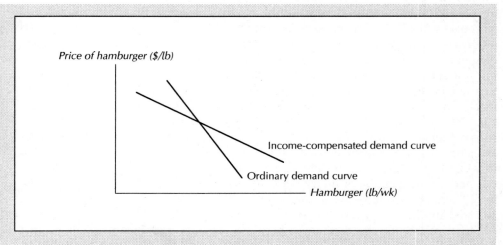

In the case of Jimmy Carter's gasoline tax proposal, there was an explicit provision for the proceeds of the tax to be returned to the people who paid it. But even without such a provision, the practical impact of a new tax would be roughly the same. After all, when the government raises more revenue from one source it needs to raise less from others. The end result is that the relevant demand curve for studying the effects of a tax on a good is the income-compensated demand curve.

As a practical matter, the distinction between the two types of demand curves is relevant only for goods for which income effects are large in relation to the corresponding substitution effects. In order for the income effect of a price change for a particular good to be large, it is necessary (but not sufficient) that the good account for a significant share of total expenditures. Many of the individual goods and services we buy, however, account for only a tiny fraction of our total expenditures. Accordingly, for such goods the distinction between the two types of demand curve will be unimportant. Even for a good that accounts for a large budget share, the income effect of a price change will sometimes be small. (The good might lie on the border between a normal and an inferior good.) For such goods, too, the distinction between ordinary and income-compensated demand curves will be of little practical significance.

ANSWERS TO IN-APPENDIX EXERCISES

A.4.1. First consider the point (0.5, 4). If we again let ΔP be 0.001 so that the new P is 4.001, the resulting Q is $2/4.001 = 0.499875$, which means that ΔQ is -0.000125. Price elasticity is therefore equal to $(4/0.5)(-0.000125/0.001) = -1$. Now consider the point (4, 0.5). If we again let ΔP be 0.001, so that the new P is 0.501, the resulting Q is $2/0.501 = 3.992$, which means that ΔQ is -0.008. Price elasticity is therefore equal to $(0.5/4)(-0.008/0.001) = -1$.

A.4.2. For $P = 4$, we have $4 = 4/\sqrt{Q}$, which yields $Q = 1$, so total expenditure is $4(1) = 4$. For $P = 3$, we have $3 = 4/\sqrt{Q}$, which yields $Q = \frac{16}{9}$, so total expenditure is $(3)(\frac{16}{9}) = (\frac{16}{3})$. So with $\epsilon = 2$ total expenditure rises with a decrease in price.

CHAPTER

5

APPLICATIONS OF RATIONAL CHOICE AND DEMAND THEORIES

In the 2005–2006 academic year, annual tuition and fees at Cornell University passed the $30,000 level. The university has a special policy whereby children of its faculty who attend Cornell are required to pay only fees, which come to approximately $2500/yr. Needless to say, this policy provides a strong financial incentive for faculty children to attend Cornell.

The faculty committee on compensation argued for many years that the university should extend the same tuition benefits to faculty children who attend universities other than Cornell. The traditional response of the university was that it could not afford to make such an offer. Under prodding by economists on the committee, however, the administration eventually took a tentative step in this direction by offering to pay one-third of tuition and fees at other universities. To its surprise, this new policy not only did not cost the university any money, it actually saved a great deal because the number of faculty children attending Cornell went down significantly once the new policy was in effect. This drop opened up an equivalent number of new positions in the freshman class, and because most of these were filled by tuition-paying students, Cornell actually came out ahead. Faculty families who received the new financial aid also came out ahead, and so did the new students who otherwise would have been unable to attend Cornell. The university had overlooked the opportunity cost of allocating positions to faculty children and had failed to anticipate that so many of them would be vacated because of the new offer.

156   CHAPTER 5   APPLICATIONS OF RATIONAL CHOICE AND DEMAND THEORIES

CHAPTER PREVIEW

Cornell's tuition policy provides yet another lesson that prices affect behavior. In this chapter we consider a variety of applications and examples involving the rational choice and demand theories developed in Chapters 3 and 4. We begin with two examples—a gasoline tax and school vouchers—that illustrate how the rational choice model can be used to shed light on important economic policy questions. Next we consider the concept of consumer surplus, a measure of how much the consumer benefits from being able to buy a given product at a given price. And we will see how the rational choice model can be used to examine how price and income changes affect welfare.

Next on our agenda are two case studies that illustrate the role of price elasticity in policy analysis. We examine the effect of a fare increase implemented by the Metropolitan Atlanta Rapid Transit Authority and the effect of liquor taxes on alcohol consumption by heavy drinkers.

Finally, we consider how the rational choice model can be adapted to consider choices that have future consequences.

USING THE RATIONAL CHOICE MODEL TO ANSWER POLICY QUESTIONS

Many government policies affect not only the incomes that people receive but also the prices they pay for specific goods and services. Sometimes these effects are the deliberate aim of government policy, but on other occasions they are the unintended consequence of policies directed toward other ends. In either case, both common sense and our analysis of the rational choice model tell us that changes in incomes and prices can normally be expected to alter the ways in which consumers spend their money. And as we will see, the rational choice model can yield crucial insights not always available to policy analysts armed with only common sense.

Application: A Gasoline Tax and Rebate Policy

As an interesting historical case in point, consider a policy proposal made during the administration of President Jimmy Carter to use gasoline taxes to help limit the quantity demanded of gasoline, thereby making the United States less dependent on foreign sources of oil. One immediate objection to this proposal was that the resulting rise in gasoline prices would impose economic hardship on the poor. Anticipating this objection, the Carter administration proposed to ease the burden on the poor by using the proceeds of the gasoline tax to reduce the payroll tax (the tax used to finance Social Security). Critics immediately responded that to return the proceeds of the tax in this fashion would defeat its purpose. These critics believed that if consumers got the gas tax back in the form of higher paychecks, they would go on buying just as much gasoline as before. But as we will see, these critics were woefully in need of instruction in the basic principles of rational choice.

Let's consider an illustrative example. Suppose the current price of gasoline is $1.00/gal, about what it was when President Carter made his proposal; and suppose that a tax of $0.50/gal is imposed that results in a $0.50 rise in the price of gasoline.[1] Suppose also that a representative consumer is then given a lump-sum

---

[1]Recall from Chapter 2 that the rise in equilibrium price will be exactly the same as the tax when the supply curve for gasoline is perfectly horizontal, an assumption made here for simplicity.

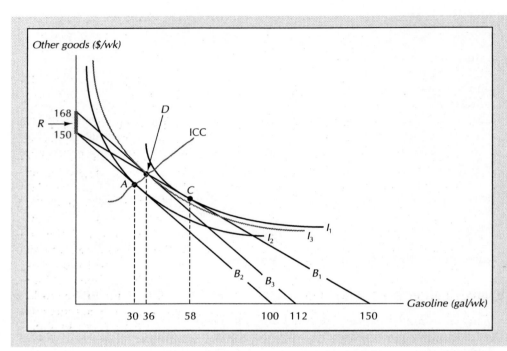

FIGURE 5.1
A Gasoline Tax and Rebate
The tax rotates the original budget constraint from B_1 to B_2. The rebate shifts B_2 out to B_3. The rebate does not alter the fact that the tax makes gasoline 50% more expensive relative to all other goods. The consumer shown in the diagram responds by consuming 22 gal/wk less gasoline.

payroll tax rebate that happens to be exactly equal to the amount of gasoline tax he pays. (Here, the term "lump-sum" means that the rebate does not vary with the amount of gasoline he consumes.) True or false: This policy will have no effect on the amount of gasoline this consumer buys. Critics of the Carter proposal would of course answer "true," but once we translate the effects of the proposal into the familiar rational choice framework, we quickly see that the correct response is "false."

To analyze the tax-and-rebate combination, let's consider a consumer whose income is \$150/wk. This consumer's budget constraint before the imposition of the tax is shown as B_1 in Figure 5.1.[2] On this budget constraint, he chooses bundle C, which contains 58 gal/wk of gasoline. His budget constraint with a \$1.50/gal price of gasoline would be B_2 if he received no rebate. On this budget constraint, he would consume bundle A, which contains only 30 gal/wk of gasoline. But how do we find the budget constraint that corresponds to a rebate equal to the amount collected from him in gasoline taxes?

The first step is to note that for any given quantity of gasoline consumed, the vertical distance between budget constraints B_1 and B_2 corresponds to the total amount of tax paid on that amount of gasoline. Thus, at 1 gal/wk of gasoline, the vertical distance between B_1 and B_2 would be \$0.50; at 2 gal/wk, it would be \$1.00; and so on.

Our next step is to trace out how the consumer's consumption will vary as a function of the size of the rebate. To do this, note that a rebate is like income from any other source, so what we really want to do is to trace out how the consumer responds to changes in income. As we saw in Chapter 4, the appropriate

---

[2]The equation for B_1 is $Y = 150 - G$, for B_2 is $Y = 150 - 1.5G$, and for B_3 is $Y = 168 - 1.5G$, where G is gasoline (gal/wk) and Y is all other goods (\$/wk).

158   CHAPTER 5 APPLICATIONS OF RATIONAL CHOICE AND DEMAND THEORIES

tool for this task is the income-consumption curve, or ICC. Accordingly, we construct the ICC through bundle A, as shown in Figure 5.1. Recall from Chapter 4 that the ICC in question is the locus of tangency points generated by a series of budget constraints parallel to B_2.

Now look at bundle D, the point where the ICC through A intersects the original budget constraint B_1. D is the equilibrium bundle on the budget constraint labeled B_3, where the price of gasoline is \$1.50/gal and the consumer has \$(150 + R)/wk = \$168/wk of income. This means that if we give the consumer a rebate of R = \$18/wk, he will consume bundle D and pay exactly \$18/wk in gasoline taxes. Note, however, that D lies well to the left of the original bundle C, which means that, despite the rebate, the consumer substantially curtails his gasoline consumption. If gasoline is a normal good, the effect of the rebate is to offset partially the income effect of the price increase. It does nothing to alter the substitution effect.

In the end, the Carter administration's tax-and-rebate proposal was never implemented, largely because of the objections of critics who lacked the economic knowledge to understand it. And as a result, the United States remains dangerously dependent on foreign oil. Indeed, with global demand for oil growing at record rates, largely because of rapid economic growth in China and India, and with heightened political instability in the Middle East, home to the world's largest stock of oil reserves, imposing a stiff tax on gasoline is an even more compelling idea now than when Carter first proposed it more than 25 years ago.

Application: School Vouchers

In recent years, there has been much discussion of the need to improve the quality of elementary and secondary education in the United States. Many policy analysts have recommended that this be accomplished by introducing more competition into the market for educational services. To this end there have been proposals that each family be given a voucher that could be used toward the tuition at any school of the family's choosing.

Such proposals contrast with the current system in most school districts, under which all families are required to pay school taxes and are then entitled to "free" tuition at the nearest public school. Under the current system, families who choose to go to private schools do not receive a refund on their school taxes. Critics of the current system complain that because tuition-charging private schools are unable to compete effectively with free public schools, public schools face little pressure to perform.

Setting aside the question of whether a voucher system would lead ultimately to higher educational quality, let us examine the likely effect of vouchers on the overall level of resources devoted to education. We can use the rational choice model to examine the educational choice confronting a representative family.

For simplicity, suppose that the quantity of education measured in terms of classroom-hours per year is fixed, and that when we speak of spending more on education, we mean not buying more hours of education but buying education of higher quality. Suppose the current tax system charges each family P_e of tax for 1 unit of public education, whether or not the family uses it, where "1 unit" is defined as a year's worth of education of the quality currently offered in the public schools. If it does not send its child to public school, the family has the option to purchase 1 or more units of education at a private school, also at the price of P_e per unit. For example, to buy 1.2 units of education at a private school

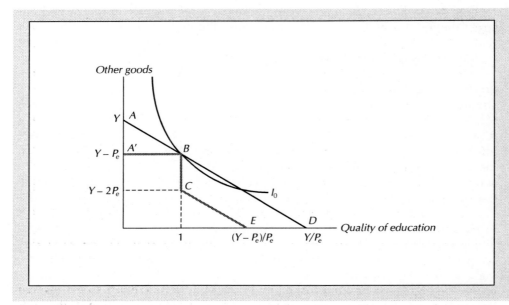

FIGURE 5.2
Educational Choice under the Current System
The family has a pretax income of Y, out of which it must pay P_e in school taxes. It is entitled to 1 unit of tuition-free public education. In lieu of public education, it may purchase at least 1 unit of private education at the price of P_e per unit. Its budget constraint is thus $A'BCE$, and its optimal bundle is B, which contains 1 unit of public education.

would mean to purchase education of 20 percent higher quality than is currently offered in the public schools. Families are required by law to provide their child with at least 1 unit of education, public or private.

Given these values, we can now derive the current budget constraint for education and other goods for a representative family whose pretax income is Y. If there were no taxes and no public schools, the family's budget constraint would be the line labeled ABD in Figure 5.2. But because each family must pay P_e in school taxes, the vertical intercept of the current budget constraint is not Y but $Y - P_e$. Since 1 unit of public education is "free," the family's budget constraint is horizontal out to 1 unit. If the family then wants to buy more than 1 unit of education under the current system, it must withdraw its child from the public school and enroll her in a private school at an additional cost of P_e per unit. This explains why the current budget constraint drops vertically by P_e at 1 unit of education. Thereafter the budget constraint continues to slope downward at the rate of P_e per unit. Thus the budget constraint for a family considering how much education to purchase is denoted by $A'BCE$ in Figure 5.2.

Note in Figure 5.2 that the nonlinear budget constraint makes a tangency solution unlikely for a family with indifference curves like the one shown. For such a family, the optimal bundle is, in effect, a corner solution in which exactly 1 unit of public education is chosen.

Let us now contrast this result with what would happen under a voucher system. Under that system, families again pay P_e in school tax, then get a voucher worth P_e, which may be used toward the purchase of either public or private education. Under the voucher system, the law still requires that families provide at least 1 unit of education for their children. The budget constraint under the voucher system will thus be given by $A'BD$ in Figure 5.3.

Compare Figures 5.2 and 5.3. Note that the principal difference produced by the voucher system is to eliminate the discontinuity at point B of the budget constraint. Parents no longer have to forfeit their school taxes when they switch

160   CHAPTER 5   APPLICATIONS OF RATIONAL CHOICE AND DEMAND THEORIES

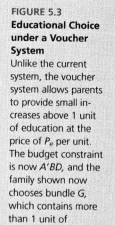

FIGURE 5.3
Educational Choice under a Voucher System
Unlike the current system, the voucher system allows parents to provide small increases above 1 unit of education at the price of P_e per unit. The budget constraint is now $A'BD$, and the family shown now chooses bundle G, which contains more than 1 unit of education.

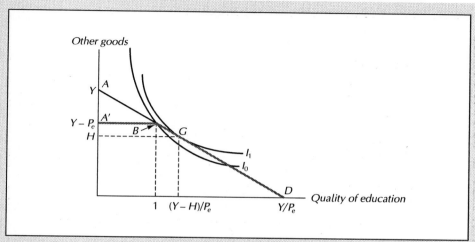

from public to private schools; they can purchase small increments in education beyond 1 unit without essentially having to "pay double." And indeed, the family in Figure 5.3 responds by choosing bundle G, which contains more than 1 unit of education. The analysis thus suggests that one effect of switching to a voucher system will be to increase the level of resources spent on educational services.

In times of budgetary stress, many people will be tempted to conclude that we should avoid any policy that will require additional resources. For these people, several cautionary notes should be stressed. First, our analysis did not take into account the possibility that competition among schools might make schools more efficient in their production of educational services. Thus, while parents might indeed choose to purchase more units of education under a voucher scheme, competition might drive the cost per unit down, making the net effect on expenditures hard to determine. Second, much of the additional resources devoted to education as a result of the voucher system would come from parents directly, not from governments. And it is by no means clear that a goal of public policy should be to prevent parents from spending more on education and less on other goods. Finally, a more complete analysis should consider the effect of additional education on economic productivity. After all, any increase in productivity that results from additional education could of course be used to offset the cost of the resources used to produce that education. In sum, our analysis in this example focuses on only one part of a much larger picture. But it is an important part, one that policymakers cannot afford to neglect.

CONSUMER SURPLUS

consumer surplus
a dollar measure of the extent to which a consumer benefits from participating in a transaction.

When exchange takes places voluntarily, economists generally assume that it makes all participants better off. Otherwise they would not have engaged in the exchange. It is often useful to have a dollar measure of the extent to which people benefit from a transaction. Such a measure, called **consumer surplus,** is particularly important for the purpose of evaluating potential government programs. It is relatively straightforward to measure the costs of, say, building a new road. But an intelligent decision about whether to build the road cannot be made without a reliable estimate of the extent to which consumers will benefit from it.

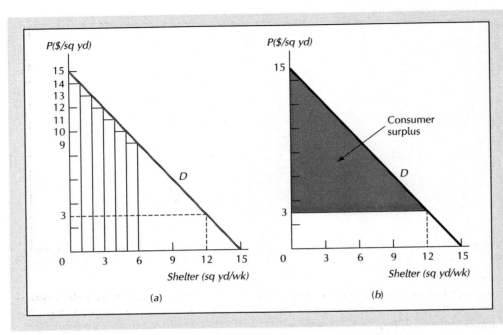

FIGURE 5.4
The Demand Curve Measure of Consumer Surplus
(a) The height of the demand curve at any quantity measures the most the consumer would be willing to pay for an extra unit of shelter. That amount minus the market price is the surplus he gets from consuming the last unit. (b) The total consumer surplus is the shaded area between the demand curve and the market price.

Using Demand Curves to Measure Consumer Surplus

The easiest way to measure consumer surplus involves the consumer's demand curve for the product. In both panels in Figure 5.4, the line labeled D represents an individual's demand curve for shelter, which sells for a market price of $3/sq yd. In panel (a), note that the most the consumer would have been willing to pay for the first square yard of shelter is $14. Since shelter costs only $3/sq yd, this means that he obtains a surplus of $11 from his purchase of the first square yard of shelter each week. The most he would be willing to pay for the second square yard of shelter is $13, so his surplus from the purchase of that unit will be smaller, only $10. His surplus from the third unit is smaller still, at $9. For shelter or any other perfectly divisible good, the height of the individual's demand curve at any quantity represents the most the consumer would pay for an additional unit of it.[3] In this example, if we subtract the purchase price of $3/sq yd from that value and sum the resulting differences for every quantity out to 12 sq yd/wk, we get roughly the shaded area shown in panel (b). (If we

---

[3]These statements about willingness-to-pay are literally true only if the demand curve we are talking about is an income-compensated demand curve like the one discussed in the Appendix to Chapter 4 (see page 147). If the demand curve shown were an ordinary demand curve of the sort we have been using, it would tell us that the consumer would be willing to buy 1 unit at a price of $14, 2 units at a price of $13, and so on. From this it would not be strictly correct to conclude that, having already paid $14 for the first unit, the consumer would then be willing to spend an *additional* $13 for the second unit. If the income effect of the demand for the good is positive, the fact that the consumer is now $14 poorer than before means that he would be willing to pay somewhat less than $13 for the second unit. But since income effects for most goods are small, it will generally be an acceptable approximation to measure consumer surplus using the ordinary demand curve. In a widely cited article, Robert Willig has argued that the demand curve method will almost always yield an acceptable approximation of the true value of consumer benefits. See R. Willig, "Consumer Surplus without Apology," *American Economic Review*, 66, 1976: 589–597.

162   CHAPTER 5   APPLICATIONS OF RATIONAL CHOICE AND DEMAND THEORIES

FIGURE 5.5
The Loss in Consumer Surplus from an Oil Price Increase
At a price of $2/gal, consumer surplus is given by the area of triangle *AEF*. At a price of $3/gal, consumer surplus shrinks to the area of triangle *ACD*. The loss in consumer surplus is the difference between these two areas, which is the area of the shaded region.

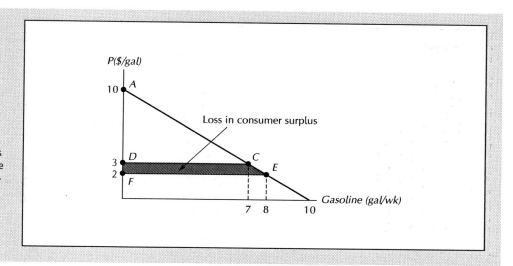

use infinitesimal increments along the horizontal axis, we get exactly the shaded area.) This shaded area represents the individual's consumer surplus from the purchase of 12 sq yd/wk of shelter.

EXAMPLE 5.1

An individual's demand curve for gasoline is given by $P = 10 - Q$, where P is the price of gasoline ($/gal), and Q is the quantity she consumes (gal/wk). If the individual's weekly income is $1000 and the current price of gasoline is $2/gal, by how much will her consumer surplus decline if an oil import restriction raises the price to $3/gal?

At a price of $2/gal, she consumes only 8 gallons of gasoline per week, which amounts to less than 2 percent of her income. The income effect of the price increase is therefore likely to be insignificant, so we can use the demand curve approximation to measure her consumer surplus before and after the price increase. (See footnote 3.) Figure 5.5 displays her demand curve. Her consumer surplus at the price of $2/gal is given by the area of the triangle *AEF* in Figure 5.5, CS = $\frac{1}{2}(10 - 2)8 = \$32$/wk. Following the price increase, her consumption falls from 8 to 7 gal/wk, and her surplus shrinks to the area of the triangle *ACD*, CS' = $\frac{1}{2}(10 - 3)7 = \$24.50$/wk. Her loss in consumer surplus is the difference between these two areas, which is the area of the trapezoid *DCEF*, the shaded region in Figure 5.5. This area is equal to CS − CS' = 32 − 24.5 = $7.50/wk.

EXERCISE 5.1

By how much would consumer surplus shrink in Example 5.1 if the price of gasoline rose from $3/gal to $4/gal?

Application: Two-Part Pricing

Economic reasoning suggests that a voluntary exchange will take place between a buyer and a seller if and only if that exchange makes both parties better off.

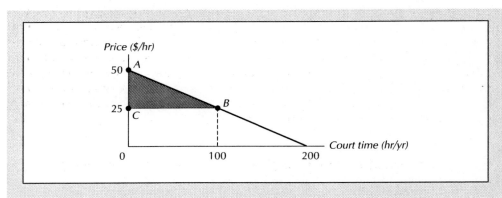

FIGURE 5.6
An Individual Demand Curve for Tennis Court Time
At a price of $25/hr, John receives $1250/yr (the shaded area) of consumer surplus from renting court time. The maximum annual membership fee the club can charge is $1250.

On the buyer's side, we may say that willingness to exchange depends on the buyer's expectation of receiving consumer surplus from the transaction.

Economic theory does not tell us very much about how the gains from exchange will be divided between the buyer and the seller. Sometimes the buyer will be in an advantageous bargaining position, enabling her to capture most of the benefits. Other times the buyer's options will be more limited, and in these cases, her consumer surplus is likely to be smaller. Indeed, as Economic Naturalist 5.1 illustrates, the seller can sometimes design a pricing strategy that captures *all* the consumer surplus.

Why do some tennis clubs have an annual membership charge in addition to their hourly court fees?

A suburban tennis club rents its courts for $25 per person per hour. John's demand curve for court time, $P = 50 - \frac{1}{4}Q$, where Q is measured in hours per year, is given in Figure 5.6. Assuming there were no other tennis clubs in town, what is the maximum annual membership fee John would be willing to pay for the right to buy court time for $25/hr?

The answer to this question is the consumer surplus John receives from being able to buy as much court time as he wants at the $25/hr price. This is equal to the area of triangle *ABC* in Figure 5.6, which is $CS = \frac{1}{2}(50 - 25)100 = \$1250/yr$. If the club charged a fee higher than that, John would be better off not renting any court time at all.

Why do many tennis clubs have both annual membership fees and court rental fees?

ECONOMIC NATURALIST 5.1

EXERCISE 5.2

In Economic Naturalist 5.1 how much would the maximum annual membership fee be if the club charged only $20/hr for court time?

164   CHAPTER 5   APPLICATIONS OF RATIONAL CHOICE AND DEMAND THEORIES

two-part pricing a pricing scheme that consists of a fixed fee and a marginal charge for each unit purchased (also called two-part tariffs).

Economic Naturalist 5.1 sheds light on many of the pricing practices we observe throughout the economy. Many amusement parks, for example, charge a fixed admission fee in addition to a charge for each ride. Many telephone companies charge a fixed monthly fee in addition to charges based on actual calls made. And some shopping clubs charge a fixed membership fee for the right to buy items carried in their stores or catalogs. Pricing schemes such as these are often called **two-part pricing**. Their effect is to transfer a portion of the consumer surplus from the buyer of the product to the seller.

ECONOMIC NATURALIST 5.2

Why do some amusement parks charge *only* a fixed admission fee, with no additional charge even for rides with long lines?

The price of a one-day pass at Disney's Magic Kingdom is $44 for children under 10. This pass includes unlimited access to all rides and attractions in the theme park, the only catch being that on certain rides—such as the popular Space Mountain roller coaster—waiting lines can be more than an hour long. Given persistent excess demands for some rides at a price of zero, why doesn't Disney charge an additional fee for each use of its most popular rides?

Economic theory predicts that the price of any good or service will rise in the face of excess demand. Long waiting lines like the ones described above thus pose a challenge for economists. In this case, a possible explanation may be that the people who have to pay for the rides (parents) are different from the ones who demand them (their children). Since their parents are paying, children want to ride the most thrilling rides whether the price is $0 or $5 per ride. At a price high enough to eliminate waiting lines, it would be possible to go on the most popular rides dozens of times a day, and many children would want to do exactly that. Parents could always ration access by saying no, of course. But not many parents look forward to a vacation in which they must spend the entire day saying no to their children. For these parents, Disney's current pricing policy is perhaps an ideal solution. It enables them to say to their children, "Go on whichever rides you want, as many times as you want," and then allow waiting lines to perform the essential rationing function.

Why doesn't Disney charge extra for its most popular rides?

OVERALL WELFARE COMPARISONS

The concept of consumer surplus helps us identify the benefits (or costs) of changes that occur in particular markets. Often we will want to assess whether consumers are better or worse off as a result of changes not just in one market but in many. Here too our model of rational choice lets us draw a variety of useful inferences. Consider the following example.

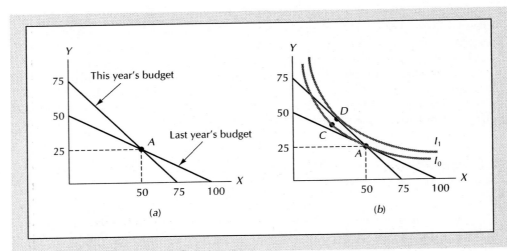

FIGURE 5.7
Budget Constraints for 2 Years
(a) If the consumer's budget constraint for this year contains the same bundle he bought last year (bundle A), he will be at least as well off this year as last. (b) If, in addition, relative prices are different in the two years, he will necessarily be able to buy a better bundle this year (bundle D).

EXAMPLE 5.2

Jones spends all his income on two goods: X and Y. The prices he paid and the quantities he consumed last year are as follows: $P_X = 10$, $X = 50$, $Y_Y = 20$, and $Y_Y = 25$. This year P_X and P_Y are both 10, and Jones's income is $750. Assuming his tastes do not change, in which year was Jones better off, last year or this?

To answer this question, it is helpful to begin by comparing Jones's budget constraints for the 2 years. To do this, we note first that his income last year was equal to what he spent, namely, $P_X X + P_Y Y = 1000$. For the prices given, we thus have the budget constraints shown in Figure 5.7a.

In Figure 5.7a, we see that Jones's budget constraint for this year contains the very same bundle he bought last year. Since his tastes have not changed, this tells us he cannot be worse off this year than last. After all, he can still afford to buy the same bundle as before. But our standard assumptions about preference orderings enable us to draw an even stronger inference. In particular, if his indifference curves have the usual convex shape, we know that an indifference curve—call it I_0—was tangent to last year's budget constraint at the point A in Figure 5.7b. We also know that this year's budget constraint is steeper than last year's, which tells us that part of I_0 must lie inside this year's budget triangle. On I_0, bundle A is equally preferred to bundle C. And because more is better, we know that D is preferred to C. It thus follows that D is preferred to A, and so we know that Jones was able to purchase a bundle of goods this year that he likes better than the one he bought last year. It follows that Jones was better off this year than last.

EXERCISE 5.3

Jones spends all his income on two goods: X and Y. The prices he paid and the quantities he consumed last year are as follows: $P_X = 15$, $X = 20$, $P_Y = 25$, and $Y = 30$. This year the prices have changed ($P_X = 15$ and $P_Y = 20$), and Jones's income is now $900. Assuming his tastes have not changed, in which year was Jones better off, last year or this?

166   CHAPTER 5   APPLICATIONS OF RATIONAL CHOICE AND DEMAND THEORIES

FIGURE 5.8
Rising Housing Prices and the Welfare of Homeowners
When the price of housing doubles, your budget constraint becomes B_2, which also contains your original bundle A. Because C, the optimal bundle on B_2, lies on a higher indifference curve than A, the effect of the housing price increase is to make you better off.

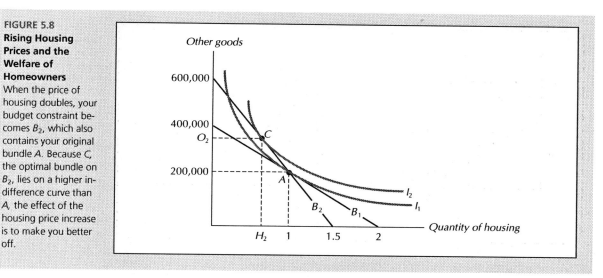

Application: The Welfare Effects of Changes in Housing Prices

Consider the following two scenarios:

1.   You have just purchased a house for $200,000. The very next day, the prices of all houses, including the one you just bought, double.

2.   You have just purchased a house for $200,000. The very next day, the prices of all houses, including the one you just bought, fall by half.

In each case, how does the price change affect your welfare? (Are you better off before the price change or after?)

I recently asked a class of first-year graduate students in economics these questions. The overwhelming majority responded that you are better off as a result of the price increase in scenario 1, but worse off as a result of the price drop in scenario 2. Although most students seemed very confident about these two responses, only one turns out to be correct.

To see why, let us first consider the case in which all housing prices double. Suppose your total wealth just before purchasing your house was $400,000. Let the size of your current house correspond to 1 unit of housing and let the price of other goods (the composite good) be 1. Your original budget constraint under scenario 1 will then correspond to the line labeled B_1 in Figure 5.8. Its vertical intercept, $400,000, is the maximum amount you could have spent on other goods. Its horizontal intercept, 2 units of housing, corresponds to the maximum quantity of housing you could have bought (that is, a house twice as large as your current house). On B_1, the equilibrium at A represents your original purchase. At A, you have 1 unit of housing and $200,000 left for other goods.

After the price of your house doubles, your budget constraint becomes the line labeled B_2 in Figure 5.8. To calculate the vertical intercept of B_2, note that your current house can now be sold for $400,000, which, when added to the $200,000 you had left over after buying your house, yields a maximum of $600,000 available for other goods. The horizontal intercept of B_2 tells us that when the price of housing doubles to $400,000/unit, your $600,000 will buy a maximum of only 1.5 units of housing. Note finally that on B_2 your optimal bundle is C, which

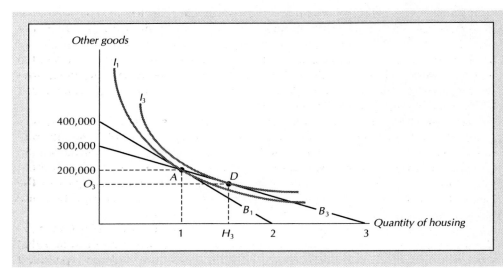

FIGURE 5.9
Falling Housing Prices and the Welfare of Homeowners
When the price of housing falls by half, your budget constraint becomes B_3, which also contains your original bundle A. Because D, the optimal bundle on B_3, lies on a higher indifference curve than A, the effect of the housing price drop is to make you better off.

contains $H_2 < 1$ units of housing and $O_2 > \$200,000$ worth of other goods. And since bundle C lies on a higher indifference curve than bundle A, you are better off than before the price increase.

Not surprisingly, when the price of housing goes up, your best response is to buy fewer units of housing and more units of other goods. Note that you are insulated from the harm of the income effect of the price increase because the price increase makes the house you own more valuable.

So far, so good. Now let us consider what for many students was the more troubling case—namely, scenario 2, in which housing prices fall by half. Again adopting the units of measure used in scenario 1, your budget constraint following the fall in housing prices is the line labeled B_3 in Figure 5.9. To get its vertical intercept, note that sale of your current house will now yield only $\$100,000$, which, when added to the $\$200,000$ you already have, makes a maximum of $\$300,000$ available for the purchase of other goods. To calculate the horizontal intercept of B_3, note that when the price of housing falls to $\$100,000$, your $\$300,000$ will now buy a maximum of 3 units of housing. Given the budget constraint B_3, the best affordable bundle is the one labeled D, which contains $H_3 > 1$ units of housing and $O_3 < 200,000$ units of other goods. As in scenario 1, the effect of the relative price change is again to move you to a higher indifference curve. This time, however, your direction of substitution is the opposite of the one in scenario 1: Because housing is now cheaper than before, you respond by purchasing more units of housing and fewer units of other goods.

In each scenario, note that your new budget constraint contains your original bundle, which means that you have to be at least as well off after the price change as before. Note also that in each case the change in relative prices means that your new budget constraint contains bundles that lie beyond your original indifference curve, making it possible to achieve a better outcome in each scenario.

Application: A Bias in the Consumer Price Index

The consumer price index (CPI) measures changes in the "cost of living," the amount a consumer must spend to maintain a given standard of living. Published each month by the Bureau of Labor Statistics, the CPI is calculated by first computing the cost of a representative bundle of goods and services during a reference period and then dividing that cost into the current cost of the same bundle. Thus, if it cost $100 to buy the representative bundle in the reference period and $150 to buy the same bundle today, the CPI would be 1.5. Announcing this figure, government spokespersons would explain that it meant the cost of living had increased by 50 percent compared with the reference period.

What the CPI fails to take into account, however, is that when the prices of different goods rise by different proportions, consumers do not generally buy the same bundle of goods they used to buy. Instead, the typical pattern is to substitute away from those goods whose prices have risen the most. By reallocating their budgets in this fashion, consumers are able to escape at least part of the harmful effects of price increases. Because the CPI fails to take substitution into account, it tends to overstate increases in the cost of living.

A simple example using the rational choice model makes this point unmistakably clear. Suppose the only goods in the economy were rice and wheat and that the representative consumer consumed 20 lb/mo of each in the reference period. If rice and wheat each cost $1/lb in the reference period, what will be the CPI in the current period if rice now costs $2/lb and wheat costs $3/lb? The cost of the reference period bundle at reference period prices was $40, while at current prices the same bundle now costs $100. The CPI thus takes the value of $100/$40 = 2.5. But is it really correct to say that the cost of living is now 2.5 times what it was?

To consider an extreme case, suppose our representative consumer regarded rice and wheat as perfect one-for-one substitutes, meaning that her indifference curves are negatively sloped 45° lines. In Figure 5.10, her original bundle is denoted as A and her original indifference curve (which coincides exactly with her original budget constraint) is labeled I_0. Now suppose we ask, how much income would she need in the current period to achieve the same level of satisfaction she achieved in the reference period? At the new prices, the slope of her budget constraint is no longer −1, but −3/2. With a budget constraint with this new slope, she could reach her original indifference curve most cheaply by buying the bundle labeled C in Figure 5.10. And since the cost of C at current prices is only $80, we can say that the cost of maintaining the original level of satisfaction has gone up by a factor of only 2.0, not 2.5.

In general, we can say that the extent to which the CPI overstates the cost of living will go up as substitution possibilities increase. The bias will also be larger when there are greater differences in the rates of increase of different prices.

Quality Change: Another Bias in the CPI?

Gathering data on the prices of goods and services might seem like a straightforward task. In practice, however, it is complicated by the existence of discounts, rebates, and other promotional offers in which the actual transaction price may be substantially different from the official list price.

Yet important as they are, accurate price data are not sufficient for estimating changes in the cost of living. We must also account for changes in the quality of what we buy. And this, unfortunately, turns out to be a far more complicated task than measuring changes in prices.

A brief look at the automobile industry illustrates the difficulty. The U.S. Department of Commerce reported that the average price paid for a new vehicle in 1994 was $19,675, a 5.1 percent increase over 1993, and a 72.8 percent increase

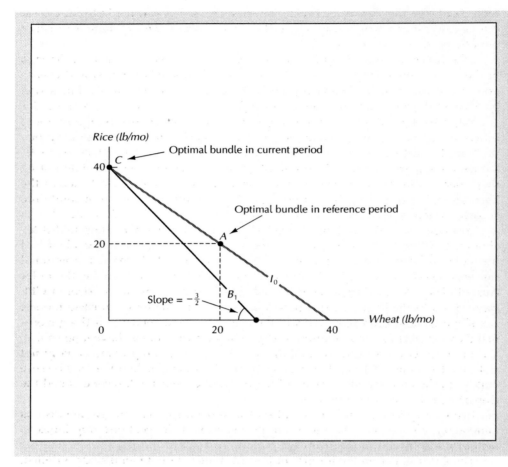

FIGURE 5.10
The Bias Inherent in the Consumer Price Index
For this consumer, rice and wheat are perfect substitutes. When the price of each was $1/lb, she bought 20 lb/mo of each in the reference period, for a total expenditure of $40/mo. If the current prices of rice and wheat are $2/lb and $3/lb, respectively, the expenditure required to buy the original bundle is $100/mo. The CPI is the ratio of these two expenditures, $100/$40 = 2.5. But the consumer can attain her original indifference curve, I_0, by buying bundle C, which costs only $80 at current prices. The cost of maintaining the original level of satisfaction has thus risen by a factor of only 2.0.

over 1984.[4] During that same 10-year span, the CPI rose only 42.6 percent. Does this mean that the prices of cars rose much more rapidly during that period than those of other goods and services? Not necessarily. After all, cars produced in 1994 came with many features not found on earlier models. For example, whereas approximately 90 percent of cars sold in the United States in 1994 came equipped with air bags and about 40 percent with antilock brakes, virtually none had these features in 1984. The number of cars with convenience equipment such as rear window defrosters and power windows once confined to luxury models rose more than 50 percent during the same decade.

The Department of Commerce now calculates a special automotive CPI, which deducts the cost of such additional features in an effort to measure changes in the prices of comparably equipped cars. This index rose only 32.2 percent between 1984 and 1994—or about 10 percent *less* than the overall CPI.

Although these adjustments obviously help, they capture only a small part of the automobile quality changes that have been occurring in recent years. For example, the automotive CPI made no allowance for the fact that 1995 cars had achieved a 40 percent reduction in hydrocarbon emissions and a 60 percent

---

[4]The data in this section are drawn from Csaba Csere, "Do Cars Cost Too Much, Or Do We Just Like Costly Cars?" *Car and Driver*, June 1995, p. 9.

reduction in oxides of nitrogen relative to 1984 cars. Nor did the index allow for the fact that cars are much more reliable, crashworthy, and corrosion resistant than they were a decade earlier.

The pace of auto quality improvement is vividly illustrated by a comparison of the 1995 Honda Civic DX sedan—one of the company's smallest and cheapest cars during that model year—with Honda's top-of-the-line Accord sedan from 1982. Besides having a bevy of safety features not found on the older Accord, the '95 Civic had a larger interior; a quieter, cleaner-burning, yet more powerful engine (102 horsepower versus 75); better tires and brakes; and a much more sophisticated suspension. The '95 Civic accelerated from 0 to 60 mph in 9.1 seconds, compared with 12.2 seconds for the '82 Accord; the '95 Civic got 40 miles per gallon on the highway, while the '82 Accord got only 32. Whereas the '95 Civic's finish will survive six northern winters in near-showroom condition, similar exposure left the '82 Accord riddled with rust. The '82 Accord had a sticker price of $8995, but since it was in short supply, many dealers sold it for about $10,000. The '95 Civic had a sticker price of $12,360, and most dealers sold it at a substantial discount. So even with the passage of 13 years, the nominal dollar transaction price was not much higher for the Civic than for the older Accord. The '95 Civic's sticker price, adjusted for changes in the overall CPI, translates into $8852 in 1982 dollars—in effect, a much better car for less money.

If the Civic–Accord comparison is representative, it seems that the government's attempts to adjust for automobile quality improvements have fallen short. With the growth of global competition, quality has been improving rapidly not just in automobiles but in other goods and services as well. And we may be sure that, as in the auto industry, many of the relevant changes will have escaped the Department of Commerce's notice.

Failure to account fully for quality of improvements has the same effect as failure to account for substitution. Both cause the official cost-of-living index to overstate the true increase in prices.

The CPI has extremely important implications for the federal budget deficit, for this is the index used to determine the cost-of-living adjustments received by Social Security recipients and beneficiaries of a host of other government programs. Even a slight upward bias in the CPI can swell the budget deficit by many billions of dollars.

USING PRICE ELASTICITY OF DEMAND

In the sphere of applied economic analysis, few tools are more important than the concept of price elasticity of demand. In this section we examine applications of this concept in two very different settings.

Application: The MARTA Fare Increase

To cover a rising budget deficit in 1987, the Metropolitan Atlanta Rapid Transit Authority raised its basic fare from 60 to 75 cents/ride. In the 2 months following the fare increase, total system revenues rose 18.3 percent in comparison with the same period a year earlier.[5] Assuming a linear demand curve and that the observed

---

[5]See Bert Roughton, Jr., "MARTA Sees Ridership Dip with Fare Hike," *Atlanta Constitution*, October 8, 1987, p. 7.

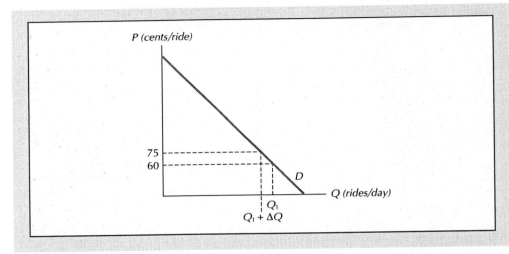

P (cents/ride)

75

60

D

Q (rides/day)

Q_1

$Q_1 + \Delta Q$

FIGURE 5.11
The MARTA Fare Increase
Knowing the percentage change in total expenditure and the percentage change in price enables us to calculate the price elasticity of demand.

changes in ridership are the result of the fare increase, what do these figures tell us about the original price elasticity of demand for rides on the MARTA system? If Q_1 denotes the original quantity of riders and ΔQ the change in riders due to the fare increase, and if ΔP and P_1 denote the price change and original price, respectively, we want to use the information given to calculate the expression $\epsilon = (\Delta Q/Q_1)/(\Delta P/P_1)$. Suppose the demand curve for rides on MARTA is as shown by the curve labeled D in Figure 5.11. The fact that total revenues went up by 18.3 percent may be expressed as follows:

$$\frac{75(Q_1 + \Delta Q) - 60Q_1}{60Q_1} = 0.183, \tag{5.1}$$

where $\Delta Q < 0$ is the fall in ridership. Equation 5.1 reduces to

$$\frac{15Q_1 + 75\Delta Q}{60Q_1} = 0.183, \tag{5.2}$$

which, in turn, solves for

$$\frac{\Delta Q}{Q_1} = -0.0536. \tag{5.3}$$

Since we know that $\Delta P/P_1 = \frac{15}{60} = 0.25$, this tells us that $\epsilon = -0.0536/0.25 = -0.2144$. The demand for MARTA rides thus turns out to be highly inelastic with respect to price, which is consistent with the fact that the fare increase led to a substantial increase in total expenditure.

EXERCISE 5.4

In the example just discussed, suppose that MARTA had raised its fare from $1.00 to $1.10 and that, in response, system revenue rose by 2 percent. What would that tell us about the elasticity of demand for MARTA tickets at the original price of $1.00? (Again assume that the demand curve for tickets is linear.)

172   CHAPTER 5   APPLICATIONS OF RATIONAL CHOICE AND DEMAND THEORIES

Application: The Price Elasticity of Demand for Alcohol

How does the consumption of alcoholic beverages respond to changes in their price? For many decades, the conventional wisdom on this subject responded, "not very much." Unfortunately, however, estimates of the price elasticity of demand for alcohol tend to be highly unreliable. The problem is that liquor prices usually don't vary sufficiently to permit an accurate estimate of their effects.

In a careful study,[6] Philip Cook made use of some previously unexploited data on significant changes in alcohol prices. He suggested that the price elasticity of demand for alcohol may be much higher than we thought.

Cook's method was to examine changes in alcohol consumption that occur in response to changes in state liquor taxes. Of the 48 contiguous states, 30 license and tax the private sale of liquor. Periodically, most of these states increase their nominal liquor taxes to compensate for the effects of inflation. The pattern is for the real value of a state's liquor tax to be highest right after one of these tax increases, then to erode steadily as the cost of living rises over the next several years. The fact that taxes are not adjusted continuously to keep their real value constant provides the real price variability we need to estimate the responsiveness of alcohol purchases to price changes.

There were 39 liquor tax increases in Cook's 30-state sample during the period 1960–1975. In 30 of these 39 cases, he found that liquor consumption declined relative to the national trend in the year following the tax increase. His estimate of the price elasticity of demand was −1.8, a substantially higher value than had been found in previous studies.

Cook's interpretation of his findings provides an interesting case study in the factors that govern price elasticity. One salient fact about the alcohol market, he noted, is that heavy drinkers, though a small fraction of the total population, account for a large fraction of the total alcohol consumed. This fact has led many people to expect that alcohol consumption would be unresponsive to variations in price. The common view of heavy drinkers, after all, is that they drink primarily out of habit, not because of rational deliberations about price. Stated another way, analysts always expected the substitution effect to be small for these people. But even if the substitution effect were zero for heavy drinkers, there would remain the income effect to consider. The budget share devoted to alcohol tends to be large among heavy drinkers for two reasons. The obvious one is that heavy drinkers buy a lot of liquor. Less obvious, perhaps, is that their incomes tend to be significantly smaller than average. Many heavy drinkers have difficulty holding steady jobs and often cannot work productively in the jobs they do hold. The result is that the income effect of a substantial increase in the price of liquor forces many heavy drinkers to consume less. In support of this interpretation, Cook observed that mortality from cirrhosis of the liver declines sharply in the years following significant liquor tax increases. This is a disease that for the most part afflicts only people with protracted histories of alcohol abuse, and clinical experience

---

[6]Philip J. Cook, "The Effect of Liquor Taxes on Drinking, Cirrhosis, and Auto Accidents," in *Alcohol and Public Policy*, Mark Moore and Dean Gerstein (eds.), Washington, DC: National Academy Press, 1982.

reveals that curtailed drinking can delay or prevent its onset in long-term heavy drinkers.

THE INTERTEMPORAL CHOICE MODEL

The choices we have considered thus far have involved trade-offs between alternatives in the present—the choice between food now and clothing now, between travel now and stereo equipment now, and so on. There was no hint in any of these choices that the alternative chosen today might affect the menu of alternatives available in the future.

Yet such effects are a prominent feature of many of our most important decisions. Our task in this section is to enlarge the basic consumer choice model in Chapter 3 to accommodate them.

Intertemporal Consumption Bundles

When deciding what to do with their incomes, people may either consume them all now or save part for the future. The question we want to be able to answer is, "How would rational consumers distribute their consumption over time?" To keep the analysis manageable, it is helpful to begin by supposing that there are only two time periods, namely, *current* and *future*. In the standard, or *atemporal*, choice model in Chapter 3, the alternatives were different goods that could be consumed in the current period—apples now versus oranges now, etc. In our simple *intertemporal choice model*, the alternatives instead will be *current consumption* (denoted C_1) versus *future consumption* (denoted C_2). Each of these is an amalgam—the functional equivalent of the composite good (see Chapter 3). For the sake of simplicity, we set aside the question of how to apportion current and future consumption among the various specific consumption goods.

In the atemporal choice model, any bundle of goods can be represented as a point in a simple two-dimensional diagram. We use an analogous procedure in the intertemporal choice model. In Figure 5.12, for example, current consumption of $6000 combined with future consumption of $6000 is represented by the bundle E. Bundle D represents current consumption of $3000 and future consumption of $9000.

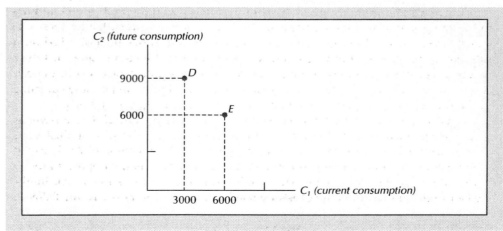

FIGURE 5.12
Intertemporal Consumption Bundles
Alternative combinations of current and future consumption are represented as points in the C_1, C_2 plane. By convention, the horizontal axis measures current consumption; the vertical axis, future consumption.

174   CHAPTER 5   APPLICATIONS OF RATIONAL CHOICE AND DEMAND THEORIES

FIGURE 5.13
The Intertemporal Budget Constraint
For every dollar by which current consumption is reduced, it is possible to increase future consumption by $1.2.

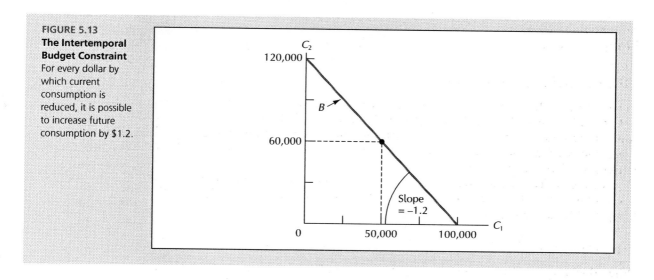

The Intertemporal Budget Constraint

Suppose you receive $50,000 income in the current period and $60,000 income in the future period. Suppose also that if you deposit some of your income from the current period in a bank, you can receive your principal plus 20 percent in the future period. Similarly, if you wish to borrow against your future income, you may receive $1 in the current period for every $1.20 you must repay in the future period. (See Figure 5.13.) To construct your intertemporal budget constraint, first note that you can always merely consume your income in each period, so $C_1 = \$50,000$ and $C_2 = \$60,000$ must be a point on your intertemporal budget constraint. Another option is to deposit all $50,000 (maximum lending) and thus receive $1.2(50,000) = \$60,000$ in addition to your $60,000 future income for $C_2 = \$120,000$ future consumption with no current consumption ($C_1 = 0$). Yet another option is to borrow $\$60,000/1.2 = \$50,000$ (maximum borrowing) in addition to your $50,000 current income for $C_1 = \$100,000$ current consumption with no future consumption ($C_2 = 0$). The equation for your intertemporal budget constraint is $C_2 = \$120,000 - 1.2C_1$, or, equivalently, $1.2C_1 + C_2 = \$120,000$.

In general, suppose you receive M_1 of your income in the first period and M_2 in the second, and can either borrow or lend at the interest rate r. Under these circumstances, what is the most you can consume in the future period? Maximum future consumption occurs when you set all your current income aside for future use. Setting aside M_1 in the current period at the interest rate r means your deposit will grow to $M_1(1 + r)$ by the future period. So the most you can possibly consume in the future is that amount plus your future income, or $M_1(1 + r) + M_2$.

What is the most you could consume in the current period? The answer is your current income plus the maximum amount you can borrow against your future income. The most you can borrow against a future income of M_2 is called the **present value** of M_2, denoted PV(M_2). It is the amount that, if deposited today at the interest rate r, would be worth exactly M_2 in the future period. Accordingly, we can find the present value of M_2 by solving $\text{PV}(M_2)(1 + r) = M_2$ for PV(M_2):

present value   the present value of a payment of X dollars T years from now is $X/(1 + r)^T$, where r is the annual rate of interest.

$$\text{PV}(M_2) = \frac{M_2}{1 + r} \qquad (5.4)$$

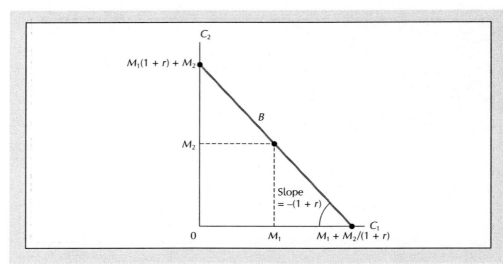

FIGURE 5.14
Intertemporal Budget Constraint with Income in Both Periods, and Borrowing or Lending at the Rate r
The opportunity cost of $1 of present consumption is $(1 + r)$ dollars of future consumption. The horizontal intercept of the intertemporal budget constraint is the present value of lifetime income, $M_1 + M_2/(1 + r)$.

For example, if M_2 were $110,000 and the interest rate were 10 percent (that is, $r = 0.10$), the present value of M_2 would be $110,000/1.1 = $100,000. Present value is a simple equivalence relationship between sums of money that are payable at different points in time. If $r = 0.10$, then $100,000 today will be worth $110,000 in the future. By the same token, $110,000 in the future is worth $100,000 today when the interest rate is 10 percent.

It is not necessary, of course, to borrow or save the maximum amounts possible. The consumer who wishes to shift some of her future income into the current period can borrow any amount up to the maximum at the rate of $1/(1 + r)$ dollars today for every dollar given up in the future. Or, she can save any amount of her current income and get back $(1 + r)$ dollars in the future for every dollar not consumed today. The intertemporal budget constraint, shown as the locus B in Figure 5.14, is thus again the straight line that joins the maximum current consumption and maximum future consumption points. And its slope will again be $-(1 + r)$. As in the atemporal model, here too the slope of the budget constraint may be interpreted as a relative price ratio. This time it is the ratio of the prices of current and future consumption. Current consumption has a higher price than future consumption because of the opportunity cost of the interest forgone when money is spent rather than saved. It is conventional to refer to the horizontal intercept of the intertemporal budget constraint as the *present value of lifetime income.*

EXERCISE 5.5

You have $50,000 of current income and $42,000 of future income. If the interest rate between the current and future period is 5 percent, what is the present value of your lifetime income? What is the maximum amount you could consume in the future? What is the equation describing your intertemporal budget constraint?

176   CHAPTER 5   APPLICATIONS OF RATIONAL CHOICE AND DEMAND THEORIES

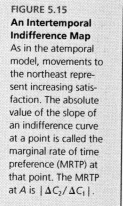

FIGURE 5.15
An Intertemporal Indifference Map
As in the atemporal model, movements to the northeast represent increasing satisfaction. The absolute value of the slope of an indifference curve at a point is called the marginal rate of time preference (MRTP) at that point. The MRTP at A is $|\Delta C_2/\Delta C_1|$.

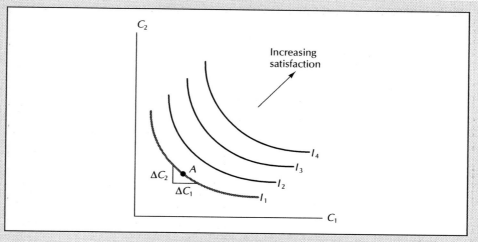

As in the atemporal case considered in Chapter 3, the intertemporal budget constraint is a convenient way of summarizing the consumption bundles that someone is *able* to buy. And again as before, it tells us nothing about which particular combination a person will *choose* to buy.

Intertemporal Indifference Curves

To discover which bundle the consumer will select from those that are feasible, we need some convenient way of representing the consumer's preferences over current and future consumption. Here again the analytical device is completely analogous to one we used in the atemporal case. Just as a consumer's preferences over two current consumption goods may be captured by an indifference map, so too may his preferences over current and future goods be represented in this fashion. In Figure 5.15, the consumer is indifferent between the bundles that lie on the locus I_1, each of which is less desirable than the bundles on I_2, and so on.

The absolute value of the slope of the intertemporal indifference curve at any point is the marginal rate of substitution between future and current consumption. At point A in Figure 5.15, it is given by $|\Delta C_2/\Delta C_1|$, and this ratio is also referred to as the **marginal rate of time preference (MRTP)** at A.[7] If $|\Delta C_2/\Delta C_1| > 1$ at A, the consumer is said to exhibit *positive time preference* at that point. This means that he requires more than 1 unit of future consumption to compensate him for the loss of a unit of current consumption. If $|\Delta C_2/\Delta C_1| < 1$ at a point, he is said to exhibit *negative time preference* at that point. Such a person is willing to forgo 1 unit of current consumption in return for less than 1 unit of future consumption. Finally, if $|\Delta C_2/\Delta C_1| = 1$ at a point, the consumer is said to have *neutral time preference* at that point. With neutral time preference, present and future consumption trade off against one another at the rate of 1 to 1.

marginal rate of time preference   the number of units of consumption in the future a consumer would exchange for 1 unit of consumption in the present.

---
[7]In calculus terms, the marginal rate of time preference is given by $|dC_2/dC_1|$.

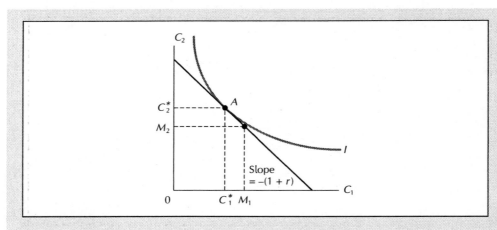

FIGURE 5.16
The Optimal Intertemporal Allocation
As in the atemporal model, the optimal intertemporal consumption bundle (bundle A) lies on the highest attainable indifference curve. Here, that occurs at a point of tangency.

As in the atemporal case, it appears justified to assume that the marginal rate of time preference declines as one moves downward along an indifference curve. The more current consumption a person already has, the more she will be willing to give up in order to obtain an additional unit of future consumption. For most of us then, the question of whether time preference is positive, negative, or neutral will be a matter of where we happen to be on our indifference maps. The scion of a wealthy family who is unable to borrow against the $5 billion he is due to inherit in 2 years very likely has strongly positive time preference. By contrast, the primitive farmer whose food stocks are perishable is likely to have negative time preference in the wake of having harvested a bumper crop.

The optimal allocation between current and future consumption is determined exactly as in the atemporal model. The consumer selects the point along his budget constraint that corresponds to the highest attainable indifference curve. If the intertemporal indifference curves have the conventional convex shape, we ordinarily get a tangency solution like the one shown in Figure 5.16. If the MRTP is everywhere larger than (or everywhere smaller than) the slope of the budget constraint, corner solutions result, just as in the atemporal case.

Note in Figure 5.16 that the marginal rate of time preference at the optimal bundle (C_1, C_2) is positive, because the absolute value of the slope of the budget constraint is $1 + r > 1$. In the example pictured in the diagram, the consumer has the same income in each time period, but consumes slightly more in period 2.

The optimal allocation will of course be different for different consumers. The optimum shown in Figure 5.17a, for example, is for a consumer whose preferences are much more heavily tilted in favor of future consumption. The one shown in Figure 5.17b, by contrast, is for a consumer who cares much more about present consumption. But in each case, note that the slope of the indifference curve at the optimal point is the same. As long as consumers can borrow and lend at the interest rate r, the marginal rate of time preference at the optimal bundle will be $(1 + r)$ (except, of course, in the case of corner solutions). For interior solutions, positive time preference is the rule, regardless of the consumer's preferences.

It is conventional to assume that both current and future consumption are normal goods. Thus an increase in the present value of lifetime income, all other factors constant, will cause both current and future consumption to rise.

178   CHAPTER 5 APPLICATIONS OF RATIONAL CHOICE AND DEMAND THEORIES

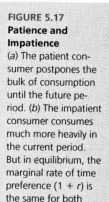

FIGURE 5.17
Patience and Impatience
(a) The patient consumer postpones the bulk of consumption until the future period. (b) The impatient consumer consumes much more heavily in the current period. But in equilibrium, the marginal rate of time preference $(1 + r)$ is the same for both types of consumers.

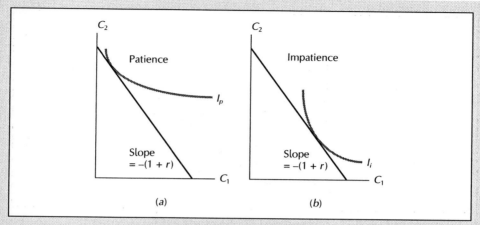

EXAMPLE 5.3

You have current income of $100,000 and future income of $154,000, and can borrow and lend at the rate $r = 0.1$. Under these conditions, you consume exactly your income in each period. True or false: An increase in r to $r = 0.4$ will cause you to save some of your current income.

Line B in Figure 5.18 is the original budget constraint. Its horizontal intercept is the present value of lifetime income when $r = 0.1$: $100,000 + $154,000/1.1 = $240,000. Its vertical intercept is future income plus $(1 + r)$ times current income: $154,000 + (1.1)($100,000) = $264,000. The optimal bundle occurs at A, by assumption, which implies that the MRTP at A is 1.1. When the interest rate rises to 0.4, the intertemporal budget constraint becomes B'. Its horizontal intercept is $100,000 + $154,000/1.4 = $210,000. Its vertical intercept is $154,000 + (1.4)($100,000) = $294,000. Because the MRTP at A is less than the absolute value of the slope of the budget constraint B', it follows that the consumer will be better off by consuming less in the present and more in the future than he did at A. The new bundle is shown at D in Figure 5.18.

Application: The Permanent Income and Life-Cycle Hypotheses

Economists once assumed that a person's current consumption depends primarily on her current income. Thus if a consumer received a windfall roughly equal to her current income, the prediction was that her consumption would roughly double.

In the 1950s, however, Milton Friedman, Franco Modigliani, Richard Brumberg, and others argued that the intertemporal choice model suggests otherwise.[8] To

---

[8]See Franco Modigliani and R. Brumberg, "Utility Analysis and the Consumption Function: An Interpretation of Cross-Section Data," in K. Kurihara (ed.), *Post Keynesian Economics*, London: Allen & Unwin, 1955; and Milton Friedman, *A Theory of the Consumption Function*, Princeton, NJ: Princeton University Press, 1957.

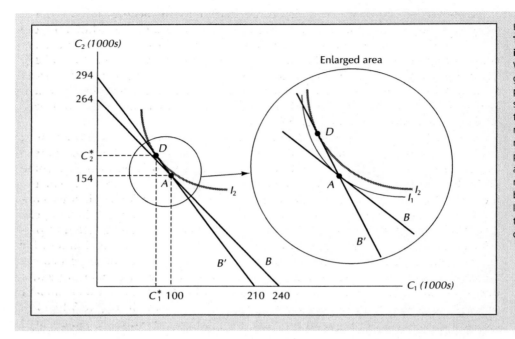

FIGURE 5.18
The Effect of a Rise in the Interest Rate
When the interest rate goes up, the intertemporal budget constraint rotates about the current endowment point. If the current endowment point (A) was optimal at the lower interest rate, the new optimal bundle (D) will have less current consumption and more future consumption.

illustrate, consider a consumer with current and future incomes both equal to 120, who can borrow and lend at the rate $r = 0.2$. The locus labeled B in Figure 5.19 is the consumer's intertemporal budget constraint, and the optimal bundle along it is denoted by A. Note that the horizontal intercept of B is the present value of life-time income, namely, $120 + (120/1.2) = 220$.

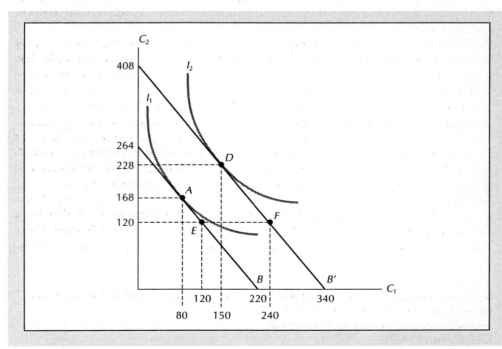

FIGURE 5.19
Permanent Income, not Current Income, is the Primary Determinant of Current Consumption
The effect of a rise in current income (from 120 to 240) will be felt as an increase not only in current consumption (from 80 to 150), but also in future consumption (from 168 to 228).

180   CHAPTER 5 APPLICATIONS OF RATIONAL CHOICE AND DEMAND THEORIES

Notice what happens when this consumer's current income rises from 120 to 240. His budget constraint is now the locus labeled B', and the optimal bundle is D. The effect of increasing current income is thus to increase not only current consumption (from 80 to 150) but future consumption as well (from 168 to 228). Because intertemporal indifference curves exhibit diminishing marginal rates of time preference,[9] the consumer generally does best not to concentrate too much of his consumption in any one period. By spreading his windfall over both periods, he is able to achieve a better outcome.

Friedman's *permanent income hypothesis* says that the primary determinant of current consumption is not current income but what he called **permanent income**. In terms of our simple intertemporal choice model, permanent income is simply the present value of lifetime income. (Following the increase in current income in Figure 5.19, permanent income is $240 + 120/1.2 = 340$.) When we consider that in reality the future consists of not just one but many additional periods, it becomes clear that current income constitutes only a small fraction of permanent income. (If there were 10 future periods we were concerned about, for example, then a 10 percent increase in current income would cause permanent income to increase by just over 2 percent.)[10] Accordingly, Friedman argued, a given proportional change in current income should give rise to a much smaller proportional change in current consumption, just as we saw in Figure 5.19. (The *life-cycle hypothesis* of Modigliani and Brumberg tells essentially the same story.)

permanent income
the present value of lifetime income.

Factors Accounting for Differences in Time Preference

Uncertainty regarding the future is one reason to prefer current to future consumption. In countries at war, for example, people often live as though there were no tomorrow, as indeed for many of them there will not be. By contrast, a peaceful international climate, secure employment, stable social networks, good health, and a variety of similar factors tend to reduce uncertainty about the future, in the process justifying greater weight on future as opposed to current consumption.

Intertemporal indifference maps, like the atemporal variety, will also vary according to the disposition of the individual. My first son, for example, has strongly positive time preferences in most situations. (His indifference curves are very steep with respect to the current consumption axis.) Ever since he was a small boy, he always ate his favorite part of his meal first, then worked his way through to his least favored items. Only with pressure would he eat his vegetables at all, and even then he always ate them last. My second son is the polar opposite case. He always starts with the foods he likes least, carefully husbanding his favorite items for the end of his meal. This contrast in their behavior at the dinner table pervades virtually every other aspect of their lives.

Time preference depends also on the specific circumstances of the choice at hand. Experimental studies have isolated certain situations in which most people have strongly positive time preference, others in which they show strongly negative time preference. Carnegie-Mellon University economist George

---

[9]Diminishing marginal rate of time preference is the intertemporal analog of diminishing marginal rate of substitution in the atemporal model.

[10]Again, we assume an interest rate of $r = 0.2$.

Loewenstein, for example, told experimental subjects to imagine they had won a kiss from their favorite movie star and then asked them when they would most like to receive it. Even though getting it right away was one of the options, most subjects elected to wait an average of several days. These choices imply negative time preference, and Loewenstein explained that most subjects simply wanted a little while to savor the anticipation of the kiss.[11]

Loewenstein also told a group of subjects to imagine that they were going to receive a painful electric shock and then asked them when they would like to receive it. This time most subjects chose to get it right away. They apparently wanted to spend as little time as possible dreading the shock. But since an electric shock is a "bad" rather than a "good," these choices too imply negative time preference.

While negative time preferences are occasionally observed in individual cases and can be invoked among many people by suitably chosen experiments, by far the more common case is for a general preference for present over future consumption. We can be sure, for example, that if we put a can of honey-roasted cashews in front of Loewenstein's experimental subjects, not many of them would want to wait a few days to anticipate the pleasure of eating them. On the contrary, the nuts would probably disappear in short order, even if that meant spoiling dinner an hour away.

Nineteenth-century economist Eugen von Böhm-Bawerk suggested that one reason for such behavior is that current consumption opportunities confront our senses directly, whereas future ones can only be imagined. The pleasure of eating the roasted nuts, for example, is both intense and immediate. Even those people who would strongly prefer the meal to the nuts often lack the self-control to wait. Böhm-Bawerk believed that our "faulty telescopic faculty" was no good reason to assign greater weight to current than to future pleasures. Uncertainty aside, he felt that people would reap greater satisfaction from their lives if they weighed the present and the future equally.

SUMMARY

- In this chapter our primary focus was on applications of the rational choice and demand theories developed in Chapters 3 and 4. We also considered the concept of consumer surplus, which measures the amount by which a consumer benefits by being able to buy a given product at a given price. We saw that consumer surplus is well approximated by the area bounded above by the individual demand curve and below by the market price. Two-part pricing structures are a device by which a portion of consumer surplus is transferred from the buyer to the seller.

- The rational choice model is also useful for evaluating the welfare effects of price and income changes.

It suggests why the consumer price index, the government's measure of changes in the cost of living, may often overstate the true cost of achieving a given level of satisfaction.

- The intertemporal choice model is, in every essential respect, analogous to the atemporal choice model in Chapter 3. In the two-dimensional case, it begins with a commodity graph that depicts current and future consumption levels of a composite good. The consumer's initial endowment is the point, (M_1, M_2), that corresponds to current and future income. If the consumer can borrow and lend at the rate r, his intertemporal budget constraint is then the line passing through the endowment point with

[11]See George Loewenstein, "Anticipation and the Valuation of Delayed Consumption," *Economic Journal*, 97, September 1987: 666–684.

182   CHAPTER 5   APPLICATIONS OF RATIONAL CHOICE AND DEMAND THEORIES

a slope of $-(1 + r)$. The opportunity cost of a unit of current consumption is $1 + r$ units of future consumption. The horizontal intercept of the intertemporal budget constraint is the present value of all current and future income, which is also called the present value of lifetime wealth.

* The consumer's intertemporal preferences are represented with an indifference map with essentially the same properties as in the atemporal case. A consumer is said to exhibit positive, neutral, or negative time preference at a point if his marginal rate of time preference (the absolute value of the slope of his indifference curve) at that point is greater than 1, equal to 1, or less than 1, respectively. In the case of

interior solutions, equilibrium occurs at a tangency between the intertemporal budget constraint and an indifference curve. Because the slope of the intertemporal budget constraint exceeds 1 when $r > 0$, consumers will exhibit positive time preference in equilibrium, irrespective of the shape of their indifference curves.

* An important application of the intertemporal choice model is to the study of decisions about how much to save. The permanent income and life-cycle hypotheses employ the model to demonstrate that it is the present value of lifetime wealth, not current income alone, that governs current consumption (and hence current savings).

QUESTIONS FOR REVIEW

1. Explain in your own words why a gasoline tax whose proceeds are refunded to the consumer in a lump-sum amount will nonetheless reduce the consumption of gasoline.

2. Explain in your own words what a two-part pricing scheme is and why sellers might use one.

3. Do you think a college education has a high- or low-price (tuition) elasticity of demand?

4. Explain in your own words why even long-term heavy drinkers might be highly responsive to increases in the price of alcohol.

5. Explain why 1 plus the interest rate in the intertemporal choice model is analogous to the relative price

ratio in the consumer choice model discussed in Chapter 3.

6. Bus services are generally more energy efficient than individuals using cars to commute to work. However, the trend over the past 30 years has been a decline in the proportion of commuters taking buses despite an increase in real energy prices. Why?

7. Jennifer, who earns an annual salary of $20,000, wins $25,000 in the lottery. Explain why she most likely will not spend all her winnings during the next year.

PROBLEMS

1. Using a diagram like Figure 5.2, explain why, under our current method of educational finance, a rich family is much more likely than a poor family to send its children to a private school.

2. When the price of gasoline is $1/gal, you consume 1000 gal/yr. Then two things happen: (1) The price of gasoline rises to $2/gal and (2) a distant uncle dies, with the instruction to his executor to send you a check for $1000/yr. If no other changes in prices or income occur, do these two changes leave you better off than before?

3. Larry demands strawberries according to the schedule $P = 4 - (Q/2)$, where P is the price of strawberries ($/pint) and Q is the quantity (pint/wk). Assuming that the income effect is negligible, how much will he be hurt if the price of strawberries goes from $1/pint to $2/pint?

4. The only video rental club available to you charges $4 per movie per day. If your demand curve for movie rentals is given by $P = 20 - 2Q$, where P is the rental price

($/day) and Q is the quantity demanded (movies per year), what is the maximum annual membership fee you would be willing to pay to join this club?

5. Jane spent all her income on hot dogs and caviar. Her demand curve for caviar was inelastic at all prices for caviar. Unfortunately, an accident at a nuclear power plant caused the supply of caviar to fall and the price to rise. What happened to Jane's consumption of hot dogs? Explain. (*Note:* You should assume that the accident had no effect on the price of hot dogs or Jane's preference for caviar.)

6. Jones spends all his income on two goods, X and Y. The prices he paid and the quantities he consumed last year are as follows: $P_X = 15$, $X = 20$, $P_Y = 25$, and $Y = 30$. If the prices next year are $P_X = 6$ and $P_Y = 30$, and Jones's income is 1020, will he be better or worse off than he was in the previous year? (Assume that his tastes do not change.)

7. Smith lives in a world with two time periods, this period and the next period. His income in each period, which he receives at the beginning of each period, is $210. If the interest rate, expressed as a fraction, is 0.05 per time period, what is the present value of his lifetime income? Draw his intertemporal budget constraint. On the same axes, draw Smith's intertemporal budget constraint when $r = 0.20$.

8. Suppose Smith from Problem 7 views current and future consumption as perfect, one-for-one substitutes for one another. Find his optimal consumption bundle.

9. Suppose Smith from Problem 7 views current and future consumption as one-to-one complements. Find his optimal consumption bundle.

10. Karen earns $75,000 in the current period and will earn $75,000 in the future
   a. Assuming that these are the only two periods, and that banks in her country borrow and lend but at an interest rate $r = 0$, draw her intertemporal budget constraint.
   b. Now suppose banks offer 10 percent interest on funds deposited during the current period, and offer loans at this same rate. Draw her new intertemporal budget constraint.

11. Find the present value of $50,000 to be received after 1 year if the annual rate of interest is
   a. 8 percent
   b. 10 percent
   c. 12 percent

12. Crusoe will live this period and the next period as the lone inhabitant of his island. His only income is a crop of 100 coconuts that he harvests at the beginning of each period. Coconuts not consumed in the current period spoil at the rate of 10 percent per period.
   a. Draw Crusoe's intertemporal budget constraint. What will be his consumption in each period if he regards future consumption as a perfect, one-for-one substitute for current consumption?
   b. What will he consume each period if he regards 0.8 unit of future consumption as being worth 1 unit of current consumption?

13. Kathy earns $55,000 in the current period and will earn $60,000 in the future period. What is the maximum interest rate that would allow her to spend $105,000 in the current period? What is the minimum interest rate that would allow her to spend $120,500 in the future period?

14. Smith receives $100 of income this period and $100 next period. At an interest rate of 10 percent, he consumes all his current income in each period. He has a diminishing marginal rate of time preference between consumption next period and consumption this period. *True or false:* If the interest rate rises to 20 percent, Smith will save some of his income this period. Explain.

184   CHAPTER 5   APPLICATIONS OF RATIONAL CHOICE AND DEMAND THEORIES

15. At current prices, housing costs $50 per unit and the composite good has a price of 1 per unit. A wealthy benefactor has given Joe, a penniless person, 1 unit of housing and 50 units of the composite good. Now the price of housing falls by half. *True or false:* Joe is better off as a result of the price change. Explain.

*16. Tom and Karen are economists. In an attempt to limit their son Harry's use of the family car, they charge him a user fee of 20 cents/mile. At that price he still uses the car more than they would like, but they are reluctant to antagonize him by simply raising the price further. So Tom and Karen ask him the following question: What is the minimum increase in your weekly allowance you would accept in return for having the fee raised to 40 cents/mile? Harry, who is a known truth-teller and has conventional preferences, answers $10/wk.
   a.   If Tom and Karen increase Harry's allowance by $10/wk and charge him 40 cents/mile, will he drive less than before? Explain.
   b.   Will the revenue from the additional mileage charges be more than, less than, or equal to $10/wk? Explain.

*17. All book buyers have the same preferences, and under current arrangements, those who buy used books at $22 receive the same utility as those who buy new books at $50. The annual interest rate is 10 percent, and there are no transaction costs involved in the buying and selling of used books. Each new textbook costs m to produce and lasts for exactly 2 years.
   a.   What is the most a buyer would pay for the use of a new book for 1 yr?
   b.   How low would m have to be before a publisher would find it worthwhile to print books with disappearing ink—ink that vanishes 1 yr from the point of sale of a new book, thus eliminating the used-book market? (Assume that eliminating the used-book market will exactly double the publisher's sales.)

*18. Herb wants to work exactly 12 hr/wk to supplement his graduate fellowship. He can either work as a clerk in the library at $6/hr or tutor first-year graduate students in economics. Pay differences aside, he is indifferent between these two jobs. Each of three first-year students has a demand curve for tutoring given by $P = 10 - Q$, where P is the price in dollars per hour, and Q is the number of hours per week. If Herb has the option of setting a two-part tariff for his tutoring services, how many hours per week should he tutor and how many hours should he work in the library? If he does any tutoring, what should his rate structure be?

†19. Cornell is committed to its current policy of allowing the children of its faculty to attend the university without paying tuition. Suppose the demand curve of Cornell faculty children (CFCs) for slots in other universities is given by $P = 10 - 5Q_0$, where P is the tuition price charged by other universities (in thousands of dollars) and Q_0 is the number of CFCs who attend those universities. Cornell is now considering a proposal to subsidize some proportion k of the tuition charged to CFCs who attend other universities. Suppose Cornell knows that it can fill all its available slots with non-CFCs who pay tuition at the rate of $15,000/yr. Assuming that all CFCs who do not attend other universities will go to Cornell, what value of k will maximize Cornell's tuition revenues, net of outside subsidies, if the tuition price at all other universities is $8000/yr?

†20. How will your answer to the preceding problem differ if the tuition charged by outside universities is $4000/yr? What is the economic interpretation of a value of k greater than 1?

*21. Harry runs a small movie theater, whose customers all have identical tastes. Each customer's reservation price for the movie is $5, and each customer's demand curve

---

*Problems marked with an asterisk (*) are more difficult.
†Problems marked with a dagger (†) are most easily solved using calculus.

for popcorn at his concession stand is given by $P_c = 4 - Q_c$, where P_c is the price of popcorn in dollars and Q_c is the amount of popcorn in quarts. If the marginal cost of allowing another patron to watch the movie is zero, and the marginal cost of popcorn is \$1, at what price should Harry sell tickets and popcorn if his goal is to maximize his profits? (Assume that Harry is able to costlessly advertise his price structure to potential patrons.)

ANSWERS TO IN-CHAPTER EXERCISES

5.1. Initial consumer surplus at $P = \$3$ (and $Q = 7$ gal/wk) is $CS = \frac{1}{2}(10 - 3)7 = \$24.50$/wk. Consumer surplus at the higher price $P' = \$4$ (and $Q' = 6$ gal/wk) is $CS' = \frac{1}{2}(10 - 4)6 = \$18$/wk. The loss in consumer surplus is given by the area of $DCEF$, which equals $24.5 - 18 = \$6.50$/wk.

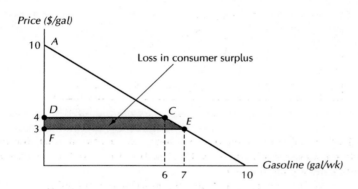

5.2. The maximum membership fee is now given by the area of triangle $AB'C'$, which is $CS = \frac{1}{2}(50 - 20)120 = \$1800$/yr.

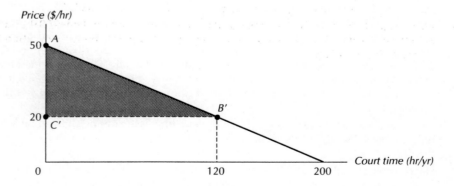

5.3. The two budget lines and last year's optimal bundle are shown in the following diagram. A closer look at the tangency point (enlarged area) shows that this year Jones can now afford to purchase a bundle he prefers to the one he bought last year.

186   CHAPTER 5   APPLICATIONS OF RATIONAL CHOICE AND DEMAND THEORIES

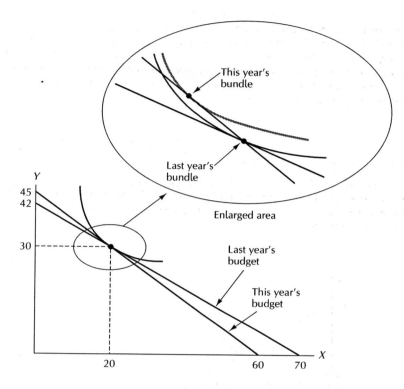

5.4. Again let P_1 and Q_1 denote the original price and quantity, and ΔP and ΔQ denote the respective changes, with $\Delta Q < 0$. The fact that the new total revenue is 2 percent higher than before tells us that

$$[1.10(Q_1 + \Delta Q) - 1.00(Q_1)] = 0.02[1.00(Q_1)].$$

Rearranging terms, we have

$$0.08Q_1 = -1.10\Delta Q,$$

which solves for

$$\Delta Q/Q_1 = -0.08/1.10.$$

And since we know that $\Delta P/P_1 = 0.10$, we have

$$\epsilon = (\Delta Q/Q_1)/(\Delta P/P_1) = (-0.08/1.10)/0.10 = -0.727.$$

5.5. PV = \$50,000 + \$42,000/1.05 = \$90,000. Maximum future consumption = 50,000(1.05) + \$42,000 = \$94,500. The equation for your intertemporal budget constraint is $C_2 = \$94,500 - 1.05C_1$.

CHAPTER

9

PRODUCTION

M any people think of production as a highly structured, often mechanical process whereby raw materials are transformed into finished goods. And without doubt, a great deal of production—like a mason's laying bricks for the walls of a house—is of roughly this sort. Economists emphasize, however, that production is also a much more general concept, encompassing many activities not ordinarily thought of as such. We define it as *any activity that creates present or future utility*.

Thus, the simple act of telling a joke constitutes production. Woody Allen (Figure 9.1) tells the story of the man who complains to his analyst that his brother thinks he's a chicken. "Why don't you tell him he's *not* a chicken?" asks the analyst, to which the man responds, "I can't, I need the eggs." Once a joke is told, it leaves no more tangible trace than a pleasant memory. But under the economic definition of production, Woody Allen is as much a production worker as the artisan whose chisel and lathe mold an ashwood log into a Louisville Slugger baseball bat. The person who delivers a singing telegram is also engaged in production; so is the doctor who gives my child a tetanus shot; the lawyer who draws up my will; the people who collect my garbage on Wednesday mornings; the postal worker who delivers my tax return to the IRS; and even the economists who write about production.

288   CHAPTER 9   PRODUCTION

FIGURE 9.1
A Production Worker
Phillippe Halsman
© Halsman Estate.

CHAPTER PREVIEW

In our discussions of consumer choice during the preceding chapters, an existing menu of goods and services was taken for granted.But where do these goods and services come from? In this chapter we will see that their production involves a decision process very similar to the one we examined in earlier chapters. Whereas our focus in earlier chapters was on the economic decisions that underlie the demand side of the market relationship, our focus in the next seven chapters is on the economic decisions that underlie the supply side.

In this chapter we describe the production possibilities available to us for a given state of technology and resource endowments. We want to know how output varies with the application of productive inputs in both the short run and the long run. Answers to these questions will set the stage for our efforts in the next chapter to describe how firms choose among technically feasible alternative methods of producing a given level of output.

THE INPUT-OUTPUT RELATIONSHIP, OR PRODUCTION FUNCTION

There are several ways to define production. One definition, mentioned above, is that it is any activity that creates present or future utility. Production may be equivalently described as a process that transforms inputs (factors of production) into outputs. (The two descriptions are equivalent because output is something that creates present or future utility.) Among the inputs into production, economists have traditionally included land, labor, capital, and the

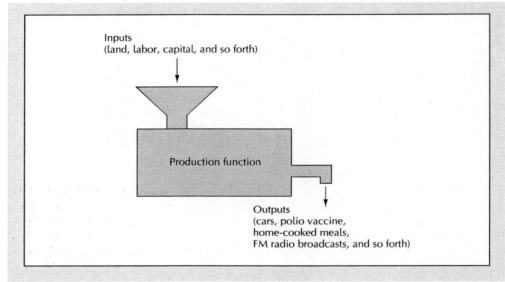

FIGURE 9.2
The Production Function
The production function transforms inputs like land, labor, capital, and management into output. The box in the diagram embodies the existing state of technological knowledge. Because knowledge has been accumulating over time, we get more output from a given combination of inputs today than we would have gotten in the past.

more elusive category called entrepreneurship.[1] To this list, it has become increasingly common to add such factors as knowledge or technology, organization, and energy.

A **production function** is the relationship by which inputs are combined to produce output. Schematically, it may be represented as the box in Figure 9.2. Inputs are fed into it, and output is discharged from it. The box implicitly embodies the existing state of technology, which has been improving steadily over time. Thus, a given combination of productive inputs will yield a larger number of cars with today's technology than with the technology of 1970.

A production function may also be thought of as a cooking recipe. It lists the ingredients and tells you, say, how many pancakes you will get if you manipulate the ingredients in a certain way.[2]

Yet another way of describing the production function is to cast it in the form of a mathematical equation. Consider a production process that employs two inputs, capital (K) and labor (L), to produce meals (Q). The relationship between K, L, and Q may be expressed as

$$Q = F(K, L), \tag{9.1}$$

where F is a mathematical function that summarizes the process depicted in Figure 9.2. It is no more than a simple rule that tells how much Q we get when we employ specific quantities of K and L. By way of illustration, suppose the

production function the relationship that describes how inputs like capital and labor are transformed into output.

---

[1]"Entrepreneurship" is defined as "the process of organizing, managing, and assuming responsibility for a business enterprise" (*Random House College Dictionary*). An entrepreneur is thus, by definition, a risk-taker.

[2]In some recipes, the ingredients must be mixed in fixed proportions. Other recipes allow substitution between ingredients, as in a pancake recipe that allows milk and oil to be substituted for eggs. Production functions can be of either of these two types.

290   CHAPTER 9 PRODUCTION

TABLE 9.1
The Production Function Q = 2KL
The entries in the table represent output, measured in meals per week, and are calculated using the formula $Q = 2KL$.

		Labor (person-hours/wk)				
		1	**2**	**3**	**4**	**5**
	1	2	4	6	8	10
Capital	**2**	4	8	12	16	20
(equipment-hours/wk)	**3**	6	12	18	24	30
	4	8	16	24	32	40
	5	10	20	30	40	50

production function for meals is given by $F(K, L) = 2KL$, where K is measured in equipment-hours per week,[3] L is measured in person-hours per week, and output is measured in meals per week. For example, 2 equipment-hr/wk combined with 3 person-hr/wk would yield $2(2)(3) = 12$ meals/wk with this particular production function. The relationship between K, L, and weekly output of meals for the production function $Q = 2KL$ is summarized in Table 9.1.

Intermediate Products and Value Added

Capital (as embodied, for example, in the form of stoves and frying pans) and labor (as embodied in the services of a chef) are clearly by themselves insufficient to produce meals. Raw foodstuffs are also necessary. The production process described by Equation 9.1 is one that transforms raw foodstuffs into the finished product we call meals. In this process, foodstuffs are **intermediate products,** ones that are transformed into something more valuable by the activity of production. Strictly speaking, the output of this process is not the meals themselves, but the *value added* to the raw foodstuffs. For example, if a chef and her equipment transformed $50 worth of raw foodstuffs into meals with a total value of $150, the resulting output would be measured as the $100 of value added.

intermediate products products that are transformed by a production process into products of greater value.

For the sake of simplicity, we will ignore the complication of intermediate goods in the examples we discuss in this chapter. But this feature could be built into all these examples without changing any of our essential conclusions.

Fixed and Variable Inputs

The production function tells us how output will vary if some or all of the inputs are varied. In practice, there are many production processes in which the quantities of at least some inputs cannot be altered quickly. The FM radio broadcast transmission of classical music is one such process. To carry it out, complex electronic equipment is needed, and also a music library and a large transmission tower. Records and compact discs can be purchased in a matter of hours. But it may take weeks to acquire the needed equipment to launch a new station, and months or even years to purchase a suitable location and construct a new transmission tower.

---

[3]Here, 1 frying pan-hr/wk is 1 frying pan used for 1 hour during the course of a week. Thus, a frying pan that is in use for 8 hr/day for each day of a 5-day workweek would constitute 40 frying pan-hr/wk of capital input.

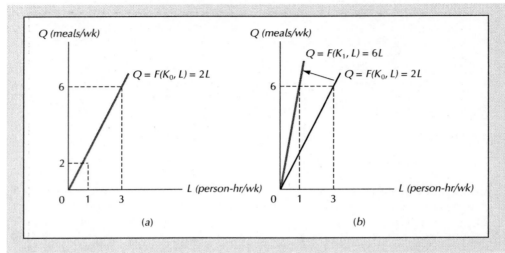

FIGURE 9.3
A Specific Short-Run Production Function
Panel *a* shows the production function, $Q = 2KL$, with K fixed at $K_0 = 1$. Panel *b* shows how the short-run production function shifts when K is increased to $K_1 = 3$.

The **long run** for a particular production process is defined as the shortest period of time required to alter the amounts of *every* input. An input whose quantity can be altered is called a **variable input.** One whose quantity cannot be altered—except perhaps at prohibitive cost—within a given time period is called a **fixed input** with respect to that time period. In the long run, all inputs are variable inputs, by definition. The **short run,** by contrast, is defined as that period during which one or more inputs cannot be varied. In the classical music broadcast example, compact discs are variable inputs in the short run, but the broadcast tower is a fixed input. If sufficient time elapses, however, even it becomes a variable input. In some production activities, like those of a street-corner hot dog stand, even the long run does not involve an extended period of time. We begin in the next section by considering short-run production and then we move on to long-run production in the following section.

long run the shortest period of time required to alter the amounts of all inputs used in a production process.

variable input an input that can be varied in the short run.

fixed input an input that cannot vary in the short run.

short run the longest period of time during which at least one of the inputs used in a production process cannot be varied.

Production in the Short Run

Consider again the production process described by $Q = F(K, L) = 2KL$, the simple two-input production function described in Table 9.1. And suppose we are concerned with production in the short run—here, a period of time in which the labor input is variable but the capital input is fixed, say, at the value $K = K_0 = 1$. With capital held constant, output becomes, in effect, a function of only the variable input, labor: $F(K, L) = 2K_0L = 2L$. This means we can plot the production function in a two-dimensional diagram, as in Figure 9.3*a*. For this particular $F(K, L)$, the short-run production function is a straight line through the origin whose slope is 2 times the fixed value of K: Thus, $\Delta Q / \Delta L = 2K_0$. In Figure 9.3*b*, note that the short-run production rotates upward to $F(K_1, L) = 6L$ when K rises to $K_1 = 3$.

EXERCISE 9.1

Graph the short-run production function for $F(K, L) = \sqrt{K}\sqrt{L}$ when K is fixed at $K_0 = 4$.

292   CHAPTER 9   PRODUCTION

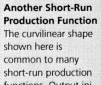

FIGURE 9.4
Another Short-Run Production Function
The curvilinear shape shown here is common to many short-run production functions. Output initially grows at an increasing rate as labor increases. Beyond $L = 4$, output grows at a diminishing rate with increases in labor.

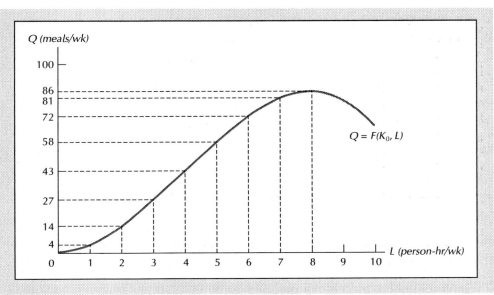

As you saw in Exercise 9.1, the graphs of short-run production functions will not always be straight lines. The short-run production function shown in Figure 9.4 has several properties that are commonly found in production functions observed in practice. First, it passes through the origin, which is to say that we get no output if we use no variable input. Second, initially the addition of variable inputs augments output at an increasing rate: moving from 1 to 2 units of labor yields 10 extra units of output, while moving from 2 to 3 units of labor gives 13 additional units. Finally, the function shown in Figure 9.4 has the property that beyond some point ($L = 4$ in the diagram), additional units of the variable input give rise to smaller and smaller increments in output. Thus, the move from 5 to 6 units of labor yields 14 extra units of output, while the move from 6 to 7 units of labor yields only 9. For some production functions, the level of output may actually decline with additional units of the variable input beyond some point, as happens here for $L > 8$. With a limited amount of capital to work with, additional workers may eventually begin to get in one another's way.

The property that output initially grows at an increasing rate may stem from the benefits of division of tasks and specialization of labor. With one employee, all tasks must be done by the same person, while with two or more employees, tasks may be divided and employees may better perform their dedicated tasks. (Similar logic applies to specializing in one task within any period of time.)

The final property noted about the short-run production function in Figure 9.4—that beyond some point, output grows at a diminishing rate with increases in the variable input—is known as the **law of diminishing returns.** And although it too is not a universal property of short-run production functions, it is extremely common. The law of diminishing returns is a short-run phenomenon. Formally, it may be stated as follows:

law of diminishing returns if other inputs are fixed, the increase in output from an increase in the variable input must eventually decline.

If equal amounts of a variable input are added and all other inputs are held fixed, the resulting increments to output will eventually diminish.

Why can't all the world's people be fed from the amount of grain grown in a single flowerpot?

The law of diminishing returns suggests that no matter how much labor, fertilizer, water, seed, capital equipment, and other inputs were used, only a limited amount of grain could be grown in a single flowerpot. With the land input fixed at such a low level, increases in other inputs would quickly cease to have any effect on total output.

ECONOMIC NATURALIST 9.1

Employing the logic of Economic Naturalist 9.1, the British economist Thomas Malthus argued in 1798 that the law of diminishing returns implied eventual misery for the human race. The difficulty is that agricultural land is fixed and, beyond some point, the application of additional labor will yield ever smaller increases in food production. The inevitable result, as Malthus saw it, is that population growth will drive average food consumption down to the starvation level.

Whether Malthus's prediction will be borne out in the future remains to be seen. But he would never have imagined that food production per capita would grow more than twenty-fold during the ensuing two centuries. Note carefully, however, that the experience of the last 200 years does not contradict the law of diminishing returns. What Malthus did not foresee was the explosive growth in agricultural technology that has far outstripped the effect of a fixed supply of land. Still, the ruthless logic of Malthus's observation remains. No matter how advanced our technology, if population continues to grow, it is just a matter of time before limits on arable land spell persistent food shortages.

The world's population has grown rapidly during the years since Malthus wrote, more than doubling during the last 50 years alone. Are we in fact doomed to eventual starvation? Perhaps not. As the late economist Herbert Stein once famously remarked, "If something can't go on forever, it won't." And indeed, population specialists now predict that the earth's population will peak by the year 2070 and then begin to decline.[4] There is thus a good chance that we will escape the dire fate that Malthus predicted.

Technological improvements in production are represented graphically by an upward shift in the production function. In Figure 9.5, for example, the curves labeled F_1 and F_2 are used to denote the agricultural production functions in 1805 and 2005, respectively. The law of diminishing returns applies to each of these curves, and yet the growth in food production has kept pace with the increase in labor input during the period shown.

Total, Marginal, and Average Products

Short-run production functions like the ones shown in Figures 9.4 and 9.5 are often referred to as **total product curves.** They relate the total amount of output to the quantity of the variable input. Also of interest in many applications is the

total product curve a curve showing the amount of output as a function of the amount of variable input.

---

[4] See "The End of World Population Growth," Wolfgang Lutz, Warren Sanderson and Sergei Sherbov, *Nature*, 412, August 2, 2001: 543–545.

294   CHAPTER 9   PRODUCTION

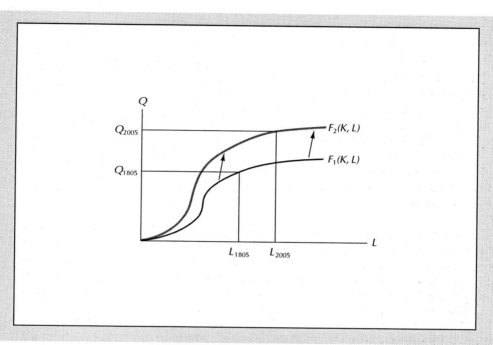

marginal product of a variable input. It is defined as *the change in the total product that occurs in response to a unit change in the variable input (all other inputs held fixed).* A business manager trying to decide whether to hire or fire another worker has an obvious interest in knowing what the **marginal product** of labor is.

marginal product change in total product due to a 1-unit change in the variable input.

More formally, if ΔL denotes a small change in the variable input, and ΔQ denotes the resulting change in output, then the marginal product of L, denoted MP_L, is defined as

$$MP_L = \frac{\Delta Q}{\Delta L}. \qquad (9.2)$$

Geometrically, the marginal product at any point is simply the slope of the total product curve at that point, as shown in the top panel of Figure 9.6.[5] For example, the marginal product of labor when $L = 2$ is $MP_{L=2} = 12$. Likewise, $MP_{L=4} = 16$ and $MP_{L=7} = 6$ for the total product curve shown in Figure 9.6. Note, finally, that MP_L is negative for values of L greater than 8.

The marginal product curve itself is plotted in the bottom panel in Figure 9.6. Note that it rises at first, reaches a maximum at $L = 4$, and then declines, finally becoming negative for values of L greater than 8. Note in the diagram that the maximum point on the marginal product curve corresponds to the inflection point on the total product curve, the point where its curvature switches from convex (increasing at an increasing rate) to concave (increasing at a decreasing rate). Note also that the marginal product curve reaches zero at the value of L at which the total product curve reaches a maximum.

As we will see in greater detail in later chapters, the importance of the marginal product concept lies in the fact that decisions about running an enterprise most naturally arise in the form of decisions about *changes*. Should we hire another

---

[5]The formal definition of the marginal product of a variable input is given by $MP(L) = \partial F(K, L)\partial L$.

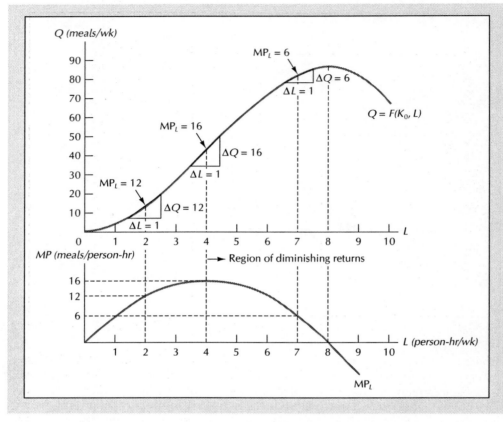

FIGURE 9.6
The Marginal Product of a Variable Input
At any point, the marginal product of labor, MP_L is the slope of the total product curve at that point (top panel). For the production function shown in the top panel, the marginal product curve (bottom panel) initially increases as labor increases. Beyond $L = 4$, however, the marginal product of labor decreases as labor increases. For $L > 8$ the total product curve declines with L, which means that the marginal product of labor is negative in that region.

engineer or accountant? Should we reduce the size of the maintenance staff? Should we install another copier? Should we lease another delivery truck?

To answer such questions intelligently, we must compare the benefit of the change in question with its cost. And as we will see, the marginal product concept plays a pivotal role in the calculation of the benefits when we alter the level of a productive input. Looking at Figure 9.6, we may identify a range of values of the variable input that a rational manager would never employ. In particular, as long as labor commands a positive wage, such a manager would never want to employ the variable input in the region where its marginal product is negative ($L > 8$ in Figure 9.6). Equivalently, he would never employ a variable input past the point where the total product curve reaches its maximum value (where $MP_L = 0$).

EXERCISE 9.2

What is the marginal product of labor when $L = 3$ in the short-run production function shown in Figure 9.3a? When $L = 1$? Does this short-run production function exhibit diminishing returns to labor?

The **average product** of a variable input is defined as the total product divided by the quantity of that input. Denoted AP_L, it is thus given by

$$AP_L = \frac{Q}{L}.$$
(9.3)

average product total output divided by the quantity of the variable input.

296   CHAPTER 9   PRODUCTION

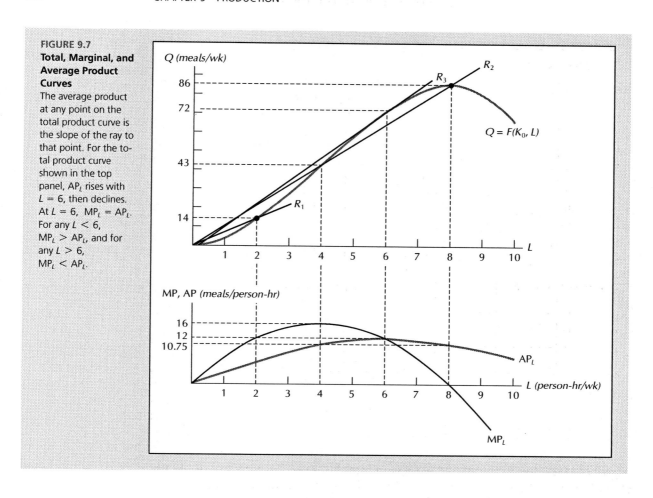

FIGURE 9.7
Total, Marginal, and Average Product Curves
The average product at any point on the total product curve is the slope of the ray to that point. For the total product curve shown in the top panel, AP_L rises with $L = 6$, then declines. At $L = 6$, $MP_L = AP_L$. For any $L < 6$, $MP_L > AP_L$, and for any $L > 6$, $MP_L < AP_L$.

When the variable input is labor, the average product is also called labor productivity.

Geometrically, the average product is the slope of the line joining the origin to the corresponding point on the total product curve. Three such lines, R_1, R_2, and R_3, are drawn to the total product curve shown in the top panel in Figure 9.7. The average product at $L = 2$ is the slope of R_1, which is $\frac{14}{2} = 7$. Note that R_2 intersects the total product curve in two places—first, directly above $L = 4$, and then directly above $L = 8$. Accordingly, the average products for these two values of L will be the same—namely, the slope of R_2, which is $\frac{43}{4} = \frac{86}{8} = 10.75$. R_3 intersects the total product curve at only one point, directly above $L = 6$. The average product for $L = 6$ is thus the slope of R_3, $\frac{72}{6} = 12$.

EXERCISE 9.3

For the short-run production function shown in Figure 9.3a, what is the average product of labor at $L = 3$? At $L = 1$? How does average product compare with marginal product at these points?

The Relationships among Total, Marginal, and Average Product Curves

Because of the way the total, marginal, and average products are defined, systematic relationships exist among them. The top panel in Figure 9.7 shows a total product curve and three of the rays whose slopes define the average product of the variable input. The steepest of the three rays, R_3, is tangent to the total product curve at $L = 6$. Its slope, $\frac{72}{6} = 12$, is the average product of labor at $L = 6$. The marginal product of labor at $L = 6$ is defined as the slope of the total product curve at $L = 6$, which happens to be exactly the slope of R_3, since R_3 is tangent to the total product curve. Thus $AP_{L=6} = MP_{L=6}$, as shown in the bottom panel by the fact that the AP_L curve intersects the MP_L curve for $L = 6$.

For values of L less than 6, note in the top panel in Figure 9.7 that the slope of the total product curve is larger than the slope of the ray to the corresponding point. Thus, for $L < 6$, $MP_L > AP_L$, as reflected in the bottom panel. Note also in the top panel that for values of L greater than 6, the slope of the total product curve is smaller than the slope of the ray to the corresponding point. This means that for $L > 6$, we have $AP_L > MP_L$, as shown in the bottom panel in Figure 9.7.

Note finally in Figure 9.7 that for extremely small values of L, the slope of the ray to the total product curve becomes indistinguishable from the slope of the total product curve itself. This tells us that for $L = 0$, average and marginal products are the same, which is reflected in the bottom panel in Figure 9.7 by the fact that both curves emanate from the same point.[6]

The relationship between the marginal and average product curves may be summarized as follows: *When the marginal product curve lies above the average product curve, the average product curve must be rising; and when the marginal product curve lies below the average product curve, the average product curve must be falling. The two curves intersect at the maximum value of the average product curve.* A moment's reflection on the definitions of the two curves makes the intuitive basis for this relationship clear. If the contribution to output of an additional unit of the variable input exceeds the average contribution of the variable inputs used thus far, the average contribution must rise. This effect is analogous to what happens when a student with a 3.8 grade point average joins a fraternity whose other members have an average GPA of 2.2: The new member's presence causes the group's GPA to rise. Conversely, adding a variable input whose marginal product is less than the average product of existing units is like adding a new fraternity member with a GPA of 1.7. Here, the effect is for the existing average to fall.[7]

---

[6]For the production function shown, that point happens to be the origin, but in general it need not be.

[7]Mathematically, the result that MP intersects AP at the maximum value of AP can be shown by noting that the necessary condition for a maximum of AP is that its first partial derivative with respect to L be zero:

$$\partial(Q/L)/\partial L = [L(\partial Q/\partial L) - Q]/L^2 = 0,$$

from which it follows that $\partial Q/\partial L = Q/L$.

298   CHAPTER 9   PRODUCTION

EXERCISE 9.4

Consider a short-run production process for which $AP_{L=10} = 7$ and $MP_{L=10} = 12$. Will $AP_{L=10.1}$ be larger or smaller than $AP_{L=10}$ for this process?

The Practical Significance of the Average-Marginal Distinction

The distinction between average and marginal products is of central importance to anyone who must allocate a scarce resource between two or more productive activities. The specific question is, How should the resource be allocated in order to maximize total output? The following examples make clear the issues posed by this problem and the general rule required to solve it.

Read through the following scenario carefully and try to answer the question posed at the end:

> Suppose you own a fishing fleet consisting of a given number of boats, and can send your boats in whatever numbers you wish to either of two ends of an extremely wide lake, east or west. Under your current allocation of boats, the ones fishing at the east end return daily with 100 pounds of fish each, while those in the west return daily with 120 pounds each. The fish populations at each end of the lake are completely independent, and your current yields can be sustained indefinitely. Should you alter your current allocation of boats?

Most people, especially those who have not had a good course in microeconomics, answer confidently that the current allocation should be altered. Specifically, they say that the fishing fleet owner should send more boats to the west side of the lake. Yet, as the following example illustrates, even a rudimentary understanding of the distinction between the average and marginal products of a productive resource makes clear that this response is not justified.

EXAMPLE 9.1

In the fishing fleet scenario just described, suppose the relationship between the number of boats sent to each end and the number of pounds caught per boat is as summarized in Table 9.2. Suppose further that you have four boats in your fleet, and that two currently fish the east end while the other two fish the west end. (Note that all of these suppositions are completely consistent with the facts outlined in the scenario.) Should you move one of your boats from the east end to the west end?

From the entries in Table 9.2, it follows that your total output under the current allocation is 440 pounds of fish per day (100 pounds from each of the two boats at the east end, 120 from each of the two at the west end). Now suppose you transfer one boat from the east end to the west end, which means you now have three boats in the west and only one in the east. From the figures in Table 9.2, we see that your total output will now be only 430 pounds per day, or 10 pounds per day less than under the current allocation. So, no, you should not move an extra boat to the west end. Neither, for that matter, should you send one of the west end boats to the east end. Loss of a boat from the west end would reduce the total daily catch at that end by 110 pounds (the difference between the 240 pounds caught by two boats and the 130 that would be caught by one), which

Number of boats	East end			West end			TABLE 9.2
	AP	TP	MP	AP	TP	MP	**Average Product, Total Product, and Marginal Product (lb/day) for Two Fishing Areas**
0	0	0		0	0		The average catch per
			100			130	boat is constant at 100
1	100	100		130	130		pounds per boat for boats
			100			110	sent to the east end of
2	100	200		120	240		the lake. The average
			100			90	catch per boat is a
3	100	300		110	330		declining function of the
			100			70	number of boats sent to
4	100	400		100	400		the west end.

is more than the extra 100 pounds you would get by having an extra boat at the east end. The current allocation of two boats to each end is optimal.

Example 9.1 is an instance of an important class of problems in which managers must decide how to allocate an input across several alternative processes used for producing a given product. *The general rule for allocating an input efficiently in such cases is to allocate the next unit of the input to the production activity where its marginal product is highest.* This form of the rule applies to resources, such as boats, that are not perfectly divisible, and also to cases in which the marginal product of a resource is always higher in one activity than in another.[8] For a resource that is perfectly divisible, and for activities for which the marginal product of the resource is not always higher in one than in the others, the rule is to *allocate the resource so that its marginal product is the same in every activity.*

Many people, however, "solve" these kinds of problems by allocating resources to the activity with the highest *average* product, or by trying to equalize *average* products across activities. The reason that this particular wrong answer often has appeal is that people often focus on only part of the relevant production process. By sending only two boats to the west end, the average catch at that end is 20 pounds per day greater than the average catch per boat at the east end. But note that if you send a third boat to the west end, that boat's contribution to the total amount of fish caught at the west end will be only 90 pounds per day (the difference between the 330 pounds caught by three boats and 240 pounds caught by two). What people often tend to overlook is that the third boat at the west end catches some of the fish that would otherwise have been caught by the first two.

As the figures in Table 9.2 illustrate, the opportunity cost of sending a third boat to the west end is the 100 pounds of fish that will no longer be caught at the east end. But since that third boat will add only 90 pounds to the daily catch at the west end, the best that can be done is to keep sending two boats to each end of the lake. The fact that either of the two boats currently fishing at the east end could catch 10 pounds per day more by moving to the west end is no cause for concern to a fishing fleet owner who understands the distinction between average and marginal products.

---

[8]See Example 9.2.

EXERCISE 9.5

Explain why we cannot necessarily conclude that you should throw more fastballs in the following scenario: You are a baseball pitcher who throws two different kinds of pitches: fastball and curve. Your team statistician tells you that at the current rate at which you employ these pitches, batters hit .275 against your curve, only .200 against your fastball. Should you alter your current mix of pitches?

Example 9.1 produced what economists call an *interior solution*—one in which each of the production activities is actually employed. But not all problems of this sort have interior solutions. As the next example will make clear, there are cases in which one activity simply dominates the other.

EXAMPLE 9.2

Same as the fishing fleet Example 9.1, except now the marginal product of each boat sent to the west end of the lake is equal to 120 lb/day.

The difference between this example and Example 9.1 is that this time there is no drop-off in the rate at which fish are caught as more boats are sent to the west end of the lake. So this time the average product of any boat sent to the west end is identical to its marginal product. And since the marginal product is always higher for boats sent to the west end, the optimal allocation is to send all four boats to that end.

Cases such as the one illustrated in Example 9.2 are by no means unusual. But by far the more common, and more interesting, production decisions are the ones that involve interior solutions such as the one we saw in Example 9.1, where some positive quantity of the productive input must be allocated to each activity.

EXAMPLE 9.3

Suppose that from the last seconds you devoted to Problem 1 on your first economics exam you earned 4 extra points, while from the last seconds devoted to Problem 2 you earned 6 extra points. The total number of points you earned on these two questions were 20 and 12, respectively, and the total time you spent on each was the same. The total number of points possible on each problem was 40. How—if at all—should you have reallocated your time between problems?

The rule for efficient allocation of time spent on exams is the same as the rule for efficient allocation of any resource: the marginal product of the resource should be the same in each activity. From the information given, the marginal product of your time spent on Problem 2 was higher than the marginal product of your time spent on Problem 1. Even though the average product of your time spent on Problem 1 was higher than on Problem 2, you would have scored more points if you had spent less time on Problem 1 and more time on Problem 2.

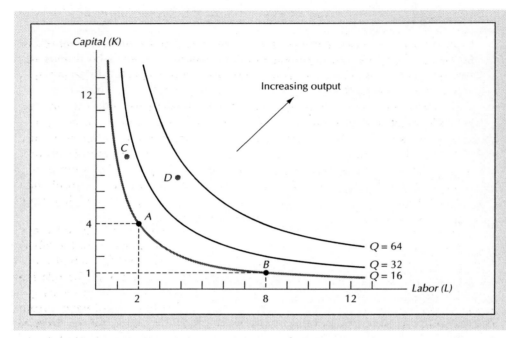

FIGURE 9.8
Part of an Isoquant Map for the Production Function $Q = 2KL$
An isoquant is the set of all (L, K) pairs that yield a given level of output. For example, each (L, K) pair on the curve labeled $Q = 32$ yields 32 units of output. The isoquant map describes the properties of a production process in much the same way as an indifference map describes a consumer's preferences.

PRODUCTION IN THE LONG RUN

The examples discussed thus far have involved production in the short run, where at least one productive input cannot be varied. In the long run, by contrast, all factors of production are by definition variable. In the short run, with K held fixed in the production function $Q = F(K, L)$, we were able to describe the production function in a simple two-dimensional diagram. With both K and L variable, however, we now require three dimensions instead of two. And when there are more than two variable inputs, we require even more dimensions.

This creates a problem similar to the one we encountered in Chapter 3 when the consumer was faced with a choice between two or more products: We are not very adept at graphical representations involving three or more dimensions. For production with two variable inputs, the solution to this problem is similar to the one we adopted in Chapter 3.

To illustrate, consider again the production function we discussed earlier in this chapter:

$$Q = F(K, L) = 2KL, \qquad (9.4)$$

and suppose we want to describe all possible combinations of K and L that give rise to a particular level of output—say, $Q = 16$. To do this, we solve $Q = 2KL = 16$ for K in terms of L, which yields

$$K = \frac{8}{L}. \qquad (9.5)$$

The (L, K) pairs that satisfy Equation 9.5 are shown by the curve labeled $Q = 16$ in Figure 9.8. The (L, K) pairs that yield 32 and 64 units of output are shown in Figure 9.8 as the curves labeled $Q = 32$ and $Q = 64$, respectively. Such

302   CHAPTER 9   PRODUCTION

isoquant   the set of all input combinations that yield a given level of output.

curves are called **isoquants,** and are defined formally as *all combinations of variable inputs that yield a given level of output.*[9]

Note the clear analogy between the isoquant and the indifference curve of consumer theory. Just as an indifference map provides a concise representation of a consumer's preferences, an *isoquant map* provides a concise representation of a production process.

On an indifference map, movements to the northeast correspond to increasing levels of satisfaction. Similar movements on an isoquant map correspond to increasing levels of output. A point on an indifference curve is preferred to any point that lies below that indifference curve, and less preferred than any point that lies above it. Likewise, any input bundle on an isoquant yields more output than any input bundle that lies below that isoquant, and less output than any input bundle that lies above it. Thus, bundle C in Figure 9.8 yields more output than bundle A, but less output than bundle D.

The only substantive respect in which the analogy between isoquant maps and indifference maps is incomplete has to do with the significance of the labels attached to the two types of curves. From Chapter 3 recall that the actual numbers assigned to each indifference curve were used to indicate only the relative rankings of the bundles on different indifference curves. The number we assign to an isoquant, by contrast, corresponds to the actual level of output we get from an input bundle along that isoquant. With indifference maps, we are free to relabel the indifference curves in any way that preserves the original ranking of bundles. But with isoquant maps, the labels are determined uniquely by the production function.

The Marginal Rate of Technical Substitution

marginal rate of technical substitution (MRTS) the rate at which one input can be exchanged for another without altering the total level of output.

Recall from our discussion of consumer theory in Chapter 3 that the marginal rate of substitution is the rate at which the consumer is willing to exchange one good for another along an indifference curve. The analogous concept in production theory is called the **marginal rate of technical substitution,** or **MRTS.** It is the rate at which one input can be exchanged for another without altering output. In Figure 9.9, for example, the MRTS at A is defined as the absolute value of the slope of the isoquant at A, $|\Delta K/\Delta L|$.

In consumer theory, we assumed that the marginal rate of substitution diminishes with downward movements along an indifference curve. For most production functions, the MRTS displays a similar property. Holding output constant, the less we have of one input, the more we must add of the other input to compensate for a one-unit reduction in the first input.

A simple but very important relationship exists between the MRTS at any point and the marginal products of the respective inputs at that point. In a small neighborhood of point A in Figure 9.9, suppose we reduce K by ΔK and augment L by an amount ΔL just sufficient to maintain the original level of output. If MP_{KA} denotes the marginal product of capital at A, then the reduction in output caused by the loss of ΔK is equal to $MP_{KA}\Delta K$. Using MP_{LA} to denote the marginal product of L at A, it follows similarly that the gain in output resulting from the extra ΔL is equal to $MP_{LA}\Delta L$. Finally, since the reduction in output

---

[9]"Iso" comes from the Greek word for "same," which also appears, for example, in the meteorological term "isobars," meaning lines of equal barometric pressure.

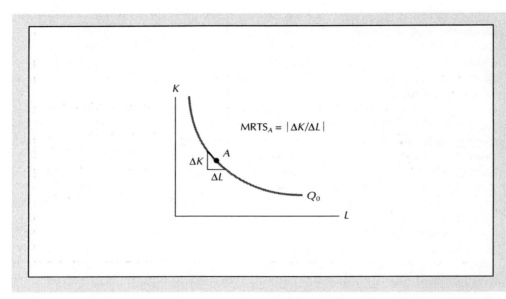

FIGURE 9.9
The Marginal Rate of Technical Substitution
The MRTS is the rate at which one input can be exchanged for another without altering total output. The MRTS at any point is the absolute value of the slope of the isoquant that passes through that point. If ΔK units of capital are removed at point A, and ΔL units of L are added, output will remain the same at Q_0 units.

from having less K is exactly offset by the gain in output from having more L, it follows that

$$MP_{KA}\Delta K = MP_{LA}\Delta L. \tag{9.6}$$

Cross-multiplying, we get

$$\frac{MP_{LA}}{MP_{KA}} = \frac{\Delta K}{\Delta L}, \tag{9.7}$$

which says that the MRTS at A is simply the ratio of the marginal product of L to the marginal product of K. This relationship will have an important application in the next chapter, where we will take up the question of how to produce a given level of output at the lowest possible cost.

EXERCISE 9.6

Given a firm's current level of capital and labor inputs, the marginal product of labor for its production process is equal to 3 units of output. If the marginal rate of technical substitution between K and L is 9, what is the marginal product of capital?

In consumer theory, the shape of the indifference curve tells us how the consumer is willing to substitute one good for another. In production theory, an essentially similar story is told by the shape of the isoquant. Figure 9.10 illustrates the extreme cases of inputs that are perfect substitutes (a) and perfect complements (b). Figure 9.10a describes a production process in which cars and gasoline are combined to produce trips. The input of gasoline comes in two brands, Texaco and Amoco, which are perfect substitutes for one another. We can substitute 1 gallon of Amoco for 1 gallon of Texaco and still produce the same number of trips as before. The MRTS between Texaco and Amoco remains constant at 1 as we move downward along any isoquant.

304   CHAPTER 9   PRODUCTION

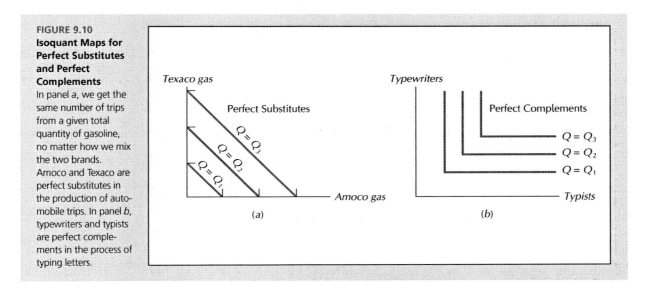

FIGURE 9.10
Isoquant Maps for Perfect Substitutes and Perfect Complements
In panel *a*, we get the same number of trips from a given total quantity of gasoline, no matter how we mix the two brands. Amoco and Texaco are perfect substitutes in the production of automobile trips. In panel *b*, typewriters and typists are perfect complements in the process of typing letters.

Figure 9.10*b* describes a production process for typing letters using the two inputs of typewriters and typists. In this process, the two inputs are perfect complements. Here, inputs are most effectively combined in fixed proportions. Having more than one typewriter per typist doesn't augment production, nor does having more than one typist per typewriter.

RETURNS TO SCALE

A question of central importance for the organization of industry is whether production takes place most efficiently at large scale rather than small scale (where "large" and "small" are defined relative to the scale of the relevant market). This question is important because the answer dictates whether an industry will end up being served by many small firms or only a few large ones.

The technical property of the production function used to describe the relationship between scale and efficiency is called *returns to scale.* The term tells us what happens to output when all inputs are increased by exactly the same proportion. Because returns to scale refer to a situation in which all inputs are variable, *the concept of returns to scale is an inherently long-run concept.*

A production function for which any given proportional change in all inputs leads to a more than proportional change in output is said to exhibit **increasing returns to scale.** For example, if we double all inputs in a production function with increasing returns to scale, we get more than twice as much output as before. As we will see in Chapters 12 and 13, such production functions generally give rise to conditions in which a small number of firms supply most of the relevant market.

Increasing returns to scale often result from the greater possibilities for specialization in large organizations. Adam Smith illustrated this point by describing the division of labor in a pin factory.[10]

increasing returns to scale the property of a production process whereby a proportional increase in every input yields a more than proportional increase in output.

---

[10]Adam Smith, *The Wealth of Nations,* New York: Everyman's Library, 1910 (1776), Book 1, p. 5.

One man draws out the wire, another straightens it, a third cuts it, a fourth points it, a fifth grinds it at the top for receiving the head; to make the head requires two or three distinct operations. . . . I have seen a small manufactory . . . of this kind where only ten men were employed . . . [who] could, when they exerted themselves, make among them about twelve pounds of pins in a day. There are in a pound upwards of four thousand pins of middling size. Those ten persons, therefore, could make among them upwards of forty-eight thousand pins in a day. Each person, therefore, making a tenth part of forty-eight thousand pins might be considered as making four thousand eight hundred pins in a day. But if they had all wrought separately and independently . . . they could not each of them have made twenty, perhaps not one pin in a day. . . .

The airline industry is often cited as a modern example of an industry with increasing returns to scale. Industry professionals have long stressed that having a large number of flights helps an airline fill each flight by feeding passengers from its incoming flights to its outgoing flights. Local airport activities also exhibit increasing returns to scale. As a consequence of the law of large numbers,[11] moreover, it follows that maintenance operations, flight crew scheduling, and other inventory-related activities are all accomplished more efficiently on a large scale than on a small scale. Similarly, ticket-counter space, ticket agents, reservations equipment, baggage-handling equipment, ground crews, and passenger-boarding facilities are all resources that are utilized more efficiently at high activity levels than at low activity levels. Increasing returns to scale in commercial air transport constitute the underlying explanation for why the industry has been moving toward ever larger airlines in the last decade.

A production function for which a proportional change in all inputs causes output to change by the same proportion is said to exhibit **constant returns to scale.** In such cases, doubling all inputs results in a doubling of output. In industries in which production takes place under constant returns to scale, large size is neither an advantage nor a disadvantage.

Finally, a production function for which a proportional change in all inputs causes a less than proportional change in output is said to exhibit **decreasing returns to scale.** Here large size is a handicap, and we do not expect to see large firms in an industry in which production takes place with decreasing returns to scale. As we will see in Chapter 11, the constant and decreasing returns cases often enable many sellers to coexist within the same narrowly defined markets.

A production function need not exhibit the same degree of returns to scale over the entire range of output. On the contrary, there may be increasing returns to scale at low levels of output, followed by constant returns to scale at intermediate levels of output, followed finally by decreasing returns to scale at high levels of output. The isoquant map for such a production function is discussed after the following Economic Naturalist example.

constant returns to scale the property of a production process whereby a proportional increase in every input yields an equal proportional increase in output.

decreasing returns to scale the property of a production process whereby a proportional increase in every input yields a less than proportional increase in output.

Why do builders use prefabricated frames for roofs but not for walls?

When construction crews build a wood-frame house, they usually construct framing for the walls at the construction site. By contrast, they often buy prefabricated framing for the roof. Why this difference?

ECONOMIC
NATURALIST
9.2

---

[11]See Chapter 6.

306   CHAPTER 9   PRODUCTION

There are two key differences between wall framing and roof framing: (1) cutting the lumber for roof framing involves many complicated angle cuts, whereas the right-angle cuts required for wall framing are much simpler; and (2) sections of roof framing of a given size are all alike, whereas wall sections differ according to the placement of window and door openings. Both properties of roof framing lead to substantial economies of scale in production. First, the angle cuts they require can be made much more rapidly if a frame or "jig" can be built that guides the lumber past the saw-blade at just the proper angle. It is economical to set up such jigs in a factory where thousands of cuts are made each day, but it usually does not pay to use this method for the limited number of cuts required at any one construction site. Likewise, automated methods are easy to employ for roof framing by virtue of its uniformity. The idiosyncratic nature of wall framing, by contrast, militates against the use of automated methods.

So the fact that there are much greater economies of scale in the construction of roof framing than wall framing helps account for why wall framing is usually built at the construction site while roof framing is more often prefabricated.

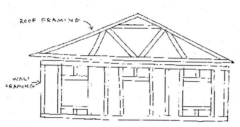

Why do builders build custom frames for walls but use prefabricated frames for roofs?

Showing Returns to Scale on the Isoquant Map

A simple relationship exists between a production function's returns to scale and the spacing of its isoquants.[12] Consider the isoquant map in Figure 9.11. As we move outward into the isoquant map along the ray labeled R, each input grows by exactly the same proportion. The particular production function whose isoquant map is shown in the diagram exhibits increasing returns to scale in the region from A to C. Note, for example, that when we move from A to B, both inputs double while output goes up by a factor of 3; likewise, when we move from B to C, both inputs grow by 50 percent while output grows by 100 percent. In the region from C to F, this same production function exhibits constant returns to scale. Note, for example, that when we move from D to E, both inputs grow by 25 percent and output also grows by 25 percent. Finally, the production function whose isoquant map is shown in Figure 9.11 exhibits decreasing returns to scale in the region to the northeast of F. Thus, when we move from F to G, both inputs increase by 16.7 percent while output grows by only 11.1 percent.

The Distinction between Diminishing Returns and Decreasing Returns to Scale

It is important to bear in mind that decreasing returns to scale have nothing whatsoever to do with the law of diminishing returns. Decreasing returns to scale refer to what happens when *all* inputs are varied by a given proportion. The law of

---

[12]The discussion in this section applies to *homothetic* production functions, an important class of production functions defined by the property that the slopes of all isoquants are constant at points along any ray.

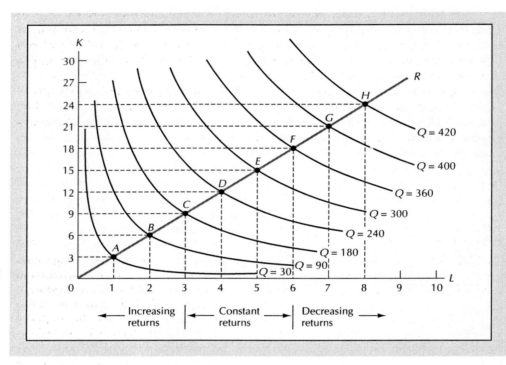

FIGURE 9.11
Returns to Scale Shown on the Isoquant Map
In the region from *A* to *C*, this production function has increasing returns to scale. Proportional increases in input yield more than proportional increases in output. In the region from *C* to *F*, there are constant returns to scale. Inputs and output grow by the same proportion in this region. In the region northeast of *F*, there are decreasing returns to scale. Proportional increases in both inputs yield less than proportional increases in output.

diminishing returns, by contrast, refers to the case in which one input varies while all others are held fixed. As an empirical generalization, it applies with equal force to production functions having increasing, constant, or decreasing returns to scale.

The Logical Puzzle of Decreasing Returns to Scale

If the production function $Q = F(K, L)$ is a complete description of the corresponding production process, it is difficult to see how any production function could ever exhibit decreasing returns to scale in practice. The difficulty is that we ought to be able to duplicate the process used to produce any given level of output, and thereby achieve constant returns to scale. To illustrate, suppose first that $Q_0 = F(K_0, L_0)$. If we now want to produce $2Q_0$ units of output, we can always do so by again doing what we did the first time—namely, by again combining K_0 and L_0 to get Q_0 and adding that to the Q_0 we already have. Similarly, we can get $3Q_0$ by carrying out $F(K_0, L_0)$ three times in succession. Simply by carrying out the process again and again, we can get output to grow in the same proportion as inputs, which means constant returns to scale. And for reasons similar to the ones discussed above for the airline industry, it will often be possible to do even better than that.

In cases in which it is not possible to at least double our output by doubling both K and L, we seem forced to conclude that there must be some important input besides K and L that we are failing to increase at the same time. This input is variously referred to as "organization" or "communication," the idea being that when a firm gets past a certain size, it somehow starts to get out of control.

Frank: Microeconomics
an/ Behavior, Sixth E/ition

III. The Theory of the Firm
an/ Market Structure

9. Pro/uction

© The McGraw–Hill
Companies, 2005

201

308   CHAPTER 9   PRODUCTION

Others claim that it is the shortage of managerial or entrepreneurial resources that creates bottlenecks in production. If there is indeed some unmeasured input that is being held fixed as we expand K and L, then we are still in the short run by definition. And there is no reason to expect to be able to double our output by doubling only *some* of our inputs.

The Appendix to this chapter considers several mathematical extensions of production theory. Topics covered include applications of the average-marginal distinction, specific mathematical forms of the production function, and a mathematical treatment of returns to scale in production.

SUMMARY

- Production is any activity that creates current or future utility. A production function summarizes the relationship between inputs and outputs. The short run is defined as that period during which at least some inputs are fixed. In the two-input case, it is the period during which one input is fixed, the other variable.

- The marginal product of a variable input is defined as the change in output brought forth by an additional unit of the variable input, all other inputs held fixed. The law of diminishing returns says that beyond some point the marginal product declines with additional units of the variable input.

- The average product of a variable input is the ratio of total output to the quantity of the variable input. Whenever marginal product lies above average product, the average product will increase with increases in the variable input. Conversely, when marginal product lies below average product, average product will decline with increases in the variable input.

- An important practical problem is that of how to allocate an input across two productive activities in such a way as to generate the maximum possible output. In general, two types of solutions are possible. A corner solution occurs when the marginal product of the input is always higher in one activity than in the other. In that case, the best thing to do is to concentrate all the input in the activity where it is most productive.

- An interior solution occurs whenever the marginal product of the variable input, when all of it is placed in one activity, is lower than the marginal product of the first unit of the input in the other activity. In this case, the output-maximizing rule is to distribute the input across the two activities in such a way that its marginal product is the same in both. Even experienced decision makers often violate this simple rule. The pitfall to be on guard against is the tendency to equate not marginal but average products in the two activities.

- The long run is defined as the period required for all inputs to be variable. The actual length of time that corresponds to the short and long runs will differ markedly in different cases. In the two-input case, all of the relevant information about production in the long run can be summarized graphically by the isoquant map. The marginal rate of technical substitution is defined as the rate at which one input can be substituted for another without altering the level of output. The MRTS at any point is simply the absolute value of the slope of the isoquant at that point. For most production functions, the MRTS will diminish as we move downward to the right along an isoquant.

- A production function is said to exhibit constant returns to scale if a given proportional increase in all inputs produces the same proportional increase in output. A production function is said to exhibit decreasing returns to scale if a given proportional increase in all inputs results in a smaller proportional increase in output. And, finally, a production function is said to exhibit increasing returns to scale if a given proportional increase in all inputs causes a greater proportional increase in output. Production functions with increasing returns to scale are also said to exhibit economies of scale. Returns to scale constitute a critically important factor in determining the structure of industrial organization.

QUESTIONS FOR REVIEW

1. List three examples of production that a noneconomist might not ordinarily think of as production.

2. Give an example of production in which the short run lasts at least 1 year.

3. Why should a person in charge of hiring productive inputs care more about marginal products than about average products?

4. A wag once remarked that when a certain government official moved from New York to California, the average IQ level in both states went up. Interpret this remark in the context of the average-marginal relationships discussed in the chapter.

5. How is an isoquant map like an indifference map? In what important respect do the two constructs differ?

6. Distinguish between diminishing returns to a variable input and decreasing returns to scale.

7. *True or false:* If the marginal product is decreasing, then the average product must also be decreasing. Explain.

8. A factory adds a worker and subsequently discovers that the average product of its workers has risen. *True or false:* The marginal product of the new worker is less than the average product of the plant's workers before the new employee's arrival.

9. Currently, 2 units of labor and 1 unit of capital produce 1 unit of output. If you double both the inputs (4 units of labor and 2 units of capital), what can you conclude about the output produced under constant returns to scale? Decreasing returns to scale? Increasing returns to scale?

PROBLEMS

1. Graph the short-run total Product curves for each of the following production functions if K is fixed at $K_0 = 4$.
   a. $Q = F(K, L) = 2K + 3L$.
   b. $Q = F(K, L) = K^2L^2$.

2. Do the two production functions in Problem 1 obey the law of diminishing returns?

3. Suppose the marginal product of labor is currently equal to its average product. If you were one of ten new workers the firm was about to hire, would you prefer to be paid the value of your average product or the value of your marginal product? Would it be in the interests of an employer to pay you the value of your average product?

4. The following table provides partial information on total product, average product, and marginal product for a production function. Using the relationships between these properties, fill in the missing cells.

Labor	Total product	Average product	Marginal product
0	0		
1	180	180	180
2	320	160	140
3	420	140	100
4	480	120	60

310   CHAPTER 9   PRODUCTION

5. The Philadelphia Police Department must decide how to allocate police officers between West Philadelphia and Center City. Measured in arrests per hour, the average product, total product, and marginal product in each of these two areas are given in the table below. Currently the police department allocates 200 police officers to Center City and 300 to West Philadelphia. If police can be redeployed only in groups of 100, how, if at all, should the police department reallocate its officers to achieve the maximum number of arrests per hour?

Number of police	West Philly			Center City		
	AP	TP	MP	AP	TP	MP
0	0	0		0	0	
			40			45
100	40	40		45	45	
			40			35
200	40	80		40	80	
			40			25
300	40	120		35	105	
			40			15
400	40	160		30	120	
			40			5
500	40	200		25	125	

6. Suppose a crime wave hits West Philadelphia, so that the marginal product and average product of police officers are now 60 arrests per hour for any number of police officers. What is the optimal allocation of 500 police officers between the two areas now?

7. A firm's short-run production function is given by

$$Q = \tfrac{1}{2}L^2 \qquad \text{for } 0 \le L \le 2$$

and

$$Q = 3L - \tfrac{1}{4}L^2 \qquad \text{for } 2 < L \le 7.$$

    a. Sketch the production function.
    b. Find the maximum attainable production. How much labor is used at that level?
    c. Identify the ranges of L utilization over which the marginal product of labor is increasing and decreasing.
    d. Identify the range over which the marginal product of labor is negative.

8. Each problem on an exam is worth 20 points. Suppose that from the last seconds you devoted to Problem 10 on the exam you earned 2 extra points, while from the last seconds devoted to Problem 8 you earned 4 extra points. The total number of points you earned on these two problems were 8 and 6, respectively, and the total time you spent on each was the same. How—if at all—should you have reallocated your time between them?

9. Suppose capital is fixed at 4 units in the production function $Q = KL$. Draw the total, marginal, and average product curves for the labor input.

10. Identify the regions of increasing, constant, and decreasing returns to scale on the isoquant map shown.

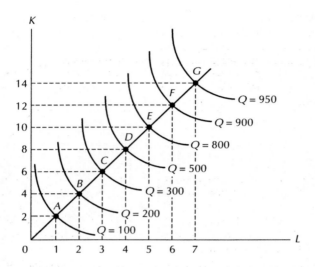

11. When Paul Samuelson switched from physics to economics, Robert Solow is said to have remarked that the average IQ in both disciplines went up. A bystander responded that Solow's claim must be wrong because it implies that the average IQ for academia as a whole (which is a weighted average of the average IQ levels for each discipline) must also have gone up as a result of the switch, which is clearly impossible. Was the bystander right? Explain.

ANSWERS TO IN-CHAPTER EXERCISES

9.1. For $K = 4$, $Q\sqrt{4}\sqrt{L} = 2\sqrt{L}$.

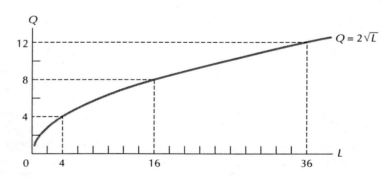

9.2. The slope of the total product curve in Figure 9.3a is 2 for all values of L. So $MP_{L=3} = 2$.

9.3. The slope of the ray to any point on the total product curve is 2, and so $AP_{L=3} = 2$. When the total product curve is a ray, as here, $AP_L = MP_L$ is constant for all values of L.

9.4. Because $AP_{L=10} < MP_{L=10}$, AP will rise when L increases, and so $AP_{L=10.1} > AP_{L=10}$.

312   CHAPTER 9   PRODUCTION

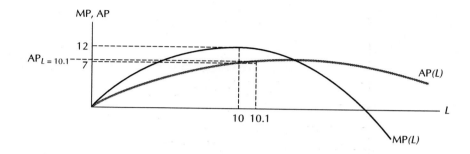

9.5. We cannot say that the pitcher should throw more fastballs without first knowing how a change in the proportion of pitches thrown would alter the effectiveness of both types of pitches. In particular, throwing more fastballs is likely to decrease the effectiveness not only of the additional fastballs thrown, but of all other fastballs as well. And if this loss exceeds the gain from switching from curves to fastballs, more fastballs should not be thrown.

9.6. From the relationship $MP_L/MP_K = MRTS$, we have $3/MP_K = 9$, which yields $MP_K = \frac{1}{3}$.

APPENDIX

9

MATHEMATICAL EXTENSIONS OF PRODUCTION THEORY

APPLICATION: THE AVERAGE-MARGINAL DISTINCTION

Suppose that when your tennis opponent comes to the net, your best response is either to lob (hit the ball over his head) or to pass (hit the ball out of reach on either side). Each type of shot is more effective if it catches your opponent by surprise. Suppose that someone who lobs all the time will win a given point only 10 percent of the time with a lob, but that someone who virtually never lobs wins the point on 90 percent of the rare occasions when he does lob. Similarly, suppose that someone who tries passing shots all the time wins any given point only 30 percent of the time with a passing shot, but that someone who virtually never tries to pass wins 40 percent of the time when he does try. Suppose, finally, that the rate at which each type of shot becomes less effective with use declines linearly with the proportion of times a player uses it. What is the best proportion of lobs and passing shots to use when your opponent comes to the net?[1]

The payoffs from the two types of shots are summarized graphically in Figure A.9.1. Here, the "production" problem is to produce the greatest possible percentage of winning shots when your opponent comes to the net. $F(L)$ tells you the percentage of points you will win with a lob as a function of the proportion of times you lob (L). $F(L)$ is thus, in effect, the average product of L. $G(L)$ tells you the percentage of points you will win with a passing shot, again as a function of the proportion of times you lob. The negative slope of $F(L)$ reflects the fact that lobs become less effective the more you use them. Similarly, the positive slope

---

[1]This example was suggested by Harvard psychologists Richard Herrnstein and James Mazur, in "Making Up Our Minds: A New Model of Economic Behavior," *The Sciences*, November/December 1987: 40–47.

314   CHAPTER 9 APPENDIX   MATHEMATICAL EXTENSIONS OF PRODUCTION THEORY

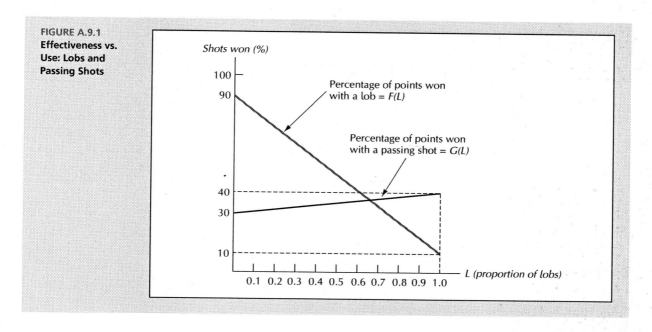

FIGURE A.9.1
Effectiveness vs. Use: Lobs and Passing Shots

of $G(L)$ says that passing shots become more effective the more you lob. Your problem is to choose L^*, the best proportion of times to lob.

To find the optimal value of L, we must first discover how the percentage of total points won, denoted P, varies with L. For any value of L, P is simply a weighted average of the percentages won with each type of shot. The weight used for each type of shot is simply the proportion of times it is used. Noting that $(1 - L)$ is the proportion of passing shots when L is the proportion of lobs, we have

$$P = LF(L) + (1 - L)G(L). \qquad (A.9.1)$$

The expression $LF(L)$ is the percentage of total points won on lobs. $(1 - L)G(L)$, similarly, is the percentage of total points won on passing shots. From Figure A.9.1, we see that the algebraic formulas for $F(L)$ and $G(L)$ are given by $F(L) = 90 - 80L$ and $G(L) = 30 + 10L$. Substituting these relationships into Equation A.9.1 gives

$$P = 30 + 70L - 90L^2, \qquad (A.9.2)$$

which is plotted in Figure A.9.2. The value of L that maximizes P turns out to be $L^* = 0.389$, and the corresponding value of P is 43.61 percent.[2]

Note in Figure A.9.3 that at the optimal value of L, the likelihood of winning with a lob is almost twice as high (58.9 percent) as that of winning with a passing shot (33.9 percent). Many people seem to find this state of affairs extremely uncomfortable—so much so that they refuse to have anything to do with it. In

---

[2]The calculus trained student can find L^* without having to plot P as a function of L simply by solving

$$dP/dL = 70 - 180L = 0,$$

which yields $L^* = \frac{7}{18} = 0.389$, which, upon substitution into Equation A.9.2, yields $P = 43.61$.

APPLICATION: THE AVERAGE-MARGINAL DISTINCTION

315

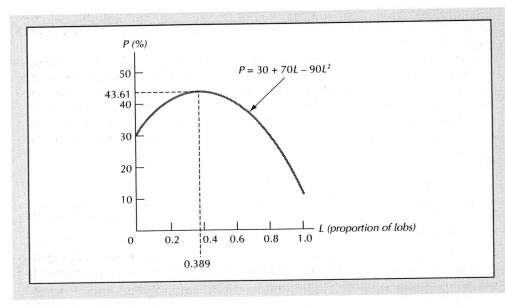

FIGURE A.9.2
The Optimal Proportion of Lobs

$$P = 30 + 70L - 90L^2$$

extensive experimental studies, Harvard psychologists Richard Herrnstein and James Mazur found that people tend to divide their shots not to maximize their overall chances of winning, but to equate the *average product* of each type. Note in Figure A.9.3 that this occurs when $L = 2/3$, at which point the percentage of points won with either shot is 36.7. At this value of L, however, the *marginal product* of a passing shot will be much higher than for a lob, because it will

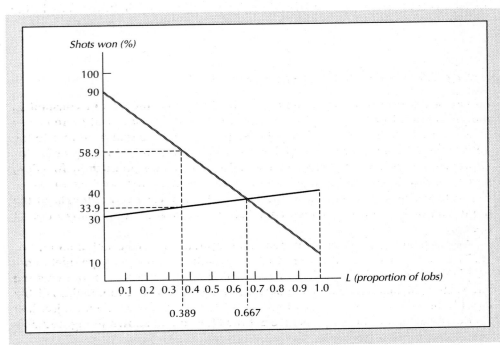

FIGURE A.9.3
At the Optimizing Point, the Likelihood of Winning with a Lob is Much Greater than of Winning with a Passing Shot

316   CHAPTER 9 APPENDIX   MATHEMATICAL EXTENSIONS OF PRODUCTION THEORY

strongly increase the effectiveness of all your *other* lobs. (Of course, an extra passing shot will also reduce the effectiveness of your other passing shots, but by a much smaller margin.)

The situation here is analogous to the allocation example involving the fishing boats mentioned in Chapter 9. There is no more reason to want the average return to each tennis shot to be the same than there is to want the average product on each end of the lake to be the same. And yet the tendency to equate average rather than marginal products is a very common pitfall, one that even experienced maximizers have to be on guard against. Let us consider one final example.

EXAMPLE A9.1

True or false? The best football coach is the one who always chooses the play that will gain the most yardage.

If you answered "true," you have not been paying attention. The best coach is the one who selects the best mix of plays, just as the best tennis player is the one who selects the best mix of shots. In the National Football League, passing plays gain almost twice as much yardage, on the average, as running plays. Why don't coaches call more passes? Because the passing game loses effectiveness if it is used too frequently. From the big difference in average gains for the two types of plays, it is apparent that most coaches are aware that the run is necessary to set up the pass. But many ostensibly expert commentators seem completely oblivious to this point. Trailing by 4 points with 20 seconds to go with fourth and goal at the 4-yard line, a team is more likely to score a touchdown if it throws the ball. However, a team will win more games over the long run if it nonetheless uses a running play in this situation every once in a while. But let a coach call a running play and fail in this situation, and both the fans in the stands and the announcers in the booth will insist that he is an idiot.

ISOQUANT MAPS AND THE PRODUCTION MOUNTAIN

Previously, we derived isoquants algebraically by holding output constant in the production function and then solving for K in terms of L. But there is also a geometric technique for deriving the isoquant map, one that is similar to the derivation of the indifference map discussed in the Appendix to Chapter 3. This approach begins with a three-dimensional graph of the production function, perhaps something like the one shown in Figure A.9.4. It resembles the sloping surface of a mountain. The value on the Q axis measures the height of the mountain, or total output, which continues to increase as we employ more of K or L.

Suppose in Figure A.9.4 we were to fix output at some constant amount, say, Q_0. That is, suppose we cut the production mountain with a plane parallel to the KL plane, Q_0 units above it. The line labeled AB in Figure A.9.4 represents the intersection of that plane and the surface of the production mountain. All the input bundles that lie on AB yield an output level of Q_0. If we then project line AB downward onto the KL plane, we get the Q_0 isoquant shown in Figure A.9.5.

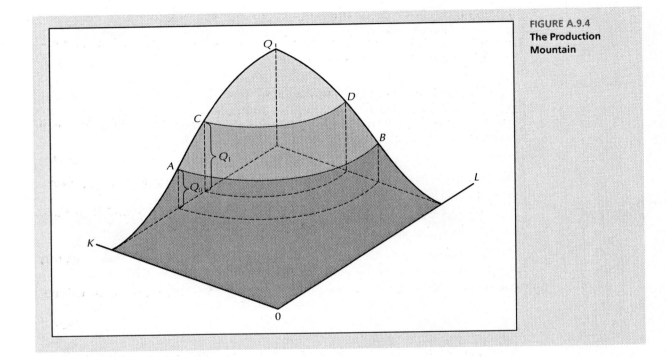

FIGURE A.9.4
The Production Mountain

As defined in Chapter 9, an isoquant is a locus of K, L pairs that produce the same level of output.

Suppose we then intersect the production mountain with another plane, this time Q_1 units above the KL plane. In Figure A.9.4, the second plane intersects the production mountain along the line labeled CD. It represents the locus of all input bundles that yield output level Q_1. Projecting CD down onto the KL plane, we thus get the isoquant labeled Q_1 in Figure A.9.5. In like fashion, we can generate an entire isoquant map corresponding to the production function $Q = F(K, L)$.

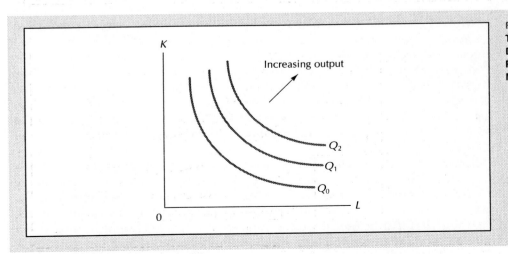

FIGURE A.9.5
The Isoquant Map Derived from the Production Mountain

318   CHAPTER 9 APPENDIX MATHEMATICAL EXTENSIONS OF PRODUCTION THEORY

SOME EXAMPLES OF PRODUCTION FUNCTIONS

In this section we will examine two of the many different production functions that are commonly used in economic analysis.

The Cobb-Douglas Production Function

Perhaps the most widely used production function of all is the Cobb-Douglas, which in the two-input case takes the form

$$Q = mK^\alpha L^\beta, \tag{A.9.3}$$

where α and β are numbers between zero and 1, and m can be any positive number.

To generate an equation for the Q_0 isoquant, we fix Q at Q_0 and then solve for K in terms of L. In the Cobb-Douglas case, this yields

$$K = \left(\frac{m}{Q_0}\right)^{-1/\alpha} (L)^{-\beta/\alpha}. \tag{A.9.4}$$

For the particular Cobb-Douglas function $Q = K^{1/2}L^{1/2}$, the Q_0 isoquant will be

$$K = \frac{Q_0^2}{L}. \tag{A.9.5}$$

A portion of the isoquant map for this particular Cobb-Douglas production function is shown in Figure A.9.6.

The number assigned to each particular isoquant in Figure A.9.6 is exactly the level of output to which it corresponds. For example, when we have 2 units of K and 2 units of L, we get $Q = \sqrt{2}\sqrt{2} = 2$ units of output. Recall from Chapter 3 that the numbers we used to label the indifference curves on an indifference map conveyed information only about *relative* levels of satisfaction. All that was required of our indexing scheme in that context was that the

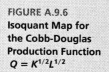

FIGURE A.9.6
Isoquant Map for the Cobb-Douglas Production Function $Q = K^{1/2}L^{1/2}$

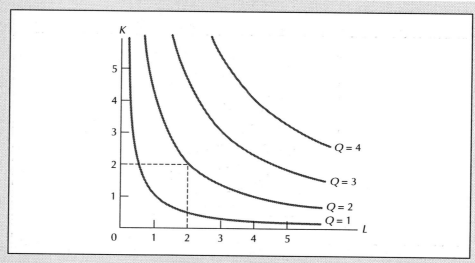

order of the numbers we assigned to the indifference curves reflect the proper ranking of the corresponding satisfaction levels. With isoquants, the situation is altogether different. We have, in effect, no choice about what labels to assign to them.

Calculus-trained students can easily verify the following expressions for the marginal products of labor and capital in the Cobb-Douglas case:

$$\text{MP}_K = \frac{\partial Q}{\partial K} = \alpha m K^{\alpha-1} L^{\beta} \qquad (A.9.6)$$

and

$$\text{MP}_L = \frac{\partial Q}{\partial L} = \beta m K^{\alpha} L^{\beta-1}. \qquad (A.9.7)$$

The Leontief, or Fixed-Proportions, Production Function

The simplest among all production functions that are widely used is the *Leontief*, named for the Nobel laureate Wassily Leontief, who devised it. For the two-input case, it is given by

$$Q = \min (aK, bL). \qquad (A.9.8)$$

If you are unfamiliar with this curious functional form, its interpretation is simply that Q is equal to either aK or bL, whichever of the two is smaller. Suppose, for example, that $a = 2$, $b = 3$, $K = 4$, and $L = 3$. Then, $Q = \min(2 \times 4, 3 \times 3) = \min(8, 9) = 8$. The isoquant map for $Q = \min (2K, 3L)$ is shown in Figure A.9.7.

To see why the Leontief is also called the fixed-proportions production function, note first in Figure A.9.7 that if we start with 3 units of K and 2 units of L, we get 6 units of output. If we then add more L—so that we have, say, 3 units

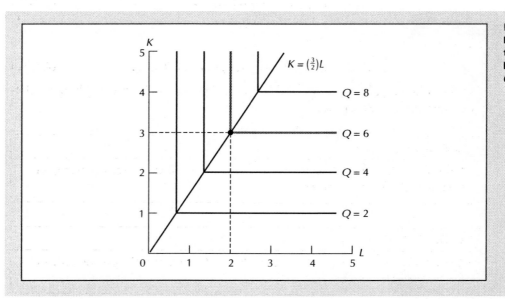

FIGURE A.9.7
Isoquant Map for the Leontief Production Function
$Q = \min (2K, 3L)$

320   CHAPTER 9 APPENDIX   MATHEMATICAL EXTENSIONS OF PRODUCTION THEORY

of L instead of 2—we still get only $Q = \min(2 \times 3, 3 \times 3) = \min(6, 9) = 6$ units of output. By the same token, adding more K when we are at $K = 3$ and $L = 2$ will not lead to any additional output. In the Leontief case, K and L are used most effectively when $aK = bL$—in the example at hand, when $2K = 3L$. In Figure A.9.7, the locus of points for which $2K = 3L$ is shown as the ray $K = (^3/_2)L$. It is along this ray that the cusps of all the right-angled isoquants of this Leontief production function will lie.

Recall from Chapter 3 that in the case of perfect complements, the indifference curves had the same right-angled shape as the isoquants for the Leontief production function. This meant that the MRS was infinite on the vertical arm of the indifference curve, zero on the horizontal arm, and undefined at the cusp. For exactly parallel reasons, the MRTS in the Leontief case will be infinite on the vertical arm of the isoquant, zero on the horizontal, and undefined at the cusp.

A MATHEMATICAL DEFINITION OF RETURNS TO SCALE

Mathematically, to increase all inputs in the same proportion means simply to multiply all inputs by the same number $c > 1$. By way of illustration, consider the production function we discussed in Chapter 9, $Q = F(K, L) = 2KL$. For this particular function, when we multiply each input by c we get

$$F(cK, cL) = 2(cK)(cL) = c^2 2KL = c^2 F(K, L). \qquad (A.9.9)$$

The result of multiplying each input by c in this production function is thus to multiply the original output level by c^2. Output thus grows more than in proportion to input growth in this case [with proportional growth, we would have had output equal to $cF(K, L)$], so this production function has increasing returns to scale. Thus, for example, if $c = 2$ (a doubling of each input), we get $F(2K, 2L) = 2(2K)(2L) = 4(2KL)$, a quadrupling of output.

Drawing on these observations, the definitions of our three cases may be summarized as follows:

$$\text{Increasing returns: } F(cK, cL) > cF(K, L); \qquad (A.9.10)$$
$$\text{Constant returns: } F(cK, cL) = cF(K, L); \qquad (A.9.11)$$

and

$$\text{Decreasing returns: } F(cK, cL) < cF(K, L). \qquad (A.9.12)$$

The following two exercises will help cement your ability to apply these definitions to specific examples.

EXERCISE A.9.1

Does the production function $Q = \sqrt{K}\,\sqrt{L}$ have increasing, constant, or decreasing returns to scale?

EXERCISE A.9.2

Does the production function $Q = K^{1/3}L^{1/3}$ have increasing, constant, or decreasing returns to scale?

In the case of the Cobb-Douglas production function, $Q = mK^\alpha L^\beta$, Equations A.9.10 through A.9.12 imply a simple relationship between the parameters α and β and the degree of returns to scale. Specifically, if $\alpha + \beta > 1$, there are increasing returns to scale; $\alpha + \beta = 1$ means constant returns to scale; and $\alpha + \beta < 1$ means decreasing returns to scale. To illustrate for the constant returns case, suppose $Q = F(K, L) = mK^\alpha L^\beta$, with $\alpha + \beta = 1$. Then we have

$$F(cK, cL) = m(cK)^\alpha (cL)^\beta, \qquad (A.9.13)$$

which reduces to

$$c^{(\alpha + \beta)}mK^\alpha L^\beta = cmK^\alpha L^\beta = cF(K, L), \qquad (A.9.14)$$

which, by Equation A.9.11, is the defining characteristic of constant returns to scale.

PROBLEMS

*1. Do the following production functions have increasing, decreasing, or constant returns to scale? Which ones fail to satisfy the law of diminishing returns?
   a. $Q = 4K^{1/2}L^{1/2}$
   b. $Q = aK^2 + bL^2$
   c. $Q = \min(aK, bL)$
   d. $Q = 4K + 2L$
   e. $Q = K^{0.5}L^{0.6}$
   f. $Q = K_1^{0.3}K_2^{0.3}L^{0.3}$

*2. What is the marginal product of labor in the production function $Q = 2K^{1/3}L^{1/3}$ if K is fixed at 27?

3. Can the Cobb-Douglas production function be used to portray a production process in which returns to scale are increasing at low output levels and are constant or decreasing at high output levels?

4. Suppose that a firm with the production function
$$Q = \min(2K, 3L)$$
is currently using 6 units of capital and 5 units of labor. What are the marginal products of K and L in this case?

5. The average number of yards gained by a college football team on a passing play is $8 + 12r$, where r is the fraction of their total plays that are running plays. Their average gain per running play is $10 - 8r$. What is their optimal fraction of running plays? At this value of r, what is the average gain per pass? The average gain per run? (This problem and the next one are similar to the tennis example considered earlier.)

6. Suppose you are a baseball pitcher with two pitches, fastball and curve. Your opponents' batting averages against these two pitches are as shown in the diagram on the next page. If your goal is to minimize your opponents' overall batting average, what is the optimal proportion of fastballs? At this proportion, what are opponents' batting averages against your two pitches?

---

*This problem is most easily solved using the calculus definition of marginal product.

322   CHAPTER 9 APPENDIX   MATHEMATICAL EXTENSIONS OF PRODUCTION THEORY

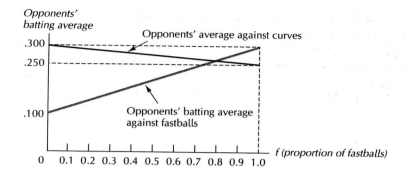

ANSWERS TO IN-APPENDIX EXERCISES

A.9.1. $F(K, L) = \sqrt{K}\sqrt{L}$, so $F(cK, cL) = \sqrt{cK}\sqrt{cL} = \sqrt{c^2}\sqrt{K}\sqrt{L} = cF(K, L)$, and so it has constant returns to scale.

A.9.2. $F(K, L) = K^{1/3}L^{1/3}$, so $F(cK, cL) = (cK)^{1/3}(cL)^{1/3} = c^{2/3}K^{1/3}L^{1/3} = c^{2/3}F(K, L) < cF(K, L)$, and so it has decreasing returns to scale.

CHAPTER

10

COSTS

Just after finishing college, I was a high school math and science teacher in Sanischare, a small village in eastern Nepal. During my two years there, one of the country's few roads was in the process of being built through Sanischare. Once the right-of-way was cleared and the culverts and bridges laid in, the next step was to spread gravel over the roadbed. As at almost every other stage of the process, the methods employed at this step were a page torn from another century. The Nepalese workmen squatted by the side of the road in the blazing sun, tapping away at large rocks with their hammers. In a 12-hour day, each worker would produce a small mound of gravel, not enough to cover even one running foot of roadbed. But there were a lot of people working, and eventually the job was done.

In the United States, of course, we build roads very differently. We do not hire people to hammer rocks into gravel by hand. Instead, we have huge machines that pulverize several tons of rock each minute. The reason for this difference seemed obvious to me at the time: Nepal, being a very poor country, simply couldn't afford to buy the expensive equipment used in the industrialized nations. But this explanation, I now realize, is wrong. As we will see, it still would have made sense for Nepal to make gravel with manual labor even if it had had vast surplus revenues in its national treasury, because labor is very cheap relative to capital equipment there.

324   CHAPTER 10   COSTS

CHAPTER PREVIEW

In this chapter our goal is to translate the theory of production developed in Chapter 9 into a coherent theory of costs. In Chapter 9 we established the relationship between the quantities of inputs employed and the corresponding level of output, but here we will forge the link between the quantity of output produced and the cost of producing it.

Our first step will be to tackle the question of how costs vary with output in the short run. This question turns out to be more involved than it sounds, for there are seven different types of costs to keep track of, namely, total cost, variable cost, fixed cost, marginal cost, average total cost, average variable cost, and average fixed cost. This array sounds bewildering at first, but the links between the different cost concepts are actually clear and simple. And each turns out to be important for the study of firm behavior, which is our principal concern in the chapters to follow.

Of even greater importance for the structure and conduct of industry is the question of how costs vary with output in the long run. Here, we will begin with the question of how to produce a given level of output—say, a mile of road, either here or in some other country—at the lowest possible cost. A given quantity can be produced many ways: We need to find the cheapest way, the most appropriate method for existing factor prices. The answer to this question enables us to explore how costs are related to returns to scale in production.

COSTS IN THE SHORT RUN

To see how costs vary with output in the short run, it is convenient to begin with a simple production example of the sort we discussed in Chapter 9. Suppose Kelly's Cleaners washes bags of laundry using labor (L) and capital (K). Labor is purchased in the open market at a wage rate $w = \$10/$person-hr.[1] Capital is fixed in the short run. The relationship between the variable input and the total number of bags washed per hour is summarized in Table 10.1. Note that output initially grows at an increasing rate with additional units of the variable input (as L grows from 0 to 4 units), then grows at a diminishing rate (as L grows from 4 to 8 units).

The total cost of producing the various levels of output is simply the cost of all the factors of production employed. If Kelly owns his own capital, its implicit rental value is an opportunity cost, the money Kelly could have earned if he had sold his capital and invested the proceeds in, say, a government bond (see Chapter 1). Suppose Kelly's capital is fixed at 120 machine-hr/hr, the rental value of each of which is $r = \$0.25/$machine-hr,[2] for a total capital rental of $30/hr. This cost is **fixed cost (FC)**, which means that it does not vary in the short run as the level of output varies. More generally, if K_0 denotes the amount of capital and r is its rental price per unit, we have

fixed cost (FC) cost that does not vary with the level of output in the short run (the cost of all fixed factors of production).

$$FC = rK_0.$$

(10.1)

---

[1] A person-hour is one person working for 1 hour. In Chapter 14 we will consider how input prices are determined. For the present, we simply take them as given.

[2] A machine-hour is one machine working for 1 hour. To say that Kelly's capital is fixed at 120 machine-hr/hr means that he has 120 machines that can operate simultaneously.

Quantity of labor (person-hr/hr)	Quantity of output (bags/hr)
0	0
1	4
2	14
3	27
4	43
5	58
6	72
7	81
8	86

TABLE 10.1
The Short-Run Production Function for Kelly's Cleaners
The entries in each row of the right column tell the quantity of output produced by the quantity of variable input in the corresponding row of the left column. This production function initially exhibits increasing, then diminishing, returns to the variable input.

Other examples of fixed cost might include property taxes, insurance payments, interest on loans, and other payments to which the firm is committed in the short run and which do not vary as the level of output varies. Business managers often refer to fixed costs as *overhead costs*.

Variable cost (VC) is defined as the total cost of the variable factor of production at each level of output.[3] To calculate VC for any given level of output in this example, we simply multiply the amount of labor needed to produce that level of output by the hourly wage rate. Thus, the variable cost of 27 bags/hr is ($10/ person-hr) (3 person-hr/hr) = $30/hr. More generally, if L_1 is the quantity of labor required to produce an output level of Q_1 and w is the hourly wage rate, we have

variable cost (VC) cost that varies with the level of output in the short run (the cost of all variable factors of production).

$$VC_{Q1} = wL_1. \tag{10.2}$$

Note the explicit dependence of VC on output in the notation on the left-hand side of Equation 10.2, which is lacking in Equation 10.1. This is to emphasize that variable cost depends on the output level produced, whereas fixed cost does not.

Total cost (TC) is the sum of FC and VC. If Kelly wishes to wash 43 bags/hr, the total cost of doing so will be $30/hr + ($10/person-hr) (4 person-hr/hr) = $70/hr. More generally, the expression for total cost of producing an output level of Q_1 is written

total cost (TC) all costs of production: the sum of variable cost and fixed cost.

$$TC_{Q1} = FC + VC_{Q1} = rK_0 + wL_1. \tag{10.3}$$

Table 10.2 shows fixed, variable, and total cost for corresponding output levels for the production function given in Table 10.1. The relationships among the various cost categories are most clearly seen by displaying the information graphically, not in tabular form. The short-run production function from Table 10.1 is plotted in Figure 10.1. Recall from Chapter 9 that the initial region of upward curvature ($0 \leq L \leq 4$) of the production function corresponds to increasing returns to the variable input. Beyond the point $L = 4$, the production function exhibits diminishing returns to the variable input.

---

[3]In production processes with more than one variable input, variable cost refers to the cost of *all* such inputs.

326   CHAPTER 10   COSTS

TABLE 10.2

Outputs and Costs
The fixed cost of capital is $30/hr, and the cost per unit of the variable factor (L) is $10/hr. Total cost is calculated as the sum of fixed cost and variable cost.

Q	FC	VC	TC
0	30	0	30
4	30	10	40
14	30	20	50
27	30	30	60
43	30	40	70
58	30	50	80
72	30	60	90
81	30	70	100
86	30	80	110

Graphing the Total, Variable, and Fixed Cost Curves

Not surprisingly, the shape of the variable cost curve is systematically related to the shape of the short-run production function. The connection arises because the production function tells us how much labor we need to produce a given level of output, and this quantity of labor, when multiplied by the wage rate, gives us variable cost. Suppose, for example, we want to plot the variable cost of producing 58 units of output. (See Figures 10.1, 10.2.) We first note from the production function shown in Figure 10.1 that 58 units of output require 5 units of labor, which, at a wage rate of $10/person-hr, gives rise to a variable cost of (5)(10) = $50/hr. So in Figure 10.2, the output level of 58 is plotted against a variable cost of $50/hr. Similarly, note from the production function that 43 units of output require 4 units of labor, which, at the $10 wage rate, gives rise in Figure 10.2 to a variable cost of $40/hr. In like fashion, we can generate as many additional points on the variable cost curve as we choose.

Of particular interest is the relationship between the curvature of the production function and that of the variable cost curve. Note in Figure 10.1 that $L = 4$ is the point at which diminishing returns to the variable factor of production

FIGURE 10.1

Output as a Function of One Variable Input
This production process shows increasing returns to the variable input up to the variable input up to $L = 4$, and diminishing returns thereafter.

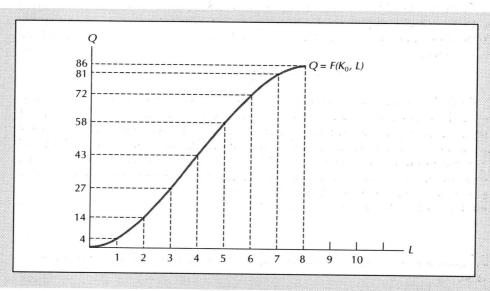

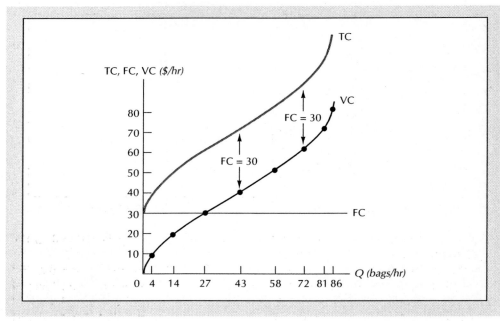

FIGURE 10.2
The Total, Variable, and Fixed Cost Curves
These curves are for the production function for Kelly's cleaners, shown in Figure 10.1. The variable cost curve passes through the origin, which means that the variable cost of producing zero units of output is equal to zero. The TC curve, which is the sum of the FC and VC curves, is parallel to the VC curve and lies $FC = 30$ units above it.

set in. For values of L less than 4, there are increasing returns to L, which means that increments in L produce successively larger increments in Q in that region. Put another way, in this region a given increase in output, Q, requires successively smaller increments in the variable input, L. As a result, variable cost grows at a diminishing rate for output levels less than 43. This is reflected in Figure 10.2 by the concave shape of the variable cost curve for output levels between 0 and 43.

Once L exceeds 4 in Figure 10.1, we enter the region of diminishing returns. Here, successively larger increments in L are required to produce a given increment in Q. In consequence, variable cost grows at an increasing rate in this region. This is reflected in the convex shape of the variable cost curve in Figure 10.2 for output levels in excess of 43.

Because fixed costs do not vary with the level of output, their graph is simply a horizontal line. Figure 10.2 shows the fixed, variable, and total cost curves (FC, VC, and TC) for the production function shown in Figure 10.1. Note in the figure that the variable cost curve passes through the origin, which means simply that variable cost is zero when we produce no output. The total cost of producing zero output is equal to fixed costs, FC. Note also in the figure that the vertical distance between the VC and TC curves is everywhere equal to FC. This means that the total cost curve is parallel to the variable cost curve and lies FC units above it.

Suppose the production function is given by $Q = 3KL$, where K denotes capital and L denotes labor. The price of capital is \$2/machine-hr, the price of labor is \$24/person-hr, and capital is fixed at 4 machine-hr/hr in the short run. Graph the TC, VC, and FC curves for this production process.

EXAMPLE 10.1

Unlike the production process shown in Figure 10.1, the process in this example is one in which there are everywhere constant returns to the variable factor of

Frank: Microeconomics
an/ Behavior, Sixth E/ition

III. The Theory of the Firm
an/ Market Structure

10. Costs

© The McGraw–Hill
Companies, 2005

221

328   CHAPTER 10   COSTS

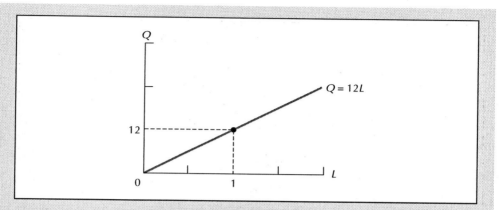

production. As shown in Figure 10.3, output here is strictly proportional to the variable input.

To derive the total cost function from this production function, we must first discover how much capital and labor are required to produce a given level of output in the short run. Since K is fixed at 4 machine-hr/hr, the required amount of labor input is found by solving $Q = 3KL = 3(4)L$ for $L = Q/12$. The total cost of producing Q units of output per hour is therefore given by

$$\text{TC}(Q) = (\$2/\text{machine-hr})(4 \text{ machine-hr}/\text{hr})$$
$$+ (\$24/\text{person-hr})\left(\frac{Q}{12} \text{ person-hr}/\text{hr}\right) = \$8/\text{hr} + \$2Q/\text{hr}. \quad (10.4)$$

The \$8/hr expenditure on capital constitutes fixed cost. Variable cost is total cost less fixed cost, or

$$\text{VC}_Q = 2Q. \quad (10.5)$$

The total, variable, and fixed cost curves are plotted in Figure 10.4.

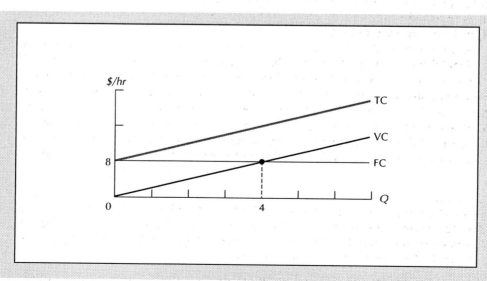

EXERCISE 10.1

Same as Example 10.1 except the price of capital r = $4/machine-hr.

Other Short-Run Costs

Average fixed cost (AFC) is fixed cost divided by the quantity of output. For the production function shown in Table 10.1, for example, the average fixed cost of washing 58 bags/hr is ($30/hr) ÷ (58 bags/hr) = $0.517/bag. More generally, the average fixed cost of producing an output level of Q_1 is written

average fixed cost (AFC) fixed cost divided by the quantity of output.

$$AFC_{Q1} = \frac{FC}{Q_1} = \frac{rK_0}{Q_1}. \qquad (10.6)$$

Note in Equation 10.6 that, unlike FC, AFC depends on the level of output produced.

Average variable cost (AVC) is variable cost divided by the quantity of output. If Kelly washes 72 bags/hr, his AVC will be ($10/person-hr) (6 person-hr/hr) ÷ 72 bags/hr = $0.833/bag. The average variable cost of producing an output level Q_1 may be written as

average variable cost (AVC) variable cost divided by the quantity of output.

$$AVC_{Q1} = \frac{VC_{Q1}}{Q_1} = \frac{wL_1}{Q_1} \qquad (10.7)$$

Average total cost (ATC) is total cost divided by the quantity of output. And since total cost is the sum of total fixed cost and total variable cost, it follows that ATC is the sum of AFC and AVC. For example, the ATC of washing 58 bags/hr is ($30/hr) ÷ (58 bags/hr) + ($10/person-hr) (5 person-hr/hr) ÷ (58 bags/hr) = $0.517/bag + $0.862/bag = $1.379/bag. The average total cost of producing Q_1 units of output is given by

average total cost (ATC) total cost divided by the quantity of output.

$$ATC_{Q1} = AFC_{Q1} + AVC_{Q1} = \frac{rK_0 + wL_1}{Q_1}. \qquad (10.8)$$

Marginal cost (MC), finally, is the change in total cost that results from producing an additional unit of output.[4] In going from 58 to 72 bags/hr, for example, total costs go up by $10/hr, which is the cost of hiring the extra worker needed to achieve that increase in output. Since the extra worker washes an extra 14 bags/hr, the marginal cost of the additional output in per-bag terms is ($10/hr) ÷ (14 bags/hr) = $0.714/bag. More generally, if ΔQ denotes the change in output from an initial level of Q_1, and ΔTC_{Q1} denotes the corresponding change in total cost, marginal cost at Q_1 is given by

marginal cost (MC) change in total cost that results from a 1-unit change in output.

$$MC_{Q1} = \frac{\Delta TC_{Q1}}{\Delta Q} \qquad (10.9)$$

Because fixed cost does not vary with the level of output, the change in total cost when we produce ΔQ additional units of output is the same as the change in variable cost. Thus an equivalent expression for marginal cost is

---

[4]In calculus terms, the definition of marginal cost is simply $MC_Q = dTC_Q/dQ$.

CHAPTER 10   COSTS

$$MC_{Q1} = \frac{\Delta VC_{Q1}}{\Delta Q},$$
(10.10)

where ΔVC_{Q1} represents the change in variable cost when we produce ΔQ units of additional output.

Graphing the Short-Run Average and Marginal Cost Curves

Since FC does not vary with output, average fixed cost declines steadily as output increases. Suppose McGraw-Hill's fixed costs in producing this textbook were approximately $200,000. If only 1000 copies were produced, its average fixed cost would be $200/book. But if the publisher produces 20,000 copies, AFC will fall to $10/book. McGraw-Hill's best-selling economics principles text, by Campbell McConnell and Stanley Brue, is considerably longer than this book, and yet its average fixed cost comes to little more than $1/book. The process whereby AFC falls with output is often referred to as "spreading overhead costs."

For the fixed cost curve FC shown in the top panel in Figure 10.5, the corresponding average fixed cost curve is shown in the bottom panel as the curve labeled AFC. Like all other AFC curves, it takes the form of a rectangular hyperbola. As output shrinks toward zero, AFC grows without bounds, and it falls ever closer to zero as output increases. Note that the units on the vertical axis of the AFC curve are dollars per unit ($/unit) of output, and that the vertical axis of the FC curve, by contrast, is measured in dollars per hour ($/hr).

Geometrically, average variable cost at any level of output Q, which is equal to VC/Q, may be interpreted as the slope of a ray to the variable cost curve at Q. Notice in the top panel in Figure 10.5 that the slope of a ray to the VC curve declines with output up to the output level Q_2; thereafter it begins to increase. The corresponding average variable cost curve, shown in the bottom panel in Figure 10.5, therefore reaches its minimum value at Q_2, the output level at which the ray R_2 is tangent to the variable cost curve. Beyond that point, the AVC curve increases with output.

The graph of the ATC curve is generated in an analogous fashion. For any level of output, ATC is the slope of the ray to the total cost curve at that output level. For the total cost curve in the top panel in Figure 10.5, the corresponding ATC curve is plotted in the bottom panel of the diagram. Note that the minimum point on ATC in the bottom panel occurs at Q_3, the output level for which the ray R_1 is tangent to the TC curve in the top panel.

Recall that because TC = FC + VC, it follows that ATC = AFC + AVC (simply divide both sides of the former equation by output). This means that the vertical distance between the ATC and AVC curves at any level of output will always be the corresponding level of AFC. Thus the vertical distance between ATC and AVC approaches infinity as output declines toward zero, and shrinks toward zero as output grows toward infinity. Note also in Figure 10.5 that the minimum point on the AVC curve occurs for a smaller unit of output than does the minimum point on the ATC curve. Because AFC declines continuously, ATC continues falling even after AVC has begun to turn upward.

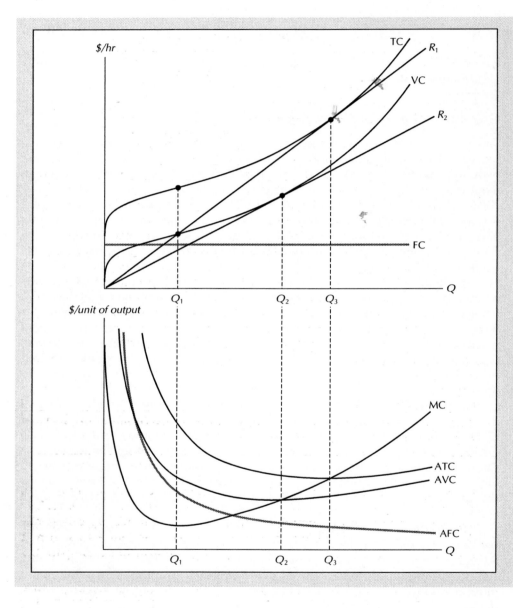

FIGURE 10.5
The Marginal, Average Total, Average Variable, and Average Fixed Cost Curves
The MC curve intersects the ATC and AVC curves at their respective minimum points.

Construct a table showing the average fixed costs, average variable cost, average total cost, and marginal cost using the information in Table 10.1 for Kelly's Cleaners. Then graph these average costs.

We calculate the average fixed cost as fixed costs divided by quantity $AFC = FC/Q$, average variable cost as variable cost divided by quantity $AVC = VC/Q$, and average total cost as total cost divided by quantity $ATC = TC/Q$. We calculate marginal cost by finding the difference in total cost and dividing by the difference in quantity: $MC = \Delta TC/\Delta Q$ to fill in the table below. The average cost curves are illustrated in Figure 10.6.

EXAMPLE 10.2

332   CHAPTER 10   COSTS

Outputs and Costs

Q	AFC	AVC	ATC	MC*
0	∞	–	∞	
				2.50
4	7.50	2.50	10.00	
				1.0
14	2.14	1.43	3.57	
				0.77
27	1.11	1.11	2.22	
				0.63
43	0.70	0.93	1.63	
				0.67
58	0.52	0.86	1.38	
				0.71
72	0.42	0.83	1.25	
				1.11
81	0.37	0.86	1.23	
				2.0
86	0.35	0.93	1.28	

*The marginal cost entries are placed between the lines of the table to indicate that each entry represents the cost per bag of moving from the preceding output level to the next.

EXERCISE 10.2

If FC takes the value 20, what is the vertical distance between the ATC and AVC curves in Figure 10.5 when $Q = 10$?

$\sqrt{AC} = 10$
$ATC =$

In terms of its role in the firm's decision of how much output to produce, by far the most important of the seven cost curves is the *marginal cost curve*. The reason, as we will see in the coming chapters, is that the firm's typical operating decision involves the question of whether to expand or contract its current level of output. To make this decision intelligently, the firm must compare the

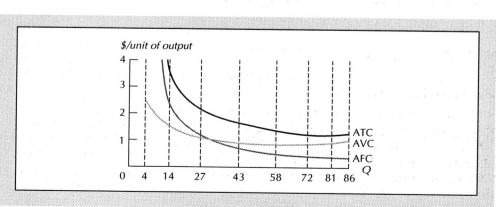

FIGURE 10.6
Quantity vs. Average Costs
ATC is the sum of AVC and AFC. AFC is declining for all values of Q.

relevant costs and benefits. The cost of expanding output (or the savings from contracting) is by definition equal to marginal cost.

Geometrically, marginal cost at any level of output may be interpreted as the slope of the total cost curve at that level of output. And since the total cost and variable cost curves are parallel, marginal cost is also equal to the slope of the variable cost curve. (Recall that the variable cost component is all that varies when total cost varies, which means that the change in total cost per unit of output must be the same as the change in variable cost per unit of output.)

Notice in the top panel in Figure 10.5 that the slope of the total cost curve decreases with output up to Q_1, and rises with output thereafter.[5] This tells us that the marginal cost curve, labeled MC in the bottom panel, will be downward sloping up to Q_1 and upward sloping thereafter. Q_1 is the point at which diminishing returns set in for this production function, and diminishing returns are what account for the upward slope of the short-run marginal cost curve.

At the output level Q_3, the slope of the total cost curve is exactly the same as the slope of the ray to the total cost curve (the ray labeled R_1 in the top panel in Figure 10.5). This tells us that marginal cost and average total cost will take precisely the same value at Q_3. To the left of Q_3, the slope of the total cost curve is smaller than the slope of the corresponding ray, which means that marginal cost will be smaller than average total cost in that region. For output levels in excess of Q_3, the slope of the total cost curve is larger than the slope of the corresponding ray, so marginal cost will be larger than average total cost for output levels larger than Q_3. These relationships are reflected in the average total cost and marginal cost curves shown in the bottom panel in Figure 10.5. Notice that the relationship between the MC and AVC curves is qualitatively similar to the relationship between the MC and ATC curves. One common feature is that MC intersects each curve at its minimum point. Both average cost curves have the additional property that *when MC is less than average cost (either ATC or AVC), the average cost curve must be decreasing with output; and when MC is greater than average cost, average cost must be increasing with output.*

Note also that both of these relationships are very much like the ones among marginal and average product curves discussed in Chapter 9. They follow directly from the definition of marginal cost. Producing an additional unit whose cost exceeds the average (either total or variable) cost incurred thus far has the effect of pulling the average cost up. Conversely, an extra unit whose cost is less than the average will necessarily pull down the average.

Finally, note in the bottom panel in Figure 10.5 that the units on the vertical axis of the marginal cost curve diagram are again dollars per unit ($/unit) of output, the same as for the three short-run average cost curves. All four of these curves can thus be displayed in a single diagram. But you must never, *ever*, attempt to place any of these four curves on the same axes with the total cost, variable cost, or fixed cost curves. The units measured along the vertical axes are simply not compatible.

Suppose output is given by the production function $Q = 3KL$, where K denotes capital and L denotes labor. The price of capital is $2/machine-hr, the price of labor is $24/person-hr, and capital is fixed at 4 units in the short run (this is the same   EXAMPLE 10.3

---

[5]A point at which the curvature changes is called an *inflection point*.

334   CHAPTER 10   COSTS

production function and input prices as in Example 10.1). Graph the ATC, AVC, AFC, and MC curves.

Recall from Example 10.1 that the total cost curve for this process is given by

$$TC_Q = 8 + 2Q. \tag{10.11}$$

Marginal cost is the slope of the total cost curve, which here is equal to $2/unit of output:

$$MC_Q = \frac{\Delta TC_Q}{\Delta Q} = 2. \tag{10.12}$$

Average variable cost is given by VC_Q/Q, which is also $2/unit of output:

$$AVC_Q = \frac{2Q}{Q} = 2. \tag{10.13}$$

When marginal cost is constant, as in this production process, it will always be equal to AVC.

Average fixed cost is given by

$$AFC_Q = \frac{8}{Q}, \tag{10.14}$$

and average total cost is given by

$$ATC_Q = 2 + \frac{8}{Q}, \tag{10.15}$$

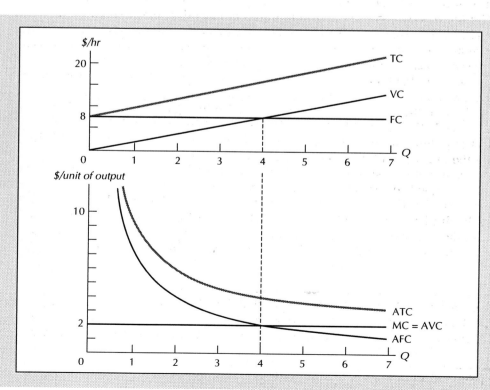

FIGURE 10.7
Cost Curves for a Specific Production Process
For production processes with constant marginal cost, average variable cost and marginal cost are identical. Marginal cost always lies below ATC for such processes.

in this example. The marginal and average cost curves are as shown in the bottom panel in Figure 10.7, where the top panel reproduces the corresponding total, variable, and fixed cost curves.

ALLOCATING PRODUCTION BETWEEN TWO PROCESSES

In Chapter 9, we saw that the problem of allocating a fixed resource between two production activities is solved by the allocation that equates the marginal product of the resource in each. There is a very closely related problem that can be solved with the cost concepts developed in this chapter. Here, the problem is to divide a given production quota between two production processes in such a way as to produce the quota at the lowest possible cost.

Let Q_T be the total amount to be produced, and let Q_1 and Q_2 be the amounts produced in the first and second processes, respectively. And suppose the marginal cost in either process at very low levels of output is lower than the marginal cost at Q_T units of output in the other (which ensures that both processes will be used).[6] *The values of Q_1 and Q_2 that solve this problem will then be the ones that result in equal marginal costs for the two processes.*

To see why, suppose the contrary—that is, suppose that the cost-minimizing allocation resulted in higher marginal costs in one process than in the other. We could then shift one unit of output from the process with the higher marginal cost to the one with the lower. Because the result would be the same total output as before at a lower total cost, the initial division could not have been the cost-minimizing one.

In Chapter 9 we saw that two production processes could have equal marginal products even though their average products differed substantially. Here, too, it is possible for two production processes to have equal marginal costs even though their average costs differ markedly. The cost-minimizing condition does not require average cost levels in the two processes to be the same, and indeed, in practice, they will often take substantially different values.

Suppose production processes A and B give rise to the following marginal and average total cost curves:

EXAMPLE 10.4

$$MC^A = 12Q^A, \qquad ATC^A = 16/Q^A + 6Q^A,$$
$$MC^B = 4Q^B, \qquad ATC^B = 240/Q^B + 2Q^B,$$

where the superscripts denote processes A and B, respectively. What is the least costly way to produce a total of 32 units of output?

The minimum-cost condition is that $MC^A_{Q^A} = MC^B_{Q^B}$, with $Q^A + Q^B = 32$. Equating marginal costs, we have

$$12Q^A = 4Q^B. \tag{10.16}$$

Substituting $Q^B = 32 - Q^A$ into Equation 10.16, we have

$$12Q^A = 128 - 4Q^A, \tag{10.17}$$

---

[6]Suppose the marginal cost at $Q = Q_T$ using production function A were less than the marginal cost at $Q = 0$ for production process B: $MC^A_{Q_T} < MC^B_0$. Then the cheapest way of producing Q_T would be to use only process A.

336   CHAPTER 10   COSTS

FIGURE 10.8
The Minimum-Cost Production Allocation
To produce a given total output at minimum cost, it should be allocated across production activities so that the marginal cost of each activity is the same.

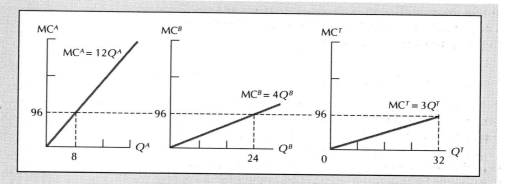

which solves for $Q^A = 8$. $Q^B = 32 - 8 = 24$ takes care of the remaining output, and at these output levels, marginal cost in both plants will be \$96/unit of output (see Figure 10.8). The line $MC^T = 3Q^T$ is the horizontal sum of MC^A and MC^B.[7] We can also see the output that equates marginal cost by summarizing the marginal cost information in a table as below.

Q	MC^A	MC^B	MC^T
0	0	0	0
8	96	32	24
16	192	64	48
24	288	96	72
32	384	128	96

The average total cost values that correspond to this allocation are $ATC^A = \$50$/unit of output and $ATC^B = \$58$/unit of output. From the average total cost curves we can deduce total cost curves in this example (just multiply ATC by Q).[8] They are given by $TC^A = 16 + 6(Q^A)^2$ and $TC^B = 240 + 2(Q^B)^2$. The cost-minimizing allocation results in $TC^A = \$400$ and $TC^B = \$1392$, illustrating that the cost-minimizing allocation does not require equality of total costs either.

EXERCISE 10.3

Same as Example 10.4 except the total output is 12.

THE RELATIONSHIP AMONG MP, AP, MC, AND AVC

In Chapter 9, we saw that the marginal product curve cuts the average product curve at the maximum value of the AP curve. And in this chapter, we saw that the marginal cost curve cuts the average variable cost curve at the minimum value of the AVC curve. There is a direct link between these relationships. To see

[7]MC^T is found by solving $Q^T = Q^A + Q^B = MC/12 + MC/4 = MC/3$ for $MC^T = 3Q^T$.
[8]Note that $MC^A = dTC^A/dQ^A = d[16 + 6(Q^A)^2]/dQ^A = 12Q^A$ and $MC^B = dTC^B/dQ^B = d[240 + 2(Q^B)^2]/dQ^B = 4Q^B$.

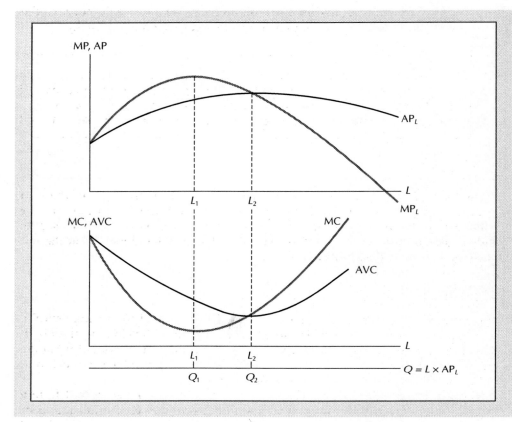

FIGURE 10.9
The Relationship among MP, AP, MC, and AVC
Normally, the MC and AVC curves are plotted with Q on the horizontal axis. In the bottom panel, they are shown as functions of L. The value of Q that corresponds to a given value of L is found by multiplying L times the corresponding value of AP_L. The maximum value of the MP curve, at $L = L_1$, top panel, corresponds to the minimum value of the MC curve, at $Q = Q_1$, bottom panel. Similarly, the maximum value of the AP curve, at $L = L_2$, top panel, corresponds to the minimum value of the AVC curve, at $Q = Q_2$, bottom panel.

the connection, note first that from the definition of marginal cost we have $MC = \Delta VC/\Delta Q$. When labor is the only variable factor, $\Delta VC = \Delta wL$ so that $\Delta VC/\Delta Q$ is equal to $\Delta wL/\Delta Q$. If wage rates are fixed, this is the same as $w\Delta L/\Delta Q$. And since $\Delta L/\Delta Q$ is equal to $1/MP$, it follows that

$$MC = \frac{w}{MP}. \tag{10.18}$$

In similar fashion, note from the definition of average variable cost that $AVC = VC/Q = wL/Q$, and since L/Q is equal to $1/AP$, it follows that

$$AVC = \frac{w}{AP}. \tag{10.19}$$

From Equation 10.18, we see that the minimum value of marginal cost corresponds to the maximum value of MP. Likewise, it follows from Equation 10.19 that the minimum value of AVC corresponds to the maximum value of AP. The top panel in Figure 10.9 plots the AP and MP curves as functions of L. The bottom panel uses Equations 10.18 and 10.19 to plot the corresponding MC and AVC curves as functions of L. (Normally, the MC and AVC curves are plotted as functions of Q. The value of Q that corresponds to a given value of L in the bottom panel may be calculated by multiplying L times the corresponding value of AP_L.) Note that the MP curve in the top panel takes its maximum value at $L = L_1$, and that the minimum value of the MC curve in the bottom panel occurs at the output level (Q_1) that corresponds to $L = L_1$. Note also that the AP curve in the top panel takes its

338   CHAPTER 10   COSTS

maximum value at $L = L_2$, and that the minimum value of the AVC curve in the bottom panel occurs at the output level (Q_2) that corresponds to $L = L_2$.

EXERCISE 10.4

For a production function at a given level of output in the short run, the marginal product of labor is greater than the average product of labor. How will marginal cost at that output level compare with average variable cost?

$MC < AVC$

COSTS IN THE LONG RUN

In the long run all inputs are variable by definition. If the manager of the firm wishes to produce a given level of output at the lowest possible cost and is free to choose any input combination she pleases, which one should she choose? As we will see in the next section, the answer to this question depends on the relative prices of capital and labor.

Choosing the Optimal Input Combination

No matter what the structure of industry may be—monopolistic or atomistically competitive, capitalist or socialist, industrialized or less developed—the objective of most producers is to produce any given level and quality of output at the lowest possible cost. Equivalently, the producer wants to produce as much output as possible from any given expenditure on inputs.

Let us begin with the case of a firm that wants to maximize output from a given level of expenditure. Suppose it uses only two inputs, capital (K) and labor (L), whose prices, measured in dollars per unit of input per day, are $r = 2$ and $w = 4$, respectively. What different combinations of inputs can this firm purchase for a total expenditure of $C = \$200/\text{day}$? Notice that this question has the very same structure as the one we encountered in the theory of consumer behavior in Chapter 3 ("With an income of M, and facing prices of P_X and P_Y, what combinations of X and Y can the consumer buy?"). In the consumer's case, recall, the answer was easily summarized by the budget constraint. The parallel information in the case of the firm is summarized by the **isocost line**, shown in Figure 10.10

isocost line   a set of input bundles each of which costs the same amount.

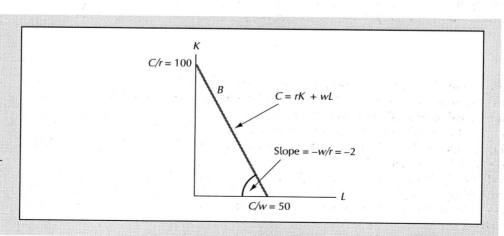

FIGURE 10.10
The Isocost Line
For given input prices ($r = 2$ and $w = 4$ in the diagram), the isocost line is the locus of all possible input bundles that can be purchased for a given level of total expenditure C ($\$200$ in the diagram). The slope of the isocost line is the negative of the input price ratio, $-w/r$.

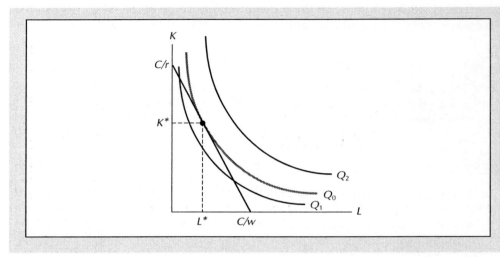

FIGURE 10.11
The Maximum Output for a Given Expenditure
A firm that is trying to produce the largest possible output for an expenditure of C will select the input combination at which the isocost line for C is tangent to an isoquant.

for the example given. Any of the input combinations on the locus labeled B can be purchased for a total expenditure of \$200/day. Analogously to the budget constraint case, the slope of the isocost line is the negative of the ratio of the input prices, $-w/r$.

EXERCISE 10.5

If $w = 3$ and $r = 6$, draw the isocost lines that correspond to total expenditure of \$90 and \$180 per unit of time.

The analytic approach for finding the maximum output that can be produced for a given cost turns out to be very similar to the one for finding the optimal consumption bundle. Just as a given level of satisfaction can be achieved by any of a multitude of possible consumption bundles (all of which lie on the same indifference curve), so too can a given amount of output be produced by any of a host of different input combinations (all of which lie on the same isoquant). In the consumer case, we found the optimum bundle by superimposing the budget constraint onto the indifference map and locating the relevant point of tangency.[9] Here, we superimpose the isocost line onto the isoquant map. In Figure 10.11, the tangency point (L^*, K^*) is the input combination that yields the highest possible output (Q_0) for an expenditure of C.

As noted, the problem of producing the largest output for a given expenditure is solved in essentially the same way as the problem of producing a given level of output for the lowest possible cost. The only difference is that in the latter case we begin with a specific isoquant (the one that corresponds to the level of output we are trying to produce), then superimpose a map of isocost lines, each corresponding to a different cost level. In our first exercise, cost was fixed and output varied; this time, output is fixed and costs vary. As shown in

---

[9]Except, of course, in the case of corner solutions.

340   CHAPTER 10   COSTS

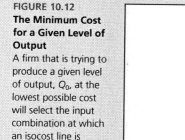

FIGURE 10.12
The Minimum Cost for a Given Level of Output
A firm that is trying to produce a given level of output, Q_0, at the lowest possible cost will select the input combination at which an isocost line is tangent to the Q_0 isoquant.

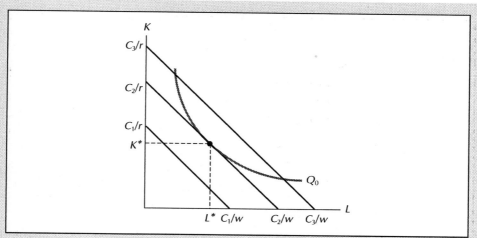

Figure 10.12, the least-cost input bundle (L^*, K^*) corresponds to the point of tangency between an isocost line and the specified isoquant (Q_0).

Recall from Chapter 9 that the slope of the isoquant at any point is equal to $-MP_L/MP_K$, the negative of the ratio of the marginal product of L to the marginal product of K at that point. (Recall also from Chapter 9 that the absolute value of this ratio is called the marginal rate of technical substitution.) Combining this with the result that minimum cost occurs at a point of tangency with the isocost line (whose slope is $-w/r$), it follows that

$$\frac{MP_L^*}{MP_K^*} = \frac{w}{r'} \tag{10.20}$$

where K^* and L^* again denote the minimum-cost values of K and L. Cross-multiplying, we have

$$\frac{MP_L^*}{w} = \frac{MP_K^*}{r}. \tag{10.21}$$

Equation 10.21 has a straightforward economic interpretation. Note first that MP_{L^*} is simply the extra output obtained from an extra unit of L at the cost-minimizing point. w is the cost, in dollars, of an extra unit of L. The ratio MP_{L^*}/w is thus the extra output we get from the last dollar spent on L. Similarly, MP_{K^*}/r is the extra output we get from the last dollar spent on K. In words, Equation 10.21 tells us that when costs are at a minimum, the extra output we get from the last dollar spent on an input must be the same for all inputs.

It is easy to show why, if that were not the case, costs would not be at a minimum. Suppose, for example, that the last units of both labor and capital increased output by 4 units. That is, suppose $MP_L = MP_K = 4$. And again, suppose that $r = \$2$ and $w = \$4$. We would then have gotten only 1 unit of output for the last dollar spent on L, but 2 units for the last dollar spent on K. We could reduce spending on L by a dollar, increase spending on K by only 50 cents, and get the same output level as before, saving 50 cents in the process. Whenever the ratios of marginal products to input prices differ across inputs, it will always

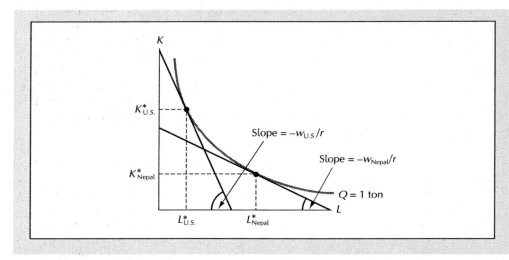

FIGURE 10.13
Different Ways of Producing 1 Ton of Gravel
Countries where labor is cheap relative to capital will select labor-intensive techniques of production. Those where labor is more expensive will employ relatively more capital-intensive techniques.

be possible to make a similar cost-saving substitution in favor of the input with the higher MP/P ratio.[10]

More generally, we may consider a production process that employs not two but N inputs, $X_1, X_2, \ldots, X_N$. In this case, the condition for production at minimum cost is a straightforward generalization of Equation 10.21:

$$\frac{\mathrm{MP}_{X_1}}{P_{X_1}} = \frac{\mathrm{MP}_{X_2}}{P_{X_2}} = \ldots = \frac{\mathrm{MP}_{X_N}}{P_{X_N}} \qquad (10.22)$$

Why is gravel made by hand in Nepal but by machine in the United States?

For simplicity, suppose that only two inputs—capital (K) and labor (L)—are involved in the transformation of rocks into gravel. (In the language of Chapter 9, rocks are an

"intermediate product.") And suppose that any of the input combinations on the isoquant labeled $Q = 1$ ton in Figure 10.13 will yield 1 ton of gravel. Thus, the combination labeled ($L^*_{U.S.}$, $K^*_{U.S.}$) might correspond to the highly capital-intensive technique used in the United States and (L^*_{Nepal}, K^*_{Nepal}) to the highly labor-intensive technique used in Nepal.

The reason the chosen techniques differ between countries is not that the United States is richer, as I had originally thought when I taught in Nepal; rather, it is that the relative prices of labor and capital differ so dramatically in the two countries. In

Why is gravel made by hand in Nepal?

ECONOMIC NATURALIST 10.1

---

[10]Again, this statement is true except in the case of corner solutions.

342   CHAPTER 10 COSTS

Nepal, labor is cheaper than in almost any other nation. While I was living there, I paid 10 cents for a haircut and chiropractic neck adjustment (both administered by the same person). Wages in the United States, by contrast, are among the highest in the world. Construction equipment is traded in world markets and, aside from shipping costs, its price does not differ much from one country to another. If the price of capital, r, is roughly the same in the two countries and the price of labor, w, is much higher in the United States, it follows that the isocost line is much flatter in Nepal. And as shown in Figure 10.13, this fact alone is sufficient to account for the dramatic difference in production techniques.

EXERCISE 10.6

Suppose capital and labor are perfect complements in a one-to-one ratio. That is, suppose that $Q = \min (L, K)$. Currently, the wage is $w = 5$ and the rental rate is $r = 10$. What is the minimum cost and method of producing $Q = 20$ units of output? Suppose the wage rises to $w' = 20$. If we keep total cost the same, what level of output can now be produced and what method of production (input mix) is used?

EXERCISE 10.7

Repeat the previous exercise but now suppose capital and labor are perfect substitutes in a one-to-one ratio: $Q = K + L$.

Why do unions support minimum wage laws so strongly?

ECONOMIC NATURALIST 10.2

American labor unions have historically been among the most outspoken proponents of minimum wage legislation. They favor not only higher levels of the minimum wage, but also broader coverage. Yet almost all members of the Teamsters, AFL-CIO, or United Auto Workers unions already earn substantially more than the minimum wage, and so are not directly affected by changes in the legislation. Why, then, do these unions devote such great effort and expense to lobbying in favor of minimum wages?

One reason might be that their members are genuinely concerned about the economic well-being of workers less fortunate than themselves. No doubt many do feel such concern. But there are other disadvantaged groups—many of them even more deserving of help than low-wage workers—on whose behalf the unions might also have lobbied. Why doesn't the AFL-CIO work just as hard, for example, trying to get extra benefits for homeless children or for the physically handicapped?

An understanding of the condition for production at minimum cost helps answer these questions. Note first that, on the average, union workers tend to be more

Why do union members, who earn substantially more than the minimum wage, favor increasing the minimum wage?

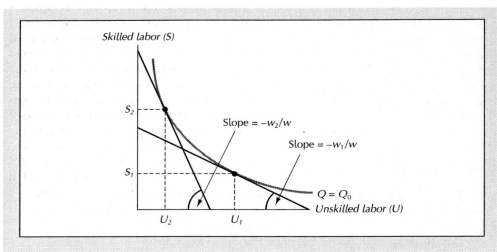

FIGURE 10.14
The Effect of a Minimum Wage Law on Employment of Skilled Labor
Unskilled labor and skilled labor are substitutes for one another in many production processes. When the price of unskilled labor rises, the slope of the isocost line rises, causing many firms to increase their employment of skilled (unionized) labor.

skilled than nonunion workers. Unskilled labor and skilled labor are substitutes for one another in many production processes, giving rise to isoquants shaped something like the one shown in Figure 10.14. What mix of the two skill categories the firm chooses to use will depend strongly on relative prices. Figure 10.14 shows the least costly mix for producing $Q = Q_0$ both before and after the enactment of the minimum wage statute. The wage rate for skilled labor is denoted by w. The prelegislation price of unskilled labor is w_1, which rises to w_2 after enactment of the law. The immediate effect is to increase the absolute value of the slope of the isocost line from w_1/w to w_2/w, causing the firm to increase its employment of skilled labor from S_1 to S_2, simultaneously reducing its employment of unskilled (nonunion) labor from U_1 to U_2.

Although most union workers are not affected directly by the minimum wage laws, these laws have the indirect consequence of increasing the demand for union labor.[11] Even if unions lacked their avowed concern for the well-being of unskilled, largely nonunion workers, there would thus be little mystery why unions devote so much of their resources in support of extensions of minimum wage legislation.

Why would a bathroom equipment manufacturer bake the image of a housefly onto the center of its ceramic urinals?

The substitution of capital for labor is sometimes motivated not by a change in factor prices, but by the introduction of new ideas. Consider, for example, the "official toilet project" initiated by Jos van Bedaf, then head manager of cleaning for the Schiphol airport in Amsterdam.[12] His problem was that the airport men's rooms, which were used by more than 100,000 patrons a year, had a tendency to become messy and smelly despite frequent cleanings. Mr. van Bedaf's solution was not to intensify the efforts of

ECONOMIC NATURALIST 10.3

---

[11]Note that this example assumes that the firm will produce the same level of output after the minimum wage hike as before. As we will see in the next chapter, however, the firm will generally produce less output than before. If the output reduction is large enough, it could offset the firm's switch to skilled labor.

[12]This example is based on Stefan Verhagen, "Fly in the Pot," *Cornell Business*, April 21, 1992.

344   CHAPTER 10 COSTS

How does the image of a housefly reduce airport maintenance costs?

maintenance crews but to make a minor change in the restroom equipment. Specifically, he requested that his sanitation equipment manufacturer supply the airport with urinals with the image of a housefly baked onto the center of each fixture's glazed ceramic surface. His theory was that the presence of this target would cause patrons to be much more accurate in their use of the facilities. The result? Dramatically cleaner facilities and a 20 percent reduction in cleaning costs. A national newspaper in the Netherlands rated the Schiphol facilities first on a list of clean restrooms.

The Relationship between Optimal Input Choice and Long-Run Costs

Given sufficient time to adjust, the firm can always buy the cost-minimizing input bundle that corresponds to any particular output level and relative input prices. To see how the firm's costs vary with output in the long run, we need only compare the costs of the respective optimal input bundles.

output expansion path the locus of tangencies (minimum-cost input combinations) traced out by an isocost line of given slope as it shifts outward into the isoquant map for a production process.

The curve labeled EE in Figure 10.15 shows the firm's **output expansion path.** It is the set of cost-minimizing input bundles when the input price ratio is fixed at w/r. Thus, when the price of K is r and the price of L is w, the cheapest way to produce Q_1 units of output is to use the input bundle S, which contains K_1^* units of K, L_1^* units of L, and costs TC_1. The bundle S is therefore one point on the output expansion path. In like fashion, the output level Q_2 is associated with bundle T, which has a total cost of TC_2, Q_3 is associated with U, which costs TC_3; and so on. In the theory of firm behavior, the long-run expansion path is the analog to the income-consumption curve in the theory of the consumer.

To go from the long-run expansion path to the long-run total cost curve, we simply plot the relevant quantity-cost pairs from Figure 10.15. Thus, the output level Q_1 corresponds to a long-run total cost of TC_1, Q_2 to TC_2, and so on. The result is the curve labeled LTC in the top panel in Figure 10.16. In the long run there is no need to distinguish among total, fixed, and variable costs, since all costs are variable.

The LTC curve will always pass through the origin, because in the long run the firm can liquidate all of its inputs. If the firm elects to produce no output, it need not retain, or pay for, the services of any of its inputs. The shape of the LTC curve shown in the top panel looks very much like that of the short-run total cost curve shown in Figure 10.2. But this need not always be the case, as we will presently see. For the moment, though, let us take the shape of the LTC curve in the top panel in Figure 10.15 as given and ask what it implies for the long-run average and marginal cost curves.

Analogously to the short-run case, long-run marginal cost (LMC) is the slope of the long-run total cost curve:

$$LMC_Q = \frac{\Delta LTC_Q}{\Delta Q} \tag{10.23}$$

In words, LMC is the cost to the firm, in the long run, of expanding its output by 1 unit.

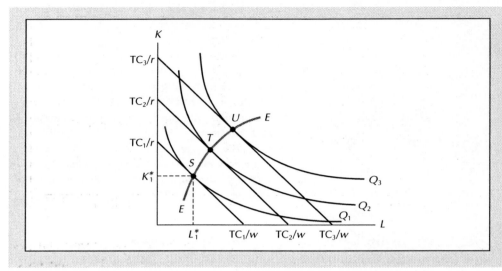

FIGURE 10.15
The Long-Run Expansion Path
With fixed input prices r and w, bundles S, T, U, and others along the locus EE represent the least costly ways of producing the corresponding levels of output.

Long-run average cost (LAC) is the ratio of long-run total cost to output:

$$LAC_Q = \frac{LTC_Q}{Q}. \qquad (10.24)$$

Again, there is no need to discuss the distinctions among average total, fixed, and variable costs, since all long-run costs are variable.

The bottom panel in Figure 10.16 shows the LAC and LMC curves that correspond to the LTC curve shown in the top panel. The slope of the LTC curve is diminishing up to the output level Q_1 and increasing thereafter, which means

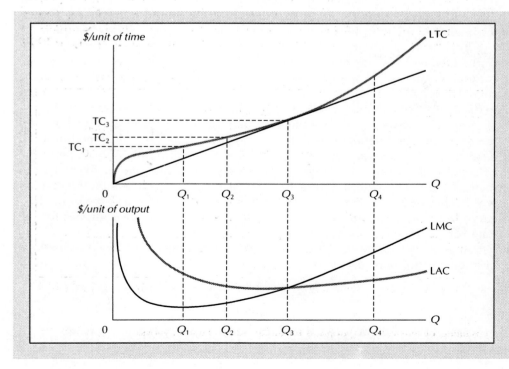

FIGURE 10.16
The Long-Run Total, Average, and Marginal Cost Curves
In the long run, the firm always has the option of ceasing operations and ridding itself of all its inputs. This means that the long-run total cost curve (top panel) will always pass through the origin. The long-run average and long-run marginal cost curves (bottom panel) are derived from the long-run total cost curves in a manner completely analogous to the short-run case.

346   CHAPTER 10   COSTS

FIGURE 10.17
The LTC, LMC, and LAC Curves with Constant Returns to Scale
(a) With constant returns, long-run total cost is strictly proportional to output. (b) Long-run marginal cost is constant and equal to long-run average cost.

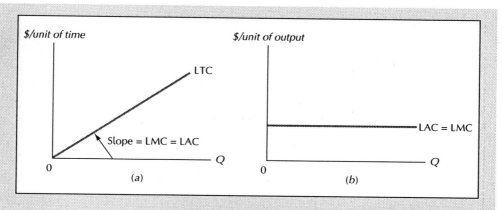

that the LMC curve takes its minimum value at Q_1. The slope of LTC and the slope of the ray to LTC are the same at Q_3, which means that LAC and LMC intersect at that level of output. And again as before, the traditional average-marginal relationship holds: LAC is declining whenever LMC lies below it, and rising whenever LMC lies above it.

For a constant returns to scale production function, doubling output exactly doubles costs.[13] Tripling all inputs triples output and triples costs, and so on. For the case of constant returns to scale, long-run total costs are thus exactly proportional to output. As shown in Figure 10.17a, the LTC curve for a production function with constant returns to scale is a straight line through the origin. Because the slope of LTC is constant, the associated LMC curve is a horizontal line, and is exactly the same as the LAC curve (Figure 10.17b).

When the production function has decreasing returns to scale, a given proportional increase in output requires a greater proportional increase in all inputs and hence a greater proportional increase in costs. The LTC, LMC, and LAC curves for a production function with decreasing returns to scale are shown in Figure 10.18.

FIGURE 10.18
The LTC, LAC, and LMC Curves for a Production Process with Decreasing Returns to Scale
Under decreasing returns, output grows less than in proportion to the growth in inputs, which means that total cost grows more than in proportion to growth in output.

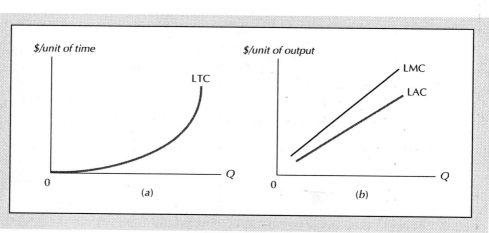

[13]Assuming, of course, that input prices remain the same as output varies.

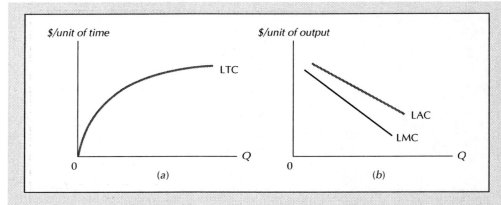

FIGURE 10.19
The LTC, LAC, and LMC Curves for a Production Process with Increasing Returns to Scale
With increasing returns, the large-scale firm has lower average and marginal costs than the smaller-scale firm.

For the particular LTC curve shown in Figure 10.18a, the associated LAC and LMC curves happen to be linear (Figure 10.18b), but this need not always happen. The general property of the decreasing returns case is that it gives rise to an upward-curving LTC curve and upward-sloping LAC and LMC curves. Note yet another application of the average-marginal relationship: the fact that LMC exceeds LAC ensures that LAC must rise with output.

Consider, finally, the case of increasing returns to scale. Here, output grows more than in proportion to the increase in inputs. In consequence, long-run total cost rises less than in proportion to increases in output, as shown in Figure 10.19a. The accompanying LAC and LMC curves are shown in Figure 10.19b. The distinguishing feature of the LAC and LMC curves under increasing returns to scale is not the linear form shown in this particular example, but the fact that they are downward sloping.

The production processes whose long-run cost curves are pictured in Figures 10.17, 10.18, and 10.19 are "pure cases," exhibiting constant, decreasing, and increasing returns to scale, respectively, over their entire ranges of output. As discussed in Chapter 9, however, the degree of returns to scale of a production function need not be the same over the whole range of output.

LONG-RUN COSTS AND THE STRUCTURE OF INDUSTRY

As noted in the preview to this chapter, long-run costs are important because of their effect on the structure of industry. A detailed elaboration of this role will be the subject of the coming chapters. Here, a brief overview of the key issues will help set the stage for that discussion.

When, as in Figure 10.20a, there are declining long-run average costs throughout, the tendency will be for a single firm to serve the market. If two firms attempted to serve such a market, with each producing only part of the total output sold, each would have higher average costs than if one of them alone served the market. The tendency in such a market will be for the firm that happens to grow larger to have a cost advantage that enables it to eliminate its rival. Markets characterized by declining long-run average cost curves are for this reason often referred to as **natural monopolies.**

Consider now the LAC curve shown in Figure 10.20b. The minimum point on this curve occurs at the output level Q_0. At that output level, the firm achieves

natural monopoly an industry whose market output is produced at the lowest cost when production is concentrated in the hands of a single firm.

CHAPTER 10   COSTS

FIGURE 10.20
LAC Curves Characteristic of Highly Concentrated Industrial Structures
(a) LAC curves that slope downward throughout tend to be characteristic of natural monopolies. Unit costs are lowest when only one firm serves the entire market. (b) U-shaped LAC curves whose minimum points occur at a substantial share of total market output are characteristic of markets served by only a small handful of firms.

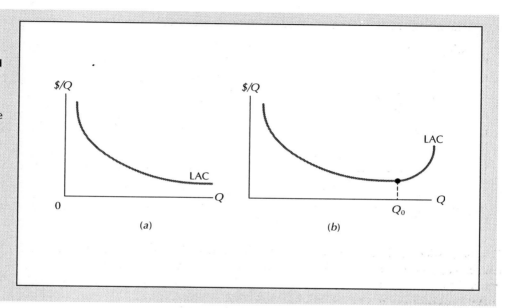

its lowest possible unit cost of production. The output level Q_0 may be called the *minimum efficient scale:* the level of production required for LAC to reach its minimum level. If Q_0 constitutes a substantial share of industry output—more than, say, 20 percent—the industry will tend to be dominated by a small handful of firms. As in the natural monopoly case, a large number of small firms would be unlikely to survive in such a market, since each would have much higher average costs than larger firms. By contrast to the natural monopoly case, however, the upturn in the LAC beyond Q_0 will make it difficult for a single firm to serve the entire market. Markets served by firms with LACs like the one in Figure 10.20b are likely to be "highly concentrated," which means that a small number of firms will tend to account for the lion's share of all output sold.

The long-run average cost curve associated with a market served by many firms is likely to take one of the three forms shown in Figure 10.21. If Q_0, the minimum point on the U-shaped average cost curve in panel *a,* constitutes only a small fraction of total industry output, we expect to see an industry populated by numerous firms, each of which produces only a small percentage of total industry output. Small size is also not a disadvantage when the production process is one that gives rise to a horizontal LAC curve like the one shown in panel *b.* For such processes, all firms—large or small—have the same unit costs of production. For the upward-sloping LAC curve shown in panel *c* in Figure 10.21, small size is not only compatible with survival in the marketplace but positively required, since large firms will always have higher average costs than smaller ones. As a practical matter, however, it is very unlikely that there could ever be an LAC curve that is upward sloping even at extremely small levels of output. (Imagine, for example, the unit costs of a firm that tried to produce $\frac{1}{100}$ of a pound of sugar.)

The relationship between market structure and the shape of the long-run average cost curve derives from the fact that, in the face of competition, market

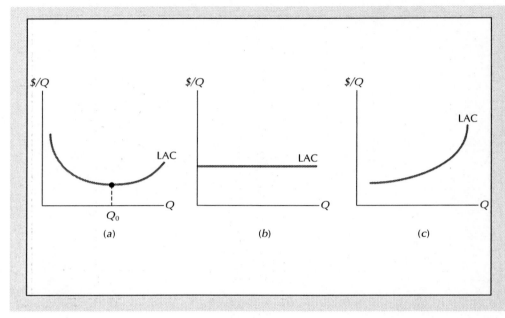

FIGURE 10.21
LAC Curves Characteristic of Unconcentrated Industry Structures
The requirement for survival in any market is that a firm have the lowest possible unit costs. If the minimum point of a U-shaped LAC (Q_0 in panel a) occurs at a small fraction of market output, or if LAC is everywhere flat or rising (panels b and c, respectively), then small size and survival are compatible. Each firm will tend to produce only a small share of total market output.

survival requires firms to have the lowest unit costs possible under existing production technology. Whether that happens at low or high levels of output depends entirely on the shape of the LAC curve.

THE RELATIONSHIP BETWEEN LONG-RUN AND SHORT-RUN COST CURVES

One way of thinking of the LAC curve is as an "envelope" of all the short-run average total cost (ATC) curves. Suppose the ATC curves that correspond to 10,000 different levels of K were drawn in a diagram like Figure 10.22. If we then took a string and molded it to the outer contour of these ATC curves, it would trace out the shape of the LAC curve. In Figure 10.22, note that for the output level at which a given ATC is tangent to the LAC, the long-run marginal cost (LMC) of producing that level of output is the same as the short-run marginal cost (SMC). Thus, $LMC(Q_1) = SMC(Q_1)$, $LMC(Q_2) = SMC(Q_2)$, and $LMC(Q_3) = SMC(Q_3)$ (see footnote 14). Note also that each point along a given ATC curve, except for the tangency point, lies above the corresponding point on the LAC curve. Note, finally, that at the minimum point on the LAC curve in Figure 10.22 ($Q = Q_2$), the long-run and short-run marginal and average costs all take exactly the same value.

Some intuition about the ATC-LAC relationship for a given ATC curve is afforded by noting that to the left of the ATC-LAC tangency, the firm has "too much" capital, with the result that its fixed costs are higher than necessary; and

---

[14]These relationships are developed in greater detail in the Appendix to this chapter.

350   CHAPTER 10   COSTS

FIGURE 10.22

The Family of Cost Curves Associated with a U-Shaped LAC

The LAC curve is the "outer envelope" of the ATC curves. LMC = SMC at the Q value for which the ATC is tangent to the LAC. At the minimum point on the LAC, LMC = SMC = ATC = LAC.

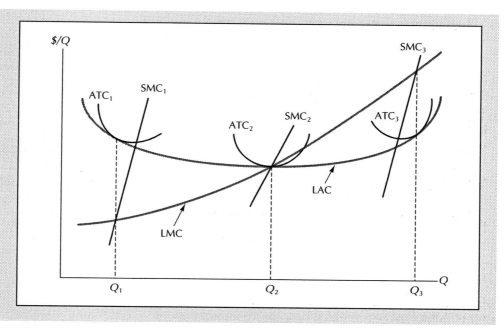

that to the right of the tangency, the firm has "too little" capital, so that diminishing returns to labor drive its costs up. Only at the tangency point does the firm have the optimal quantities of both labor and capital for producing the corresponding level of output.

The Appendix to this chapter considers the relationship between long-run and short-run costs in greater detail. It also develops the calculus approach to cost minimization.

SUMMARY

- Of all the topics covered in an intermediate microeconomics text, students usually find the material on cost curves by far the most difficult to digest. And for good reason, since the sheer volume of specific concepts can easily seem overwhelming at first encounter. It is important to bear in mind, therefore, that all the various cost curves can be derived from the underlying production relationships in a simple and straightforward manner.

- Short-run cost curves, for example, all follow directly from the short-run production function. All short-run production functions we have discussed involved one fixed factor and one variable factor, but the theory would be exactly the same in the case of more than one fixed input. Short-run total costs are decomposed into fixed and variable costs, which

correspond, respectively, to payments to the fixed and variable factors of production. Because of the law of diminishing returns, beyond some point we require ever larger increments of the variable input to produce an extra unit of output. The result is that short-run marginal cost, which is the slope of the short-run total cost curve, is increasing with output in the region of diminishing returns. Diminishing returns are also responsible for the fact that short-run average total and variable cost curves—which are, respectively, the slopes of the rays to the short-run total and variable cost curves—eventually rise with output. Average fixed costs always take the form of a rectangular hyperbola, approaching infinity as output shrinks toward zero, and falling toward zero as output grows increasingly large.

* The problem of allocating a given production quota to two different production facilities is similar to the problem of allocating an available input across two different facilities. In the latter case, the goal is to maximize the amount of output that can be produced with a given amount of input. In the former, it is to produce a given level of output at the lowest total cost. The solution is to allocate the production quota so that the marginal cost is the same in each production process. This solution does not require that average costs be the same in each process, and in practice, they often differ substantially.

* The optimal input bundle for producing a given output level in the long run will depend on the relative prices of the factors of production. These relative prices determine the slope of the isocost line, which is the locus of input bundles that can be purchased for a given total cost. The optimal input bundle will be the one that lies at the point of tangency between an isocost line and the desired isoquant. At the cost-minimizing point, the ratio of the marginal product of an input to its price will be the same for every input. Put another way, the extra output obtained from the last dollar spent on one input must be the same as the extra output obtained from the last dollar spent on any other input. Still another way of stating the minimum-cost condition is that the marginal rate of technical substitution at the optimizing bundle must be the same as the slope of the isocost line.

* These properties of production at minimum cost help us understand why methods of production often differ sharply when relative factor prices differ sharply. We saw, for example, that it helps explain why developing countries often use labor-intensive techniques while their industrial counterparts choose much more capital-intensive ones, and why labor unions often lobby on behalf of increased minimum wages, even though virtually all of their members earn more than the minimum wage to begin with.

* For a given level of output, long-run total costs can never be larger than short-run total costs for the simple reason that we have the opportunity to adjust all of our inputs in the long run, only some of them in the short run. The slope of the long-run average cost curve is a direct reflection of the degree of returns to scale in production. When there are increasing returns, LAC declines with output. With decreasing returns, by contrast, LAC rises with output. And finally, constant returns in production give rise to a horizontal LAC. A U-shaped LAC is one that corresponds to a production process that exhibits first increasing, then constant, and finally decreasing returns to scale. No matter what its shape, the LAC curve will always be an envelope of the corresponding family of ATC curves, each of which will be tangent to the LAC at one and only one point. At the output levels that correspond to these points of tangency, LMC and the corresponding SMC will be the same.

* The relationship between market structure and long-run costs derives from the fact that survival in the marketplace requires firms to have the lowest costs possible with available production technologies. If the LAC curve is downward sloping, lowest costs occur when only one firm serves the market. If the LAC curve is U-shaped and its minimum point occurs at a quantity that corresponds to a substantial share of total market output, the lowest costs will occur when only a few firms serve the market. By contrast, if the minimum point on a U-shaped LAC curve corresponds to only a small fraction of total industry output, the market is likely to be served by many competing firms. The same will be true when the LAC curve is either horizontal or upward sloping.

QUESTIONS FOR REVIEW

1. What is the relationship between the law of diminishing returns and the curvature of the variable cost curve?

2. What is the relationship between the law of diminishing returns and the slope of the short-run marginal cost curve?

3. In which production process is fixed cost likely to be a larger percentage of short-run total costs, book publishing or landscape gardening?

4. Why does the short-run MC curve cut both the ATC and AVC curves at their minimum points?

5. If the LAC curve is rising beyond some point, what can we say about the degree of returns to scale in production?

6. Why should the production of a fixed amount of output be allocated between two production activities so that the marginal cost is the same in each?

352   CHAPTER 10   COSTS

PROBLEMS

1. The Preservation Embalming Company's cost data have been partially entered in the table below. Following the sudden and unexpected death of the company's accountant, you are called on to fill in the missing entries.

Bodies embalmed	Total cost	Fixed cost	Variable cost	ATC	AVC	AFC	MC
0	24	24	0	–	–	–	
							16
1	40	24	16				
							34
2	74	24	50				
							34
3	108	24	84				
							52
4	160	24	136				
							60
5	220	24	196		39.2		
							42
6	262	24	238		47		

2. Sketch the short-run TC, VC, FC, ATC, AVC, AFC, and MC curves for the production function

$$Q = 3KL,$$

where K is fixed at 2 units in the short run, with $r = 3$ and $w = 2$. *[handwritten: Q = 6L]*

3. When the average product of labor is the same as the marginal product of labor, how will marginal cost compare with average variable cost? *[handwritten: Same]*

4. A firm has access to two production processes with the following marginal cost curves: $MC_1 = 0.4Q$ and $MC_2 = 2 + 0.2Q$. *[handwritten: Q_1 = 6, Q_2 = 2]*
   a. If it wants to produce 8 units of output, how much should it produce with each process? *[handwritten: MC is same, min 2.4]*
   b. If it wants to produce 4 units of output? *[handwritten: MC = 1.6]*

5. A firm uses two inputs, K and L, in its production process and finds that no matter how much output it produces or how input prices vary, it always minimizes its costs by buying only one or the other of the two inputs. Draw this firm's isoquant map.

6. A firm finds that no matter how much output it produces and no matter how input prices vary, it always minimizes its costs by buying half as many units of capital as of labor. Draw this firm's isoquant map.

7. A firm purchases capital and labor in competitive markets at prices of $r = 6$ and $w = 4$, respectively. With the firm's current input mix, the marginal product of capital is 12 and the marginal product of labor is 18. Is this firm minimizing its costs? If so, explain how you know. If not, explain what the firm ought to do. *[handwritten: $\frac{MP_K}{P_K} = \frac{MP_L}{P_L}$; less capital, more labor]*

8. A firm has a production function $Q = F(K, L)$ with constant returns to scale. Input prices are $r = 2$ and $w = 1$. The output-expansion path for this production function at these input prices is a straight line through the origin. When it produces 5 units of output, it uses 2 units of K and 3 units of L. How much K and L will it use when its long-run total cost is equal to 70?

9. A firm with the production function $Q = F(K, L)$ is producing an output level Q^* at minimum cost in the long run. How will its short-run marginal cost when K is fixed compare with its short-run marginal cost when L is fixed?

10. A firm employs a production function $Q = F(K, L)$ for which only two values of K are possible, K_1 and K_2. Its ATC curve when $K = K_1$ is given by $ATC_1 = Q^2 - 4Q + 6$. The corresponding curve for $K = K_2$ is $ATC_2 = Q^2 - 8Q + 18$. What is this firm's LAC curve?

11. If a firm's LMC curve lies above its SMC curve at a given level of output, what will be the relationship between its ATC and LAC curves at that output level?

*12. A firm has a long-run total cost function:

$$LRTC(Q) = Q^3 - 20Q^2 + 220Q.$$

Derive expressions for long-run average cost and marginal cost, and sketch these curves.

*13. For the long-run total cost function

$$LRTC(Q) = Q^2 + 10,$$

sketch ATC, AVC, AFC, and MC.

ANSWERS TO IN-CHAPTER EXERCISES

10.1. The variable cost curve is the same as before; the FC and TC curves are shifted upward by 8 units. (See the following graph.)

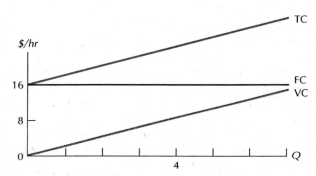

10.2. The vertical distance between the ATC and AVC curves is AFC. So we have $ATC_{10} - AVC_{10} = FC/10 = 20/10 = 2$.

10.3. Equating marginal costs, we have $12Q^A = 4Q^B$. Substituting $Q^B = 12 - Q^A$ yields $12Q^A = 48 - 4Q^A$, which solves for $Q^A = 3$. $Q^B = 12 - 3 = 9$ takes care of remaining output, and at these output levels, marginal cost in both plants will be \$36/unit of output.

10.4. When marginal product lies above average product, marginal cost lies below average variable cost. (See Figure 10.9.)

10.5.

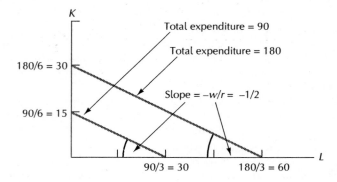

---

*These problems are most easily solved using the calculus definition of marginal cost.

354   CHAPTER 10   COSTS

10.6. To produce 20 units of output, we will need $L = K = 20$. As $r = 10$ and $w = 5$, costs are

$$C = 10K + 5L = 200 + 100 = 300,$$

which may be rewritten as $K = 30 - \frac{1}{2}L$ in slope-intercept form. When the wage rises to $w = 20$, keeping costs at $C = 300$ requires that we find the point at which $K = L$ on the new isocost curve

$$C = 10K + 20L = 300,$$

which may be rewritten as $K = 30 - 2L$ in slope-intercept form. Setting $K = L$, we have

$$10K + 20L = 300 = 10L + 20L = 300 = 30L = 300, \text{ so } L = 10.$$

Thus, $L = K = 10$ and we produce $Q = 10$.

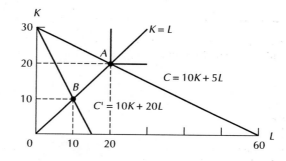

10.7. To produce 20 units of output, we will need $L = 20$ or $K = 20$. Since $r = 10$ and $w = 5$, costs are

$$C = \min\{10K, 5L\} = \min\{200, 100\} = 100.$$

When the wage rises to $w = 20$, keeping costs at $C = 100$ implies that

$$Q = \max\left\{\frac{100}{r}, \frac{100}{w}\right\} = \max\{10, 5\} = 10.$$

Thus, we use no labor ($L = 0$), all capital ($K = 10$), and produce $Q = 10$.

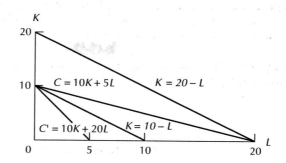

APPENDIX

10

MATHEMATICAL EXTENSIONS OF THE THEORY OF COSTS

THE RELATIONSHIP BETWEEN LONG-RUN AND SHORT-RUN COST CURVES

Let us consider first in greater detail the relationship between long- and short-run total costs. Recall that the LTC curve is generated by plotting the Q value for a given isoquant against the corresponding total cost level for the isocost line tangent to that isoquant. Thus, for example, in Figure A.10.1, $Q = 1$ is associated with a long-run total cost of LTC_1, $Q = 2$ with LTC_2, and so on.

When K is variable, as it and all other factors are in the long run, the expansion path is given by the line $0E$. Now suppose, however, that K is fixed at K_2^*, the level that is optimal for the production of $Q = 2$. The short-run expansion path will then be the horizontal line through the point $(0, K_2^*)$, which includes the input bundles X, T, and Z. The short-run total cost of producing a given level of output—say, $Q = 1$—is simply the total cost associated with the isocost line that passes through the intersection of the short-run expansion path and the $Q = 1$ isoquant (point X in Figure A.10.1), namely, STC_1.

Note in Figure A.10.1 that short- and long-run total costs take the same value for $Q = 2$, the output level for which the short- and long-run expansion paths cross. For all other output levels, the isocost line that passes through the intersection of the corresponding isoquant and the short-run expansion path will lie above the isocost line that is tangent to the isoquant. Thus, for all output levels other than $Q = 2$, short-run total cost will be higher than long-run total cost.

The short- and long-run total cost curves that correspond to the isoquant map of Figure A.10.1 are shown in Figure A.10.2. Note in Figure A.10.1 that the closer output is to $Q = 2$, the smaller the difference will be between long-run

356   CHAPTER 10 APPENDIX   MATHEMATICAL EXTENSIONS OF THE THEORY OF COSTS

FIGURE A.10.1
The Short-Run and Long-Run Expansion Paths
The long-run expansion path is the line of OE. With K fixed at K_2^*, the short-run expansion path is a horizontal line through the point $(0, K_2^*)$. Because K_2^* is the optimal amount of K for producing 2 units of output, the long-run and short-run expansion paths intersect at T. The short-run total cost of producing a given level of output is the cost associated with the isocost line that passes through the intersection of the relevant isoquant and the short-run expansion path. Thus, for example, STC_3 is the short-run total cost of producing 3 units of output.

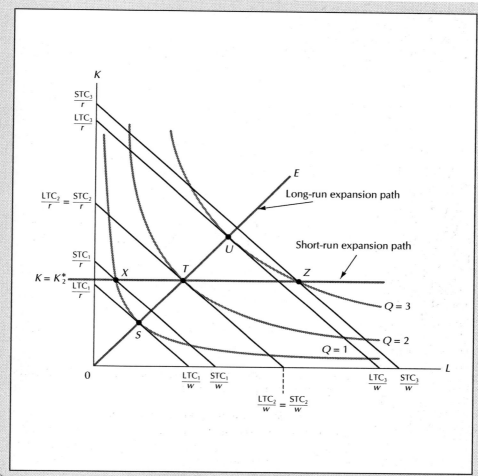

FIGURE A.10.2
ThE LTC and STC Curves Associated with the Isoquant Map in Figure A.10.1
As Q approaches 2, the level of output for which the fixed factor is at its optimal level, STC_Q approaches LTC_Q. The two curves are tangent at $Q = 2$.

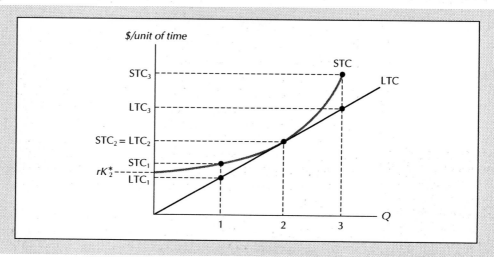

THE RELATIONSHIP BETWEEN LONG-RUN AND SHORT-RUN COST CURVES   357

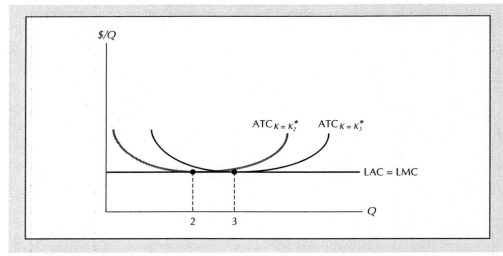

FIGURE A.10.3
The LAC, LMC, and Two ATC Curves Associated with the Cost Curves from Figure A.10.2
Short-run average cost is tangent to long-run average cost at the same output level for which the corresponding LTC and STC curves are tangent.

and short-run total cost. This property is reflected in Figure A.10.2 by the fact that the STC curve is tangent to the LTC curve at $Q = 2$: The closer Q is to 2, the closer STC_Q is to STC_2. Note also in Figure A.10.2 that the STC curve intersects the vertical axis at rK_2^*, the fixed cost associated with K_2^* units of K.

The production process whose isoquant map is shown in Figure A.10.1 happens to be one with constant returns to scale. Accordingly, its long-run average and marginal cost curves will be the same horizontal line. The position of this line is determined by the slope of the LTC curve in Figure A.10.2. The associated ATC curve will be U-shaped and tangent to the LAC curve at $Q = 2$, as shown in Figure A.10.3.

There are short-run cost curves not just for $K = K_2^*$, but for every other level of the fixed input as well. For example, the short-run average cost curve when K is fixed at K_3^* (the optimal amount of K for producing $Q = 3$) is shown in Figure A.10.3 as the curve labeled $ATC_{K=K_3^*}$. Like the ATC curve associated with K_2^*, it too is U-shaped, and is tangent to the LAC curve at $Q = 3$. The ATC curves will in general be U-shaped and tangent to the LAC curve at the output level for which the level of the fixed input happens to be optimal.

A similar relationship exists in the case of production processes that give rise to U-shaped LAC curves. For such a process, the LAC curve and three of its associated ATC curves are shown in Figure A.10.4. When the LAC curve is U-shaped, note that the tangencies between it and the associated ATC curves do not in general occur at the minimum points on the ATC curves. The lone exception is the ATC curve that is tangent to the minimum point of the U-shaped LAC (ATC_2 in Figure A.10.4). On the downward-sloping portion of the LAC curve, the tangencies will lie to the left of the minimum points of the corresponding ATC curves; and on the upward-sloping portion of the LAC curve, the tangencies will lie to the right of the minimum points.

In the text, we noted that one way of thinking of the LAC curve is as an "envelope" of all the ATC curves, like the one shown in Figure A.10.4. At the output level at which a given ATC is tangent to the LAC, the long-run marginal cost (LMC) of producing that level of output is the same as the short-run marginal cost (SMC). To see why this is so, recall that the tangency point represents

358   CHAPTER 10 APPENDIX   MATHEMATICAL EXTENSIONS OF THE THEORY OF COSTS

FIGURE A.10.4
The Family of Cost Curves Associated with a U-Shaped LAC
The LAC curve is the "outer envelope" of the ATC curves, LMC = SMC at the Q value for which the ATC is tangent to the LAC. At the minimum point on the LAC, LMC = SMC = ATC = LAC.

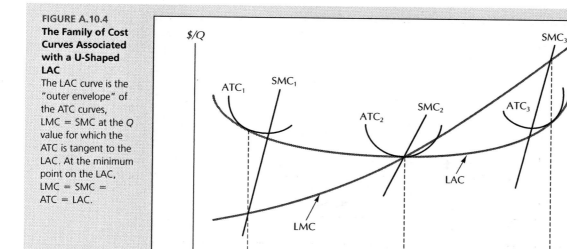

the quantity level that is optimal for the fixed factor level that corresponds to the particular ATC curve. If we change output by a very small amount in the short run—by either increasing or reducing the amount of the variable input—we will end up with an input mix that is only marginally different from the optimal one, and whose cost is therefore approximately the same as that of the optimal mix. Accordingly, for output levels very near the relevant tangency point, SMC and LMC are approximately the same.

Note also in Figure A.10.4 that the SMC curves are always steeper than the LMC curve. The reason is implicit in our discussion of why LMC and SMC are nearly the same in a neighborhood of the tangency points. Starting at a tangency point—say, at Q_1 in Figure A.10.4—suppose we want to produce an extra unit of output in the short run. To do so, we will have to move from an input mix that is optimal to one that contains slightly more L and slightly less K than would be optimal for producing $Q_1 + 1$ in the long run. So the cost of that extra unit will be higher in the short run than in the long run, which is another way of saying $SMC_{Q_1+1} > LMC_{Q_1+1}$.

Now suppose that we start at Q_1 and want to produce 1 unit of output less than before. To do so, we will have to move to an input bundle that contains less L and more K than would be optimal for producing $Q_1 - 1$. In consequence, our cost savings will be smaller in the short run than they would be in the long run, when we are free to adjust both L and K. This tells us that $LMC_{Q_1-1} > SMC_{Q_1+1}$. To say that LMC exceeds SMC whenever output is less than Q_1, but is less than SMC when output is greater than Q_1, is the same thing as saying that the LMC curve is less steep than the SMC curve at Q_1.

EXERCISE A.10.1

Consider a production function $Q = F(K, L)$ for which only two values of K are possible. These two values of K give rise to the ATC curves shown in the diagram. What is the LAC curve for this firm?

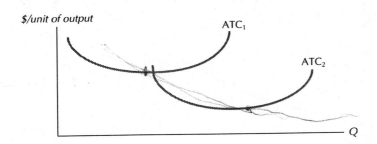

THE CALCULUS APPROACH TO COST MINIMIZATION

Using the Lagrangian technique discussed in the Appendix to Chapter 3, we can show that the equality of MP/P ratios (Equation 10.22 on p. 341) emerges as a necessary condition for the following cost-minimization problem:

$$\min_{K, L} P_K K + P_L L \qquad \text{subject to } F(K, L) = Q_0. \qquad (A.10.1)$$

To find the values of K and L that minimize costs, we first form the Lagrangian expression:

$$\pounds = P_K K + P_L L + \lambda[F(K, L) - Q_0]. \qquad (A.10.2)$$

The first-order conditions for a minimum are given by

$$\frac{\partial \pounds}{\partial K} = P_K + \frac{\lambda \partial F}{\partial K} = 0, \qquad (A.10.3)$$

$$\frac{\partial \pounds}{\partial L} = P_L + \frac{\lambda \partial F}{\partial L} = 0, \qquad (A.10.4)$$

and

$$\frac{\partial \pounds}{\partial \lambda} = F(K, L) - Q_0 = 0. \qquad (A.10.5)$$

Dividing Equation A.10.3 by Equation A.10.4 and rearranging terms, we have

$$\frac{\partial F/\partial K}{P_K} = \frac{\partial F/\partial L}{P_L}, \qquad (A.10.6)$$

which is the result of Equation 10.21 in Chapter 10. (As an exercise, derive the same result by finding the first-order conditions for a maximum level of output subject to a cost limit of C.)

An alternative to the Lagrangian technique is to solve the production function constraint in Equation A.10.1 for K in terms of L, then substitute the result back into the expression for total cost. To illustrate this alternative approach, consider the following example.

EXAMPLE A10.1

For the production function $Q = F(K, L) = \sqrt{K}\sqrt{L}$ with $P_K = 4$ and $P_L = 2$, find the values of K and L that minimize the cost of producing 2 units of output.

Our problem here is to minimize $4K + 2L$ subject to $F(K, L) = \sqrt{K}\sqrt{L} = 2$. Here the production function constraint is $Q = 2 = \sqrt{K}\sqrt{L}$, which yields $K = 4/L$. So our problem is to minimize $4(4/L) + 2L$ with respect to L. The first-order condition for a minimum is given by

$$\frac{d[(16/L) + 2L]}{dL} = 2 - \frac{16}{L^2} = 0,$$

(A.10.7)

which yields $L = 2\sqrt{2}$. Substituting back into the production function constraint, we have $K = 4/(2\sqrt{2}) = \sqrt{2}$.

PROBLEMS

1. A firm produces output with the production function
   $$Q = \sqrt{K}\sqrt{L},$$
   where K and L denote its capital and labor inputs, respectively. If the price of labor is 1 and the price of capital is 4, what quantities of capital and labor should it employ if its goal is to produce 2 units of output?

2. Sketch LTC, LAC, and LMC curves for the production function given in Problem 2. Does this production function have constant, increasing, or decreasing returns to scale?

3. Suppose that a firm has the following production function:
   $$Q(K, L) = 2L\sqrt{K}.$$
   a. If the price of labor is 2 and the price of capital is 4, what is the optimal ratio of capital to labor?
   b. For an output level of $Q = 1000$, how much of each input will be used?

4. A firm with the production function
   $$Q(K, L) = 2L\sqrt{KL}$$
   is currently utilizing 8 units of labor and 2 units of capital. If this is the optimal input mix, and if total costs are equal to 16, what are the prices of capital and labor?

5. For a firm with the production function
   $$Q(K, L) = 3 \ln K + 2 \ln L,$$
   find the optimal ratio of capital to labor if the price of capital is 4 and the price of labor is 6.

ANSWER TO IN-APPENDIX EXERCISE

A.10.1.   The LAC curve (bottom panel) is the outer envelope of the two ATC curves (top panel).

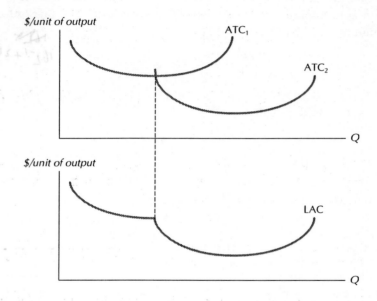

CHAPTER

11

PERFECT COMPETITION

I magine yourself a member of the Colorado state legislature. You have been asked to vote for a bill whose purpose is to alleviate poverty among farmers in a rural county. Farmers in that county rent their farmland from landowners and are allowed to keep the proceeds from the sale of the crops they grow. Because of limited rainfall, their crops are usually meager, resulting in very low incomes for the average worker. The bill under consideration would authorize public funds to construct an irrigation system that would double the crop yields on the land in the county.

You strongly favor the objective of the bill and are about to vote in favor of it when you meet with your legislative aide, an intern who majored in economics in college. She urges you in the strongest possible terms not to vote for the bill. She concedes that the project would double crop yields, and she too is sympathetic to the goal of providing improved conditions for farmers. Even so, she insists that the bill would have little or no long-run effect on the earnings of farmers. Your aide has given you sound advice on similar matters in the past, and you decide to hear her out.

CHAPTER PREVIEW

In this chapter we will develop the analytical tools necessary for our hypothetical state legislator to assess his aide's advice, including a model of price and output determination in perfectly competitive markets. Our first step will be to characterize the competitive firm's objective as that of earning the highest possible profit. This is clearly not the only goal a firm might pursue, but we will see several reasons why firms might often behave as if profit were all they cared about.

We will then consider the four conditions that define a perfectly competitive market: (1) the existence of a standardized product, (2) price-taking behavior on the part of firms, (3) perfect long-run mobility of factors of production, and (4) perfect information on the part of consumers and firms. It turns out that none of these conditions is likely to be satisfied in practice for any industry. Nonetheless, we will see that the economic model of perfect competition often generates useful insights even when its structural preconditions are only approximately satisfied.

Next, using the cost curves discussed in Chapter 10, we will derive the necessary condition for profit maximization in the short run. The rule calls for the firm to produce an output level at which its short-run marginal cost is equal to the price of the product. We will see that implementation of this rule fortunately does not require that firms have a detailed understanding of the economist's concept of marginal cost.

From the individual firm's supply decision, we will move to the issue of industrywide supply. The technique for generating the industry supply schedule turns out to be closely analogous to the one for aggregating individual demand curves into a market demand curve: we simply add the individual firms' supply curves horizontally.

The industry short-run supply and demand curves interact to determine the short-run market price, which forms the basis for output decisions by individual firms. We will see that a firm's short-run profitability acts as a signal governing the movement of resources into and out of the industry—more specifically, that profits prompt resources to enter while losses prompt them to leave.

We will see that in the long run, if tastes and technology are unchanging, a competitive industry whose firms have U-shaped LAC curves will settle at an equilibrium price equal to the minimum value of the LAC curve. And we will also see that, under certain conditions, it will not be possible in such a market for anyone to enter into additional transactions that would benefit some people without at the same time harming some others.

THE GOAL OF PROFIT MAXIMIZATION

In studying not only perfect competition but also a variety of other market structures, economists traditionally assume that the firm's central objective is to maximize profit. Two things must be said about this assumption. The first is to clarify just what is meant by the term "profit," and the second is to explain why it often makes sense to assume that firms try to maximize it.

Profit—or, more precisely, *economic profit*—is defined as the difference between total revenue and total cost, where total cost includes all costs—both explicit and implicit—associated with resources used by the firm. This definition is significantly different from the one used by accountants and many other noneconomists, which does not subtract opportunity or implicit costs from total revenue. *Accounting profit* is simply total revenue less all explicit costs incurred.

To illustrate the distinction, suppose a firm produces 100 units of output per week by using 10 units of capital and 10 units of labor. Suppose the weekly price of each factor is $10/unit, and the firm owns its 10 units of capital. If output sells for $2.50/unit, the firm's total revenue will be $250/wk. To calculate the week's economic profit, we subtract from $250 the $100 spent on labor (an explicit cost) and the $100 opportunity cost of capital (an implicit cost), which leaves $50. (Under the assumption that the firm could have rented its capital to some other firm at the weekly rate of $10/unit, the $100 opportunity cost is simply the earnings forgone by using the capital in its own operation.) The week's accounting profit for this firm, by contrast, is $150, the difference between the $250 total revenue and the $100 out-of-pocket expenditure for labor.

Accounting profit may be thought of as the sum of two components: (1) *normal profit*, which is the opportunity cost of the resources owned by the firm (in this example, $100), and (2) economic profit, as defined above (here, $50). Economic profit is profit over and above the normal profit level.

The importance of the distinction between accounting and economic profits is driven home forcefully—if a bit fancifully—by the following example.

Cullen Gates runs a miniature golf course in Valdosta, Georgia. He rents the course and equipment from a large recreational supply company and supplies his own labor. His monthly earnings, net of rental payments, are $800, and he considers working at the golf course just as attractive as his only other alternative, working as a grocery clerk for $800/mo.

Now Cullen learns that his Uncle Bill has given him some land in New York City (the parcel bounded by the streets shown in Figure 11.1). The land has been cleared, and Cullen discovers that a construction company is willing to install and maintain a miniature golf course on it for a payment of $4000/mo. Cullen also commissions a market survey, which reveals that he would collect $16,000/mo in revenue by operating a miniature golf course there. (After all, there are many more potential golfers in Manhattan than in Valdosta.) After deducting the $4000/mo payment to the construction company, this would leave him with $12,000/mo free and clear. Given these figures, and assuming that the cost of living is the same in New York as in Valdosta, should Cullen, a profit maximizer, switch his operation to Manhattan?

EXAMPLE 11.1

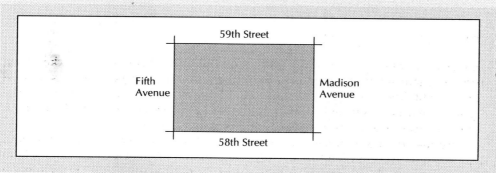

FIGURE 11.1 Potential Site for a Manhattan Miniature Golf Course

CHAPTER 11   PERFECT COMPETITION

Since he is a profit maximizer, he should switch to Manhattan only if his economic profit there will be higher than in Valdosta. Suppose, however, that Cullen is unfamiliar with the concept of economic profit and instead compares his accounting profits in the two locations. In Valdosta, his accounting profit is $800/mo, the amount he has left over after paying all his bills. In Manhattan, the corresponding figure will be $12,000/mo. On this comparison, he would quickly forsake Valdosta for New York.

If he compares economic profits, however, he will reach precisely the opposite conclusion. In Valdosta, his economic profit is zero once we account for the opportunity cost of his labor. (He could have earned $800/mo as a grocery clerk, exactly the amount of his accounting profit.) To calculate what his economic profits would be in New York, we must deduct from his $12,000/mo accounting profits not only the $800 monthly opportunity cost of his labor, but also the opportunity cost of his land. Few locations on earth command higher land prices than midtown Manhattan. Suppose we conservatively estimate that Cullen's land would sell for $100,000,000 in today's real estate market, and suppose that the interest rate is 1 percent/mo. The opportunity cost of devoting the land to a miniature golf course will then be $(0.01) \times (\$100,000,000) = \$1,000,000/mo$, which makes his monthly economic profit in Manhattan equal to $\$12,000 - \$800 - \$1,000,000 = -\$988,800$. Thus, if we assign any reasonable value to the opportunity cost of his land, it will obviously be better for Cullen to sell or rent it to someone else and remain in Valdosta. The reason Manhattan real estate is so expensive is that people can build skyscrapers on it and charge high rents to a multitude of tenants. To build a miniature golf course in midtown Manhattan would be like wearing diamonds on the soles of your shoes.

EXERCISE 11.1

In Example 11.1, how low would the monthly interest rate have to be before Cullen should relocate to Manhattan?

Let's turn now to the assumption of profit maximization. To predict what any entity—a firm, person, committee, or government—will do under specific conditions, some sort of assumption must be made about its goals. After all, if we know where people want to go, it's much easier to predict what they'll do to get there. Economists assume that the goal of firms is to maximize economic profit; then they try to discover what specific behaviors contribute to that objective.

Numerous challenges have been raised to the profit-maximization assumption. Some critics say the firm's goal is to maximize its chances of survival; others believe that it wants to maximize total sales or total revenues; and some even claim that firms don't try to maximize anything at all.

One reason for such skepticism is that examples abound in which the managers of firms appear incompetent and too poorly informed to take the kinds of actions required for maximizing profit. It is important to understand, however, that the assumption of profit maximization is not refuted by the existence of incompetent managers. On the contrary, a case can be made that, even in a world in which the actions of firms are initially random, there will be a long-run tendency for profit-maximizing behavior eventually to dominate.[1]

The argument is directly analogous to Charles Darwin's theory of evolution by natural selection, and it goes roughly as follows. First, in a world of random action, some firms will, purely by chance, come much closer than others to profit-maximizing behavior. The result will be that the former firms will have greater surplus revenues at their disposal, which will enable them to grow faster than their rivals. The other side of this coin is that firms whose behavior deviates most sharply from profit maximization are the ones most likely to go bankrupt. In the animal kingdom, food is an essential resource for survival, and profit plays a parallel role in the competitive marketplace. Those firms with the highest profits are often considerably more likely to survive. The evolutionary argument concludes that, over long periods of time, behavior will tend toward profit maximization purely as a result of selection pressures in the competitive environment.

But the forces in support of profit maximization are not limited to the unintentional pressures of natural selection. They also include the actions of people who are very consciously pursuing their own interests. Bankers and other moneylenders, for example, are eager to keep their risks to a minimum, and for this reason, they prefer to do business with highly profitable firms. In addition to having more internal resources, such firms thus have easier access to external sources of capital to finance their growth. Another important force supporting profit-maximizing behavior is the threat of an outside takeover. The price of shares of stock in a firm is based on the firm's profitability (more on this point in Chapter 15), with the result that shares of stock of a non-profit-maximizing firm will often sell for much less than their potential value. This creates an opportunity for an outsider to buy the stock at a bargain price and then drive its price upward by altering the firm's behavior.

Another pressure in favor of profit maximization is that the owners of many firms compensate their managers in part by giving them a share of the firm's profits. This provides a clear financial incentive for managers to enhance profitability whenever opportunities arise for them to do so.

Let us note, finally, that the assumption of profit maximization does not imply that firms conduct their operations in the most efficient conceivable manner at all times. In the world we live in there are not only many intelligent, competent managers, but also a multitude who possess neither of these attributes. Needless to say, not every task can be assigned to the most competent person in the universe. In a sensible world, the most important tasks will be carried out by the best managers, the less important tasks by less competent ones. So the mere fact that we often observe firms doing silly things does not establish that they are not maximizing profits. To maximize profits means simply to do the best one can under the circumstances, and that will sometimes mean having to muddle along with uninspired managers.

Taken as a whole, the foregoing observations lend support to the assumption of profit maximization. We might even say that they place the burden of proof on those who insist that firms do not maximize profits. But they obviously

---

[1]See, for example, Armen Alchian, "Uncertainty, Evolution, and Economic Theory," *Journal of Political Economy*, 1950.

do not establish conclusively that firms always pursue profit at the expense of all other goals. This remains an empirical question, and in the chapters to come we will see some evidence that firms sometimes fall short. Even so, the assumption of profit maximization is a good place to begin our analysis of firm behavior, and there is no question but that it provides useful insights into how firms respond to changes in input or product prices, taxes, and other important features of their operating environments.

THE FOUR CONDITIONS FOR PERFECT COMPETITION

To predict how much output a competitive firm will produce, economists have developed the *theory of perfect competition.* Four conditions define the existence of a perfectly competitive market. Let us consider each of them in turn.

1. Firms Sell a Standardized Product In a perfectly competitive market, the product sold by one firm is assumed to be a perfect substitute for the product sold by any other. Interpreted literally, this is a condition that is rarely if ever satisfied. Connoisseurs of fine wines, for example, insist that they can tell the difference between wines made from the same variety of grape grown on estates only a few hundred meters apart. It is also difficult to speak of a market for even such a simple commodity as shirts, because shirts come in so many different styles and quality levels. If we define the market sufficiently narrowly, however, it is sometimes possible to achieve a reasonable degree of similarity among the products produced by competing firms. For instance, "Midwestern spring wheat" may not be exactly the same on different farms, but it is close enough that most buyers don't care very much which farm the wheat comes from.

2. Firms Are Price Takers This means that the individual firm treats the market price of the product as given. More specifically, it must believe that the market price will not be affected by how much output it produces. This condition is likely to be satisfied when the market is served by a large number of firms, each one of which produces an all but imperceptible fraction of total industry output. But a large number of firms are not always necessary for price-taking behavior. Even if there are only two firms in the market, for example, each may behave as a price taker if it believes that other firms stand ready to enter its market at a moment's notice.

3. Factors of Production Are Perfectly Mobile in the Long Run One implication of this condition is that if a firm perceives a profitable business opportunity at a given time and location, it will be able to hire the factors of production it needs in order to take advantage of it. Similarly, if its current venture no longer appears attractive in relation to alternative business ventures, it is free to discharge its factors of production, which will then move to industries in which opportunities are stronger. Of course, no one believes that resources are perfectly mobile. Labor, in particular, is not likely to satisfy this condition. People buy homes, make friends, enroll their children in schools, and establish a host of other commitments that make it difficult to move from one place to another. Nonetheless, the perfect mobility assumption is often reasonably well satisfied in practice, especially if we take into account that it is not always necessary for labor to move geographically in order for it to be mobile in an economic sense. Indeed, the firm can often move to the worker, as happened when New England shoe and textile factories relocated in the South in order to employ the less expensive labor available there.

4. Firms and Consumers Have Perfect Information   A firm has no reason to leave its current industry if it has no way of knowing about the existence of more profitable opportunities elsewhere. Similarly, a consumer has no motive to switch from a high-priced product to a lower-priced one of identical quality unless she has information about the existence of the latter. Here too the required condition is never satisfied in a literal sense. The world is sufficiently complex that there will inevitably be relevant features of it hidden from view. As a practical matter, the assumption of perfect information is usually interpreted to mean that people can acquire most of the information that is most relevant to their choices without great difficulty. Even this more limited condition will fail in many cases. As we saw in Chapter 8, people often have the relevant information right at their fingertips and yet fail to make sensible use of it. These observations notwithstanding, we will see that the state of knowledge is often sufficient to provide a reasonable approximation to the perfect information condition.

To help assess whether the assumptions underlying the model of perfect competition are hopelessly restrictive, it is useful to compare them to the assumptions that underlie the physicist's model of objects in motion. If you have taken a high school or college physics course, then you know (or once knew) that a force applied to an object on a frictionless surface causes that object to accelerate at a rate inversely proportional to its mass. Thus, a given force applied to a 10-kilogram object will cause that object to accelerate at twice the rate we observe when the same force is applied to a 20-kilogram object.

To illustrate this theory, physics teachers show us films of what happens when various forces are applied to a hockey puck atop a large surface of dry ice. These physicists understand perfectly well that there is an easily measured amount of friction between the puck and the dry ice. But they are also aware that the friction levels there are so low that the model still provides reasonably accurate predictions.

In the kinds of situations we are most likely to encounter in practice, friction is seldom as low as between a puck and a dry ice surface. This will be painfully apparent to you, for example, if you have just taken a spill from your Harley Sportster on an asphalt road. But even here the physicist's laws of motion apply, and we can make adjustments for friction in order to estimate just how far a fallen rider will slide. And even where the model cannot be calibrated precisely, it tells us that the rider will slide farther the faster he was going when he fell, and that he will slide farther if the pavement is wet or covered with sand or gravel than if it is clean and dry.

With the economic model of perfect competition, the issues are similar. In some markets, most notably those for agricultural products, the four conditions come close to being satisfied. The predictions of the competitive model in these cases are in many ways as precise as those of the physicist's model applied to the puck on dry ice. In other markets, such as those for garbage trucks or earth-moving equipment, at least some of the conditions are not even approximately satisfied. But even in these cases, the competitive model can tell us something useful if we interpret it with sufficient care.

370   CHAPTER 11   PERFECT COMPETITION

THE SHORT-RUN CONDITION FOR PROFIT MAXIMIZATION

The first question we want our model of competitive firm behavior to be able to answer is, "How does a firm choose its output level in the short run?" Under the assumption that the firm's goal is to maximize economic profit, it will choose that level of output for which the difference between total revenue and total cost is largest.

Consider a firm with the short-run total cost curve labeled TC in the top panel in Figure 11.2. Like many of the firms we discussed in Chapter 10, this firm experiences first increasing, then decreasing, returns to its variable input, which produces the familiar pattern of curvature in its total cost curve. Suppose this firm can sell its output at a price of $P_0 = \$18/\text{unit}$. Its total revenue per week will then be \$18/unit of output times the number of units of output sold each week. For example, if the firm sells no output, it earns zero total revenue; if it sells 10 units of output per week, it earns \$180/wk; if it sells 20 units/wk, it earns \$360/wk; and so on. So for the perfectly competitive firm, which can sell as much or as little output as it chooses at a constant market price, total revenue is exactly proportional to output. For the firm in this example, the total revenue

FIGURE 11.2
Revenue, Cost, and Economic Profit
The total revenue curve is the ray labeled TR in the top panel. The difference between it and total cost (TC in the top panel) is economic profit (Π_Q in the bottom panel). At $Q = 0$, $\Pi_Q = -FC = -30$. Economic profit reaches a maximum (\$12.60/wk) for $Q = 7.4$.

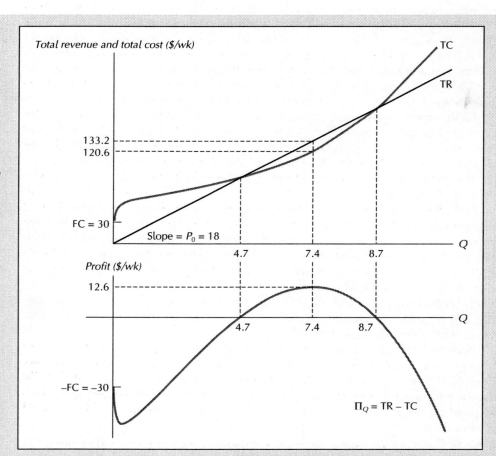

Frank: Microeconomics
an/ Behavior, Sixth E/ition

III. The Theory of the Firm
an/ Market Structure

11. Perfect Competition

© The McGraw–Hill
Companies, 2005

263

THE SHORT-RUN CONDITION FOR PROFIT MAXIMIZATION

371

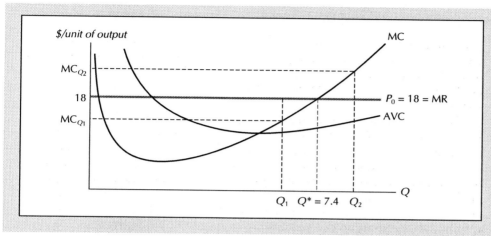

FIGURE 11.3
The Profit-Maximizing Output Level in the Short Run
A necessary condition for profit maximization is that price equal marginal cost on the rising portion of the marginal cost curve. Here, this happens at the output level $Q^* = 7.4$.

curve is the line labeled TR in the top panel in Figure 11.2. It is a ray whose slope is equal to the product price, $P_0 = 18$.

The bottom panel in Figure 11.2 plots the difference between TR and TC, which is the curve labeled Π_Q, the notation traditionally used in economics to represent economic profit. Here, Π_Q is positive for output levels between $Q = 4.7$ and $Q = 8.7$, and reaches a maximum at $Q = 7.4$. For output levels less than 4.7 or greater than 8.7, the firm is earning economic losses, which is simply another way of saying that its economic profits are negative for those values of Q.

In the bottom panel in Figure 11.2, note also that the vertical intercept of the profit curve is equal to $-\$30/$wk, the negative of the firm's fixed cost. When the firm produces no output, it earns no revenue and incurs no variable cost but must still pay its fixed costs, so its profit when $Q = 0$ is simply $-$FC. If there were no positive output level for which the firm could earn higher profit than $-$FC, its best option would be to produce zero output in the short run.

The maximum profit point can also be characterized in terms of the relationship between output price and short-run marginal cost. Output price, which is equal to the slope of the total revenue curve, is also called **marginal revenue (MR)**.[2] Marginal revenue is formally defined as *the change in revenue that occurs when the sale of output changes by 1 unit*. In the cost-benefit language of Chapter 1, MR is the benefit to the firm of selling an additional unit of output. If the firm wants to maximize its profit, it must weigh this benefit against the cost of selling an extra unit of output, which is its marginal cost.

marginal revenue the change in total revenue that occurs as a result of a 1-unit change in sales.

The short-run marginal and average variable cost curves that correspond to the TC curve in Figure 11.2 are shown in Figure 11.3, where we again suppose that the firm can sell its output at a price of $P_0 = \$18/$unit. To maximize its economic profit, the firm should follow this rule: Provided P_0 is larger than the minimum value of AVC (more on the reason for this condition below), *the firm should produce a level of output for which marginal revenue, $P_0 = 18$, is equal to marginal cost on the rising portion of the MC curve*. For the particular cost curves shown in Figure 11.3, $P_0 = 18$ is indeed larger than the minimum value of AVC, and is equal to marginal

[2]As we will see in the next chapter, output price and marginal revenue are *not* the same for a monopolist.

CHAPTER 11   PERFECT COMPETITION

cost at the quantity level $Q^* = 7.4$. The requirement that marginal revenue intersect marginal cost on the rising portion of marginal cost implies that marginal revenue intersects marginal cost from above. Thus marginal revenue lies below marginal cost past this point of intersection, and the firm has no incentive to expand output beyond this point (additional units would reduce profits).

As the following exercise demonstrates, the definitions of MR and MC tell us something about the relative values of the slopes of the TR and TC curves at the maximum-profit point in Figure 11.2.

EXERCISE 11.2

How do the slopes of the TC and TR curves compare at $Q = 7.4$ in Figure 11.2?

Why is "price = marginal cost" a necessary condition for profit maximization? Suppose we picked some other level of output, say, Q_1, that is less than $Q^* = 7.4$. The benefit to the firm of selling an additional unit of output will be $P_0 = \$18$ (its marginal revenue). The addition to total cost of producing an extra unit of output at Q_1 will be its marginal cost at the level of output, MC_{Q1}, which in Figure 11.3 is clearly less than \$18. It follows that for any level of output on the rising portion of the MC curve to the left of $Q^* = 7.4$, the benefit of expanding (as measured by marginal revenue) will be greater than the cost of expanding (as measured by marginal cost). This amounts to saying that profit will increase when we expand output from Q_1.

Now consider any level of output to the right of $Q^* = 7.4$, such as Q_2. At Q_2, the benefit of contracting output by 1 unit will be the resulting cost savings, which is marginal cost at that level of output, namely, MC_{Q2}. (Note here that we are using the term "benefit" to refer to the avoidance of a cost.) The cost to the firm of contracting output by 1 unit will be its marginal revenue, $P_0 = 18$, the loss in total revenue when it sells 1 unit less. (Here, not getting a benefit is a cost.) Since $MC_{Q2} > \$18$, the firm will save more than it loses when it contracts output by 1 unit. It follows that for any output level greater than $Q^* = 7.4$, the firm's profit will grow when it contracts output. The only output level at which the firm cannot earn higher profit by either expanding or contracting is $Q^* = 7.4$, the level for which the cost of any move is exactly equal to its benefit.[3]

---

[3]The firm's problem is to maximize $\Pi = PQ - TC_Q$, where TC_Q is the short-run total cost of producing Q units of output. The first-order condition for a maximum is given by

$$\frac{dp}{dQ} = P - \frac{dTC_Q}{dQ} = P - MC_Q = 0,$$

which gives the condition $P = MC_Q$. The second-order condition for a maximum is given by

$$\frac{d^2p}{dQ^2} = \frac{-dMC_Q}{dQ} < 0$$

or

$$\frac{dMC_Q}{dQ} > 0,$$

which tells us why we must be at a point on the rising portion of the marginal cost curve.

THE SHORT-RUN CONDITION FOR PROFIT MAXIMIZATION   373

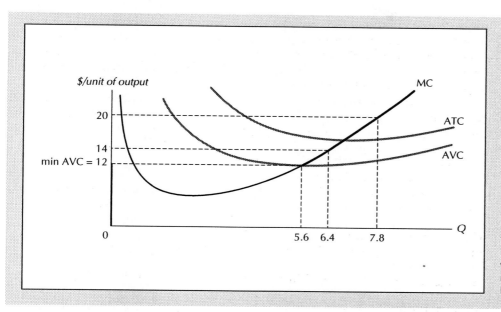

FIGURE 11.4
The Short-Run Supply Curve of a Perfectly Competitive Firm
When price lies below the minimum value of average variable cost (here $12/unit of output), the firm will make losses at every level of output, and will keep its losses to a minimum by producing zero. For prices above min AVC, the firm will supply that level of output for which $P = MC$ on the rising portion of its MC curve.

The Shutdown Condition

Recall that the rule for short-run profit maximization is to set price equal to marginal cost, provided price exceeds the minimum value of average variable cost. Why must price be greater than the minimum point of the AVC curve? The answer is that unless this condition is met, the firm will do better to shut down—that is, to produce no output—in the short run. To see why, note that the firm's *average revenue (AR)* per unit of output sold is simply the price at which it sells its product. (When price is constant for all levels of output, average revenue and marginal revenue are the same.)[4] If average revenue is less than average variable cost, the firm is taking a loss on each unit of output it sells. The firm's total revenue (average revenue times quantity) will be less than its total variable cost (AVC times quantity), and this means that it would do better by not producing any output at all. Shutting down in this context means simply to produce zero output in the short run. The firm will resume production if price again rises above the minimum value of AVC, the trigger point for its **shutdown condition.**

As we saw in Figure 11.2, a firm that produces zero output will earn economic profit equal to the negative of its fixed costs. If the price of its product is less than the minimum value of its average variable costs, it would have even greater economic losses if it produced a positive level of output.

The two rules—(1) that price must equal marginal cost on a rising portion of the marginal cost curve and (2) that price must exceed the minimum value of the average variable cost curve—together define the short-run supply curve of the perfectly competitive firm. The firm's supply curve tells how much output the firm wants to produce at various prices. As shown by the heavy locus in Figure 11.4,

shutdown condition if price falls below the minimum of average variable cost, the firm should shut down in the short run.

---

[4]Note that $AR = TR/Q = PQ/Q = P.$

it is the rising portion of the short-run marginal cost curve that lies above the minimum value of the average variable cost curve (which is \$12/unit of output in this example). Below $P = 12$, the supply curve coincides with the vertical axis, indicating that the firm supplies zero output when price is less than min AVC. For prices above 12, the firm will supply the output level for which $P = MC$. Thus, prices of 14 and 20 will cause this firm to supply 6.4 and 7.8 units of output, respectively. The competitive firm acts here as both a price taker and a profit maximizer: taking the market price as given, it chooses the level of output that maximizes economic profit at that price.

Note in Figure 11.4 that the firm supplies positive output whenever price exceeds min AVC, and recall that average variable cost is less than average total cost, the difference being average fixed cost. It follows that no matter how small AFC is, there will be a range of prices that lie between the AVC and ATC curves. For any price in this range, the firm supplies the level of output for which $P = MC$, which means that it will lose money because P is less than ATC. For example, the firm whose cost curves are shown in Figure 11.4 cannot cover all its costs at a price of \$14. Even so, its best option is to supply 6.4 units of output per week, because it would lose even more money if it were to shut down. Being able to cover variable costs does not assure the firm of a positive level of economic profit. But it is sufficient to induce the firm to supply output in the short run.

Note also in Figure 11.4 that the firm's short-run supply curve is upward sloping. This is because the relevant portion of the firm's short-run marginal cost curve is upward sloping, which, in turn, is a direct consequence of the law of diminishing returns.

THE SHORT-RUN COMPETITIVE INDUSTRY SUPPLY

The short-run supply curve for a competitive industry is generated in a manner analogous to the one we used to generate the market demand curve in Chapter 5. In this case we simply announce a price and then add together the amounts each firm wishes to supply at that price. The resulting sum is industry supply at that price. Additional points on the industry supply curve are generated by pairing other prices with the sums of individual firm supplies at those prices.

Figure 11.5 illustrates the procedure for one of the simplest cases, an industry consisting of only two firms. At a price of \$2/unit of output, only firm 1 (left panel) wishes to supply any output, and so its offering, $Q_1 = 2$ units of output per week, constitutes the entire industry supply at $P = 2$ (right panel). At $P = 3$, firm 2 enters the market (center panel) with an offering of $Q_2 = 4$. Added to firm 1's offering at $P = 3$—namely, $Q_1 = 3$—the resulting industry supply at $P = 3$ is $Q = 7$ (right panel). In like fashion, we see that industry supply at $P = 7$ is $Q = 7 + 8 = 15$. In Chapter 5, we saw that the market demand curve is the horizontal summation of the individual consumer demand curves. Here, we see that the market supply curve is the horizontal summation of the individual firm supply curves.

The horizontal summation of an individual firm's supplies into industry supply has a simple form when the firms in the industry are all identical. Suppose n firms each have supply curve $P = c + dQ_i$. To add up the quantities for the n firms into industry supply, we rearrange the firm supply curve $P = c + dQ_i$ to

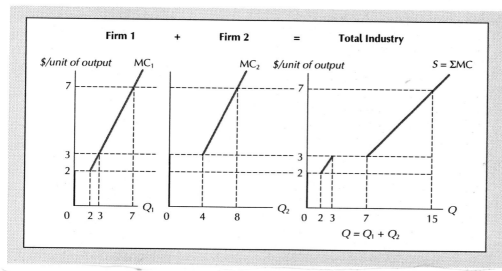

FIGURE 11.5

The Short-Run Competitive Industry Supply Curve

To get the industry supply curve (right panel), we simply add the individual firm supply curves (left and center panels) horizontally.

$$Q = Q_1 + Q_2$$

express quantity alone on one side $Q_i = (c/d) + (1/d)P$. Then industry supply is the sum of the quantities supplied Q_i by each of the n firms,

$$Q = nQ_i = n\left(-\frac{c}{d} + \frac{1}{d}P\right) = -\frac{nc}{d} + \frac{n}{d}P.$$

$$\frac{Q + nc/d}{n/d}$$

We can then rearrange industry supply $Q = -(nc/d) + (n/d)P$ to get it back in the form of price alone on one side: $P = c + (d/n)Q$. The intuition is that each one unit supplied by the industry is $1/n$ unit for each firm to supply. These calculations suggest a general rule for constructing the industry supply curve when firms are identical. If we have n individual firm supply curves $P = c + dQ_i$, then the industry supply curve is $P = c + (d/n)Q$.

Suppose an industry has 200 firms, each with supply curve $P = 100 + 1000Q_i$. What is the industry supply curve?

                                                                   EXAMPLE 11.2

First, we need to rearrange the representative firm supply curve $P = 100 + 1000Q_i$ to have quantity alone on one side:

$$Q_i = -\frac{1}{10} + \frac{1}{1000}P.$$

Then we multiply by the number of firms $n = 200$:

$$Q = nQ_i = 200Q_i = 200\left(-\frac{1}{10} + \frac{1}{1000}P\right) = -20 + \frac{1}{5}P.$$

Finally, we rearrange the industry supply curve $Q = -20 + (\frac{1}{5})P$ to have price alone on one side $P = 100 + 5Q$ to return to the slope-intercept form.

EXERCISE 11.3

Suppose an industry has 30 firms, each with supply curve $P = 20 + 90Q_i$. What is the industry supply curve?

CHAPTER 11 PERFECT COMPETITION

SHORT-RUN COMPETITIVE EQUILIBRIUM

The individual competitive firm must choose the most profitable level of output to produce in response to a given price. But where does that price come from? As we saw in Chapter 2, it comes from the intersection of the supply and demand curves for the product. Recall that at the equilibrium price sellers are selling the quantity they wish to sell and buyers are buying the quantity they wish to buy.

In the left panel in Figure 11.6, the curve labeled D is the market demand curve for a product sold in a perfectly competitive industry. The curve labeled S is the corresponding short-run industry supply curve, the horizontal summation of the relevant portions of the individual short-run marginal cost curves.[5] These two curves intersect to establish the short-run competitive equilibrium price, here denoted $P^* = \$20$/unit of output. $P^* = 20$, in turn, is the price on which individual firms base their output decisions.

The conditions confronting a typical firm are shown in the right panel in Figure 11.6. The demand curve facing this firm is a horizontal line at $P^* = 20$. This means that it can sell as much or as little as it chooses at the market price of $20/unit. Put another way, any single firm can sell as much as it wants to without affecting the market price. If a firm charged more than the $20, it would sell no output at all because buyers would switch to a competing firm that sells for $20. A firm could charge less than $20, of course, but would have no motive to do so if its objective were to maximize economic profit, since it can already sell as much as it wants to at $20. The result is that even though the market demand curve is

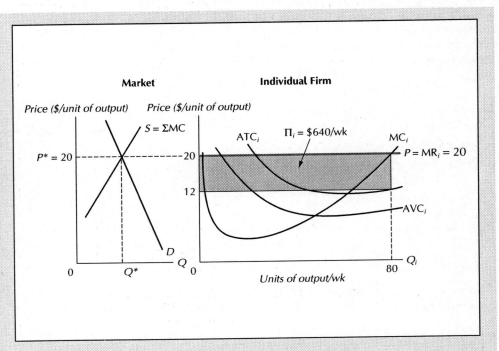

FIGURE 11.6
Short-Run Price and Output Determination under Pure Competition
The short-run supply and demand curves intersect to determine the short-run equilibrium price, $P^* = 20$ (left panel). The firm's demand curve is a horizontal line at $P^* = 20$ (right panel). Taking $P^* = 20$ as given, the firm maximizes economic profit by producing $Q_i^* = 80$ units/wk, for which it earns an economic profit of $\Pi_i = \$640$/wk (the shaded rectangle in the right panel).

[5]Here, the "relevant portions" are those that lie above the respective values of min AVC.

downward sloping, the demand curve facing the individual firm is perfectly elastic. (Recall from the definition of price elasticity in Chapter 5 that a horizontal demand curve has infinite price elasticity, which is what "perfectly elastic" means.)

In the right panel in Figure 11.6, the representative firm maximizes its profit by equating $P^* = \$20/\text{unit}$ to marginal cost at an output level of $Q_i^* = 80$ units/wk. At that output level its total revenue is $P^*Q_i^* = \$1600/\text{wk}$ and its total costs are $\text{ATC}_{Q_i^*}Q_i^* = (\$12/\text{unit})(80 \text{ units/wk}) = \$960/\text{wk}$. Its economic profit is the difference between total revenue and total cost, $\$1600/\text{wk} - \$960/\text{wk} = \$640/\text{wk}$, and is represented by the shaded rectangle denoted Π_i. Equivalently, profits can be calculated as the difference between price ($\$20/\text{unit}$) and average total cost ($\$12/\text{unit}$) times the quantity sold (80 units/week).

Recall that the opportunity cost of resources owned by the firm constitutes part of the cost included in its average total cost curve. This is why we say that total revenues over and above total costs constitute economic profit. If the firm's revenue were exactly equal to its total cost, it would earn only a normal profit—which is to say, zero economic profit.

Facing a price equal to average total cost implies that total cost equals total revenue, and the firm earns zero economic profits. Thus price equal to the minimum of average total cost can be called the breakeven point—the lowest price at which the firm will not suffer negative profits in the short run.

The situation portrayed in Figure 11.6 and Table 11.1 is one in which the short-run equilibrium price enables the firm to make a positive economic profit. Another possibility is that the short-run supply and demand curves will intersect at an equilibrium price that is sufficiently high to induce firms to supply output, but not high enough to enable them to cover all their costs. This situation is shown in Figure 11.7 and Table 11.1. In the left panel, supply and demand intersect at a

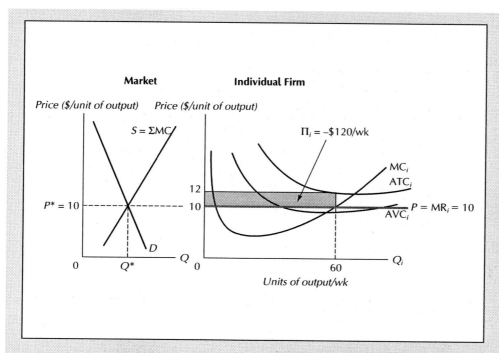

FIGURE 11.7
A Short-Run Equilibrium Price that Results in Economic Losses
The short-run supply and demand curves sometimes intersect to produce an equilibrium price $P^* = \$10/\text{unit}$ of output (left panel) that lies below the minimum value of the ATC curve for the typical firm (right panel), but above the minimum point of its AVC curve. At the profit-maximizing level of output, $Q_i^* = 60$ units/wk, the firm earns an economic loss of $\Pi_i = -\$120/\text{wk}$.

378   CHAPTER 11   PERFECT COMPETITION

TABLE 11.1
Economic Profits versus Economic Losses
At a price of 20, the firm earns economic profits, but at a price of 10, it suffers economic losses.

Q	ATC	MC	$\pi(P = 20)$	$\pi(P = 10)$
40	14	6	240	−160
60	12	10	480	−120
80	12	20	640	−160
100	15	31	500	−500

price $P^* = \$10$/unit of output, which lies above the minimum value of the AVC curve of the firm shown in the right panel, but below that firm's ATC curve at the profit-maximizing level of output, $Q_i^* = 60$ units of output per week. The result is that the firm makes an economic loss of $P^*Q_i^* - ATC_{Q_i^*}Q_i^* = -\$120$/wk. This loss is shown in the right panel in Figure 11.7 by the shaded rectangle labeled Π_i. Note that this loss is less than $-$ TFC, the value of economic profit when output is zero. Thus it makes sense to produce even when economic profit falls below zero in the short run.

EXERCISE 11.4

If the short-run marginal and average variable cost curves for a competitive firm are given by MC = 2Q and AVC = Q, how many units of output will the firm produce at a market price of P = 12? At what level of fixed cost will this firm earn zero economic profit?

THE EFFICIENCY OF SHORT-RUN COMPETITIVE EQUILIBRIUM

allocative efficiency a condition in which all possible gains from exchange are realized.

One of the most attractive features of competitive markets is the fact that they result in **allocative efficiency,** which means that they fully exploit the possibilities for mutual gains through exchange. To illustrate, let us consider the short-run equilibrium pictured in the left panel of Figure 11.8, and suppose that the cost curves pictured in the right panel are the same for each of 1000 firms in the industry.

In a competitive market in the short run, consumers give firms money, which firms use to buy variable inputs to produce the output that goes to consumers. To say that the competitive equilibrium leaves no room for further mutually beneficial exchange is the same thing as saying that there is no way for any producer and consumer to agree to a private transaction at any price other than $10. Of course, consumers would gladly pay less than $10 for an additional unit of output. But since $10 is equal to the value of the resources required to produce another unit (MC_i in the right panel of Figure 11.8), no firm would be willing to respond. Firms, for their part, would gladly produce an extra unit of output if the price were higher than $10. But with 100,000 units of output already in the market, there are no consumers left who are willing to pay more than $10 (left panel of Figure 11.8). At the short-run competitive equilibrium price and quantity, the value of the resources used to produce the last unit of output (as measured by short-run marginal cost) is exactly equal to the value of that unit of output to consumers (as measured by the price they are willing to pay for it). Firms may wish that prices were higher, and consumers may complain that prices are too high already. But two parties have no incentive to trade at any price other than the equilibrium price.

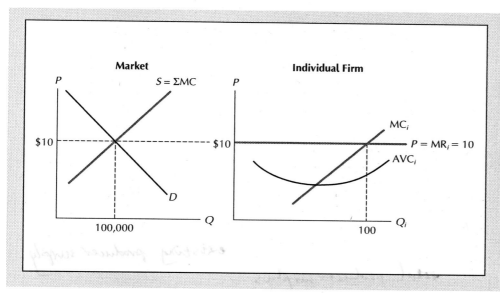

FIGURE 11.8
Short-Run Competitive Equilibrium Is Efficient
At the equilibrium price and quantity, the value of the additional resources required to make the last unit of output produced by each firm (MC in the right panel) is exactly equal to the value of the last unit of output to buyers (the demand price in the left panel). This means that further mutually beneficial trades do not exist.

PRODUCER SURPLUS

To say that a competitive market is efficient is to say that it maximizes the net benefits to its participants. In policy analysis, it is often useful to estimate the actual amount by which people and firms gain from their participation in specific markets. Suppose, for example, that a Third World government knows it can open up new markets for seafood by building a road from its coast to an interior region. If its goal is to use the country's resources as efficiently as possible, its decision about whether to build the road will depend on whether the benefits people and firms reap from these new markets exceed the cost of building the road.

In Chapter 4 we discussed the concept of consumer surplus as a measure of the benefit to the consumer of engaging in a market exchange. An analogous measure exists for producers. Economists call it **producer surplus,** and it measures how much better off the firm is as a result of having supplied its profit-maximizing level of output. It may seem tempting to say that the firm's producer surplus is simply its economic profit, but that will not generally be the case. To see why, first recall that in the short run if the firm produces nothing, it will sustain a loss equal to its fixed cost. If the price exceeds the minimum value of AVC, however, it can do better by supplying a positive level of output. How much better? The firm's gain compared with the alternative of producing nothing is the difference between total revenue and total variable cost at the output level where $P = MC$. Now recall that economic profit is the difference between total revenue and total cost and that total cost differs from variable cost by fixed cost; it follows that producer surplus is the sum of economic profit and fixed cost.[6] Diagrammatically, it is the area of the shaded rectangle shown in the left panel in Figure 11.9. In the short run, producer surplus is thus larger than economic

producer surplus the dollar amount by which a firm benefits by producing a profit-maximizing level of output.

---

[6]If $\Pi = TR - TC$ and $TC = VC + FC$, then producer surplus = $TR - VC = TR - TC + FC = \Pi + FC$.

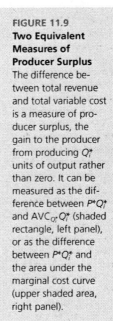

FIGURE 11.9
Two Equivalent Measures of Producer Surplus
The difference between total revenue and total variable cost is a measure of producer surplus, the gain to the producer from producing Q_i^* units of output rather than zero. It can be measured as the difference between $P^*Q_i^*$ and $AVC_{Q_i^*}Q_i^*$ (shaded rectangle, left panel), or as the difference between $P^*Q_i^*$ and the area under the marginal cost curve (upper shaded area, right panel).

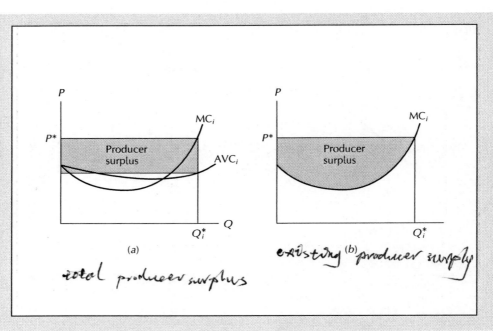

profit, because the firm would lose more than its economic profit if it were prevented from participating in the market.

The right panel in Figure 11.9 shows an equivalent way of representing producer surplus. The alternative measure makes use of the fact that variable cost at any level of output is equal to the area under the marginal cost curve (below the shaded area in the right panel). To see why this is so, note that the variable cost of producing 1 unit of output is equal to marginal cost at 1 unit, MC_1; VC for 2 units is the sum of MC_1 and MC_2, and so on, so that $VC_Q = MC_1 + MC_2 + \cdots + MC_Q$, which is just the area under the MC curve. Hence the difference between the total revenue and total variable cost may also be expressed as the upper shaded area in the right panel in Figure 11.9.

Which of the two ways of measuring producer surplus is most useful will depend on the specific context at hand. If we are interested in the change in an existing producer surplus, the method shown in the right panel in Figure 11.9 will usually be easiest to work with. But when we want to measure total producer surplus, it will often be easier to calculate the surplus by using the method shown in the left panel.

To measure aggregate producer surplus for a market, we simply add the producer surplus for each firm that participates. In cases where each firm's marginal cost curve is upward sloping for the bulk of its range, aggregate producer surplus will be well approximated by the area between the supply curve and the equilibrium price line, P^*, as shown in Figure 11.10.

Recall from Chapter 4 that a rough approximation of consumer surplus for the market as a whole is given by the area between the demand curve and the equilibrium price line, as indicated by the shaded upper triangle in Figure 11.11.[7]

---

[7] Recall that this measure of consumer surplus is most accurate when income effects are small.

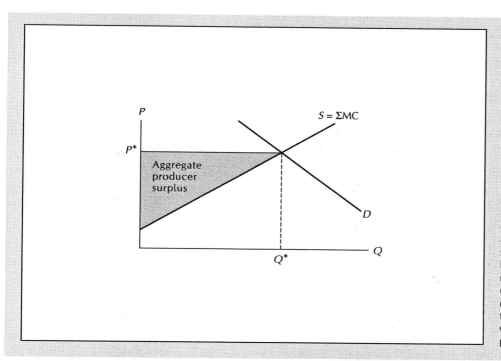

FIGURE 11.10
Aggregate Producer Surplus When Individual Marginal Cost Curves are Upward Sloping Throughout
For any quantity, the supply curve measures the minimum price at which firms would be willing to supply it. The difference between the market price and the supply price is the marginal contribution to aggregate producer surplus at that output level. Adding these marginal contributions up to the equilibrium quantity Q^*, we get the shaded area, which is aggregate producer surplus.

The total benefits from exchange in the marketplace may be measured by the sum of consumer and producer surpluses.

Suppose there are two types of users of fireworks: careless and careful. Careful users never get hurt, but careless ones sometimes injure not only themselves, but also innocent bystanders. The short-run marginal cost curves of each of the 1000

EXAMPLE 11.3

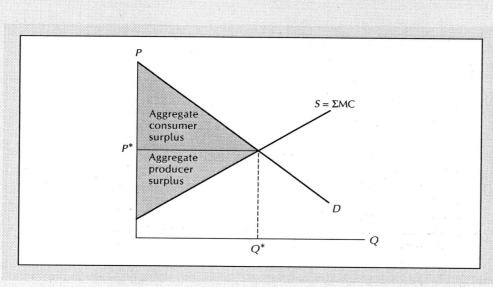

FIGURE 11.11
The Total Benefit from Exchange in a Market
The sum of aggregate producer surplus (shaded lower triangle) and consumer surplus (shaded upper triangle) measures the total benefit from exchange.

382   CHAPTER 11   PERFECT COMPETITION

$2 \bullet \bar{2} \bar{E} \; 40$
$Q = 20000$

FIGURE 11.12
Producer and Consumer Surplus in a Market Consisting of Careful Fireworks Users
The upper shaded triangle is consumer surplus ($200,000/yr). The lower shaded triangle is producer surplus ($200,000/yr). The total benefit of keeping this market open is the sum of the two, or $400,000/yr.

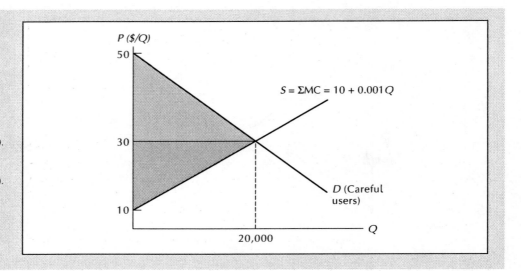

firms in the fireworks industry are given by $MC = 10 + Q$, where Q is measured in pounds of cherry bombs per year and MC is measured in dollars per pound of cherry bombs. The demand curve for fireworks by careful users is given by $P = 50 - 0.001Q$ (same units as for MC). Legislators would like to continue to permit careful users to enjoy fireworks. But since it is impractical to distinguish between the two types of users, they have decided to outlaw fireworks altogether. How much better off would consumers and producers be if legislators had the means to effect a partial ban?

If the entire fireworks market is banned completely, the total of consumer and producer surplus will be zero. So to measure the benefits of a partial ban, we need to find the sum of consumer and producer surplus for a fireworks market restricted to careful users. To generate the supply curve for this market, we simply add the marginal cost curves of the individual firms horizontally, which results in the curve labeled S in Figure 11.12. The demand curve for careful users would intersect S at an equilibrium price of $30 and an equilibrium quantity of 20,000 lb/yr.

By outlawing the sale of fireworks altogether, legislators eliminate producer and consumer surplus values given by the areas of the two shaded triangles in Figure 11.12, which add to $400,000/yr. In the language of cost-benefit analysis, this is the cost imposed on producers and careful users. The benefit of the ban is whatever value the public assigns to the injuries prevented (net of the cost of denying careless users the right to continue). It is obviously no simple matter to put a dollar value on the pain and suffering associated with fingers blown off by cherry bombs. In Chapter 14, we will discuss how at least rough estimates have been attempted in similar situations. But even in the absence of a formal quantitative measure of the value of injuries prevented, the public can ask itself whether the forgone surplus of $400,000/yr is a reasonable price to pay. Because virtually every state legislature has enacted a ban on the private sale and use of fireworks, the answer to this question seems to be an emphatic yes.

> **EXERCISE 11.5**
>
> What would the sum of consumer and producer surplus be in Example 11.3 if the demand curve for careful users were instead given by $P = 30 - 0.001Q$?

ADJUSTMENTS IN THE LONG RUN

The firm's objective, in both the long run and the short run, is to earn the highest economic profit it can. In the preceding section we saw that a firm will sometimes find it in its interest to continue supplying output in the short run even though it is making economic losses. In the long run, however, a firm would prefer to go out of business if it could not earn at least a normal profit in its current industry.

Suppose that industry supply and demand intersect at the price level $P = 10$, as shown in the left panel in Figure 11.13. The cost curves for a representative firm are shown in the right panel in Figure 11.13. At $Q = 200$, the price of $10/unit of output exceeds ATC_2, with the result that the firm earns economic profit of $600 each time period. This profit is indicated by the shaded rectangle.

The situation depicted in Figure 11.13 is inherently unstable. The reason is that positive economic profit creates an incentive for outsiders to enter the industry. Recall that the average total cost curves already include the opportunity cost of the capital that a firm requires to do business. This means that an outsider can buy everything needed to duplicate the operations of one of the existing firms in the industry, and in the process earn an economic profit of $600 each time period.

As additional firms enter the industry, their short-run marginal cost curves are added to those of existing firms, which shifts the industry supply curve to the right. If only one firm entered the industry, there would be no significant effect on price. And with price virtually the same as before, each firm in the industry would continue to earn economic profits of $600 per time period. These

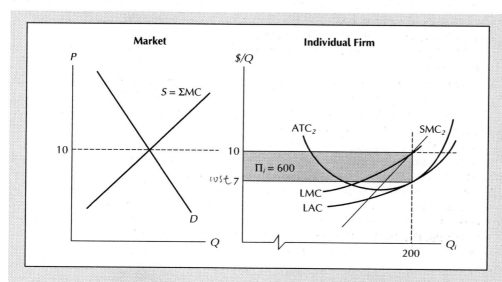

FIGURE 11.13
A Price Level that Generates Economic Profit
At the price level $P = $10/unit$, the firm has adjusted its plant size so that $SMC_2 = LMC = 10$. At the profit-maximizing level of output, $Q = 200$, the firm earns an economic profit equal to $600 each time period, indicated by the area of the shaded rectangle.

FIGURE 11.14
A Step along the Path toward Long-Run Equilibrium
Entry of new firms causes supply to shift rightward, lowering price from 10 to 8. The lower price causes existing firms to adjust their capital stocks downward, giving rise to the new short-run cost curves ATC_3 and SMC_3. As long as price remains above short-run average cost (here, $ATC_3 = 5$), economic profits will be positive ($\Pi = \$540$ per time period), and incentives for new firms to enter will remain.

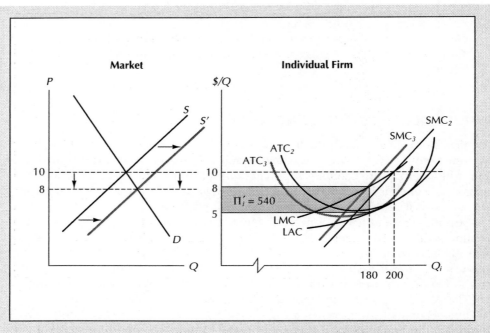

profits will continue to act as a carrot to lure additional firms into the industry, and the accumulating rightward supply shift will gradually cause price to fall.

The left panel in Figure 11.14 portrays the rightward shift in industry supply that results from a significant amount of entry. The new supply schedule, S', intersects the demand schedule at $P = 8$, and this lower price level gives firms an incentive to readjust their capital stocks. In the right panel in Figure 11.14, note that the amount of capital that gives rise to the short-run cost curves ATC_3 and SMC_3 is optimal for the price level $P = 8$. Note also that the profit-maximizing level of output for $P = 8$ is $Q = 180$, and that this results in an economic profit of 540 per time period, as indicated by the shaded rectangle.

Note that the adjustment by existing firms to the lower price level shifts each of their short-run marginal cost curves to the left. In terms of its effect on the industry supply curve, this adjustment thus works in the opposite direction from the adjustment caused by the entry of new firms. But the *net* effect of the two adjustments must be to shift industry supply to the right. If it were not, price wouldn't have fallen in the first place, and there would have been no reason for existing firms to reduce their capital stocks.

Even after the adjustments described above take place, new and existing firms in the industry continue to earn positive economic profits. The new profit level is lower than before, but will still act as an incentive for additional entry into the industry. Further entry sets off yet another round of adjustment, as the continuing fall in price renders existing capital stocks too large. For industries whose firms have U-shaped long-run average cost curves, entry, falling prices, and capital stock adjustment will continue until these two conditions are met: (1) Price reaches the minimum point on the LAC curve (P^* in the right panel in Figure 11.15), and (2) all firms have moved to the capital stock size that gives

THE INVISIBLE HAND   385

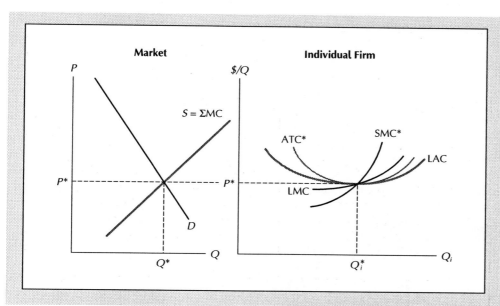

FIGURE 11.15
The Long-Run Equilibrium under Perfect Competition
If price starts above P^*, entry keeps occurring and capital stocks of existing firms keep adjusting until the rightward movement of the industry supply curve causes price to fall to P^*. At P^*, the profit-maximizing level of output for each firm is Q_i^*, the output level for which $P^* = SMC^* = LMC = ATC^* = LAC$. Economic profits of all firms are equal to zero.

rise to a short-run average total cost curve that is tangent to the LAC curve at its minimum point (ATC* in the right panel in Figure 11.15). Note in the right panel in Figure 11.15 that once all firms have reached this position, economic profit for each will be zero. The short-run marginal cost curve in the right panel is like the short-run marginal cost curve of all other firms in the industry, and when these curves are added horizontally, we get the industry supply curve shown in the left panel, which intersects the market demand curve at the long-run equilibrium price of P^*. This is the long-run competitive equilibrium position for the industry. Once it is reached, there will be no further incentive for new firms to enter the industry, because existing firms will all be earning an economic profit of zero.

In discussing the movement toward long-run competitive equilibrium, we began with an initial situation in which price was above the minimum value of long-run average cost and existing firms were all earning an economic profit. Suppose we had instead started with a situation in which price was below the minimum value of LAC. In that case, existing firms would be earning negative economic profits (that is, economic losses), which would be an incentive for some of them to leave the industry. The exodus would shift the supply curve leftward, causing an increase in price and movements by existing firms to adjust their capital stocks upward. This process would continue until all firms have once again settled into the long-run equilibrium position portrayed in the right panel in Figure 11.15.

THE INVISIBLE HAND

As Adam Smith saw clearly more than two centuries ago, it is the invisible hand of the self-interest motive—in particular, the carrot of economic profit, or the stick of economic losses—that drives competitive industries to their respective long-run equilibrium positions. But even though no firm consciously intends to

386   CHAPTER 11   PERFECT COMPETITION

promote the general social welfare, there are some remarkably attractive features of long-run competitive equilibrium. Thus, as Smith described the actions of an industrialist,

> he intends only his own security; and by directing that industry in such a manner as its produce may be of the greatest value, he intends only his own gain; and he is in this, as in many other cases, led by an invisible hand to promote an end which was no part of his intention. Nor is it always the worse for the society that it was no part of it. By pursuing his own interest, he frequently promotes that of the society more effectually than when he really intends to promote it.[8]

In what sense is the long-run equilibrium in competitive markets attractive from the perspective of society as a whole? For one thing, price is equal to marginal cost, both long-run and short-run, which means that the equilibrium is efficient in the sense previously discussed: it exhausts all possibilities for mutually beneficial trades. The last unit of output consumed is worth exactly the same to the buyer as the resources required to produce it. Moreover, price is equal to the minimum point on the long-run average cost curve, which means that there is no less costly way of producing the product. Finally, all producers earn only a normal rate of profit, which is the opportunity cost of the resources they have invested in their firms. The public pays not a penny more than what it cost the firms to serve them.

Even more remarkable than these efficiency properties is the sheer volume of activity that is coordinated by the market mechanism. Throughout the dead of Ithaca winters, a food truck sits parked outside the Cornell dormitories all night, so that at 3 A.M. any student can take a few steps outside and purchase a fresh cup of coffee for 75 cents. No students had to instruct the operator of that truck to be there, or tell him where to buy paper cups or propane gas for his portable stove. A store near my house will sell me a new cartridge for my printer at a moment's notice, or a new carbide-tipped blade for the radial arm saw that sits in my

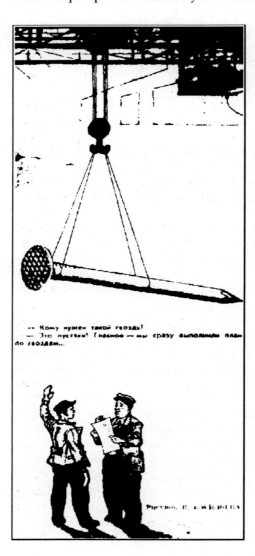

"Who needs a nail as big as that?"
"Who cares? The important thing is we fulfilled the plan for nails in one fell swoop."

---

[8]Adam Smith, *The Wealth of Nations*, Chapter 2 http://www.online-literature.com/view.php/wealth_nations/24?term=invisible%20hand.

garage. The butcher shop at my supermarket has fresh rabbit on Fridays and Saturdays, and a truck arrives each morning at dawn carrying fresh swordfish caught in the waters off the coast of Maine. On only a few hours' notice, several airlines stand ready to carry me to New York, Los Angeles, or Cedar Rapids, Iowa. All this activity, and much, much more, takes place without any central coordination at all, the result of a multitude of economic agents each acting in search of an economic profit.

In controlled economies, resources are allocated not by markets but by central planning committees. Because of natural limits on the amount of information such committees can process, they are unable to specify in exact detail the characteristics of the goods called for by their plans. Workers and managers in controlled economies are therefore often able to interpret their production orders in self-serving ways.

The famous Russian cartoon reprinted on the preceding page, for example, shows the response of the manager of a roofing nail factory who was called on by the plan to deliver 10,000 pounds of roofing nails for the month of August. He alertly discovered that the easiest way to fulfill his quota was to produce a single 10,000-pound nail.

Whatever other faults it may have, the market system cannot be accused of producing products that people don't want to buy. In the market system, the consumer is sovereign, and firms that fail to provide what consumers want face economic extinction.[9] The question of whether central plans are more efficient than market incentives was a hotly debated issue for most of the twentieth century. But no longer. Before their demise in the late 1980s, controlled economies all over the globe introduced marketlike incentives in a desperate attempt to revive their lagging production totals.

This is not to say that competitive markets lead to the best possible outcome in every instance. On the contrary, in later chapters we will see that market systems fall short in a variety of ways.

Moreover, the efficiency claims on behalf of competitive allocations are conditional on the initial distribution of resources among members of society. Markets are efficient at producing what people demand in the marketplace, and what gets produced depends on how much income specific people have. If you do not believe that the underlying distribution of resources is fair, there is no compelling reason for you to approve of the pattern of goods and services served up by competitive markets. But one need not take a naively optimistic view of the competitive process to appreciate its truly awesome power to draw order from complexity.

APPLICATION: THE COST OF EXTRAORDINARY INPUTS

The Irrigation Project

We are in a position now to return to the question with which we began this chapter, namely, whether a state-supported irrigation system that doubles crop yields will raise the incomes of poor farmers. Recall that the farmers in question live in an isolated county and rent their farm parcels from landowners.

---

[9]Harvard economist John Kenneth Galbraith challenged this view. We will consider his arguments in Chapter 13.

388   CHAPTER 11 PERFECT COMPETITION

First, let's consider the current situation in which no irrigation system exists. Farmers here may be viewed as the operators of small competitive firms. They rent land, supply their own labor, and keep the proceeds from selling their grain in a market so large that their own offerings have no appreciable effect on the price of grain, which is, say, $10/bushel. For the sake of simplicity, let us ignore the cost of seed, tools, and other minor inputs.

Suppose that an individual farmer can farm 40 acres and that without irrigation the land will yield 30 bushels of grain per acre per year. His total revenue from the sale of his grain will then be $12,000/yr, from which he must deduct the rent for his land. How will that rent be determined?

Suppose the alternative to working as a farmer is to work in a factory for $6000/yr, and that factory work is generally regarded as neither more nor less pleasant than farming. If the land rent were only, say, $5000/yr for a 40-acre parcel, then all the county's workers would prefer farming to working in the factories, because their net earnings would be $7000 instead of $6000. Assuming that there are many more factory workers than could farm the county's limited supply of farmland, there would be excess demand for farm parcels at a rental price of $5000/yr. Factory workers would bid against one another, and the bidding would continue until the rental price for a 40-acre parcel reached $6000/yr. At that price, a farmer would have $6000 left over from the sale of his crops, which would leave him indifferent between the options of farming and factory work. The land rent could never exceed $6000 for very long under these conditions, for if it did, net farm incomes would fall below $6000/yr and everyone would want factory work instead of farming.

Now let's see what happens with the introduction of the irrigation project. With grain yields now 60 bushels/acre instead of 30, a 40-acre farm will produce $24,000 in annual total revenue instead of $12,000. If the land rent remained at its original $6000/yr level, a farmer would earn $18,000/yr instead of $6000. Indeed, it was the prospect of such a dramatic rise in farm incomes that has attracted so much support for the irrigation bill in the first place.

What the supporters of the bill have failed to recognize, however, is that land rents will not remain at $6000/yr after the introduction of the irrigation system. Needless to say, factory workers would bid vigorously for an opportunity to rent a farm parcel that would raise their income from $6000 to $18,000/yr. In the face of this bidding pressure, the rental price of farmland will continue to rise until it reaches a level of $18,000/yr. (If it were only $17,000, for example, a factory worker could switch to farming and raise his annual income from $6000 to $7000.) Once the annual rent for a 40-acre parcel reaches $18,000, the balance between farm and factory opportunities will be restored.

Recall that our hypothetical state legislator's aide recommended against the irrigation project on the grounds that it would not raise the incomes of farmers in the long run. She perceived correctly that the beneficiaries of the state-supported irrigation project would be not the impoverished farmers but the owners of the land. On the view that these owners already have high incomes, there is no social purpose served by spending tax dollars to increase their incomes further.[10]

---

[10]Of course, the irrigation project would still be attractive if its cost were less than the value of the extra grain that resulted.

THE LONG-RUN COMPETITIVE INDUSTRY SUPPLY CURVE   389

This example illustrates the important idea that strong forces tend to equalize the average total costs of different firms in a competitive industry. Here, land prices adjusted to bring the average costs of the irrigated farms into balance with the average costs of growing crops elsewhere.

An Efficient Manager

Suppose one firm is like all others except that it employs an extraordinarily efficient manager. This manager is so efficient that the firm earns $500,000 of economic profit each year in an industry in which the economic profit of the other firms hovers very close to zero. Because this manager receives the same salary as all other managers, the firm that employs her has much lower costs than all other firms in the industry. But that creates a strong incentive for some other firm to bid this manager away by offering her a higher salary.

Suppose a new firm offered her $300,000 more than her current annual salary and she accepted. That new firm would then earn an economic profit of $200,000/yr. That's not as good as an economic profit of $500,000/yr, but it is $200,000/yr better than the normal profit her original employer will earn without her.

Still other firms would have an incentive to offer even more for this manager. Theory tells us that the bidding should continue until the cost savings for which she is responsible are entirely incorporated into her salary—that is, until her salary is $500,000/yr higher than the salary of an ordinary manager. And once her salary is bid up to that level, the firm that hires her will no longer enjoy a cost advantage over the other firms in the industry. The existence of such competitive bidding for inputs makes it plausible to assume that all the firms in a competitive industry have roughly the same average total costs in equilibrium.

EXERCISE 11.6

Suppose all firms in an industry have "competent" managers and earn zero economic profit. The manager of one of the firms suddenly leaves and the firm finds that only incompetent applicants respond when the position is advertised at the original salary of $50,000/yr (which is the going rate for competent managers in this industry). Under an incompetent manager paid this salary, the firm will experience an economic loss of $20,000/yr. At what salary would it make sense for this firm to hire an incompetent manager?

THE LONG-RUN COMPETITIVE INDUSTRY SUPPLY CURVE

We saw that the short-run supply curve for a perfectly competitive industry is the horizontal summation of the short-run marginal cost curves of its individual firms. But the corresponding long-run supply curve for a competitive industry is not the horizontal summation of the long-run marginal cost curves of individual firms. Our task in the next sections is to derive the long-run supply curve for competitive industries operating under a variety of different cost conditions.

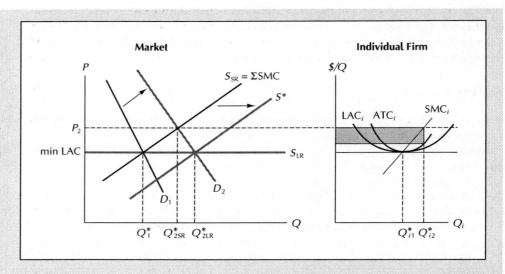

FIGURE 11.16
The Long-Run Competitive Industry Supply Curve
When firms are free to enter or leave the market, price cannot depart from the minimum value of the LAC curve in the long run. If input prices are unaffected by changes in industry output, the long-run supply curve is S_{LR}, a horizontal line at the minimum value of LAC.

Long-Run Supply Curve with U-Shaped LAC Curves

What does the long-run supply curve look like in an industry in which all firms have identical U-shaped long-run average cost (LAC) curves? Suppose, in particular, that these LAC curves are like the one labeled LAC_i in the right panel in Figure 11.16. Suppose the demand curve facing the industry is initially the one labeled D_1 in the left panel. Given this demand curve, the industry will be in long-run equilibrium when each firm installs the capital stock that gives rise to the short-run marginal cost curve labeled SMC_i in the right panel. The number of firms in the industry will adjust so that the short-run supply curve, denoted S_{SR} in the left panel, intersects D_1 at a price equal to the minimum value of LAC_i. (If there were more firms than that or fewer, each would be making either an economic loss or a profit.)

Now suppose demand shifts rightward from D_1 to D_2, intersecting the short-run industry supply curve at the price P_2. The short-run effect will be for each firm to increase its output from Q_{i1}^* to Q_{i2}^*, which will lead to an economic profit measured by the shaded rectangle in the right panel in Figure 11.16. With the passage of time, these profits will lure additional firms into the industry until the rightward supply shift (to S^* in the left panel) again results in a price of min LAC. The long-run response to an increase in demand, then, is to increase industry output by increasing the number of firms in the industry. As long as the expansion of industry output does not cause the prices of capital, labor, and other inputs to rise, there will be no long-run increase in the price of the product.[11]

If demand had shifted to the left from D_1, a parallel story would have unfolded: Price would have fallen in the short run, firms would have adjusted their offerings, and the resulting economic losses would have induced some firms to leave the industry. The exodus would shift industry supply to the left until price had again risen to min LAC. Here again the long-run response to a shift in demand

---

[11]More follows on what happens when changes in industry output cause changes in input prices.

is accommodated by a change in the number of firms. With U-shaped LAC curves, there is no tendency for a fall in demand to produce a long-run decline in price.

In summary, the long-run supply curve for a competitive industry with U-shaped LAC curves and constant input prices is a horizontal line at the minimum value of the LAC curve. In the long run, all the adjustment to variations in demand occurs not through changing prices but through variations in the number of firms serving the market. Following possibly substantial deviations in the short run, price shows a persistent tendency to gravitate to the minimum value of long-run average cost.

Industry Supply When Each LAC Curve Is Horizontal

As in the case of U-shaped LAC curves, the long-run industry supply curve when each firm's LAC curve is horizontal will again be a horizontal line (again assuming that input prices do not change with changes in industry output). But there is one salient difference between the two cases: When firms have identical U-shaped LAC curves, we can predict that each firm will produce the quantity that corresponds to the minimum point on its LAC. We thus get an industry composed of firms that all produce the same level of output.

In the case of horizontal LAC curves, by contrast, there is simply no unique minimum-cost point. LAC is the same at any level of output, which leads to an indeterminacy not present in the earlier case. We just cannot predict what the size distribution of firms will look like in the case of horizontal LAC curves. There may be a handful of large firms, many small ones, or a mixture of different sizes. All we can say with confidence is that price in the long run will gravitate toward the value of LAC.

How Changing Input Prices Affect Long-Run Supply

In our analysis of cost curves in Chapter 10, which forms the basis of our analysis of supply under perfect competition, an important assumption was that input prices do not vary with the amount of output produced. For a single firm whose input purchases constitute only a small fraction of the total input market, this assumption is plausible. In many cases, moreover, even the entire industry's demands for inputs constitute only a small share of the overall input market. For example, even if the insurance industry issues 20 percent more policies this year than last, it employs such a small percentage of the total available supplies of secretaries, computers, executives, and other inputs that the prices of these inputs should not be significantly affected. So here too we may reasonably assume that input prices do not depend on output.

But there are at least some industries in which the volume of inputs purchased constitutes an appreciable share of the entire input market. The market for commercial airliners, for example, consumes a significant share of the total amount of titanium sold each year. In such cases, a large increase in industry output will often be accompanied by significant increases in input prices.

When that happens, we have what is known as a **pecuniary diseconomy**, a bidding up of input prices when industry output increases.[12] Even though

pecuniary diseconomy a rise in production cost that occurs when an expansion of industry output causes a rise in the prices of inputs.

---

[12]A *pecuniary diseconomy* thus implies that input prices will fall when industry output contracts.

392   CHAPTER 11   PERFECT COMPETITION

FIGURE 11.17
Long-Run Supply Curve for an Increasing Cost Industry
When input prices rise with industry output, each firm's LAC curve will also rise with industry output (left panel). Thus the firm's LAC curve when industry output is Q_2 lies above its LAC curve when industry output is Q_1 (left panel). Firms will still gravitate to the minimum points on their LAC curves (Q_i^*, left panel), but because this minimum point depends on industry output, the long-run industry supply curve (S_{LR}, right panel) will now be upward sloping.

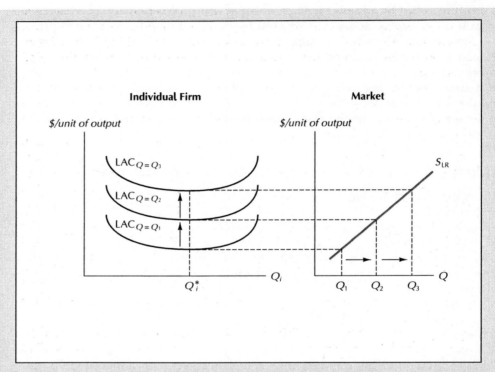

the industry can expand output indefinitely without using more inputs per unit of output, the minimum point on each firm's LAC curve is nonetheless a rising function of industry output. For example, note in the left panel in Figure 11.17 that the firm's LAC curve for an industry output of Q_2 lies above its LAC curve for an industry output of $Q_1 < Q_2$, and that the LAC curve for an industry output of $Q_3 > Q_2$ lies higher still. To each industry output level there corresponds a different LAC curve, because input prices are different at every level of industry output. The long-run supply curve for such an industry will trace out the minimum points of these LAC curves. Thus, on the long-run industry supply curve (S_{LR}, right panel), Q_1 corresponds to the minimum point on the firm's LAC curve when industry output is Q_1 (left panel); Q_2 corresponds to the minimum point for the LAC curve for Q_2; and so on. With pecuniary diseconomies, the long-run supply curve will be upward sloping even though each individual firm's LAC curve is U-shaped. Pecuniary diseconomies also produce an upward-sloping industry supply curve when each firm's LAC curve is horizontal. Competitive industries in which rising input prices lead to upward-sloping supply curves are called *increasing cost industries*.

There are also cases in which the prices of inputs may fall significantly with expanding industry output. This will happen, for example, if inputs are manufactured using technologies in which there are substantial economies of scale. A dramatic increase in road building, for example, might facilitate greater exploitation of economies of scale in the production of earthmoving equipment, resulting in a lower price for that input. Such cases are called *pecuniary economies,* and give rise to a downward-sloping long-run industry supply curve, even where each firm's LAC curve is either horizontal or U-shaped. Competitive industries in which falling input prices lead to downward-sloping supply curves are called *decreasing cost industries.*

Why do color photographs cost less than black-and-white photographs?

When I was a boy, color photographs were a luxury, costing several times as much as black and white. Today, the photo-processing shop near my house charges $14.91 to develop and print a 36-exposure roll of black-and-white film, but only $6.99 for the same size roll of color film. This fall in the relative price of color photos has occurred despite the fact that the color process remains more complex than the one for black and white.

If color processing is more complex than black and white, why does it cost less? The answer is in part because of economies of scale in the production of the machinery used to make both types of prints. When color photography was in its infancy, film was expensive and the colors tended to fade rapidly, so most people used black and white. The high volume of black-and-white photo processing, in turn, made it possible to produce processing machines cheaply because of economies of scale. As the price of color film declined over time and its quality rose, more people began to use it and the demand for color-processing equipment gradually grew. And again because of economies of scale in the production of processing equipment, this led to a fall in the cost of an important input for color printmaking—a pecuniary economy. At the same time, the decline in production of black-and-white processing equipment led to an increase in its price—a pecuniary diseconomy.

Why do color photos cost less than black-and-white ones?

The resulting changes in the equilibrium prices and quantities of the two types of prints are roughly as shown in Figure 11.18. Note that the relative positions of the two supply curves are the same for both years. This means that the printmaking industry would be willing to supply any given total quantity of black-and-white prints for a lower price than for the same quantity of color prints in both years. It is the change in demand patterns, together with downward-sloping supply curves in both markets, that explains the observed reversal in relative prices.

ECONOMIC NATURALIST 11.1

THE ELASTICITY OF SUPPLY

In Chapter 5 we defined the price elasticity of demand as a measure of the responsiveness of the quantity demanded to variations in price. An analogous concept exists for measuring the responsiveness of the quantity supplied to variations in price. Naturally, it is called the **price elasticity of supply.** Suppose we are at a point (Q, P) on the industry supply curve shown in Figure 11.19, where

price elasticity of supply the percentage change in quantity supplied that occurs in response to a 1 percent change in product price.

FIGURE 11.18
Pecuniary Economies and the Price of Color and Black-and-White Photos
Because of economies of scale in the production of equipment used to process film, the long-run supply curves of both color and black-and-white prints are downward sloping. In 1955, when the quality of color film was poor, most people demanded black and white, resulting in lower prices. In 2005, by contrast, demand for color is much greater than for black and white. The result is that color prints are now less expensive than black and white, even though color-processing equipment remains more complicated.

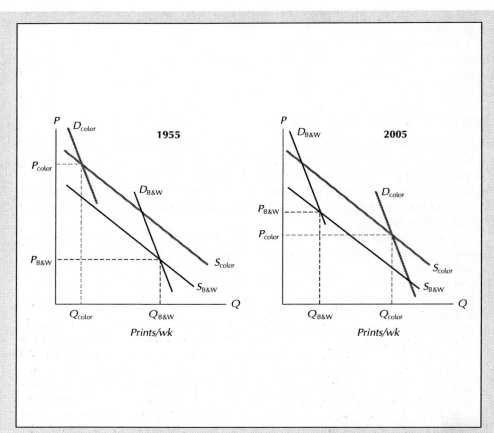

a change in price of ΔP gives rise to a change of ΔQ in the quantity supplied. The price elasticity of supply, denoted ϵ^S, is then given by

$$\epsilon^S = \frac{\Delta Q}{\Delta P}\frac{P}{Q} \text{ (see footnote 13 below).} \tag{11.1}$$

As in the case of elasticity of demand, supply elasticity has a simple interpretation in terms of the geometry of the industry supply curve. When ΔP is small, the ratio $\Delta P/Q$ is the slope of the supply curve, which means that the ratio $\Delta Q/\Delta P$ is the reciprocal of that slope. Thus the price elasticity of supply may be interpreted as the product of the ratio of price to quantity and the reciprocal of the slope of the supply curve:

$$\epsilon^S = \frac{P}{Q}\frac{1}{\text{slope}}. \tag{11.2}$$

---

[13]In calculus terms, supply elasticity is defined by

$$\epsilon^S = \frac{P}{Q}\frac{dQ}{dP}.$$

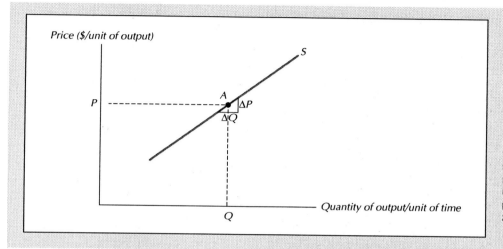

FIGURE 11.19
The Elasticity of Supply
At point *A*, the elasticity of supply is given by $\epsilon^s = (\Delta Q/\Delta P)(P/Q)$. Because the short-run supply curve is always upward sloping, the short-run elasticity of supply will always be positive. In the long run, elasticity of supply can be positive, zero, or negative.

Because of the law of diminishing returns, the short-run competitive industry supply curve will always be upward sloping, which means that the short-run elasticity of supply will always be positive. For industries with a horizontal long-run supply curve, the long-run elasticity of supply is infinite. Output can be expanded indefinitely without a change in price. Because of pecuniary economies and diseconomies, long-run competitive industry supply curves may also be either downward or upward sloping in specific cases. The corresponding long-run elasticities of supply in these cases will be either negative or positive.

As noted earlier, most industries employ only a relatively small share of the total volume of inputs traded in the marketplace, which means that modest variations in industry output should have no significant effect on input prices in most industries. In practical applications of the competitive model, therefore, most economists adopt the working hypothesis that long-run supply curves are horizontal. Of course, this hypothesis can always be modified when there is evidence that pecuniary economies or diseconomies are important.

APPLYING THE COMPETITIVE MODEL

As noted earlier in the chapter, economists recognize that no industries strictly satisfy the four requirements for perfect competition—a standardized product, firms as price takers, perfect factor mobility, and perfect information. For practical purposes, the important question is how far an industry can fall short of these conditions before general tendencies of the competitive model fail to apply. Unfortunately, there are no hard-and-fast rules for making this judgment. In industries where entry and exit are especially easy—such as the airline industry—a firm may behave as a price taker even in a market in which it is the only competitor.[14] In industries in which entry and exit are more difficult, even

---

[14]At a limited number of large airports, entry is difficult even in the airline industry. For these airports to accommodate carriers, new capacity will have to be built, which could take years or even decades.

CHAPTER 11 PERFECT COMPETITION

the existence of a relatively large number of established firms does not guarantee price-taking behavior. In the short run, especially, firms may be able to work out tacit agreements to restrain price competition even when there are extranormal profits.

Despite this difficulty, experience has shown that many of the most important long-run properties of the competitive model apply in most industries, with the notable exception of those where the government erects legal barriers to entry (for example, by requiring a government license in order to participate in a market, as used to be the case in the airline industry).

By way of illustration, let's consider three brief applications that highlight some of the insights afforded by the perfectly competitive model.

Price Supports as a Device for Saving Family Farms

At the beginning of the twentieth century, more than 20 percent of the U.S. labor force earned its living by farming. Today, the corresponding figure is less than 3 percent. This change is obviously not the result of a dramatic decline in food consumption. Rather, it is one of the many consequences of farming methods having become vastly more productive during this century.

As farm machinery has grown larger and more sophisticated, the size of land parcel at which long-run average cost curves cease declining has grown ever larger. Where family farms of fewer than 100 acres were once common in the American heartland, large corporate farms with several thousand acres have increasingly become the norm.

In terms of the competitive model developed in this chapter, the family farm may be thought of as a firm whose capital stock gives rise to the short-run cost curves denoted ATC_F and SMC_F in Figure 11.20. The corresponding cost curves for the corporate farm are denoted ATC_C and SMC_C. Competition has the effect of driving the long-run equilibrium price toward P^*, the minimum point on the LAC curve. At P^*, corporate farms earn a normal profit while family farms, with their higher costs, earn economic losses of Π_F, as measured by the shaded rectangle in Figure 11.20.

Despite the intense determination of many family farmers to remain on the land, large losses are simply not sustainable over a period of many years. Most

FIGURE 11.20
Cost Curves for Family and Corporate Farms
With the availability of modern farming methods, large farms have much lower unit costs than small ones. A price that covers cost for large corporate farms will produce large economic losses for family farms.

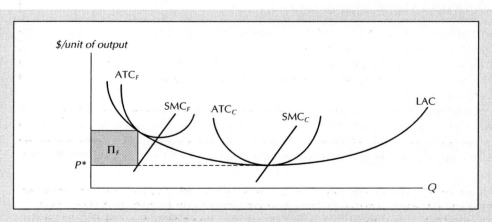

APPLYING THE COMPETITIVE MODEL   397

farmers remain well past the time they are no longer able to earn a profit equal to the opportunity cost of their land. Many remain even long after they have ceased to earn the opportunity cost of their own labor. And a substantial number hang on by borrowing away most of the value of their only significant asset, their farmland. But credit cannot be extended without limit, and in the absence of government intervention, the long-run tendency has been for family farmers to leave the industry, selling whatever land they still own to the more efficient corporate farms.

Contrary to the stylized assumptions of the model of perfect competition, this process of resource mobility is far from perfect. Family farming is a way of life, one that people do not readily abandon when the terms of trade turn against them. There is great sympathy among American voters for the plight of family farmers. We don't like to witness scenes on the nightly news of families huddled tearfully together as the auctioneer sells off the last of their possessions. We appreciate that these families have worked hard all their lives in an era when many others earn their living by selling crack or robbing convenience stores. Our sympathy for the family farmers has been translated by Congress into legislative programs designed to enable them to remain on their farms.

Price supports for agricultural products are among the most important of these programs. The details of the support programs are highly complex, but for the purpose of our analysis it will suffice to say that the government announces a price for a given product and then stands ready to buy whatever private buyers fail to purchase.[15] One of the most important, if not always explicitly stated, goals of the price support programs is to keep prices high enough to prevent small family farms from going bankrupt.

Sad to say, these programs have failed miserably. Sadder still, even the most cursory understanding of competitive market dynamics would have made clear to Congress why this outcome was inevitable. To illustrate, suppose the price support is set at P_G in a market in which the unsupported price would have been P^*. In Figure 11.21, we see that the short-run effect is to cause family farms to

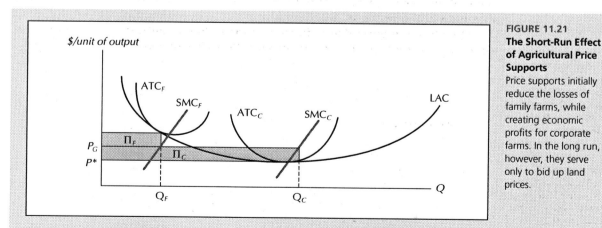

FIGURE 11.21
The Short-Run Effect of Agricultural Price Supports
Price supports initially reduce the losses of family farms, while creating economic profits for corporate farms. In the long run, however, they serve only to bid up land prices.

---

[15]Recent agricultural price support programs, such as the loan deficiency program, work by paying farmers the difference between a specified target price and the actual market price. Under these programs, the price paid by buyers can actually be lower than the unregulated equilibrium price.

increase their output to Q_F, and to cause corporate farms to increase theirs to Q_C. At these output levels, family farms will earn an economic loss indicated by the color rectangle labeled Π_F in Figure 11.21, while corporate farms earn an economic profit indicated by the shaded rectangle Π_C.

In the short run, to the extent the new loss is smaller than the previous loss suffered by family farmers, the price support has had the intended effect of helping the family farmer. But the relief is destined to be transitory. To see why, note first that the same price support that reduces the short-run losses of family farms generates positive profits for corporate farms. We know, however, that positive profits are not sustainable in an industry in which there is freedom of entry. They will lure outsiders to bid for farmland so that they too may earn more than a normal rate of return. The effect of this bidding will be to cause land prices to rise to the point where corporate farms no longer earn economic profits. But with land prices higher than before, the cost curves of all farms, corporate and family, shift upward. For owners, some of the sting of these economic losses is mitigated by the greater implicit value of their land. But for the many farm families who rent their land, there is no such compensation.

As technology continues to advance, and with it the scale of the most efficient farms, the stage is now set for another round of distress for family farms and the attendant pressure to increase the government price support level. A treadmill has been set in motion whereby the price support keeps escalating, only to set off another round of escalation in land prices. As a policy for protecting the long-term economic viability of family farms, the agricultural price support program could hardly have been more ill conceived.

Economists are not in a position to tell Congress whether trying to preserve the existence of the family farm is a worthwhile goal. That is a political question. But given that Congress has decided to pursue this objective, economists can give advice about what policies are most likely to be effective. The price supports failed because of the competitive bidding for land that was induced by them. Their long-run effect was to drive up the price of land, while doing little to ensure the survival of small family farms. A much more direct and efficient way to aid family farmers would be to reduce their income taxes; or, in the case of more extreme need, to give them outright cash grants.

The Illusory Attraction of Taxing Business

As noted in Chapter 2, political leaders often find it easier to propose new taxes on business than to collect additional taxes from individuals. Proposals to tax business usually include statements to the effect that "wealthy corporations can better afford to pay extra taxes than struggling workers can." But as we saw in Chapter 2, a tax placed on the product sold by an industry will in general be passed on, at least in part, to consumers.

Let us examine a perfectly competitive industry in which individual firms have identical U-shaped LAC curves like the one labeled LAC_i in the right panel in Figure 11.22. In the most common case, moderate variations in the industry's output will have no appreciable effect on its input prices, with the result that the long-run supply curve for this industry will be a horizontal line at the minimum point of LAC_i (the curve labeled S_{LR} in the left panel). If D is the market demand curve, then the equilibrium price will be P^*.

APPLYING THE COMPETITIVE MODEL   399

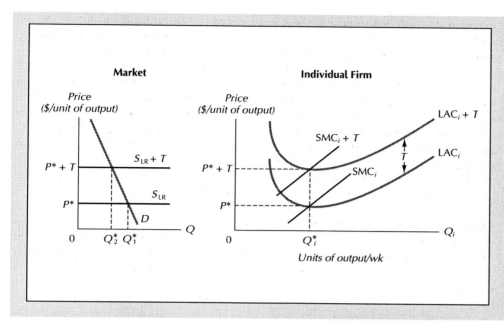

FIGURE 11.22
The Effect of a Tax on the Output of a Perfectly Competitive Industry
A tax of T dollars per unit of output raises the LAC and SMC curves by T dollars (right panel). The new long-run industry supply curve is again a horizontal line at the minimum value of LAC (left panel). Equilibrium price rises by T dollars (left panel), which means that 100 percent of the tax is passed on to consumers.

Now suppose a tax of T dollars is collected on each unit of output sold in the market. The effect of this tax is to shift the LAC and SMC curves of each firm upward by T dollars (right panel in Figure 11.22). The new long-run industry supply curve is again a horizontal line at the minimum value of the LAC curve—this time the curve $S_{LR} + T$ in the left panel in Figure 11.22. The effect of the tax is to increase the price of the product by exactly T dollars. Industry output contracts from Q_1^* to Q_2^* (left panel), and this contraction is achieved by firms leaving the industry.

Thus we see that, for competitive industries whose firms have U-shaped LAC curves, and whose input prices are fixed (the most empirically relevant case), the burden of a tax on output falls entirely on consumers. As we will see in later chapters, there are a variety of legitimate reasons for taxing the output of specific industries. But the claim that corporations have more money than people do is simply not one of these reasons. Claims to the contrary are fraudulent, and an economically literate population would be unlikely to reelect politicians who defend taxing business on this ground.

If constant cost competitive industries are able to pass on 100 percent of taxes to buyers, why do industry lobbyists oppose taxes so strongly? Note in Figure 11.22 that one effect of a tax is to reduce total industry output. This reduction is achieved by some firms going out of business. Bankruptcy is never a pleasant experience for the owners of a firm, and on this account it is far from surprising that industry trade associations are so strongly opposed to new taxes.

The Adoption of Cost-Saving Innovations

The economist's emphasis on the competitive firm as a price taker sometimes creates the impression that competitive firms do little more than passively respond to impersonal price signals served up by the environment. This impression is

CHAPTER 11 PERFECT COMPETITION

deeply misleading. While it is true, for example, that an individual trucker can do little to affect trucking rates set in the open market, there is a great deal he can and must do to ensure his continued survival.

The short-run response to the dramatic fuel price increases of the 1970s automatically led to just the sorts of adjustments predicted by the competitive model: short-term losses, exit from the industry, gradually rising prices, and a gradual restoration of profitability for surviving firms. But the change in the environment also created opportunities that some firms actively exploited to their own advantage. A case in point is illustrated in the following Economic Naturalist.

ECONOMIC NATURALIST 11.2

Why did 18-wheel cargo trucks suddenly begin using airfoils in the mid-1970s?

Before 1970, the profile of the typical 18-wheel semi tractor-trailer truck was like the one shown in the top drawing below. The broad, flat expanse of the top of the trailer was directly exposed to the force of the oncoming wind, which at highway speeds was substantial. But diesel fuel cost only $0.30/gal in 1970, and so the penalty from having to run the engine a little harder was not large in those days.

With diesel prices over $1/gal by the early 1980s, however, that penalty became much more important—so much so that entrepreneurs devised ways of reducing it. One of the most successful innovations was the simple airfoil that now adorns the cab of virtually every large truck on the road. Shown in the bottom drawing on the right, its purpose is to deflect the wind to the top of the trailer. The profile of today's semi is still no aerodynamic masterpiece, but truckers estimate that the reduced wind resistance increases their mileage by 15 percent at highway speeds.

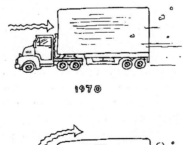

1970

1985

Why did airfoils suddenly appear on large trucks in the mid-1970s?

The truckers who were first to install the airfoils did so at a time when the industry price level was determined by the higher costs of running trucks that lacked them. As a result, these early adopters earned economic profits from their efforts. As time passed, however, more and more trucks began to sport the devices, and the industry price level gradually declined in response to the lower costs they made possible. At this point in history, it is rare to see an 18-wheeler that lacks an airfoil. By now it is safe to assume that the resultant cost savings have been fully reflected in lower trucking rates. The result is that the owner of a truck must now install an airfoil merely to be able to earn a normal rate of profit. Those who fail to install them pay the penalty of earning economic losses.

The lesson of this example is that the entrepreneur who earns economic profits is the one who adopts cost-saving innovations ahead of the competition. It is the search for such innovations that keeps even the price-taking firm from being merely a passive reactor to economic forces beyond its control.

SUMMARY

* The assumed objective of the firm is to maximize its economic profit. Competitive pressures in the marketplace may render this a plausible assumption, even though it seems to impute an unrealistically high degree of purposefulness to the actions of many managers. Economic profit is the difference between total revenue and cost—both explicit and implicit—of all resources used in production. Economic profit is not to be confused with accounting profit, which is the difference between total revenue and the explicit cost of resources used.

* The economic model of perfect competition assumes a standardized product, price-taking behavior on the part of the firms, perfect mobility of resources, and perfect information on the part of buyers and firms. In this sense, it is similar to the physicist's model of motion on frictionless surfaces. Both models describe idealized conditions that are rarely if ever met in practice, and yet each generates useful predictions and explanations of events we observe in the world.

* The rule for profit maximization in the short run is to produce the level of output for which price is equal to short-run marginal cost on the rising portion of that curve. If price falls below the minimum value of average variable cost, the firm does best to produce no output in the short run. The individual firm's short-run supply curve is thus the rising portion of its short-run marginal cost curve that lies above the minimum point of its average variable cost curve.

* The short-run industry supply curve is the horizontal summation of the individual firms' supply curves. It intersects the industry demand curve to determine the short-run equilibrium price. The individual competitive firm's demand curve is a horizontal line at the equilibrium price. If that price happens to lie above the minimum value of the long-run average cost curve, each firm will earn positive economic profit. If price is less than that value, each will suffer economic losses.

* Long-run adjustments consist not only of alterations in the size of existing firms' capital stocks, but also of entry and exit of firms. Where firms have identical U-shaped LAC curves, the long-run equilibrium price will be the minimum value of that LAC curve, and each firm will produce the corresponding quantity.

* Both long-run and short-run equilibrium positions are efficient in the sense that the value of the resources used in making the last unit of output is exactly equal to the value of that output to the buyer. This means that the equilibrium position exhausts all possibilities for mutually beneficial exchange. The long-run equilibrium has two additional attractive features: (1) Output is produced at the lowest possible unit cost, and (2) the seller is paid only the cost of producing the product. No economic profit is extracted from the buyer.

* Under perfect competition with constant input prices, the long-run industry supply curve is a horizontal line, not only when LAC curves are horizontal, but also when they are U-shaped. When input prices are an increasing function of industry output, the industry supply curves in both cases will be upward sloping. When input prices decline with industry output, the competitive industry supply curve will be downward sloping.

* The effect of competition for the purchase of unusually high-quality inputs is to raise the price of those inputs until they no longer enable the firm that employs them to earn an economic profit. This is an extremely important part of the long-run adjustment process, and failure to account for it lies behind the failure of many well-intended economic policies.

* Even price-taking firms must actively seek out means of reducing their costs of doing business. To the early adopters of cost-saving innovations goes a temporary stream of economic profit, while late adopters must suffer through periods of economic losses.

QUESTIONS FOR REVIEW

1. What is the difference between economic profit and accounting profit, and how does this difference matter for actual business decisions?

2. Under what conditions will we expect firms to behave as price takers even though there are only a small number of other firms in the industry?

3. Would the market for dry cleaning be perfectly competitive in large cities such as San Francisco or New York City? Why or why not? How about in a small city such as Athens, Ohio, or Meredith, New Hampshire?

CHAPTER 11 PERFECT COMPETITION

4. A firm's total revenue curve is given by TR = $aQ - 2Q^2$. Is this a perfectly competitive firm? Explain why or why not. *No*

5. Does the fact that a business manager may not know the definition of marginal cost contradict the theory of perfect competition? *No*

6. *True or false:* If marginal cost lies below average fixed cost, the firm should shut down in the short run. Explain. *false*

7. What do economists mean when they say that the short-run competitive equilibrium is efficient?

8. *True or false:* In a constant cost industry, a tax of a constant, fixed amount on each unit of output sold will not affect the amount of output sold by a perfectly competitive firm in the long run. Explain. *true*

9. Suppose all firms in a competitive industry are operating at output levels for which price is equal to long-run marginal cost. *True or false:* This industry is necessarily in long-run equilibrium. *false*

10. *True or false:* Consumer surplus is the area between the demand curve and the price line. For a perfectly competitive firm the demand curve equals the price line. Thus, a perfectly competitive industry produces no consumer surplus. *false*

11. Why are pecuniary economies and diseconomies said to be the exception rather than the rule?

12. Would you expect a firm that adopts cost-saving innovations faster than 80 percent of all firms in its industry to earn economic profits? If so, will there be any tendency for these profits to be bid away?

PROBLEMS

1. A competitive firm has the cost structure described in the following table. Graph the marginal cost, average variable cost, and average total cost curves. How many units of output will it produce at a market price of 32? Calculate its profits and show them in your graph.

Q	ATC	AVC	MC
1	44	4	8
2	28	8	16
4	26	16	32
6	31	24	48
8	37	32	64

2. If the short-run marginal and average variable cost curves for a competitive firm are given by SMC = $2 + 4Q$ and AVC = $2 + 2Q$, how many units of output will it produce at a market price of 10? At what level of fixed cost will this firm earn zero economic profit?

3. Each of 1000 identical firms in the competitive peanut butter industry has a short-run marginal cost curve given by

$$SMC = 4 + Q.$$

If the demand curve for this industry is

$$P = 10 - \frac{2Q}{1000},$$

Q = 2000

P = 6

what will be the short-run loss in producer and consumer surplus if an outbreak of aflatoxin suddenly makes it impossible to produce any peanut butter?

4. Assuming the aflatoxin outbreak in Problem 3 persists, will the long-run loss in producer and consumer surplus be larger than, smaller than, or the same as the short-run loss?

5. A perfectly competitive firm faces a price of 10 and is currently producing a level of output at which marginal cost is equal to 10 on a rising portion of its short-run marginal cost curve. Its long-run marginal cost is equal to 12. Its short-run average variable cost is equal to 8. The minimum point on its long-run average cost curve is equal to 10. Is this firm earning an economic profit in the short run? Should it alter its output in the short run? In the long run, what should this firm do?

6. All firms in a competitive industry have long-run total cost curves given by

$$\text{LTC}_Q = Q^3 - 10Q^2 + 36Q, \qquad LAC$$

where Q is the firm's level of output. What will be the industry's long-run equilibrium price? (*Hint:* Use either calculus or a graph to find the minimum value of the associated long-run average cost curve.) What will be the long-run equilibrium output level of the representative firm?

7. Same as Problem 6, except now

$$\text{LTC}_Q = Q^2 + 4Q.$$

Could any firm actually have this particular LTC curve? Why or why not?

8. The marginal and average cost curves of taxis in Metropolis are constant at \$0.20/mile. The demand curve for taxi trips in Metropolis is given by $P = 1 - 0.00001Q$, where P is the fare, in dollars per mile, and Q is measured in miles per year. If the industry is perfectly competitive and each cab can provide exactly 10,000 miles/yr of service, how many cabs will there be in equilibrium and what will be the equilibrium fare?

9. Now suppose that the city council of Metropolis decides to curb congestion in the downtown area by limiting the number of taxis to 6. Applicants participate in a lottery, and the six winners get a medallion, which is a permanent license to operate a taxi in Metropolis. What will the equilibrium fare be now? How much economic profit will each medallion holder earn? If medallions can be traded in the marketplace and the rate of interest is 10 percent/yr, how much will the medallions sell for? (*Hint:* How much money would you have to deposit in a bank to earn annual interest equal to the profit made by a taxi medallion?) Will the person who buys a medallion at this price earn a positive economic profit?

10. Merlin is like all other managers in a perfectly competitive industry except in one respect: Because of his great sense of humor, people are willing to work for him for half the going wage rate. All other firms in the industry have short-run total cost curves given by

$$\text{STC}_Q = M + 10Q + wQ^2 \text{ (see footnote 16)},$$

where M is the salary paid to ordinary managers and w is the going wage rate for the industry. If all firms in the industry face an output price of 28, and if $w = 2$, how much more will Merlin be paid than the other managers in the industry? *40.5*

11. You are the owner/manager of a small competitive firm that manufactures house paints. You and all your 1000 competitors have total cost curves given by

$$\text{TC} = 8 + 2Q + 2Q^2,$$

and the industry is in long-run equilibrium.

Now you are approached by an inventor who holds a patent on a process that will reduce your costs by half at each level of output.

a. What is the most you would be willing to pay for the exclusive right to use this invention? *16.25*

b. Would the inventor be willing to sell at that price?

12. In the short run, a perfectly competitive firm produces output using capital services (a fixed input) and labor services (a variable input). At its profit-maximizing level of output, the marginal product of labor is equal to the average product of labor.

---

[16] The associated marginal cost curve is $d\text{STC}_Q/dQ = \text{MC}_Q = 10 + 2wQ$.

CHAPTER 11   PERFECT COMPETITION

    a.   What is the relationship between this firm's average variable cost and its marginal cost? Explain.

    b.   If the firm has 10 units of capital and the rental price of each unit is \$4/day, what will be the firm's profit? Should it remain open in the short run?

13. A firm in a competitive industry has a total cost function of $TC = 0.2Q^2 - 5Q + 30$, whose corresponding marginal cost curve is $MC = 0.4Q - 5$. If the firm faces a price of 6, what quantity should it sell? What profit does the firm make at this price? Should the firm shut down?

14. The demand for gasoline is $P = 5 - 0.002Q$ and the supply is $P = 0.2 + 0.004Q$, where P is in dollars and Q is in gallons. If a tax of \$1/gal is placed on gasoline, what is the incidence of the tax? What is the lost consumer surplus? What is the lost producer surplus?

15. Suppose that bicycles are produced by a perfectly competitive, constant cost industry. Which of the following will have a larger effect on the long-run price of bicycles: (1) a government program to advertise the health benefits of bicycling, or (2) a government program that increases the demand for steel, an input in the manufacture of bicycles that is produced in an increasing cost industry?

16. Suppose a representative firm in a perfectly competitive, constant cost industry has a cost function $TC = 4Q^2 + 100Q + 100$.

    a.   What is the long-run equilibrium price for this industry?

    b.   If market demand is given by the function $Q = 1000 - P$, where P denotes price, how many firms will operate in this long-run equilibrium?

    c.   Suppose the government grants a lump-sum subsidy to each firm that manufactures the product. If this lump-sum subsidy equals 36, what would be the new long-run equilibrium price for the industry?

17. The domestic supply and demand curves for Jolt coffee beans are given by $P = 10 + Q$ and $P = 100 - 2Q$, respectively, where P is the price in dollars per bushel, and Q is the quantity in millions of bushels per year. The United States produces and consumes only a trivial fraction of world Jolt bean output, and the current world price of \$30/bushel is unaffected by events in the U.S. market. Transportation costs are also negligible.

    a.   How much will U.S. consumers pay for Jolt coffee beans, and how many bushels per year will they consume?

    b.   How will your answers to part (a) change if Congress enacts a tariff of \$20/bushel?

    c.   What total effect on domestic producer and consumer surplus will the tariff have? How much revenue will the tariff raise?

18. An Australian researcher has discovered a drug that weakens a sheep's wool fibers just above the sheep's skin. The drug sharply reduces the cost of shearing (cutting the wool off) sheep because the entire coat pulls off easily in one piece. The world wool market is reasonably close to the model of perfect competition in both the product and factor sides. Trace out all of the effects of the introduction of this new drug.

ANSWERS TO IN-CHAPTER EXERCISES

11.1. Let r^* be the monthly interest rate for which Cullen's economic profit would be zero. Then r^* must satisfy \$16,000 - \$4,000 - \$800 - r^* (\$100,000,000) = 0, which yields $r^* = 0.000112$, or 0.0112 percent/mo. Cullen should relocate only if the interest rate is lower than r^*.

11.2. Marginal cost is the slope of the total cost curve, and marginal revenue is the slope of the total revenue curve. At the maximum profit point, $Q = 7.4$, the slopes of these two curves are exactly the same.

11.3. First, we need to rearrange the representative firm supply curve $P = 20 + 90Q_i$ to have quantity alone on one side.

$$Q_i = -\frac{2}{9} + \frac{1}{90}P.$$

Then we multiply by the number of firms $n = 30$.

$$Q = nQ_i = 30Q_i = 30\left(-\frac{2}{9} + \frac{1}{90}P\right) = -\frac{20}{3} + \frac{1}{3}P.$$

Finally, we rearrange the industry supply curve $Q = -\frac{20}{3} + \frac{1}{3}P$ to have price alone on one side, $P = 20 + 3Q$, to return to slope-intercept form.

11.4. Short-run profit maximization for a perfectly competitive firm occurs at the quantity where price equals marginal cost, $P = MC$, provided $P > $ min AVC (otherwise, the firm shuts down). Since marginal cost is $MC = 2Q$, the market price $P = 12$ equals marginal cost $12 = 2Q$ at quantity $Q = 6$. Note that min AVC $= 0$ here. We can express profits (with fixed costs separated out) as $\pi = (P - AVC)Q - FC$. Since average variable cost is $AVC = Q = 6$, the firm would earn profits of

$$\pi = (12 - 6)6 - FC = 36 - FC.$$

Thus, with fixed cost FC $= 36$, the firm would earn zero profits.

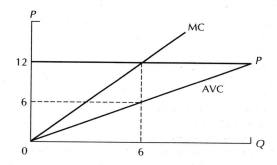

11.5. Total surplus is equal to the sum of the two shaded triangles shown below, which is $100,000/yr.

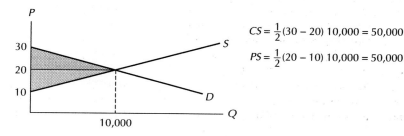

$$CS = \frac{1}{2}(30 - 20)\,10,000 = 50,000$$

$$PS = \frac{1}{2}(20 - 10)\,10,000 = 50,000$$

11.6. If the firm pays an incompetent manager only $30,000, it will continue to earn zero economic profit. It cannot pay any more than that without suffering an economic loss.

CHAPTER

12

MONOPOLY

Virtually every movie theater charges different admission prices to movie-goers who belong to different groups. Students pay one price, adults another, senior citizens still another. Some theaters sell "ten-packs" of movie tickets at a much lower unit price than the tickets they sell at the door. And people who attend showings at the dinner hour sometimes pay much less than those who attend evening showings. None of these practices would be expected under our model of perfect competition, which holds that all buyers pay a single price for a completely standardized product (the so-called *law of one price*).

The same theater operators who charge different ticket prices to different groups follow quite another practice when it comes to the sale of concession items. Here, the law of one price almost always prevails. Students, adults, senior citizens, major league baseball players, the clergy, service station attendants, and all other patrons pay exactly the same price for their popcorn. The same observation applies to the prices of soft drinks and candy. These prices, however, are usually much higher than we see for the same items sold in grocery stores and other retail establishments, certainly far greater than any reasonable measure of the marginal cost of providing them.

Both behaviors—charging differential admission prices on the one hand and uniformly high concession prices on the other—are, as we will see, perfectly consistent with what the economic model predicts about the single seller of a good or service.

408   CHAPTER 12   MONOPOLY

CHAPTER PREVIEW

In this chapter, our task will be to examine the market structure that least resembles perfect competition—namely, *monopoly*, the case of a market served by a single seller of a product with no close substitutes. We will discuss five factors that lead to this market structure: (1) control over key inputs, (2) economies of scale, (3) patents, (4) network economies, and (5) government licenses. We will then see that the monopolist's rule for maximizing profits in the short run is the same as the one used by perfectly competitive firms. The monopolist will expand output if the gain in revenue exceeds the increase in costs, and will contract output if the loss in revenue is smaller than the reduction in costs.

Next, we will examine the monopolist's behavior when confronted with the options of selling in several separate markets. Here again, the logic of cost-benefit analysis will provide a convenient framework for analyzing the firm's decision about whether to alter its current behavior.

Our next step will be to examine the efficiency properties of the standard monopoly equilibrium. We will see that, unlike the perfectly competitive case, the monopoly equilibrium does not exhaust the potential gains from exchange. In general, the value to society of an additional unit of output will exceed the cost to the monopolist of the resources required to produce it. We will see that this finding has often been interpreted to mean that monopoly is less efficient than perfect competition. We will also see, however, that this interpretation is of only limited practical significance because the conditions that give rise to monopoly are rarely compatible with those required for perfect competition.

Our policy focus in the chapter will be on the question of how the government should treat natural monopolies—markets characterized by downward-sloping long-run average cost curves. We will consider five policy alternatives: (1) state ownership, (2) private ownership with government price regulation, (3) competitive bidding by private firms for the right to be the sole provider of service, (4) vigorous enforcement of antitrust laws designed to prevent monopoly, and finally, (5) a complete *laissez-faire*, or hands-off, policy. Problems are inherent in each alternative, and we will see that the best policy generally will be different in different circumstances.

DEFINING MONOPOLY

A monopoly is a market structure in which a single seller of a product with no close substitutes serves the entire market. This definition could hardly appear any simpler, and yet it turns out to be exceedingly difficult to apply in practice. Consider the example of movie theaters with which the chapter began. Is a local movie house a monopoly under our definition? In smaller cities, at least, it is likely to be the only one showing a given film at a given time. Whether it is a monopoly obviously depends on what we mean by a close substitute. If, for example, the theater is currently showing *Halloween Part 8*, there are likely to be a rich variety of close substitutes for its product. Indeed, literally hundreds of low-grade blood-and-gore films are released each year, and the potential patrons of such films generally do not have to look far if they are dissatisfied with the films available at any particular theater.

But what about a theater that is in the midst of an exclusive 6-month, first-run engagement of the latest *Spiderman* film? For fans of this series, there is really no close substitute. Those who want to see it while the excitement level surrounding its release is still high have only one seller to deal with.

The key feature that differentiates the monopoly from the competitive firm is the price elasticity of demand facing the firm. In the case of the perfectly competitive firm, recall, price elasticity is infinite. If a competitive firm raises its price only slightly, it will lose all its sales. A monopoly, by contrast, has significant control over the price it charges.

Empirically, one practical measure for deciding whether a firm enjoys significant monopoly power is to examine the cross-price elasticity of demand for its closest substitutes. In one famous antitrust case, the DuPont Corporation was charged with having an effective monopoly on the sale of cellophane. Even though the company sold more than 80 percent of all cellophane traded, it was able to defend itself against this charge by arguing that the cross-price elasticities between cellophane and its close substitutes—at the time, mainly waxed paper and aluminum foil—were sufficiently high to justify lumping all of these flexible-wrap products into a single market. DuPont sold less than 20 percent of total industry output under this broader market definition. In a controversial decision, the court deemed that small enough to sustain effective competition.

This is not to say, however, that cross-price elasticity provides a clear, unambiguous measure that distinguishes a product with close substitutes from one without. While there may not be anything quite like the latest *Spiderman* movie, there have always been lots of alternative ways to entertain oneself for 2 hours. For the person whose heart is set on seeing *Spiderman,* the theater operator is a monopolist, but for the person merely out in search of a good movie, the same theater operator faces stiff competition. The difference between perfect competition and monopoly often boils down to the question of which of these two types of buyers is more numerous. As in so many other cases in economics, the task of distinguishing between competition and monopoly remains as much an art as a science.

Note carefully that the distinction between monopoly and competition does not lie in any difference between the respective price elasticities of the *market* demand curves for the two cases. On the contrary, the market price elasticity of demand for products supplied by competitive firms is often much smaller than the price elasticity of demand facing a monopolist. The price elasticity of demand is smaller for wheat than for Polaroid cameras, even though wheat is produced under nearly perfectly competitive conditions while Polaroid's patents make it the only legal seller in most of its markets. *The important distinction between monopoly and competition is that the demand curve facing the individual competitive firm is horizontal (irrespective of the price elasticity of the corresponding market demand curve), while the monopolist's demand curve is simply the downward-sloping demand curve for the entire market.*

FIVE SOURCES OF MONOPOLY

How does a firm come to be the only one that serves its market? Economists discuss five factors, any one or combination of which can enable a firm to become a monopoly. Let's consider these factors in turn.

1. Exclusive Control over Important Inputs   The Perrier Corporation of France sells bottled mineral water. It spends millions of dollars each year advertising

410   CHAPTER 12   MONOPOLY

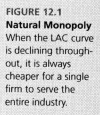

FIGURE 12.1
Natural Monopoly
When the LAC curve is declining through-out, it is always cheaper for a single firm to serve the entire industry.

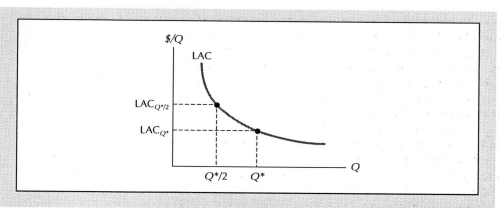

the unique properties of this water, which are the result, it says, of a once-in-eternity confluence of geological factors that created their mineral spring. In New York State, the Adirondack Soft Drink Company offers a product that is essentially tap water saturated with carbon dioxide gas. I am unable to tell the difference between Adirondack Seltzer and Perrier. But others feel differently, and for many of them there is simply no satisfactory substitute for Perrier. Perrier's monopoly position with respect to these buyers is the result of its exclusive control over an input that cannot easily be duplicated.

A similar monopoly position has resulted from the deBeers Diamond Mines' exclusive control over most of the world's supply of raw diamonds. Synthetic diamonds have now risen in quality to the point where they can occasionally fool even an experienced jeweler. But for many buyers, the preference for a stone that was mined from the earth is not a simple matter of greater hardness and refractive brilliance. They want *real* diamonds, and deBeers is the company that has them.

Exclusive control of key inputs is not a guarantee of permanent monopoly power. The preference for having a real diamond, for example, is based largely on the fact that mined diamonds have historically been genuinely superior to synthetic ones. But assuming that synthetic diamonds eventually do become completely indistinguishable from real ones, there will no longer be any basis for this preference. And as a result, the deBeers' control over the supply of mined diamonds will cease to confer monopoly power. New ways are constantly being devised of producing existing products, and the exclusive input that generates today's monopoly is likely to become obsolete tomorrow.

2. Economies of Scale   When the long-run average cost curve (given fixed input prices) is downward sloping, the least costly way to serve the market is to concentrate production in the hands of a single firm. In Figure 12.1, for example, note that a single firm can produce an industry output of Q^* at an average cost of LAC_{Q^*}, while with two firms sharing the same market, average cost rises to $LAC_{Q^*/2}$. A market that is most cheaply served by a single firm is called a *natural monopoly*. A frequently cited example is the provision of local telephone service.

Recall from Chapter 11 that it is possible for the LAC curve to be downward sloping even in the absence of economies of scale. This can happen, for example, if the price of an important input falls significantly when industry output expands (a *pecuniary economy,* in the language of Chapter 11). Note carefully, however, that this case is *not* one that gives rise to natural monopoly. Input prices here depend on the level of industry output, not on the output of any one firm. Pecuniary economies will apply with equal force whether one or many firms serve the market.

Strictly speaking, then, it is the degree of returns to scale, not the slope of the LAC curve, that determines whether we have a natural monopoly. With fixed input prices, of course, there is always a one-to-one relationship between returns to scale and the slope of the LAC curve (see Chapter 10).

3. Patents Most countries of the world protect inventions through some sort of patent system. A patent typically confers the right to exclusive benefit from all exchanges involving the invention to which it applies. There are costs as well as benefits to patents. On the cost side, the monopoly it creates usually leads, as we will see, to higher prices for consumers. On the benefit side, the patent makes possible a great many inventions that would not otherwise occur. Although some inventions are serendipitous, most are the result of long effort and expense in sophisticated research laboratories. If a firm were unable to sell its product for a sufficiently high price to recoup these outlays, it would have no economic reason to undertake research and development in the first place. Without a patent, competition would force price down to marginal cost, and the pace of innovation would be slowed dramatically. The protection from competition afforded by a patent is what makes it possible for the firm to recover its costs of innovation. In the United States, the life of a patent is 17 years, a compromise figure that is too long for many inventions, too short for many others. In particular, there is a persuasive argument that the patent life should be extended in the prescription drug industry, where the testing and approval process often consumes all but a few years of the current patent period.[1]

4. Network Economies On the demand side of many markets, a product becomes more valuable as greater numbers of consumers use it.[2] A vivid early illustration was the VHS technology's defeat of the competing Beta format in home video recorders. The attraction of VHS over the initial versions of Beta was that it permitted longer recording times. Beta later corrected this deficiency, and on most important technical dimensions became widely regarded by experts as superior to VHS. Yet the initial sales advantage of VHS proved insuperable. Once the fraction of consumers owning VHS passed a critical threshold, the reasons for choosing it became compelling—variety and availability of tape rentals, access to repair facilities, the capability to exchange tapes with friends, and so on.

In extreme cases, such *network economies* function like economies of scale as a source of natural monopoly. Microsoft's Windows operating system, for example, achieved its dominant market position on the strength of powerful network economies. Because Microsoft's initial sales advantage gave software developers a strong incentive to write for the Windows format, the inventory of available

---

[1]Henry Grabowski, *Drug Regulation and Innovation,* Washington, DC: American Enterprise Institute, 1976.

[2]See, for example, Joseph Farrell and Garth Saloner, "Standardization, Compatibility, and Innovation," *Rand Journal of Economics,* 16, 1985: 70–83.; and M. L. Katz and Carl Shapiro, "Systems Competition and Network Effects," *Journal of Economic Perspectives,* Spring 1994: 93–115.

412   CHAPTER 12   MONOPOLY

HELLO, THIS IS BILL GATES. REMEMBER, NOBODY HAS A MONOPOLY ON SAFETY, SO BUCKLE UP!

software in the Windows format is by now vastly larger than for any competing operating system. And although general-purpose software such as word processors and spreadsheets continues to be available for multiple operating systems, specialized professional software and games usually appear first in the Windows format and often only in that format. This software gap has given people a good reason for choosing Windows, even if, as in the case of many Apple Macintosh users, they believe a competing system is otherwise superior. The end result is that more than 90 percent of the world's personal computers now run Microsoft's Windows operating system. If that's not a pure monopoly, it comes awfully close.

5. Government Licenses or Franchises   In many markets, the law prevents anyone but a government-licensed firm from doing business. At rest areas on the Massachusetts Turnpike, for example, not just any fast-food restaurant is free to set up operations. The Turnpike Authority negotiates with several companies, chooses one, and then grants it an exclusive license to serve a particular area. As someone who likes Whoppers better than Big Macs, I am happy that the MassPike chose Burger King over McDonald's. But their choice is bound to disappoint many other buyers. The Turnpike's purpose in restricting access in the first place is that there is simply not room for more than one establishment in these locations. In such cases, the government license as a source of monopoly is really a scale economy acting in another form. But government licenses are also required in a variety of other markets, such as the one for taxis, where scale economies do not seem to be an important factor. To raise revenues, many college campuses (such as Ohio State) sell exclusive rights to vending machine sales (such as only Coke or only Pepsi).

Government licenses are sometimes accompanied by strict regulations that spell out what the licensee can and cannot do. Where the government gives a chain restaurant an exclusive license, for example, the restaurant will often be required to charge prices no more than, say, 10 percent higher than it charges in its unregulated outlets. In other cases, the government simply charges an extremely high fee for the license, virtually forcing the licensee to charge premium prices. This is the practice of some airport authorities, who essentially auction their terminal counter space to the highest bidders. Your annoyance at having to pay $5 for a hot dog in LaGuardia Airport is thus more properly focused on the Port Authority of New York than on the vendor.

By far the most important of the five factors for explaining monopolies that endure in the long run is economies of scale. Production processes are likely to change over time, which makes exclusive control over important inputs only a transitory source of monopoly. Patents too are inherently transitory. Network economies, once firmly entrenched, can be as persistent a source of natural monopoly as economies of scale. Strictly speaking, network economies work through the demand side of the market by affecting what buyers are willing to pay for a product. But they may be equivalently conceptualized on the supply side as yet another feature of product quality. The more people who own the product, the higher its effective quality level. It may thus be said of a product that benefits from network economies that any given quality level can be produced at lower cost as sales volume increases. Viewed in this way, network economies are just another form of economies of scale in production, and that's how we shall view them in the discussion that follows. Government licenses can persist for extended periods, but many of these licenses are themselves merely an implicit recognition of scale economies that would lead to monopoly in any event.

Information as a Growing Source of Economies of Scale

In 1984, at the dawn of the personal computing age, approximately 80 percent of the cost of a personal computer was accounted for by its hardware, only 20 percent by its software. Only six years later, those percentages were exactly reversed. Now all but a tiny fraction of the total costs of bringing a personal computer to market are associated in one way or another with the production of information. Although this transformation has been especially dramatic in the case of personal computers, an essentially similar transformation has been occurring for most other products as well.

The distinctive feature about information is that virtually all costs associated with the production of information are fixed—in contrast to hardware, for which a large share of production costs are roughly proportional to the volume of production. The upshot is that the production of information-rich products is often characterized by enormous economies of scale.

Because the concept of economies of scale refers to the long run by definition, the preceding paragraph's reference to economies of scale and fixed costs in the same breath might seem inconsistent. After all, fixed costs are expenditures associated with fixed inputs, and as we saw in Chapter 9, no inputs are fixed in the long run.

As a practical matter, however, large one-time costs, including product research and other costs associated with generating information, are often incurred before a product is launched. Typically these costs never recur, even during a product life cycle spanning several decades. Strictly speaking, these costs are not fixed, since the inputs used for generating the information could be varied in principle. Yet when the product is launched, there is simply no economic reason for varying them. So for practical purposes these costs are essentially fixed. In any case, the important point is that the firm's long-run average cost curve is likely to be downward sloping whenever a substantial share of its total cost is associated with initial investments in information.

A case in point is the microprocessor that powers personal computers and a growing array of other products. The fixed investment required to produce the latest Intel Pentium chip is roughly $2 billion. Once the chip has been designed

414   CHAPTER 12   MONOPOLY

and the manufacturing facility built, however, the marginal cost of producing each chip is only a few cents. It is hardly a surprise, therefore, that Intel currently supplies more than 80 percent of all microprocessors sold today.

Economies of scale have always been an important feature of the modern industrial landscape. But as more and more of the value embedded in products consists of information, the importance of economies of scale can only grow further.

With this brief overview of the causes of monopoly in mind, let us turn now to the question of what the consequences of monopoly are. In order to do this, we will proceed in much the same fashion as we did in our study of the competitive firm. That is, we will examine the firm's output decision and ask whether it leads to a situation in which all possible gains from exchange are exhausted. It will turn out that the answer to the latter question is generally no. But in formulating a government policy to improve on the results of unregulated monopoly, we will see that it is critical to understand the original source of monopoly.

THE PROFIT-MAXIMIZING MONOPOLIST

As in the competitive case, we assume that the monopolist's goal is to maximize economic profit. And again as before, in the short run this means to choose the level of output for which the difference between total revenue and short-run total cost is greatest. The case for this motive is less compelling than in the case of perfect competition. After all, the monopolist's survival is less under siege than the competitor's, and so the evolutionary argument for profit maximization applies with less force in the monopoly case. Nonetheless, we will explore just what behaviors follow from the monopolist's goal of profit maximization.

The Monopolist's Total Revenue Curve

The key difference between the monopolist and the perfect competitor is the way in which total, and hence marginal, revenue varies with output. Recall from Chapter 11 that the demand curve facing the perfect competitor is simply a horizontal line at the short-run equilibrium market price—call it P^*. The competitive firm is a price taker, typically because its own output is too small to have any discernible influence on the market price. Under these circumstances, the perfectly competitive firm's total revenue curve is a ray with slope P^*, as shown in Figure 12.2.

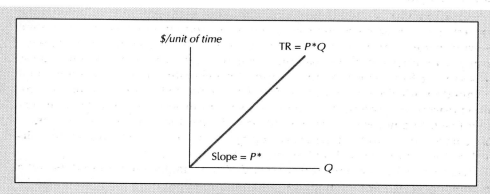

FIGURE 12.2
The Total Revenue Curve for a Perfect Competitor
Price for the perfect competitor remains at the short-run equilibrium level P^* irrespective of the firm's output. Its total revenue is thus the product of P^* and the quantity it sells: $TR = P^*Q$.

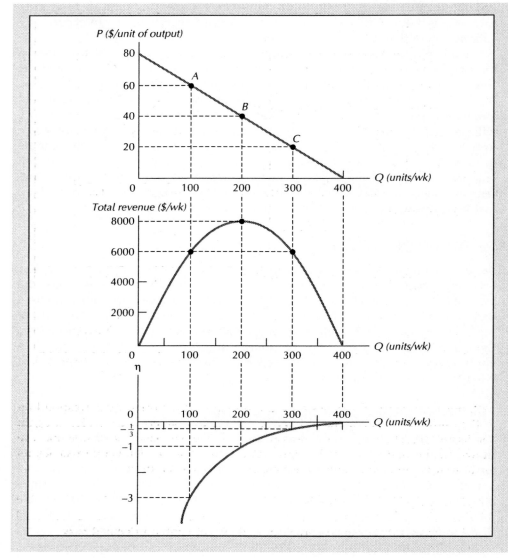

FIGURE 12.3
Demand, Total Revenue, and Elasticity
For the monopolist to increase sales, it is necessary to cut price (top panel). Total revenue rises with quantity, reaches a maximum value, and then declines (middle panel). The quantity level for which the price elasticity of demand is unity corresponds to the midpoint of the demand curve, and at that value total revenue is maximized.

Now consider a monopolist with the downward-sloping demand curve $P = 80 - \left(\frac{1}{5}\right) Q$ pictured in the top panel in Figure 12.3. For this firm too, total revenue is the product of price and quantity. At point A on its demand curve, for example, it sells 100 units of output per week at a price of $60/unit, giving a total revenue of $6000/wk. At B, it sells 200 units at a price of $40, so its total revenue at B will be $8000/wk, and so on. The difference between the monopolist and the competitor is that for the monopolist to sell a larger amount of output, it must cut its price—not only for the marginal unit but for all preceding units as well. As we saw in Chapter 5, the effect of a downward-sloping demand curve is that total revenue is no longer proportional to output sold. As in the competitive case, the monopolist's total revenue curve (middle panel in Figure 12.3) passes through the origin, because in each case selling no output generates no revenue. But as price falls, total revenue for the monopolist does not rise linearly

416   CHAPTER 12   MONOPOLY

FIGURE 12.4

Total Cost, Revenue, and Profit Curves for a Monopolist
Economic profit [$\Pi(Q)$ in the bottom panel] is the vertical distance between total revenue and total cost (TR and TC in the top panel). Note that the maximum-profit point, $Q^* = 175$, lies to the left of the output level at which TR is a maximum ($Q = 200$).

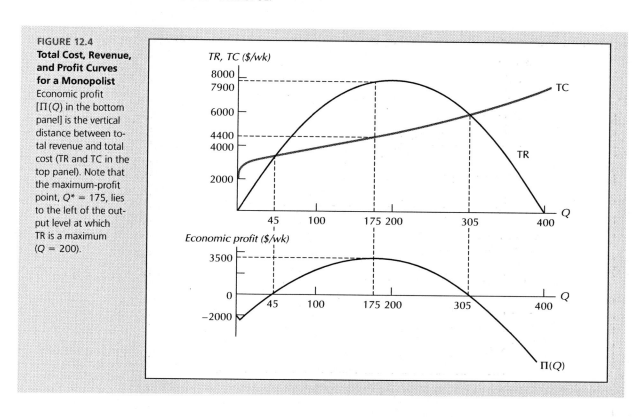

with output. Instead, it reaches a maximum value at the quantity corresponding to the midpoint of the demand curve (*B* in the top panel), after which it again begins to fall. The corresponding values of the price elasticity of demand are shown in the bottom panel in Figure 12.3. Note that total revenue reaches its maximum value when the price elasticity of demand is unity. 统一价

EXERCISE 12.1   ◯

> Sketch the total revenue curve for a monopolist whose demand curve is given by *P* = 100 − 2*Q*.

The top panel in Figure 12.4 portrays the short-run total cost curve and total revenue curve for a monopolist facing the demand curve shown in Figure 12.3. Economic profit, plotted in the bottom panel, is positive in the interval from $Q = 45$ to $Q = 305$, and is negative elsewhere. The maximum profit point occurs at $Q^* = 175$ units/wk, which lies to the left of the output level for which total revenue is a maximum ($Q = 200$).

Notice in Figure 12.4 that the vertical distance between the short-run total cost and total revenue curves is greatest when the two curves are parallel (when $Q = 175$). Suppose this were not the case. For example, suppose that at the maximum-profit point the total cost curve were steeper than the total revenue curve. It would then be possible to earn higher profits by producing less output, because costs would go down by more than the corresponding reduction in total revenue. Conversely, if the total cost curve were less steep than the total revenue curve, the monopolist could earn higher profits by expanding output, because total revenue would go up by more than total cost.

Marginal Revenue

The slope of the total cost curve at any level of output is by definition equal to marginal cost at that output level. By the same token, the slope of the total revenue curve is the definition of *marginal revenue*.[3] As in the case of the perfectly competitive firm, we can think of marginal revenue as the change in total revenue when the sale of output changes by 1 unit. More precisely, suppose ΔTR_Q is the change in total revenue that occurs in response to a small change in output, ΔQ. Marginal revenue, denoted MR_Q, is then given by

$$MR_Q = \frac{\Delta TR_Q}{\Delta Q}. \qquad (12.1)$$

Using this definition, a profit-maximizing monopolist in the short run will choose that level of output Q^* for which

$$MC_{Q^*} = MR_{Q^*} \quad \text{(see footnote 4),} \qquad (12.2)$$

provided marginal revenue intersects marginal cost from above. Equation 12.2 defines the **optimality condition for a monopolist.** The monopolist wants to sell all units for which marginal revenue exceeds marginal cost, so marginal revenue should lie above marginal cost prior to the intersection (for some cost structures, marginal cost may decline initially and then increase, leading to two intersections of marginal cost and marginal revenue).

Recall that the analogous condition for the perfectly competitive firm is to choose the output level for which price and marginal cost are equal. Recalling that marginal revenue and price (P) are exactly the same for the competitive firm (when such a firm expands output by 1 unit, its total revenue goes up by P), we see that the profit-maximizing condition for the perfectly competitive firm is simply a special case of Equation 12.2.

In the case of the monopoly firm, marginal revenue will always be less than price.[5] To see why, consider the demand curve pictured in Figure 12.5, and suppose that the monopolist wishes to increase output from $Q_0 = 100$ to $Q_0 + \Delta Q = 150$ units/wk. His total revenue from selling 100 units/wk is ($60/unit) (100 units/wk) = $6000/wk. To sell an additional $\Delta Q = 50$ units/wk, he must cut his price to $60 - \Delta P = $50/unit, which means his new total revenue will be ($50/unit)(150 units/wk), which is equal to $7500/wk. To calculate marginal revenue, we simply subtract the original total revenue, $6000/wk, from the new total revenue, and divide by the change in output, $\Delta Q = 50$ units/wk. This yields $MR_{Q_0 = 100} = (\$7500/\text{wk} - \$6000/\text{wk})/(50\,\text{units/wk}) = \$30/\text{unit}$, which is clearly less than the original price of $60/unit.

optimality condition for a monopolist a monopolist maximizes profit by choosing the level of output where marginal revenue equals marginal cost.

---

[3]In calculus terms, marginal revenue is defined as the derivative $d\text{TR}/dQ$.

[4]This condition can also be justified by noting that the first-order condition for maximum profit is given by

$$\frac{d\Pi}{dQ} = \frac{d(\text{TR} - \text{TC})}{dQ} = MR - MC = 0.$$

[5]There is actually one exception to this claim, namely, the case of the perfectly discriminating monopolist, discussion of which follows.

418   CHAPTER 12   MONOPOLY

FIGURE 12.5

Changes in Total Revenue Resulting from a Price Cut

The area of rectangle *A* ($1000/wk) is the loss in revenue from selling the previous output level at a lower price. The area of rectangle *B* ($2500/wk) is the gain in revenue from selling the additional output at the new, lower price. Marginal revenue is the difference between these two areas ($2500 − $1000 = $1500/wk) divided by the change in output (50 units/wk). Here MR equals $30/unit, which is less than the new price of $50/unit.

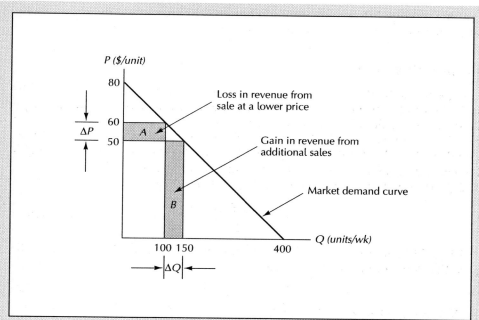

Another useful way of thinking about marginal revenue is to view it as the sum of the gain in revenue from new sales and the loss in revenue from selling the previous output level at the new, lower price. In Figure 12.5, the area of rectangle *B* ($2500/wk) represents the gain in revenue from the additional sales at the lower price. The area of rectangle *A* ($1000/wk) represents the loss in revenue from selling the original 100 units/wk at $50/unit instead of $60. Marginal revenue is the difference between the gain in revenue from additional sales and the loss in revenue from sales at a lower price, divided by the change in quantity. This yields ($2500/wk − $1000/wk)/(50 units/wk), which is again equal to $30/unit.

To explore how marginal revenue varies as we move along a straight-line demand curve, consider the demand curve pictured in Figure 12.6, and suppose that the monopolist wishes to increase output from Q_0 to $Q_0 + \Delta Q$ units. His total revenue from selling Q_0 units is $P_0 Q_0$. To sell an additional ΔQ units, he must cut his price to $P_0 - \Delta P$, which means his new total revenue will be $(P_0 - \Delta P)(Q_0 + \Delta Q)$, which is equal to $P_0 Q_0 + P_0 \Delta Q - \Delta P Q_0 - \Delta P \Delta Q$. To calculate marginal revenue, simply subtract the original total revenue, $P_0 Q_0$, from the new total revenue, and divide by the change in output, ΔQ. This leaves $MR_{Q_0} = P_0 - (\Delta P / \Delta Q) Q_0 - \Delta P$, which is clearly less than P_0. As ΔP approaches zero, the expression for marginal revenue thus approaches[6]

$$MR_{Q_0} = P_0 - \frac{\Delta P}{\Delta Q} Q_0. \tag{12.3}$$

---

[6]Note that when ΔP shrinks toward zero, the corresponding ΔQ does so as well. Because ΔP and ΔQ are both positive here, the ratio $\Delta P / \Delta Q$ is simply the negative of the slope of the demand curve.

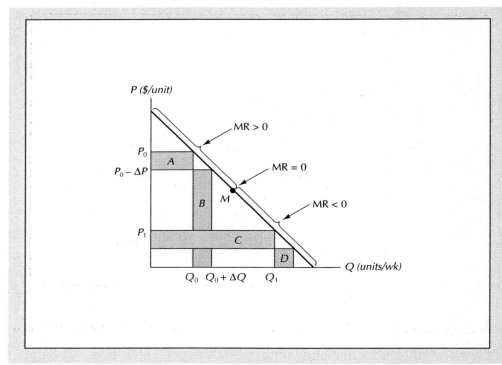

FIGURE 12.6
Marginal Revenue and Position on the Demand Curve
When Q is to the left of the midpoint (M) of a straight-line demand curve (for example, $Q = Q_0$), the gain from added sales (area B) outweighs the loss from a lower price for existing sales (area A). When Q is to the right of the midpoint (for example, $Q = Q_1$), the gain from added sales (area D) is smaller than the loss from a lower price for existing sales (area C). At the midpoint of the demand curve, the gain and the loss are equal, which means marginal revenue is zero.

Equation 12.3 makes intuitive sense if we think of ΔQ as being a 1-unit change in output; P_0 would then be the gain in revenue from the sale of that extra unit, and $(\Delta P/\Delta Q)Q_0 = \Delta P Q_0$ would be the loss in revenue from the sale of the existing units at the lower price. We see again in Equation 12.3 that marginal revenue is less than price for all positive levels of output.

The fact that area B is larger than area A in Figure 12.6 means that marginal revenue is positive at Q_0. Once output moves past the midpoint (M in Figure 12.6) on a straight-line demand curve, however, the marginal revenue of a further expansion will be negative. Thus, the area of rectangle C is larger than the area of rectangle D in Figure 12.6, which means that marginal revenue at the output level Q_1 is less than zero.

Marginal Revenue and Elasticity

Yet another useful relationship links marginal revenue to the price elasticity of demand at the corresponding point on the demand curve. Recall from Chapter 5 that the price elasticity of demand at a point (Q, P) is given by

$$\epsilon = \frac{\Delta Q}{\Delta P} \frac{P}{Q}. \tag{12.4}$$

In Equation 12.4, the terms ΔQ and ΔP have opposite signs, because the demand curve is downward sloping. By contrast, recall that the ΔQ and ΔP terms in Equation 12.3, which also represent changes in P and Q as we move along the demand curve, are both positive. Suppose we redefine ΔQ and ΔP

420   CHAPTER 12   MONOPOLY

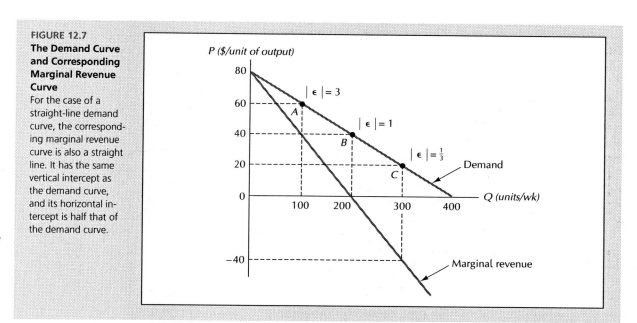

FIGURE 12.7
The Demand Curve and Corresponding Marginal Revenue Curve
For the case of a straight-line demand curve, the corresponding marginal revenue curve is also a straight line. It has the same vertical intercept as the demand curve, and its horizontal intercept is half that of the demand curve.

from Equation 12.4 so that both of these terms are positive. That equation then becomes

$$|\epsilon| = \frac{\Delta Q}{\Delta P}\frac{P}{Q}. \tag{12.5}$$

The purpose of making both ΔQ and ΔP positive is to be able to relate Equation 12.5 back to Equation 12.3. If we now solve Equation 12.5 for $\Delta P/\Delta Q = P/(Q|\epsilon|)$ and substitute into Equation 12.3, we get

$$\text{MR}_Q = P\left(1 - \frac{1}{|\epsilon|}\right). \tag{12.6}$$

Equation 12.6 tells us that the less elastic demand is with respect to price, the more price will exceed marginal revenue.[7] It also tells us that in the limiting case of infinite price elasticity, marginal revenue and price are exactly the same. (Recall from Chapter 11 that price and marginal revenue are the same for the competitive firm, which faces a horizontal, or infinitely elastic, demand curve.)

Graphing Marginal Revenue

Equation 12.6 also provides a convenient way to plot the marginal revenue values that correspond to different points along a demand curve. To illustrate, consider the straight-line demand curve in Figure 12.7, which intersects the vertical axis at a price value of $P = 80$. The elasticity of demand is infinite at that point, which means that $\text{MR}_0 = 80(1 - 1/|\epsilon|) = 80$. Although marginal revenue will

---

[7]Equation 12.6 can be derived using calculus as follows:

$$\text{MR} = \frac{d\text{TR}}{dQ} = \frac{d(PQ)}{dQ} = P + Q\frac{dP}{dQ} = P\left(1 + \frac{Q}{P}\frac{dP}{dQ}\right) = P\left(1 + \frac{1}{\epsilon}\right) = P\left(1 - \frac{1}{|\epsilon|}\right).$$

generally be less than price for a monopolist, the two are exactly the same when quantity is zero. The reason is that at zero output there are no existing sales for a price cut to affect.

Now suppose we move, say, one-quarter of the way down the demand curve to point A, (100, 60). At that point, $|\epsilon| = 3$. Thus we have $MR_{100} = (60)(1 - \frac{1}{3}) = 40$.

Halfway down the demand curve, at point B, (200, 40), $|\epsilon| = 1$, which gives us $MR_{200} = (40)(1 - \frac{1}{1}) = 0$. This confirms our earlier finding (Chapter 5) that total revenue is at a maximum at the midpoint of a straight-line demand curve, where elasticity is unity.

Finally, consider point C, (300, 20), which is three-fourths of the way down the demand curve. Here $|\epsilon| = \frac{1}{3}$, so we have $MR_{300} = (20)[1 - (1/\frac{1}{3})] = (20)(-2) = -40$. Thus, at $Q = 300$, the effect of selling an extra unit of output is to reduce total revenue by $40/wk.

Filling in additional points in the same fashion, we quickly see that the marginal revenue curve associated with a straight-line demand curve is itself a straight line, one whose slope is twice that of the demand curve. The marginal revenue curve cuts the horizontal axis just below the midpoint of the demand curve, and for all quantities larger than that marginal revenue is negative. Note that all points to the right of the midpoint of the demand curve have price elasticity values less than 1 in absolute value. The fact that marginal revenue is negative in this region thus fits our observation from Chapter 5 that a cut in price will reduce total revenue whenever demand is inelastic with respect to price.

Find the marginal revenue curve that corresponds to the demand curve $P = 12 - 3Q$.   EXAMPLE 12.1

The marginal revenue curve will have the same intercept as and twice the slope of the demand curve, which gives us $MR = 12 - 6Q$, as plotted in Figure 12.8.

The general formula for a linear demand curve is $P = a - bQ$, where a and b are positive numbers. The corresponding marginal revenue curve will be $MR = a - 2bQ$ (see footnote 8).

EXERCISE 12.2

Sketch demand and marginal revenue curves for a monopolist whose market demand curve is given by $P = 100 - 2Q$.

Graphical Interpretation of the Short-Run Profit Maximization Condition

Recall from Chapter 11 the graphical representation of the maximum-profit point for the competitive firm in the short run. An analogous graphical representation exists for the monopolist. Consider a monopolist with the demand, marginal revenue, and

---

[8]Note that total revenue for the demand curve $P = a - bQ$ is given by $TR = aQ - bQ^2$. The corresponding marginal revenue curve is

$$MR = \frac{dTR}{dQ} = a - 2bQ.$$

422   CHAPTER 12   MONOPOLY

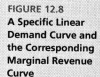

FIGURE 12.8
A Specific Linear Demand Curve and the Corresponding Marginal Revenue Curve
The marginal revenue curve has the same vertical intercept and twice the slope of the corresponding linear demand curve.

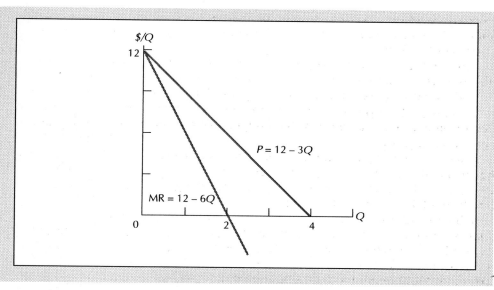

$$\dfrac{840}{20} = 42$$

short-run cost curves pictured in Figure 12.9. The profit-maximizing level of output for this firm is Q^*, the one for which the marginal revenue and marginal cost curves intersect. At that quantity level, the monopolist can charge a price of P^*, and by so doing will earn an economic profit equal to the shaded rectangle labeled Π.

EXAMPLE 12.2

A monopolist faces a demand curve of $P = 100 - 2Q$ and a short-run total cost curve of $TC = 640 + 200$. The associated marginal cost curve is $MC = 20$. What is the profit-maximizing price? How much will the monopolist sell, and how much economic profit will it earn at that price?

The marginal revenue curve for this demand curve is $MR = 100 - 4Q$. Marginal cost is the slope of the total cost curve, which is constant at 20 in this example. Setting $MR = MC$, we have $100 - 4Q = 20$, which yields the profit-maximizing quantity, $Q^* = 20$. Plugging $Q^* = 20$ back into the demand curve, we get the profit-maximizing price, $P^* = 60$. This solution is shown graphically in Figure 12.10, which also displays the average total cost curve for the monopolist. Note that at Q^* the ATC is 52, which means the monopolist earns an economic profit of $60 - 52 = 8$ on each unit sold. With $Q^* = 20$, that makes for a total economic profit of 160.

Note in Figure 12.10 that the monopolist's fixed cost was irrelevant to the determination of the profit-maximizing output level and price. This makes sense intuitively, because fixed cost has no bearing on the gains and losses that occur when output changes.

EXERCISE 12.3

How would the profit-maximizing price and quantity change in Example 12.2 if the monopolist's total cost curve were instead given by $TC = 640 + 40Q$? The associated marginal cost curve is $MC = 40$.

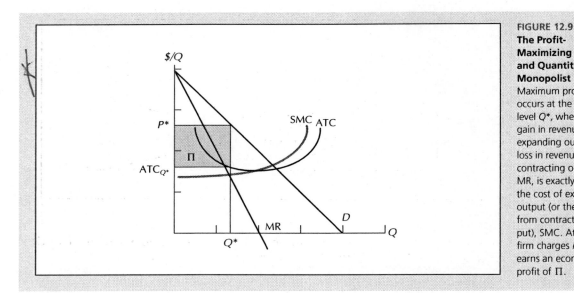

FIGURE 12.9
The Profit-Maximizing Price and Quantity for a Monopolist
Maximum profit occurs at the output level Q^*, where the gain in revenue from expanding output (or loss in revenue from contracting output), MR, is exactly equal to the cost of expanding output (or the savings from contracting output), SMC. At Q^*, the firm charges P^* and earns an economic profit of Π.

A Profit-Maximizing Monopolist Will Never Produce on the Inelastic Portion of the Demand Curve

If a monopolist's goal is to maximize profits, it follows directly that she will never produce an output level on the inelastic portion of her demand curve. If she were to increase her price at such an output level, the effect would be to increase total revenue. The price increase would also reduce the quantity demanded, which, in turn, would reduce the monopolist's total cost. Since economic profit is the difference between total revenue and total cost, profit would necessarily increase in response to a price increase from an initial position on the inelastic portion of the demand curve. The profit-maximizing level of output

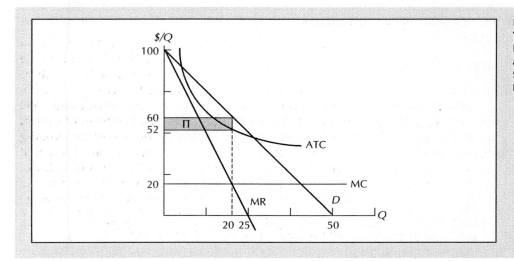

FIGURE 12.10
The Profit-Maximizing Price and Quantity for Specific Cost and Demand Functions

424   CHAPTER 12   MONOPOLY

FIGURE 12.11
**A Monopolist Who
Should Shut Down
in the Short Run**
Whenever average
revenue (the price
value on the demand
curve) is lower than
average variable cost
for every level of out-
put, the monopolist
does best to cease
production in the
short run.

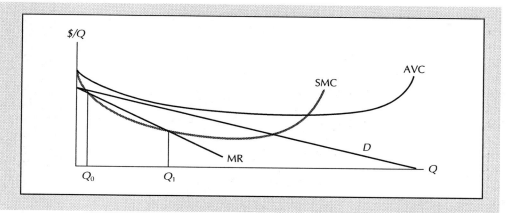

must therefore lie on the elastic portion of the demand curve, where further price
increases would cause both revenue and costs to go down.

The Profit-Maximizing Markup

The profit-maximization condition MR = MC can be combined with Equation 12.6,
which says MR = $P[1 - (1/|\epsilon|)]$, to derive the profit-maximizing markup for the
monopolist:

$$\frac{P - MC}{P} = \frac{1}{|\epsilon|},$$

(12.7)

which is the difference between price and marginal cost, expressed as a fraction of
the profit-maximizing price. For example, if the price elasticity of demand facing a
monopolist were equal to -2, the profit-maximizing markup would be $\frac{1}{2}$, which
implies that the profit-maximizing price is twice marginal cost. Equation 12.7 tells
us that the profit-maximizing markup grows smaller as demand grows more elastic. In the limiting case of infinitely elastic demand, the profit-maximizing markup
is zero (which implies P = MC), the same as in the perfectly competitive case.

The Monopolist's Shutdown Condition

In the case of the perfectly competitive firm, we saw that it paid to shut down
in the short run whenever the price fell below the minimum value of average
variable cost (AVC). The analogous condition for the monopolist is that there
exist no quantity for which the demand curve lies above the average variable
cost curve. The monopolist whose demand, marginal revenue, SMC, and AVC
curves are shown in Figure 12.11, for example, has no positive level of output
for which price exceeds AVC, and so the monopolist does best by ceasing
production in the short run. He will then sustain a short-run economic loss equal
to his fixed costs, but he would do even worse at any positive level of output.

Another way of stating the shutdown condition for a monopolist is to say
that he should cease production whenever average revenue is less than average
variable cost at every level of output. Average revenue is simply another name
for price—the value of P along the monopolist's demand curve.[9]

---

[9]More formally, note that average revenue = $TR/Q = PQ/Q = P$.

Figure 12.11 also illustrates the important point that MR = MC is a necessary, but not sufficient, condition for maximum profit. Note in the figure that marginal revenue is equal to marginal cost at the output level Q_0. Why isn't this the maximum-profit point? Recall that in the case of the perfectly competitive firm, the maximum-profit condition called for price to equal marginal cost on a rising portion of the marginal cost curve, above the minimum point on the AVC curve. A somewhat different condition applies in the case of the monopolist. In Figure 12.11, note that at Q_0 the MR curve intersects the MC curve from below.[10] This means not only that Q_0 is not the maximum-profit point, but that it actually corresponds to a *lower* profit level than any of the other output levels nearby. For example, consider an output level just less than Q_0. At any such output level the gains from contracting output (MC) will exceed the losses (MR), so the firm does better to contract from Q_0. Now consider an output level just slightly larger than Q_0. For such an output level, the gains from expanding (MR) exceed the costs (MC), so the firm does better to expand. Thus, when the firm is at Q_0, it can earn higher profits by either contracting *or* expanding. Q_0 is called a *local minimum* profit point.[11]

Note also in Figure 12.11 that the MR curve intersects the MC curve a second time at the output level Q_1. This time the intersection occurs from above, and you can easily show as an exercise that Q_1 yields higher profits than any of the other output levels close by. (The argument runs exactly parallel to the one in the preceding paragraph.) We refer to points like Q_1 as *local maximum* profit points. But although Q_1 yields more profit than any nearby output level, the firm fails to cover its average variable cost at the level of output, and so does better simply to produce nothing at all. The point Q^* we saw earlier in Figure 12.9 is both a local maximum profit point and a *global maximum* profit point, the latter designation indicating that no other output level, including zero, yields higher profit. For a monopolist, a global maximum profit point might occur either on the rising or on the falling portion of the MC curve. But it must be at a point where the MR curve intersects the MC curve from above.

EXERCISE 12.4

Find the optimal price and quantity for the monopolist described by the information on the following table.

Q	P	MR	SMC	AVC
0	100	100	150	150
15	86	71	71	107
25	75	50	41	84
34	66	33	33	72
50	50	0	63	63

---

[10]To "intersect from below at Q_0" means that as Q approaches Q_0 from the left, MR lies below MC and then crosses MC when $Q = Q_0$.

[11]The second-order condition for maximum profit is given by

$$\frac{d(\text{MR} - \text{MC})}{dQ} = \frac{d\text{MR}}{dQ} - \frac{d\text{MC}}{dQ} < 0,$$

which says simply that the slope of the marginal revenue curve must be less than the slope of the marginal cost curve.

426   CHAPTER 12   MONOPOLY

To recapitulate briefly, we have seen that the monopolist behaves like a perfectly competitive firm in the sense that each chooses an output level by weighing the benefits of expanding (or contracting) output against the corresponding costs. For both the perfect competitor and the monopolist, marginal cost is the relevant measure of the cost of expanding output. Fixed costs are irrelevant for short-run output decisions in both cases. For both the monopolist and perfect competitor, the benefits of expanding output are measured by their respective values of marginal revenue. For the competitor, marginal revenue and price are one and the same. For the monopolist, by contrast, marginal revenue is less than price. The competitor maximizes profit by expanding output until marginal cost equals price. The monopolist maximizes profit by expanding output until marginal cost equals marginal revenue, and thus chooses a lower output level than if he had used the competitor's criterion. Both the monopolist and the perfect competitor do best to shut down in the short run if price is less than average variable cost for all possible levels of output.

A MONOPOLIST HAS NO SUPPLY CURVE

As we saw in Chapter 11, the competitive firm has a well-defined supply curve. It takes market price as given and responds by choosing the output level for which marginal cost and price are equal. At the industry level, a shifting demand curve will trace out a well-defined industry supply curve, which is the horizontal summation of the individual firm supply curves.

There is no similar supply curve for the monopolist. The reason is that the monopolist is not a price taker, which means that there is no unique correspondence between price and marginal revenue when the market demand curve shifts. Thus, a given marginal revenue value for one demand curve can correspond to one price, while the same value of marginal revenue for a second demand curve corresponds to a different price. As a result, it is possible to observe the monopolist producing Q_1^* and selling at P^* in one period, and then selling Q_2^* at P^* in another period.

To illustrate, consider a monopolist with a demand curve of $P = 100 - Q$ and with the same cost curves as in Example 12.2, in particular with $MC = 20$. The marginal revenue curve for this monopolist is given by $MR = 100 - 2Q$, and equating MR to MC yields a profit-maximizing output level of $Q^* = 40$. The corresponding profit-maximizing price is $P^* = 60$. Note that this is the same as the profit-maximizing price we saw for the monopolist in Example 12.2, even though the demand curve here lies to the right of the earlier one.

When the monopolist's demand curve shifts, the price elasticity of demand at a given price generally will also shift. But these shifts need not occur in the same direction. When demand shifts rightward, for example, elasticity at a given price may either increase or decrease, and the same is true when demand shifts leftward. The result is that there can be no unique correspondence between the price a monopolist charges and the amount she chooses to produce. And hence we say that the monopolist has no supply curve. Rather, she has a *supply rule*, which is to equate marginal revenue and marginal cost.

ADJUSTMENTS IN THE LONG RUN

In the long run, the monopolist is of course free to adjust all inputs, just as the competitive firm is. What is the optimal quantity in the long run for a monopolist with a given technology? The best the monopolist can do is to produce the quantity for

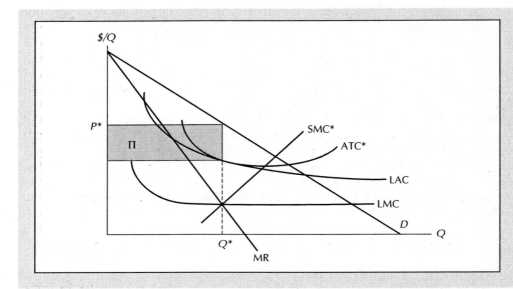

FIGURE 12.12
Long-Run Equilibrium for a Profit-Maximizing Monopolist
The profit-maximizing quantity in the long run is Q^*, the output level for which LMC = MR. The profit-maximizing price in the long run is P^*. The optimal capital stock in the long run gives rise to the short-run marginal cost curve SMC*, which passes through the intersection of LMC and MR.

which long-run marginal cost is equal to marginal revenue. In Figure 12.12, that will mean choosing a capital stock that gives rise to the short-run average and marginal cost curves labeled ATC* and SMC*. For that level of capital stock, the short-run marginal cost curve passes through the intersection of the long-run marginal cost and marginal revenue curves. Q^* will be the profit-maximizing quantity in the long run, and it will sell at a price of P^*. For the conditions pictured in Figure 12.12, the long-run economic profit level, Π, will be positive, and is indicated by the area of the shaded rectangle.

As we saw in Chapter 11, economic profits tend to vanish in the long run in perfectly competitive industries. This tendency will sometimes be present for monopoly. To the extent that the factors that gave rise to the firm's monopoly position come under attack in the long run, there will be downward pressure on its profits. For example, competing firms may develop substitutes for important inputs that were previously under the control of the monopolist. Or in the case of patented products, competitors may develop close substitutes that do not infringe on existing patents, which are in any event only temporary.

But in other cases there may be a tendency for monopoly profits to persist even in the long run. The firm shown in Figure 12.12, for example, has a declining long-run average cost curve, which means that it may enjoy a persistent cost advantage over potential rivals. In such natural monopolies, economic profits may be highly stable over time. And the same, of course, may be true for a firm whose monopoly comes from having a government license. Persistent economic profits are indeed one of the major policy concerns about monopoly, as we will discuss further later in the chapter.

PRICE DISCRIMINATION

Our discussion thus far has assumed that the monopolist sells all its output at a single price. In reality, however, monopolists often charge different prices to different buyers, a practice that is known as *price discrimination*. The movie

428   CHAPTER 12   MONOPOLY

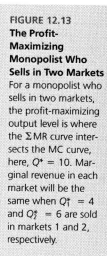

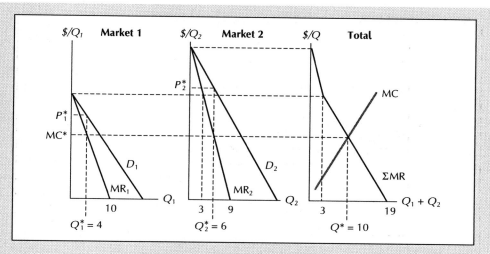

theater discount tickets discussed at the beginning of this chapter constitute one example. In the following sections, we analyze how the profit-maximizing monopolist behaves when it is possible to charge different prices to different buyers. When price discrimination is possible, a monopolist can transfer some of the gains from consumers into its own profits. However, we will see that not all the higher profits under price discrimination come at the expense of consumers. Efficiency is enhanced as the monopolist expands output toward the level at which demand intersects marginal cost.

Sale in Different Markets

Suppose the monopolist has two completely distinct markets in which she can sell her output. Perhaps she is the only supplier in the domestic market for her product, and the only one in a foreign market as well. If she is a profit maximizer, what prices should she charge and what quantities should she sell in each market?

Suppose the demand and marginal revenue curves for the two markets are as given in the left and middle panels in Figure 12.13. First note that if the monopolist is maximizing profit, her marginal revenue should be the same in each market. (If it weren't, she could sell 1 unit less in the market with lower MR and 1 unit more in the market with higher MR, and in the process increase her profit.) Given that MR in the two markets must be the same, the profit-maximizing total quantity will be the one for which this common value is the same as marginal cost. Graphically, the solution is to add the marginal revenue curves horizontally across the two markets, and produce the level of output for which the resulting curve intersects the marginal cost curve. In the right panel in Figure 12.13, the optimal total output is indicated by $Q^* = 10$ units. $Q_1^* = 4$ of it is sold in market 1 at a price of P_1^*, and the remaining $Q_2^* = 6$ in market 2 at a price of P_2^*.

EXAMPLE 12.3   A monopolist has marginal costs $MC = Q$ and home market demand $P = 30 - Q$. The monopolist can also sell to a foreign market at a constant price $P_F = 12$. Find and graph the quantity produced, quantity sold in the home market, quantity sold in

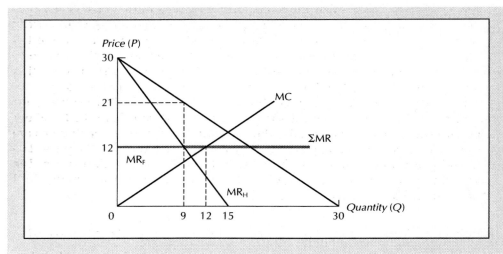

FIGURE 12.14
A Monopolist with a Perfectly Elastic Foreign Market
The curve ΣMR follows MR_H as long as $MR_H \geq MR_F$, and then follows MR_F. The profit-maximizing output level is where the ΣMR curve intersects the MC curve, here $Q^* = 12$.

the foreign market, and price charged in the home market. Explain why the monopolist's profits would fall if it were to produce the same quantity but sell more in the home market.

The linear demand curve $P = 30 - Q$ has associated marginal revenue $MR = 30 - 2Q$. The profit-maximizing level of output for a monopolist selling to segmented markets occurs where ΣMR = MC. The horizontal sum of the marginal revenues across markets is the home marginal revenue function MR_H up to home output where $MR_F = MR_H$, and then the foreign marginal revenue function $MR_F = 12$ for any further units (see Figure 12.14). Total marginal revenue equals marginal cost at $MR_F = MC$, which solves for $Q = 12$. Marginal cost for this level of output equals home marginal revenue at $30 - 2Q_H = 12$, so $Q_H = 9$ with the remaining units sold abroad:

$$Q_F = Q - Q_H = 12 - 9 = 3.$$

In the home market, the monopolist charges

$$P_H = 30 - Q_H = 30 - 9 = 21.$$

Any further units sold at home would yield marginal revenue less than 12. Since sales to the foreign market yield a constant marginal revenue of 12, shifting sales to the home market would decrease profits due to the lost marginal revenue for each unit shifted.

EXERCISE 12.5 ◯

Suppose a monopolist sells in two separate markets, with demand curves given by $P_1 = 10 - Q_1$ and $P_2 = 20 - Q_2$, respectively. If her total cost curve is given by TC = 5 + 2Q (for which the associated marginal cost curve is given by MC = 2), what quantities should she sell and what prices should she charge in the two markets?

Note in Exercise 12.5 that the monopolist who sells in two markets charges a higher price in the market where demand is less elastic with respect to price.[12] Charging different prices to buyers in completely separate markets is often referred to as *third-degree price discrimination*. There is no special significance to the term "third-degree" beyond the fact that this type of price discrimination happened to have been the third one that appeared in an early taxonomy.

Examples of third-degree price discrimination abound. This textbook, for instance, is also offered in an international student edition that sells for about one-third the price of the domestic edition. Because the incomes of students are generally much lower in foreign markets than in the United States, the price elasticity of demand tends to be much higher in foreign than in U.S. markets. The price that maximizes profits in the U.S. market would discourage most Third World students from buying.

ECONOMIC NATURALIST 12.1

Why do some doctors and lawyers offer discounts to people with low incomes?

In medicine, law, dentistry, and other professions, many practitioners set their fees on a "sliding scale"—in effect, selling their services to low-income consumers at significant discounts. This practice is often said to stem from professionals' concerns

Why do doctors often set lower fees for poor patients?

about the economic hardships confronting the poor. Such concerns are no doubt often heartfelt. But note also that the services offered by these professionals are normal goods, which means that the demand curves of low-income customers lie well below those of their wealthier counterparts. Sliding-scale fees may thus also be viewed as attempts by professionals to increase their profits by tailoring their prices to elasticity differences among different groups of buyers. A similar pattern is observed in the market for movie tickets, in which it is common for theater owners to set lower prices for students, senior citizens, and other groups believed to have higher price elasticities of demand.

Notice also that price discrimination is feasible only when it is impossible, or at least impractical, for buyers to trade among themselves. If students in other lands could trade with those in the United States, for example, it would not be possible to sell essentially the same book for $30 in Calcutta and $100 in New York. Entrepreneurial students would buy $30 books abroad and sell them to U.S. students for, say, $95; others, hoping to get in on the action, would cut price even further, and eventually the price differential would vanish. Buying at a low price from one source and reselling at a higher price is often called **arbitrage.** Where arbitrage is practical, large price differentials for a single product cannot persist. Arbitrage ensures, for example, that the price of gold in London can never differ significantly from the price of gold in New York.

arbitrage the purchase of something for costless risk-free resale at a higher price.

---

[12]This result follows from Equation 12.6, which says that MR $= P(1 - 1/|\epsilon|)$. Setting $MR_1 = MR_2$ yields $P_1/P_2 = (1 - 1/|\epsilon_2|)/(1 - 1/|\epsilon_1|)$. Hence the higher price will be charged to customers with the lower price elasticity of demand.

Why do theater owners offer student discounts on admission tickets but not on popcorn?

Arbitrage is practical in some cases but not in others. Student discounts on tickets enable theater operators to segment their markets because it is not possible for one person to see a movie at a low price and then sell the experience to someone else at a higher price. By the same token, it is practical for lawyers and doctors to charge different people different prices on the basis of differences in price elasticity of demand. But such market segmentation is more difficult for products like popcorn. If theater operators attempted to sell popcorn for $1 to students and for $3 to adults, some enterprising student would seize the arbitrage opportunity, selling popcorn to disgruntled adults for only $2. And under the pressure of competition from other arbitrageurs, the price differential would fall until the price differential was barely sufficient to make it worth the students' while to engage in the transaction.

ECONOMIC NATURALIST 12.2

Why do theater owners give student discounts on tickets but not on snacks?

The Perfectly Discriminating Monopolist

First-degree price discrimination is the term used to describe the largest possible extent of market segmentation. To illustrate, suppose a monopolist has N potential customers, each one of whom has a downward-sloping demand curve like the one labeled D_i in Figure 12.15. What is the most revenue the monopolist could extract from the sale of Q' units of output to such a customer? If the

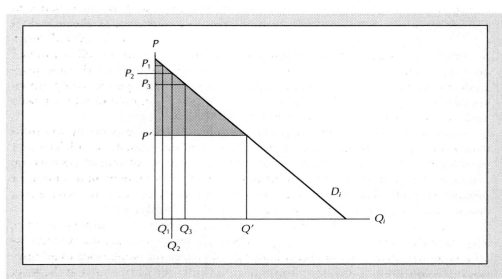

FIGURE 12.15
Perfect Price Discrimination
If the monopolist can sell each unit of output at a different price, he will charge the maximum the buyer is willing to pay for each unit. In this situation, the monopolist captures all the consumer surplus.

432   CHAPTER 12   MONOPOLY

FIGURE 12.16
The Perfectly Discriminating Monopolist
The marginal revenue curve for the monopolist who can discriminate perfectly is exactly the same as his demand curve. The profit-maximizing output is Q*, the one for which the SMC and demand curves intersect. Economic profit (Π) is given by the shaded area.

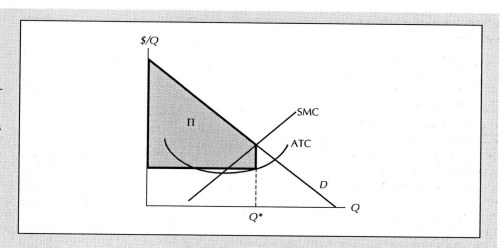

monopolist had to sell all units at the same price, the best he could do would be to charge P', which would yield a total revenue of $P'Q'$. But if he can charge different prices for different units of output, he can do much better. For example, he can sell the first Q_1 units at a price of P_1, the next $Q_2 - Q_1$ units at a price of P_2, and so on. If the intervals into which the monopolist can partition the product are arbitrarily small, this form of pricing will augment total revenue by the area of the shaded triangle in Figure 12.15.

Had the monopolist been forced to charge a single price for all units, that shaded triangle would have been consumer surplus. When he is able to charge different prices for each unit, however, the monopolist captures all the consumer surplus. The consumer pays the maximum he would have been willing to pay for each unit, and as a result receives no surplus.

How much output will a profit-maximizing, perfectly discriminating monopolist produce? As always, the rule is to equate marginal revenue to marginal cost. Figure 12.16 portrays the demand, short-run marginal, and average total cost curves for a perfectly discriminating monopolist. But what is the marginal revenue curve for this monopolist? *It is exactly the same as his demand curve.* Because he can discriminate perfectly, he can lower his price to sell additional output without having to cut price on the output originally sold. Price and marginal revenue are one and the same, just as in the case of perfect competition. The best this firm can do is to produce $Q*$ units of output, each of which it sells at the highest price each of its buyers is willing to pay.

There are two salient points of comparison between the perfectly discriminating monopolist and the monopolist who cannot discriminate at all. The first is that the perfect discriminator produces a higher level of output because he need not be concerned with the effect of a price cut on the revenue from output produced thus far. He can cut price to the people who would not otherwise buy, and maintain higher prices to those who are willing to pay them.

A second important difference is that there generally is positive consumer surplus under the nondiscriminating monopolist, but none under the perfect discriminator. Because the nondiscriminator must charge the same price to all buyers, there is pressure on him not to set his price too high. If he sets it at the level the least elastic demanders are willing to pay, he will lose the patronage of all others. As a result, the monopolist will not do this, and the least elastic deman-ders end up paying a price well below their respective reservation prices—hence the consumer surplus.

Perfect price discrimination is a never-attained theoretical limit. If a cus-tomer's demand curve were tattooed on his forehead, it might be possible for a seller to tailor each price to extract the maximum possible amount from every buyer. But in general, the details of individual demand are only imperfectly known to the seller. Merchants often estimate individual elasticity on the basis of information known about groups to which the individual belongs. A catalog merchant, for example, may print special editions with higher prices for mailing into high-income zip codes like 90213 (Beverly Hills, California).

Perhaps the closest thing we see to an in-depth assessment of individual elas-ticities is in the behavior of merchants in bazaars in the Middle East. The shrewd camel trader has had many years of experience in trying to assess how much a buyer with a given demographic and psychological profile is willing to pay. His stock in trade is to interpret the incongruous gesture, the furtive eye movement. But even here, the wily buyer may know how to conceal his eagerness to own the camel.

Second-Degree Price Discrimination

Yet another form of price discrimination is the practice by which many sellers post not a single price, but a schedule along which price declines with the quantity you buy. Thus, many electric utilities employ what are called *declining tail-block rate structures* by which the first, say, 300 kilowatt-hours per month are billed at 10 cents each, the next 700 at 8 cents, and all quantities over 1000 kilowatt-hours/mo at 5 cents each. Such rate structures are a form of *second-degree price discrimination*.

Figure 12.17 illustrates the effect of such a rate structure for a consumer with the demand curve labeled D_i. In comparison with the alternative of charging a

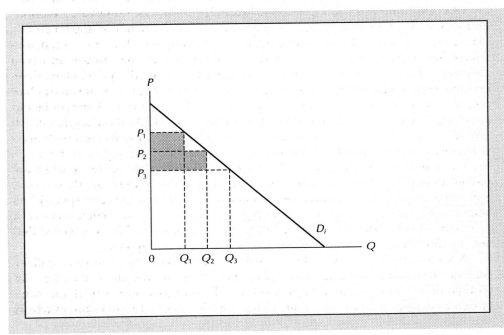

FIGURE 12.17
Second-Degree Price Discrimination
The seller offers the first block of consumption (0 to Q_1) at a high price (P_1), the second block (Q_1 to Q_2) at a lower price (P_2), the third block (Q_2 to Q_3) at a still lower price (P_3), and so on. Even though second-degree price discrimination makes no attempt to tailor rates to the char-acteristics of individu-als or specific groups, it often enables the monopolist to capture a substantial share of consumer surplus (the shaded area).

price of P_3 for every unit, the quantity discount scheme increases the consumer's total payment by an amount equal to the shaded area.

Second-degree price discrimination is like first-degree in that it tries to extract consumer surplus from each buyer. The two principal differences are these: (1) The same rate structure is available to every consumer under second-degree schemes, which means that they make no attempt to tailor charges to elasticity differences among buyers; and (2) the limited number of rate categories tends to limit the amount of consumer surplus that can be captured under second-degree schemes. First-degree schemes get the whole triangle, whereas Figure 12.17 shows that second-degree schemes capture only part of it.

The Hurdle Model of Price Discrimination

Every seller would like to practice perfect price discrimination. The difficulty, as noted earlier, is that sellers lack the information on individual demand curves necessary to do so. Yet another important form of price discrimination consists of a technique whereby the firm induces the most elastic buyers to identify themselves. This is the *hurdle model of price discrimination*. The basic idea is that the seller sets up a hurdle of some sort and makes a discount price available to those buyers who elect to jump over it. The logic is that those buyers who are most sensitive to price will be more likely than others to jump the hurdle.

One example of a hurdle is a rebate form included in the product package. Here, jumping over the hurdle means filling in the form, finding a stamp and an envelope, and then getting to the post office to mail it in. The firm's hope is that people who don't care much about price will be less likely than others to bother going through this process. If so, then people whose demands are less elastic end up paying the "regular" price, while those with more elastic demands pay the lower discount price.

It is a rare product whose seller does not use the hurdle model of differential pricing. Booksellers offer only high-priced hardback editions in the first year of publication. Buyers who don't care strongly about price buy these editions when they first come out. Others wait a year or two and then buy the much less expensive softcover edition. Here, the hurdle is having to endure the wait. Appliance sellers offer regular "scratch-'n-dent" sales at which machines with trivial cosmetic imperfections are sold for less than half their regular price. Here, there are two common hurdles: having to find out when and where the sale takes place and having to put up with a scratch or dent (which most of the time will be out of sight). Airlines offer "super-saver" discounts of up to half off the regular coach fare. Here also there are two common hurdles: having to make reservations a week or more in advance and having to stay over a Saturday night. Many retailers include discount coupons in their newspaper ads. Here, the hurdles are having to read the ads, clip the coupons, and get to the store before they expire. Some sellers post signs behind the counter saying "Ask about our special low price." Here, the hurdle is merely having to do the asking. But even this trivial hurdle can be remarkably effective, because many well-heeled buyers would find asking about a special price too unseemly even to contemplate.

None of these schemes perfectly segregates high-elasticity from low-elasticity buyers. For instance, there are some people who wait for the January white sales to buy their towels even though they would buy just as many if the sales weren't offered. But on the whole, the hurdles seem to function much as

THE EFFICIENCY LOSS FROM MONOPOLY   435

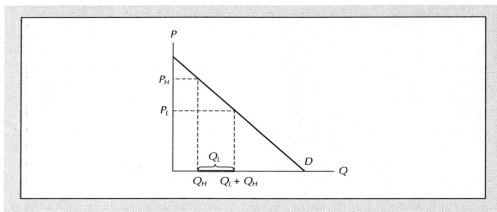

FIGURE 12.18
A Perfect Hurdle
When a hurdle is perfect, the only buyers who become eligible for the discount price (P_L) by jumping it are those who would not have been willing to pay the regular price (P_H). A perfect hurdle also imposes no significant costs on those who jump it.

intended. A perfect hurdle would be one that imposes only a negligible cost on the buyers who jump it, yet perfectly separates buyers according to their elasticity of demand. Analytically, the effect of such a hurdle is portrayed in Figure 12.18, where P_H represents the "regular" price and P_L represents the discount price. With a perfect hurdle, none of the people who pay the discount price has a reservation price greater than or equal to the regular price, which means that all of them would have been excluded from the market had only the regular price been available.

The hurdle model need not be limited to the two-price version depicted in Figure 12.18. On the contrary, many sellers have developed it into a highly complex art form involving literally dozens of price-hurdle combinations. On its Los Angeles–Honolulu route alone, for example, United Airlines offers dozens of different fares, each with its own set of restrictions. But no matter how simple or complex the scheme may be, its goal is the same—to give discounts to customers who would not otherwise buy the product.

The hurdle model is like first-degree price discrimination in that it tries to tailor prices to the elasticities of individual buyers. The principal difference is that even in its most sophisticated form, the hurdle model cannot hope to capture all the consumer surplus.

THE EFFICIENCY LOSS FROM MONOPOLY

Recall from Chapter 11 the claim that perfect competition led to an efficient allocation of resources. This claim was based on the observation that in long-run competitive equilibrium, there are no possibilities for additional gains from exchange. The value to buyers of the last unit of output is exactly the same as the market value of the resources required to produce it.

How does the long-run equilibrium under monopoly measure up by the same criteria? Not very well, it turns out. To illustrate, consider a monopolist with constant long-run average and marginal costs and the demand structure shown in Figure 12.19. The profit-maximizing quantity for this monopolist is Q^*, which he will sell at a price of P^*. Note that at Q^*, the value of an additional unit of output to buyers is P^*, which is greater than the cost of producing an additional unit, LMC. This means that the single-price monopolist does not exhaust all possible gains from exchange. As we saw earlier, if it were possible

436   CHAPTER 12   MONOPOLY

FIGURE 12.19
The Welfare Loss from a Single-Price Monopoly
A monopolist who charges a single price to all buyers will produce Q^* and sell at P^*. A competitive industry operating under the same cost conditions would produce Q_C and sell at P_C. In comparison with the perfectly competitive outcome, single-price monopoly results in a loss of consumer surplus equal to the area of $\Pi + S_1$. Since the monopolist earns Π, the cost to society is S_1—called the deadweight loss from monopoly.

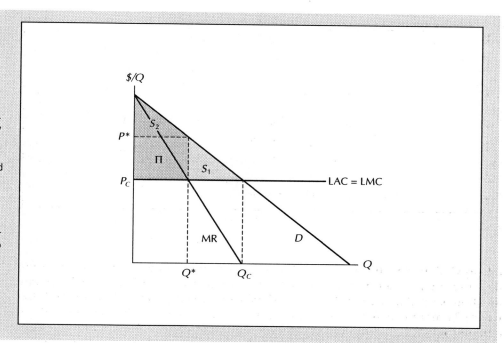

for the monopolist to charge different prices to every buyer, output would expand to Q_C, which is the same amount we would see in a perfectly competitive industry under the same demand and cost conditions. If output did expand from Q^* to Q_C because of perfect price discrimination, the gain in producer surplus would be equal to the combined areas of the triangles labeled S_1 and S_2. Under perfect competition, the triangle S_1 would be part of consumer surplus. The cost to society of having such an industry served by a single-price monopolist, rather than by perfectly competitive sellers, will be the loss of that consumer surplus.

Thus, in pure efficiency terms, the perfectly discriminating monopolist and the perfectly competitive industry lead to the same result. The difference is that in the former case all the benefit comes in the form of producer surplus, in the latter case all in the form of consumer surplus. The efficiency loss from monopoly is the result of failure to price discriminate perfectly. This loss (the area of triangle S_1 in Figure 12.19) is called the *deadweight loss from monopoly*.

In the preceding analysis, it made sense to speak of the welfare loss from having monopoly rather than competition because the cost structure was one that is compatible with the existence of perfect competition. But with that kind of cost structure, only legal barriers could prevent the emergence of competition. The existence of economic profits (Π in Figure 12.19) would lure competitors into the industry until price and quantity were driven to P_C and Q_C, respectively.

Suppose the reason for having a monopoly with a flat LAC curve is that the firm enjoys patent protection for its product. Can we now say that the welfare loss from having a single-price monopoly is equal to the lost consumer surplus measured in Figure 12.19? Before answering, we must first ask, "What is the alternative to the current situation?" If it is a society without patent protection, we may well have never gotten the product in the first place, so it hardly makes sense to complain that, compared with pure competition, monopoly produces a welfare loss. True enough, the patent-protected single-price monopoly does not exhaust all possible gains from trade. But with the patent-protected monopoly, we do get a consumer surplus plus producer surplus of $S_2 + \Pi$, whereas we might have gotten nothing at all without the patent protection.

PUBLIC POLICY TOWARD NATURAL MONOPOLY

These observations make clear that the relevant question is not whether monopoly is efficient in comparison with some unattainable theoretical ideal, but how it compares with the alternatives we actually confront. This question is nowhere more important than in the case of natural monopoly.

To keep the analysis simple, consider a technology in which total cost is given by

$$TC = F + MQ, \tag{12.8}$$

where Q is the level of output. And suppose the demand and marginal revenue curves for a single-price monopolist producing with this technology are as shown in Figure 12.20. The theoretical ideal allocation for this market would be to produce a quantity of Q^{**} and sell it at marginal cost, which here is equal to M. By contrast, the single-price monopoly produces only Q^* and sells it for P^*.

There are basically two objections to the equilibrium price-quantity pair of the single-price natural monopoly: (1) the *fairness objection,* which is that the producer earns an economic profit (Π); and (2) the *efficiency objection,* which is that price is above marginal cost, resulting in lost consumer surplus (S).

Policymakers may respond in a variety of ways to the fairness and efficiency objections. The five options considered below account for the most important alternatives.

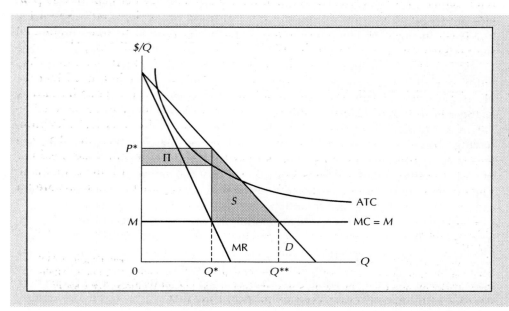

FIGURE 12.20
A Natural Monopoly
The two main objections to single-price natural monopoly are that it earns economic profit (Π) and that it results in the loss of consumer surplus (S).

438   CHAPTER 12   MONOPOLY

Drawing by Schrier. Copyright © 1981 Saturday Review, Inc.

"And then, after many years of business failures, Bertram finally made his fortune selling signs to the postal system saying 'Sorry, this window closed.'"

1. State Ownership and Management

Efficiency requires that price be equal to marginal cost. The difficulty this creates is that, for natural monopoly, marginal cost is below average total cost. Because private firms are not able to charge prices less than average cost and remain in business in the long run, the single-price firm has no alternative but to charge more than marginal cost. An option for getting around this particular difficulty is to have the state take over the industry. The attractive feature of this option is that the government is not bound, the way a private firm is, to earn at least a normal profit. It would thus be able to set a price equal to marginal cost, and absorb the resulting economic losses out of general tax revenues.

But there are also unattractive features of state ownership. Foremost among them is the fact that it often seems to weaken incentives for cost-conscious, efficient management. As Harvard University economist Harvey Leibenstein has emphasized, an organization's costs depend not just on its technology, but also on the vigor with which it pursues efficiency. In Leibenstein's phrase, an organization that does not act energetically to curb costs is said to exhibit **X-inefficiency.**[13]

X-inefficiency a condition in which a firm fails to obtain maximum output from a given combination of inputs.

X-inefficiency is by no means the exclusive province of government. In widely varying degrees, it is found in private firms as well. Leibenstein argued that the extent to which X-inefficiency is a problem will depend on economic incentives, which suggests a theoretical reason for believing that it is likely to be more widespread in government. When a private firm cuts a dollar from its costs, its profit goes up by a dollar. By contrast, when the person in charge of a government agency cuts a dollar from her agency's budget, the effect is merely to shrink her fiefdom.

Several noted scholars have argued that the goal of most bureaucrats is to maximize their operating budgets.[14] This is not to deny that bureaucrats are for

---

[13]Harvey Leibenstein, "Allocative Efficiency vs. X-Efficiency," *American Economic Review,* June 1966: 392–415.

[14]See, for example, William Niskanen, *Bureaucracy and Representative Government,* Chicago: Aldine-Atherton, 1971; and Gordon Tullock, *The Politics of Bureaucracy,* Washington, DC: Public Affairs Press, 1965. But for a contrasting view, see Albert Breton and Ronald Wintrobe, *The Logic of Bureaucratic Conduct,* Cambridge: Cambridge University Press, 1982.

the most part sincere, dedicated public servants. But it is perhaps only human nature for a bureaucrat to think that her particular agency has the most important mission in government, and to lobby accordingly on its behalf.

Below we will consider some quantitative evidence that bears on the relative efficiency of state-managed and private firms. Even common experience, however, provides some relevant natural experiments. Each spring in northern U.S. cities, for example, municipal road crews repair the potholes left by winter while, at the same time, the parking lots of supermarkets, shopping centers, and other nongovernment road surfaces are under repair by private paving companies. The contrast between the two groups is often striking. It is common to see seven members of an eight-man municipal road crew leaning on their shovels smoking cigarettes, giving occasional advice to the newcomer among them as he lazily tamps asphalt into the holes. The private crews who work the parking lots, though often only half as large, usually fill many more potholes per day.

Another illuminating case study in the effects of state management is the Department of Motor Vehicles. Try to remember the last time you visited the DMV in person. Would you ever go there again if you didn't have to? If you are like most people, you came away with the impression that a manager of even very modest talents could have devised some way of performing that service more expeditiously. We may safely speculate that few people would elect to live in a society in which the DMV was in charge of a substantial share of productive activity.

Despite the X-inefficiency problem, state-operated natural monopoly may be the best solution in some cases.[15] But there are other policy alternatives that offer many of the same benefits with fewer apparent costs.

2. State Regulation of Private Monopolies

One such alternative is to leave ownership in private hands, while providing guidelines or regulations that limit pricing discretion. The stereotypical example of this approach is public regulation of private companies that provide electricity, water, and telephone service.

The main form of government price regulation employed in the United States is known as *rate-of-return regulation,* in which prices are set to allow the firm to earn a predetermined rate of return on its invested capital. Ideally, this rate of return would allow the firm to recover exactly the opportunity cost of its capital, which is to say, it would ideally be the same as the competitive rate of return on investment.

In practice, however, regulatory commissions can never be certain what the competitive rate of return will be in any period. If the rate they set lies below the competitive return, the firm will have an incentive to reduce the quality of its service, and eventually to go out of business. By contrast, if regulators set too high a rate of return, prices will be higher than necessary and the firm will earn an extra-normal profit. Neither of these outcomes is attractive, but regulatory commissions have traditionally decided that the problems caused by an insufficient rate of return are far more serious than those caused by an excessive one.

---

[15]See Elliott D. Sclar, *You Don't Always Get What You Pay For,* Ithaca, NY: Cornell University Press, 2000.

440   CHAPTER 12   MONOPOLY

Harvey Averch and Leland Johnson were the first to explore in detail the consequences of a regulatory rate of return set higher than the cost of capital.[16] Their conclusion, in a nutshell, is that this practice gives the firm an incentive to substitute capital for other inputs in a way that inflates the cost of doing business. If the regulated utility's goal is to maximize profit, the behavioral path it will follow will be to make its "rate base"—the invested capital on which it earns the allowed rate of return—as large as possible. If the regulated monopolist can borrow capital at 8 percent/yr and is allowed to earn 10 percent/yr on each dollar invested, it can clear $20,000 of extra profit for every extra $1,000,000 of borrowed funds it invests.

At least two important distortions follow from the discrepancy between the allowed rate of return and the actual cost of capital. The first we may call the *gold-plated water cooler effect*. It refers to the fact that the regulated monopolist has an incentive to purchase more capital equipment than is actually necessary to produce any given level of output. Faced with a choice between buying a regular water cooler, for example, and a more expensive gold-plated one, the regulated monopolist has an incentive to opt for the latter. To illustrate, suppose that the allowed rate of return on capital were 10 percent a year and the actual cost of capital only 8 percent. If a gold-plated water cooler costs $1000 more than a regular one, the monopolist would then earn $20 higher profit each year by installing the more expensive water cooler. Regulatory commissions try to prevent the purchase of unnecessary equipment, but the complexities of day-to-day operations are too great to allow every decision to be monitored carefully.

A second distortion induced by rate-of-return regulation is peculiar to the monopolist who serves more than one separate market, and we may call it the *cross-subsidy effect*. Because the allowed rate of return exceeds the cost of capital, such a monopolist has an incentive to sell below cost in the more elastic market, and cross-subsidize the resulting losses by selling above cost in the less elastic market. The idea is that the below-cost price in the elastic market boosts sales by more than the above-cost price in the less elastic market curtails them. The resulting increase in output increases the requirements for capital to produce it, and hence increases the profits allowed by regulation.

To illustrate, consider the regulated monopolist whose demand and cost curves for two markets are shown in Figure 12.21. The ATC curves are constructed to include the allowed rate of profit, which exceeds the cost of capital. Thus, when the monopolist is earning a zero profit in terms of the cost curves shown in Figure 12.21, he is really earning

$$\Pi = (r^a - r^c)K, \tag{12.9}$$

where r^a is the allowed rate of return, r^c the actual cost of capital, and K the size of the total capital stock. To maximize profit, the monopolist thus wants to make K as big as possible, which in turn means making the sum of the outputs sold in the two markets as large as possible. To do that, he will set

---

[16]Harvey Averch and Leland Johnson, "Behavior of the Firm under Regulatory Constraint," *American Economic Review*, December 1962: 1052–1069. See also R. M. Spann, "Rate of Return Regulation and Efficiency in Production: An Empirical Test of the Averch-Johnson Thesis," *Bell Journal of Economics*, Spring 1974: 38–52.

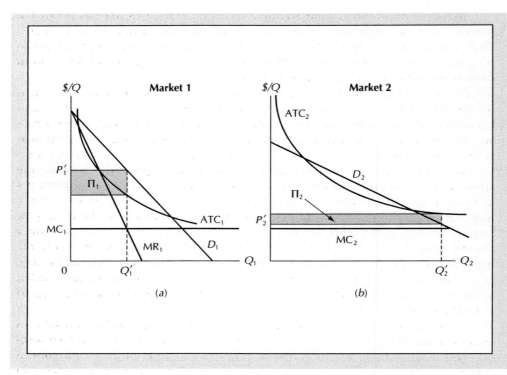

FIGURE 12.21
Cross-Subsidization to Boost Total Output
A regulated monopolist is generally allowed to earn a rate of return that exceeds the actual cost of capital, which provides an incentive to acquire as much capital as possible. To increase output (thereby to increase the required capital stock), the monopolist can sell above cost in his less elastic market (market 1 in panel a) and use the resultant profits ($\Pi_1 > 0$) to subsidize the losses ($\Pi_2 < 0$) sustained by selling below cost in his more elastic market.

MR = MC in the market with the less elastic demand (market 1 in panel a) and use the profits earned in that market (Π_1) to subsidize a price below average cost in the market with more elastic demand (market 2 in panel b). The aim, again, is to boost sales in the latter market by more than they are curtailed in the former. By selling the largest possible output, the monopolist is able to employ the largest possible capital stock, and thereby is able to earn the largest possible profit.

Regulatory pitfalls have not prevented governments in virtually every part of the world from continuing to intervene in the price and output decisions of important natural monopolies like electric utilities and local telephone service. Whether these interventions do more good than harm, in purely economic terms, remains an unsettled question. But they clearly seem to serve an important psychological function on behalf of a public that feels understandably uncomfortable about not having a buffer between itself and the sole supplier of a critical good or service.

3. Exclusive Contracting for Natural Monopoly

In the title of a widely quoted article, UCLA economist Harold Demsetz asked the disarmingly simple question, "Why Regulate Monopoly?"[17] His point was that even though cost conditions may dictate that a market be served by a single

---

[17]Harold Demsetz, "Why Regulate Monopoly?" *Journal of Law and Economics*, April 1968: 55–65.

442   CHAPTER 12   MONOPOLY

supplier, there can still be vigorous competition to see who gets to *be* that supplier. In Demsetz's proposal, the government would specify in detail the service it wanted provided—fire protection, garbage collection, postal delivery, whatever— and then call for private companies to submit bids to supply the service. And to the low bidder would then go the contract.

This scheme has been tried with success in a number of different municipalities. The city of Scottsdale, Arizona, for example, has its fire protection services provided by a private contractor selected in this fashion. And the residents of Oakland, California, have their garbage collected each week not by municipal garbage workers but by the Oakland Scavenger Company, a private, profit-seeking firm. In both instances, the costs incurred in providing service are approximately half the cost of comparable services provided directly by municipal governments. In the fire protection case, moreover, there is hard evidence that the cost reductions are not achieved through reductions in the quality of service. Profit-seeking fire insurance companies, whose survival depends on their ability to assess risks accurately, charge no more for fire insurance in Scottsdale than they do in communities with municipal fire departments.[18] The advantage of private contracting for the provision of natural monopoly services is that it takes production out of the hands of bureaucrats, who are often not very good at keeping costs down.

The political scientist Elliott Sclar cautions, however, that the advantages of contracting for public services are often more apparent than real (see footnote 15). Most contracts with private suppliers, for example, contain contingency clauses that allow higher fees in the event of unforeseen changes in circumstances. The government employees who monitor the implementation of private contracts may be unable to keep these extra fees under tight control. Added to that is the problem of corruption. Public contracts in practice may often go not to the firm that submits the lowest bid but to the one that pays the highest bribe.

Even if we abstract from these problems, private contracting may not be an attractive option in many cases. Because the contract must specify the details of the service to be provided, it must go into extraordinary detail in the case of a complex service, such as telecommunications. Moreover, it must make provisions for how new contractors are to be selected. In the case of electric utilities, changing contractors necessarily involves the transfer of a vast, complex array of generation and distribution equipment. At what price should this equipment be sold? By the time all the *i*'s are dotted and the *t*'s crossed, the exclusive contracts for providing monopoly service may be so detailed as to be indistinguishable from direct economic regulation.

4. Vigorous Enforcement of Antitrust Laws

A major element in the policy arsenal for dealing with monopoly is the nation's antitrust laws. The most important of these are the Sherman Act (1890), which makes it illegal "to monopolize, or attempt to monopolize . . . any part of the

---

[18]For an extended survey of studies comparing private costs and public costs, see E. S. Savas, *Privatizing the Public Sector*, Chatham, NJ: Chatham House Publishers, 1982.

trade or commerce among the several States . . . ," and the Clayton Act (1914), one of whose provisions prevents corporations from acquiring shares in a competitor where the effect would be to "substantially lessen competition or create a monopoly."

In interpreting the antitrust laws, the U.S. Justice Department has developed guidelines that prohibit mergers between competing companies whose combined market share would exceed some predetermined fraction of total industry output. These guidelines are applied with highly varying degrees of zeal under different political administrations. As a general rule, Democrats have been far less tolerant of mergers than Republicans have.

In the case of industries with declining long-run average cost curves, the cost of production will be much higher if we are served by many firms rather than by only a few. The most vigorous supporters of the antitrust laws insist that the laws will not impede the formation of natural monopolies. But as we will see in Chapter 13, they may substantially postpone the time when economies of scale are fully realized.

One response to this difficulty would be to apply the antitrust laws to prevent only those mergers where significant cost savings would not be realized. The government is not in a good position, however, to distinguish one type of case from another. Congress was well aware of this, and explicitly ruled out consideration of cost savings as a rationale for allowing mergers. The result is that antitrust policy impedes all consolidations, even those that would lead to substantial reductions in cost.

5. A Laissez-Faire Policy toward Natural Monopoly

As a fifth and final alternative for dealing with natural monopoly, let us consider the possibility of laissez faire, or doing nothing—just letting the monopolist produce whatever quantity she chooses and sell it at whatever price the market will bear. The obvious objections to this policy are the two we began with, namely, the fairness and efficiency problems. In this section, however, we will see that there may be at least some circumstances in which these problems are of only minimal importance.

Consider, in particular, a natural monopolist who uses the hurdle model of differential pricing. To keep the discussion simple, let's suppose she charges a regular price and also a discount price, the latter available to customers who clear some hurdle, such as mailing in a rebate form. How does the presence of this differential pricing device affect the fairness and efficiency objections to natural monopoly?

Consider first the efficiency objection. Recall that the problem is that the single-price monopolist charges a price above marginal cost, which excludes many potential buyers from the market, ones who value the product more highly than the value of the resources required to produce it.

For illustrative purposes, let's examine a natural monopolist with a total cost curve given by $F + MQ$ and a linear demand curve given by $P = A - BQ$. Figure 12.22a shows the demand and marginal cost curves for such a monopolist. If she is a single-price profit maximizer, she will produce Q^* and sell for P^*. But if she is able to charge one price to the buyers along the upper part of the demand curve and a lower price to all other buyers (Figure 12.22b), her

444   CHAPTER 12   MONOPOLY

FIGURE 12.22
The Efficiency Losses from Single-Price and Two-Price Monopoly
By being able to offer a discount price to the most elastic portion of the demand curve, the two-price monopolist (panel *b*) expands the market, thereby causing a much smaller efficiency loss (area *Z*, panel *b*) than in the case of the single-price monopolist (area *W*, panel *a*).

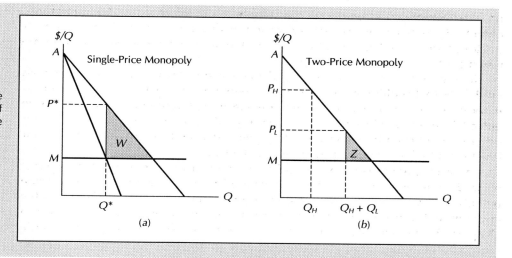
(a)   (b)

profit-maximizing strategy will be to sell Q_H at the price P_H and $Q_H + Q_L$ at the price P_L.[19]

Note that the efficiency loss associated with the two-price monopolist (lost consumer surplus, which is the area of triangle Z in panel *b*) is much smaller than the corresponding loss for the single-price monopolist (the area of triangle W in panel *a*).

In general, the more finely the monopolist can partition her market under the hurdle model, the smaller the efficiency loss will be. As noted earlier, it is common in most firms to see not one but a whole menu of different discount prices, each with a different set of restrictions (the deeper the discount, the more stringent the restriction). Given the wide latitude many firms have to expand

---

[19]For the single-price monopolist the profit function is given by

$$\Pi_1 = (A - BQ)Q - F - MQ.$$

The first-order condition for a maximum is given by

$$\frac{d\Pi_1}{dQ} = A - 2BQ - M = 0,$$

which yields a profit-maximizing quantity of $Q' = (A - M)/2B$, and a corresponding price of $P' = (A + M)/2$.

The profit function for the two-price monopolist, by contrast, is given by

$$\Pi_2 = (A - BQ_H)Q_H + (A - BQ_H - BQ_L)Q_L - F - M(Q_H + Q_L).$$

The first-order conditions for a maximum are given by

$$\frac{\partial \Pi_2}{\partial Q_H} = A - 2BQ_H - BQ_L - M = 0$$

and

$$\frac{\partial \Pi_2}{\partial Q_L} = A - BQ_H - 2BQ_L - M = 0,$$

which can be solved for

$$Q_H = \frac{A - M}{3B} = Q_L \quad \text{and} \quad P_L = \frac{A + 2M}{3} \quad \text{and} \quad P_H = \frac{2A + M}{3}.$$

(handwritten annotations:) $TC = F + MQ$ $P = A - BQ$

their markets through hurdle pricing, the efficiency problem of natural monopoly will often be of only secondary importance.

What about the fairness problem? First, what *is* this problem? The popular perception of it is that the monopolist transfers resources from people who desperately need them (namely, poor consumers) to others who have more than they need to begin with (namely, wealthy shareholders). We will see below that, defined in this particular way, the problem is sometimes less serious than it appears.

The more general question of what constitutes a fair distribution of society's resources is a deep philosophical one, well beyond the scope of our discussion here. At the very least, however, we can say that no firm is entitled to acquire, through force or coercion, the power to extract excessive resources from other persons. But suppose the monopolist has become the lone seller in her market through completely benevolent means. This is not implausible. As a natural monopolist, her costs are by definition lower than if other firms also served the same market. And perhaps her cheerful and courteous service has also helped entrench her position. Does she then create an injustice by charging prices in excess of marginal cost?

Certainly consumers would be happier to pay only the marginal cost of production. But marginal cost is less than average cost in a natural monopoly, and so it is not possible for *everyone* to pay marginal cost and have the supplier remain in business. At best, *some* consumers can pay prices close to marginal cost, but others will have to pay substantially more. Even so, if the monopolist is earning an economic profit, we know that buyers are paying more, on the average, than the cost of the resources required to serve them. How can this be defended in the name of fairness?

Earlier we saw that hurdle pricing makes the monopoly allocation more efficient. It would be an exaggeration to say that the same hurdle model makes the existence of monopoly profits seem completely fair. But it does help mitigate some of the most serious objections to them.

Consider first the source of a given dollar of monopoly profit. From which buyers does this dollar come? It is straightforward to show that it cannot have come from the discount price buyer. Typical discount prices range from 15 to 50 percent off the so-called regular price, and seldom do more than half of all buyers pay the discount price. Taking an illustrative case in which the discount is 30 percent and half of all buyers receive it, we see that the monopolist's revenue would fall by 15 percent if everyone paid the discount price. Very few firms would remain profitable in the face of a 15 percent decline in total revenue.

It follows that if the monopolist is earning economic profit, the source of that profit is the buyer who pays the regular price. The fact that this buyer could have paid a discount price if he had been willing to jump the requisite hurdle tells us that the burden imposed on him is no greater than the trouble of jumping the hurdle. This is obviously not the same as saying that the regular-price buyer makes a voluntary charitable contribution to the monopolist. But it does take at least some of the sting out of the notion that the monopolist's customers are being cruelly victimized.

So much for the source of monopoly profit. What about its disposition? Who gets it? If we assume a corporate income tax rate of 40 percent, 40 cents of each dollar of monopoly profits goes to the U.S. Treasury. The remainder is paid out

446   CHAPTER 12   MONOPOLY

to shareholders, either directly through dividends or indirectly by reinvesting it into the company. Granted, the average income of shareholders is greater than that of citizens as a whole. But there are many low-income shareholders in the United States. Most employee pension funds, for example, are invested in the stock market, as are the private insurance holdings of many low-income individuals. So a considerable fraction of any dollar of monopoly profit will wind up in the hands of low-income shareholders.

But to take the worst possible case from a distributional point of view, let us suppose that what is left of the dollar of monopoly profit goes entirely to the wealthiest resident of Manhattan. Assume that she pays federal income tax at the rate of 33 percent on the 60 cents that the federal government hasn't already taken, leaving 40 cents. State and local income and sales taxes will claim an additional 7 cents, leaving only 33 cents in the hands of our wealthy shareholder.

To summarize then, the source of a dollar in monopoly profit is the regular-price buyer, someone who could have paid a discount price had he but taken a little extra trouble. Of that dollar, 60 cents goes to the federal treasury and another 7 cents to state and local governments. The disposition of more than two-thirds of the dollar is thus subject to governmental control. The remainder becomes income in the hands of shareholders, at least some of whom have low incomes to begin with. So it is by no means clear that the economic profit associated with natural monopoly creates distributional inequities of the sort commonly perceived.

Hurdles, of course, are seldom perfect. Inevitably they screen out some buyers who will not buy at the regular price. And much of the time, real resources must be expended in order to jump over these hurdles. Mailing in a rebate coupon may not take a lot of time, but the time it takes could certainly be better spent. And in at least some cases, tax avoidance will keep the government from collecting as much as the tax tables specify.

So what are we to conclude from this brief analysis of the five policy options for dealing with natural monopoly? The short answer is that each has problems. None completely eliminates the difficulties that arise when a single seller serves the market. Sometimes the least costly solution will be competitive contracting, other times direct state ownership. Regulation will continue to play a role in specific industries, particularly the traditional public utilities. And despite their many shortcomings, antitrust laws serve the public well by discouraging price-fixing and other anticompetitive practices. But in some cases, particularly those in which the monopolist has devised means of richly segmenting the market, the best option may be simply not to intervene at all.

Does Monopoly Suppress Innovation?

One of the most enduring topics of conversation among economic conspiracy buffs is the notion that monopolists deprive consumers of a spectrum of enormously valuable technological innovations. Who has not heard, for example, of how the lightbulb manufacturers have conspired to prevent revolutionary new designs for long-lasting lightbulbs from reaching the market?

Is the suppression of innovation yet another cost of monopoly that we ought to have considered in our analysis of public policy options? As the following example will make clear, the logic of profit maximization suggests that monopolists may not always be so eager to suppress innovation.

Suppose the current lightbulb design lasts 1000 hours. Now the lightbulb monopolist discovers how to make a bulb that lasts 10,000 hours for the same per-bulb cost of production. Will the monopolist introduce the new bulb?

EXAMPLE 12.4

Suppose we measure the quantity produced by the monopolist not as lightbulbs per se, but as the number of bulb-hours of lighting services. Thus, if the cost of producing the current design is, say, $1.00/bulb-hr, then the cost of the new design is only $0.10/bulb-hr. In Figure 12.23, D represents the market demand curve for lighting and MR the associated marginal revenue curve.

Note that the profit-maximizing price and quantity for the current design, whose marginal cost is $1/bulb-hr, are P_1 and Q_1, respectively. For the new design, whose marginal cost is $0.10/bulb-hr, the profit-maximizing price and quantity are P_2 and Q_2. The monopolist's profit under the current design is the area of the rectangle $ABCE$. For the new design, the corresponding profit value is the area of the rectangle $FGHK$. And because the monopolist's profit is higher under the new design, it has every incentive to make that design available. Indeed, as some of you may recall, the availability of just such an efficient new lightbulb was announced several years ago.

This example does not imply that the monopolist's incentives to introduce innovations will always and everywhere be the same as a competitive firm's. But it should caution us against uncritical acceptance of claims that monopolists always deprive consumers of the benefits of the latest available technology.

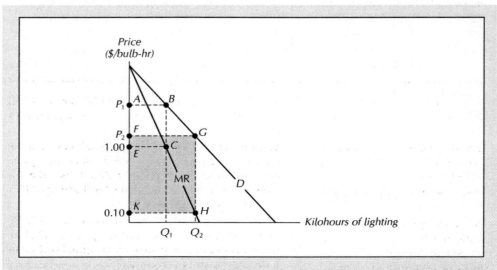

FIGURE 12.23
Does Monopoly Suppress Innovation?
The cost of producing the new, efficient lightbulb, at $0.10/bulb-hr, is only one-tenth the cost of producing the current design, $1/bulb-hr. Because the monopolist's profits with the efficient design (area of *FGHK*) exceed its profits with the current design (area of *ABCE*), it will offer the new design.

448   CHAPTER 12   MONOPOLY

SUMMARY

* Monopoly is the name given to the market structure in which a single firm serves the entire market. Five factors, acting alone or in combination, give rise to monopoly: (1) control over key inputs, (2) economies of scale, (3) patents, (4) network economies, and (5) government licenses. In the long run, by far the most important of these is economies of scale, in part because it also helps explain network economies and government licenses.

* Because the monopolist is the only seller in the market, his demand curve is the downward-sloping market demand curve. Unlike the perfect competitor, who can sell as much as he chooses at the market price, the monopolist must cut price in order to expand his output. The monopolist's rule for maximizing profits is the same as the one used by perfectly competitive firms. It is to expand output if the gain in revenue (marginal revenue) exceeds the increase in costs (marginal cost), and to contract if the loss in revenue is smaller than the reduction in costs. The pivotal difference is that marginal revenue is less than price for the monopolist, but equal to price for the perfect competitor.

* When the monopolist can sell in several separate markets, he distributes output among them so that marginal revenue is the same in each. Here again, the familiar logic of cost-benefit analysis provides a convenient framework for analyzing the firm's decision about whether to alter its current behavior.

* Unlike the perfectly competitive case, the monopoly equilibrium generally does not exhaust the potential gains from exchange. In general, the value to society of an additional unit of output will exceed the cost to the monopolist of the resources required to produce it. This finding has often been interpreted to mean that monopoly is less efficient than perfect competition. But this interpretation is of only limited practical significance, because the conditions that give rise to monopoly—in particular, economies of scale in production—are rarely compatible with those required for perfect competition.

* Our policy focus in the chapter was on the question of how the government should treat natural monopolies—markets characterized by downward-sloping long-run average cost curves. We considered five policy alternatives: (1) state ownership, (2) private ownership with government price regulation, (3) competitive bidding by private firms for the right to be the sole provider of service, (4) vigorous enforcement of antitrust laws designed to prevent monopoly, and finally (5) a complete laissez-faire, or hands-off, policy. Problems arise with each of these alternatives, and the best policy will in general be different in different circumstances. The laissez-faire stance is most attractive in markets where the monopolist is able to employ the hurdle model of differential pricing. Allowing buyers to decide for themselves whether to become eligible for a discount price softens both the efficiency and fairness objections to natural monopoly.

QUESTIONS FOR REVIEW

1. What five factors give rise to monopoly? In the long run, why is economies of scale the most important factor?

2. If the United States has thousands of cement producers but a small town has only one, is this cement producer a monopolist? Explain.

3. When is marginal revenue less than price for a monopolist? Explain.

4. Why does a profit-maximizing monopolist never produce on an inelastic portion of the demand curve? Would a revenue-maximizing monopolist ever produce on the inelastic portion of the demand curve?

5. Why is an output level at which MR intersects MC from below never the profit-maximizing level of output?

6. What effect will the imposition of a 50 percent tax on economic profit have on a monopolist's price and output decisions? (*Hint:* Recall that the assumed objective is to choose the level of output that maximizes economic profit.)

7. Suppose the elasticity of demand is $\eta = -3$. By how much does price exceed marginal cost? How does this markup of price over marginal cost compare with perfect competition?

8. *True or false:* A lump-sum tax on a monopolist will always increase the price charged by the monopolist and lower the quantity of output sold.

9. *True or false:* If a monopolist faces a perfectly horizontal demand curve, then the dead-weight loss to the economy is zero.

10. What forces work against X-inefficiency in privately owned monopolies?

11. How does the hurdle method of price discrimination mitigate both the efficiency and fairness problems associated with monopoly?

PROBLEMS

1. You are a self-employed profit-maximization consultant specializing in monopolies. Five firms are currently seeking your advice, and although the information they have supplied to you is incomplete, your expert knowledge allows you to go back and make a definite recommendation in each case. Select one of the following recommendations for each firm in the short run:
   a. Remain at the current output level.
   b. Increase output.
   c. Reduce output.
   d. Shut down.
   e. Go back and recalculate your figures because the ones supplied can't possibly be right.

Firm	P	MR	TR	Q	TC	MC	ATC	AVC	Your recommendation
A	3.90	3.00		2000	7400	2.90		3.24	b MR>MC, P>AVC
B	5.90			10000		5.90	4.74	4.24	C
C		9.00	44000	4000		9.00	11.90	10.74	A P>AVC
D	35.90	37.90		5000		37.90	35.90		e P<MR
E	35.00		3990	1000	3300		at min value	23.94	e

$TR = QP = 100Q - Q^2$ NR $MR = 100 - 2Q$ $MR = MC$
$100 - 2Q = 2Q$
$Q = 25, P = 15$
$TR - TC = 509$

2. A monopolist has a demand curve given by $P = 100 - Q$ and a total cost curve given by $TC = 16 + Q^2$. The associated marginal cost curve is $MC = 2Q$. Find the monopolist's profit-maximizing quantity and price. How much economic profit will the monopolist earn?

3. Now suppose the monopolist in Problem 2 has a total cost curve given by $TC = 32 + Q^2$. The corresponding marginal cost curve is still $MC = 2Q$, but fixed costs have doubled. Find the monopolist's profit-maximizing quantity and price. How much economic profit does the monopolist earn?

4. Now suppose the monopolist in Problem 2 has a total cost curve given by $TC = 16 + 4Q^2$. The corresponding marginal cost curve is now $MC = 8Q$, and fixed costs are back to the original level. Find the monopolist's profit-maximizing quantity and price. How much economic profit does the monopolist earn?

$MR_n = MR_F = 60$ 5. Now suppose the monopolist in Problem 2 also has access to a foreign market in which he can sell whatever quantity he chooses at a constant price of 60. How much $100 - 2Q = 60$ will he sell in the foreign market? What will his new quantity and price be in the $Q_h = 20$, $MC = MR$ original market?

$2Q = 60$
$Q_{total} = 30$
$Q_F = 30 - 20 = 10$
$P_h = 100 - 20 = 80$

6. Now suppose the monopolist in Problem 2 has a long-run marginal cost curve of $MC = 20$. Find the monopolist's profit-maximizing quantity and price. Find the efficiency loss from this monopoly.

450   CHAPTER 12   MONOPOLY

[handwritten: MR=MC]

[handwritten: P=MC]   *[handwritten: TR=100Q-10Q²   MR=100-20Q   20=100-20Q, Q=4]*

[handwritten: P=60]

7. Suppose a perfectly discriminating monopolist faces market demand $P = 100 - 10Q$ and has constant marginal cost MC = 20 (with no fixed costs). How much does the monopolist sell? How much profit does the monopolist earn? What is the maximum per-period license fee the government could charge the firm and have the firm still stay in business?

8. The demand by senior citizens for showings at a local movie house has a constant price elasticity equal to -4. The demand curve for all other patrons has a constant price elasticity equal to -2. If the marginal cost per patron is \$1 per showing, how much should the theater charge members of each group?

[handwritten: $MR = P(1 - \frac{1}{|\eta|})$]

[handwritten: $P = \frac{MC}{1 - 1/|\eta|}$]

9. During the Iran–Iraq war, the same arms merchant often sold weapons to both sides of the conflict. In this situation, a different price could be offered to each side because there was little danger that the country offered the lower price would sell arms to its rival to profit on the difference in prices. Suppose a French arms merchant has a monopoly of Exocet air-to-sea missiles and is willing to sell them to both sides. Iraq's demand for Exocets is $P = 400 - 0.5Q$ and Iran's is $P = 300 - Q$, where P is in millions of dollars. The marginal cost of Exocets is MC = Q. What price will be charged to each country?

[handwritten: $P_S = \frac{4}{3}, P_A = $]

10. If you have ever gone grocery shopping on a weekday afternoon, you have probably noticed some elderly shoppers going slowly down the aisles checking their coupon book for a coupon that matches each of their purchases. How is this behavior explained by the hurdle model of price discrimination?

[handwritten: $MC = MR = 10 \times (1 - \frac{1}{2}) = 5$]

11. A monopolist's price is \$10. At this price the absolute value of the elasticity of demand is 2. What is the monopolist's marginal cost?

12. Suppose the government imposed a price ceiling on a monopolist (an upper bound on the price the monopolist can charge). Let $\bar{P}$ denote the price ceiling, and suppose the monopolist incurs no costs in producing output. *True or false:* If the demand curve faced by the monopolist is inelastic at the price $\bar{P}$, then the monopolist would be no better off if the government removed the price ceiling. *[handwritten: false]*

13. *The New York Times*, a profit-maximizing newspaper, faces a downward-sloping demand schedule for advertisements. When advertising for itself in its own pages (for example, an ad saying "Read Maureen Dowd in the Sunday *Times*"), is the opportunity cost of a given-size ad simply the price it charges its outside advertisers? Explain.

*14. Crazy Harry, a monopolist, has a total cost curve given by TC = 5Q + 15. He sets two prices for his product, a regular price, P_H, and a discount price, P_L. Everyone is eligible to purchase the product at P_H. To be eligible to buy at P_L, it is necessary to present a copy of the latest Crazy Harry newspaper ad to the salesclerk. Suppose the only buyers who present the ad are those who would not have been willing to buy the product at P_H.
    a.   If Crazy Harry's demand curve is given by $P = 20 - 5Q$, what are the profit-maximizing values of P_H and P_L?
    b.   How much economic profit does Harry make?
    c.   How much profit would he have made if he had been forced to charge the same price to all buyers?
    d.   Are buyers better or worse off as a result of Harry's being able to charge two prices?

15. An author has signed a contract in which the publisher promises to pay her \$10,000 plus 20 percent of gross receipts from the sale of her book. *True or false:* If both the publisher and the author care only about their own financial return from the project, then the author will prefer a higher book price than will the publisher.

16. A film director has signed a contract in which the production studio promises to pay her \$1,000,000 plus 5 percent of the studio's rental revenues from the film, all of whose costs of production and distribution are fixed. *True or false:* If both the director and the studio care only about their own financial return from the project, then the director will prefer a lower film rental price than will the studio.

---

*This problem is most easily solved using the calculus method described in footnote 19.

ANSWERS TO IN-CHAPTER EXERCISES

12.1.

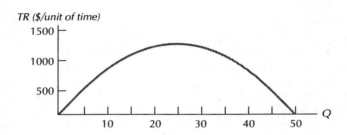

12.2.

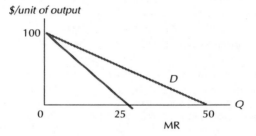

12.3. MC = 40 = 100 − 4Q, which solves for $Q^* = 15$, $P^* = 100 − 2Q^* = 70$.

12.4. The profit-maximizing level of output for a single-price monopolist occurs where MR = MC. Marginal revenue equals marginal cost at both $Q = 15$ and $Q = 34$, but $Q = 34$ has marginal revenue intersect from above and thus is the maximal one. However, even at $Q = 34$, price does not cover average variable cost ($66 = P <$ AVC = 72). The average variable cost curve lies everywhere above the demand curve (see figure), so the firm can do no better than earn profits equal to negative of the fixed costs. Thus, the optimal quantity is $Q = 0$: the firm should shut down!

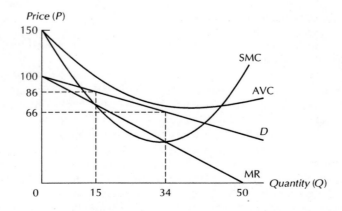

12.5. $MR_1 = 10 − 2Q_1$ (left panel), and $MR_2 = 20 − 2Q_2$ (center panel), so the horizontal summation of the MR curves is given by ΣMR (right panel). The profit-maximizing

452   CHAPTER 12   MONOPOLY

quantity is 13, 4 of which should be sold in market 1, the remaining 9 in market 2. The profit-maximizing prices are $P_1^* = 6$ and $P_2^* = 11$.

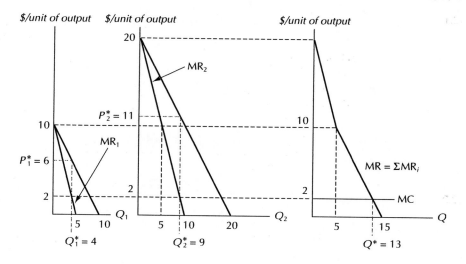

CHAPTER

13

IMPERFECT COMPETITION: A GAME-THEORETIC APPROACH

T he story is told of three lawyers and three economists who meet one morning as they arrive at the 30th Street Station in Philadelphia to catch the Metroliner for New York, where they are scheduled to attend the annual meetings of the Law and Economics Association. Each lawyer buys a one-way ticket. To their surprise, however, they notice that the economists standing in the adjacent ticket line buy only a single ticket among them. "What are they up to?" one of the lawyers wonders aloud to his colleagues as the six men take their seats on the train.

Shortly after the train pulls out, the lawyers notice the conductor punching tickets in the car ahead. At this point, the three economists quickly crowd into one of the lavatories at the back of the car. Presently, the conductor comes by and collects each lawyer's ticket and, on his way to the next car, knocks on the door of the occupied lavatory, saying "Tickets, please." The door opens a crack, and a hand reaches out to present a ticket, which the conductor dutifully punches and returns.

Four days later, the men arrive at Penn Station for their return journey. Inspired by the economists, the lawyers buy only a single ticket, cackling to themselves at their cleverness. But this time they are puzzled to notice that the economists don't buy any tickets at all.

The six men board the train, and at first sight of the approaching conductor, the three lawyers hurriedly sequester themselves in one of the lavatories. At this, the three economists get up and proceed to the rear of the car. Two of them go into the other lavatory while the third knocks on the door of the lawyers' lavatory, saying, "Tickets please." One of the lawyers holds their ticket out the door, which the economist collects and then joins his colleagues.

454   CHAPTER 13   IMPERFECT COMPETITION: A GAME-THEORETIC APPROACH

CHAPTER PREVIEW

As the parable of the lawyers and the economists illustrates, the payoff to an action often depends not only on the action itself, but also on how it relates to actions taken by others in the same environment. In previous chapters, we viewed economic decision makers as confronting an environment that is essentially passive. In the perfectly competitive environment of Chapter 11, for example, firms were assumed to ignore the actions of their adversaries. And in the monopoly environment of Chapter 12, the firm simply had no rivals to worry about. Both perfect competition and monopoly represent idealized forms. They are useful for generating insights about general tendencies but are rarely, if ever, encountered in practice. Our task in this chapter is to describe and explore the hybrid forms of industrial organization we deal with on a daily basis—namely, oligopoly and monopolistic competition.

We will begin by introducing some elementary concepts from the mathematical theory of games. We will then apply these concepts to analyze the behavior of oligopolists, comparing several simple models in which firms make alternative assumptions about the behavior of their rivals. After considering a traditional model of monopolistic competition, we will discuss a simple spatial model of monopolistic competition in which customers have particular locations or product characteristics that they most prefer. In this situation, we will see, firms tend to compete most intensively for the buyers of products that are most similar to their own.

AN INTRODUCTION TO THE THEORY OF GAMES

At the market equilibrium price, worldwide demand for coffee is inelastic with respect to price. Thus when a frost destroys half the crop in a country that exports a large share of the world's coffee, the price of coffee may rise so much that local farmers actually earn higher profits than if there had been no frost. If coffee growers could earn more by selling less coffee, why do they need to wait for a frost to kill half their crop? Why not just plant less coffee in the first place?

The answer, of course, is that while it might be in the interests of farmers as a whole to curtail production, no individual farmer would ever have an incentive to do so. Each individual farmer, after all, does best if all others *except* him cut back. That way he gets to sell the same quantity as before at the new higher price. In a competitive industry like coffee farming, the existence of many small independent producers makes it difficult to organize conspiracies to curtail output.

Such collusion might seem less difficult to accomplish among oligopolists—that is, in industries served by only a small number of firms. But although successful collusion sometimes does work to the benefit of firms in such industries, it usually turns out to be surprisingly difficult to sustain. Indeed, a recurring theme in the economics of oligopoly is that what it pays each firm to do individually often turns out to be harmful to the interests of firms taken as a whole.

The basic problem confronting colluding oligopolists has the same structure as the prisoner's dilemma game we saw in Chapter 7. Recall that in the original story used to illustrate the prisoner's dilemma, two prisoners are held in separate cells for a serious crime that they did in fact commit. The prosecutor, however, has only enough hard evidence to convict them of a minor offense, for

AN INTRODUCTION TO THE THEORY OF GAMES 455

		Prisoner *Y*	
		Confess	**Remain silent**
Prisoner *X*	**Confess**	5 years for each	0 years for *X* 20 years for *Y*
	Remain silent	20 years for *X* 0 years for *Y*	1 year for each

TABLE 13.1
The Prisoner's Dilemma
The dominant strategy for each prisoner is to confess. Yet when each confesses, each does worse than if each had remained silent.

which the penalty is, say, a year in jail. Each prisoner is told that if one confesses while the other remains silent, the confessor will go scot-free while the other spends 20 years in prison. If both confess, they will get an intermediate sentence, say, 5 years. These payoffs are summarized in Table 13.1. The two prisoners are not allowed to communicate with one another.

Situations like the prisoner's dilemma may be analyzed using the mathematical theory of games developed by John von Neumann and Oskar Morgenstern during the 1940s.[1] This theory begins by describing the three elements common to all games: (1) the players, (2) the list of possible strategies, and (3) the payoffs that correspond to each combination of strategies. In Table 13.1, the two players in the game are prisoner *X* and prisoner *Y*. Each player has two strategies: confess and remain silent. The payoffs to each combination of strategies are the sentences they receive, which are summarized in the *payoff matrix* shown in Table 13.1.

Some games, like the prisoner's dilemma, have a **dominant strategy,** which means a strategy that produces better results no matter what strategy the opposing player follows. The dominant strategy in the prisoner's dilemma is to confess. No matter what *Y* does, *X* gets a lighter sentence by speaking out: if *Y* too confesses, *X* gets 5 years instead of 20; and if *Y* remains silent, *X* goes free instead of spending a year in jail. The payoffs are perfectly symmetric, so *Y* also does better to confess, no matter what *X* does. The difficulty is that when each behaves in a self-interested way, both do worse than if each had shown restraint. Thus, when both confess, they get 5 years, instead of the 1 year they could have gotten by remaining silent.

dominant strategy the strategy in a game that produces better results irrespective of the strategy chosen by one's opponent.

To illustrate the analogy between the prisoner's dilemma and the problem confronting oligopolists who are trying to collude, let us consider two firms that are the sole providers of mineral water in a given market. Suppose the market demand curve takes the specific form $P = 20 - Q$, and that each firm can produce mineral water from its own spring at zero marginal cost. Suppose the two firms are considering a collusive agreement under which each produces half the monopoly output and offers it for sale at the monopoly price. For the specific demand curve assumed, the monopoly quantity (that is, the quantity for which $MR = MC = 0$) is 10, and the monopoly price is also 10. If the firms enter into and abide by this agreement, each will sell 5 units at a price of 10, giving each an economic profit of 50. On a strict profit criterion, there is no possibility for each firm to do better than that.

---

[1]See John von Neumann and Oskar Morgenstern, *Theory of Games and Economic Behavior*, 3rd ed., Princeton, NJ: Princeton University Press, 1953.

456   CHAPTER 13 IMPERFECT COMPETITION: A GAME-THEORETIC APPROACH

TABLE 13.2

Profits to Cooperation and Defection

The dominant strategy is for each firm to defect, for by so doing it earns higher profit no matter which option its rival chooses. Yet when both defect, each earns less than when each cooperates.

		Firm 1	
		Cooperate ($P = 10$)	Defect ($P = 9$)
Firm 2	**Cooperate** ($P = 10$)	$\Pi_1 = 50$ $\Pi_2 = 50$	$\Pi_1 = 99$ $\Pi_2 = 0$
	Defect ($P = 9$)	$\Pi_1 = 0$ $\Pi_2 = 99$	$\Pi_1 = 49.50$ $\Pi_2 = 49.50$

Yet this does not assure that each firm will abide by the agreement. Note that the payoff to each firm depends on the combination of behaviors they choose. Each firm has two options—namely, to abide by the agreement or to defect. For the sake of discussion, suppose that to defect means to cut price by 1 unit, from 10 to 9. If one firm abides by the agreement while the other defects, what will happen? Since the two firms are selling identical products, the defecting firm will capture the entire market because of its lower price. Selling 11 units at a price of 9, it will earn a profit of 99; the trusting cooperator sells no output and thus earns zero profit.

If both firms defect, they will end up splitting the 11 units of output sold at a price of 9, and each will make an economic profit of 49.50. Since each firm has two options—(1) cooperate, by charging 10 as agreed; and (2) defect, by charging 9—there are four possible combinations of behavior. These combinations, and the profits that result from each, are summarized in Table 13.2.

Note in the table that it is a dominant strategy for each firm to defect. That is, each firm gets a higher payoff by defecting, no matter which option the other firm chooses. To illustrate, consider the choice facing firm 2. It says to itself, "Suppose firm 1 cooperates; which choice is best for me?" By cooperating when firm 1 cooperates, the firms end up in the upper left cell of the profit matrix in Table 13.2, which means each earns 50. But if firm 2 defects, the result will be the lower left cell, where it would end up earning 99. Now firm 2 says, "Suppose firm 1 defects. Which choice is best for me this time?" If firm 2 cooperates, we get the upper right cell of the profit matrix, where it earns 0. But if firm 2 defects, it earns 49.50. Thus, no matter which choice firm 1 makes, firm 2 earns higher profit by defecting.

By exactly parallel reasoning, defection is also a dominant strategy for firm 1. Note, however, that when each firm defects, each does worse than if each had cooperated. In this situation, behavior that is in the interest of each individual firm adds up to a result that is not in the interest of firms generally.

As this example is set up, the firms don't do much worse when each defects than when each cooperates. But firms that find it in their interest to defect once are likely to find it in their interest to do so again. If one now charges 8 while the other remains at 9, for example, the former will earn a profit of 96, while the latter earns 0. A firm need not feel a compelling desire to outdo its rival in order for defection to be an attractive option. On the contrary, its motive may be purely self-protective, the very rational fear that its rival will defect. The resulting process of competitive price-cutting will terminate only when price has plummeted all the way down to marginal cost. At that point, neither firm earns any profit at all. So the cost of failing to abide by a cooperative agreement can be high indeed.

AN INTRODUCTION TO THE THEORY OF GAMES 457

		Firm 1	
		Don't advertise	**Advertise**
Firm 2	**Don't advertise**	$\Pi_1 = 500$ $\Pi_2 = 500$	$\Pi_1 = 750$ $\Pi_2 = 0$
	Advertise	$\Pi_1 = 0$ $\Pi_2 = 750$	$\Pi_1 = 250$ $\Pi_2 = 250$

TABLE 13.3
Advertising as a Prisoner's Dilemma
When advertising's main effect is brand switching, the dominant strategy is to advertise heavily (lower right cell), even though firms as a whole would do better by not advertising (upper left cell).

Oligopolists compete not only along the price dimension, but through the use of advertising as well. And here too the interests of an individual firm often conflict with the interests of firms taken as a whole, as the following Economic Naturalist illustrates.

Why do cigarette companies advertise "too much"?

When a firm advertises its product, its demand increases for two reasons. First, people who never used that type of product before learn about it, leading some to buy it. Second, other people who already consume a different brand of the same product may switch brands because of advertising. The first effect boosts sales for the industry as a whole. The second merely redistributes existing sales among firms.

The American cigarette industry is one in which the most important effect of advertising is believed to be brand-switching. In such industries, the decision whether to advertise often confronts individual firms with a prisoner's dilemma. Table 13.3 shows the profits to a hypothetical pair of cigarette producers under the four possible combinations of their advertise/don't advertise decisions. If both firms advertise (lower right cell), each earns a profit of only 250, as compared with a profit of 500 each if neither advertises (upper left cell). So it is clearly better for neither firm to advertise than for both to advertise.

Yet note the incentives confronting the individual firm. Firm 1 sees that if firm 2 doesn't advertise, firm 1 can earn higher profits by advertising (750) than by not advertising (500). Firm 1 also sees that if firm 2 does advertise, firm 1 will again earn more by advertising (250) than by not advertising (0). It is thus a dominant strategy for firm 1 to advertise. And because the payoffs are symmetric, it is also a dominant strategy for firm 2 to advertise. So here too when each firm does what is rational from its own point of view, firms as a group do worse than if they had acted in concert.

Congress passed a law forbidding the advertising of cigarettes on television as of January 1, 1971. Its stated purpose was to protect people from messages that might persuade them to consume a product that has been proved hazardous to human health. The law seems to have achieved this purpose, at least in part, as evidenced by the subsequent decline in

ECONOMIC NATURALIST 13.1

Why do cigarette companies advertise so much?

458   CHAPTER 13   IMPERFECT COMPETITION: A GAME-THEORETIC APPROACH

the proportion of Americans who smoke. But the law has also had an unintended effect, which was to solve—at least temporarily—the prisoner's dilemma confronting American cigarette manufacturers. In the year before the law's enactment, cigarette manufacturers spent more than $300 million advertising their products. The corresponding figure for the following year was more than $60 million smaller, and much of that difference translated into higher profits for the industry. The advertising ban thus accomplished for the cigarette manufacturers what the imperatives of individual profit seeking could not—an effective way of limiting the advertising arms race. In the succeeding years, however, competitive pressures have led cigarette manufacturers to increase their expenditures on forms of advertising that remain legal, thereby eroding their profit windfall.

The Nash Equilibrium Concept

When, as in the prisoner's dilemma, both parties have a dominant strategy in a game, the equilibrium for the game occurs when each plays the dominant strategy. But there are many games in which not every player has a dominant strategy. Consider, for example, the variation on the advertising game shown in Table 13.4. No matter what firm 2 does, firm 1 does better to advertise; so advertise is the dominant strategy for firm 1. But now the same cannot be said of firm 2. If firm 1 advertises, firm 2 does best also to advertise. But if firm 1 does not advertise, firm 2 does best not to advertise. In contrast to the prisoner's dilemma, here the best strategy for firm 2 depends on the particular strategy chosen by firm 1.

Even though firm 2 does not have a dominant strategy in this game, we can say something about what is likely to happen. In particular, firm 2 is able to predict that firm 1 will advertise because that is a dominant strategy for firm 1. And since firm 2 knows this, it knows that its own best strategy is also to advertise. In this game, the lower right cell is called a **Nash equilibrium**,[2] which is defined as a combination of strategies such that each player's strategy is the best he can choose given the strategy chosen by the other player. Thus, at a Nash equilibrium, neither player has any incentive to deviate from its current strategy. Note that when each player follows his dominant strategy in a prisoner's dilemma, the result is a Nash equilibrium. But as we have seen, a Nash equilibrium does not require both players to have a dominant strategy.

Nash equilibrium the combination of strategies in a game such that neither player has any incentive to change strategies given the strategy of his opponent.

TABLE 13.4
A Game in Which Firm 2 Has No Dominant Strategy
Firm 1's dominant strategy is to advertise. But firm 2 has no dominant strategy. If firm 1 advertises, firm 2 does best also to advertise, but if firm 1 does not advertise, firm 2 does best not to advertise.

		Firm 1	
		Don't advertise	Advertise
Firm 2	**Don't advertise**	$\Pi_1 = 500$ $\Pi_2 = 400$	$\Pi_1 = 750$ $\Pi_2 = 100$
	Advertise	$\Pi_1 = 200$ $\Pi_2 = 0$	$\Pi_1 = 300$ $\Pi_2 = 200$

[2]After John F. Nash, the American mathematician who introduced the concept in 1951.

EXERCISE 13.1

Does either firm have a dominant strategy in the game below? Does the game have a Nash equilibrium?

		Firm 1	
		High research budget	Low research budget
Firm 2	High research budget	$\Pi_1 = 200$ $\Pi_2 = 40$	$\Pi_1 = 60$ $\Pi_2 = 100$
	Low research budget	$\Pi_1 = 0$ $\Pi_2 = 30$	$\Pi_1 = 40$ $\Pi_2 = 80$

The Maximin Strategy

In the game shown in Table 3.4, we saw that if firm 1 follows its dominant strategy by advertising, firm 2 will also do better by advertising. So if firm 2 believes that firm 1 will act rationally, firm 2's best option is to advertise. But firm 2 may not be sure that firm 1 will choose rationally. In that case firm 2 might want at least to consider the possibility that firm 1 will choose not to advertise. In that case, if firm 2 advertises it will earn a profit of 0, far worse than the 400 it would earn by not advertising.

When firm 2 does not have a dominant strategy of its own and is uncertain about firm 1's choice, what should it do? The answer depends on both the likelihood it assigns to firm 1's possible choices and how its own payoffs are affected by those choices. Under the circumstances, it is extremely difficult to predict what firm 2 will do.

Suppose, however, that firm 2 takes an extremely cautious approach when confronted with such uncertainty. It might then choose to follow what is called the **maximin strategy,** which means to choose the option that maximizes the lowest possible value of its own payoff. Referring again to Table 13.4, note that if firm 2 chooses not to advertise, the lowest payoff it can receive is 100 (which will happen if firm 1 advertises). But if firm 2 chooses to advertise, the lowest payoff it can receive is 0 (which will happen if firm 1 chooses not to advertise). So if we know that firm 2 follows the maximin strategy in this situation, we can predict that it will choose not to advertise.

maximin strategy
choosing the option that makes the lowest payoff one can receive as large as possible.

Strategies for Repeated Play in Prisoner's Dilemmas

Games discussed thus far have involved only two players. But these games are easily extended to cover multiple players. In the multi-player prisoner's dilemma, for example, the two strategy choices are again cooperate and defect, and defecting is again a dominant strategy for every player. And the defining condition of the game continues to be that each player receive a higher payoff when each cooperates than when each defects.

To say that the costs of failing to cooperate are high in prisoner's dilemmas is simply another way of saying that there are powerful financial incentives to

460   CHAPTER 13   IMPERFECT COMPETITION: A GAME-THEORETIC APPROACH

find some way to hold collusive agreements together. What the potential participants to a collusive agreement need is some way to penalize those who defect, thereby making it in their material interests not to do so. When a prisoner's dilemma confronts parties who will interact only once, this turns out to be very difficult to achieve. But when the participants expect to interact repeatedly in the future, new possibilities emerge.

Experimental research in the 1960s identified a very simple strategy that proves remarkably effective at keeping potential defectors in check.[3] The strategy is called *tit-for-tat*, and it works as follows: The first time you interact with someone, you cooperate. In each subsequent interaction you simply do what that person did in the previous interaction. Thus, if your partner defected on your first interaction, you would then defect on your next interaction with her. If she then cooperates, your move next time will be to cooperate as well.

Tit-for-tat is described as a "nice" strategy because of the propensity of players to cooperate on the first interaction. If two tit-for-tat players interact together over a long period of time, the result will be cooperation in each and every interaction. Tit-for-tat is also a "tough" strategy, however, because those who follow it always stand ready to punish defectors in the next interaction. Finally, it is a "forgiving" strategy, in the sense that a player is willing to cooperate with a former defector once she shows evidence of willingness to cooperate.

University of Michigan political scientist Robert Axelrod conducted an extensive analysis of how well the tit-for-tat strategy performs against other strategies for playing the repeated prisoner's dilemma game.[4] In an early round of Axelrod's computer simulations, tit-for-tat was the most successful strategy, in the sense that people who followed it earned more, on the average, than those using any of the other strategies tested. Axelrod then published this finding and invited experts from all over the world to try to design a better strategy. His challenge produced a host of ingenious counterstrategies. Axelrod found, however, that even these strategies, many of which had been put together for the specific purpose of defeating tit-for-tat, did not survive against it.

The success of tit-for-tat requires a reasonably stable set of players, each of whom can remember what other players have done in previous interactions. It also requires that players have a significant stake in what happens in the future, for it is only the fear of retaliation that keeps people from defecting. When these conditions are met, cooperators can identify one another and discriminate against defectors.

The conditions called for by the tit-for-tat strategy are often met in human populations. Many people do interact repeatedly, and most keep track of how others treat them. Axelrod has assembled persuasive evidence that these forces help explain how people actually behave. Perhaps the most impressive of all this evidence comes from accounts of the "live-and-let-live" system that developed in the trench warfare in Europe during World War I. In many areas of the war, the same enemy units lay encamped opposite one another in the trenches over a period of several years. Units were often closely matched, with the result that neither side had much hope of quickly defeating the other. Their choices were

---

[3]See Anatol Rapoport and A. Chammah, *Prisoner's Dilemma*, Ann Arbor: University of Michigan Press, 1965.

[4]Robert Axelrod, *The Evolution of Cooperation*, New York: Basic Books, 1984.

to fight intensively, with both sides sustaining heavy casualties, or to exercise restraint.

The conditions of interaction described by historian Tony Ashworth in his account of the trench fighting closely resemble those required for the success of tit-for-tat.[5] The identities of the players were more or less stable. Interactions between them were repeated, often several times daily, for extended periods. Each side could easily tell when the other side defected from the strategy. And each side had a clear stake in keeping its future losses to a minimum.

There is little doubt that tit-for-tat often did emerge as the strategy of choice for both Allied and German fighting units in World War I. Although strongly discouraged as a matter of official policy, restraint was sometimes conspicuously apparent. Referring to night patrol squads operating out of the trenches, Ashworth writes:

> both British and Germans on quiet sectors assumed that should a chance face-to-face encounter occur, neither patrol would initiate aggression, but each would move to avoid the other. Each patrol gave peace to the other where aggression was not only possible, but prescribed, provided, of course, the gesture was reciprocated, for if one patrol fired so would the other.[6]

In the words of one of the participants in the conflict:

> We suddenly confronted, round some mound or excavation, a German patrol. . . . We were perhaps twenty yards from one another, fully visible. I waved a weary hand, as if to say, what is the use of killing each other? The German officer seemed to understand, and both parties turned and made their way back to their own trenches.[7]

Often, bombardments would occur only at specified times of day and would be directed away from the most vulnerable positions. Mealtimes and hospital tents, for example, were usually tacitly off limits.

The conditions discussed by Axelrod help to explain not only when people will cooperate, but also when they are most likely to *refrain* from cooperation. For example, he notes that mutual restraint in trench warfare began to break down once the end of the war was clearly in sight.

As in warfare, so, too, in the world of business. Companies pay their bills on time, Axelrod suggests, not because it is the right thing to do but because they require future shipments from the same suppliers. When future interactions appear unlikely, this tendency to cooperate often breaks down: "[An] example is the case where a business is on the edge of bankruptcy and sells its accounts receivable to an outsider called a 'factor.' This sale is made at a very substantial discount because

> once a manufacturer begins to go under, even his best customers begin refusing payment for merchandise, claiming defects in quality, failure to meet specifications, tardy delivery, or what-have-you. The great enforcer of morality in commerce is the continuing relationship, the belief that one will have to do business again with this customer, or this supplier, and when a failing company loses this automatic enforcer, not even a strong-arm factor is likely to find a substitute.[8]

---

[5]Tony Ashworth, *Trench Warfare: The Live and Let Live System*, New York: Holmes and Meier, 1980.

[6]Ibid., p. 103.

[7]Herbert Read, quoted in ibid., p. 104.

[8]Mayer, quoted in Axelrod, op. cit., pp. 59, 60.

462   CHAPTER 13 IMPERFECT COMPETITION: A GAME-THEORETIC APPROACH

One additional requirement for the success of tit-for-tat is that there not be a known, fixed number of future interactions. Indeed, if players know exactly how many times they will interact, then mutual cooperation on every move cannot be a Nash equilibrium. To see why, suppose each firm knew it was going to interact with its rival for, say, exactly 1000 more times. Each would then know that the other would defect on the last interaction, because there would be no possibility of being punished for doing so. But since each firm realizes that, it will also have no reason not to defect on the 999th interaction. After all, a defection will occur on the 1000th interaction no matter what it does on the round before. The same argument can be applied step-by-step back to the first interaction, with the result that the tit-for-tat strategy completely unravels.

The unraveling problem does not arise if there is not a known, fixed number of interactions.[9] If we suppose, for example, that there is always some positive probability that a further interaction will ensue, then no interaction can ever be identified as being the last one, which means the threat of future punishment will always have at least some force. In the situations in which most firms find themselves (an exception being the bankruptcy case cited earlier), it seems plausible to assume that there will always be some probability of interaction in the future.

Is it inevitable, then, that the tit-for-tat strategy will produce widespread collusion among firms? By no means. One difficulty is that tit-for-tat's effectiveness depends on there being only two players in the game. In competitive and monopolistically competitive industries there are generally many firms, and even in oligopolies there are often several. When there are more than two firms, and one defects this period, how do the cooperators selectively punish the defector next period? By cutting price? That will penalize everyone, not just the defector. Even if there are only two firms in an industry, the problem remains that some other firm may enter the industry. So the would-be cooperators have to worry not only about each other, but also about the entire list of firms that might decide to compete with them. Each firm may see this as a hopeless task and decide to defect now, hoping to reap at least some extra-normal profit in the short run.

We will consider the threat of potential entry in greater detail in the sections to follow. For the moment, we may note that, as a purely empirical matter, cartel agreements and other forms of collusion have occurred frequently in the past but have tended to be highly unstable. Apparently the practical problems involved in implementing tit-for-tat in the environments confronting firms make it very difficult to hold collusive agreements together for long.

Sequential Games

The games we have considered so far have been ones in which both players must pick their strategies simultaneously. Each player had to choose his strategy knowing only the incentives facing his opponent, not the opponent's actual choice of strategy. But in many games, one player moves first, and the other is then able to choose his strategy with full knowledge of the first player's choice.

---

[9]Another way the unraveling problem is avoided is if there is some positive probability that others will follow the tit-for-tat strategy even though, strictly speaking, it is not rational for them to do so. See David Kreps, Paul Milgrom, John Roberts, and Robert Wilson, "Rational Cooperation in Finitely Repeated Prisoner's Dilemmas," *Journal of Economic Theory*, 27, 1982: 245–252.

This description roughly fits the circumstances in which the United States and the former Soviet Union (USSR) found themselves during much of the cold war.

At that time, the military strategies of both nations were based on the doctrine of mutually assured destruction (MAD). The idea behind MAD was simple: Both sides maintained sufficiently large and well-defended nuclear arsenals to ensure that each would be able to retaliate if the other launched a first strike. The prospect of a devastating counterstrike, according to the MAD theory, is what prevented each side from even considering a first strike.

The fact that neither side ever launched a first strike is interpreted by some people as evidence that the MAD strategy must have worked. And yet there is an apparent logical flaw in the strategy, one that suggests the real source of restraint must lie elsewhere. To appreciate the problem, put yourself in the shoes of a U.S. president who has just learned that the Russians have launched a first strike. At that moment, you know that the MAD strategy has already failed. For whatever reason, the threat of a counterstrike did not in fact deter the Russian first strike. Do you now order a counterstrike anyway? You realize that to do so will only increase the likelihood of total world destruction. True enough, American interests have been grievously damaged by the attack. But at that point, a counterstrike will only damage them further.

The logical difficulty with MAD is thus that each side knows perfectly well that once a first strike has already been launched, it will not be in the other side's interest to retaliate. And since each party knows this, the threat of a counterstrike loses all power to deter.

Or at least so it seems in theory. Perhaps the threat deters because each side fears the other might not respond rationally once it is the victim of a first strike. (A casual review of the American and Soviet leaders of the post–World War II period lends at least some credence to this interpretation.) But whether or not MAD is an effective defense strategy, its apparent flaw is troubling. The same logic that exposed this flaw suggests a simple way to repair it. It is to install a so-called doomsday machine—a tamper-proof device that will *automatically* retaliate once a first strike has been launched. Once each side became aware the other had such a device in place, the MAD strategy would be complete and a first strike truly would become unthinkable.

To see how economists treat sequential games analytically, suppose the former Soviet Union was considering whether to launch a nuclear strike against the United States. This decision may be portrayed in a "game tree" diagram like the one shown in Figure 13.1. If the first move is the USSR's, the game starts at point A. The first two branches of the game tree represent the USSR's alternatives of attacking and not attacking. If it attacks, then the United States finds itself at point B on the top branch of the game tree, where it must decide whether or not to strike back. If the United States retaliates, we end up at point D, where the payoffs are -100 for each country. If the United States does not retaliate, we end up at point E, where the payoffs are 100 for the USSR and -50 for the United States. (The units of these payoffs are purely arbitrary. The values chosen are intended to reflect each country's hypothetical relative valuation of the different outcomes.) The bottom half of the game tree represents the alternative in which the USSR does not attack. If the USSR chooses this alternative, the United States finds itself at point C, where it again faces a decision about whether or not to launch missiles at the USSR. For argument's sake, suppose that the payoffs to the two countries under each alternative are shown on the bottom two branches

464   CHAPTER 13 IMPERFECT COMPETITION: A GAME-THEORETIC APPROACH

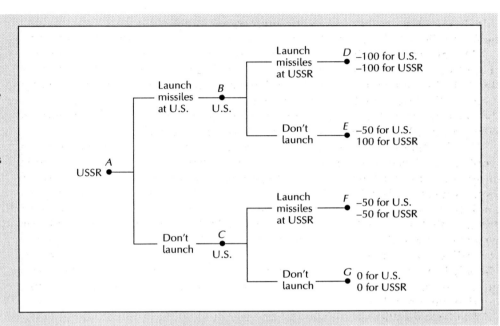

FIGURE 13.1

Nuclear Deterrence as a Sequential Game

If the USSR attacks, the best option for the United States is not to retaliate (point *E*). If the USSR doesn't attack, the best option for the United States is also not to attack (point *G*). Since the USSR gets a higher payoff at *E* than at *G*, it will attack. If the United States is believed to be a payoff maximizer, its threat to retaliate against a first strike will not be credible.

of the game tree at points *F* and *G*, respectively. Given the assumed payoffs for each of the four possible outcomes of the game tree, the USSR can analyze what the United States will do under each alternative. If the USSR attacks (point *B*), the best option open to the United States is not to retaliate (point *E*). If the USSR does not attack (point *C*), the best option for the United States is also not to attack (point *G*). The USSR thus knows that if the United States is a payoff maximizer, the game will end at point *E* if the USSR attacks at point *G* if the USSR does not attack. And since the USSR has a higher payoff at point *E*, it does best to attack. The United States may threaten to retaliate, but as long as its adversaries believe it is a payoff maximizer, such threats will lack credibility.

Now suppose that the United States could install a "doomsday machine"— a device that would automatically retaliate in the event of an attack by the USSR. The effect would be to eliminate the bottom half of the top branch of the game tree in Figure 13.1. The USSR would then know that if it attacked, the game would end at point *D*, where the USSR gets a payoff of −100. And since this is worse than the outcome if the USSR does not attack (point *G*), the best option open to the USSR would then be to leave its missiles in their silos.

ECONOMIC NATURALIST 13.2

Why might a company make an investment it knew it would never use?

The Sears Tower in Chicago is currently the tallest building in the United States. This status endows the building with a special form of prestige, enabling its owners to command higher rents than in otherwise similar office buildings. Now, suppose that company *X* is considering whether to build an even taller building. Suppose it knows that any firm that has permanent ownership of the tallest building will earn a large economic profit. Its concern, naturally, is that Sears (or some other firm) may build a still taller building, which would substantially diminish company *X*'s payoff.

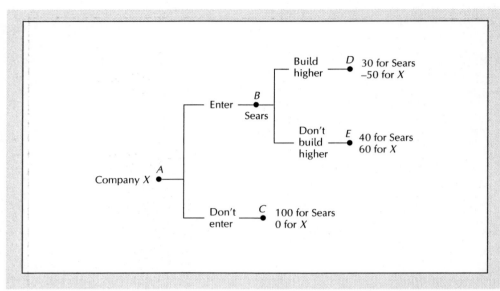

FIGURE 13.2
The Decision to Build the Tallest Building
If company X builds a skyscraper taller than the Sears Tower, Sears must decide whether to build higher (point D) or yield its status as the tallest building (point E). Because Sears earns a higher payoff at E than at D, it will not build higher. And since X knows that, it will enter the market despite Sears's threat to build a taller building.

Both Sears and company X realize that they are participants in a sequential game of the type pictured in Figure 13.2. The game starts at point A, where X must decide whether to enter with a taller building. If it does not, Sears will receive a payoff of 100, X a payoff of 0. If X enters, however, the game moves to point B, where Sears must decide whether to build higher or stand pat. Suppose that if Sears builds higher, its payoff will be 30, while X will earn a payoff of -50; and that if Sears does not build higher, its payoff will be 40, while X will get a payoff of 60. Sears naturally wants X not to enter. It may even announce its intention to build a taller building in the event that X enters. But as long as X knows the payoffs facing Sears, it can conclude that the best option open to Sears once X enters is to stand pat. The Nash equilibrium of this sequential game is point E, where X enters and Sears stands pat.

Now suppose that before Sears had originally built its tower, it had the option of building a platform atop the building on which it could build an addition that would make the building taller. Building this platform costs 10 units, but reduces the cost of building a taller building by 20 units. If Sears had installed this platform, the sequential game between it and company X would then be as portrayed by the game tree in Figure 13.3. Sears's payoff at point D is now 40 (it saves 20 on building costs less the 10-unit cost of the platform). Its payoffs at C and E are each 10 units less than in Figure 13.2 (reflecting the cost of the platform). Despite the small magnitude of these changes in payoffs, the presence of the platform dramatically alters the outcome of the game. This time X can predict that if it enters with the tallest building, it will be in Sears's interest to add to its existing building, which means that X will receive a payoff of -50. As a result, X will not find it worthwhile to enter this market, and so the game will end at point C. The payoff to Sears at C is 90 (the original 100 minus the 10-unit cost of building the platform). Its 10-unit investment in the platform thus increases its net payoff by 50 (the difference between the 90-unit payoff it receives with the platform and the 40-unit payoff it would have received without it).[10]

---

[10]Microsoft Internet Explorer versus Netscape and Barnes and Noble versus Borders are more recent examples of strategic entry deterrence games.

FIGURE 13.3
Strategic Entry Deterrence
Had it originally built a platform atop its building at a cost of 10 units, Sears would have reduced the cost of building a taller building by 20 units. Then company X would have calculated that it would not be worthwhile to build a taller building, because it then would have been in Sears's interest to respond with an addition. The Nash equilibrium of the altered game occurs at point C.

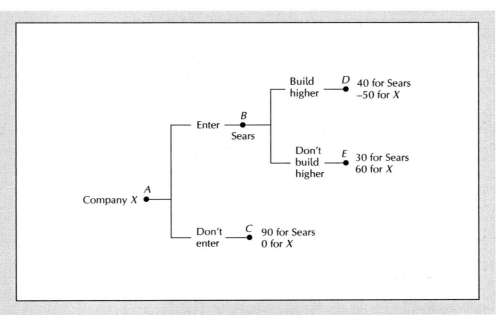

The platform investment just discussed is an example of what economists call *strategic entry deterrence*. When such investments are effective, it is because they change potential rivals' expectations about how the firm will respond when its market position is threatened.

Why would a firm build a factory with more capacity than it would ever need?

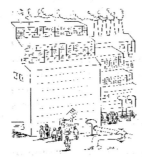

Why might a firm build a bigger factory than it needed?

Larger production facilities typically have higher fixed costs and lower marginal costs than smaller ones. So the question can be rephrased as follows: Why might it be in a firm's interest to have a factory with very low marginal cost, even if the result were to make its total cost higher than for a smaller facility?

A possible answer is that the larger factory constitutes another example of strategic entry deterrence. If potential entrants knew that an incumbent firm had extremely low marginal cost, they could predict that it would be in the incumbent's interest to remain in business even at a price level too low for entrants to earn a normal profit. In that case, it would not be rational for rivals to enter the market. And their absence, in turn, would enable the incumbent to charge a price sufficiently high to cover the costs of the larger facility.

SOME SPECIFIC OLIGOPOLY MODELS

If a firm is considering a change in its output level or selling price, there are many possible assumptions it could make about the reactions of its rivals. It could assume, for example, that its rivals will continue producing at their current levels of output. Alternatively, it could assume that they would continue to charge their current prices. Or it could assume that they would react in various specific ways to its own price and output changes. In the sections that follow, we explore the implications of each alternative assumption.

The Cournot Model

We begin with the simplest case, the so-called **Cournot model**, in which each firm assumes that its rivals will continue producing at their current levels of output. Named for the French economist Auguste Cournot, who introduced it in 1838, this model describes the behavior of two firms that sell bottled water from mineral springs. A two-firm oligopoly is called a *duopoly,* and the Cournot model is sometimes referred to as the *Cournot duopoly model,* although its conclusions can easily be generalized to more than two firms.

Cournot model oligopoly model in which each firm assumes that rivals will continue producing their current output levels.

The central assumption of the Cournot model is that each duopolist treats the other's quantity as a fixed number, one that will not respond to its own production decisions. This is a weak form of interdependence, indeed, but we will see that even it leads to an outcome in which the behavior of each firm substantially affects its rival.

Suppose the total market demand curve for mineral water is given by

$$P = a - b(Q_1 + Q_2), \tag{13.1}$$

where a and b are positive numbers and Q_1 and Q_2 are the outputs of firms 1 and 2, respectively. Cournot assumed that the water could be produced at zero marginal cost, but this assumption is merely for convenience. Essentially similar conclusions would emerge if each firm had a constant positive marginal cost.

Let us look first at the profit-maximization problem facing firm 1. Given its assumption that firm 2's output is fixed at Q_2, the demand curve for firm 1's water is given by

$$P_1 = (a - bQ_2) - bQ_1, \tag{13.2}$$

which is rewritten to emphasize the fact that firm 1 treats Q_2 as given.

As Equation 13.2 shows, we get the demand curve for firm 1 by subtracting bQ_2 from the vertical intercept of the market demand curve. The idea is that firm 2 has skimmed off the first Q_2 units of the market demand curve, leaving firm 1 the remainder to work with.

If Q_2 were equal to zero, firm 1 would have the entire market demand curve to itself, as is indicated by D in Figure 13.4. If Q_2 is positive, we get firm 1's demand curve by shifting the vertical axis of the demand diagram rightward by Q_2 units. Firm 1's demand curve is that portion of the original demand curve that lies to the right of this new vertical axis, and for this reason it is sometimes called a *residual demand curve.* The associated marginal revenue curve is labeled MR_1. Firm 1's rule for profit maximization is the same as for any other firm that faces a downward-sloping demand curve, namely, to equate marginal revenue and marginal cost. Marginal cost in this example is assumed to be zero, so the profit-maximizing level of output for firm 1 is that level for which its marginal revenue curve takes the value of zero.

The equilibrium outputs for a Cournot duopoly can be deduced from the residual demand diagram. Given that firm 2 is producing Q_2, firm 1 maximizes its profits by producing where marginal revenue equals marginal cost. Marginal revenue for firm 1 is given by $MR_1 = (a - bQ_2) - 2bQ_1$. Marginal revenue has

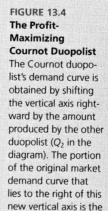

FIGURE 13.4
The Profit-Maximizing Cournot Duopolist
The Cournot duopolist's demand curve is obtained by shifting the vertical axis rightward by the amount produced by the other duopolist (Q_2 in the diagram). The portion of the original market demand curve that lies to the right of this new vertical axis is the demand curve facing firm 1. Firm 1 then maximizes profit by equating marginal revenue and marginal cost, the latter of which is zero.

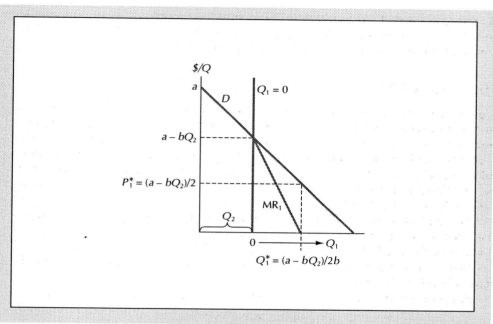

twice the slope as demand, so marginal revenue intersects zero marginal cost at half the distance from the $Q_1 = 0$ axis to the horizontal intercept of the demand curve. By symmetry (the two firms are identical so they must behave the same), $Q_2 = Q_1$, which means that each of the three segments shown on the horizontal axis in Figure 13.4 has the same length. And this implies that each firm produces output equal to one-third of the distance from the origin to the horizontal intercept of the demand curve. The demand curve $P = a - bQ$ has a horizontal intercept of $Q = a/b$; hence, $Q_1 = Q_2 = a/(3b)$. A more general approach is to set marginal revenue equal to marginal cost and solve for the output of firm 1 in terms of the output of firm 2.[11]

$$Q_1^* = \frac{a - bQ_2}{2b} \tag{13.3}$$

reaction function   a curve that tells the profit-maximizing level of output for one oligopolist for each amount supplied by another.

Economists often call Equation 13.3 firm 1's **reaction function,** and denote it by $Q_1^* = R_1(Q_2)$. This notation is suggestive because the reaction function tells how firm 1's quantity will react to the quantity level offered by firm 2.

Because the Cournot duopoly problem is completely symmetric, firm 2's reaction function has precisely the same structure:

$$Q_2^* = R_2(Q_1) = \frac{a - bQ_1}{2b}. \tag{13.4}$$

---

[11]For example, this more general approach is needed if firms are asymmetric (not identical) and thus would not produce the same level of output.

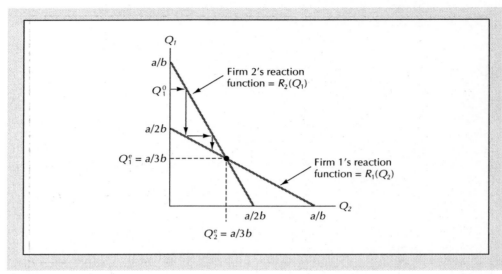

FIGURE 13.5
Reaction Functions for the Cournot Duopolists
The reaction function for each duopolist gives its profit-maximizing output level as a function of the other firm's output level. The duopolists are in a stable equilibrium at the point of intersection of their reaction functions.

The two reaction functions are plotted in Figure 13.5. To illustrate the workings of the reaction function concept, suppose firm 1 initially produced a quantity of Q_1^0. Firm 2 would then produce the level of output that corresponds to Q_1^0 on its reaction function. Firm 1 would respond to that output level by picking the corresponding point on its own reaction function. Firm 2 would then respond by picking the corresponding point on its reaction function, and so on. The end result of this process is a stable equilibrium at the intersection of the two reaction functions. When both firms are producing $a/3b$ units of output, neither wants to change.[12] These output levels thus constitute a Nash equilibrium for the Cournot duopolists.

How profitable are the Cournot duopolists? Since their combined output is $2a/3b$, the market price will be $P = a - b(2a/3b) = a/3$. At this price, each will have total revenue equal to $(a/3)(a/3b) = a^2/9b$. And since neither firm has any production costs, total revenues and economic profits here are one and the same.

Cournot duopolists face a market demand curve given by $P = 56 - 2Q$, where Q is total market demand. Each can produce output at a constant marginal cost of 20/unit. Graph their reaction functions and find the equilibrium price and quantity.

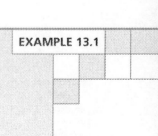

EXAMPLE 13.1

Figure 13.6a shows the residual demand curve facing firm 1 when firm 2 produces Q_2 units. Firm 1's marginal revenue curve has the same vertical intercept as its demand curve and is twice as steep. Thus the equation for firm 1's marginal revenue curve is $MR_1 = 56 - 2Q_2 - 4Q_1$. Equating MR_1 to marginal cost (20), we

---

[12]To solve algebraically for firm 1's equilibrium level of output, we substitute $Q_1^* = Q_2^*$ into its reaction function and solve:

$$R_1(Q_2^*) = \frac{a - bQ_2^*}{2b} = \frac{a - bQ_1^*}{2b} = Q_1^*,$$

which yields $Q_1^* = a/3b$.

FIGURE 13.6
Deriving the Reaction Functions for Specific Duopolists
Panel *a* shows the profit-maximizing output level for firm 1 (Q_1^*) when firm 2 produces Q_2. That and the parallel expression for firm 2 constitute the reaction functions plotted in panel *b*.

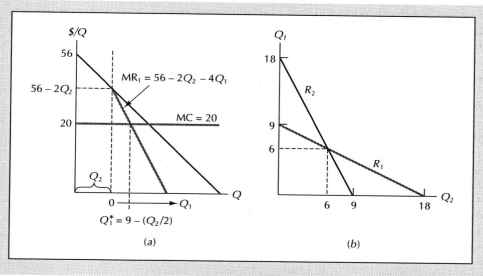

solve for firm 1's reaction function, $Q_1^* = R_1 = 9 - (Q_2/2)$. By symmetry, firm 2's reaction function is $R_2 = 9 - (Q_1/2)$. The two reaction functions are shown in Figure 13.6*b*, where they intersect at $Q_1 = Q_2 = 6$. Total market output will be $Q_1 + Q_2 = 12$. Consulting the market demand curve, we see that the market price will be $P = 56 - 2(12) = 32$

EXERCISE 13.2

Repeat Example 13.1 with the two firms facing a market demand curve of $P = 44 - Q$.

You may be wondering why the Cournot duopolists assume that their own production decisions will be ignored by their rivals. If so, you have asked a penetrating question, the same one posed by Cournot's critic, the French economist Joseph Bertrand. Let's now consider his alternative solution to the duopoly problem.

The Bertrand Model

Bertrand model oligopoly model in which each firm assumes that rivals will continue charging their current prices.

Bertrand's insight was that from the buyer's perspective, what really counts is how the prices charged by the two firms compare. Since the duopolists are selling identical mineral water, every buyer will naturally want to buy from the seller with the lower price. The **Bertrand model** proposed that each firm chooses its price on the assumption that its rival's price would remain fixed. On its face, this assumption seems no more plausible than Cournot's, and since prices and quantities correspond uniquely along market demand curves, it may seem natural to wonder whether Bertrand's assumption even leads to a different outcome. On investigation, however, the outcomes turn out to be very different indeed.

To illustrate, suppose the market demand and cost conditions are the same as in the Cournot example. And suppose firm 1 charges an initial price of P_0^1. Firm 2 then faces essentially three choices: (1) it can charge more than firm 1, in which case it will sell nothing; (2) it can charge the same as firm 1, in which case the two firms will split the market demand at that price; or (3) it can sell at a marginally lower price than firm 1, in which case it will capture the entire market demand at that price. The third of these options will always be by far the most profitable.[13]

As in the Cournot model, the situations of the duopolists are completely symmetric in the Bertrand model, which means that the option of selling at a marginally lower price than the competition will be the strategy of choice for both firms. Needless to say, there can be no stable equilibrium in which each firm undersells the other. The back-and-forth process of price-cutting will continue until it reaches its natural economic limit—namely, marginal cost, which in the mineral spring example is zero. (If instead we had considered an example in which both firms have the same positive marginal cost, price would have fallen to that value.) Once each firm has cut its price to marginal cost, it will have no incentive to cut further. With each firm selling at marginal cost, the duopolists will share the market equally.

Bertrand duopolists face a market demand curve given by $P = 56 - 2Q$. Each can produce output at a constant marginal cost of 20/unit. Find the equilibrium price and quantity.

EXAMPLE 13.2

The solution is both firms price at marginal cost $P = MC = 20$. Industry output is determined by market demand: $20 = 56 - 2Q$ implies $Q = 18$. The firms split the market equally, so each firm produces half of industry output $Q_1 = Q_2 = Q/2 = 9$.

EXERCISE 13.3

If the market demand curve facing Bertrand duopolists is given by $P = 10 - Q$ and each has a constant marginal cost of 2, what will be the equilibrium price and quantity for each firm?

So we see that a seemingly minor change in the initial assumptions about firm behavior—that each duopolist takes its rival's price, not quantity, as given—leads to a sharply different equilibrium. Now we consider how another small change in the initial assumptions about firm behavior can lead to yet another equilibrium.

The Stackelberg Model

In 1934, the German economist Heinrich von Stackelberg asked the simple but provocative question, "What would a firm do if it knew its only rival were a naive Cournot duopolist?" The answer is that it would want to choose its own output level by taking into account the effect that choice would have on the output level of its rival.

---

[13]In the case of a price only infinitesimally smaller than firm 1's price, firm 2's profit will be virtually twice as large under option 3 as under option 2.

472   CHAPTER 13   IMPERFECT COMPETITION: A GAME-THEORETIC APPROACH

FIGURE 13.7
The Stackelberg Leader's Demand and Marginal Revenue Curves
When firm 1 knows firm 2 is a Cournot duopolist, it can take account of the effect of its own behavior on firm 2's quantity choice. The result is that it knows exactly what its demand curve will be.

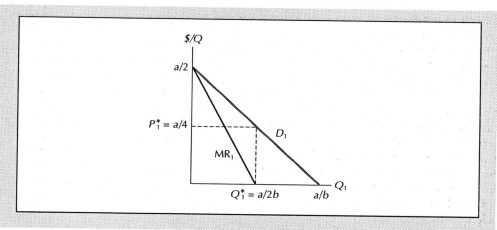

Returning to the Cournot model, suppose firm 1 knows that firm 2 will treat firm 1's output level as given. How can it make strategic use of that knowledge? To answer this question, recall that firm 2's reaction function is given by $Q_2^* = R_2(Q_1) = (a - bQ_1)/2b$. Knowing that firm 2's output will depend on Q_1 in this fashion, firm 1 can then substitute $R_2(Q_1)$ for Q_2 in the equation for the market demand curve, which yields the following expression for its own demand curve:

$$P = a - b[Q_1 + R_2(Q_1)] = a - b\left(Q_1 + \frac{a - bQ_1}{2b}\right) = \frac{a - bQ_1}{2} \qquad (13.5)$$

This demand curve and the associated marginal revenue curve are shown as D_1 and MR_1 in Figure 13.7. Since marginal cost is assumed to be zero in the mineral spring example, firm 1's profit-maximizing output level will be the one for which MR_1 is zero, namely, $Q_1^* = a/2b$. The market price will be $a/4$.

EXAMPLE 13.3

A Stackelberg leader and follower face a market demand curve given by $P = 56 - 2Q$. Each can produce output at a constant marginal cost of 20/unit. Find the equilibrium price and quantity.

The solution is found by substituting firm 2's reaction function $Q_2 = 9 - Q_1/2$ into the demand facing firm 1, $P = (56 - 2Q_2) - 2Q_1$, to find $P = 38 - Q_1$ with corresponding marginal revenue $MR_1 = 38 - 2Q_1$. Setting marginal revenue equal to marginal cost yields firm 1's output $Q_1 = 9$. Inserting firm 1's output into firm 2's reaction function yields firm 2's output $Q_2 = \frac{9}{2}$. Total industry output is $Q = Q_1 + Q_2 = \frac{27}{2}$, with price $P = 56 - 2Q = 56 - 27 = 29$.

EXERCISE 13.4

The market demand curve for a Stackelberg leader and follower is given by $P = 10 - Q$. If each has a marginal cost of 2, what will be the equilibrium price and quantity for each?

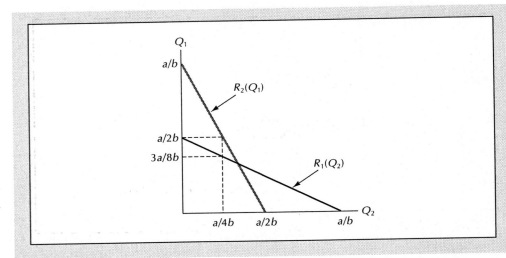

FIGURE 13.8
The Stackelberg Equilibrium
In the Stackelberg model, firm 1 ignores its own reaction function from the Cournot model. It chooses its own quantity to maximize profit, taking into account the effect that its own quantity will have on the quantity offered by firm 2.

For obvious reasons, firm 1 is referred to as a *Stackelberg leader. Stackelberg follower* is the term used to describe firm 2. To help place the Stackelberg leader's behavior in clearer perspective, let's again consider the graph of the two firms' Cournot reaction functions, reproduced here as Figure 13.8. As we saw in Figure 13.7, $a/2b$ is the best output for firm 1 to produce once it takes into account that firm 2 will respond to its choice according to the reaction function $R_2(Q_1)$. Once firm 1 produces $a/2b$, firm 2 will consult R_2 and respond by producing $a/4b$. Now here is the crucial step. If firm 1 thought that firm 2 would stay at $a/4b$ no matter what, its best bet would be to consult its own reaction function and produce the corresponding quantity, namely, $3a/8b$. By doing so, it would earn more than by producing $a/2b$. The problem is that firm 1 realizes that if it cuts back to $3a/8b$, this will elicit a further reaction from firm 2, culminating in a downward spiral to the intersection point of the two reaction functions. Firm 1 would do better to move to $3a/8b$ if it could somehow induce firm 2 to remain at $a/4b$. But it cannot. The best option open to firm 1 is therefore to grit its teeth and stay put at $a/2b$.

Comparison of Outcomes

Now that we have considered three different types of behavior for duopolists, let's compare the outcomes of the different models. A monopoly confronting the same demand and cost conditions as Cournot duopolists would have produced $a/2b$ units of output at a price of $a/2$, earning an economic profit of $a^2/4b$ (see Figure 13.9). The interdependence between the Cournot duopolists thus causes price to be one-third lower and total quantity to be one-third higher than the corresponding values in the monopoly case.[14] Whereas the equilibrium price and quantity in the Cournot model differed by only a factor of one-third from those

---

[14]As a fraction of the output for a perfectly competitive industry, industry output under a Cournot duopoly is $N/(N+1)$ with N firms. As the number of firms N becomes large, the Cournot industry output (and therefore price and profit) approaches that of a perfectly competitive industry. In this sense, Cournot duopoly is truly between monopoly and perfect competition.

FIGURE 13.9
Comparing Equilibrium Price and Quantity
The monopolist would maximize profit where marginal revenue equals zero, since there are no marginal production costs. The equilibrium price will be higher, and the equilibrium quantity lower, than in the Cournot case.

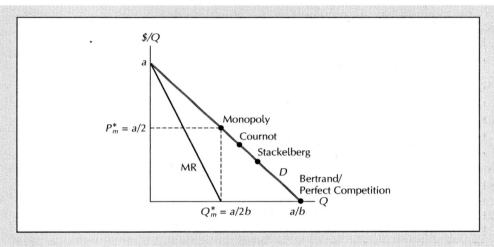

in the monopoly case, in the Bertrand model they are precisely the same as in the competitive case.[15]

How well should the Stackelberg duopolists do? Naturally, the leader fares better since it is the one strategically manipulating the behavior of the follower. Referring to Figure 13.7 we see that firm 1's profit is $a^2/8b$, which is twice that of firm 2. As it happens, this is exactly what firm 1 would have earned had it and firm 2 colluded to charge the monopoly price, $a/2$, and split the market evenly (see Figure 13.9). The combined output of the two firms in the Stackelberg case is $3a/4b$, which is slightly higher than in the Cournot case, with the result that the market price, $a/4$, is slightly lower than in the Cournot case ($a/3$). The results of the four possibilities considered thus for are summarized in Table 13.5.

The Stackelberg model represents a clear improvement over the Cournot and Bertrand models in that it allows at least one of the firms to behave strategically. But why should only one firm behave in this fashion? If firm 1 can make strategic use of its rival's reaction function, why can't firm 2 do likewise? Suppose, in fact, that both firms try to be Stackelberg leaders. Each will then ignore its own reaction function and produce $a/2b$, with the result that total industry output and price will be a/b and 0, respectively, the same as in the Bertrand model.

TABLE 13.5
Comparison of Oligopoly Models
All four models assume a market demand curve of $P = a - bQ$ and marginal cost equal to zero. (Of course, if marginal cost is not zero, the entries will be all different from the ones shown.)

Model	Industry output Q	Market price P	Industry profit Π
Shared monopoly	$Q_m = a/(2b)$	$P_m = a/2$	$\Pi_m = a^2/(4b)$
Cournot	$(4/3)Q_m$	$(2/3)P_m$	$(8/9)\Pi_m$
Stackelberg	$(3/2)Q_m$	$(1/2)P_m$	$(3/4)\Pi_m$
Bertrand	$2Q_m$	0	0
Perfect competition	$2Q_m$	0	0

---

[15]If firms choose capacity and then price, the outcome matches the Cournot equilibrium. See David Kreps and Jose Scheinkman, "Quantity Precommitment and Bertrand Competition Yield Cournot Outcomes," *Bell Journal of Economics*, 14, 1983: 326–337.

From the standpoint of consumers, this is a very desirable outcome, of course. But for the owners of the firms, universal strategic behavior leads to the worst possible outcome.

Contestable Markets

In a widely discussed book, economists William Baumol, John Panzer, and Robert Willig suggested that oligopolies and even monopolies will sometimes behave much like perfectly competitive firms.[16] The specific condition under which this will happen, according to their theory, is that entry and exit be perfectly free. With costless entry, a new firm will quickly enter if an incumbent firm dares to charge a price above average cost. The name "contestable markets" refers to the fact that when entry is costless, we often see a contest between potential competitors to see which firms will serve the market.

Costless entry does not mean that it costs no money to obtain a production facility to serve a market. It means that there are no *sunk* costs associated with entry and exit. The most important piece of equipment required to provide air service in the New York–London market, for example, is a wide-bodied aircraft, which carries a price tag of almost $100 million. This is a hefty investment, to be sure, but it is not a sunk cost. If a firm wants to leave the market, it can sell or lease the aircraft to another firm, or make use of it in some other market. Contrast this case with that of a cement producer, which must spend a similar sum to build a manufacturing facility. Once built, the cement plant has essentially no alternative use. The resources that go into it are sunk costs, beyond recovery if the firm suddenly decides it no longer wants to participate in that market.

Why are sunk costs so important? Consider again the contrast between the air service market and the cement market. In each case we have a local monopoly. Because of economies of scale, there is room for only one cement factory in a given area and only one flight at a given time of day. Suppose in each case that incumbent firms are charging prices well in excess of average costs, and that in each case a new firm enters and captures some of the excess profit. And suppose, finally, that the incumbents react by lowering their prices, with the result that all the firms, entrants and incumbents alike, are losing money. In the cement market case, the entrant will then be stuck with a huge capital facility that will not cover its costs. The airline case, by contrast, carries no similar risk. If the market becomes unprofitable, the entrant can quickly pull out and deploy its asset elsewhere.

The contestable market theory is like other theories of market structure in saying that cost conditions determine how many firms will end up serving a given market. Where there are economies of scale, we expect to see only a single firm. Where there are U-shaped LAC curves whose minimum points occur at a substantial fraction of industry output, we expect only a few firms. With constant costs, there may be many firms. Where the contestable market theory differs from others is in saying that there is no clear relationship between the *actual* number of competitors in a market and the extent to which price and quantity

---

[16]William Baumol, John Panzer, and Robert Willig, *Contestable Markets and the Theory of Industry Structure*, San Diego, CA: Harcourt Brace Jovanovich, 1982. For an accessible summary, see Baumol, "Contestable Markets: An Uprising in the Theory of Industry Structure," *American Economic Review*, 72, March 1982: 1–15.

476   CHAPTER 13   IMPERFECT COMPETITION: A GAME-THEORETIC APPROACH

resemble what we would see under perfect competition. Where the threat of entry is credible, incumbent firms are simply not free to charge prices that are significantly above cost.

Critics of the contestable market theory counter that there are important sunk costs involved in participation in *every* market.[17] Granted, in the airline case it is possible to lease an aircraft on a short-term basis; but that alone is not sufficient to start a viable operation. Counter space must be obtained at the airport terminal; potential passengers must be alerted to the existence of the new service, usually with an expensive advertising campaign. Reservations, baggage handling, and check-in facilities must be arranged. Ground service contracts for the aircraft must be signed, and so on. Each step involves irretrievable commitments of resources, and they add up to enough to make a brief stay in the market very costly indeed. The fiercest critics contend that so long as there are any sunk costs involved in entry and exit, the contestable market theory breaks down.

All the returns are not in yet on the contestable market theory. The critics have raised some formidable objections, but there do appear to be at least some settings where the insights hold up. In the intercity bus market, for example, either Greyhound or Trailways is likely to be the only firm providing service in any given city-pair market. Traditional theories of market structure suggest that prices would be likely to rise steeply during holiday weekends, when substantially larger numbers of people travel. What we see in many markets, however, is that small charter bus companies offer special holiday service at fares no higher than normal. These companies often do little more than post a few leaflets on college campuses, stating their prices and schedules and giving a telephone number to call for reservations. The circumstances of the intercity bus industry come very close to the free entry ideal contemplated by the contestable market theory, and the results are much as it predicts. Much more remains to be said about just when the threat of entry will be a significant disciplining force, a subject we consider in more detail in the next section.

Competition When There Are Increasing Returns to Scale

Consider an example of a duopoly in an industry with increasing returns to scale. How would two firms survive in such an industry, whose cost conditions make it a natural monopoly? It is easy enough to imagine two firms starting out at an early stage of a new product's development, each serving a largely different segment of the market. But now suppose the industry has matured, and a single, nationwide market exists for the product. Should we expect that one firm will drive the other out of business and take over the role of natural monopolist? And if so, what price will it charge?

To make our discussion concrete, suppose that the technology is one with constant marginal cost and declining average total cost, as shown in Figure 13.10. For simplicity, suppose that the size of the total market is fixed at Q_0. With two firms in the industry, each producing half that amount, average cost is AC'. If there were only one firm, its average cost would be only AC_0. By what process do we expect that one firm might eliminate the other?

---

[17]W. G. Shepherd, "Contestability vs. Competition," *American Economic Review*, 74, September 1984: 572–587.

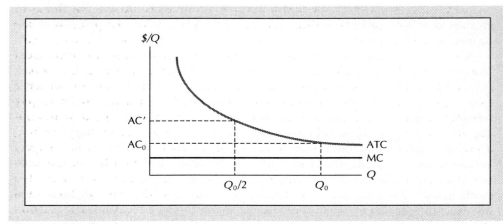

FIGURE 13.10
Sharing a Market with Increasing Returns to Scale
With two firms in the market, costs are higher than with one. Yet there may be no tendency for one firm to drive the other out of business.

The obvious strategy for the two firms would be to merge. The difficulty is that Justice Department antitrust guidelines do not permit mergers between firms whose combined share of the market exceeds a small fraction of total market output. Here, the combined share would be 100 percent, making approval all but impossible.

A second alternative is that one of the firms will announce a preemptive price cut, hoping to drive the other out of business. Suppose, for example, that it charges AC_0, what its average cost would be if in fact its strategy proved successful. How will its rival respond? It can either match the price cut and again split the market or refuse and sell nothing. Since its marginal cost is less than AC_0, it will do better by matching. At that price, however, both firms will lose money; and if the price holds, it is just a matter of time before one of them goes out of business. It might take a long time, though, and even the surviving firm could suffer substantial losses in the interim.

More important, from the perspective of the firm considering whether to initiate a price cut, there is no assurance that it would be the one to survive. So if we view the decision from the point of view of the firm, initiating a price war looks like a very risky proposition indeed. Without the threat of entry, it is easy to see why a live-and-let-live strategy might be compellingly attractive.

But let us suppose, for the sake of discussion, that one firm does somehow manage to capture the entire market, and suppose further that potential entrants face substantial sunk costs if they enter this market. Will the surviving firm then be free to charge the monopoly price?

For the same reasons a duopolist would be reluctant to initiate a price war, an outsider would be wary about entering the industry to face a possibly ruinous battle with the incumbent firm. It may be possible, though, for an outside firm to write contracts with buyers. If it offered a lower price than the incumbent firm, it could then assure itself of the entire market. But an outside firm realizes that it would be in the interest of the incumbent to match or beat any price it could offer. The potential entrant, after all, must charge enough to cover its prospective sunk costs if entry into the market is to be profitable, whereas the incumbent need only cover its variable costs. Of course, the incumbent would be delighted to cover *all* its costs. But rather than be driven from the market, it would be rational for the incumbent to accept a price that just barely covered its variable costs.

CHAPTER 13   IMPERFECT COMPETITION: A GAME-THEORETIC APPROACH

Because of this asymmetry, it will never pay a new firm to take the initiative to enter a natural monopolist's market (unless the new firm happens, for some reason, to have a substantial cost advantage). Any money it spent on market surveys, contract negotiations, and the like would be lost as soon as the incumbent made a better offer, which would always be in the incumbent's interest to do.

There is one remaining avenue along which the threat of entry might serve to discipline an incumbent natural monopolist. Although it would never pay a potential entrant to incur expenses to try to penetrate this type of market, it might very well pay *buyers* in the market to bear the expense of approaching a potential entrant. If the buyers absorb this expense, they can again expect that the incumbent will agree to offer a competitive price on the product. (If the incumbent does not, they can simply sign an agreement to buy from the outside firm.) So if it is practical for buyers to act collectively at their own expense to negotiate with potential entrants, even an incumbent natural monopolist may be forced to sell at close to a competitive price. By way of illustration, most local governments act as purchasing agents for their communities by negotiating contracts with potential monopoly suppliers of community services.

In markets for privately sold goods, buyers are often too numerous to organize themselves to act collectively in this fashion. Few people want to go to a town meeting every night to discuss negotiations with potential suppliers of countless different products. Where it is impractical for buyers to organize direct collective action, it may nonetheless be possible for private agents to accomplish much the same objective on their behalf.

Certain department stores, for example, might be interpreted as acting in this role. The Sears, Roebuck chain built its early success by delivering on its slogan, "Quality at a fair price." Its function was to act as a purchasing agent for the community, negotiating contracts with single-source suppliers. It earned a reputation for driving hard bargains with these suppliers and for passing the savings along to its customers. Why should it and other department stores pass such savings along in the form of lower prices? Merchants are in competition with one another not only for the sale of products produced by natural monopolists, but for an enormous list of competitively produced products as well. To have a reputation for delivering quality merchandise at reasonable prices is an essential element in the marketing strategies of many of these merchants, and consumers are the ultimate beneficiaries.

THE CHAMBERLIN MODEL OF MONOPOLISTIC COMPETITION

Monopolistic competition, a market structure that is close to perfect competition, occurs if many firms serve a market with free entry and exit, but in which one firm's products are not perfect substitutes for the products of other firms. The degree of substitutability between products then determines how closely the industry resembles perfect competition.

The traditional economic model of monopolistic competition was developed independently during the 1930s by Edward Chamberlin and by the late Cambridge economist Joan Robinson. It begins with the assumption of a clearly defined "industry group," which consists of a large number of producers of products that are close, but imperfect, substitutes for one another. The market for men's dress shirts provides a convenient illustration. Shirts made by Gant serve essentially the same purpose as those made by Van Heusen, Sero, Ralph Lauren, Arrow, or Sears-Roebuck. And yet, for many consumers, it is hardly a matter of indifference which brand they buy.

Two important implications follow from these assumptions about industry structure. The first is that because the products are viewed as close substitutes, each firm will confront a downward-sloping demand schedule. Someone who has a particular liking for Gant shirts would be willing to pay more for one than for a shirt from some other manufacturer. But let Gant raise its price sufficiently and even these buyers will eventually switch to another brand. The second implication, which follows from the assumption of a large number of independent firms, is that each firm will act as if its own price and quantity decisions have no effect on the behavior of other firms in the industry. And because the products are close substitutes, this in turn means that each firm perceives its demand schedule as being highly elastic.

A fundamental feature of the Chamberlin model is the perfect symmetry of the position of all firms in the industry. In metaphorical terms, the Chamberlinian firm may be thought of as one of many fishing boats, each of which has a number of fishing lines in the water. If any one boat were to set its hooks with a more alluring bait while others used the same bait as before, the effect would be for the innovator to increase its share of the total catch by a substantial margin. After all, its lines have become more attractive not only in absolute terms, but also relative to the lines of other boats. Because the situation is perfectly symmetric, however, if it makes sense for one boat to use more attractive bait, so will it for others. Yet when all use better bait, the innovator's lines are no more attractive in relative terms than before. Accordingly, the addition to its total catch will be much smaller than if others had held to their original behavior.

The analogy between the fishing example and pricing behavior by the Chamberlinian monopolistically competitive firm is complete. In contemplating the demand for its own product, the firm assumes that its competitors do not respond in any way to its price and quantity decisions. Like the operators of the fishing boats, the firm is correct in assuming that a change in its own behavior will not *cause* others to change theirs. Yet the symmetry between firms assures that if it makes sense for one firm to alter its price, it will make sense for all others to do likewise.

The result is that the firm really confronts two different demand curves—one that describes what will happen when it alone changes its price and a second that describes what will happen when all prices change in unison. Thus, for example, the curve *dd* in Figure 13.11 represents the demand curve facing the Chamberlinian firm if it alone varies its price; the curve *DD* is the demand curve when all firms change prices together. At an initial situation in which all firms charge P', each will sell Q'. If only one firm lowers its price to P'', it will sell Q'''. But if others match its price cut, each will sell only Q''.

It is important to stress that individual firms need not fail to realize that the prices of similarly situated firms tend to move together. On the contrary, each firm may be perfectly aware of that. But it also realizes that its own price movements are not what *cause* other firms to change their behavior. When it is thinking about the consequences of a price move, therefore, it is forced to think in

CHAPTER 13   IMPERFECT COMPETITION: A GAME-THEORETIC APPROACH

FIGURE 13.11
The Monopolistic Competitor's Two Demand Curves
The demand facing any one firm will be more elastic if others hold prices constant (*dd*) than if all firms vary prices in unison (*DD*).

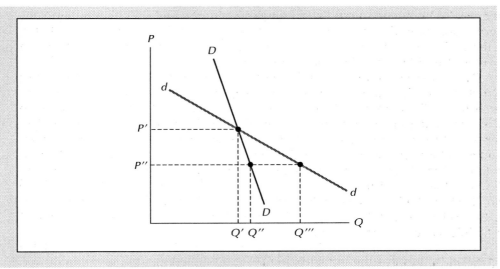

terms of movements along *dd*, not along the demand curve that describes what happens when all prices change in unison (*DD*).[18]

Chamberlinian Equilibrium in the Short Run

For illustrative purposes, let us consider the monopolistically competitive firm whose demand (the *dd* curve), marginal revenue, average total cost, and short-run marginal cost curves are portrayed in Figure 13.12. Following precisely the same argument we employed in the case of the pure monopoly, we can easily show that the short-run profit-maximizing quantity is Q^*, the one for which the marginal revenue curve intersects the short-run marginal cost curve. The profit-maximizing price is P^*, the value that corresponds to Q^* on the demand curve *dd*.

In Figure 13.12, note also that the demand curve *DD* intersects the demand curve *dd* at the profit-maximizing price, P^*. This is yet another consequence of the fundamental symmetry that exists within Chamberlinian firms. The *DD* curve, recall, is the locus along which each firm's quantity would move with price if the prices of all firms moved in unison. The *dd* curve, by contrast, is the locus along which the firm's quantity will move with price when the prices of all other firms are fixed. Because the situation confronting each firm is the same, if P^* is the profit-maximizing price for one, it must also be for the rest. The price level at which other firms' prices are fixed along *dd* is thus P^*, which implies that at P^* on *dd*, the price of *every* firm will be P^*. And this is why *dd* intersects *DD* at P^*.

Chamberlinian Equilibrium in the Long Run

As in the perfectly competitive case, the fact that there are economic profits in the short run will have the effect of luring additional firms into the monopolistically

---

[18]The issue here is much the same as the one confronting participants in the prisoner's dilemma. Each person may know that it is rational for the other person to defect and may therefore expect him to do so. But each person also knows that his own behavior will not affect what the other person does.

THE CHAMBERLIN MODEL

481

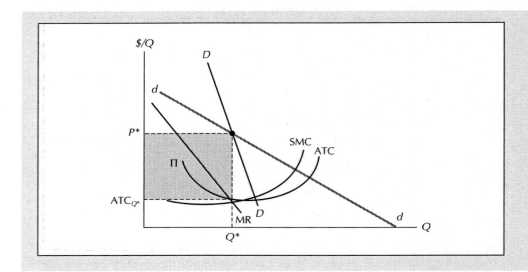

FIGURE 13.12
Short-Run Equilibrium for the Chamberlinian Firm
The Chamberlinian monopolistically competitive firm maximizes economic profit in the short run by equating marginal revenue and short-run marginal cost. Economic profit is Π the area of the shaded rectangle.

competitive industry. What is the effect of the entry of these firms? In the competitive case, we saw that it was to shift the industry supply curve rightward, causing a reduction in the short-run equilibrium price. Put another way, the effect of entry in the perfectly competitive model is to cause each firm's horizontal demand curve to shift downward. In the Chamberlin model, the analogous effect is to shift each firm's demand curve to the left. More precisely, on the assumption that each firm competes on an equal footing for a share of total industry demand, the effect of entry is to cause an equal proportional reduction in the quantity that each firm can sell at any given price. Each firm in the market essentially claims an equal share of industry demand, and with more firms in the industry, that share necessarily declines.

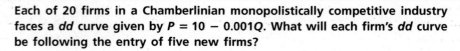

EXERCISE 13.5

Each of 20 firms in a Chamberlinian monopolistically competitive industry faces a *dd* curve given by $P = 10 - 0.001Q$. What will each firm's *dd* curve be following the entry of five new firms?

Following the leftward shift in demand caused by entry, each firm has the opportunity to readjust the size of its capital stock and to choose its new profit-maximizing level of output. If extra-normal profit still remains, entry will continue.

The long-run equilibrium position is one in which the demand curve *dd* has shifted left to the point that it is tangent to the long-run average cost curve (and tangent as well to the associated short-run average cost curve). Note in Figure 13.13 that Q^*, the profit-maximizing level of output by the MR = MC criterion, is exactly the same as the output level for which the *dd* curve is tangent to the long- and short-run average cost curves. This is no mere coincidence. We can argue independently of the MR = MC condition that the tangency point must be the maximum-profit point. At that point, the firm earns zero economic profit,

Frank: Microeconomics
an/ Behavior, Sixth E/ition | III. The Theory of the Firm
an/ Market Structure | 13. Imperfect Competition:
A Game–Theoretic
Approach | © The McGraw–Hill
Companies, 2005 | 373

FIGURE 13.13
**Long-Run
Equilibrium in the
Chamberlin Model**
Entry occurs, shifting
dd leftward until it be-
comes tangent to the
LAC curve. The firm
produces Q*, sells for
P*, and earns zero
economic profit.

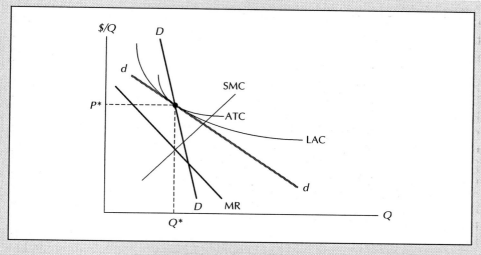

while at any other output level, average cost would exceed average revenue, which means that economic profit would be negative.

Note again in Figure 13.13 that the demand curve *DD* intersects *dd* at the equilibrium price P* for the reasons discussed earlier. If all firms raised price from P*, each would move upward along *DD*, and each would earn an economic profit. But in the absence of a binding collusive agreement, it would not be in the interest of any firm to maintain its price above P*, because at any such price its marginal revenue (along the MR curve associated with *dd*) would exceed its marginal cost. At any price above P*, it could earn higher profits by cutting price and selling more output. The only stable outcome is the tangency point shown in Figure 13.13.

Perfect Competition versus Chamberlinian Monopolistic Competition

There are several obvious points of comparison between the long-run equilibrium positions of perfect competition and Chamberlinian monopolistic competition. First, competition meets the test of allocative efficiency, while monopolistic competition does not. Under competition, price is exactly equal to long-run marginal cost, which means that there are no unexploited possibilities for mutual gains through exchange. Under monopolistic competition, by contrast, price will exceed marginal cost, even in the long run. This means that there will be people in society who value an additional unit of output more highly than the value of the resources required to produce it. If monopolistic competitors could come up with a way to cut price to such buyers without cutting price on existing sales, they would gladly do so, making everyone better off in the process. As we saw in the case of the monopolist, such selective price cutting is sometimes possible. But it is inherently imperfect, and on this account monopolistic competition is destined to fall short of perfect competition on the narrow efficiency standard.

Some economists also argue that monopolistic competition is less efficient than perfect competition because in the former case firms do not produce at the minimum points of their long-run average cost (LAC) curves. This is not a very telling comparison, however, because other aspects of the two cases are so different. The relevant question is whether people who currently buy from monopolistic competitors would be happier if all products were exactly the same and cost a little less. This is not an easy question, and, lacking an answer to it, we cannot conclude that monopolistic competition is inefficient merely because firms don't produce at the minimum points of their LAC curves.

There is at least one important sense, related to the discussion in the preceding paragraph, in which the Chamberlin model is strikingly more realistic than the competitive model. In the perfectly competitive case, recall, price and marginal cost are the same in equilibrium. This implies that the firm should react with sleepy-eyed indifference to an opportunity to fill a new order at the current market price. In the monopolistically competitive case, by contrast, price exceeds marginal cost, which implies that the firm should greet a new order at the current market price with enthusiasm. Periods of temporary shortages apart, we know of very few instances of the former reaction. Almost every businessperson who ever lived is delighted to accept new orders at the current market price.

In terms of long-run profitability, finally, the equilibrium positions of both the perfect competitor and the Chamberlinian monopolistic competitor are precisely the same. Freedom of entry in each case holds long-run economic profit at zero. By the same token, freedom of exit assures that there will be no long-run economic losses in either case.

Criticisms of the Chamberlin Model

The late Nobel laureate George Stigler and others criticized the Chamberlin model on a variety of grounds. First of all, there is the difficulty of defining what is meant by the amorphous concept of "industry group." The Chamberlinian concept envisions a group of products that are different from one another in some unspecified way, yet equally likely to appeal to any given buyer. Stigler complained that it is impossible, as a practical matter, to draw operational boundaries between groups of products in this fashion. Viewed from one perspective, a product like Coca-Cola is unique unto itself. (Recall the angry customer reaction when Coke made a slight alteration in its traditional formula, and the company's subsequent decision to reintroduce "Coke Classic.") Viewed slightly differently, however, Coke is a substitute for Pepsi, which is a substitute for milk, which in turn is a substitute for ice cream. But ice cream is a substitute for chocolate cake, which certainly doesn't *seem* like a substitute for Coca-Cola. Pushed to its logical extreme, Stigler argued, the Chamberlinian product group quickly expands to include virtually every consumer product in the economy.

From a methodological perspective, Stigler joined Milton Friedman in arguing that a theory should be judged not by the descriptive accuracy of its assumptions, but by its ability to predict responses to changes in the economic environment. (See Chapter 1.) Stigler believed that Chamberlin's theory significantly complicates the theory of perfect competition, without appreciably altering its most important predictions. With respect to many specific issues, this charge has clear merit. Both theories, for example, predict that economic profit will attract entry, which will both reduce prices and eliminate profit in the long run.

But the most telling criticism of the Chamberlin model is not that it too closely resembles the competitive model, but that in at least one very important respect it does not depart sufficiently from it. The problem lies with the critical assumption that each firm has an equal chance to attract any of the buyers in an industry. In some cases, this description is reasonably accurate, but in many other instances it clearly falls short. In the breakfast cereal industry, for example, the person who buys Fruit-'n-Fiber might consider switching to Grape-Nuts or Shredded Wheat, but wouldn't dream of switching to Captain Crunch or Fruit Loops.

In recent years, research on the theory of monopolistic competition has focused on models that incorporate the specific features of a product that make buyers choose it over all others. In contrast with the Chamberlin model, these models produce conclusions that often differ sharply with those of the perfectly competitive model. This alternative way of thinking about monopolistic competition was discussed in the text and is the basis for the model that follows.

A Spatial Interpretation of Monopolistic Competition

As noted earlier, the extent to which one monopolistically competitive firm's product is an effective substitute for another's determines how closely their industry will resemble perfect competition. One concrete way of thinking about lack of complete substitutability is distance. Gas across town is not a perfect substitute for gas at the nearest corner, especially not when your tank is nearly empty.

Imagine yourself a resident of a small island nation with a large lake in the middle of it. Business activity there is naturally restricted to the doughnut-shaped piece of land that constitutes the island's periphery. There is considerable specialization of labor on your island. People toil all day at their respective tasks and then take their evening meals at restaurants. People on your island lack the customary preference for culinary diversity. Instead, you and your neighbors prefer to eat baked potatoes and grilled beefsteak every night. Meals in any given restaurant are produced under increasing returns to scale—the more meals produced, the lower the average cost per meal.

How many restaurants should there be in this island nation? We are tempted to say only one, thereby keeping the cost per meal to a minimum. If the circumference of the island were, say, only 300 yards, this would almost surely be the correct answer. But for a much larger island, the direct cost of meals is not likely to be the only item of concern to you and your fellow residents. You will also care about the cost of getting to and from the nearest restaurant. If the island were 300 miles around, for example, the cost savings from having only a single restaurant could hardly begin to compensate for the travel costs incurred by those who live on the far side of the island.

The market for evening meals on this island is in one respect the same as the markets we have considered in earlier chapters: A single, standardized meal is served in every restaurant. But the type of food served is not the only important characteristic of a meal. Buyers care also about *where* the meal is served. When products differ along one or more important dimensions—location, size, flavor, quality, and so on—we immediately confront the general question of how much product diversity there should be. Should an economy have 5 different brands of cars, 10, or 50? How many different kinds of tennis racquets should there be?

To help fix ideas, suppose there are initially four restaurants evenly spaced around the periphery of the island, as represented by the heavy black squares in Figure 13:14. Suppose the circumference of the island is 1 mile. The distance between adjacent restaurants will then be $\frac{1}{4}$ mile, and no one can possibly live more than $\frac{1}{8}$ mile away from the nearest restaurant, the one-way trip length required for someone who lives exactly halfway between two restaurants.

THE CHAMBERLIN MODEL

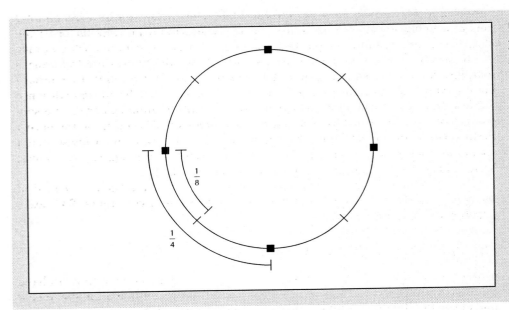

FIGURE 13.14
An Industry in Which Location Is the Important Differentiating Feature
Restaurants (heavy black squares) are the same except for their geographic location. Each person dines at the restaurant closest to home. If the circumference of the loop is 1 mile, this means that the distance between restaurants will be $\frac{1}{4}$ mile, giving rise to a maximum one-way trip length of $\frac{1}{8}$ mile.

To fill out the structure of the environment, suppose there are L consumers scattered uniformly about the circle, and suppose the cost of travel is t dollars per mile. Thus, for example, if t were equal to \$24/mile, the transportation cost incurred by someone who lives $d = \frac{1}{16}$ mile from the nearest restaurant would be the product of the round-trip distance $(2d)$ and the unit travel cost (t): $2td = 2(\$24/\text{mile})(\frac{1}{16}\text{ mile}) = \$3$.

Suppose further that each consumer will eat exactly 1 meal/day at the restaurant for which the total price (which is the price charged for the meal plus transportation costs) is lowest. And suppose, finally, that each restaurant has a total cost curve given by

$$TC = F + MQ. \qquad (13.6)$$

Recall from earlier chapters that the total cost curve in Equation 13.6 is one in which there is a fixed cost F and a constant marginal cost M. Here, F may be thought of as the sum of equipment rental fees, opportunity costs of invested capital, and other fixed costs associated with operating a restaurant; and M is the sum of the labor, raw material, and other variable costs incurred in producing an additional meal.

Recall also that average total cost (ATC) is simply total cost divided by output. With a total cost function given by $TC = F + MQ$, average total cost is thus equal to $F/Q + M$. This means that the more customers that are served in a given location, the lower the average total cost will be.

Suppose, for example, that each of our four restaurants has a total cost curve, measured in dollars per day, given by $TC = 50 + 5Q$, where Q is the number of meals it serves each day. If the population, L, is equal to 100 persons, each restaurant will serve $(100/4) = 25$ meals/day, and its total cost will be given by $TC = 50 + 5(25) = \$175/\text{day}$. Average total cost in each restaurant will be $TC/25 = (\$175/\text{day})/(25 \text{ meals/day}) = \$7/\text{meal}$. By comparison, if there were only two restaurants, each would serve 50 meals/day and have an average total cost of only \$6/meal.

486   CHAPTER 13 IMPERFECT COMPETITION: A GAME-THEORETIC APPROACH

What will be the average cost of transportation when there are four restaurants? This cost will depend on unit transportation costs (t) and on how far apart the restaurants are. Recall that the distance between adjacent restaurants will be $\frac{1}{4}$ mile when there are four restaurants. Some people will live right next door to a restaurant, and for these people the transportation cost will be zero. With four restaurants, the farthest someone can live from a restaurant is $\frac{1}{8}$ mile, the one-way distance for a person who lives halfway between two adjacent restaurants. For this person, the round-trip will cover $\frac{1}{4}$ mile; and if t is again equal to \$24/mile, the travel cost for this patron will be (\$24/mile)($\frac{1}{4}$ mile) = \$6. Since people are uniformly scattered about the loop, the average round-trip will be halfway between these two extremes; it will thus cover a distance of $\frac{1}{8}$ mile, and its cost will be \$3.

The *overall average cost per meal* is the sum of average total cost (\$7/meal in the four-restaurant example) and average transportation cost (here, \$3/meal), which comes to \$10/meal.

The Optimal Number of Locations

If unit transportation cost (t) were zero, it would then clearly be optimal to have only a single restaurant, because that would minimize the overall average cost per meal. But if transportation cost were sufficiently high, a single restaurant would not be optimal because the average patron would have to travel too great a distance. The optimal number of locations is thus the result of a trade-off between the start-up and other fixed costs (F) of opening new locations, on the one hand, and the savings from lower transportation costs, on the other.

What is the best number of outlets to have? Our strategy for answering this question will be to ask whether the overall average cost per meal served (average total cost plus average transportation cost) would decline if we had one more restaurant than we have now. If so, we should add another restaurant and ask the same question again. Once the overall average cost stops declining, we will have reached the optimal number of restaurants.

To illustrate, suppose we increase the number of restaurants in our earlier example from four to five. How will this affect overall average cost? Again supposing that the restaurants are evenly spaced around the loop, each will now attract only one-fifth of the island's 100 inhabitants, which means that each will serve 20 meals/day. The ATC for each restaurant will thus be $[50 + 5(20)]/20 =$ \$7.50/meal. up \$0.50/meal from the previous value. (Recall that ATC with four restaurants was \$7/meal.) The distance between adjacent restaurants is $\frac{1}{5}$ mile when there are five restaurants. This means that the average one-way trip with five restaurants is $\frac{1}{20}$ mile, which in turn means that the average round-trip length is $\frac{1}{10}$ mile. Average transportation cost is thus ($\frac{1}{10}$ mile)(\$24/mile) = \$2.40. Note that this is \$0.60 less than the previous average transportation cost of \$3, reflecting the decline in average trip length. Adding average total cost and average transportation cost, we see that the overall average cost with five restaurants is \$7.50 + \$2.40 = \$9.90/meal.

EXERCISE 13.6

In the preceding example, what is the overall average cost per meal if we add a sixth restaurant around the loop?

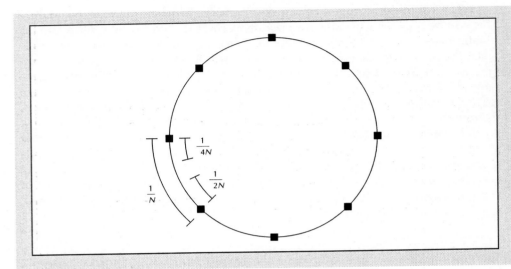

FIGURE 13.15
Distances with N Outlets
With N outlets, the distance between adjacent outlets will be 1/N. The farthest a person can live from an outlet is 1/2N. And the average one-way distance people must travel to reach the nearest outlet is 1/4N. The average round-trip distance is 1/2N.

Your calculation in Exercise 13.6 demonstrates that overall average cost per meal goes up when we increase the number of restaurants from five to six. And since the overall average cost declined when we moved from four to five, this means the optimal number of restaurants for our island nation is five.

We can make the preceding analysis more general by supposing that there are N outlets around the loop, as shown by the heavy black squares in Figure 13.15. Now the distance between adjacent outlets will be $1/N$, and the maximum one-way trip length will be half that, or $1/2N$. If we again suppose that people are uniformly distributed around the loop, it follows that the average one-way distance to the nearest outlet is $1/4N$ (which is halfway between 0, the distance of the person closest to a given outlet, and $1/2N$, the distance of the person farthest from it). The average round-trip distance is twice the average one-way distance, and is thus equal to $1/2N$.

Because the distance between restaurants declines as the number of restaurants grows, the total transportation cost, denoted C_{trans}, will be a decreasing function of the number of outlets. Since transportation cost is t dollars per person per mile traveled, total transportation cost will be the product of the cost per mile (t), population (L), and the average round-trip length ($\frac{1}{2N}$):

$$C_{trans} = tL\frac{1}{2N}. \tag{13.7}$$

The total cost of meals served, denoted C_{meals}, also depends on both population and the number of outlets. It is given by

$$C_{meals} = LM + NF, \tag{13.8}$$

where the first term on the right reflects the fact that each of the L people eats a meal whose marginal cost is M, and the second term is the total fixed cost for N outlets. The object is to choose N to minimize the sum of the two types of costs, $C_{trans} + C_{meals}$.

488   CHAPTER 13   IMPERFECT COMPETITION: A GAME-THEORETIC APPROACH

FIGURE 13.16
The Optimal Number of Outlets
Total transportation cost (C_{trans}) declines with the number of outlets (N), while total cost of meals served (C_{meals}) increases with N. The optimal number of outlets (N*) is the one that minimizes the sum of these costs.

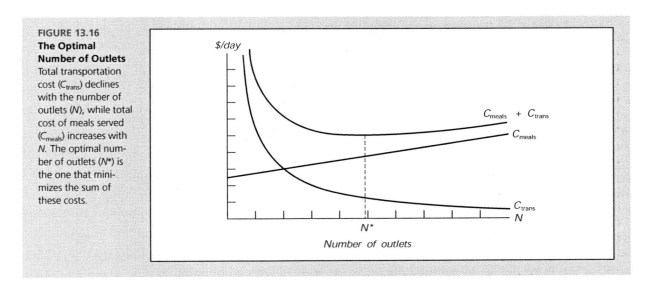

The two cost functions and their sum are shown graphically in Figure 13.16, where N* denotes the cost-minimizing number of outlets.[19]

The slope of the C_{meals} curve is equal to F, which represents the cost of an additional outlet. The slope of the C_{trans} curve is equal to $-tL/2N^2$ and represents the savings in transportation cost from adding an additional outlet.[20] If the slope of C_{meals} is less than the absolute value of the slope of C_{trans}, the reduction in transportation cost from adding another outlet will more than compensate for the extra fixed cost from adding that outlet. The optimal number of outlets, N*, is the one for which the slope of the C_{meals} curve is the same as the absolute value of the slope of the C_{trans} curve. N* must thus satisfy

$$\frac{tL}{2N^{*2}} = F, \tag{13.9}$$

which yields

$$N^* = \sqrt{\frac{tL}{2F}}. \tag{13.10}$$

---

[19]These functions are plotted as if N were a continuous variable, not an integer. For industries involving large numbers of firms, the continuous approximation will introduce only minimal error.

[20]This slope is found by taking the derivative

$$\frac{d(C_{trans})}{dN} = \frac{-tL}{2N^2},$$

again treating N as if it were continuously variable. Students who haven't had calculus can convince themselves that this expression is correct by letting ΔN be, say, 0.001 and then calculating the resulting change in C_{trans},

$$\Delta C_{trans} = \frac{tL}{2(N + 0.001)} - \frac{tL}{2N} = \frac{-0.001tL}{2N(N + 0.001)}.$$

The ratio $\Delta C_{trans}/\Delta N$ is thus

$$\frac{\Delta C_{trans}}{0.001} = \frac{-tL}{2N(N + 0.001)} \approx \frac{-tL}{2N^2}.$$

This expression for the optimal number of outlets has a straightforward economic interpretation. Note first that if transportation cost rises, N^* will also rise. This makes sense because the whole point of adding additional outlets is to economize on transportation costs. Note that N^* also increases with population density, L. The more people there are who live on each segment of the loop, the more people there are who will benefit if the average distance to the nearest outlet becomes shorter. And note, finally, that N^* declines with F, the start-up cost of an additional outlet, which is also just as expected.

Applying Equation 13.10 to our restaurant example in which $L = 100$, $t = 24$, and $F = 50$, we get $N^* = \sqrt{(2400/100)} = 4.9$. Needless to say, it is impossible to have 4.9 restaurants, so we choose the integer nearest 4.9, namely, 5. And indeed, just as our earlier calculations indicated, having five restaurants results in a lower overall average cost than does having either four or six.

EXERCISE 13.7

How would N^* change in the preceding example if there were 400 people on the island instead of 100?

Will the independent actions of private, profit-seeking firms result in the optimal number of outlets around the loop? This question sounds very simple, but turns out to be exceedingly difficult to answer. We now know that under some conditions there will tend to be more than the optimal number, while under other conditions there will be fewer.[21] But for the moment let us note that the number of outlets that emerges from the independent actions of profit-seeking firms will in general be related to the optimal number of outlets in the following simple way: Any environmental change that leads to a change in the optimal number of outlets (here, any change in population density, transportation cost, or fixed cost) will lead to a change in the same direction in the equilibrium number of outlets. For example, a fall in transportation cost will tend to decrease both the optimal number of outlets and the number of outlets we actually observe in practice.

Why are there so many fewer grocery stores in most cities now than there were in 1930? And why do residential neighborhoods in New York City have more grocery stores than residential neighborhoods in Los Angeles?

Grocery retailing, like other forms of retailing, is characterized by strong economies of scale. It thus confronts the usual trade-off between direct production cost, on the one hand, and transportation cost, on the other. Throughout this century, changing patterns of automobile ownership have affected the pattern of grocery store size and location in the United States. In 1920, most families did not own cars and had to do their shopping on foot. In terms of our expression for the optimal number of outlets (Equation 13.10), this meant a high value of t, unit transportation cost. Today, of

ECONOMIC NATURALIST 13.4

---

[21]A detailed technical discussion of some of the relevant issues can be found in Avinash Dixit and Joseph Stiglitz, "Monopolistic Competition and Optimal Product Diversity," *American Economic Review*, 1977: 297–308; and A. Michael Spence, "Product Selection, Fixed Costs, and Monopolistic Competition," *Review of Economic Studies*, 1976: 217–235.

Why are grocery stores closer together in New York City than in Los Angeles?

course, virtually every family has a car, which has led people to take advantage of the lower prices that are possible in larger stores. One exception to this general pattern is Manhattan. Even today, most Manhattan residents do not own cars. Moreover, population density is extremely high there, which means a high value of L in Equation 13.10. The combined effect of high values of L and t is that very few Manhattan residents have to walk more than two blocks to get to their nearest grocery store. The total population in Los Angeles is also very high, but it is spread out over a much larger area, and most families own at least one automobile. As a result, Los Angeles grocery stores are both larger and farther apart than their New York City counterparts.

The Analogy to Product Characteristics

The power of the spatial interpretation of monopolistic competition is that it can be applied not only to geographic location, but also to a variety of other product characteristics. Consider, for example, the various airline flights between any two cities on a given day. People have different preferences for traveling at various times of day, just as they have different preferences about where to eat or shop. Figure 13.17 depicts an air-travel market (for example, Kansas City to Minneapolis) with four flights per day, scheduled at midnight, 6 A.M., noon, and 6 P.M. With the choice of an airline flight, just as with the choice of a place to dine, people will tend to select the alternative that lies closest to their most preferred option. Thus, a person who would most prefer to go at 7 P.M. will

FIGURE 13.17
A Spatial Interpretation of Airline Scheduling
In a market with four flights per day, there is no traveler for whom there is not a flight leaving within 3 hours of his most preferred departure time.

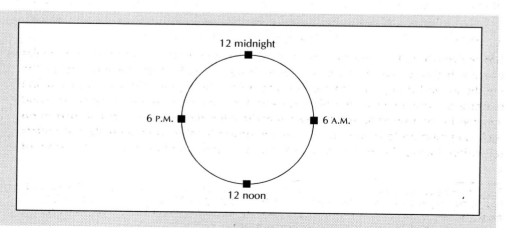

probably choose the 6 P.M. flight. In terms of our spatial model, having to wait for a flight is the analog of having to travel a certain distance in order to get to a store.

Why not have a flight leaving every 5 minutes, so that no one would be forced to travel at an inconvenient time? The answer again has to do with the trade-off between cost and convenience. The larger an aircraft is, the lower its average cost per seat is. If people want frequent flights, airlines are forced to use smaller planes and charge higher fares. Conversely, if people didn't care when they traveled, the airline could use the largest possible aircraft (in today's fleet, the 450-seat Boeing 747) and fly at whatever interval was required to accumulate enough passengers to fill the plane. (In the Paducah, Kentucky–Klamath Falls, Oregon market, that would mean one flight every other February 29!) But most passengers have schedules to keep and are willing to pay a little extra for more conveniently timed flights. The result is the same sort of compromise we saw in the restaurant and grocery store examples.

Virtually every consumer product can be interpreted fruitfully within the context of the spatial model. In the automobile market, for example, the available permutations of turbo versus nonturbo, automatic versus standard, coupe versus convertible, sedan versus station wagon, two doors versus four doors, bucket seats versus bench seats, air conditioned versus not air conditioned, metallic indigo versus forest green, and so on, lead to an extraordinarily large number of possibilities. It would be considerably cheaper, of course, if we had only a single standard model. But people are willing to pay a little extra for variety, just as they are willing to pay a little extra for a more conveniently located store. In the parlance of the spatial model, car manufacturers are said to "locate" their models in a "product-space." Their aim is to see that few buyers are left without a choice that lies "close" to the car that would best suit them. Similar interpretations apply to cameras, stereos, vacations, bicycles, wristwatches, wedding bands, and virtually every other good for which people have a taste for variety.

Paying for Variety

Variety, as we have seen, is costly. Many critics claim that market economies serve up wastefully high degrees of product variety. Wouldn't the world be a better place, these critics ask, if we had a simpler array of products to choose from, each costing less than the highly specific models we see today? The extra costs of product variety may indeed seem an unnecessary burden imposed on consumers who neither desire nor can easily afford it. In a slightly more detailed model of spatial competition, however, these problems appear much less serious.

In our simple model, we assumed that each buyer faced the same unit transportation cost. This assumption is unrealistic even in models where the only dimension of variety is geographic location. Buyers who own automobiles, for example, will have much lower transportation costs than those who don't; likewise, buyers whose time is worth little, in opportunity cost terms, have lower transportation costs than those whose time is more valuable. The issue is the same for product variety. Those who care a lot about special product features will have higher "transport costs" than those who do not, which means simply that people in the former group are willing to pay more than others for a product whose special features suit their particular tastes.

492   CHAPTER 13   IMPERFECT COMPETITION: A GAME-THEORETIC APPROACH

FIGURE 13.18
Distributing the Cost of Variety
The buyers who care most about variety will generally choose the model with premium features. By pricing its models differently, the seller recovers most of the extra costs of variety from the buyers who are most responsible for their incurrence.

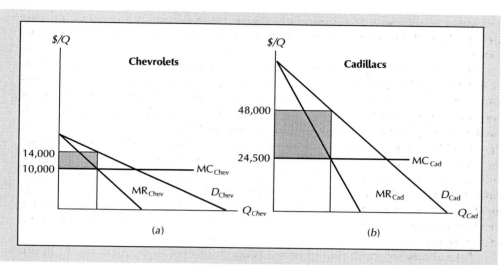

It is also true, as a general proposition, that the demand for variety increases sharply with income. In the language of Chapter 5, variety is a luxury, not a necessity. The association between income and the demand for variety plays a pivotal role in the way most producers market their products. To illustrate, consider the array of automobiles offered by General Motors, ranging from the subcompact Chevrolet Cavalier to the full-sized Cadillac Seville STS. All these cars incorporate a variety of specialized features, which are the result of costly research and development. The research and development costs are largely fixed, which gives rise to a substantial scale economy in the production of cars. If GM (or any other company) could sell more cars in a given year, it could produce each of them at a lower cost.

When marginal cost lies below average cost, it is not possible to charge each buyer a price equal to marginal cost and still earn a normal profit. (Recall from Chapter 10 that a firm's average cost includes a normal rate of profit.) As we saw in Chapter 12, the firm with a scale economy has an incentive to expand its market by setting price close to marginal cost if it can do that without altering its prices on existing sales. But we also saw that if some buyers pay prices below average cost, others must pay prices above it.

The car manufacturer's response to this situation is to set the prices of its better models above average cost, while pricing its lesser models below average cost. Panels *a* and *b* in Figure 13.18 for example, show the cost and demand conditions for Chevrolets and Cadillacs, respectively. The marginal cost of producing a Cadillac is only slightly higher than that of producing a Chevrolet. The basic design innovations are available to the company for both cars, and the hardware produced for the Cadillac is only slightly more costly than that used in the Chevrolet. But because the buyers who care most about variety are willing to pay much more for a Cadillac than for a Chevrolet, the company can set sharply different prices for the two models. In an average year, the surplus of total revenue above variable cost for all models (which is the sum of the two shaded rectangles in Figure 13.18) is just about enough to cover the company's research and development and other fixed costs.

Variety is costly, just as the critics claim. But the cost of variety is not distributed evenly among all buyers. In the example above, it was paid by the buyers of Cadillacs, not by the buyers of Chevrolets. By the same token, people who buy the BMW 325i enjoy almost all the important advantages of the extensive BMW research program for about $6000 less than the people who buy the BMW 330i, which differs from the 325i only in having a slightly larger engine. Even by the yardstick used by critics of the market system, this seems a better outcome than the one they urge, which is that all buyers have a standardized "people's car." Under current marketing arrangements, people who don't place high value on variety get to enjoy it at the expense of those who care most about having it. The alternative would be to deny variety to the people who care most about it, without producing real cost savings for the buyers who would be satisfied with a standardized product. Even Volkswagen, which once touted the virtues of a single, standardized model, now offers several dozen versions of its Golf, Jetta, and Passat lines.

Similar pricing strategies affect recovery of the costs of variety in virtually every industry. Consider again the restaurant industry. In a city in which most people have cars, which is to say in virtually every city, the cheapest way to provide restaurant meals would be to have a single restaurant with only one item on the menu. An army of chefs would labor over gigantic cauldrons of peas and mashed potatoes, while others operated huge ovens filled with roasting chickens. But people don't want the same meal every night, any more than they all want the same kind of car. Even in small cities like Ithaca, New York, we have Indian, Mexican, Thai, Chinese, Japanese, Korean, Greek, Italian, French, Cajun, Vietnamese, and Spanish restaurants in addition to the usual domestic fare and fast-food chains.

How are the extra costs of all this variety apportioned? Most restaurants price the different items on their menus in differing multiples of marginal cost. Alcoholic beverages, desserts, and coffee, in particular, are almost always priced at several times marginal cost, whereas the markup on most entrees is much smaller. Most restaurants also offer some sort of daily specials, entrees that are priced very close to marginal cost. The result is that the diner who wants to economize on the cost of eating out, either because he has low income or for whatever other reason, will order only the basic meal, taking before-dinner drinks and dessert and coffee at home (or doing without those extras). Such diners end up paying a price not much more than the marginal cost of being served. Other diners who are willing or able to do so will purchase the more costly option of having the entire package at the restaurant. The diners who pursue the latter strategy are much more likely than others to be the ones who feel strongly about variety (again, because the demand for variety is strongly linked to income). Under current marketing arrangements, they are the ones who end up paying most of its cost. Those who care less about variety are still able to enjoy a lamb vindaloo dinner one night and Szechuan chicken the next; and if they don't order drinks and dessert, they pay little more than they would have to in a standardized soup kitchen.

As a final illustration of how the costs of variety are apportioned in monopolistically competitive markets, consider the case of airline ticket pricing. As discussed earlier, the important dimension of variety here is the timing of flights. Not all travelers have equally pressing demands for frequently scheduled flights. Some are willing to pay substantially extra for a slightly earlier departure time, while others would wait a week rather than pay even $5 more. To the extent that airlines use smaller, more costly (per seat) aircraft in order to offer more frequent flights, it is to accommodate the needs of the former group.

Who pays the added costs of the smaller flights? Virtually every airline employs the hurdle model of differential pricing described in Chapter 12. The particular variant the airlines use offers discounts of approximately 50 percent to passengers who satisfy two restrictions: (1) they must buy their tickets in advance, usually 7 days before flight time; and (2) their journey must include a Saturday night. The effect of these two restrictions together is to eliminate most travelers who demand maximum travel flexibility. In particular, business travelers, whose schedules tend to be much tighter than those of vacation travelers, almost always end up paying the regular coach fare under the current marketing system. By contrast, very few vacation travelers fail to qualify for at least some form of discount.

If it is largely the scheduling demands of business travelers that dictate the use of smaller, more costly aircraft, this apportioning of the costs appears not only fair but also efficient. Discount tickets enable airlines to attract passengers who would not fly otherwise, and these passengers make possible the use of larger, less costly aircraft. Business travelers end up getting the frequent service they want, and leisure travelers are not forced to pay the added costs of it.[22]

Historical Note: Hotelling's Hot Dog Vendors

In Harold Hotelling's seminal paper on the spatial model of monopolistic competition,[23] he discussed the problem of two hot dog vendors who are free to position themselves wherever they wish along a stretch of beach. Suppose the beach is 1 mile long and bounded at each end by some natural obstacle. Suppose also that the vendors charge the same price, customers are evenly distributed along the beach, and each customer buys one hot dog from the nearest vendor. If the vendors' goal is to sell as many hot dogs as possible, where should they position themselves?

Suppose, as in Figure 13.19, that vendor 1 stands at point A and vendor 2 stands at point B, where both A and B are $\frac{1}{4}$ mile from the midpoint of the beach located at C. In this configuration, all customers to the left of C are closest to vendor 1 and will buy from him, while those to the right of C will buy from vendor 2. Each vendor thus gets half the market. The greatest one-way distance any customer has to travel is $\frac{1}{4}$ mile, and the average one-way distance between customers and their nearest vendor is half that, or $\frac{1}{8}$ mile.

Mathematically inclined readers can verify that A and B are in fact the locations that minimize average travel distance for all consumers. And yet these locations are clearly not optimal from the perspective of either vendor. To see why, suppose vendor 1 were to move 10 steps toward B. The customers to the left of C would continue to find him the closest vendor. But now those customers less than 5 steps to the right of C—people who used to be closest to vendor 2—will suddenly find themselves switching to vendor 1. Moving farther to the right will increase vendor 1's sales still further. Vendor 1 will maximize his sales by

---

[22]For a more detailed discussion of this issue, see R. Frank, "When Are Price Differentials Discriminatory?" *Journal of Policy Analysis and Management*, 2, Winter 1983: 238–255.

[23]Harold Hotelling, "Stability in Competition," *The Economic Journal*, 39, 1929: 41–57.

THE CHAMBERLIN MODEL   495

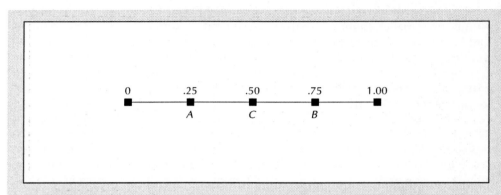

FIGURE 13.19
The Hot Dog Vendor Location Problem
Each hot dog vendor does best by positioning himself at the center of the beach, even though that location does not minimize the average distance that their customers must travel.

positioning himself as close as he can get to vendor 2 on the side of vendor 2 that is closer to the center of the beach.

Vendor 2, of course, can reason in the same fashion, so his strategy will be perfectly symmetric: He will try to get as close to vendor 1 on the side of vendor 1 that is closest to the center. And when both vendors behave in this fashion, the only stable outcome is for each to locate at C, the center of the beach. At C, each gets half of the market, just as he did originally. But the average distance that customers must travel is now $\frac{1}{4}$ mile, twice what it was when the vendors were located at A and B.

Having both vendors at the middle of the beach is thus not optimal from the vantage point of customers, and yet neither vendor would be better off if he were to move unilaterally. The hot dog vendor location problem is thus not one of those cases in which Adam Smith's invisible hand guides resources so as to produce the greatest good for all.

Application: A Spatial Perspective on Political Competition

When former Alabama Governor George Corley Wallace ran for president as a third-party candidate in 1968, he often complained to his audiences that "there's not a dime's worth of difference between the Republican and Democratic candidates." Richard Nixon and Hubert Humphrey were those candidates, but Wallace preferred to call them "Tweedledum" and "Tweedledee." Although Wallace surely exaggerated the similarities between Nixon and Humphrey, his assessment nonetheless captures an essential truth about the American two-party political system, namely, that it tends to nominate presidential candidates whose positions on most major issues are remarkably similar.

This tendency is easily understood once we recognize the analogy between the political

"The Democratic Party today changed its name to 'The Republican Party'."

FIGURE 13.20
A Political Location Problem
A candidate positioned at *A* will be most attractive to Democrats, one at *B* most attractive to Republicans. But in a general election involving voters from both parties, the candidates standing closer to *C* will attract more voters.

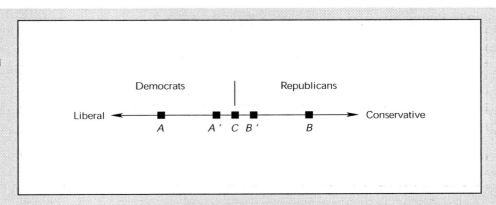

location problem and Hotelling's hot dog vendor location problem. Instead of having a beach, we now have a political spectrum ranging from left (liberal) to right (conservative) (see Figure 13.20). Voters to the left of the midpoint of the political spectrum classify themselves as liberal, increasingly so the farther left they are. Those to the right of the midpoint are increasingly conservative as we move farther to the right. To simplify discussion, suppose all voters to the left of the midpoint belong to the Democratic party, while all to the right are Republicans.

In an election involving only Democrats, a candidate positioned at *A* (the midpoint of the liberal half of the spectrum) would attract the greatest number of voters. Similarly, an election involving only Republicans would tend to favor a candidate positioned at *B*, the midpoint of the conservative half of the spectrum. Yet voters in each party know that their nominee must stand for general election before the voters of both parties. And so the most extreme members of each party have an incentive to set their own preferences aside in favor of a candidate located closer to the center of the overall political spectrum, someone like *A'* for the Democrats or *B'* for the Republicans.

In practice, the extent to which extremists in each party actually follow this prudent course varies from election to election. Occasionally the major parties do nominate candidates like Barry Goldwater or George McGovern, neither of whom would be mistaken for a centrist. Still, the location model's prediction that the nominees of the major parties will tend to be moderates corresponds remarkably well with the broad historical record.

CONSUMER PREFERENCES AND ADVERTISING

In perfectly competitive markets it would never pay a producer to advertise her product. Being only one of many producers of identical products, the firm that advertised would attract only an insignificant share of any resulting increase in demand. In monopolistically competitive and oligopolistic markets, the incentives are different. Because products are differentiated, producers can often shift their demand curves outward significantly by advertising.

How does advertising affect the efficiency with which markets allocate resources? In the description of the world offered by rational choice theory, producers are essentially agents of consumers. Consumers vote with their purchase dollars, and producers are quick to do their bidding. This description has been called the *traditional sequence*, and Harvard economist John Kenneth Galbraith is one of its most prominent critics. In its place, he proposed a *revised sequence* in which the producer, not the consumer, sits in the driver's seat. In Galbraith's scheme, the corporation decides which products are cheapest and most convenient to produce, and then uses advertising and other promotional devices to create a demand for them.

Galbraith's revised sequence recasts Adam Smith's invisible hand in an unflattering new light. Smith's story, recall, was that producers motivated only by self-interest would provide the products that best meet consumers' desires. Those who behaved otherwise would fail to attract customers and go out of business. If Galbraith is correct, however, this story is turned on its head: It is like saying the all-too-visible hand of Madison Avenue guides consumers to serve the interests of large corporations.

Galbraith's revised sequence is not without intuitive appeal. Many people are understandably skeptical, for example, when an economist says that the purpose of advertising is to make consumers better informed. The plain fact, after all, is that this is often anything but its intent. For example, the celebrity milk mustache is surely not part of a process whereby we become more knowledgeable about the nutritional merits of milk consumption.

But for all the obvious hype in advertising messages, the Galbraith view of the process overlooks something fundamental: It is easier to sell a good product than a bad one. All an advertisement can reasonably hope to accomplish is to induce the consumer to *try* the product. If it is one she tries and likes, she will probably buy it again and again. She will also recommend it to friends. If it is one she doesn't like, however, the process usually ends there. Even if a firm were to succeed in getting *everyone* to try it once, it still wouldn't be able to maintain a profitable, ongoing venture.

Imagine two alternative products, one that meets real human needs but is costly to produce, and another that meets no real need but is somewhat cheaper. Which of these two types would a profit-hungry producer do best to advertise? Given the importance of repeat business and word-of-mouth endorsements, the first will generally be more attractive, and by a compelling margin. The fact that it costs more to produce will not deter consumers unless its extra benefits do not justify those extra costs.

New products go through extensive market testing before they ever land on the shelves. Millions of dollars are spent analyzing test subjects' reactions to them. In the end, most products that enter this testing process never see the light of day. Only when a firm has concrete evidence that a product is likely to be well received does it dare to commit the millions of dollars required for an intensive national advertising campaign.

Firms that fail to adopt this posture often pay sharp penalties. The Lotus software company, for example, spent more than $10 million advertising *Jazz*, its spreadsheet program for the Apple Macintosh, even though it had clear evidence that the program lacked specific features that many users deemed vital. The Lotus ads were incredibly sophisticated, and no doubt succeeded in selling a fair number of programs. And yet *Jazz*'s main rival, Microsoft's *Excel*, a much better product, quickly captured the market with only a small fraction of Lotus' advertising outlays.

Advertising and other efforts to persuade consumers are best viewed as part of a pump-priming process. Given the enormous costs, it usually pays to promote only those products that consumers are likely to want to purchase repeatedly, or to speak well of to their friends. And in fact there is clear evidence that most firms follow

498   CHAPTER 13   IMPERFECT COMPETITION: A GAME-THEORETIC APPROACH

"To paraphrase the great Vince Lombardi, packaging isn't everything, it's the __only__ thing."

precisely this strategy. Frozen-dinner producers advertise their fancy ethnic entrees, not their chicken pot pies. Publishers advertise books that seem likely to become best-sellers, not their titles with more limited appeal. Motion picture studios tout the movies they hope will become blockbusters, not their low-budget films.

Because producers have an incentive to advertise only those products that consumers are most likely to find satisfying, the so-called traditional sequence is more plausible than Galbraith and other critics make it out to be. True enough, where the quality differences between competing goods are small, advertising may have a significant influence on which brand a consumer chooses. But as a first approximation, it still makes sense to assume that consumers have reasonably well-defined notions of what they like, and that producers spend much effort on trying to cater to those notions.

This is not to say, however, that market incentives lead to the amount of advertising that is best from society's point of view. As we saw earlier in this chapter, strategic competition between rivals may sometimes lead firms to spend excessively on advertising.

SUMMARY

- The characteristic feature of oligopolistic markets is interdependence among firms. The interdependencies among oligopolistic firms are often successfully analyzed using the mathematical theory of games. The three basic elements of any game are the players, the set of possible strategies, and the payoff matrix. A Nash equilibrium occurs when each player's strategy is optimal given the other player's choice of strategy. A strategy is called dominant if it is optimal no matter what strategy the other player chooses.

- The incentives facing firms who attempt to collude are similar to the ones facing participants in the prisoner's dilemma. The difficulty in holding cartels together is that the dominant strategy for each member is to cheat on the agreement. Repeated interactions between a very small number of firms can support collusive behavior under circumstances in which strategies like tit-for-tat are effective.

* Incumbent firms may sometimes act strategically to deter potential rivals from entering their markets. Often this involves incurring higher costs than would otherwise be necessary.

* The basic idea of the theory of contestable markets is that when the cost of entry and exit is very low, the mere threat of entry can be sufficient to produce an allocation similar to the one we see under perfect competition. Critics of this theory have stressed that there are almost always nontrivial sunk costs associated with entry and exit, and that even small sunk costs leave considerable room for strategic entry deterrence.

* There is not always a strong tendency for natural monopoly to emerge from the interaction of a small number of firms, each of which produces under sharply increasing returns to scale. Here too the role of sunk costs turns out to be important. It may sometimes be necessary for buyers to take certain initiatives if they are to secure the least costly of the potentially available options.

* In the Cournot model, each firm takes the *quantities* produced by its rivals as given; in the Bertrand model, by contrast, each firm takes its rivals' *prices* as given. Although the behavioral orientation of firms sounds very much the same in these two cases, the results are strikingly different. The Cournot model yields a slightly lower price and a slightly higher quantity than we would see if the firms colluded to achieve the monopoly outcome. By contrast, the Bertrand model leads to essentially the same outcome we saw under perfect competition.

* A slightly more sophisticated form of interdependence among firms is assumed in the Stackelberg model, in which one firm plays a leadership role and its rivals merely follow. This model is similar in structure to the Cournot model, except that where the Cournot firms took one another's quantities as given, the Stackelberg leader strategically manipulated the quantity decisions of its rivals.

* Monopolistic competition is defined by two simple conditions: (1) the existence of numerous firms each producing a product that is a close, but imperfect, substitute for the products of other firms; and (2) free entry and exit of firms. In the spatial model of monopolistic competition, customers have particular locations or product characteristics they most prefer. The result is that firms tend to compete most intensively for the consumers of products most similar to their own.

* A central feature of the spatial model of monopolistic competition is the trade-off between the desire for lower cost, on the one hand, and greater variety or locational convenience, on the other. The optimum degree of product diversity depends on several factors. Greater diversity is expected with greater population density and higher transportation costs (where, in the general case, "transportation costs" measure willingness to pay for desired product features). Optimal product diversity is negatively related to the start-up costs of adding new product characteristics or locations. The market metes out a certain rough justice in that the costs of additional variety tend to be borne most heavily by those to whom variety is most important.

QUESTIONS FOR REVIEW

1. What is the fundamental difference among the Cournot, Bertrand, and Stackelberg models of oligopoly?

2. How is the problem of oligopoly collusion similar in structure to the prisoner's dilemma?

3. What is the difficulty with the tit-for-tat strategy as a possible solution to the oligopoly collusion problem?

4. Does the equilibrium in the Cournot model satisfy the definition of a Nash equilibrium?

5. What role does the assumption of sunk costs play in the theory of contestable markets?

6. Describe the trade-off between cost and variety.

7. How is the optimal degree of product variety related to population density? To transportation cost? To the fixed costs of offering new products?

PROBLEMS

1. The market demand curve for mineral water is given by $P = 15 - Q$. If there are two firms that produce mineral water, each with a constant marginal cost of 3 per unit, fill in the entries for each of the four duopoly models indicated in the table. (In the Stackelberg model, assume that firm 1 is the leader.)

500   CHAPTER 13   IMPERFECT COMPETITION: A GAME-THEORETIC APPROACH

Model	Q_1	Q_2	$Q_1 + Q_2$	P	Π_1	Π_2	$\Pi_1 + \Pi_2$
Shared monopoly							
Cournot							
Bertrand							
Stackelberg							

2. The market demand curve for a pair of Cournot duopolists is given as $P = 36 - 3Q$, where $Q = Q_1 + Q_2$. The constant per unit marginal cost is 18 for each duopolist. Find the Cournot equilibrium price, quantity, and profits.

3. Solve the preceding problem for Bertrand duopolists.

4. The market demand curve for a pair of duopolists is given as $P = 36 - 3Q$, where $Q = Q_1 + Q_2$. The constant per unit marginal cost is 18 for each duopolist. Find the equilibrium price, quantity, and profit for each firm, assuming the firms act as a Stackelberg leader and follower, with firm 1 as the leader.

5. Because of their unique expertise with explosives, the Zambino brothers have long enjoyed a monopoly of the U.S. market for public fireworks displays for crowds above a quarter of a million. The annual demand for these fireworks displays is $P = 140 - Q$. The marginal cost of putting on a fireworks display is 20. A family dispute broke the firm in two. Alfredo Zambino now runs one firm and Luigi Zambino runs the other. They still have the same marginal costs, but now they are Cournot duopolists. How much profit has the family lost?

6. While grading a final exam a professor discovers that two students have virtually identical answers. He talks to each student separately and tells them that he is sure that they shared answers, but he cannot be sure who copied from whom. He offers each student a deal—if they both sign a statement admitting to the cheating, each will be given an F for the course. If only one signs the statement, he will be allowed to withdraw from the course and the other nonsigning student will be expelled from the university. Finally, if neither signs the statement they will both get a C for the course because the professor does not have enough evidence to prove that cheating has occurred. Assuming the students are not allowed to communicate with one another, set up the relevant payoff matrix. Does each student have a dominant strategy?

7. Suppose A and B know that they will interact in a prisoner's dilemma exactly four times. Explain why the tit-for-tat strategy will not be an effective means for assuring cooperation.

8. Firm 1 and firm 2 are automobile producers. Each has the option of producing either a big car or a small car. The payoffs to each of the four possible combinations of choices are as given in the following payoff matrix. Each firm must make its choice without knowing what the other has chosen.

		Firm 1	
		Big car	Small car
Firm 2	Big car	$\Pi_1 = 400$ $\Pi_2 = 400$	$\Pi_1 = 800$ $\Pi_2 = 1000$
	Small car	$\Pi_1 = 1000$ $\Pi_2 = 800$	$\Pi_1 = 500$ $\Pi_2 = 500$

   a.   Does either firm have a dominant strategy?

   b.   There are two Nash equilibria for this game. Identify them.

9. Suppose we have the same payoff matrix as in Problem 8 except now firm 1 gets to move first and knows that firm 2 will see the results of this choice before deciding which type of car to build.

   a.   Draw the game tree for this sequential game.

   b.   What is the Nash equilibrium for this game?

10. The state has announced its plans to license two firms to serve a market whose demand curve is given by $P = 100 - Q$. The technology is such that each can pro-duce any given level of output at zero cost, but once each firm's output is chosen, it cannot be altered.

   a.   What is the most you would be willing to pay for one of these licenses if you knew you would be able to choose your level of output first (assuming your choice was observable by the rival firm)?

   b.   How much would your rival be willing to pay for the right to choose second?

*11. Firm 1 and firm 2 are competing for a cable television franchise. The present value of the net revenues generated by the franchise is equal to R. Each firm's probability of winning the franchise is given by its proportion of the total spent by the two firms on lobbying the local government committee that awards the franchise. That is, if I_1 and I_2 represent the lobbying expenditures of firms 1 and 2, respectively, then firm 1's probability of winning is given by $I_1/(I_1 + I_2)$, while firm 2's probability of winning is $I_2/(I_1 + I_2)$. If each firm assumes that the other firm's spending is independent of its own, what is the equilibrium level of spending for each firm?

12. State whether true or false and briefly expain why: If a business owner is delighted to accept additional orders at the current price, he or she cannot have been a profit-maximizing, perfectly competitive producer.

13. A toll road commission is planning to locate garages for tow trucks along a 100-mile circular highway. Each garage has a fixed cost of $5000 per day. Towing jobs are equally likely along any point of the highway and cost per mile towed is $50. If there were 5000 towing jobs per day, what number of garages would minimize the sum of the fixed costs and towing costs?

14. The 1000 residents of Great Donut Island are all fishermen. Every morning they go to the nearest port to launch their fishing boats and then return in the evening with their catch. The residents are evenly distributed along the 10-mile perimeter of the island. Each port has a fixed cost of $1000/day. If the optimal number of ports is 2, what must be the per mile travel cost?

ANSWERS TO IN-CHAPTER EXERCISES

13.1 Regardless of firm 1's strategy, firm 2 does best with a big research budget. The choice of a big research budget is thus a dominant strategy for firm 2. Firm 1 does not have a dominant strategy. If firm 2 chooses a low research budget, then firm 1 does best by choosing a low research budget. But if firm 2 chooses a high research budget, then firm 1 does best by choosing a high research budget. Since firm 1 can predict that firm 2 will choose a high research budget, firm 1's best strategy is to choose a high research budget. The combination of "High research budget—High research budget" is a Nash equilibrium.

---

*This problem requires the use of calculus maximization techniques.

CHAPTER 13   IMPERFECT COMPETITION: A GAME-THEORETIC APPROACH

13.2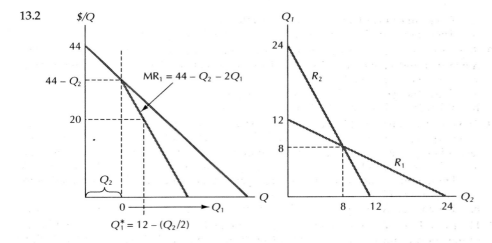

13.3 Price will settle at marginal cost, and so $P = 2$. The corresponding market demand, $Q = 8$, will be shared equally by the two firms: $Q_1 = Q_2 = 4$.

13.4 Firm 2's marginal revenue curve is given by $10 - Q_1 - 2Q_2$. Setting $MR = MC = 2$, we have firm 2's reaction function, $R_2(Q_1) = Q_2^* = 4 - (Q_1/2)$. Substituting into firm 1's demand function, we get $P_1 = 10 - Q_1 - 4 + (Q_1/2) = 6 - (Q_1/2)$, and the corresponding marginal review curve, $MR_1 = 6 - Q_1$. $MR_1 = MC = 2$ solves for $Q_1^* = 4$. This means that Q_2 will be 2 units, for a total market output of 6 units. The market price will be $10 - 6 = 4$.

13.5 Each firm initially got $\frac{1}{20} = 5$ percent of total demand, but will now get only $\frac{1}{25} = 4$ percent. This means that at every price, the quantity demanded will be 20 percent lower than before (see the graph below). The new dd curve is $P = 10 - 0.00125Q$.

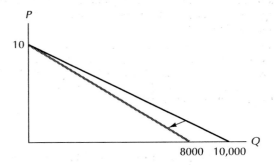

13.6 With six restaurants the average round-trip distance is $\frac{1}{12}$ mile, which yields an average transportation cost of $2. On average, each restaurant will attract 100/6 people per day, which yields an ATC of $[50 + 5(100/6)]/(100/6) = \$8/\text{day}$. Overall average cost with six restaurants is thus $10/day.

13.7 N^* will now be $\sqrt{[(24)(400)/100]} \approx 9.8$, so there should now be 10 restaurants.

CHAPTER

17

EXTERNALITIES, PROPERTY RIGHTS, AND THE COASE THEOREM

At the corner of 22nd and M Streets, NW, in Washington, D.C., stands a venerable restaurant called Blackie's House of Beef. During the real estate boom of the 1970s, this location emerged as a prime site for the construction of high-rise commercial buildings. With the passage of each month, the opportunity cost of continuing to operate a one-story restaurant on that site continued to soar. And yet the owners of Blackie's were of no mind to abandon their location. The restaurant had been the family business for many years, and the family was determined to see it continue.

Eventually they came up with a creative solution. They negotiated a multimillion-dollar agreement whereby, without disturbing a single brick in the restaurant, a high-rise structure would be constructed on stilts *above* the restaurant. Blackie's is still open for business, a quaint, old-world country inn nestled beneath a high-rise Marriott Hotel. In a similar multimillion-dollar transaction, a developer purchased the rights to build a new skyscraper astraddle the Museum of Modern Art in midtown Manhattan.

In most jurisdictions, owning a piece of property confers the right to exclude anyone from constructing a building in the airspace above it. But a similar right does not extend to all other forms of activity in the same airspace. For example, hundreds of thousands of American houses are located beneath commercial flight paths between major cities, and each day thousands of airliners use the airspace above these houses without paying a penny. This pattern of rights is not a matter of historical accident. It has emerged, as we will see, as a means of making the most efficient use of property when it is difficult to negotiate agreements on a case-by-case basis.

614   CHAPTER 17   EXTERNALITIES, PROPERTY RIGHTS, AND THE COASE THEOREM

CHAPTER PREVIEW

Our subjects in this chapter are externalities and property rights. We will begin with a series of examples illustrating what happens when an action by one party harms another and the parties are able to negotiate costlessly with one another. Next we will consider a related set of examples in which negotiation is costly. We will then apply the principles that emerge from these examples to a variety of questions regarding the design of property rights. Should the owner of a dock be allowed to exclude a boater from tying up during a storm? When should a person be allowed to exclude others from walking across his land? Or from blocking his view? Should pastureland be owned privately or in common? Should a developer be allowed to construct an office building over someone else's property without her consent? Should airplanes be allowed to fly over houses? The answers to such questions, we will see, depend on the kinds of accommodations people would reach among themselves if they were free to negotiate costlessly with one another.

Next we will apply the theory of property rights and externalities to the topic of contests for relative position. We will conclude this chapter with an examination of taxation as a possible solution to the problem of negative externalities.

THE RECIPROCAL NATURE OF EXTERNALITIES

In the first edition of this text (1991), I began this section with the following sentence:

> One of the great injustices of academic life is that Ronald H. Coase[1] has never been awarded the Nobel Prize in economics.

I was thus delighted when I learned that Coase was at last awarded the prize in 1992. Now an emeritus professor at the University of Chicago Law School, Coase is the author of the most influential and widely cited economics paper of the post-war era. Titled "The Problem of Social Cost,"[2] this paper profoundly changed the way economists, legal scholars, political philosophers, and others think about externalities and the legal and social institutions that have evolved to deal with them.

Coase began with an example involving a doctor whose ability to examine patients was disrupted by the noise of machinery operated by a confectioner (candy maker) in an adjacent building. Historically, the economic and legal view toward such a situation was simple and clear: The confectioner's noise was harming the doctor and it ought to be restrained. Coase's seminal insight was that this view completely overlooks the reciprocal nature of the problem. True enough, the confectioner's noise does harm the doctor. *But if we prevent the noise, we harm the confectioner.* After all, the confectioner makes the noise, not for the purpose of harming the doctor, but in pursuit of his own livelihood. In such situations, there will be harm to *someone*, no matter what happens. Whether the harm caused to the doctor by the noise is greater than the harm that would be caused to the confectioner if he were prohibited from making it is strictly an empirical question. The common interest of each party, Coase recognized, is to avoid the larger of these two unpleasant outcomes.

---

[1]Rhymes with "dose."

[2]*Journal of Law and Economics*, 3, 1960: 144–171.

Legal regime	Outcome	Net benefit		
		Doctor	Confectioner	Total
Liable	Confectioner shuts down to avoid liability payment	60	0	60
Not liable	Doctor pays confectioner P to shut down, $40 \leqslant P \leqslant 60$	$60 - P$	P	60

TABLE 17.1
Outcome and Payoff Summary for Example 17.1
The gain to the confectioner from operating is 40. The loss to the doctor from the noise is 60. The efficient outcome is for the confectioner to shut down, and this happens under both legal regimes.

The earlier, one-sided view of externalities led to a legal tradition in which the confectioner was generally held liable for any damage his noise caused to the doctor. Coase pointed out, however, that if the doctor and the confectioner were able to negotiate costlessly with one another, the most efficient outcome would occur regardless of whether the confectioner was liable. His simple and elegant argument in support of this claim is illustrated in the following series of numerical examples.

EXAMPLE 17.1

Suppose the benefit to the confectioner of continuing to make noise is 40, while the cost of the noise to the doctor is 60 (see footnote 3). If the confectioner's only alternative to making the noise is to produce nothing, what will happen if he is made liable for the noise damage? (To be liable for the damage means being required to compensate the doctor for any damage caused by the noise.)

The confectioner will examine his two options—shutting down or compensating the doctor—and choose the one that makes him best off. If he stays open, he will earn 40, but will have to pay 60 to the doctor, for a net loss of 20. If he shuts down, his net gain is 0, and since this is clearly better than losing 20, he will discontinue operation.

Alternatively, suppose the confectioner had not been liable for noise damage. That is, suppose the law grants him the right to continue operating without compensation to the doctor. Coase argued that in this case the doctor will pay the confectioner to shut down. If the confectioner stays open, he will gain only 40 while the doctor will lose 60. But the doctor can compensate the confectioner for the loss of shutting down and still have enough left over to be better off than if the confectioner had stayed open. Suppose, for example, the doctor pays the confectioner 50 to shut down. The confectioner's net gain will now be 10 more than if he had stayed open. And the doctor's net gain of 10 is 10 more than if the noise had continued.

If P denotes the payment the doctor makes to the confectioner to compensate him for shutting down, we know that P must be at least 40 (what the confectioner would get by staying open) and no larger than 60 (what the doctor would get if there were no noise). The net results under the two legal regimes (confectioner liable versus confectioner not liable) are summarized in Table 17.1.

---

[3]The numerical cost and benefit values used in this and in the following examples represent the present values of all current and future costs and benefits to the parties in question.

TABLE 17.2
Outcome and Payoff Summary for Example 17.2
The gain to the confectioner from operating is 60. The loss to the doctor from the confectioner's noise is 40. The efficient outcome is for the confectioner to continue operating, and this happens under both legal regimes.

Legal regime	Outcome	Net benefit		
		Doctor	Confectioner	Total
Liable	Confectioner stays open and pays doctor 40	40	20	60
Not liable	Confectioner stays open; doctor shuts down	0	60	60

Note that because the gain to the confectioner of operating his machinery (40) is smaller than the noise damage it imposes on the doctor (60), the most efficient outcome is for the confectioner to shut down. Example 17.1 makes clear that if both the doctor and confectioner are rational and can negotiate costlessly with one another, this will happen regardless of whether the confectioner is liable for noise damage. On efficiency grounds, the legal regime is thus a matter of complete indifference here. On distributional grounds, however, the parties will be anything but neutral about liability. If the confectioner is not liable, his gain is $P \geq 40$, whereas he will be forced to shut down and earn nothing if he is liable. The doctor's net gain will be 60 if the confectioner is liable, but only $60 - P$ if the confectioner is not liable.

EXAMPLE 17.2

Same as Example 17.1, except now the benefit to the *confectioner* of operating is 60, the benefit to the doctor in a noise-free environment only 40. Assume that the doctor must shut down if the noise continues.

This time the efficient outcome is for the confectioner to continue operating, since his gain exceeds the cost he imposes on the doctor. If he is not liable for noise damages, the confectioner will stay open and the doctor's best option will be to shut down. Alternatively, if the confectioner is liable for noise damage, he will again continue to operate and pay the doctor 40 to compensate him for his losses. The net results for this example are summarized in Table 17.2. Note that, as in Example 17.1, both legal regimes lead to the most efficient outcome, but have very different distributional consequences.

The preceding examples assumed that the only alternatives open to two parties were either to continue operations in the current form or to shut down entirely. In practice, however, one or both parties often face a broader range of alternatives. As the following examples will illustrate, here too the ability to negotiate costlessly leads to efficient outcomes.

EXAMPLE 17.3

Same as Example 17.1, except now the *confectioner* has access to a soundproofing device that will completely eliminate the noise from his machines. The cost of the device is 20, which means that if he installs it his net gain from operating will fall from 40 to 20. As in Example 17.1, the doctor will gain 60 if there is no noise, 0 if there is noise.

If the confectioner is liable for noise damage, his best option will be to install the soundproofing. His alternatives are either to shut down or to pay the doctor 60 in noise damages, and each of these is clearly worse. If the confectioner is not liable, it will be in the doctor's interest to pay the confectioner to install the

Legal regime	Outcome	Net benefit		
		Doctor	Confectioner	Total
Liable	Confectioner installs soundproofing at own expense	60	20	80
Not liable	Doctor pays confectioner P to install soundproofing, $20 \leqslant P \leqslant 60$	$60 - P$	$20 + P$	80

TABLE 17.3
Outcome and Payoff Summary for Example 17.3
The gain to the confectioner from operating without soundproofing is 40. Soundproofing costs 20. The loss to the doctor from the confectioner's noise is 60. The efficient outcome is for the confectioner to install soundproofing and to continue operating, and this happens under both legal regimes.

soundproofing. His alternative, after all, is to shut down or to endure the noise damage. The minimum payment that would be acceptable to the confectioner to install the soundproofing is 20, its cost. The most the doctor would be willing to pay for him to install it is 60, the amount the doctor would lose if it weren't installed. Again letting P denote the payment from the doctor to the confectioner, the outcomes and payoffs for the two legal regimes are as summarized in Table 17.3.

Let us now consider what happens when the doctor too has some adjustment he can make to escape the damage caused by the confectioner's noise.

Same as Example 17.3, except now the doctor can escape the noise damage by moving his examination room to the other side of his office. The noisy room in which he now examines patients could then be used for storage. The cost to the doctor of this rearrangement is 18.

EXAMPLE 17.4

With this new option available, the doctor is the one who is able to eliminate the noise damage at the lowest possible cost. If the confectioner is liable for noise damage, he will offer the doctor a payment P to compensate him for rearranging his office. The payment must be at least 18, or else the doctor would not make the accommodation. (Recall that, with the confectioner liable, the doctor has the option of being fully compensated for any noise damage.) And the payment cannot exceed 20, or else the confectioner could install soundproofing and solve the problem on his own. If the confectioner is not liable for noise damage, the doctor will rearrange his office at his own expense. The outcomes and payoffs for this example are summarized in Table 17.4. Note that we again get the efficient outcome no matter which legal regime we choose. Note also that the choice of legal regime again affects the distribution of costs and benefits, only this time by a much smaller margin than in Example 17.3. The difference is that each party now has a relatively inexpensive method for solving the noise problem unilaterally. In Example 17.3, the doctor lacked such an alternative, making the confectioner's bargaining power very strong when he was not liable for noise damage. In this example, by contrast, the confectioner cannot extract a large payment from the doctor for keeping quiet because the doctor can solve the noise problem on his own.

The patterns revealed in the preceding examples may be stated formally as:

The Coase Theorem: When the parties affected by externalities can negotiate costlessly with one another, an efficient outcome results no matter how the law assigns responsibility for damages.

618   CHAPTER 17   EXTERNALITIES, PROPERTY RIGHTS, AND THE COASE THEOREM

TABLE 17.4

Outcome and Payoff Summary for Example 17.4

The gain to the confectioner from operating without soundproofing is 40. Soundproofing costs 20. The loss to the doctor from the confectioner's noise is 60. The doctor can rearrange his office to eliminate the noise problem at a cost of 18. The efficient outcome is for the doctor to rearrange his office, and this happens under both legal regimes.

Legal regime	Outcome	Net benefit		
		Doctor	Confectioner	Total
Liable	Confectioner pays doctor P to rearrange his office, $18 \leq P \leq 20$	$42 + P$	$40 - P$	82
Not liable	Doctor rearranges, his office at his own expense	42	40	82

In the wake of its publication, Coase's classic paper became a subject of great controversy. Many took him to be saying that there is no real role for government in solving problems related to pollution, noise, and other externalities. By this interpretation, Coase's message seemed to be that if government stays out of the way, people will always come up with efficient solutions on their own. And yet Coase stated clearly that this conclusion holds only for a world in which parties can negotiate with one another at relatively low cost. He recognized that there are many important externalities for which this assumption is not satisfied. At the simplest level, time and energy are required for negotiation, and when the potential benefits are small, it may simply not be worth it. Alternatively, there are situations in which a single polluter causes damage to a large number of people. Negotiating with large groups is inherently difficult and costly, and each person in the group faces strong incentives to escape these costs. Another serious barrier to negotiation is the problem of how to divide the surplus. Recall from Example 17.3 that the efficient outcome was for the doctor to pay the confectioner to install soundproofing. The minimum payment acceptable to the confectioner was 20, the cost of the soundproofing. The most the confectioner could hope to extract from the doctor was 60, the value to the doctor of eliminating the noise. The doctor would naturally like to pay only 20, and the confectioner would like to get 60. If each takes a hard line in the discussion, animosities may emerge and the possibility of a deal may break down altogether. For these and a host of other reasons, negotiations are often costly. When they are, it matters very much indeed which legal regime we choose, as the following examples will illustrate.

EXAMPLE 17.5

As in Example 17.2, suppose that the gain to the doctor in a noise-free environment is 40, while the gain to the confectioner from unfettered operations is 60. Suppose also that the confectioner has access to a soundproofing device that eliminates all noise damage at a cost of 20. And suppose, finally, that it costs the doctor and confectioner 25 to negotiate a private agreement between themselves. For negotiation to be a worthwhile alternative, they must be able to share this cost in some way that makes each of them better off than if they did not negotiate.

If the confectioner is made liable for noise damage, he will install the soundproofing. His next-best alternative, after all, is to pay the doctor 40 in noise damages,[4] and the installation of soundproofing costs him only 20. Because being liable gives the confectioner an incentive to install the soundproofing on his own,

---
[4]For the confectioner to operate and pay noise damages to the doctor, it is not necessary for them to incur the cost of negotiating a private agreement.

Legal regime	Outcome	Net benefit		
		Doctor	Confectioner	Total
Liable	Confectioner installs soundproofing at his own expense	40	40	80
Not liable	Confectioner does not install soundproofing; doctor shuts down	0	60	60

TABLE 17.5
Outcome and Payoff Summary for Example 17.5
The gain to the confectioner from operating without soundproofing is 60. Soundproofing costs 20. The loss to the doctor from the confectioner's noise is 40. The cost of negotiating a private agreement is 25. The efficient outcome is for the confectioner to install soundproofing, but this happens only when he is made liable for noise damage.

there is no need for him to negotiate an agreement with the doctor, and thus no need to incur the cost of negotiation.

But now suppose that the confectioner is not liable for noise damage. If there were no costs of negotiation, the doctor would pay the confectioner P, where $20 \leq P \leq 40$, to install soundproofing. If it costs 25 to negotiate an agreement, however, then it is no longer possible for the doctor to compensate the confectioner for installing soundproofing. The soundproofing makes it possible for the doctor to gain 40, which is insufficient to cover both the cost of the soundproofing (20) and the cost of negotiating the agreement (25), which total 45. When it is costly to negotiate, we no longer get the efficient outcome irrespective of which legal regime we choose. In this example, for which the relevant data are summarized in Table 17.5, we get the most efficient result only if the confectioner is liable.

In Example 17.5, the total gain for society as a whole is 80 if the confectioner is liable, only 60 if he is not liable. But as the following example will illustrate, the existence of barriers to negotiation does not guarantee that we will always get an efficient outcome by making parties liable for the damage caused by external effects.

Same as Example 17.5, except the confectioner no longer has a soundproofing option; instead, the doctor has the option of avoiding the noise by rearranging his office, which will cost him 18.

EXAMPLE 17.6

If the confectioner is not liable for noise damage, this is exactly what the doctor will do. But if the confectioner is liable, the cost of negotiation now stands in the way of his paying the doctor to rearrange his office. The sum of negotiating costs (25) and rearrangement costs (18) comes to 43, which is 3 more than the 40 that will be saved by avoiding the noise. So if he is liable, the best option available to the confectioner is simply to continue operating and pay the doctor 40 for the noise damage.[5] Here, unlike Example 17.5, we get the efficient outcome when the confectioner is not liable. The data for Example 17.6 are summarized in Table 17.6.

EXERCISE 17.1

How would the entries in Table 17.6 be affected if the cost of negotiation were 20 instead of 25?

---

[5]Again, making a liability payment does not require the parties to incur the costs of negotiation.

TABLE 17.6
Outcome and Payoff Summary for Example 17.6
The gain to the confectioner from operating is 60. The loss to the doctor from the confectioner's noise is 40. The doctor can escape the noise by rearranging his office at a cost of 18. The cost of negotiating a private agreement is 25. The efficient outcome is for the doctor to rearrange his office, but this happens only when the confectioner is not liable for noise damage.

Legal regime	Outcome	Net benefit		
		Doctor	Confectioner	Total
Liable	Confectioner operates and pays doctor 40 for noise damage	40	20	60
Not liable	Doctor rearranges his office at his own expense	22	60	82

Application: External Effects from Nuclear Power Plants

Although Austria itself has had a law banning nuclear power plants since 1978, it is surrounded by countries that operate a total of 41 such plants. Two of these plants, located just 35 miles from the Austrian border with Slovakia, share important design features with the ill-fated Chernobyl plant that in 1986 experienced the worst nuclear accident in history. Thus the citizens of Austria were understandably concerned about their vulnerability to a similar mishap.

In a remarkably bold application of the reasoning Coase suggested, Austrian officials offered in January 1991 to provide Slovakia (then part of Czechoslovakia) with free electric power as an inducement to shut down the two Soviet-designed reactors.[6] Austrian Economics Minister Wolfgang Scheussel estimated that the cost of the replacement power would be about $350 million annually.

Czech Premier Marian Calfa expressed interest in the Austrian offer and pledged that a working group would study it. In the years since the proposal was initially made, however, no agreement has been reached to implement it. As this experience illustrates, the costs of negotiation sometimes stand in the way even of agreements that would substantially benefit both parties.

Coase's observation that people will reach efficient outcomes when they can negotiate costlessly has widespread application. In many situations, after all, the costs of negotiation are small relative to the benefits of reaching agreements about externalities. But the more far-reaching implications of Coase's work lie in the pattern illustrated in Examples 17.5 and 17.6, where we find the seeds of a very powerful theory of law and social institutions. Boiled down to its essence, the theory can be stated as the following rule:

> Efficient laws and social institutions are the ones that place the burden of adjustment to externalities on those who can accomplish it at least cost.

One of the immediate implications of this rule is that the best laws regarding harmful effects cannot be identified unless we know something about how much it costs different parties to avoid harmful effects. If, as in Example 17.5, the emitter of noise has lower costs, we get an efficient outcome by making him liable for damages. But if the person adversely affected by the noise has a lower cost of avoidance, as in Example 17.6, we do better by not making the noisemaker liable.

The efficiency rule finds application in a rich variety of situations, several of which we examine in the sections that follow.

---

[6]See Michael Z. Wise, "Prague Offered Payoff to Shut Nuclear Plant," *The Washington Post*, January 30, 1991.

PROPERTY RIGHTS

Private Property Laws and Their Exceptions

No free-market economy can function successfully without laws that govern the use of private property. Among other things, these laws describe how people can lawfully acquire different types of property—by inheriting it, purchasing it, or receiving it as a gift, but not by theft or other means that entail the use of force. In most cases, these laws grant owners of property the right to exclude others from using it without permission. Yet hosts of detailed exceptions sharply limit this right to exclude. As the following Economic Naturalist examples suggest, these exceptions are not random. Rather, they follow a systematic pattern, one that the insights of Coase help us to understand.

Why does the law permit airlines to operate flights over private land without permission?

Think back to the discussion with which we began this chapter about the rights to use airspace over various parcels of land. For a developer to build a hotel in the airspace above my land, he must first secure my permission, which I will grant only in return for a substantial payment. But even in the aftermath of the terrorist attacks of September 11, 2001, the law permits commercial airliners to fly over my land without payment whenever they choose. Why this distinction?

Note first that each case involves an externality—the visual blight and inconvenience of having a hotel overhead in the first case, the noise and possible danger from the airplanes in the second. The cost to me of the first externality is much larger than the second, but that alone cannot account for why we treat the two cases differently, since the benefits to the developer from erecting a building over my land are also likely to be great. The crucial distinction is that individual negotiation is much more practical in the case of the developer than in the case of the airlines. In the former case, there are only two parties involved, and the benefits from an efficient outcome are likely to be large enough to justify the costs of negotiation. So in this case, we can feel confident of achieving an efficient outcome most of the time if we define property rights to exclude developers from building in the airspace above our houses. In the airline case, by contrast, the benefits of flying over any single house are small, and in any event, the cost of negotiating with all the potentially affected parties would be prohibitive. Because the total benefits of overflight are large relative to the total costs imposed on homeowners, we get an efficient outcome here if property rights do not permit landowners to exclude planes from flying overhead.

Should commercial aircraft be allowed to fly over private land without the property owner's permission?

There are exceptions to this general principle, however, and these too provide an illuminating illustration of the Coasian efficiency rule. The most conspicuous exception involves approach and takeoff lanes to and from airports near major metropolitan areas. Jets fly low to the ground just after takeoff and just before landing, and the noise that reaches property below is often deafening. In these situations, local ordinances commonly prohibit landings and takeoffs during the hours when it is most costly (difficult) for property owners to adjust to noise—namely, the hours when most of them are sleeping. Here again, negotiation on an individual basis is impractical, and the best we can do is to define rights to achieve the lowest cost of accommodation.

622   CHAPTER 17   EXTERNALITIES, PROPERTY RIGHTS, AND THE COASE THEOREM

FIGURE 17.1
Lakeshore Property and the Law of Trespass
The cost of getting from *A* to *C* without crossing *C*'s property is much higher than by the direct route along the lakeshore. For this reason, the law does not allow lakeshore homeowners to exclude people from walking across their property.

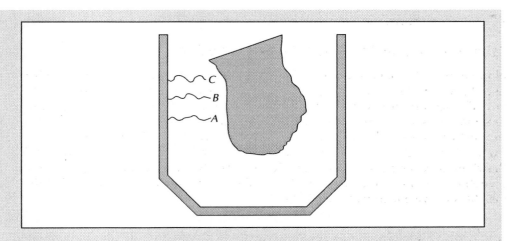

ECONOMIC NATURALIST 17.2

Should trespassing on waterfront property be permitted?

Why does the law of trespass not apply along waterfront property?

In many cultures of the world, people regard a stranger walking across their land as an intrusion. The trespasser, in the economist's parlance, confers a negative externality on the property owner. Such externalities might be dealt with in a variety of ways. Most of my neighbors, for example, have built fences across their yards to prevent people from taking shortcuts across their property. Some even post signs saying to beware of violent dogs. In most jurisdictions, it is perfectly lawful to take such steps to exclude others from using your property. And yet the laws of my community do not afford the same rights to people who own cottages on the shore of nearby Cayuga Lake. On the contrary, they explicitly permit any citizen to walk across any parcel of land located along the lakeshore.

This distinction exists not because the owners of lakeshore property value their privacy any less than others do. Rather, it is because the cost of not being able to cross a person's land along the lakeshore is so much higher than it is elsewhere. To illustrate, suppose that *A*, *B*, and *C* in Figure 17.1 are three lakeshore properties and that someone at *A* wants to visit someone at *C*. Access to lakeshore properties by road involves travel from the main highway down long, steep, often treacherous driveways. Lacking the ability to cross *B*'s property, *A* would have to ascend his driveway out to the main road, travel to *C*'s driveway, and then make the trip down it. Because the costs of this circuitous routing are so much larger than the costs of the direct path along the lakeshore, the law of trespass makes an exception for these properties. Their owners consider an occasional unwelcome disturbance a small price to pay for the additional convenience of being able to travel freely along the lakeshore.

By contrast, the right to cross someone's property in my neighborhood would be worth relatively little. The streets are all close together, so there is always a relatively easy way to get where you want to go without having to take shortcuts. With respect to potential trespass on both the lakeshore and other properties, negotiation is prohibitively costly on a case-by-case basis. So the law of property defines rights of access in the way that, on average, leads to an efficient outcome. It gives most property owners the right to exclude, but withholds that right from the owners of lakeshore property.

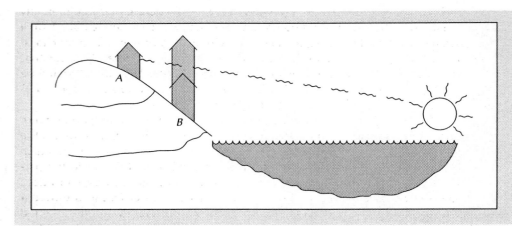

FIGURE 17.2
The Value of an Unobstructed View
It is efficient for *B* to build a two-story house if and only if the extra value of the taller house to *B* is greater than the value to *A* of maintaining his view.

Why are property laws often suspended during storms?

On the 13th day of November 1804, the Ploof family went sailing on Vermont's Lake Champlain. A sudden violent storm came up, making it impossible for them to get back to their home port. In desperation, they took refuge by tying up at a dock on an island in the lake. The dock was owned by a Mr. Putnam, who sent his servant down to order the Ploofs off his property. The Ploofs cast off into the storm, and shortly thereafter their sloop was destroyed, injuring several family members. The Ploofs later filed a successful damage suit against Putnam. The court decided that although Putnam would ordinarily have the right to exclude people from using his dock, the circumstances of the storm created an exception. Note that in deciding the case this way, the Vermont court was mimicking the result that dock owners and boat owners would generally reach for themselves if it were possible to negotiate costlessly and dispassionately during a storm. The value of the dock to a boater in distress is almost certainly higher than the value to the owner of being able to exclude him, and the Vermont court chose to define the state's laws of property with this observation in mind.

Does a property owner always have the right to exclude strangers from using his dock?

ECONOMIC NATURALIST 17.3

Why do building height limits vary from city to city?

Consider the situation pictured in Figure 17.2. Resident *A* owns a house on a hillside overlooking the sea and places high value on being able to watch the sunset from his living room window. Now *B* purchases the property below *A* and is considering which of two houses to build. The first is a one-story house that would leave *A*'s view intact. The second is a two-story design that would completely block *A*'s view. Suppose the gain to *A* from an unobstructed view is 100, the gain to *B* from having a one-story house is 200, and the gain to *B* from a two-story house is 280. If the laws of property let people build houses of any height they chose, and if negotiation between property owners were costless, which of the two houses would *B* build?

To answer this question, first note that the increase in *B*'s gain from having the taller house is 80, which is 20 less than the cost to *A* from the loss of his view. The

ECONOMIC NATURALIST 17.4

Why are zoning laws more strict in San Francisco than in most Midwest cities?

efficient outcome is thus for *B* to build the one-story house. And that is exactly what would happen if the two parties could negotiate costlessly. Rather than see *B* build the taller house, it will be in *A*'s interest to compensate *B* for choosing the shorter version. To do so, he will have to give *B* at least 80, for that is what *B* gives up by not having the two-story house. The most *A* would be willing to give *B* is 100, since that is all the view is worth to *A*. For some payment *P*, where $80 \leq P \leq 100$, *A* will get to keep his view.

Suppose, however, that negotiations between the two parties were impractical. *B* would then go ahead with the two-story house, since that is the version he values most. By comparison with the one-story design, *B* would gain 80, but *A* would lose 100. The optimal structure of property rights in this particular example would be to prohibit any building that blocks a neighbor's view.

Of course, if the valuations assigned by the parties were different, a different conclusion might follow. If, for example, *B* valued the two-story house at 300 and *A*'s view were again worth 100, the optimal structure of property rights would be to allow people to build to whatever height they choose. In either case, the optimal structure of property rights is the one that places the burden of adjustment (either the loss of a view or the loss of a preferred building design) on the party that can accomplish it at the lowest cost.

As a practical matter, the laws of property in many jurisdictions often embody precisely this principle. In cities like San Francisco, where the views of the ocean and bay are breathtakingly beautiful, strict zoning laws regulate construction that blocks an existing building's line of sight. Zoning laws in cities where there is less to look at are generally much more liberal in the kinds of buildings they permit. But even in cities that have no special view to protect, zoning laws generally limit the fraction of the lot that can be occupied by man-made structures. Most people value access to at least some sunlight, and ordinances of this sort make it possible for them to get it.

Most people who grow up in market economies like the United States take the institution of private property rights for granted. But as the preceding examples have made clear, the details of our various property laws have a great deal of economic structure. They embody sophisticated, if often implicit, calculations about how to reach the most efficient solutions to practical problems involving externalities. Indeed, as the following section illustrates, the very existence of private property may be traced to early attempts to deal with externalities.

The Tragedy of the Commons

To explore the origins of the institution of private property, it is instructive to consider, as in the next example, what would happen in a society that lacked a well-developed institution of property rights.

EXAMPLE 17.7

A village has six residents, each of whom has wealth of 100. Each resident may either invest his money in a government bond, which pays 12 percent per year, or use it to buy a year-old steer, which will graze on the village commons (there being no individually owned grazing land in this village). Year-old steers and government bonds each cost exactly 100. Steers require no effort to tend and can be sold for a price that depends on the amount of weight they gain during the year. Yearly

Number of steers	Price per 2-year-old steer
1	120
2	118
3	114
4	111
5	108
6	105

TABLE 17.7
Steer Prices as a Function of Grazing Density
As more steers graze on the commons, each steer gains less weight, resulting in a lower price per steer.

weight gain, in turn, depends on the number of steers that graze on the commons. The prices of 2-year-old steers are given in Table 17.7 as a function of the total number of steers. If village residents make their investment decisions independently, how many steers will graze on the commons?

As long as each villager cannot control access to the commons by cattle owned by others, the income-maximizing strategy will be to send an extra steer out onto the commons if and only if its price next year will be at least 112. (At that price, the gain from owning a steer is equal to the gain from buying a bond.) By this reckoning, there will be 3 steers sent onto the commons, and the rest of the villagers' money will be invested in government bonds. With this pattern of investment, village income from investment will be 14 from each of the 3 steers and 12 from each of the 3 bonds, for a total of 78.

Notice, however, that this is not the largest possible income the villagers could have earned. From the point of view of the village as a whole, the investment rule for steers should be: Send an extra steer onto the commons if and only if its marginal contribution to the value of the total herd after 1 year is greater than or equal to 112. Sending the third steer onto the commons resulted in a total herd worth $3 \times 114 = 342$, which is only 106 more than the value of a herd with only 2 steers ($2 \times 118 = 236$). Total village income is maximized by buying 4 bonds and sending 2 steers onto the commons. This pattern results in an income of 48 from bonds and 36 from steers, for a total of 84.

The reason that the invisible hand failed to produce the best social result here is that individual villagers ignored an important externality. Their criterion for deciding to send another steer was to look only at the price increase that would occur for that particular steer. They took no account of the fact that sending an extra steer would cause existing cattle to gain less weight. Pastureland is a scarce resource in this example, and the villagers failed to allocate it efficiently because they were allowed to use it for free.

The problem would be solved if individual villagers could own pastureland and exclude others from using it. Suppose, for example, the village government decided to put the pastureland up for auction. What price would it fetch? Anyone who buys the pastureland has the right to restrict the number of steers to 2, which is the income-maximizing amount. We saw that, if used in this way, the land will generate an annual income of 36 from an annual investment of 200 (the price of two steers). Had the 200 instead been used to purchase government bonds, only 24 would have been earned. Having control over the commons thus yields a surplus of 12/yr over the income available to a person able to buy only government bonds.

626   CHAPTER 17 EXTERNALITIES, PROPERTY RIGHTS, AND THE COASE THEOREM

FIGURE 17.3
The Tragedy of the Commons
When a resource, such as a fishery or a pasture, is owned in common, each user gets to keep the average product of his own productive inputs he applies to the resource. Privately owned inputs will be applied to the resource until X', the point at which their average product equals their opportunity cost, W, resulting in an economic surplus of zero. The socially optimal allocation is X^*, the level of input for which W is equal to the marginal product of privately owned inputs, and results in an economic surplus of S^*.

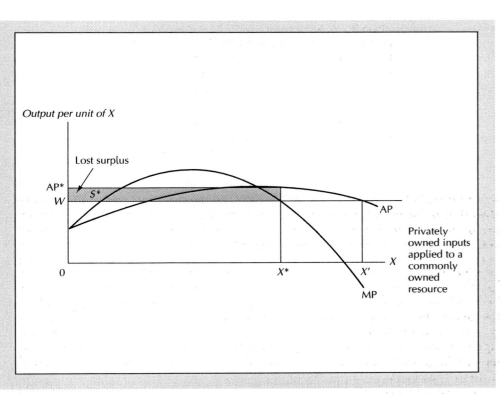

It follows that the price of the pastureland at auction will be 100 (the price of a bond that pays an income of 12/yr). If the price of pastureland were any less than 100, all investors would want to buy it instead of buying government bonds. If it sold for more than 100, every investor could do better by buying government bonds. The village government could take the 100 raised from the auction of its pastureland and distribute it among the 6 villagers, for an average payment of $\frac{100}{6}$.

EXERCISE 17.2

What grazing fee would solve the commons problem discussed in Example 17.7?

In early societies, it was a general practice for important resources such as pastureland and fisheries to be owned in common. The difficulty with such ownership schemes is that they lead to overexploitation of the resource. Figure 17.3 illustrates the problem of individual villagers who have the option of working in a factory at a wage of W/day, or of keeping all the fish they can catch from the village lake. The curve labeled AP shows how the average catch per fisherman varies with the number of fishermen, while MP shows the change in the total catch as a function of the number of fishermen. If fishermen get to keep whatever they catch, their decision rule will be to fish up to X', the point where $AP = W$. At X', the value of the total catch is exactly equal to the total income that the villagers who fished could have earned by working in the factory.

The socially optimal allocation is to fish only up to X^* in Figure 17.3, the point at which $W = MP$, and for all remaining villagers to work in the factory.

At this allocation, the villagers who fish will earn a total of S^* (the shaded area) more than they could have earned by working in the factory.

If villagers are given free access to fish in the lake, the allocation that sends X^* out to fish will not be stable. Because each fisherman will be earning more than the villagers who work in the factory, factory workers will have an incentive to switch to fishing. Switching will stop only when X' have gone out to fish, making earnings in the two alternatives the same. As in the earlier pastureland example, the additional fishermen ignore the externality they impose on the existing fishermen. Each looks only at the size of his own catch, ignoring the fact that his presence makes everyone else's catch smaller.

In order to sustain the efficient allocation, something must be done to limit access to the lake. The simplest approach is to charge people for the right to go fishing. If the fishing fee were set at $AP^* - W$ (see Figure 17.3), the optimal allocation would result automatically from the income-maximizing decisions of individual villagers. Here, as in the pasture example, the problem was that individuals overutilized a productive resource they were allowed to use for free. The invisible hand mechanism can function properly only when all resources sell for prices that reflect their true economic value.

One of the continuing sources of inefficiency in modern economies involves the allocation of resources that no single nation's property laws can govern. For instance, several species of whales have been hunted to near extinction because no international laws of property exist to restrain individual incentives to kill whales. And the Mediterranean Sea has long had serious problems with pollution because none of the many nations that border it has an economic incentive

"Gentlemen, it's time we gave some serious thought to the effects of global warming."

628   CHAPTER 17   EXTERNALITIES, PROPERTY RIGHTS, AND THE COASE THEOREM

to consider the effects of its discharges on other countries. As the world's population continues to grow, the absence of an effective system of international property rights will become an economic problem of increasing significance.

An important case in point is the trend toward global warming. Scientists now estimate that if carbon dioxide and other greenhouse gases continue to accumulate in the atmosphere at current rates, the earth's average temperature will rise by as much as 8 degrees Fahrenheit in this century—enough to melt the polar ice caps and flood thousands of square miles of coastal land. If a single agency had the power to enact globally binding environmental legislation, it would be a straightforward, albeit costly, matter to reduce the buildup of greenhouse gases. But in our world of sovereign nations, this power does not exist.

EXTERNALITIES, EFFICIENCY, AND FREE SPEECH

As the following discussion illustrates, the Coasian principles of efficiency apply not only to the design of property rights but also to the design of constitutions. In particular, they shed light on the extent to which society has an interest in protecting the right to free speech.

The First Amendment to the U.S. Constitution protects most forms of speech and expression, even those that cause intensely painful effects on others. A man once wrote to a newspaper advice columnist to confess to a cruel act he had committed decades earlier, during his senior year in high school. He and his friends had leafed through the school yearbook and picked out the photograph of the girl they agreed was the ugliest in their class. The letter writer had then called the girl on the telephone to congratulate her on her selection. During the ensuing years, he had never been able to forget her anguished groan in response. He would give anything, he said, if he could turn back the clock and recant that phone call.

Given the choice between receiving such a telephone call and being hit sharply on the arm with a stick, many people would immediately choose the latter. Had the boys hit the girl with a stick, they could have been put in jail. And yet they were perfectly within their First Amendment rights to make that phone call.

Why does our Constitution prohibit one form of harm but not the other? In the Coasian framework, the first thing to recognize is that it is highly impractical to negotiate solutions case by case to either type of harmful effect. We just cannot imagine the boys and the girl dickering about what she would be willing to pay to avoid hearing a painful remark or, for that matter, to avoid being struck with a stick. The structure of the law must therefore be guided by a judgment about which structure of rights will generate the best outcome where case-by-case negotiation is impractical.

Most people would surely agree that the world would be better if speech like the telephone prank could be prohibited. The practical question is whether it is possible to frame a law that would prevent such speech without preventing other speech that we value highly. Sadly, the answer seems to be no. Any law that prevented people from making cruel remarks to others would almost surely prohibit a great deal of highly valuable speech as well. The fear of criticism keeps many an otherwise wayward person in line, much to society's benefit. If it were practical to write a law that would permit justified criticism but prohibit criticism that is unwarranted, or even merely unkind, we might be seriously tempted to implement it. But so far, no one has come up with such a law.

Even so, the First Amendment's protection of free speech is far from absolute. For example, it does not protect a person's right to yell "Fire" in a crowded theater. Nor does it permit people to shout profanities on public street corners. Nor are we permitted to advocate the overthrow of the government by violent means. In such cases, we seem willing to say that the benefits of free speech are too small to justify its external costs.

SMOKING RULES, PUBLIC AND PRIVATE

Research studies show that exposure to cigarette smoke exhaled by others can be harmful to one's health. Such findings have lent considerable support to the recent trend toward laws that ban smoking in public places. On the plausible assumptions that (1) negotiating with strangers in public places is generally impractical and (2) the harm to nonsmokers from undesired exposure to smoke is more important than the harm to smokers from not being able to smoke in public places, such laws make good sense in the Coasian framework.

Thus far, however, no law has been proposed that would disallow smoking in private dwellings. The result is that sometimes people are exposed to smoke from their roommates. On the plausible assumption that the costs of negotiation with prospective roommates is relatively low, the following example illustrates that the lack of such laws is not likely to lead to an undesirable outcome.

Smith and Jones are trying to decide whether to share a two-bedroom apartment or to live separately in one-bedroom apartments. The rental fees are $300/mo for one-bedroom and $420/mo—or $210/mo per person—for two-bedroom apartments. Smith is a smoker and would be willing to give up $250/mo rather than give up being able to smoke at home. Jones, however, is a nonsmoker and would sacrifice up to $150/mo rather than live with a smoker. Apart from the issues of smoking and rent, the two find joint living neither more nor less attractive than living alone. Neither has an alternative roommate available. Will they live together or separately?

EXAMPLE 17.8

If they live separately, each can have things the way he wants on the smoking issue. The downside is that it is more costly to live alone. If they live together, they will save on rent, but one of them will have to compromise. Either Smith will have to give up smoking, or Jones will have to tolerate Smith's smoke. If a compromise is to be made at all, it will be made by Jones, since he is willing to pay less than Smith is to have his way. By living together, each party saves $90/mo in rent. If we ignore the possibility of negotiation, they will not live together because this savings is less than the cost to Jones of having to live with a smoker.

But suppose they are able to negotiate costlessly. The practical question then becomes whether the *total* savings in rent justifies the cost of the compromise to Jones. The total savings in rent is $180/mo, which is the difference between the $600/mo total they would pay if they lived alone and the $420 they will pay living together. And since this savings exceeds the cost to Jones by $30/mo, it should be possible to negotiate an agreement whereby the two will prefer to live together. Smith will have to give some of his $90/mo savings to Jones.

Let X denote the amount Smith gives to Jones. Since the cost to Jones of living with a smoker is $150/mo, and his savings in rent is only $90/mo, X must be at least $60/mo. Because Smith gets to continue smoking in the shared living arrangement, his $90/mo rent savings is pure gain, which means that $90/mo is the largest possible value for X. The relevant details for this example are summarized in Table 17.8.

630   CHAPTER 17   EXTERNALITIES, PROPERTY RIGHTS, AND THE COASE THEOREM

TABLE 17.8
Payoff Summary for Example 17.8
The cost to Smith of not smoking is $250/mo. The cost to Jones of living with a smoker is $150/mo. The total savings in rent from living together is $600/mo − $420/mo = $180/mo, which is $30/mo more than the least costly compromise required by shared living quarters, which is the $150/mo it costs Jones to live with a smoker.

	Net rental payment ($/mo)		Net gain ($/mo)		
	Jones	Smith	Jones	Smith	Total
Live separately	300	300	—	—	—
Live together; Smith pays Jones X to compensate for smoke, $60 \leqslant X \leqslant 90$	$210 - X$	$210 + X$	$X - 60$	$90 - X$	30

Example 17.8 drives home the point that external effects are completely reciprocal. Smith's smoking harms Jones, just as traditional discussions of the issue emphasize. But denying Smith the opportunity to smoke will harm him, at least as he sees it. When it comes to the question of sharing living quarters, the smoke problem is a quintessentially shared problem. Because people are free to make whatever living arrangements they find mutually agreeable, Jones cannot be forced to endure smoke against his wishes. And by the same token, Smith cannot be forced to give up smoking. If they are to reap the savings from living together, one party must compromise on the smoke issue, and the other must compromise financially. Unless the terms of their agreement represent a clear improvement for both parties over the alternative of living alone, there will simply be no agreement.

> **EXERCISE 17.3**
>
> **How would the entries in Table 17.8 be different if there were an exhaust system that completely eliminated the damage from smoke at a cost of $60/mo?**

POSITIVE EXTERNALITIES

The Coase theorem applies not only to negative externalities but also to positive ones. Recall from Chapter 16 the example of the beekeeper and the owner of the apple orchard. The activities of each confer positive externalities on the other, which, if ignored, will result in suboptimally small levels of both apple and honey production. But if negotiation between them is costless, the beekeeper can offer to subsidize the orchard owner for planting more trees. The orchard owner, likewise, can offer payments to induce the beekeeper to enlarge his apiary. With either positive or negative externalities, inefficiencies result only if it is costly or otherwise impractical to negotiate agreements about how to correct them.

POSITIONAL EXTERNALITIES

In many areas of endeavor, rewards are determined not by our absolute performance, but by how we perform relative to others. To be a champion swimmer, for example, what counts is not how fast you swim in absolute terms, but how your times compare with others'. As we noted earlier, Mark Spitz won seven gold medals in the 1972 Olympics, and yet his winning times would not even have qualified him for the 2000 American men's swimming team.

Situations in which rewards are determined by relative performance are often called contests. In virtually every contest, each contestant will take a variety of actions in an attempt to enhance his or her probability of winning. Indeed, to take such actions is the essence of what it means to be in a contest. Some of these actions entail only minimal costs. Swimmers, for example, sometimes shave the hair from their heads and bodies in order to glide more smoothly through the water.

But in every contest where something important is at stake, competitors almost always take much more costly steps to win. In the race for national political office, contestants spend millions on advertising. In the race for military supremacy, nations invest billions developing and building new weapons.

Because the rewards in contests are distributed according to relative position, the laws of simple arithmetic tell us that any action that increases one contestant's chances of winning must necessarily reduce the chances of others. With this observation in mind, it is instructive to think of performance-enhancing actions as giving rise to *positional externalities*. If A and B are competing for a prize that only one of them can attain, anything that helps A will necessarily harm B.

The result is that when the stakes are high, unregulated contests almost always lead to costly *positional arms races*. In the absence of effective drug regulations, for example, many linemen in the National Football League apparently now feel compelled to enhance their size and strength by using anabolic steroids. It is easy to see why. In an arena where sheer physical bulk plays a central role, failure to use these dangerous hormones might obviously jeopardize a player's position on his team.

Like so many other arms races, however, the race to grow bigger and stronger yields few real benefits for the group of contestants as a whole. After all, the contest at the line of scrimmage can have only one winner, whether each team's linemen average 300 pounds or 240. At the same time, the race imposes substantial costs. Anabolic steroids have been linked to cancer of the liver and other serious health problems.

In hockey it is standard procedure for defensemen to throw their bodies to the ice to prevent an opponent's shot from going into the net. In NCAA hockey contests, this practice seldom causes serious injury anymore, because players are now required to wear helmets with heavy wire cages over the face openings. But before the appearance of these helmets, it was a risky proposition indeed. When a hockey puck traveling at more than 100 miles/hr makes contact with a human face, the results are ugly. On objective grounds, it seems utter folly for a player to risk mutilation by throwing his face in the path of the puck. And yet few players ever hesitated to do so when the chance arose. The urge to win—to do well in relative terms—is a powerful force of human nature. In situations where the material payoffs from winning are very large, this is hardly surprising. But even when the stakes are ostensibly low—as, for example, in a nonleague high school hockey game in upstate New York—people go to extreme lengths to enhance their chances.

Given what is at stake, voluntary restraint is rarely an effective solution to positional arms races. And so governing bodies in many sports now require strict drug testing of all competing athletes. The NCAA's helmet rule, similarly, has been a face-saving solution, both literally and figuratively; without it, few players would have dared to wear a face cage on their own. (In the National Hockey League, which has no similar requirement, helmets with face cages are rarer than defensemen's front teeth.)

As a further illustration of collective restraint of positional externalities, consider the ancient practice of dueling. A gentleman once felt compelled to defend his honor by challenging the offending party to a duel with pistols at sunrise. Duelists, and the people who cared about them, soon recognized the unfettered duel as an unacceptably costly practice. Over time, rules evolved that reduced the mortality rate. For example, the distance at which the pistols were fired grew steadily longer. And pistols with spiral-grooved barrels were forbidden. (Such grooves impart a spin to the bullet, making its trajectory much more true.) With these restrictions in place, only 1 in 6 duelists was actually struck by a bullet, and only 1 in 14 died. This was still a steep price to pay, of course, and it eventually led to an outright prohibition against dueling. With firm legal sanctions in place, we are now able to maintain our honor in a variety of much less injurious ways.

One of the most important contests people face in life is the task of making sure their children enter the labor market with a good education. This task is a contest because a "good" education, like an "effective" lineman, is an inescapably *relative* concept. If an effective lineman is one who is bigger, stronger, and faster than most other linemen, a good education is one that is *better than the education that most others receive*. This relativistic aspect of our objective is what makes us vulnerable to a positional arms race of the sort we see elsewhere.

In the education context, what form does this arms race take? Because public schools are funded largely by local property taxes, educational quality and neighborhood quality are closely linked in our public school systems. Competition for position thus often involves trying to move to the best possible neighborhoods. It is common for families to endure many hardships—working long hours, accepting risky jobs, going without vacations, skimping on savings, and so on—in order to scrape together the cash needed to move into a better school district. Again, however, the laws of simple arithmetic remind us that it is not possible for *everyone* in society to move forward in relative terms. Only 10 percent of our children can occupy the top tenth of our school seats, no matter how valiantly everyone strives.

Even in contests with very low stakes, we have seen that people often accept considerable sacrifice and risk to enhance their chances of winning. The contest to launch our children well in life is a contest whose stakes are high. Any one family's efforts to move forward in relative terms impose a negative externality on others. In a variety of other contexts, we have seen that social institutions evolve to promote efficient solutions to externalities. Armed with this view, we can gain similar new insights into a variety of social institutions that restrain the positional arms race among families. The traditional explanations for many of these institutions, we will see, often raise more questions than they answer.

Limiting the Workweek

The Fair Labor Standards Act requires, among other things, that employers pay a 50 percent wage premium whenever people work more than 8 hours a day or

40 hours a week. This regulation sharply discourages overtime work, and has been defended on the grounds that, without it, monopsony employers would require workers to work unacceptably long hours.

Critics of overtime laws respond that if workers disliked working long hours, competition would result in an overtime premium even without a regulation. Alternatively, if workers wanted to work long hours, why would they support a law that discourages employers from having them do so? In the eyes of its detractors, the overtime law is either irrelevant or harmful.

Positional externalities suggest an alternative rationale for work hours regulation. If someone stays a few extra hours at work, she will increase her earnings, both in absolute and in relative terms. One result is that she will be able to afford a house in a better school district. But again, the problem is that one family's forward movement in relative terms means a backward movement for others. Rather than see their families fall behind, others will feel pressure to work longer hours themselves. In the end, these efforts are largely offsetting. As before, only 10 percent of our children can occupy seats in top-decile school districts.

By working until 8 P.M. each day, we can produce more and enjoy larger incomes than if we work only until 5 P.M. But in the process, we have less time to spend with our families and friends. It is easy to see why people might prefer to live in communities where everyone quits work at 5 P.M. And it is equally easy to see why there might be few such communities in the absence of overtime laws.

Savings

Many observers complain, correctly, that the Social Security system prevents them from deciding for themselves when and how much to save for retirement. On the traditional view that having more options is better than having fewer, it would appear better for participation in Social Security to be purely voluntary. Yet most societies have mandatory programs to supplement retirement incomes. Positional externalities may again help us to understand why.

The argument is essentially the same as in the case of hours regulation. A parent has the choice of saving some of her current income for retirement or spending that income now on a house in a better school district. As before, many parents find the second option compelling.

The aggregate effects of such choices, however, fall short of what parents intend. When everyone spends more on a house in a better school district, the result is merely to bid up the prices of those houses. In the process, no one moves forward in the educational hierarchy, and yet parents end up having too little savings for retirement. Acting as individuals, however, their only real alternative is to send their children to less desirable schools.

The Social Security system mitigates this dilemma by making a portion of each person's income unavailable for spending. It helps solve a related set of positional externalities as well. A job seeker, for example, is well advised to look as good as he or she possibly can for job interviews. Looking good, however, is not a simple matter of wearing clothes that are clean and mended. Like a good education, a tasteful appearance is a relative concept. To look good means to look better than others, and the most practical way to do that is to spend more than most others do on clothing. The rub is that this same calculus operates for everyone. In the end, we get a fruitless escalation in the amount a person has to spend on clothing merely to avoid looking shabby. Viewed from the perspective of the population as a whole, it would make sense to save more and spend less on clothing. But it would not pay any individual, acting alone, to take this step. The Social Security system, by sheltering a portion of our incomes, limits how much people spend in this and a variety of other analogous situations.

Workplace Safety

As a final illustration of positional externalities, consider the case of safety regulations in the workplace. As in the case of hours regulations, proponents of safety regulations often defend them by saying that monopsonists would otherwise force their workers to labor under unacceptably risky conditions. But as we saw in Chapter 14, this argument seriously underestimates the pressures of competition in the labor market. With these pressures in mind, critics of safety regulation say that it deprives workers of the right to decide for themselves how much safety they want to purchase in the workplace.

Once we take positional externalities into account, however, the institution of safety regulation appears less puzzling. One worker's choice of a riskier job makes it difficult for other workers to bid as effectively as before for houses in the best school districts. Feeling this pressure, they too are more likely to opt for riskier jobs. In positional terms, of course, these movements largely offset one another. People may prefer to neutralize this arms race by adopting laws that set minimum standards for workplace safety.[7]

TAXING EXTERNALITIES

Before the appearance of Coase's 1960 paper, the economics profession was wedded to the view, pioneered by the British economist A. C. Pigou, that the best solution to negative externalities is to tax them. The idea is simple. If *A* carries out an activity that imposes a cost on *B*, then taxing *A* by the amount of that cost will provide him with the proper incentive to consider the externality in his production decisions. As the following example makes clear, however, such taxes sometimes make matters worse than if we did nothing at all.

EXAMPLE 17.9

Consider again the doctor and confectioner from Examples 17.1 through 17.6. Suppose that the doctor gains 60 by operating in a noise-free environment, and that the confectioner gains 40 by operating his noisy equipment. Suppose also that the doctor can eliminate the noise problem by rearranging his office at a cost of 18. And suppose, finally, that negotiation between the doctor and confectioner is

---

[7]Whether such standards achieve their stated goal of making the workplace safer is strictly an empirical question. Some authors have argued that the bureaucratic inefficiencies of safety regulation have actually led to *reduced* safety levels. See Albert Nichols and Richard Zeckhauser, "Government Comes to the Workplace: An Assessment of OSHA," *The Public Interest, 49*, 1977: 39–69.

prohibitively costly. The tax approach calls for a tax on the confectioner equal to the damage his activity would cause, which, in the absence of a response by the doctor, means a tax of 60. How will the outcome under such a tax compare with what would have happened in its absence?

If there were costless negotiation, the confectioner could pay the doctor to rearrange his office and then operate without paying the tax, since his operation would cause no noise damage. But since negotiation is impractical, the doctor has no reason to incur this cost on his own. He knows that by doing nothing, the confectioner will face a tax of 60 if he operates, which in turn means that the confectioner's best option is to shut down. After all, his operation generates a gain of only 40 to begin with. With the confectioner no longer in operation, the doctor will gain 60 and the confectioner 0.

With no tax, however, the confectioner would have continued operations, for a gain of 40. The doctor's best response would have been to rearrange his office at a cost of 18, leaving him with a net gain of 42. Without the tax, we thus get the most efficient outcome, whereas the total gain with the tax is considerably smaller. The relevant data for this example are summarized in Table 17.9.

As Example 17.9 amply demonstrates, a tax on pollution can leave us in a worse position than if there were no tax at all. This is not surprising once we recognize that a tax on pollution has essentially the same effect as making the polluter liable for pollution damages. But this same recognition implies that taxation will not *always* be inefficient. It happened to be inefficient in Example 17.9 because the doctor happened to be the party who was best able to deal with the noise problem and the tax removed all incentive for him to do so. Suppose, to the contrary, the doctor had not had some inexpensive means of escaping the noise damage. The tax still would have led the confectioner to shut down, but this would now be the most efficient outcome. (See Example 17.1.)

Alternatively, suppose the confectioner had had some inexpensive means of eliminating the noise problem. Suppose, for example, that he could have installed soundproofing for a cost of 10. Here, too, the tax would have led to the most efficient outcome. The confectioner would have installed the soundproofing to escape the tax, and the doctor would have operated without disturbance.

Whether it is efficient to tax pollution thus depends on the particular circumstances at hand. If negotiation is costless, taxing will always lead to an efficient outcome. (But so, for that matter, will not taxing.) If negotiation is impractical, taxing pollution will still lead to an efficient outcome if the polluter has the least costly way of reducing pollution damage. Only if negotiation is impractical and the victim has the least costly means of avoiding damage will taxing pollution lead to an inefficient outcome. Taxing and not taxing will yield essentially the

TABLE 17.9
Outcome and Payoff Summary for Example 17.9
The gain to the confectioner from operating is 40. The loss to the doctor from the confectioner's noise is 60. The doctor can rearrange his office to eliminate the noise problem at a cost of 18. The efficient outcome is for the doctor to rearrange his office, and this happens only when there is no tax on the confectioner.

		Net benefit		
Legal regime	Outcome	Doctor	Confectioner	Total
Tax of 60 on confectioner	Confectioner shuts down	60	0	60
No tax or liability	Doctor rearranges his office at his own expense	42	40	82

TABLE 17.10
Cost and Emissions for Five Production Processes
Each firm has access to five alternative production processes, A–E, which vary both in cost and in the amount of pollution they produce.

Process (smoke)	A (4 tons/day)	B (3 tons/day)	C (2 tons/day)	D (1 ton/day)	E (0 tons/day)
Cost to firm X	100	190	600	1200	2000
Cost to firm Y	50	80	140	230	325

same outcomes if the costs of limiting pollution damage are roughly the same for both polluter and victim.

Suppose society has reached the judgment that the producers of pollution are in fact the ones who can mitigate its damages at the lowest cost. Society must then choose a policy that provides an incentive for the polluter to take action. One option is to set direct limits on the amount of pollution discharged. Alternatively, we could adopt a pollution tax, which means to charge polluters a fee for each unit of pollution they discharge. As the following example will demonstrate, the tax option offers a compelling advantage over the option of direct regulation.

EXAMPLE 17.10

Two firms, X and Y, have access to five different production processes, each one of which has a different cost and gives off a different amount of pollution. The daily costs of the processes and the corresponding number of tons of smoke are listed in Table 17.10. If pollution is unregulated, and negotiation between the firms and their victims is impossible, each firm will use A, the least costly of the five processes, and each will emit 4 tons of pollution per day, for a total pollution of 8 tons/day. The city council wants to cut smoke emissions by half. To accomplish this, they are considering two options. The first is to require each firm to curtail its emissions by half. The alternative is to set a tax of T on each ton of smoke emitted each day. How large would T have to be in order to curtail emissions by half? And how would the total costs to society compare under the two alternatives?

If each firm is required to cut pollution by half, each must switch from process A to process C. The result will be 2 tons/day of pollution for each firm. The cost of the switch for firm X will be 600/day − 100/day = 500/day. The cost to Y will be 140/day − 50/day = 90/day, which means a total cost for the two firms of 590/day.

How will each firm respond to a tax of T per ton of pollution? First it will ask itself whether switching from process A to B will increase its costs by more or less than T/day. If by less, it will pay to switch, because process B, which yields 1 ton less smoke, will save the firm T/day in taxes. If process B's costs exceed A's by more than T, however, the firm will not switch. It will be cheaper to stick with A and pay the extra T in taxes. If the switch from B to C pays, the firm will then ask the same question about the switch from B to C. It will keep switching until the extra costs of the next process are no longer smaller than T.

To illustrate, suppose a tax of 50/ton were levied. Firm X would stick with process A because it costs 90/day less than process B and produces only 1 ton/day of extra smoke, and thus 50/day in extra taxes. Firm Y, by contrast, will switch to process B because it costs only 30/day more and will save 50/day in taxes. But

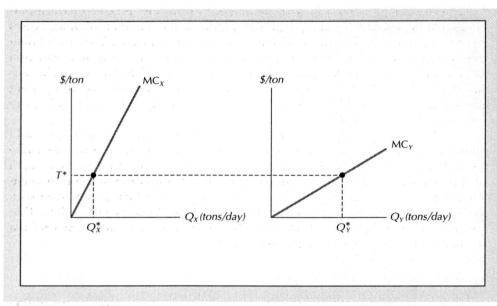

FIGURE 17.4
The Tax Approach to Pollution Reduction
MC_X and MC_Y represent the marginal cost of smoke reduction for firms X and Y, respectively. When pollution is taxed at a fixed rate, each firm reduces its emissions up to the point where the marginal cost of further reduction is exactly equal to the tax. The result is the least costly way of achieving the corresponding aggregate pollution reduction.

firm Y will not continue on to C because it costs 60/day more than B and will save only an additional 50/day in taxes. With firm X staying with A and firm Y switching to B, we get a total pollution reduction of 1 ton/day. A tax of 50/ton thus does not produce the desired 50 percent reduction in pollution.

The solution is to keep increasing the tax until we get the desired result. Consider what happens with a tax of 91/ton. This tax will lead firm X to adopt process B, firm Y to adopt process D. Total emissions will be the desired 4 tons/day. The cost to firm X will be 190/day − 100/day = 90/day, and the cost to firm Y will be 230/day − 50/day = 180/day. The total cost for both firms is thus only 270/day, or 320/day less than the cost of having each firm cut pollution by half. Note that the taxes paid by the firm are not included in our reckoning of the social costs of the tax alternative, because this money is not lost to society. It can be used to reduce whatever taxes would otherwise have to be levied on citizens.

The advantage of the tax approach is that it concentrates pollution reduction in the hands of the firms that can accomplish it in the least costly way. The direct regulatory approach of requiring each firm to cut by half took no account of the fact that firm Y can reduce pollution much more cheaply than firm X can. Under the tax approach, note that the cost of the last ton of smoke removed is the same for each firm.

More generally, suppose that there are two producers, firm X and firm Y, whose marginal costs of smoke removal are shown by the curves labeled MC_X and MC_Y, respectively, in Figure 17.4. If the goal is to reduce total smoke emissions by $Q = Q_X^* + Q_Y^*$ tons/day, a tax of T^* will accomplish that goal in the least costly way. The characteristic feature of this solution is that the marginal cost of pollution reduction would be exactly the same for all firms. If that were not the case, it would always be possible to reallocate the pollution reduction in such a way as to reduce total costs.

The direct regulatory approach (telling each firm how much to reduce pollution) could also achieve any given total pollution reduction at minimum costs if regulators knew each firm's marginal cost of reduction curve. They could then simply assign reduction quotas in such a way as to equate marginal reduction costs across firms. The difficulty is that regulatory officials will generally not have even the vaguest idea of what these curves look like. The compelling advantage of the tax approach is that it achieves efficiency without requiring any such knowledge on the part of regulators.

Recall from Chapter 16 our discussion of the efficiency losses generally caused by taxation. Another important advantage of taxing negative externalities is that it provides a means of raising government revenue that does not entail such efficiency losses. On the contrary, we have seen that the taxation of negative externalities can actually *increase* efficiency. Whether taxing negative externalities would yield enough revenue for government to carry out all its activities is an empirical question. If it would, then concerns about inefficiencies from taxation would no longer be a subject of concern.

Taxing Positional Externalities

There is considerable evidence that the utility that people get from consumption depends not only on absolute consumption levels, but on relative consumption levels as well. No one in the nineteenth century felt disadvantaged by not owning an automobile or a television set, and yet people who lack these items today are apt to feel strongly dissatisfied indeed. And their dissatisfaction is not merely a matter of envying the possessions of their neighbors. If no one owned a car, then I would not be required to have one to meet the minimal demands of social existence. But because almost everyone has a car today, it is extremely difficult to get along without one.

If relative consumption is important, it follows logically that each person's consumption imposes negative externalities on others. When any one person increases his consumption, he raises, perhaps imperceptibly, the consumption standard for others. As the British economist Richard Layard once stated, "In a poor society a man proves to his wife that he loves her by giving her a rose, but in a rich society he must give a dozen roses."

The fact that many forms of consumption generate negative externalities has important implications for tax policy. To illustrate, consider a young man's decision about how big a diamond to give his fiancée. Because the function of this gift is to serve as a token of commitment, the one he buys must necessarily cost enough to hurt. His jeweler will tell him that the custom in this country is to pay 2 months' salary for a stone and setting. If he makes $60,000/yr, he will have to come up with $10,000 or else feel like a cheapskate.

From the perspective of the economy as a whole, the outcome would be better if there were a 400 percent tax on jewelry. The after-tax price of what is now only a $2000 diamond would then rise to $10,000. In buying this smaller diamond, the young man would incur the same economic hardship as before. And since this is the essence of the gift's function, his goal would not really be compromised by the tax. Nor would the young man's fiancée suffer any real loss. Because *everyone* would now be buying smaller diamonds, the smaller stone would provide much the same satisfaction as the larger one would have. On the plus side, the government gets an additional $8000 to finance its expenditures or reduce other taxes. The only loser is the deBeers diamond cartel of South Africa, which would earn $8000 less than before the tax.

The standards that define acceptable schools, houses, wardrobes, cars, vacations, and a host of other important budget items are inextricably linked to the amounts other people spend on them. Because individual consumers typically ignore positional externalities in their choices, the result is that such commodities appear much more attractive to individuals than to society as a whole. For the same reasons that it is often efficient to tax pollution, it will be efficient to tax many of these forms of consumption. On efficiency grounds, such taxes would be an attractive substitute for existing taxes that interfere with efficient resource allocation.

SUMMARY

- When an action by one party harms another and the parties are able to negotiate costlessly with one another, the negative externalities are dealt with efficiently regardless of whether the law makes people liable for the harmful effects of their actions. This result is known as the Coase theorem.

- When negotiation is costly, it does matter how liability is assigned. In general, the most efficient outcome occurs when the law places the burden of avoiding harmful effects on the party that can accomplish it at the lowest cost.

- This general principle sheds light on a variety of questions regarding the design of property rights. It helps explain: why the owner of a dock may not legally exclude a boater from tying up during a storm; when people are allowed to exclude others from walking across their land or from blocking their view; why pastureland is more productive if owned privately rather than in common; why airplanes are allowed to fly over someone's property, while developers cannot build above it without permission. In each case, the laws of property are set up to mimic as closely as possible the kinds of accommodations people would reach for themselves if they were free to negotiate costlessly with one another.

- Similar principles apply to a variety of other governmental restraints on behavior. In the case of free speech and other constitutional liberties, the best

legal solutions turn out to be the ones that most closely resemble the solutions people would have negotiated among themselves, had it been practical to do so.

- Similar conclusions apply in situations that involve positive externalities. If negotiation is costless, people will forge agreements that result in efficient outcomes, even in cases in which one party's activities create indirect benefits to the other. And where negotiation is costly, institutions often tend to evolve that encourage activities with positive external effects.

- In contests for relative position, as in all other contests, the efforts by one contestant confer a negative externality on other contestants: anything that increases one party's odds of winning necessarily reduces the odds of others. The effect is almost always to induce some form of arms race among contestants, in which the efforts of each party serve largely to offset one another. The theory of externalities and property rights sheds light on the laws by which citizens of modern societies restrict such arms races.

- Taxation is one solution to the problem of negative externalities. Although it is not always an ideal answer, it does offer several important advantages over direct regulation in many situations. Taxation of negative externalities provides a source of governmental revenue that is largely exempt from the allocative inefficiencies we encountered in Chapter 16.

QUESTIONS FOR REVIEW

1. When negotiation costs are negligible, why is the assignment of liability for externalities irrelevant for efficiency?

2. Does the assignment of liability matter for distributional reasons?

640   CHAPTER 17   EXTERNALITIES, PROPERTY RIGHTS, AND THE COASE THEOREM

3. Suppose you are the party who can avoid a particular external effect at the lowest cost. Why might you favor a general rule that assigns liability to whichever party can avoid damage at the lowest cost?

4. Why do we permit airplanes but not real estate developers to use the airspace over private homes without prior consent?

5. Why do most property laws limit private coastal property to the waterline at high tide?

6. Give three examples of the tragedy of the commons on your campus.

7. How does the widespread existence of negative externalities alter the claim (see Chapter 16) that taxing goods lowers economic efficiency?

PROBLEMS

1. Every November, Smith and Jones each face the choice between burning their leaves or stuffing them into garbage bags. Burning the leaves is much easier but produces noxious smoke. The utility values for each person, measured in utils, are listed in the table for each of the four possible combinations of actions:

		Smith	
		Burn	Bag
Jones	Burn	Jones: 4 / Smith: 4	Jones: 8 / Smith: 2
Jones	Bag	Jones: 2 / Smith: 8	Jones: 6 / Smith: 6

a. If Smith and Jones are utility maximizers and make their decisions individually, what will they do?

b. How will your answer to part (a) differ, if at all, if Smith and Jones can make binding agreements with each other?

Now suppose the payoff matrix is as follows:

		Smith	
		Burn	Bag
Jones	Burn	Jones: 6 / Smith: 6	Jones: 8 / Smith: 2
Jones	Bag	Jones: 2 / Smith: 8	Jones: 4 / Smith: 4

c. What will they do this time if they can make binding agreements?

2. Smith can produce with or without a filter on his smokestack. Production without a filter results in greater smoke damage to Jones. The relevant gains and losses for the two individuals are listed in the table below:

	With filter	Without filter
Gains to Smith	$200/wk	$245/wk
Damage to Jones	$35/wk	$85/wk

   a. If Smith is not liable for smoke damage and there are no negotiation costs, will he install a filter? Explain carefully.
   b. How, if at all, would the outcome be different if Smith were liable for all smoke damage and the cost of the filter were $10/wk higher than indicated in the table? Explain carefully.

3. Smith can operate his sawmill with or without soundproofing. Operation without soundproofing results in noise damage to his neighbor Jones. The relevant gains and losses for Smith and Jones are listed in the table:

	Without soundproofing	With soundproofing
Gains to Smith	$150/wk	$34/wk
Damage to Jones	$125/wk	$6/wk

   a. If Smith is not liable for noise damage and there are no negotiation costs, will he install soundproofing? Explain.
   b. How, if at all, would your answer differ if the negotiation costs of maintaining an agreement were $4/wk? Explain.
   c. Now suppose Jones can escape the noise damage by moving to a new location, which will cost him $120/wk. With negotiation costs again assumed to be zero, how, if at all, will your answer to part (a) differ? Explain.

4. Smith and Jones are trying to decide whether to share an apartment. To live separately, each would have to pay $300/mo in rent. An apartment large enough to share can be rented for $450/mo. Costs aside, they are indifferent between living together and living separately except for these two problems: Smith likes to play his stereo late at night, which disturbs Jones's sleep; and Jones likes to sing in the shower at 6 A.M., which awakens Smith. Jones would sacrifice up to $80/mo rather than stop singing in the shower, and Smith would sacrifice up to $155/mo rather than stop playing his stereo late at night. Smith would tolerate Jones's singing and Jones would tolerate Smith's stereo in return for compensation payments not less than $75/mo and $80/mo, respectively.
   a. Should they live together? If so, indicate how they can split the rent so that each does better than by living alone. If not, explain why no such arrangement is feasible.
   b. Now suppose Smith wins a free pair of stereo headphones. If he wears them late at night, Jones's sleep is not disturbed. Smith likes the headphones well enough, but would be willing to pay $40/mo to keep on listening to late-night music through his speakers. How, if at all, does the existence of this new option affect your answer to part (a)? Explain carefully.

5. A and B can live separately at a rent of $400/mo each, or together at a rent of $600. Each would be willing to give up $30/mo to avoid having to give up his privacy. In addition to the loss of privacy, joint living produces two other conflicts, namely, each has a particular behavior the other finds offensive: B is a trumpet player, and A smokes cigarettes. B would be willing to pay $60/mo rather than tolerate smoking in his house and $120/mo to continue playing his trumpet. A, for his part, would

Frank: Microeconomics
an/ Behavior, Sixth E/ition

V. General Equilibrium an/
Welfare

17. Externalities, Property
Rights, an/ the Coase
Theorem

© The McGraw–Hill
Companies, 2005

423

642   CHAPTER 17   EXTERNALITIES, PROPERTY RIGHTS, AND THE COASE THEOREM

pay up to $100/mo to continue smoking and up to $90/mo to avoid listening to trum-
pet music. Will they live together? Explain carefully. Would your answer be different
if A didn't mind giving up his privacy?

6. A and B live on adjacent plots of land. Each has two potential uses for her land, the
present values of each of which depend on the use adopted by the other, as summarized in the table. All the values in the table are known to both parties.

		A	
		Apple growing	**Pig farming**
B	**Rental housing**	A: $200 B: $700	A: $450 B: $400
	Bee keeping	A: $400 B: $650	A: $450 B: $500

a. If there are no negotiation costs, what activities will the two pursue on their
land?
b. If there are negotiation costs of $150, what activities will the two pursue on their
land?
c. What is the maximum net income A can earn in parts (a) and (b) above?

7. A village has six residents, each of whom has $1000. Each resident may either invest
his money in a government bond, which pays 11 percent/yr, or use it to buy a year-
old steer, which will graze on the village commons. Year-old steers and government
bonds each cost exactly $1000. Steers require no effort to tend and can be sold for a

Number of steers	Price per 2-year-old steer
1	$1200
2	1175
3	1150
4	1125
5	1100
6	1075

price that depends on the amount of weight they gain during the year. Yearly weight
gain, in turn, depends on the number of steers that graze on the commons. The prices
of 2-yr-old steers are given in the table as a function of the total number of steers:
a. If village residents make their investment decisions independently, how many
steers will graze on the commons?
b. How many steers would graze on the commons if investment decisions were
made collectively?
c. What grazing fee per steer would result in the socially optimal number of steers?

8. A competitive fishing industry consists of five independently owned and operated
fishing boats working out of the port of Ithaca. Assume that no other fishermen fish
Cayuga Lake, and that the MC of operating a boat for 1 day is equivalent to 70
pounds of fish. (A boat left idle generates no costs.) The total catch per shoreline, in
pounds, is given in the following table as a function of the number of boats fishing
the east and west shores of the lake:

	Total catch	
Number of boats per side	East shore	West shore
1	100	85
2	180	150
3	255	210
4	320	260
5	350	300

a. If each boat owner decides independently which side of the lake to fish and all boats are in plain view of each other, how many boats would you expect to find fishing each shore on any given day? What is the net catch (that is, the total catch from both shores, less operating costs)?

b. Is this distribution of fishing craft optimal from the social point of view? If so, explain why. If not, what is the socially optimal distribution and the corresponding net catch?

9. Two firms, X and Y, have access to five different production processes, each one of which gives off a different amount of pollution. The daily costs of the processes and the corresponding number of tons of smoke are listed in the table:

Process (smoke)	A (4 tons/day)	B (3 tons/day)	C (2 tons/day)	D (1 ton/day)	E (0 tons/day)
Cost to firm X	100	120	140	170	220
Cost to firm Y	60	100	150	255	375

a. If pollution is unregulated, which process will each firm use, and what will be the total daily smoke emissions?

b. The city council wants to cut smoke emissions by half. To accomplish this, it requires a municipal permit for each ton of smoke emitted and limits the number of permits to the desired level of emissions. The permits are then auctioned off to the highest bidders. If X and Y are the only polluters, how much will each permit cost? How many permits will X buy? How many will Y buy?

c. Compare the total cost to society of this permit auction procedure to the total cost of having each firm reduce emissions by half.

10. Suppose the government attempts to restrict pollution by mandating a maximum amount that each firm can pollute. In general, this will result in a higher cost for pollution control than is necessary. Explain why.

*11. A small village has six people. Each can either fish in a nearby lagoon or work in a factory. Wages in the factory are $4/day. Fish sell in competitive markets for $1 apiece. If L persons fish the lagoon, the total number of fish caught is given by $F = 8L - 2L^2$. People prefer to fish unless they expect to make more money working in the factory.

a. If people decide individually whether to fish or work in the factory, how many will fish? What will be the total earnings for the village?

---

*This problem is most easily solved by making use of the calculus definition of marginal product given in the Appendix to Chapter 9.

644   CHAPTER 17   EXTERNALITIES, PROPERTY RIGHTS, AND THE COASE THEOREM

b. What is the socially optimal number of fishermen? With that number, what will the total earnings of the village be?

c. Why is there a difference between the equilibrium and socially optimal numbers of fishermen?

12. Once a week Smith purchases a six-pack of cola and puts it in his refrigerator for his two children to drink later. He invariably discovers that all six cans get drunk the first day. Jones also purchases a six-pack of cola once a week for his two children, but unlike Smith, he tells them that each may drink no more than three cans. Explain why the cola lasts much longer at Jones's house than at Smith's.

13. Suppose Smith owns and works in a bakery located next to an outdoor cafe owned by Jones. The patrons of the outdoor cafe like the smell that emanates from the bakery. When Smith leaves his windows open, the cafe faces the demand curve $P_C = 30 - 0.2Q_C$, while when the windows are closed, demand is given by $P_C = 25 - 0.2Q_C$. However, Smith doesn't like the street noise he hears when his windows are open, and in particular, the disutility he receives has a monetary value of 5. Assume that the cafe has a constant marginal cost of 10, and that integration (merger) is not a possibility because each owner greatly enjoys owning and operating his own establishment.

a. In the absence of a contract between the parties, do the firms behave in an efficient fashion? If not, describe the range of contracts that might emerge in response to the externality problem present in the environment. In answering this question, assume Smith understands how the bakery odor affects demand at the cafe, and Jones knows how much Smith dislikes street noise.

b. Suppose now everything is the same as above, except that given the current seating arrangement in the cafe, the cafe does not face a higher demand when the bakery windows are open. To realize this higher demand, Jones needs to make a sunk investment of 50, which moves the tables closer to the bakery. Is it wise for Jones to make this investment prior to Smith and Jones signing a contract? Explain.

c. Go back to the initial setup, but now assume that Smith's disutility from street noise equals 50 rather than 5. Further, suppose that prior to the parties agreeing on a contract Jones becomes the mayor and grants to himself the property rights concerning whether the bakery windows are left open or closed. Does this have an effect on whether the parties reach an efficient outcome? Explain.

14. Smith and Jones face the choice of driving to work early or late. If they both drive to work at the same time, each gets in the way of the other on the road, and so their daily commute takes longer and is more irritating. The monetary payoffs for each person are listed in the table below for each of the four possible combinations of actions:

		Smith	
		Early	Late
Jones	Early	Jones: 30 Smith: 30	Jones: 50 Smith: 20
	Late	Jones: 20 Smith: 50	Jones: 10 Smith: 10

a. If Smith and Jones are payoff maximizers and make their decisions individually, what will they do?

b. If Smith and Jones can make binding agreements with each other, what will they do?

15. Same as Problem 14, except now the payoff values of each person are

		Smith	
		Early	**Late**
Jones	**Early**	Jones: 30 / Smith: 30	Jones: 50 / Smith: 20
	Late	Jones: 20 / Smith: 60	Jones: 10 / Smith: 10

a. If Smith and Jones are payoff maximizers and make their decisions individually, what will they do?

b. If Smith and Jones can make binding agreements with each other, what will they do?

c. How do your answers differ from Problem 14 and why?

16. Smith loves dogs and has a pair of West Highland terriers. Jones has an incredible fear of dogs and cannot stand to be within sight of them. Smith and Jones are deciding whether to live in Arlington or Bexley. If they end up living in the same part of town, Jones will run into Smith out walking the Westies and get frightened. Thus, Jones prefers to be physically separated from Smith. The payoffs for each person are listed in the table below for each of the four possible combinations of actions:

		Smith	
		Arlington	**Bexley**
Jones	**Arlington**	Jones: 0 / Smith: 800	Jones: 500 / Smith: 900
	Bexley	Jones: 800 / Smith: 800	Jones: 0 / Smith: 900

a. If Smith and Jones are payoff maximizers and make their decisions individually, what will they do?

b. If Smith and Jones can make binding agreements with each other, what will they do?

17. Same as Problem 16, except now payoff values of each person are

		Smith	
		Arlington	**Bexley**
Jones	**Arlington**	Jones: 0 / Smith: 800	Jones: 500 / Smith: 1000
	Bexley	Jones: 600 / Smith: 800	Jones: 0 / Smith: 1000

a. If Smith and Jones are payoff maximizers and make their decisions individually, what will they do?

b. If Smith and Jones can make binding agreements with each other, what will they do?

c. How do your answers differ from Problem 17 and why?

646   CHAPTER 17   EXTERNALITIES, PROPERTY RIGHTS, AND THE COASE THEOREM

ANSWERS TO IN-CHAPTER EXERCISES

17.1. With a negotiation cost of only 20, it is now practical for the confectioner to pay the doctor to rearrange his office when the confectioner is liable. But note in the table below that it is still more efficient for the confectioner not to be liable:

Legal regime	Outcome	Net benefit		
		Doctor	Confectioner	Total
Liable	Confectioner operates and pays doctor 18 ≤ $P \leq 20$ to rearrange office	$22 + P$	$40 - P$	62
Not liable	Doctor rearranges his office at his own expense	22	60	82

17.2. Recall that the optimal number of steers is two. The grazing fee must be more than 2 to prevent a third steer from being sent out to graze. The fee cannot be more than 6 without keeping the second steer from being sent out.

17.3. Now the cost of accommodating to the smoke problem is 60, which is again less than the joint savings in rent. Let X represent Jones's contribution to the cost of the exhaust system, which means that Smith's contribution is $60 - X$. X cannot exceed 90, or else Jones will live separately; and X cannot be less than -30, or else Smith will live separately. The total gain is $180 - 60 = 120$.

	Net rental payment ($/mo)		Net gain ($/mo)		
	Jones	Smith	Jones	Smith	Total
Live separately	300	300	—	—	—
Live together and install exhaust system for smoke, $-30 \leq X \leq 90$	$210 + X$	$270 - X$	$90 - X$	$30 + X$	120

CHAPTER

18

GOVERNMENT

Local telephone companies are regulated monopolies, and so governmental regulators must rule on all their charges to the public. Historically, regulatory agencies prevented charges for directory assistance calls in the belief that such charges would "diminish the value of a vital public communications network." This conclusion, needless to say, seemed hopelessly vague to most economists. Directory assistance calls cost the phone company (and hence society) a lot of money to provide, and the economist's immediate fear is that people will be uneconomical in their use of this or any other resource for which they do not have to pay.

Some years ago, Alfred Kahn, then chairman of the New York State Public Service Commission (which regulates New York telephone companies), proposed that the companies begin charging 10 cents for every call made to directory assistance. Kahn was on leave from his post as an economics professor at Cornell, and earned cheers from his colleagues for his sensible proposal to give people an incentive to look numbers up for themselves in the phone book.

But his proposal drew a much different response from consumer advocates. These groups hired sociologists and other expert witnesses, who testified that the social fabric would deteriorate sharply if people were penalized for attempting to get in touch with one another. Other witnesses complained that the charges would impose an unacceptable burden on the poor.

Kahn's idea seemed doomed, when he proposed a brilliant amendment, one that would preserve its efficiency gains while at the same time eliminating any adverse effects on the poor. The amendment was that every telephone subscriber would be given a 30-cent credit on his or her monthly telephone bill in reflection of the costs saved on directory assistance calls. For example, someone who made one directory assistance call per month would be charged 10 cents, which, when combined with the credit, would make his monthly bill 20 cents less than before. Someone who made three directory assistance calls per month would break even, someone with four would pay 10 cents more than before, and so on. On the plausible assumption that a charge of 10 cents per call would be more likely to induce a low-income person than a high-income person to cut down on directory assistance calls, the net effect of the amended proposal was actually to increase the real purchasing power of the poor.

CHAPTER PREVIEW

The directory assistance episode illustrates two critically important points about government economic policy: (1) that distributional concerns permeate discussion of even the most seemingly trivial policies; and (2) that the most efficient solution to a public policy problem is one that enables both rich and poor alike to do better than before. Our task in this chapter is to explore two important functions of government: the provision of public goods and the direct redistribution of income. Concerns about both fairness and efficiency, we will see, are inextricably linked in both of these areas.

We will also see that the mere fact that a good has the characteristics of a public good does not mean that it must necessarily be provided by government. We will examine a variety of ingenious schemes, ranging from free commercial television to highly structured collective legal contracts, whereby public goods are provided with virtually no involvement by government.

We will see that problems similar to those that arise in connection with public goods are encountered whenever there are significant indivisibilities or economies of scale in the production of private consumption goods.

Next we will take up the question of how societies make choices between competing public projects, with particular focus on cost-benefit analysis as an alternative to majority voting schemes.

We will address a problem that plagues all mechanisms of public decision making, namely, that self-interested parties have an incentive to influence outcomes in their own favor. This problem goes by the name of rent seeking and it is often a serious threat to our social welfare.

From the problems of public choice, which themselves have important distributional overtones, we will turn to the topic of direct income transfer programs. Here our focus will be on how such transfers might be accomplished without undermining incentives to work and take risks.

PUBLIC GOODS

pure public good a good that has a high degree of nondiminishability and nonexcludability.

collective good a good that is excludable and has a high degree only of nondiminishability.

As noted in Chapter 16, public goods are those goods or services that possess, in varying degrees, the properties of *nondiminishability* and *nonexcludability*. The nondiminishability property, again, says that any one person's consumption of a public good has no effect on the amount of it available for others. Nonexcludability means that it is either impossible or prohibitively costly to exclude nonpayers from consuming the good.

Goods that have high degrees of both of these properties are often called **pure public goods,** the classic example of which is national defense. Goods that have only the nondiminishability property are sometimes referred to as **collective goods.** Collective goods are sometimes provided by government, sometimes by private companies. Most pure public goods are provided by government, but even here

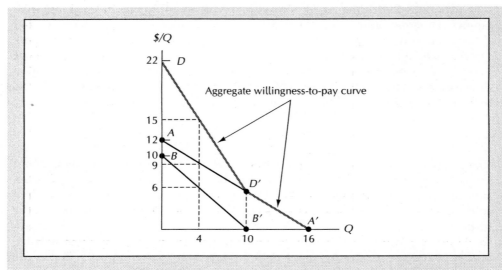

FIGURE 18.1
The Aggregate Willingness-to-Pay Curve for a Public Good
AA' and *BB'* represent the respective amounts that *A* and *B* are willing to pay for an additional unit of the public good. The aggregate willingness-to-pay curve is the vertical summation of the individual willingness-to-pay curves, the curve labeled *DD'A'*.

there are exceptional cases in which profit-seeking companies have devised schemes for providing them.

Let's begin our analysis with the case of a government trying to decide what quantity to provide of some pure public good—say, public television programming. For simplicity, imagine that there are only two citizens, *A* and *B*, and that each assigns a different value to any given quantity of the public good. In Figure 18.1, the horizontal axis measures the quantity of programming. The curve labeled *AA'* represents the amount *A* would be willing to pay for an additional unit of programming, and *BB'* represents the corresponding curve for *B*. Thus, at a level of 4 units of programming, *A* would be willing to pay $9/wk for an additional unit, while *B* would be willing to pay only $6/wk. The fact that the two willingness-to-pay curves are downward sloping reflects the fact that the more programming there already is, the less valuable an additional unit will be.

The central fact about providing any pure public good is that each person must consume the same amount of it. In markets for private goods, by contrast, each person can consume whatever amount she chooses at the prevailing price. To obtain the market demand curve for a private good, we simply added the individual demand curves horizontally. In the case of public goods, the analog to the market demand curve is the aggregate willingness-to-pay curve. It is obtained by adding the individual willingness-to-pay curves not horizontally but vertically. At $Q = 4$ units of programming in Figure 18.1, for example, *A* and *B* together are willing to pay a total of $9 + 6 = $15/wk$ for an additional unit of programming. The curve labeled *DD'A'* represents the vertical summation of the two individual willingness-to-pay curves.

EXERCISE 18.1

Ten homogeneous consumers all have individual willingness-to-pay curves $P = 12 - \frac{1}{5}Q$ for a public good—say, a concert in an open park (where *P* is measured in dollars and *Q* is measured in minutes). Construct and graph the aggregate willingness-to-pay curve. For a 30-minute concert, what is the maximum each individual would be willing to pay?

CHAPTER 18 GOVERNMENT

FIGURE 18.2
Equilibrium in a Market for Jointly Produced Products
DD' is the demand curve for pairs of drumsticks; *WW'* the demand curve for pairs of wings. Their vertical sum, *CC'D'*, is the market demand curve for chickens. The equilibrium price and quantity of chickens are determined by the intersection of this demand curve and the market supply curve.

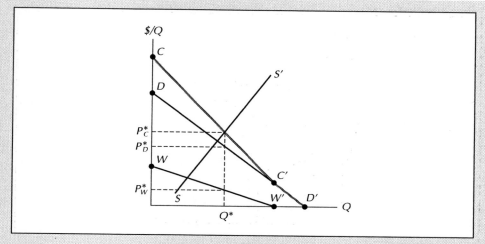

The Analogy to Joint Production

In passing, let's note the striking similarity between the procedure for generating the aggregate willingness-to-pay curve for a public good and the procedure whereby the demand curve for a product like chicken is generated from the demand curves for the various parts of a chicken. For simplicity, suppose chickens are composed of only two parts, wings and drumsticks, the demand curves for which are given by the curves labeled *WW'* and *DD'* in Figure 18.2. The horizontal axis in Figure 18.2 measures three things simultaneously: total pairs of drumsticks, total pairs of wings, and total number of chickens—because any given number of chickens will give rise to that same number of pairs of wings and drumsticks. On the simplifying assumption that wings and drumsticks are the only two chicken parts, we get the market demand curve for chickens by adding the demand curve for wings and the demand curve for drumsticks vertically. The curve labeled *CC'D'* in Figure 18.2 represents this vertical summation.

The curve labeled *SS'* in Figure 18.2 is the supply curve for chickens. Assuming the chicken industry is competitive, it is the horizontal summation of the marginal cost curves of the individual chicken producers. As in any other competitive market, equilibrium in the market for chickens occurs at the intersection of the supply and demand curves. The equilibrium quantity of chickens will be Q^*, and that quantity will give rise to Q^* pairs of drumsticks and Q^* pairs of wings. The market-clearing prices for drumsticks and wings will be P_D^* and P_W^*, respectively. These two prices sum to the equilibrium price of chickens, P_C^*.

There are several important points to note about the equilibrium in the market for jointly produced goods. First note that the equilibrium quantities of wings, drumsticks, and chicken are efficient in the Pareto sense. At Q^* the cost to society of producing another chicken is P_C^*, and this is exactly the total value that consumers place on its component parts. Any other quantity of chickens would leave open the possibility of mutual gains from exchange. Note also that the price of each chicken part cannot be determined from cost information alone, even if we know exactly the marginal cost of raising another chicken. There is simply no scientific basis for apportioning the cost of the entire bird among each

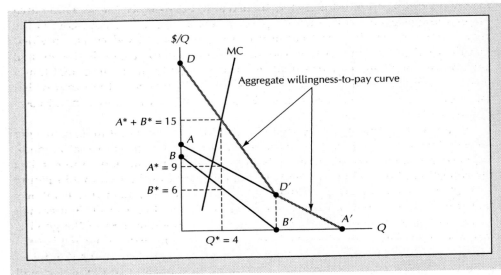

FIGURE 18.3
Optimal Provision of a Public Good
The optimal level of the public good is $Q^* = 4$, the level for which aggregate marginal willingness to pay for the good is exactly equal to its marginal cost.

of its constituent parts. Drumsticks and wings sell for their respective prices because those are the prices necessary to clear the markets for each. In a precisely analogous way, there is no correspondence between the amount that any one individual is willing to pay for a public good and its marginal cost of production.

The Optimal Quantity of a Public Good

Let's return again to our example of public television programming. Given the aggregate willingness-to-pay curve, what is the optimal quantity of programming? The answer is determined in much the same way as in the market for chickens. In Figure 18.3, the curve labeled $DD'A'$ again represents the aggregate willingness-to-pay curve for public television programming. The curve labeled MC represents the marginal cost of television programming as a function of its quantity. The intersection of these two curves establishes $Q^* = 4$, the optimal level of public television programming. At $Q^* = 4$, the amounts that A and B would be willing to pay for another unit of programming add to exactly the cost ($15/wk) of producing another unit. If this equality did not hold, we could easily show that society would be better off by either expanding or contracting the amount of programming.

EXERCISE 18.2

Consider the scenario described in Exercise 18.1, and suppose that the marginal cost of providing the concert is $MC = 2Q$. Determine the optimal length of the concert.

Paying for Q^*

We must make a slight qualification to the claim that Q^* is the optimal level of the public good in Figure 18.3. The statement is true subject to the provision that the *total* cost of Q^* does not exceed the total amount that the public would be willing to pay for it. The total willingness to pay for Q^* is the area under the aggregate willingness-to-pay curve up to Q^*. The total cost is the area under the marginal cost curve up to Q^*, plus any fixed costs. Provided that the total cost is smaller than the total willingness to pay, Q^* is the optimal level of the public good. This qualification is similar to the requirement that a profit-maximizing firm produce where $MR = MC$, subject to the proviso that total revenues cover total costs (total variable costs in the short run, all costs in the long run).

If the government is to produce Q^* units of a public good, it must somehow raise sufficient tax revenue to cover the total production costs of that amount. Suppose, for the sake of discussion, that the government's tax structure requires the collection of equal tax payments from all citizens. In the example in Figure 18.3, B's willingness to pay for the public good is smaller than A's. It follows that B will vote for the provision of Q^* only if the total cost of Q^* is less than twice the area under BB' up to Q^*. For example, if the total cost of the good is 100, and each party must be taxed equally, B will vote for it only if his total willingness to pay exceeds 50. If the amount B is willing to pay for the public good is only, say, 40, this condition will not be satisfied, and so the project will not win approval.

And yet we know that this public good is one whose benefits to all citizens add up to more than its costs. Compared with the alternative in which the public good is not provided, both A and B can be made better off by providing Q^* of it and then taxing A more heavily than B in order to pay for it. It follows that a tax structure that levies the same tax on all citizens cannot in general be Pareto efficient.

The situation here is analogous to the case in which the incomes of two spouses differ substantially. Suppose Julie earns \$100,000/yr while her husband, Bruce, earns only \$15,000. Given her income, Julie as an individual would want to spend much more than Bruce would on housing, travel, entertainment, and the many other items they consume in common. But suppose the couple adopted a rule that each had to contribute an equal share toward the purchase of such items. The result would be to constrain the couple to live in a small house, to take only inexpensive vacations, to skimp on entertainment and dining out, and so on. And so it is easy to imagine that Julie would find it attractive to pay considerably more than 50 percent for jointly consumed goods, thereby enabling both of them to consume in the manner their combined income affords.

As in the case of private goods, the willingness to pay for public goods is generally an increasing function of income. The rich, on the average, assign greater value to public goods than the poor do, not because they have different tastes but because they have more money. A tax system that taxed the poor just as heavily as the rich would result in the rich getting smaller amounts of public goods than they want. Rather than see that happen, the rich would gladly agree to a tax system that assigns them a larger share of the tax burden. It would be missing the point to criticize such a system by saying that the system is unfair because it enables the poor to enjoy the services of public goods for a smaller price. It does have this property, to be sure; but from the viewpoint of the rich, its terms are still attractive because the tax payments of the poor, though small, mean the rich end up paying less than if they had to finance public goods all by themselves.

Frank: Microeconomics
an/ Behavior, Sixth E/ition

V. General Equilibrium an/
Welfare

18. Government

© The McGraw–Hill
Companies, 2005

434

Private Provision of Public Goods

Governments are not the exclusive providers of public goods in any society. Substantial quantities of such goods are routinely provided through a variety of private channels. If it is impractical to exclude people from consuming a public good, the pressing question is, How can the good be paid for, if not by mandatory taxes?

Funding by Donation   One method for funding public goods is through voluntary donations. People donate great artworks to museums; they make contributions to listener-supported radio stations, to fund animal shelters, to research on debilitating diseases, and so on. Motives for such donations are as varied as the projects they support. Some see charitable giving as a means to achieve respect and admiration in the community.[1] Others may feel pressure to give in order to avoid social ostracism. These motives are really two sides of the same coin—social reward in the first case and social penalty in the second. Where such social forces are effective, they are a practical way of excluding nonpayers from full enjoyment of the public good.

Alternatively, people may donate because the increment to the public good that their contribution will finance is simply worth that much money to them. This motive is most likely to be important in situations in which one person's action can significantly affect the scale of the public good. Someone who lives at the end of a short dirt road in a rural area, for example, may find it worthwhile to pave the entire road at his own expense. He would naturally be happier if everyone who lived on the road chipped in. But rather than do without the road altogether, it may be worthwhile for him to pave it himself. Similarly, a person who plants a flower garden in front of her house provides a public good for neighbors to enjoy. If her own personal enjoyment from the garden exceeds its cost, pure self-interest is a sufficient motive for her to plant it.

But self-interested motives do not seem sufficient to explain why people make anonymous donations that will have no appreciable effect on the benefits they themselves receive. In the case of listener-supported radio stations, no single person's contribution will make a perceptible difference in the nature or quality of programming. The station will either continue to operate in its current form, or else improve, or else get worse—irrespective of what any one person does.

In such situations, the logic of pure self-interest seems to dictate **free riding**—abstaining in the hope that others will contribute. And yet millions of people contribute to such enterprises each year. For many of these people, the satisfaction of giving—of having contributed to the common good—is an end in itself. And as we saw in Chapter 7, there may well be important material advantages in being such a person.

The fact that public goods are often supported through voluntary contributions does not necessarily mean, however, that they are supported at socially optimal levels. Residents might be perfectly willing to pay sufficient taxes to build the socially optimal road. And yet, in the absence of taxes, the road that actually gets built is likely to be considerably smaller. Similarly, many people might strongly want society to invest more in public television programming.

free riding   choosing not to donate to a cause but still benefiting from the donations of others.

---

[1]To achieve the social benefit of charitable giving, the gift must become public knowledge. Most charitable organizations publicize their list of donors.

654   CHAPTER 18   GOVERNMENT

But these same people might be reluctant to give voluntarily as much as they would be willing to pay in taxes.

Sale of By-Products   Free-rider problems are sometimes solved by devising novel means to finance the public good. One such way is the sale of an important by-product of the public good. In the case of commercial television, for example, financing comes from sponsors, generally private corporations, who pay for the right to beam advertising messages to the audience attracted by the broadcast. The captive viewing audience is a by-product of the broadcast, and sponsors are willing to pay a lot for access to it. As the following example makes clear, however, this system does not always assure an optimal allocation of broadcast resources.

EXAMPLE 18.1

In a given time slot, a television network faces the alternative of broadcasting either the *Jerry Springer Show* or *Masterpiece Theater*. If it chooses *Springer*, it will win 20 percent of the viewing audience, but only 18 percent if it chooses *Masterpiece Theater*. Suppose those who would choose *Springer* would collectively be willing to pay $10 million for the right to see that program, while those who choose *Masterpiece Theater* would be willing to pay $30 million. And suppose, finally, that the time slot is to be financed by a detergent company. Which program will the network choose? Which program would be socially optimal?

The sponsor cares primarily about the number of people who will see its advertisements, and will thus choose the program that will attract the largest audience— here, the *Jerry Springer Show*. The fact that those who prefer *Masterpiece Theater* would be willing to pay a lot more to see it is of little concern to the sponsor. But this difference in willingness to pay is critical when it comes to determining the optimal result from society's point of view. Because the people who prefer *Masterpiece Theater* could more than compensate the *Springer* viewers for relinquishing the time slot, *Masterpiece Theater* is a Pareto-superior outcome. But unless its supporters happen to buy more soap in total than the *Springer* viewers, *Springer* will prevail. The difficulty with reliance on advertising and other indirect mechanisms for financing public goods is that there is no assurance that they will reflect the relevant benefits to society.

Development of New Means to Exclude Nonpayers   Another way to finance public goods privately is to devise cheap new ways of excluding people who do not pay for the good. In broadcast television, it was once impossible to prevent any household from tuning in to a program once it was sent out over the airwaves. With the advent of cable TV, however, households are now simple to exclude. With the ability to charge for specific programs, it is no longer necessary to make programming decisions on the basis of which program will garner the largest audience. In our *Jerry Springer* versus *Masterpiece Theater* example, a broadcasting company that can exclude nonpayers would have every incentive to show *Masterpiece Theater*, because its proponents now have a practical means of translating their greater willingness to pay into profits for the producer.

But note that whereas the outcome of pay-per-view TV is more efficient in the sense of selecting the programs the public most values, it is less efficient in one other important respect. By charging each household a fee for viewing, it discourages some households from tuning in. And since the marginal social cost of an additional household watching a program is exactly zero, it is inefficient to limit the audience in this way. Which of the two inefficiencies is more important—free TV's inefficiency in choosing between programs or pay TV's inefficiency in excluding potential beneficiaries—is an empirical question.

Private Contracts Legal contracts among private individuals offer yet another means for overcoming some of the difficulties associated with the free-rider problem. Consider, for example, the public good consisting of residential maintenance and beautification. As neighborhoods are customarily organized, it is impractical to exclude your neighbors from the benefits they will reap if you keep your house well painted and your yard neatly trimmed. Nor would it be efficient to exclude them, because their consumption of these benefits does not diminish their value to you and others in any way. In this respect, home maintenance and beautification satisfy the definition of a pure public good and, for this reason, will generally be undersupplied by private individuals.

We saw in Chapter 17 that if transactions were costless, your neighbors could subsidize your investments in home maintenance and beautification, and you could do likewise for them. Set at the proper levels, subsidies of this sort would result in the optimal levels of investment by every homeowner. But in general it is costly to negotiate such subsidies on a case-by-case basis, and so the level of investment in home maintenance often ends up being well below optimal.

The organizers of condominiums, cooperatives, and other forms of legal residential associations have come up with an effective solution to this problem. The condominium contract requires each owner to contribute a specified sum each month toward maintenance and beautification. This payment functions much like a tax in the sense that it is mandatory for all parties to the contract. The advantage is that it is less coercive than a tax in one important respect: People who wish to spend less on home maintenance are free to live elsewhere.

Similar selection may occur between neighborhoods in different school districts. One district may choose higher spending levels on schools (and higher taxes to fund them) than another district nearby. Households then self-select: Families with children choose to live in the high-tax area, and singles and retirees choose to live in the other district.[2]

The Economics of Clubs A pure public good has the property that an additional person's consumption of the good does not limit the amount of it available to others. Stated another way, the marginal cost of additional consumption of the public good is exactly zero. Many privately produced goods have the property that marginal cost, although not zero, declines sharply with the number of users accommodated. The swimming pool is a case in point. The number of swimmers it can accommodate rises in proportion to its surface area, but its cost rises much more slowly. The difference between such goods and goods that satisfy the nondiminishability criterion perfectly is thus one of degree rather than of kind.

When the marginal cost of expanding the capacity of a private good is low relative to its average cost, consumers face an economic incentive to share the purchase and use of the good. In the swimming pool example, the cost to each of 20 families

---

[2]See also the subsequent discussion of local public goods.

FIGURE 18.4
The Trade-Off between Privacy and Cost
When the marginal cost of accommodating an extra user of a consumption good is less than the average cost, consumers can save money by forming clubs that share ownership of such goods. The optimal club for members with the same tastes is one for which the marginal rate of substitution between all other goods and privacy is exactly equal to the cost of additional privacy.

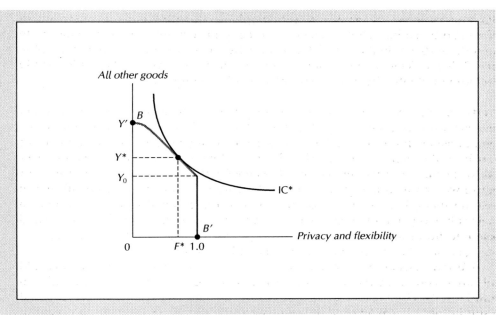

of a pool large enough for all to share will be much smaller than the cost of a pool large enough to serve the needs of only a single family. Indeed, the same statement is true of virtually any good that is not kept in continuous use by a single user. For example, most homeowners use extension ladders only once or twice a year, making it possible for several families to cut costs by sharing a single ladder.

The disadvantage of sharing, besides the fact that it requires someone to take the initiative to organize the arrangement, is that it limits both privacy and flexibility of access to the good. Thus, a homeowner might want to use the ladder on a particular Saturday afternoon, only to find it already in use by one of its other co-owners. Sometimes such inconveniences are trivial in relation to the cost savings; other times they will not be.

Opportunities for shared ownership thus confront the consumer with a variant of the standard consumer choice problem. To illustrate, consider again the choice between a privately owned pool and a shared pool. If we measure privacy and flexibility in the use of a pool on a scale from 0 to 1.0, a private pool would take the value 1.0, representing maximal privacy and flexibility. The limiting case at the other extreme is a large pool shared by infinitely many other people; the flexibility index for such a pool takes the value 0, representing virtually no privacy or flexibility.

The vertical axis in Figure 18.4 measures the amount the consumer spends on all other goods besides pools. If she buys her own private pool, at a cost of $Y' - Y_0$, she will achieve a privacy and flexibility index of 1.0. The other extreme represents a completely crowded pool, at a cost of 0 and a flexibility index of 0. Pools of intermediate size and crowdedness are represented by intermediate points on the budget constraint BB' in Figure 18.4. The consumer's best option is (F^*, Y^*), the point for which this budget constraint is tangent to an indifference curve (IC^*).

On the plausible assumption that the demand for privacy increases with income, we would predict that high-income consumers would be more likely to purchase their own pools than low-income consumers. But even consumers with very high incomes will find it attractive to participate in sharing arrangements for extremely costly consumption goods. Rather than maintain exclusive rights to operate an airplane that would sit idle on the tarmac most hours of the week, for example, even wealthy amateur pilots often choose to become members of flying clubs, the use of whose aircraft is shared with other members.

In the case of very inexpensive goods, by contrast, we would expect the demand for privacy to take precedence over the lure of cost savings even for consumers of relatively modest means. A privately owned toothbrush, like a privately owned airplane or swimming pool, is destined to remain idle for most hours of the day. Its cost per owner could be lowered substantially if it were shared by the members of a toothbrushing club. But the savings from such a transaction would be far too small to justify the sacrifice in privacy. Virtually everyone, even the poorest citizen, finds it worthwhile to maintain exclusive access to his personal toothbrush.

PUBLIC CHOICE

Whether public goods are provided by governments, charitable organizations, or private clubs, decisions must be made about the types and quantities to provide. The budget constraint confronting the group is often clear enough. The much more difficult aspect of the problem is to devise some means for translating the diverse preferences of the group's members into a single voice.

Majority Voting

One method of discerning group preferences is the majority vote. By this standard, projects favored by a majority—in either a direct referendum or a vote taken by elected representatives—are adopted and all others are abandoned. In recent years, much attention has been given to the fact that majority voting often leads to intransitivities in the ranking of alternatives. To illustrate, consider a group with three members—McCain, Biden, and Schumer—each of whom has a well-ordered ranking of three alternative projects: a new missile, a medical research project, and more aid to the poor. McCain likes the missile best, medical research next best, and aid to the poor least. Biden likes medical research best, aid to the poor next best, and the new missile least. Schumer, finally, likes aid to the poor best, a new missile next best, and medical research least. These rankings are summarized in Table 18.1.

Given these rankings, note what happens when each of the three pairs of alternatives is put to a vote. In deciding which of any pair of alternatives to vote for, each voter will naturally choose the one he prefers to the other. Thus, in a vote between a new missile and medical research, the missile will get 2 votes (McCain and Schumer); the research only 1 (Biden). In a vote between research and aid to the poor, research gets 2 votes (McCain and Biden); aid only 1 (Schumer). And finally, in a vote between aid and the missile, aid gets 2 votes (Schumer and Biden); the missile only 1 (McCain). Thus the missile defeats the research program and the research program defeats aid to the poor, and yet aid to the poor defeats the missile program! Such intransitivities were assumed not to occur in individual preference orderings, but can easily happen if social choice takes place by successive majority votes between pairs of alternatives.

TABLE 18.1
Preferences that Produce Intransitive Choices in Majority Voting
In a majority vote, the missile defeats the research program, which in turn defeats aid to the poor. And yet aid to the poor wins when paired against the missile. Majority voting schemes can lead to intransitivities even when individual preference orderings are transitive.

	McCain	Biden	Schumer
Best	Missile	Research	Aid
Second	Research	Aid	Missile
Third	Aid	Missile	Research

Agenda Manipulation The possibility of intransitivities in majority voting makes the order in which alternatives are considered by the electorate critically important. Suppose, for example, that McCain is in charge of setting the agenda for voting. His first priority will be to avoid a direct confrontation between the missile (his most favored project) and the aid project (which he knows will defeat the missile in a majority vote). He can ensure the missile's success by first conducting a vote between the aid project and the research project, followed by a vote between the winner of that election and the missile. The research project will win the first vote and will then be defeated by the missile in the second. Given power to set the agenda, either Biden or Schumer could have taken similar steps to ensure victory for either the research project or the aid project.

The Median Voter Theorem Intransitive rankings do not always result when alternatives are considered pairwise in a majority voting system. For example, we will get no intransitivities when the alternatives represent different quantities of a given public good and each voter ranks each according to how close it is to what, for her, is the optimal amount of the good. To illustrate, suppose our three voters are now considering what percentage of GNP to devote to national defense; and suppose that, as shown in Figure 18.5, the ideal percentages for McCain, Biden, and Schumer are 50, 6, and 10, respectively. Suppose, finally, that the percentages being considered for adoption are 5, 8, 11, 20, 40, and 60.

Does the power to set the order in which pairs of alternatives are considered confer the power to choose the ultimate outcome? This time the answer is no. In any pair of alternatives put to a vote, the winner will always be the one preferred by Schumer. Suppose, for instance, that 5 and 8 are put to a vote. McCain and Schumer will vote for 8 and Biden for 5, making Schumer's choice the

FIGURE 18.5
The Power of the Median Voter
The most preferred options for Biden, Schumer, and McCain are 6, 10, and 50 percent, respectively, making Schumer the median voter. No matter what pair of proposed percentages for defense is put to a vote, the one closest to Schumer's most preferred option will win.

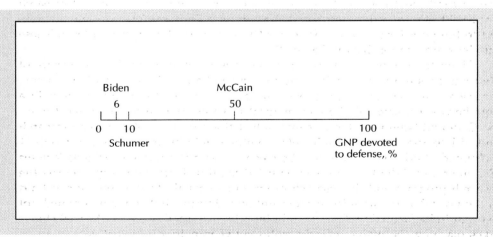

winner. If the alternatives are 20 and 60, Biden and Schumer will vote for 20 and McCain for 60, and Schumer's choice again wins. Because Schumer's most preferred outcome lies between the most preferred choices of the other two, he is the so-called **median voter** in this situation, and his vote will always prevail. The *median voter theorem* states that whenever alternatives can be ranked according to their closeness to each voter's ideal outcome, majority voting will always select the alternative most preferred by the median voter.

> **median voter** the voter whose ideal outcome lies above the ideal outcomes of half the voters.

EXERCISE 18.3

Given that the percentages of GNP under consideration for spending on national defense are again 5, 8, 11, 20, 40, and 60, which outcome will be chosen if the most preferred percentages of Biden, Schumer, and McCain are 11, 25, and 40, respectively?

The technical feature of preferences that eliminates intransitivities in the defense spending example is called **single-peakedness.** To have single-peaked preferences with respect to the share of GNP spent on defense means to have a uniquely most-preferred outcome and to rank all other outcomes in terms of their distance from it. Such preferences rule out liking 10 percent most and then ranking 30 percent better than 20 percent.

> **single-peaked preferences** preferences that exhibit a single most-preferred outcome, with other outcomes ranked lower as their distances from their most-preferred outcome increases.

In contexts like the defense example, it seems plausible to assume that preferences are indeed single-peaked. But in other contexts, such as the missile-aid-research example, preferences need not have this property. Numerous important examples occur in practice in which majority voting leads to intransitive rankings, making the power to set the agenda tantamount to the power to choose the final outcome.

Cost-Benefit Analysis

The difficulty of public choice by majority voting is not just that it sometimes leads to intransitivities. An even more serious problem is that it almost completely obscures important differences in the intensity with which different voters hold their preferences. Suppose, for example, that there are two alternatives put to a vote: (1) to allow smoking in public buildings and (2) to prohibit smoking in public buildings. If 51 percent of the voters prefer the first alternative and only 49 percent the second, the result will be to allow smoking in public buildings. But suppose the 49 percent who favor a prohibition feel very strongly about it and collectively would be willing to pay $100 million/yr in order to have it. And suppose the opponents of the prohibition are only mildly opposed; they know it will cause them some short-term inconvenience, but most of them want to quit or cut down on their smoking anyway, and they realize the ordinance will help them to do that. Collectively, the most they would be willing to pay in order to continue smoking in public buildings is only $1 million/yr. Under these circumstances, there is a simple transfer payment that makes the outcome chosen by the majority clearly Pareto inferior to the prohibition on smoking in public buildings. If the prohibitionists give the smokers $10 million/yr in exchange for agreeing to the ban, both groups will be better off than if smoking continues— the smokers by $9 million/yr, the nonsmokers by $90 million/yr.

TABLE 18.2

Willingness to Pay for Three Projects
Cost-benefit analysis chooses the project with the largest surplus of benefits over costs. If each project costs 100, the surplus will be 20 for the missile, 65 for the research program, and 35 for the aid program. The cost-benefit test will therefore choose the research program.

	McCain	Biden	Schumer	Total
Missile	100	−25	45	120
Research	35	90	40	165
Aid	−20	60	95	135

Cost-benefit analysis is an alternative to majority voting that attempts to take explicit account of how strongly people feel about each of the alternatives under consideration. Its method for measuring intensity of preference is to estimate how much people would be willing to pay in order to have the various alternatives. In the smoking example, it would immediately rule in favor of the prohibition because its benefits to its supporters (as measured by what they would be willing to pay to have it) strongly outweigh its costs to its opponents (as measured by what they would be willing to pay to avoid it).

Another advantage of cost-benefit analysis is that it would also avoid the intransitivities that often arise under majority voting. To illustrate, let's consider how it would deal with the missile-aid-research decision we discussed earlier. Table 18.2 displays hypothetical valuations assigned by McCain, Biden, and Schumer to each of the three alternatives. Positive entries in the table represent the amounts each person would pay to have a program he likes. Negative entries represent what someone would pay to avoid a program he dislikes. The entries in the first column of the table, for instance, indicate that McCain would pay 100 to have the missile program, 35 to have the medical research program, and 20 to avoid the aid program for the poor. Note that each person's ranking of the alternatives is the same in Table 18.2 as it was in Table 18.1.

To keep the discussion simple, suppose that the cost of each program is 100, but that because of budgetary shortages, only one of the three programs can be undertaken. How will cost-benefit analysis choose among them? It will pick the one for which the surplus of total benefit over cost is greatest. Again for simplicity, assume that the amounts the three voters would pay for each program accurately capture all relevant benefits. The total benefit of each program will then be the sum of what each voter would pay to have (or avoid) it. These totals are listed in the last column of Table 18.2 and reveal that the research program is the clear winner.

Note also that the research program would not have won if McCain had been able to set the agenda for a majority voting session. He would first pit the research program against the aid program, defeating it 2 to 1. And McCain's favored missile project would then defeat the research program by the same margin. Schumer, through similar agenda manipulation, could arrange for his favored aid program to emerge the winner in a majority voting sequence.

Note, finally, that if the research program did *not* get adopted, it would always be possible to construct a Pareto-preferred switch to the research program. Suppose, for example, that McCain set the agenda in a majority voting sequence, with the result that the missile program was chosen. This outcome yields a loss of 25 for Biden. By contrast, had the research program been chosen, Biden would have had a gain of 90, a net improvement of 115 for him. This improvement is big enough to enable Biden to compensate both McCain and Schumer for the losses they would suffer by switching from the missile to the research program. Suppose, for example, that Biden gives McCain 70 and

Schumer 10 for switching. Then the net benefits to McCain and Schumer will be 105 and 50, respectively, a gain of 5 each over their positions with the missile program. A similar Pareto-improving move could be constructed if we had begun with the aid program. Indeed, the cost-benefit test will in general lead to a Pareto-efficient outcome.

If cost-benefit analysis satisfies the Pareto criterion while majority voting does not (at least, not always), why do we so often use majority voting for making collective choices? One objection to cost-benefit analysis is that because it measures benefits by what people are willing to pay, it gives insufficient weight to the interests of people with little money. On this view, the poor may feel very strongly about an issue, and yet their feelings will not count for much in cost-benefit analysis since they don't translate into large willingness-to-pay values. This sounds at first like a serious objection, but as the following example clearly demonstrates, it does not survive close scrutiny.

EXAMPLE 18.2

Suppose there are only two people, R (who is rich) and P (who is poor). And suppose that R favors a public project that P opposes. In purely psychological terms, their intensity of feeling is the same. But because R has much more money, he would be willing to pay 100 to have the project, while P would be willing to pay only 10 to avoid it. If each could choose which method to use for deciding on public projects, which would each favor, cost-benefit analysis or majority rule?

At first glance, majority rule sounds attractive to P because it gives him veto power over any project he does not favor. But the first step P would take if he were given that veto power would be to yield it in exchange for a compensation payment. If R values the project at 100 and P would pay only 10 to avoid it, the most efficient outcome here is to go ahead with the project. If R gives P a compensation payment of X, where $10 \leq X \leq 100$, then each party will be better off than if P had insisted on exercising his veto. By P's own reckoning, the inconvenience of the project is less than the value to him of the compensation payment. The fact that the cost-benefit test always leads to the greatest economic surplus means that it will always be in the interests of R and P alike to use it.

Critics of cost-benefit analysis sometimes concede that it would lead to Pareto-optimal outcomes in every case if it were practical to make the needed compensation payments. But they go on to argue that such compensation payments usually are not practical on a case-by-case basis. And so, they conclude, it is unfair to make decisions on the basis of cost-benefit analysis.

This argument also fails on close examination. First, note that in most societies literally thousands of decisions are taken each year with respect to public goods and programs. Each one, if adopted, would help some people and hurt others. Almost always the individual magnitudes of the gains and losses in any one decision are extremely small, much less than 1 percent of even a poor person's annual earnings. If projects are decided by the cost-benefit criterion, the amount that winners gain on any adopted project will necessarily outweigh the amount that losers lose. Where small projects are concerned, then, the cost-benefit test is like flipping a coin that is biased in your favor. On each flip of the coin you might either win or lose, but the probability of winning exceeds the probability of losing. If both the gains and losses are small and randomly distributed among individuals, and if the coin is to be flipped thousands of times, this makes for a very attractive gamble indeed. The law of large numbers (see Chapter 6) tells us that it is virtually certain that everyone will come out a winner in the end.

But suppose that the gains and losses from each outcome are not random; that, on the contrary, the poor usually come out on the losing side of the cost-benefit test because of their inability to back up their favored programs with high willingness-to-pay values. Even if it is impractical to compensate the poor on an issue-by-issue basis, it is *still* possible to achieve a better outcome for everyone by relying on the cost-benefit criterion. The reason is that the poor can be compensated on an ongoing basis through the tax system. If the alternative is to rely on majority voting, which would allow the poor to block projects whose benefits exceed their cost, the cost-benefit criterion, together with compensation through the tax system, will deliver a preferred outcome for every party.

The only telling argument in favor of majority voting is its simplicity. It is much easier to take a majority vote than to gather detailed information about what different individuals would be willing to pay for their preferred alternatives. Much progress has been made in recent years in the design of mechanisms that induce people to reveal truthfully what their valuations are. But these mechanisms remain cumbersome, and it is a lot easier to allow people to reveal their preferences by their votes. And in many situations, of course, majority voting and cost-benefit analysis will lead to the same outcome anyway.

Local Public Goods and the Tiebout Model

Even with a perfect mechanism for choosing between alternative public goods, it is difficult to escape the need for painful compromise. One group will sincerely believe that it is society's duty to provide complete health care for every citizen; another will believe with equal sincerity that it is each individual's responsibility to provide for his own health care. Given differences of this sort, the result is often some form of compromise—partial public support for health care—that pleases neither group of voters.

With respect to public goods provided at the local level, Professor Charles Tiebout suggested that at least some of these compromises can be avoided if people are free to form communities with others of similar tastes.[3] Those who favor high levels of public goods can group together in communities in which they willingly accept the high tax rates necessary to finance these levels. And others who favor a more limited menu of public goods and services can form groups of their own and have lower tax rates.

As an empirical matter, local governments do differ widely with respect to the level of public goods they provide. Even so, there are practical difficulties with the notion of trying to tailor a local environment to precisely one's own preferences. Consider, for example, the issue of public support for the poor. People have legitimate differences over what this level of support should be. But those who favor high levels of support often take on more than they bargained for when they enact generous welfare policies at the local level. The difficulty is

[3]Charles Tiebout, "The Pure Theory of Local Expenditure," *Journal of Political Economy*, October 1956: 416–424.

that such policies attract new low-income beneficiaries from other jurisdictions with lower benefits. This, in turn, makes it necessary to raise tax rates, which leads some upper-income taxpayers to leave, further exacerbating the fiscal imbalance. The ability to form local communities of like-minded voters softens the need to compromise in some areas, but by no means eliminates it.

Rent Seeking

As a practical matter, the gains from public choices are often large and concentrated in the hands of a few, whereas the costs, while also large, are spread among many. The difficulty such situations create for the public is clear. The prospective beneficiaries of a public program have powerful incentives to lobby government in favor of it, while each of the prospective losers has too little at stake to bother about. The result, all too frequently, is that projects are approved even when their benefits do not exceed their costs.

A related difficulty arises in the case of similar projects whose benefits do exceed their costs. Because there are large gains to be had from the project, private parties are willing to spend large sums in order to enhance their odds of being chosen as its beneficiaries. Pursuit of these gains goes by the name of *rent seeking*. One consequence of rent seeking is that the expected gains from government projects are often squandered by the competition among potential beneficiaries.

Consider, for example, a local government faced with the task of awarding the local cable TV franchise. Unless the government is prepared to engage in strict rate-of-return regulation, which most local governments are not, the franchisee can expect to earn substantial monopoly profits. The likelihood of any applicant being awarded the franchise is an increasing function of the amount of money it spends lobbying local legislators. The lure of the franchise's expected profits thus causes applicants to engage in a lobbying war to win the franchise. And as the following example illustrates, such lobbying wars tend to dissipate much of the gains made possible by the project.

EXAMPLE 18.3

Three firms have met the deadline for applying for the franchise to operate the cable TV system for Cedar Rapids during the coming year. The annual cost of operating the system is 25, and the demand curve for its services is given by $P = 50 - Q$, where P is the price per subscriber per year and Q is the number of subscribers. The franchise lasts for exactly 1 year and permits the franchisee to charge whatever price it chooses. The city council will choose the applicant that spends the most money lobbying city council members. If the applicants cannot collude, how much will each spend on lobbying?

The winner will set the monopoly price for the service, which is the price that corresponds to the quantity at which marginal revenue equals marginal cost. Marginal revenue for the cable system is given by $MR = 50 - 2Q$, and marginal cost is zero by assumption. The profit-maximizing quantity will thus be 25, which gives rise to a price of 25. Total revenue will be $25(25) = 625$, which makes for a profit of $625 - 25 = 600$. If any applicant spends more on lobbying than the other two spend, it will win the franchise. If all three spend the same, each applicant will have a 1-in-3 chance of earning 600 in profit, which means an expected profit of 200. If the lobbyists could collude, each would agree to spend the same small, token amount on lobbying. But in the absence of a binding agreement, each will be strongly tempted to try to outspend the others. If each firm's spending reaches 200, each will have expected profits of zero (a one-third chance to earn 600, minus the 200 spent on lobbying). At this point, it might seem foolish to bid any further, because higher spending levels would mean an expected loss. And yet if any one of the three spent 201, while the other two stayed at 200, it would get the franchise for sure and earn a net profit of 399. The losers would each have losses of 200. Rather than face a sure loss of 200, the losers may well find it attractive to bid 201 themselves. Where this process will stop is anyone's guess.[4] The one thing that seems certain is that it will dissipate some or all of the gains that could have been had from the project. From the viewpoint of any individual firm, it is perfectly rational to lobby in this fashion for a chance to win government benefits. From the standpoint of society as a whole, however, such activity is almost completely wasteful. The efficient government is one that takes every feasible step to discourage rent seeking—for example, by selecting contractors on the basis of the price they promise to charge, not on the amount they lobby.

INCOME DISTRIBUTION

In market economies, the main means of earning income is by selling factors of production. Some people, by far the minority, earn a significant portion of their income from the ownership of stocks, bonds, and other financial instruments. Most people depend primarily on the proceeds from the sale of their own labor.

This system of distributing incomes is far from perfect, but it does have several attractive properties. First, it leads to a determinate outcome: The theory of competitive factor markets tells us that each factor will be paid the value of its marginal product, and that in long-run competitive equilibrium, these payments will add up to exactly the total product available for distribution.[5] Given the obvious potential for claims to exceed available output in any system, the fact that the marginal productivity scheme clearly identifies a feasible payment for every party is no small advantage. A second attractive feature of the marginal productivity system is that it rewards initiative, effort, and risk taking. The harder, longer, and more effectively a person works, the more she will be paid. And if she risks her capital on a venture that happens to succeed, she will reap a handsome dividend.

---

[4]The following experiment provides some relevant evidence. A $1 bill is auctioned off subject to the following rules. The bill goes to the highest bidder, who must pay the auctioneer the amount he bid. The second-highest bidder gets nothing, but must also pay the auctioneer the amount he bid. In a typical trial of this auction, the bids slowly approach 50 cents, at which point there is a pause. Then the second bidder offers more than 50 cents and the bids quickly escalate to $1. There is another pause at $1, whereafter the second bidder bids more than $1, and the bids again quickly escalate. It is not uncommon for the winning bid to exceed several dollars.

[5]Recall that long-run competitive equilibrium occurs at the minimum point of every firm's long-run average cost curve; at that point there are constant returns in production. It is a property of production functions with constant returns that $F(K, L) = K\partial F/\partial K + L\partial F/\partial L$, which says that paying each factor its marginal product will exactly exhaust the total product available.

The Rawlsian Criticism of the Marginal Productivity System

The marginal productivity system is not without flaws, however. The most common criticism is that it often generates a high degree of inequality. Those who do well in the marketplace end up with vastly more than they can spend, while those who fail often cannot meet even their basic needs. Such inequality might be easier to accept if it were strictly the result of differences in effort. But it is not. Talent plays an important role in most endeavors, and although it can be nurtured and developed if you have it, whether you have it in the first place is essentially a matter of luck.

Even having abundant talent is no guarantee of doing well. It is also necessary to have the *right* talent. Being able to hit a baseball 400 feet with consistency will earn you millions annually, while being the best fourth-grade teacher in the nation will earn you little; and being the best handball player in the world will earn you virtually nothing. The baseball star earns so much more, not because he works harder or has more talent, but because he is lucky enough to be good at something people are willing to pay a lot for.

John Rawls, a Harvard moral philosopher, constructed a cogent ethical critique of the marginal productivity system, one based heavily on the microeconomic theory of choice itself. The question he asked was "What constitutes a just distribution of income?" To answer it, he proposed the following thought experiment. Imagine that you and the other citizens of some country have been thrown together in a meeting to choose the rules for distributing income. This meeting takes place behind a "veil of ignorance," which conceals from each person any knowledge of what talents and abilities he and others have. No individual knows whether he is smart or dull, strong or weak, fast or slow, and so on—which means that no one knows which particular rules of distribution would work to his own advantage. Rawls argued that the rules people would choose in such a state of ignorance would necessarily be fair; and if the rules are fair, it follows that the distribution to which they give rise will also be fair.

What rules would people choose from behind a veil of ignorance? If the national income to be distributed were a fixed amount every year, it is likely that most would choose to give everyone an equal share. This is likely, Rawls argued, because most people are strongly risk averse. Since an unequal distribution would involve not only a chance of doing well, but also a chance of doing poorly, most people would prefer to eliminate the risk by choosing an equal distribution.

The difficulty, however, is that the total amount of income available for distribution is *not* a fixed amount every year. Rather, it depends on how hard people work, how much initiative and risk they take, and so on. If everyone were guaranteed an equal share of the national income at the outset, why would anyone work hard or take risks? Without rewards for hard work and risk taking, national income would be dramatically smaller than if such rewards existed. Of course, material rewards for effort and risk taking necessarily lead to inequality. But Rawls argues that people would be willing to accept a certain degree of inequality as long as these rewards produced a sufficiently large increase in the total amount of output available for distribution.

How much inequality? Much less than the amount produced by purely competitive factor markets, Rawls argued. The idea is that each person behind the veil of ignorance would rationally fear being in a disadvantaged position, and so each would choose distributional rules that would maximize the income of the poorest citizen. That is, additional inequality would be considered justified as long as it had the effect of raising the income of each and every citizen. Rawls's own critics responded that his proposal was unrealistically conservative—that most people would allow additional inequality if the effect, say, were to increase *most* incomes. But Rawls's basic point was that people behind a veil of ignorance would choose rules that would produce a more equal distribution of income than we get under the marginal productivity system. And since these choices define what constitutes a just distribution of income, he argued, fairness requires at least some attempt to reduce the inequality produced by the marginal productivity system.

Practical Reasons for Redistribution

The moral argument Rawls outlined has obvious force. But there are also compelling practical reasons for limiting inequality. We saw, for example, that an equal tax levied on every citizen will in general result in an inefficient level of public goods. To the extent that willingness to pay for public goods increases with income, high-income citizens will have every selfish reason to support a tax structure in which they carry a much larger share of the tax burden than the poor do. And to the extent that the public goods financed under such a tax system are equally available to persons of different income levels, the effect will be to reduce inequality.

Forces analogous to the ones that shape pay distributions within firms suggest another practical reason for income redistribution at the society level. Recall from Chapter 14 that within any single firm the tendency is for the most productive employees to be paid less than the values of their marginal products, and for the least productive employees to be paid more. The difference between a worker's wage and the value of her marginal product may be interpreted as a compensating differential that reflects her rank within the firm. Heterogeneous collections of workers will remain together in a firm only if those who hold positions of low rank are adequately compensated by those who hold high rank.

These forces in the firm are reflected at the societal level as well. It is obviously advantageous to occupy a position in the upper portion of society's income distribution. Such positions exist, however, only if there are others willing to occupy positions in the lower portion of the income distribution. Society has a clear interest in forging terms on which all members will view it as in their interests to remain part of society. If experience is any guide, social cohesion may simply not be possible without some attempt to compensate people for the implicit burden of occupying low positions in the overall distribution of income.

Fairness and Efficiency

We saw that efforts to reduce inequality may be justified on the basis of both moral and practical arguments. Some mix of such arguments has apparently been found compelling, for no modern economy leaves income distribution entirely to the marketplace. This underlying commitment to norms of equality is strong and plays a pivotal role in almost every debate on public policy.

The economist's natural advantage lies in answering questions related to efficiency. For this reason, many economists are reluctant even to discuss issues related to equity. Yet virtually every policy change will affect not only efficiency,

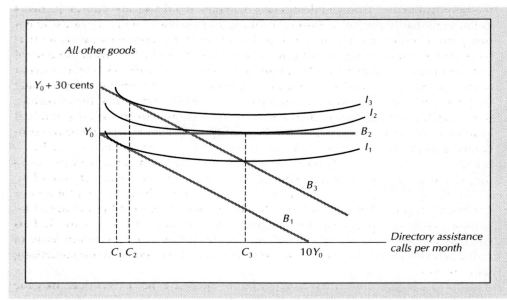

FIGURE 18.6
Charging for Directory Assistance
When directory assistance calls are free, the consumer makes C_3 of them each month. Charging 10 cents each for them cuts down on the volume of these calls substantially, enough to finance a 30 cent per month credit for every customer. The new system is more efficient than the old and places more purchasing power in the hands of the typical customer.

but also the distribution of income. And we know that most societies seem prepared to reject efficient allocations if they do not pass muster on grounds of fairness. The result is that unless economists are prepared to work within social constraints on inequality, there will be little or no audience for their policy recommendations.

During a supply interruption of some important commodity, for example, economists are almost always quick to recommend letting the price rise to market-clearing levels. We know, after all, that this policy will lead to an efficient allocation of the scarce good. The social complaint, however, is that sharply rising prices will impose an unacceptable burden on the poor. And so, in the wake of shortages, governments often reject the free market path in favor of rationing, queues, and other, more cumbersome, methods of distribution.

The unfortunate irony in this response is that inefficient solutions make the economic pie smaller for everyone, rich and poor alike. Contrary to popular impressions, the goals of fairness and efficiency need not be in conflict at all. We saw in Chapter 16 that distribution and efficiency are separable issues. Given a suitable choice of initial endowments, *any* Pareto-efficient allocation is sustainable as a competitive equilibrium. When economists recommend a policy on grounds of efficiency, they must also be prepared to explain how its distributional consequences can be altered to meet social constraints.

A case in point is the episode with which we began this chapter. The issue, recall, was whether local telephone companies should be permitted to charge for calls to directory assistance. Alfred Kahn's proposal that they should was greeted by complaints that this policy would impose unacceptable hardships on the poor. Kahn salvaged the proposal by amending it to require that every telephone subscriber be given a 30 cent credit on his telephone bill in reflection of the costs saved from having fewer directory assistance calls.

Let's examine how this amended proposal works. In Figure 18.6, the horizontal axis measures directory assistance calls per month and the vertical axis

Frank: Microeconomics
an/ Behavior, Sixth E/ition

V. General Equilibrium an/
Welfare

18. Government

© The McGraw-Hill
Companies, 2005

449

measures expenditure on all other goods. The horizontal line labeled B_2 represents the budget constraint for a consumer with a monthly income of Y_0 in the event that there is no charge for directory assistance calls. B_1 represents the same person's budget when there is a 10 cent charge for such calls. And B_3 is the budget constraint when there is a 30 cent monthly credit in addition to the 10 cent charge per call. I_1, I_2, and I_3 are indifference curves. They have the conventional shape, except that beyond some number of calls each month they turn upward, reflecting the fact that most people would not choose to make an unlimited number of calls to directory assistance even if those calls were free. For the consumer shown, failure to charge for directory assistance calls results in C_3 calls/mo. A simple 10 cent charge results in C_1 calls/mo, a sharply lower number. The 10 cent charge with 30 cent credit results in C_2 calls/mo. On the plausible assumption that 30 cents/mo is a trivial amount of income even for a poor person, C_2 and C_1 should be almost the same. The 30 cent credit is financed by the cost savings that result when the number of calls falls from C_3 to C_2. This reduction in calls enables the telephone company to run its operations with fewer switchboards and operators—resources that are freed up to do something more useful.

A social scientist from another planet might find it hard to believe that the trivial hardship of paying for directory assistance calls would have dissuaded a regulatory commission from approving the charge. Yet such is the strength of distributional concerns in public policy debate. By taking care to share the cost savings with ratepayers in the form of a conspicuous 30 cent monthly credit, an otherwise doomed policy reform was salvaged.

In many other markets, such as those for gasoline and natural gas, the distributional consequences of charging prices based on cost are much more pronounced than in the case of directory assistance calls. In such situations, of course, the distributional issue is all the more salient. The efficiency gains from charging prices that reflect costs are also much larger in these cases, and with sufficient attention to the distribution of these gains, it should be possible to reach political agreement on how to achieve them.

Methods of Redistribution

The methods by which society redistributes income are subject to the same kinds of analysis that economists bring to bear on other programs and institutions. Our principal concern here is that poorly designed redistributive programs can easily undo the very efficiency gains they were created to facilitate.

Our Current Welfare Programs   Abba Lerner, one of my former professors in graduate school, once remarked that the main problem the poor confront is that they have too little income. The solution, in his view, was disarmingly simple. We should give them some money. Traditional welfare programs, however, are much more complicated. We have food stamps, rent stamps, energy stamps, day care subsidies, aid to families with dependent children, and a host of other separate programs, each with its own administrative bureaucracy. The end result is that it takes approximately 7 tax dollars to get 1 additional dollar of income into the hands of a poor person.

High as they are, these costs are not the major problem from an efficiency standpoint. Of potentially far greater concern is the effect current programs

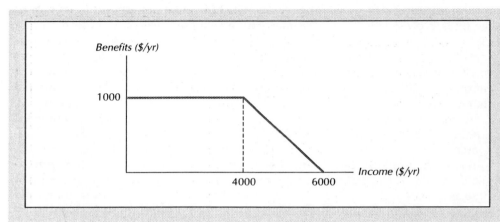

FIGURE 18.7
Benefits versus Income for a Typical Welfare Program
Persons who earn below $4000/yr receive the full benefit level of $1000/yr. For each dollar earned above $4000, benefits go down by 50 cents. Once a person's income reaches $6000/yr, all benefits cease.

have on work incentives. To illustrate the difficulty, it is necessary first to describe some of the administrative details of the programs. Each program has a full benefit level that all persons who earn less than some threshold income level are eligible to receive. Once a beneficiary begins to earn more than that threshold, his benefits are reduced by some fraction of each additional dollar earned. This fraction is called the *marginal benefit reduction rate*. Figure 18.7 shows how benefits vary with income for a program with a full benefit level of $1000/yr, a threshold income level of $4000/yr, and a marginal benefit reduction rate of 50 percent.

The real problem comes when a person participates in several welfare programs at once, as is common under our current system. Consider, for example, a person enrolled in four programs like the one shown in Figure 18.7. Once his income reaches $4000/yr, he will lose $2 in benefits (50 cents from each of the four programs) for every additional dollar he earns. Needless to say, these terms are hardly conducive to the expenditure of effort. The adverse effects on labor supply decisions are one of the most serious costs of our current welfare system.

The Negative Income Tax Milton Friedman calculated that for the cost of our current programs, every man, woman, and child now classified as poor in the United States could be given a payment of more than $8000/yr. This calculation, together with his concern about adverse effects on work incentives, led Friedman to propose a radical reform in which our entire array of current programs would be replaced by a single program he called the *negative income tax (NIT)*.

Friedman's version of the NIT starts out by giving every man, woman, and child—rich or poor—an income tax credit that is large enough to sustain a minimally adequate standard of living. Someone who earned no income would receive this credit in cash. People with earned income would then be taxed on their income at some rate less than 100 percent. The initial credit and the tax rate combine to determine a breakeven income level at which each person's tax liability exactly offsets his initial tax credit. People earning below that level would receive a net benefit payment from the government, while those earning more would make a net tax payment.

CHAPTER 18   GOVERNMENT

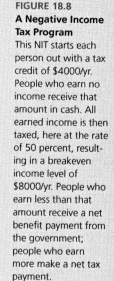

FIGURE 18.8

A Negative Income Tax Program
This NIT starts each person out with a tax credit of $4000/yr. People who earn no income receive that amount in cash. All earned income is then taxed, here at the rate of 50 percent, resulting in a breakeven income level of $8000/yr. People who earn less than that amount receive a net benefit payment from the government; people who earn more make a net tax payment.

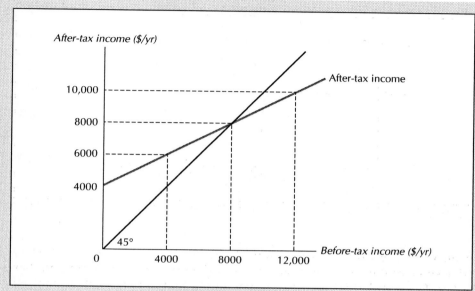

Figure 18.8 shows how the program would work with a tax credit of $4000/yr and a tax rate of 50 percent. The breakeven income level for these program values is $8000/yr. Someone earning $4000/yr would receive a net benefit payment of $2000/yr, while someone earning $12,000/yr would make a tax payment of $2000/yr.

EXERCISE 18.4

Find the breakeven income level for a program whose tax credit is $6000 and whose tax rate is 40 percent. What is the net benefit received by a person who earns $4000/yr from paid employment?

The NIT would be administered in much the same way as our current income tax is administered. One strong advantage of the NIT is thus its promise to eliminate the costly overlapping bureaucracies of our current programs. But the main attraction of the NIT to economists is that it has a much less perverse effect on work incentives than current programs do. Because the marginal tax rate confronting poor people would never exceed 100 percent under the NIT, people would be assured of having more after-tax income if they worked longer hours.

Although the incentive problem is less severe under the NIT than under our current welfare programs, it remains a serious difficulty. If the NIT is to be the *sole* means of insulating people against poverty, its payment to people with no earned income must be at least as large as the poverty threshold. And if the payment is large enough to live on, it will inevitably induce many people to stop working. The importance of this problem was confirmed by federal experiments with the NIT during the 1970s. Although the labor force withdrawals observed in these experiments were smaller than predicted by the NIT's fiercest critics, they were nonetheless substantial.

But even if the NIT induced only a handful of people to pursue lives of leisure at taxpayer expense, critics would find these people, and there would be an eager audience for reports of their doings on the nightly news. Both liberals and conservatives alike would be chagrined at the sight of NIT recipients practicing their guitars and playing volleyball on Monday mornings. In the face of such images, an NIT with a grant large enough to support able-bodied people who chose not to work would be politically unsustainable.

Public Employment for the Poor   Like the NIT, proposals for public jobs for the disadvantaged (JOBS) received much attention during the early days of the war on poverty. These proposals had the obvious appeal of not providing handouts for people who could support themselves. In the language of program advocates, the government would serve as the "employer of last resort," the guarantor of "decent employment at a decent wage" to all who were unable to find such work in the private sector.

As the sole mechanism for lifting the poor from poverty, the public jobs idea fell victim to several criticisms. Perhaps the most important was that guaranteed public employment would cause people to desert the private sector in droves. This claim was based on evidence that unskilled workers find government jobs much more attractive than private jobs with similar wages. Thousands of applicants line up when openings for menial government jobs are posted; at the same time want ads for kitchen help in the private sector often go unanswered. With the prospect of a large-scale employment migration clearly in mind, policymakers concluded that resources simply would not permit an open-ended offer of government employment at wages comparable to those in the private sector.

A second criticism was that public jobs for the disadvantaged would inevitably be make-work tasks, no more useful than Keynes's call for people to dig holes and fill them up. This criticism struck a resonant chord in the United States, where the predisposition has often been to view *all* government jobs as make-work. This attitude alone would probably have killed the JOBS proposals, even if they could somehow have been made economically feasible.

A Combination of NIT and JOBS   With a few simple changes, however, the JOBS and NIT programs can be combined in a way that eliminates many of the difficulties we encounter when each is viewed as the sole weapon against poverty.

With JOBS, for example, the government could solicit bids from private contractors to hire unskilled workers at subminimum wages to perform a variety of specified tasks. (More on these tasks in a moment.) With the wage set much lower than for private jobs, there would be no reason to fear a massive exodus from the private sector.

Having public jobs for the poor administered by private contractors chosen through competitive bidding would do much to eliminate the inefficient management that so often plagues government operations. As noted in Chapter 12, some cities have found that their costs go down by more than half, with no reductions in quality, when they provide services like fire protection and trash removal through private contractors. If the administration of JOBS were subjected to the ruthless cost-cutting pressures of private markets, there would be every reason to expect efficient performance here as well.

People with even limited skills can perform many useful services.

David Young-Wolff/PhotoEdit.

There is general agreement that, given competent management, many useful tasks can be performed by people who lack extensive experience and training. What city would not be pleased to have additional landscaping and maintenance in its parks? With proper supervision, unskilled persons can carry out such tasks. And they can transport the elderly and handicapped in specially equipped vans; fill potholes in city streets; replace burned-out street lamps; transplant seedlings in erosion control projects; remove graffiti from public places; paint government buildings; and recycle newspapers and aluminum and glass containers.

These and countless other socially useful tasks remain to be done, and could be done by people who lack the skills necessary to find employment in the private sector. Even single parents with small children could participate, by helping to staff day care centers in which their own children were enrolled.

A simple design change would also eliminate the major difficulties associated with the traditional NIT. This change would be to limit the maximum NIT payment to a figure that, like the JOBS salary, is well below the annual earnings equivalent of full-time employment at the minimum wage. With the payment held below that level, it would not be possible for people to drop out of the labor market to live at taxpayer expense. Yet when combined with earnings from the JOBS program—or, better still, with earnings from a private job—the NIT grant would lift a person above the poverty threshold (see Figure 18.9). Neither program alone can accomplish this goal without creating unacceptable side effects. But the two programs together can.

Indirect Benefits of the Combined Program   The JOBS-NIT combination would not be cheap. But neither is our current system. In addition to their direct costs and perverse work incentives, current programs impose innumerable indirect costs. Many of these take the form of regulations designed to help the poor. Because current programs cannot transfer extra income directly to the poor without undermining work incentives even further, policymakers constantly face pressure to interfere with private markets to shield the poor from price increases. As discussed in Chapter 2, for example, bureaucrats designed a Byzantine system of regulations in order to prevent gasoline price increases during the oil supply interruption of 1979. It was

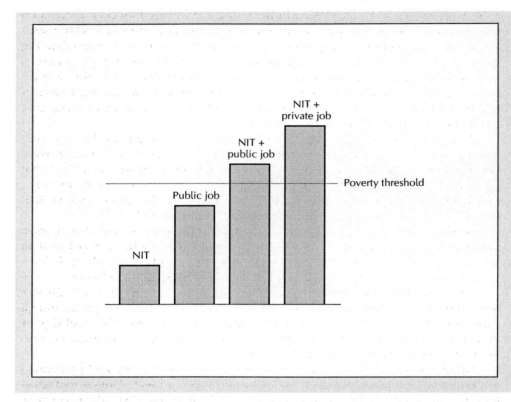

FIGURE 18.9
Income Sources in the NIT-JOBS Program
An NIT with a cash grant far too small to live on would not encourage people to drop out of the labor force. Nor would a government-sponsored job at subminimum wages lure productively employed workers out of private-sector jobs. But the combined income from both programs would be sufficient to lift people above the poverty threshold. And because of the low pay in public jobs, participants would have strong incentives to continue searching for jobs in the private sector.

common to see lines at gas stations wrap around several city blocks, and several motorists were killed or injured in disputes over who stood where in those queues.

With a combination of NIT and JOBS in place of our current welfare programs, policymakers could have transferred extra income directly to the poor in the wake of the oil shocks of 1979. And this, in turn, would have permitted us to allocate oil in the most sensible and efficient way—by the price mechanism.

Many cities have similarly adopted rent controls in the name of their concerns about the poor. Yet as any intermediate microeconomics student can readily explain, these controls cost us many dollars for every dollar they save the poor. Low-income housing deteriorates; lawyers prosper from otherwise pointless condominium conversions; couples whose children have left home continue living in eight-room apartments; desperate tenants bribe superintendents to get on waiting lists; and so on. With a combination of JOBS and NIT programs, people's incomes could be augmented directly, thereby circumventing the need for wasteful stopgap measures like rent controls.

An Objection to JOBS   Many people who think of themselves as friends of the poor will find it unpalatable to require that people perform services in return for public assistance. Some would liken this policy to forced servitude and object that it deprives poor people of their dignity.

Such objections stem from a refusal to acknowledge our true menu of policy choices. In an ideal world, liberals and conservatives alike might agree to provide generous unconditional assistance to those who cannot fend for themselves, and no assistance at all for others. In the world we live in, however, there is no reliable scheme for separating the members of these two groups. Lacking such a scheme, we are hardly in a position to offer one group benefits while denying them to the other. And no one pretends that it is possible to offer generous unconditional assistance to *everyone*. Our practical alternatives, in plain view for everyone to see, are (1) to offer very limited unconditional assistance to everyone (roughly, our current scheme) or (2) to offer more generous assistance conditional on the performance of useful tasks.

As a college student, you are unlikely to be desperately poor. But try for a moment to imagine that you are not only poor but unlucky. There are private jobs out there somewhere that pay a decent wage, but your luck is so bad that you have despaired of ever landing one. Policymakers in Washington are trying to decide what to do about you. You and they know that the choices are limited to the two alternatives mentioned. Which would *you* prefer?

Suppose you prefer the second—to perform a useful task in exchange for a living wage. That way, you reason, you can afford to live in an apartment in which your children do not eat flakes of leaded paint off the walls and doorframes. You also know that working in a government job might help you acquire skills that would enable you to get the high-wage job you really want. Finally, despite what you have heard to the contrary, you do not feel that performing a socially useful task demeans you in any way. How would you then feel if your "friends" in high places lobbied vigorously against your chosen alternative, saying that it would "rob you of your dignity"?

Liberals and conservatives have a shared interest—both moral and practical—in redistributing income in ways that do not undermine efficiency. Our current redistributive programs are for the most part both costly and ineffective. Microeconomic analysis has as much to teach us about the reform of these programs as it does about the many other important policy issues we've examined throughout this text.

SUMMARY

- Public goods are like other goods in that their value can be measured by what people would be willing to pay to have more of them. But whereas the aggregate demand curve for a private good is formed by adding the individual demand curves horizontally, the aggregate willingness-to-pay curve for a public good is the vertical summation of the corresponding individual curves. This difference arose because the quantity of a public good must be the same for every consumer. In the private case, by contrast, the price is the same for different buyers, who then select different quantities.

- There is a clear analogy between the demand for public goods and the demand for jointly produced private goods. To produce additional chicken wings, it is necessary to produce additional drumsticks. Just as the quantity of a public good must be the same for all consumers, so must the quantity of chicken wings consumed be exactly equal to the quantity of drumsticks consumed. And just as the

price one person is willing to pay for a given quantity of a public good can differ from what another is willing to pay, so will the price of drumsticks generally be different from the price of wings.

- As with private goods, the supply curve of a public good is simply the marginal cost of producing it. The optimal quantity of a public good is the level for which the aggregate willingness-to-pay curve intersects the supply curve. In order to pay for the optimal quantities of public goods it will generally be necessary for individual tax payments to vary directly with the amounts that individuals are willing to pay for public goods. To the extent that people with higher incomes demand higher quantities of public goods, the result is that both rich and poor will favor a tax system that places a larger share of the total tax burden on the rich.

- The mere fact that a good has the characteristics of a public good does not mean that it must necessarily be provided by government. There are many ingenious schemes, ranging from free commercial television to highly structured collective legal contracts, whereby public goods are provided with virtually no involvement by government.

- Problems similar to those that arise in connection with public goods are encountered whenever there are significant indivisibilities or economies of scale in the production of private consumption goods. In such situations, we saw, it is common for clubs to form in which members share the costs of important consumption goods. The trade-off confronting a potential member of such a club is between cost savings and reduced privacy in the use of the good.

- Majority voting sometimes produces intransitive rankings among projects. When it does, the power to choose the order in which different pairs of alternatives are considered is often tantamount to the power to determine the final outcome. There is a special class of issues in which majority voting is not vulnerable to agenda manipulation. With respect to single issues in which each voter ranks every alternative in terms of its distance from his ideal choice, the final outcome will be the one most preferred by the median voter, no matter what order the votes are taken in. This result is known as the median voter theorem.

- Cost-benefit analysis is a simple but very powerful alternative to majority voting. Applied in the proper way to a sufficiently large number of small decisions, it almost always satisfies the Pareto criterion.

- Even with a perfect mechanism for revealing public sentiments about the relative desirability of different public goods, there will still be difficult choices about which goods to produce. The problem is that the types of public goods strongly favored by some groups are often strongly opposed by others. If heterogeneous voters are forced to coexist in a single jurisdiction, the frequent result is a painful compromise that satisfies no one. But the need for such

compromises is greatly reduced if voters are able to group themselves into communities with relatively homogeneous tastes.

- A problem that plagues all mechanisms of public decision making is that self-interested parties have an incentive to influence outcomes in their own favor. This problem goes by the name of rent seeking and has become an increasingly serious threat to our social welfare.

- The primary mechanism for distributing income in market economies is the factor market. People sell their labor in return for a payment equal to the value of its marginal product. And they invest their savings at interest rates that are similarly linked to the marginal productivity of capital. This method of income distribution has several desirable properties on efficiency grounds—in particular, it rewards effort and the willingness to incur risk. But critics, notably John Rawls, have argued that people would never voluntarily choose to live under a process that yields such highly unequal outcomes as we see in untempered factor markets.

- In addition to the moral argument Rawls has offered, there are at least two practical reasons for income redistribution. First, the rich would favor paying more than an equal share of the total tax burden because otherwise they would end up with an inefficiently small provision of public goods. And second, redistribution may be necessary to maintain a voluntary sense of social cohesion, something as much in the interests of the rich as of the poor.

- Our current array of welfare programs is costly, not only because of bureaucratic duplication, but also because of its indirect effects on work incentives and on public policies with respect to private markets. A combination of a small negative income tax, supplemented by subminimum-wage public jobs, could transfer income to the poor without many of the unintended side effects of our current programs.

QUESTIONS FOR REVIEW

1. Why are the individual willingness-to-pay curves added vertically, not horizontally, to get the aggregate willingness-to-pay curve for a public good?

2. How are jointly produced private goods analogous to public goods?

3. Why would even rich citizens be likely to oppose having equal tax payments by rich and poor alike?

4. In what way does a private good produced under conditions of increasing returns to scale resemble a

public good? Describe the trade-off between flexibility and cost that confronts users of such goods.

5. How does majority voting lead to intransitive social rankings?

6. Describe two forms of inefficiency associated with rent seeking.

7. Why is a negative income tax, by itself, unable to solve the redistribution problem?

CHAPTER 18   GOVERNMENT

PROBLEMS

1. A government is trying to decide how much of a public good to provide. The willingness-to-pay curves for each of its two citizens are as given in the diagram. The marginal cost curve for the public good is given by MC = $Q/2$, where Q is the quantity of the good. There is also a fixed cost of 10 associated with production of the good.

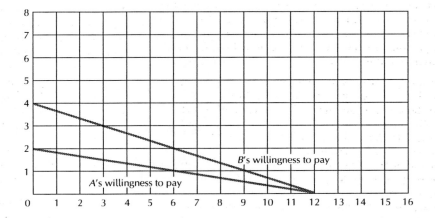

a. What is the optimal quantity of the public good?
b. If both citizens must be taxed equally to provide the good, will it receive a majority vote?

2. On the assumption that the public good described in Problem 1 is provided at the optimal level, how much should the state charge each citizen each time he or she uses the public good?

3. Ten identical consumers all have individual willingness-to-pay curves $P = 5 - \frac{1}{20}Q$ for a public good—say, local parks (where P is measured in hundreds of dollars and Q is measured in acres). Construct and graph the aggregate willingness-to-pay curve. For 50 acres of parks, what is the maximum each individual would be willing to pay?

4. Consider the scenario described in Problem 3, but now consider that the marginal cost of providing parks measured in hundreds of dollars is MC = $\frac{1}{2}Q$. Determine the optimal size of local parks.

5. Chicken wings and chicken drumsticks are jointly produced private goods. The introduction of Buffalo wings—the fast-food sensation—has led to a sharp increase in the demand for chicken wings. Show how this affects the equilibrium price and quantity of drumsticks.

6. Lumber and sawdust are joint products, whose demand functions are D_L and D_S, as shown in the diagram. The quantity axis measures the number of trees. Points on the demand schedules indicate demands for the lumber or sawdust equivalents of a given quantity of trees.
   a. Provide an economic interpretation of the fact that the demand schedule for sawdust extends below the horizontal axis.
   b. If the supply schedule for trees is as given in the diagram, show the equilibrium prices and quantities of sawdust and lumber on a graph.

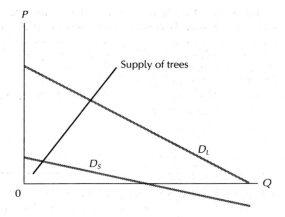

7. Viewer-supported television stations often give contributors "free" gifts for making contributions at various levels. ("Two handsome *News Hour* coffee mugs for a donation of $120.") Based on what you know about the psychology of framing decisions (see Chapter 8), explain why this practice might help stations raise more money.

8. Colleges and universities commonly name buildings and business or medical schools after substantial donors (witness Ohio State's Max Fisher School of Business and Schottenstein Center/Value City Arena). Meanwhile, few donors care to earmark their gifts for routine maintenance of university buildings. How might the social benefits of charitable giving explain these observations?

9. *True or false:* Because the issues at stake in national presidential elections are much more important than those at stake in a small village mayoral election, rational choice theory says a much larger proportion of voters will turn out in the former than in the latter. Explain.

10. *True or false:* The fact that the voter turnout is significantly greater in close presidential elections than in one-sided ones provides clear support for the proposition that voters are rational. Explain.

11. A fraternity consisting of 20 sophomores, 20 juniors, and 20 seniors is about to elect its next president. Arnold, Bo, and Chuck are the three candidates. Members of each class have the ranking schemes given in the table:

Class	Best	Next best	Last
Seniors	Arnold	Bo	Chuck
Juniors	Bo	Chuck	Arnold
Sophs	Chuck	Arnold	Bo

The tradition in the fraternity is to pit two candidates against each other and then pit the winner of that contest against the third candidate. If you were a sophomore, whom would you pair off in the preliminary round? If you were a senior?

12. Smith is a hard-hearted person who favors giving the poor only sufficient aid to keep them from going hungry. Assuming everyone else in Smith's community feels the same way he does, why might Smith nonetheless be opposed to a proposal to let each community set its own level of welfare support?

13. A. Smith, who is currently unemployed, is a participant in four welfare programs that offer daily benefits of $10 each to people with no earned income. Each program

678   CHAPTER 18   GOVERNMENT

then curtails its benefits by 50 cents for every dollar of income a recipient earns. A. Smith's identical twin brother, B. Smith, is enrolled in an experimental negative income tax program that gives him $40/day in benefits and then taxes him at the rate of 50 percent on each dollar of earned income. Now suppose A. Smith is offered a job that pays $4/hr, the same wage his brother earns.

a.   Draw the budget constraint for each twin.
b.   How many hours would they have to work before A. Smith ends up with more net cash and benefits than his brother?

ANSWERS TO IN-CHAPTER EXERCISES

18.1 The aggregate willingness-to-pay curve would be $P = 120 - 2Q$, the vertical summation of the individual willingness-to-pay curves (see graph). For $Q = 30$ minutes, each individual would be willing to pay up to $P = 12 - \frac{1}{5}Q = 12 - \frac{1}{5}(30) = \$6$, for a total of $60 from 10 consumers.

18.2 To find the optimal duration of the concert, equate the aggregate willingness-to-pay $P = 120 - 2Q$ and the marginal cost $MC = 2Q$ to find $Q = 30$ minutes.

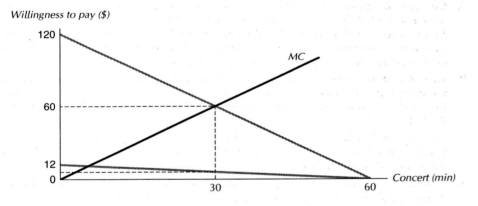

Willingness to pay ($)

18.3 Again, Schumer is the median voter. The alternative closest to his ideal percentage is 20, and this will win a majority in a vote on any pair of alternatives.

18.4 Let Y^* denote the breakeven income level. To calculate Y^*, we solve $6000 + (1 - 0.4)Y^* = Y^*$, which yields $Y^* = \$15,000/\text{yr}$. A person who earns $4000/yr would pay $0.4(\$4000) = \$1600/\text{yr}$ in taxes, and would thus receive a net annual benefit of $6000 - \$1600 = \$4400$.

part four

Macroeconomics

Part 4 studies the economy as a system in which feedbacks occur. Output is demanded by firms, by households, by the government and by foreigners. Since interest rates affect the demand for output, the financial sector interacts with the real economy. Price and wage adjustments help restore output to full capacity but monetary policy and fiscal policy also play a role. Together, all this affects inflation and unemployment. Economies are increasingly open to foreign trade and foreign capital. The balance of payments records transactions with foreigners. The dynamics of the national economy also depends on the exchange rate policy pursued. By the end of Part 4, we can explain business cycles around full capacity and long-run growth in full capacity output.

Chapter 19 introduces the macroeconomy. Chapters 20–21 develop a basic model of output determination in the short run. Chapters 22 and 23 describe money, banking and how interest rates are set. Chapter 24 examines monetary and fiscal policy. Chapter 25 introduces aggregate supply and price adjustment. Chapters 26 and 27 look at inflation and unemployment, and Chapters 28 and 29 at exchange rates and the balance of payments. Chapter 30 discusses long-run growth, Chapter 31 analyses short-run business cycles. After thirteen chapters of macroeconomics, Chapter 32 takes stock.

Contents

chapter 19

Introduction to macroeconomics

Learning outcomes

By the end of this chapter, you should understand:

1. macroeconomics as the study of the whole economy

2. internally consistent national accounts

3. the circular flow between households and firms

4. why leakages always equal injections

5. more comprehensive measures of GDP and GNP

W e now turn to the big issues, such as unemployment, inflation and economic growth. Macroeconomics sacrifices details to study the big picture.

Macroeconomics is the study of the economy as a system.

The distinction between microeconomics and macroeconomics is more than the difference between economics in the small and economics in the large, which the Greek prefixes *micro* and *macro* suggest. The purpose of their analysis is also different.

A model simplifies to focus on the key elements of a problem and think about them clearly. We could study the whole economy by piecing together a microeconomic analysis of every market but it would be hard to keep track of all the economic forces at work. Our brains do not have a big enough Pentium chip to make sense of it.

Microeconomics and macroeconomics take different approaches to keep the analysis manageable. Microeconomics stresses a detailed understanding of particular markets. To achieve this detail, many interactions with other markets are suppressed. In saying a tax on cars reduces the equilibrium quantity of cars, we ignore what the government does with the tax revenue. If government debt is reduced, interest rates and the exchange rate may fall, boosting competitiveness and car output.

Microeconomics is like looking at a horse race through a pair of binoculars. It is great for details, but sometimes we get a clearer picture of the whole race by using the naked eye. Because macroeconomics studies the interaction of different parts of the economy, it uses a different simplification to keep the analysis manageable. Macroeconomics simplifies the building blocks in order to focus on how they fit together and influence one another.

Macroeconomics stresses broad aggregates such as the total demand for goods by households or the total spending on machinery and building by firms. As in watching the horse race with the naked eye, our notion of individual details is more blurred but our full attention is on the big picture. We are more likely to notice the horse sneaking up on the rails.

336 Part 4 : Macroeconomics

19.1 The big issues

The **labour force** is people at work or looking for work. It excludes people neither working nor looking for work. The **unemployment rate** is the fraction of the labour force without a job.

Real **gross national product** (GNP) measures the income of an economy, the quantity of goods and services the economy can afford to purchase. **Economic growth** is a rise in real GNP.

The **inflation rate** is the percentage increase in the average price of goods and services.

Here are some key questions that form the theme of the analysis in Part 4.

Why did unemployment rise after the 1960s but fall in the 1990s? Did workers price themselves out of jobs by greedy wage claims? Does technical progress destroy jobs? Can the government create more jobs? These are questions we need to answer in Part 4.

What determines real GNP? Why was there a boom in the late 1990s, a slowdown after 2000 and a rise in activity after 2003? Why do some countries grow faster than others?

The price level is a weighted average of the prices households pay for goods and services. What causes inflation? Money growth, oil price rises or a budget deficit? Have we now learned how to defeat inflation?

Almost every day the media discuss inflation, unemployment and economic growth. These issues help determine elections and make people interested in macroeconomics.

19.2 The facts

We begin with some facts about unemployment, economic growth and inflation. Table 19.1 puts recent performance in perspective, showing data for the UK, the US and Germany since 1960.

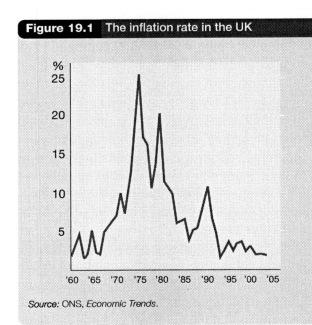

Figure 19.1 The inflation rate in the UK

Source: ONS, *Economic Trends*.

Table 19.1	Inflation, unemployment and output growth 1960–2004 (annual, %)		
	UK	**USA**	**Germany**
Unemployment			
60–73	3	5	1
73–81	6	7	3
81–90	10	7	7
90–01	7	5	7
01–04	5	5	9
Real growth			
60–73	3	4	5
73–81	1	2	2
81–90	3	3	2
90–01	2	3	3
01–04	2	3	2
Inflation			
60–73	5	3	3
73–81	15	9	5
81–90	6	5	3
90–01	3	3	3
01–04	2	2	2

Source: OECD, *Economic Outlook*.

Table 19.2	Unemployment (%)		
	1980	1989	2004
USA	7.25	5.3	5.7
Japan	2.0	2.3	5.0
France	5.8	9.4	9.5
Italy	5.6	9.8	8.5
UK	6.2	7.3	4.7
Belgium	9.3	7.5	8.5
Holland	6.0	6.9	4.7
Sweden	2.0	1.5	6.4

Source: OECD, Economic Outlook.

The two decades before 1970 were a golden age of low unemployment, rapid growth and low inflation. In the early 1970s, with the world economy booming, OPEC quadrupled the price of oil. The rest of the 1970s saw high inflation, low growth and rising unemployment. After another oil price hike in 1979–80, the 1980s were another tough period. Table 19.1 shows that it was not until the 1990s that inflation and unemployment fell. Table 19.2 gives more details on the rise and fall of unemployment, trends that few countries escaped.

Figure 19.1 takes a longer look at UK inflation, which soared in 1970s. The Thatcher government reduced inflation after 1980 but lost control in the late 1980s when it let the economy grow too rapidly, leading to more inflation. Subsequent Chancellors – John Major, Norman Lamont, Kenneth Clarke and Gordon Brown – gradually got the UK back on an even keel. Figure 19.1 explains why New Labour has stressed prudence and the avoidance of boom and bust.

19.3 An overview

The economy comprises millions of individual economic units: households, firms and the departments of central and local government. Together, their individual decisions determine the economy's total spending, income and output.

The circular flow

Initially, we ignore the government and other countries. Table 19.3 shows transactions between households and firms. Households own the factors of production (inputs to production). Households rent labour to firms in exchange for wages. Households are also the ultimate owners of firms and get their profits. Capital and land, even if held by firms, are ultimately owned by households.

The first row of Table 19.3 shows that households supply factor services to firms that use these inputs to make output. The second row shows the corresponding payments. Households earn factor incomes (wages, rents, profits), payments by firms for these factor services. The third row shows that households spend their incomes buying the output of firms, giving firms the money to pay for production inputs. Figure 19.2 shows this *circular flow* between households and firms.

The circular flow shows how real resources and financial payments flow between firms and households.

The inner loop shows flows of real resources between the two sectors. The outer loop shows the corresponding flows of money in a market economy. A centrally

Table 19.3	Transactions by households and firms
Households	Firms
Supply factor services to firms	Use factors to make output
Receive factor incomes from firms	Rent factor services from households
Buy output of firms	Sell output to households

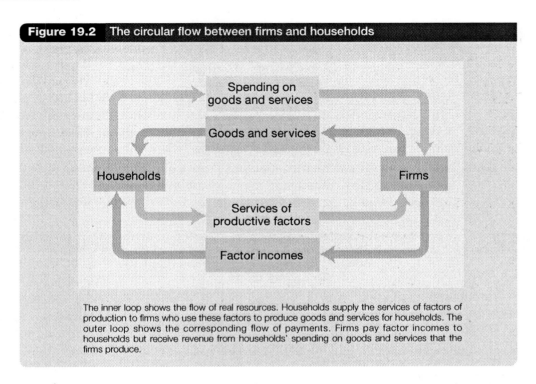

Figure 19.2 The circular flow between firms and households

The inner loop shows the flow of real resources. Households supply the services of factors of production to firms who use these factors to produce goods and services for households. The outer loop shows the corresponding flow of payments. Firms pay factor incomes to households but receive revenue from households' spending on goods and services that the firms produce.

planned economy could arrange the resource transfers on the inner loop without using the outer loop.

Figure 19.2 suggests three ways to measure economic activity in an economy: (a) the value of goods and services produced, (b) the level of factor earnings, which represent the value of factor services supplied, or (c) the value of spending on goods and services. All payments are the counterparts of real resources. For the moment, we assume all payments are spent buying real resources. Hence, we get the same estimate of total economic activity whether we use the value of production, the level of factor incomes, or spending on goods and services.

Factor incomes equal household spending if all income is spent. The value of output equals total spending on goods and services if all goods are sold. The value of output also equals the value of household incomes. Since profits are residually defined as the value of sales minus the

BOX 19-1　The second industrial revolution

The biggest mass migration in the history of the world is under way in China, whose building boom is now devouring half of worldwide concrete production. New urban apartments, office blocks, and skyscrapers are housing China's rural masses who are flocking to cities along the eastern coastline. In the next 25 years, 345 million people are going to move from the rural areas into the cities.

In 1999, the new port at Qingdao did not even exist. Now it is one of the biggest container ports in the world. Every day ships unload vast quantities of raw materials such as iron ore and oil – materials that are

going directly into the building boom – and fill up with exports from the country's ever-expanding manufacturing industry. Meanwhile the capital city, Beijing, is changing before people's eyes, with each new building battling the next for attention.

What we are observing in China is the circular flow of income. Commerce is expanding rapidly and households are responding by providing labour for construction and production. As commerce continues to expand, more labour is employed, more goods are produced and more is consumed.

Adaped from BBC News Online, 11 May 2004.

rental of factor inputs, and since profits accrue to the households that own firms, household incomes – from supplying land, labour and capital, or from profits – equals the value of output.

Our model is still very simple. What happens if firms do not sell all their output? What happens if firms sell output not to households but to other firms? What happens if households do not spend all their income? The next section answers these questions. Having done so, our conclusion will be unchanged: the level of economic activity can be measured by valuing total spending, total output or total earnings. All three methods give the same answer.

The circular flow diagram in Figure 19.2 lets us keep track of some key interactions in the economy as a whole. But the diagram is too simple. It leaves out important features of the real world: saving and investment, government spending and taxes, transactions between firms and with the rest of the world. We need a comprehensive system of national accounts.

19.4 National income accounting

Gross domestic product (GDP) measures the output made in the domestic economy, regardless of who owns the production inputs.

Value added is the increase in the value of goods as a result of the production process.

Final goods are purchased by the ultimate user, either households buying consumer goods or firms buying capital goods such as machinery. **Intermediate goods** are partly-finished goods that form inputs to a subsequent production process that then uses them up.

Measuring GDP

GDP measures the value of output in the economy. Initially we discuss a *closed economy*, not linked to the rest of the world, in which output and income are the same.

First, we extend our simple circular flow diagram. Transactions do not take place exclusively between a single firm and a single household. Firms hire labour services from households but buy raw materials and machinery from *other* firms. To avoid double counting, we use value added.

To get value added, we take the firm's output then deduct the cost of the input goods used up to make that output. Closely related is the distinction between final goods and intermediate goods. Ice cream is a final good. Steel is an intermediate good, made by one firm but used as an input by another firm. Capital goods are final goods because they are *not* used up in subsequent production. They do not fully depreciate.

An example will clarify these concepts. Study it until you have mastered them. We assume that there are four firms in the economy: a steel maker, a producer of capital goods (machines) for the car industry, a tyre maker and a car producer who sells to the final user, households. Table 19.4 calculates GDP for this simple economy.

Table 19.4 Calculating GDP

(1) Good	(2) Seller	(3) Buyer	(4) Transaction value	(5) Value added	(6) Spending on final goods	(7) Factor earnings
Steel	Steel maker	Machine maker	£ 1 000	£1 000	–	£1 000
Steel	Steel maker	Car maker	£ 3 000	£3 000	–	£3 000
Machine	Machine maker	Car maker	£ 2 000	£1 000	£2 000	£1 000
Tyres	Tyre maker	Car maker	£ 500	£ 500	–	£ 500
Cars	Car maker	Households	£ 5 000	£1 500	£5 000	£1 500
Total transactions			£11 500			
GDP			£ 7 000	£7 000	£7 000	

The steel firm makes £4000 worth of steel, one-quarter sold to the machine maker and three-quarters sold to the car maker. If the steel producer also mines the iron ore from which the steel is produced, all £4000 is value added or net output of the steel firm. This revenue is paid out in wages and rents, or remains as residual profits that also accrue to households as income. Hence the first two rows of the last column also add up to £4000. Firms have spent £4000 buying this steel output but it is not expenditure on final goods. Steel is an intermediate good, used up in later stages of the production process.

The machine maker spends £1000 buying steel input, then converts it into a machine sold to the car maker for £2000. The value added by the machine maker is £2000 less the £1000 spent on steel input. This net revenue of £1000 accrues directly or indirectly to households as income or profit. Since the car firm intends to keep the machine, the full value of £2000 is then shown under 'final expenditure'.

Like the steel producer, the tyre manufacturer makes an intermediate output that is not final expenditure. If the tyre manufacturer also owns the rubber trees from which the tyres were made, the entire output of £500 is value added and contributes to household incomes. If the tyre company bought rubber from a domestic rubber producer, we subtract the input value of rubber from the tyre manufacturer's output to get value added or net output, but add another row in the table showing the activity of the rubber producer.

The car producer spends £3000 on steel and £500 on tyres. Since both are used up during the period in which cars are made, we subtract £3500 from the car output of £5000 to get the value added of the car maker. This net revenue pays households for factor services supplied, or is paid to them as profits.

Finally, the car producer sells the car for £5000 to the final consumer – households. Only then does the car become a final good. Its full price of £5000 is final expenditure.

Table 19.4 shows that the gross value of all the transactions is £11 500. This overstates the value of the goods the economy has actually produced. For example, the £3000 that the steel producer earned by selling steel to the car producer is already included in the final value of car output. It is double-counting to count this £3000 again as output of the steel producer.

Column (5) shows the value added at each stage in the production process. £7000 is the true net output of the economy. Since each firm pays the corresponding net revenue to households either as direct factor payments or indirectly as profits, household earnings are £7000 in the last column of the table. If we add up payments made to households as income and profits we get the same measure of GDP.

Table 19.4 confirms that we also get the same answer if we measure spending on *final* goods and services. In this case final users are households buying cars and the car producer buying the (everlasting) machinery used to make cars.

Investment and saving

Investment is the purchase of new capital goods by firms. Saving is the part of income not spent buying goods and services.

This example explains value added and the distinction between intermediate and final goods. It also deals with a second complication. Total output and household income are each £7000 but households spend only £5000 on cars. What do they do with the rest of their income? And who does the rest of the spending? To resolve these issues, we need investment and saving.

Households spend £5000 on cars. Since their income is £7000, they save £2000. The car maker spends £2000 on investment, buying new machinery. Figure 19.3 shows how to amend the circular flow diagram of Figure 19.2. The bottom half

Figure 19.3 Investment, saving, and the circular flow

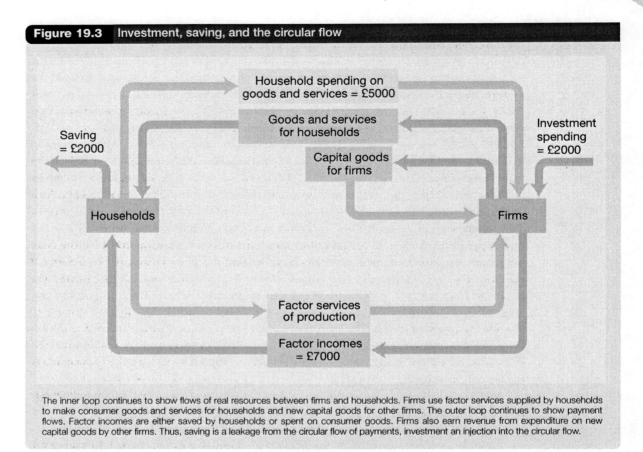

The inner loop continues to show flows of real resources between firms and households. Firms use factor services supplied by households to make consumer goods and services for households and new capital goods for other firms. The outer loop continues to show payment flows. Factor incomes are either saved by households or spent on consumer goods. Firms also earn revenue from expenditure on new capital goods by other firms. Thus, saving is a leakage from the circular flow of payments, investment an injection into the circular flow.

of Figure 19.3 shows that incomes and factor services are each £7000. But £2000 leaks out from the circular flow when households save. Only £5000 finds its way back to firms as households spending on cars.

The top half of the figure shows that £5000 is the value of output of consumer goods and of household spending on these goods. Since GDP is £7000, where does the other £2000 come from? If not from household spending, it must come from spending by firms themselves. It is the £2000 of investment expenditure made by the car producer buying machinery for car production.

The numbers in Table 19.4 relate to flows of output, expenditure and income in a particular period, such as a year. During this period the economy goes once round the inner and outer loops of Figure 19.3. On the inner loop, firms make an output of £5000 for consumption by households and an output of £2000 of capital goods for investment by firms. On the outer loop, which relates to money payments, saving is a *leakage* of £2000 from the circular flow and investment spending by firms on new machinery is an *injection* of £2000 to the circular flow.

> A leakage from the circular flow is money no longer recycled from households to firms.
> An injection is money that flows to firms without being cycled through households.

Two questions immediately arise. First, is it coincidental that household savings of £2000 exactly equal investment expenditure of £2000 by firms? Second, if not, how is the money saved by households transferred to firms to allow them to pay for investment spending?

Suppose Y denotes GDP, which also equals the value of household incomes, C denotes household spending on consumption and S saving. By definition saving is unspent income, so $Y \equiv C + S$, where the symbol ≡ means 'is identically equal to, as a matter of definition'. Since one definition of GDP is the sum of final expenditure, $Y \equiv C + I$. Putting these two definitions together

$$S \equiv I \tag{1}$$

since both are identical to $(Y - C)$.

It is thus no accident that saving and investment are each £2000 in our example. Equation (1) tells us that saving and investment are always equal, in the absence of government and foreign sectors.

Look again at the outer loop of Figure 19.3. All household spending in the top half of the figure returns to households as income in the bottom half of the figure. Investment spending by firms is matched by an income flow to households in excess of their consumer spending. Since saving is defined as the excess of income over consumption, investment and savings must always be equal.

These accounting identities follow from our definitions of investment, savings and income. *Actual* saving must equal *actual* investment. This need not mean *desired* shavings equals *desired* investment. To study that we need models of desired savings and investment, a task we begin in the next chapter.[1]

What connects the leakage of saving and the injection of investment? Since firms pay households £7000 but get only £5000 from household spending, they are borrowing £2000 to pay for the new capital goods they are buying. Since households save £2000, they are lending it to firms for investment. In a market economy, financial institutions and financial markets channel household saving to the firms that wish to borrow to invest in new capital goods.

Investment lets us deal with another problem glossed over in our simpler circular flow diagram. What happens if firms cannot sell all the output that they produce? Surely this creates a gap between the output and expenditure measures of GDP?

Final goods are goods not used up in the production process in the period. In Table 19.4 steel was an intermediate good used up in making cars and machines. Machines were a final good because the car maker could use them again in the next period. Suppose that car sales are not £5000 but only £4000. The car maker is left with £1000 worth of cars that must be stockpiled.

Inventories or **stocks** are goods currently held by a firm for future production or sale.

The car producer may hold stocks of steel, an input to production of cars in the next period, or stocks of finished cars awaiting sale to consumers in the next period.

In Chapter 6 we described stocks as *working capital*. Not used up in production and sale during the current period, stocks are classified as capital goods. Adding to stocks is investment in working capital. When stocks are depleted, we treat this as negative investment or disinvestment.

Now we can keep the national accounts straight. When the car firm sells only £4000 of the £5000 worth of cars made this period, we treat the inventory investment of £1000 by the car producer as final expenditure. As in Table 19.4, the output and expenditure measures of GDP are each £7000 including the output and expenditure on the machinery for making cars. But spending on final goods is now: car firm (£2000 on machines, £1000 on stocks), household-consumer (£4000 on cars).

[1] It helps to draw parallels with microeconomics. The demand curve shows desired purchases at any price, the supply curve desired sales at any price. In equilibrium desired purchases equal desired sales. When the price is too high there is excess supply and some desired sales are frustrated. But since every transaction has a buyer and a seller, actual purchases equal actual sales whether or not the market is in equilibrium.

This can be confusing. The trick is to distinguish between classification by commodity and classification by economic use. Steel is an intermediate commodity but that is not important. When a steel producer makes *and sells* steel we show this as production of an intermediate good. Since it has been passed on to someone else, our expenditure measure picks it up further up the chain of production and sales. But when a firm adds to its stocks we must count that as final expenditure because it will not show up anywhere else in the national accounts. The firm is temporarily adding to its capital. When it later uses up these stocks, we treat this as negative investment to keep the record straight.

We now introduce the government sector.

The government

Governments raise revenue both through direct taxes T_d on incomes (wages, rents, interest and profits) and through indirect taxes or expenditures taxes T_e (VAT, petrol duties, cigarette taxes). Taxes finance two kinds of expenditure. Government spending on goods and services G is purchases by the government of physical goods and services. It includes the wages of civil servants and soldiers, the purchase of typewriters, tanks and military aircraft, and investment in roads and hospitals.

Governments also spend money on *transfer payments* or benefits, B. These include pensions, unemployment benefit and subsidies to firms. Transfer payments are payments that do not require the provision of any goods or services in return.

Transfer payments do not affect national income or national output. They are not included in GDP. There is no corresponding net output. Taxes and transfer payments merely redistribute existing income and spending power away from people being taxed and towards people being subsidized. In contrast, spending G on goods and services produces net output, gives rise to factor earnings in the firms supplying this output, and to additional spending power of the households receiving this income. Hence government spending G on goods and services is part of GDP. It is final expenditure, since government is now an additional end user of the output.

GDP at market prices measures domestic output inclusive of indirect taxes on goods and services. GDP at basic prices measures domestic output exclusive of indirect taxes on goods and services. The former exceeds the latter by the amount of revenue raised in indirect taxes.

National income accounts aim to provide a logically coherent set of definitions and measures of national output. However, taxes drive a wedge between the price the purchaser pays and the price the seller receives. We can choose to value national output either at market prices inclusive of indirect taxes on goods and services, or at the prices received by producers after indirect taxes have been paid.

Measuring consumption C, investment I, and government spending G on goods and services at market prices inclusive of indirect taxes, the value added or net output of the economy is now

$$\text{GDP at market prices} \equiv \text{final spending} \equiv C + I + G \qquad (2)$$

Higher indirect taxes increase the price of goods and services. Although the value of output increases at market prices, the physical quantity of output is unchanged. It makes more sense to measure GDP at basic prices Thus, subtracting indirect taxes T_e,

$$Y \equiv \text{GDP at basic prices} \equiv [C + I + G] - T_e \qquad (3)$$

This measure is independent of indirect taxes. Higher tax rates increase the value of $(C + I + G)$ but also raise T_e, leaving GDP at basic prices unchanged. From now on, we use Y to denote GDP at basic prices.

Part 4 : Macroeconomics

Personal disposable income is household income after direct taxes and transfer payments. It shows how much households have available for spending and saving.

Figure 19.4 shows how direct taxes and transfer benefits affect the circular flow of payments, once we add the government sector. Household incomes at basic prices Y are supplemented by benefits B less direct taxes T_d. This gives us personal disposable income $(Y + B - T_d)$.

Hence, saving is now the part of disposable income not spent on consumption.

$$S \equiv (Y + B - T_d) - C \text{ and } Y \equiv S + C + T_d - B \qquad (4)$$

Figure 19.4 The government and the circular flow

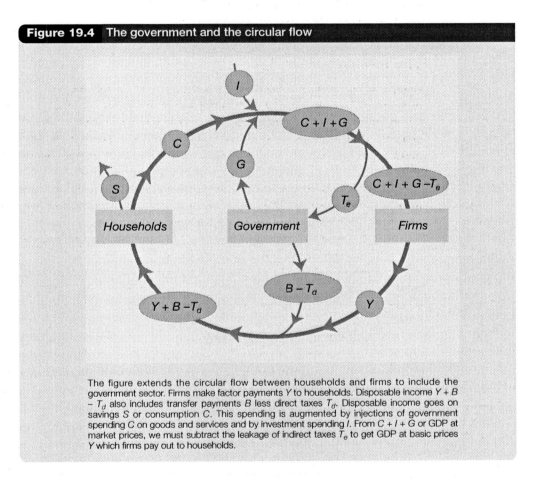

The figure extends the circular flow between households and firms to include the government sector. Firms make factor payments Y to households. Disposable income $Y + B - T_d$ also includes transfer payments B less direct taxes T_d. Disposable income goes on savings S or consumption C. This spending is augmented by injections of government spending C on goods and services and by investment spending I. From $C + I + G$ or GDP at market prices, we must subtract the leakage of indirect taxes T_e to get GDP at basic prices Y which firms pay out to households.

Round the top loop of Figure 19.4, consumption C at market prices is now supplemented by injections of investment spending I and government spending G. From $(C + I + G)$ or GDP at market prices, we subtract indirect taxes T_e to get Y or GDP at basic prices.

$$Y \equiv C + I + G - T_e \qquad (5)$$

Comparing this with the second part of equation (4)

$$S + T_d + T_e - B \equiv I + G \qquad (6)$$

Our national income accounts make sense. The left-hand side of (6) is leakages from the circular flow of payments between firms and households. Money leaks out through household savings and taxes (net of benefit subsidies) to the government. The right-hand side of (6) tells us the injections to the circular flow: investment spending by firms and government spending on goods and services. Total leakages must equal total injections, otherwise we've made a bookkeeping error and the sums will not add up. In the special case where $T_d \equiv T_e \equiv G \equiv B \equiv 0$ there is no government sector and (6) implies $S \equiv I$, as in equation (1).

Notice too that equation (6) can be rewritten as

$$T_d + T_e - B - G \equiv I - S \tag{7}$$

The left-hand side is the financial surplus of the government, total revenue minus its total spending. The right-hand side is the private sector deficit, the excess of investment spending over household saving. As a matter of definition, the private sector can run a deficit only if the government runs a surplus, and vice versa.

The foreign sector

So far we have studied a closed economy not transacting with the rest of the world. We now examine an *open economy* that deals with other countries.

Households, firms and the government may buy imports Z that are not part of domestic output and do not give rise to domestic factor incomes. These goods are not in the output measure of GDP, the *value added* by domestic producers. However, imports show up in final expenditure. There are two solutions to this problem. We could subtract the import component separately from C, I, G and X and measure only final expenditure on the domestically made bit of consumption, investment, government spending and exports. But it is easier to continue to measure total final expenditure on C, I, G and X and then subtract from this total expenditure on imports Z. It comes to exactly the same thing.

Exports (X) are domestically produced but sold abroad. Imports (Z) are produced abroad but purchased for use in the domestic economy.

Hence in an open economy we recognize foreign trade by redefining GDP at basic prices as

$$Y \equiv C + I + G + X - Z - T_e \equiv C + I + G + NX - T_e \tag{8}$$

where NX denotest net exports $(X - Z)$.

What about leakages and injections? Imports are a leakage, money not recycled to domestic firms, but exports are an injection, a revenue source not arising from domestic households. Hence, using (8) and (6)

$$S + (T_d + T_e - B) + Z \equiv I + G + X \tag{9a}$$
$$[S - I] \equiv (G + B - T_e - T_d) + NX \tag{9b}$$

Equation (9a) makes the usual point that total leakages must equal total injections. Imports are an extra leakages, exports an extra injections to the circular flow.

Equation (9b) extends (7) to an open economy. A private sector surplus $S - I$ is a leakage from the circular flow. It must be matched by an injection of the same amount. This injection can come either from a government deficit $(G + B - T_e - T_d)$ or from net exports NX, the excess of export earnings over import spending. Since our trade surplus is foreigners' trade deficit, (9b) says that the surplus of the private sector must be matched by the budget deficit of the government plus the trade deficit of foreigners.

From GDP to GNP or GNI

To complete the national accounts we must face two final problems. So far we have assumed all factors of production are domestically owned: all net domestic output accrues to domestic households as factor incomes. But this need not be so. When Nissan owns a car factory in the UK, some of the profits are sent back to Japan to be spent or saved by Japanese households.

Conversely, UK households earn income from owning foreign assets. This income from interest, dividends, profits and rents is shown in the national accounts as the flow of *property income* between countries. The net flow of property income into the UK is the excess of inflows of property income from factor services supplied abroad over the outflows of property income from factor services by foreigners in the UK.

When there is a net flow of property income between the UK and the rest of the world, the output and expenditure measure of GDP will no longer equal the total factor incomes earned by UK citizens. We use the terms *gross national product* (GNP) or *gross national income* (GNI) to measure GDP adjusted for net property income from abroad.

> **GNP (or GNI)** measures total income earned by domestic citizens regardless of the country in which their factor services were supplied. GNP (or GNI) equals GDP plus net property income from abroad.

If the UK has an inflow of £2 billion of property income from abroad but an outflow of £1 billion of property income accruing to foreigners, UK GNP, measuring income earned by UK citizens, will exceed UK GDP, measuring the value of goods produced in the UK, by £1 billion.

Table 19.5 shows actual data for UK GDP and GNP in 2003. Official statistics often decompose G, government spending on goods and services, into government consumption and government investment. Table 19.5 therefore shows data on consumption by households, consumption by government (and non-profit organizations), and on combined investment by government and private firms.

Table 19.5 UK national accounts, 2004 (£ billion, current prices)

Expenditure measure		Income measure	
At market prices:		Income source: employment	613.5
C by households	692.3	Profits and rents	245.4
C by government and non-profit organizations	259.1	Other	98.4
I by private and government	179.3	GDP at basic prices	957.3
NX	−32.4	Indirect taxes	142.6
GDP at market prices	1098.3	GDP at market prices	1099.9
Net property income from abroad	56.1		
GNP (GNI) at market prices	1154.4		

Source: ONS, *UK National Accounts*.

From GNP to national income

The final complication is depreciation.

> **Depreciation** or capital consumption is the rate at which the value of the existing capital stock declines per period as a result of usage or obsolescence.

Depreciation is a flow concept telling us how much our effective capital stock is being used up in each time period. Depreciation is an economic cost because it measures resources being used up in the production process.

Our simple example in Table 19.4 ignored depreciation completely. The machine bought by the car maker lasted for ever. We now recognize that machinery wears out. In consequence, the *net* output of the economy is lower. The part of the economy's gross output used merely to replace existing capital is not available for consumption, investment in net additions to the capital stock, government spending or exports.

> **National income** is the economy's net national product. It is calculated by subtracting depreciation from GNP at basic prices.

Similarly, we need to reduce our measure of the incomes available for spending on these goods. Thus, we subtract depreciation from GNP to get net national product (NNP) or national income.

National income measures how much the economy can spend or save, after setting aside enough resources to maintain the capital stock intact by offsetting depreciation.

We have now developed a complete set of national accounts. Figure 19.5 may keep you straight.

Figure 19.5 National income accounting: a summary

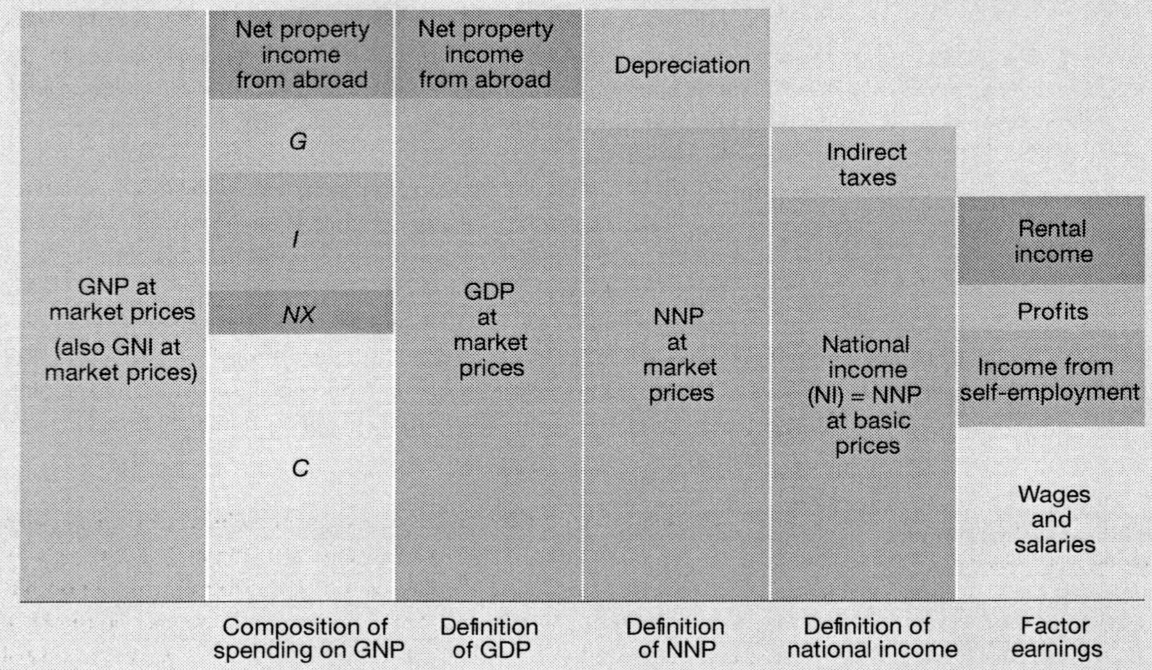

Composition of spending on GNP	Definition of GDP	Definition of NNP	Definition of national income	Factor earnings
Net property income from abroad	Net property income from abroad	Depreciation		
G			Indirect taxes	Rental income
I				Profits
NX	GDP at market prices	NNP at market prices	National income (NI) = NNP at basic prices	Income from self-employment
C				Wages and salaries

GNP at market prices (also GNI at market prices)

Now you've read this section, why not test your understanding by visiting the Online Learning Centre at www.mcgraw-hill.co.uk/textbooks/begg

---

19.5 What GNP measures

A firm's accounts show how the company is doing. Our national income accounts let us assess how the economy is doing. Just as a firm's accounts may conceal as much as they reveal, we must interpret the national income accounts with care.

We focus on GNP as a measure of economic performance. Since depreciation is rather difficult to measure, and consequently may be treated differently in different countries or during different time periods, using gross national product avoids the need to argue about depreciation.

In this section we make three points. First, we recall the distinction between nominal and real variables. Second, we show how per capita GNP can provide a more accurate picture of the standard of living of an average person in an economy. Finally, we discuss the incompleteness of GNP as a measure of the activities that provide economic welfare to members of society.

Nominal GNP measures GNP at the prices prevailing when income was earned.

Nominal and real GNP

Since it is physical quantities of output that yield people utility or happiness, it can be misleading to judge the economy's performance by looking at nominal GNP.

BOX 19-2   Hidden GNP

Gangster Al Capone, never charged with murder, was eventually convicted of tax evasion. Taxes are evaded by smugglers and drug dealers but also by gardeners, plumbers and everyone else doing things 'for cash'. Since GNP data are based on tax statistics, the 'hidden' economy is unreported.

Economists have various ways to estimate its size. One way is to count large-denomination banknotes in circulation. People with fistfuls of £50 notes are often engaged in tax evasion. Another way is to guess people's income by studying what they spend. Maria Lacko has used the stable relationship between household use of electricity and its main determinants – income and weather temperature – to estimate incomes from data on electricity consumption and temperature. She confirms two popularly held views. The hidden economy is large both in former communist economies, where the new private sector is as yet unrecorded, and in several Mediterranean countries with a history of trouble getting their citizens to pay tax.

The hidden economy (% of GNP)

Poland	34	Finland	11
Hungary	31	USA	10
Spain	21	UK	10
Greece	20	France	6
Italy	16	Japan	3

Source: M. Lacko, *Hungarian Hidden Economy in International Comparisons*, Institute of Economics, Budapest, 1996.

Real GNP, or GNP at constant prices, adjusts for inflation by measuring GNP in different years at the prices prevailing at some particular date known as the *base year*.

Table 19.6 presents a simple hypothetical example of a whole economy. Nominal GNP rises from £600 to £1440 between 1980 and 2002. If we take 1980 as the base year we can measure real GNP in 2002 by valuing output quantities in 2002 using 1980 prices. Real GNP rises only from £600 to £860. This rise of 43 per cent in real GNP gives a truer picture of the extra quantity of goods made by the economy as a whole.

Table 19.6   Nominal and real GNP

		1980	2002
Quantity	apples	100	150
	chickens	100	140
Price £	apples	2	4
	chickens	4	6
Value in	apples	200	600
Current £	chickens	400	840
	Nominal GNP	600	1440
Value in	apples	200	300
1980 £	chickens	400	560
	Real GNP	600	860

The **GNP deflator** is the ratio of nominal GNP to real GNP expressed as an index.

The GNP deflator

Chapter 2 introduced the consumer price index (CPI), an index of the average price of goods purchased by consumers. The most common measure of the inflation rate in the UK is the percentage rise in the RPI over its value a year earlier.

However, consumption expenditure is only one part of GNP, which also includes investment, government spending and net exports. To convert nominal GNP to real GNP we need to use an index showing what is happening to the price of all goods. This index is called the GNP deflator.

To express the deflator as an index, we take the ratio of nominal to real GNP and multiply by 100. In Table 19.7, nominal and real GNP coincide in the base year 1980. Their ratio is 1, the index is 100. For 2002 the ratio of nominal to real GNP is 1.674 (= 1440/860) and the index is 167.4. According to the GNP deflator, prices for the whole economy rose from 100 to 167.4, a 67.4 per cent rise from 1980 to 2002.

Table 19.7	UK GNP 1960–2000		
	1960	1980	2000
Nominal GNP (current billion)	25	227	946
GNP deflator (1995 = 100)	8	45	114
Real GNP (£billion, 1995 prices)	316	501	828

Source: ONS, *Economic Trends*.

Table 19.7 gives UK data over four decades. Nominal GNP in the UK rose from £25 billion in 1960 to over £855 billion in 1998. Without knowing what happened to the price of goods in general we cannot judge what happened to the quantity of output over the period. The second row of Table 19.8 answers this question. On average, prices in 1998 were 13 times those in 1960. Hence, the change in real GNP was much smaller than the change in nominal GNP in the same period. It is important to distinguish between nominal and real GNP.

Per capita real GNP

Real GNP is a simple measure of the real income of an economy. The annual percentage rise in real GNP tells us how fast an economy is growing. Table 19.8 shows the average annual growth rate of real GNP in three countries over two decades. The first column shows that the annual growth rate of real GNP during 1980–99 was highest in Jordan and lowest in Denmark. Although this tells us about the growth of the whole economy, we may be interested in a different question: what was happening to the standard of living of a representative person in each of these countries? To answer this question we need to examine per capita real GNP.

Table 19.8	Growth, 1980–2002 (% a year)	
	Real GNP	Per capita real GNP
Denmark	2.3	2.2
UK	2.7	2.3
Jordan	4.1	0.1

Source: World Bank, *World Development Report*.

Per capita real GNP is real GNP divided by the total population. It is real GNP per head.

For a given real GNP, the larger the population the smaller the quantity of goods and services per person. Table 19.8 shows growth of per capita real GNP. The ranking is largely reversed. To get a simple measure of the standard of living enjoyed by a person in a particular country, it is better to look at per capita real GNP, which adjusts for population, than to look at total real GNP.

Even per capita real GNP is only a crude indicator. Table 19.8 does *not* say that every person in Denmark got 2.3 per cent more goods and services each year. It shows what was happening on average. Some people's real incomes increased by a lot more, some people became absolutely poorer. The more the income distribution changes over time, the less reliable is the change in per capita real GNP as an indicator of what is happening to any particular person.

A comprehensive measure of GNP

Because we use GNP to measure the income of the economy, the coverage of GNP should be as comprehensive as possible. In practice, we encounter two problems in including all production in GDP and GNP. First, some outputs, such as noise, pollution and congestion, are 'bads'. We should subtract them from GDP and GNP. This is a sensible suggestion but hard to implement. These nuisance goods are not traded through markets, so it is hard to quantify their output or decide how to value its cost to society.

Similarly, many valuable goods and services are excluded from GNP because they are not marketed and therefore hard to measure accurately. These activities include household chores, DIY activities and unreported jobs.

BOX 19-3 'Asia propelled to brink of environmental catastrophe'

Well-run firms spend serious money on information systems that let their managers make intelligent decisions. In contrast, governments often have to make do with economic data gathered on the cheap. Many data are simply the biproduct of tax records. Published GDP data ignore valuable commodities like leisure and omit important harmful outputs like environmental pollution.

Citing a study by the Asian Development Bank, the *Financial Times* article noted that Asia would overtake the countries of the OECD as the world's biggest source of greenhouse gas pollutants by 2015. Environmental degradation means that almost 40 per cent of the region's population now live in areas prone to drought and erosion. With the Asian population set to triple in the next 20 years, and half these people living in cities, air pollution will reach new records. Nor is access to clean water much better.

Asian countries from Thailand to the Philippines have had three decades of very rapid GDP growth. Because of this success, they are often called the Asian tigers. But if national accounts had to keep a proper account of environmental depreciation, many of these countries would have much less impressive growth records. We might start calling them the Asian snails.

Source: Financial Times, 18 June 2001.

Deducting the value of nuisance outputs and adding the value of unreported and non-marketed incomes would make GNP a more accurate measure of the economy's production of goods and services. But there is another important adjustment to make before using GNP as the basis for national economic welfare. People enjoy not merely goods and services but also leisure time.

Suppose Leisurians value leisure more highly than Industrians. Industrians work more and produce more goods. Industria has a higher measured GNP. It is silly to say this proves that Leisurians have lower welfare. By choosing to work less hard they reveal that the extra leisure is worth at least as much as the extra goods they could have made by working more.

Because it is difficult and expensive to collect regular measurements on non-marketed and unreported goods and bads, and to make regular assessments of the implicit value of leisure, real GNP inevitably remains the commonest measure of economic activity. Far from ideal, it is the best measure available on a regular basis.

SUMMARY

- Macroeconomics examines the economy as a whole.

- Macroeconomics sacrifices individual detail to focus on the interaction of broad sectors of the economy. Households supply production inputs to firms that use them to make output. Firms pay factor incomes to households, who buy the output from firms. This is the circular flow.

- Gross domestic product (GDP) is the value of net output of the factors of production located in the domestic economy. It can be measured in three equivalent ways: value added in production, factor incomes including profits or final expenditure.

- Leakages from the circular flow are those parts of payment by firms to households that do not automatically return to firms as spending by households on the output of firms. Leakages are saving, taxes net of subsidies and imports. Injections are sources of revenue to firms that do not arise from household spending. Investment expenditure by firms, spending on goods and services by the government, and exports are injections. By definition, total leakages equal total injections.

- GDP at market prices values domestic output at prices inclusive of indirect taxes. GDP at basic prices measures domestic output at prices exclusive of indirect taxes. Gross national product (GNP), also called gross national income (GNI), adjusts GDP for net property income from abroad.

- National income is net national product (NNP) at basic prices. NNP is GNP minus the depreciation of the capital stock during the period. In practice, many assessments of economic performance are based on GNP since it is not hard to measure depreciation accurately.

- Nominal GNP measures income at current prices. Real GNP measures income at constant prices. It adjusts nominal GNP for changes in the GNP deflator as a result of inflation.

- Per capita real GNP divides real GNP by the population. It is a more reliable indicator of income per person in an economy but only an average measure of what people get.

- Real GNP and per capita real GNP are crude measures of national and individual welfare. They ignore non-market activities, 'bads' such as pollution, valuable activities such as work in the home, and production unreported by tax evaders. Nor do they measure the value of leisure.

- Because it is expensive – and sometimes impossible – to make regular and accurate measurements of all these activities, in practice GNP is the most widely used measure of national performance.

REVIEW QUESTIONS

Car firms buy in raw materials (steel), intermediate goods (windscreens, tyres) and labour to make cars. Windscreen and tyre companies hire workers and also buy raw materials from other industries. What is the value added of the car industry (the three firms shown below)?

Producer of	Output	Intermediate goods used	Raw materials used	Labour input
Cars	1000	250	100	100
Windscreens	150		10	50
Tyres	100		10	30

GNP at market prices is £300 billion. Depreciation is £30 billion, indirect taxes £20 billion. (a) What is national income? (b) Why does depreciation cause a discrepancy between GNP and national income? (c) Why do indirect taxes enter the calculation?

$GNP = 2000$, $C = 1700$, $G = 50$, and $NX = 40$. (a) What is investment I? (b) If exports are 350, what are imports? (c) If depreciation = 130, what is national income? (d) In this example net exports are positive. Could they be negative?

Given the data below: (a) What is 2005 GNP in 2004 prices? (b) What is the growth rate of real GNP from 2004 to 2005? (c) What is the inflation rate?

	Nominal GDP	GNP deflator
2004	2000	100
2005	2400	110

Should these be in a comprehensive measure of GNP: (a) time spent by students in lectures; (b) the income of muggers; (c) the wage paid to traffic wardens; (d) dropping litter?

Common fallacies Why are these statements wrong? (a) Unemployment benefit props up national income in years when employment is low. (b) A high per capita real GNP is always a good thing. (c) In 2002 *Crummy Movie* earned £1 billion more at the box office than *Gone With The Wind* earned 50 years ago. *Crummy Movie* is already a bigger box office success.

To check your answers to these questions, go to page 641.

To help you grasp the key concepts of this chapter check out the extra resources posted on the Online Learning Centre at www.mcgraw-hill.co.uk/ textbooks/begg. There are quick test questions, economics examples and access to Powerweb articles, all for free!

For even more exercises, recaps and examples to help you study, purchase a copy of the Economics Student Workbook. Simply visit www.mcgraw hill.co.uk/textbooks/begg and follow the links to the Workbook to buy your copy.

chapter 20

Output and aggregate demand

Learning outcomes

By the end of this chapter, you should understand:

1 actual output and potential output

2 why output is demand determined in the short run

3 short-run equilibrium output

4 consumption and investment demand

5 how aggregate demand determines short-run equilibrium output

6 the marginal propensity to consume *MPC*

7 how the size of the multiplier affects the *MPC*

8 the paradox of thrift

During 1960–2000 UK real output grew on average by 2.3 per cent a year but fluctuated around this trend. Real output actually fell during 1973–75, 1979–81 and 1989–92, but grew strongly during 1975–79, 1981–89 and 1992–2004. Words used by economists to describe these fluctuations – recession, recovery, boom and slump – are part of everyday language.

Why does real GDP fluctuate? To construct a simple model, we ignore discrepancies between national income, real GNP, and real GDP. We use income and output interchangeably. First, we distinguish *actual* output and *potential* output.

Potential output tends to grow over time as the supply of inputs grows. Population growth adds to the labour force. Investment in education, training and new machinery adds to human and physical capital. Technical advances let given inputs produce more output. Together, these explain UK average growth at 2.3 per cent a year since 1960.

> **Potential output** is the economy's output when inputs are fully employed.

We study the theory of long-run economic growth in potential output in Chapter 30. First, we focus on deviations of actual output from potential output in the short run. Since potential output changes slowly, we begin with a short-run analysis of an economy with a fixed potential output.

Potential output is not the maximum an economy can conceivably make. With a gun to our heads, we could all make more. Rather, it is the output when every market in the economy is in long-run equilibrium. Every worker wanting to work at the equilibrium wage can find a job, and every machine that can profitably be used at the equilibrium rental for capital is in use. Thus, potential output includes an allowance for 'equilibrium unemployment'. Some people do not want to work at the equilibrium wage rate. Moreover, in a constantly changing economy, some people are temporarily between jobs. Today, UK potential output probably entails an unemployment rate of about 4 per cent.

Suppose actual output falls below potential output. Workers are unemployed and firms have idle machines or spare capacity. A key issue in macroeconomics is how quickly output returns to potential output. In microeconomics, studying one market in isolation, we assumed excess supply would quickly bid the price down, eliminating excess supply to restore equilibrium. In macroeconomics, this cannot be taken for granted. Disturbances in one part of the economy induce changes elsewhere that may feed back again, exacerbating the original disturbance.

We cannot examine this issue by *assuming* that the economy is always at potential output, for then a problem could never arise. We must build a model in which departures from potential output are possible, examine the market forces then set in motion, and decide how successfully market forces restore output to potential output.

Thus our initial model has two crucial properties. First, all prices and wages are fixed at a given level. Second, at these prices and wage levels, there are workers without a job who would like to work and firms with spare capacity they could profitably use. The economy has spare resources. It is then unnecessary to analyse the supply side of the economy in detail. Any rise in demand is happily met by firms and workers until potential output is reached.

Since markets trade the smaller of supply and demand, output is demand-determined when there is excess supply and wages and prices have yet to adjust to restore long-run equilibrium. Output then depends only on aggregate demand.

Below potential output, firms happily supply whatever output is demanded. Total output is demand-determined.

Later, we shall relax the assumption that prices and wages are fixed. Not only do we want to study inflation, we also want to examine how quickly market forces, acting through changes in prices and wages, can eliminate unemployment and spare capacity. But first we must learn to walk. We postpone the analysis of price and wage adjustment until Chapter 25. Until then, we study the demand-determined model of output and employment developed by John Maynard Keynes in *The General Theory of Employment, Interest and Money*, published in 1936. Keynes used the model to explain high unemployment and low output in the Great Depression of the 1930s.

Most young economists soon became *Keynesians*, advocating government intervention to keep output close to potential output. By the 1950s, this approach was challenged by *Monetarists*, led by Milton Friedman. They argued that Keynesian analysis, although helpful in studying recession, was a poor tool for studying inflation, which Monetarists attribute to money creation. We develop an approach that uses the best insights of both Keynesians and Monetarists.

In the 1970s unemployment rose again, despite Keynesian policies. Some economists discarded Keynesian economics completely. Not only did they deny the effectiveness of government policy to stabilize output, they argued that stabilizing output may not even be desirable.

This has now prompted a fightback by *New Keynesians*, who believe that the central messages of Keynes, right all along, can be understood better by using modern microeconomics to explain the market failures that justify Keynesian intervention. To scale these peaks of economic research, we need to begin at the foothills.

Chapter 19 introduced the circular flow of income and payments between households and firms. Households buy the output of firms. Firms' revenue is ultimately returned to households. We now build a simple model of this interaction of households and firms. The next chapter adds the government and the foreign sector.

20.1 Components of aggregate demand

Without a government or a foreign sector, there are two sources of demand: consumption demand by households, and investment demand by firms. Using AD to denote aggregate demand, C for consumption demand, and I for investment demand,

$$AD = C + I \tag{1}$$

Consumption demand and investment demand are chosen by different economic groups and depend on different things.

Consumption demand

Personal disposable income is the income households receive from firms, plus transfer payments received from the government, minus direct taxes paid to the government. It is the net income households can spend or save.

Households buy goods and services from cars to cinema tickets. These consumption purchases account for about 90 per cent of personal disposable income.

With no government, disposable income is simply the income received from firms. Given its disposable income, each household plans how much to spend and to save. Deciding one decides the other. One family may save to buy a bigger house, another may spend more than its income, or 'dissave', taking the round-the-world trip it always wanted.

Many things affect consumption and saving decisions. We examine these in detail in Chapter 24. To get started, one simplification takes us a long way. We assume that, in the aggregate, households' consumption demand rises with aggregate personal disposable income.

Figure 20.1 shows real consumption and real personal disposable income in the UK. Because the scatter of points lies close to the line summarizing this relationship, our simplification is helpful. Nevertheless, the points do not lie *exactly* along the line. Our simplification omits some other influences on consumption demand that we take up in Chapter 24.

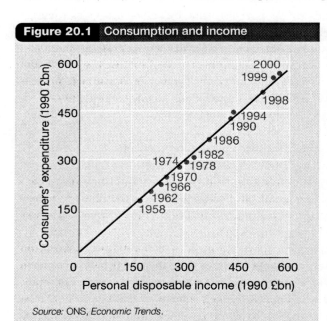

Figure 20.1   Consumption and income

Source: ONS, Economic Trends.

The consumption function

This positive relation between disposable income and consumption demand is shown in Figure 20.2 and is called the *consumption function*. The consumption function tells us how to go from personal disposable income Y to consumption demand C. If A is a positive constant, and c is a positive fraction between zero and one,

$$C = A + cY \tag{2}$$

The consumption function shows aggregate consumption demand at each level of personal disposable income.

Our bare-bones model has no government, no transfer payments and no taxes. Personal disposable income equals national income. Figure 20.2, and equation (2) then relate consumption demand to *national* income Y. The consumption function is a straight line. A straight line is completely described by

The **marginal propensity to consume** is the fraction of each extra pound of disposable income that households wish to consume.

The **saving function** shows desired saving at each income level.

its intercept – the height at which it crosses the vertical axis – and its slope – the amount it rises for each unit we move horizontally to the right.

The intercept is *A*. We call this *autonomous* consumption demand. Autonomous means unrelated to income. Households wish to consume *A* even if income *Y* is zero.[1] The slope of the consumption function is the marginal propensity to consume.

In Figure 20.2 and equation (2), the marginal propensity to consume *MPC* is *c*. If income rises by £1, desired consumption rises by £*c*.

Saving is income not consumed. Figure 20.2 and equation (2) imply what when income *Y* is zero, saving is *–A*. Households are dissaving, or running down their assets.

Since a fraction *c* of each pound of extra income is consumed, a fraction $(1 - c)$ of each pound of income is saved. The *marginal property to save MPS* is $(1 - c)$. Since an extra pound of income leads either to extra desired consumption or to extra desired saving, $MPC + MPS = 1$. Figure 20.3 shows the *saving function* corresponding to the consumption function in Figure 20.2.

Note too that, using equation (2) and the definition of saving $Y \equiv C + S$, we can deduce the saving function shown in Figure 21.3. It must be

$$S = -A + (1 - c) Y \qquad (3)$$

Adding (2) and (3), the left-hand side gives desired consumption plus desired saving, the right hand side gives income *Y*, as it should. Planned saving is the part of income not planned to be spent on consumption.

Figure 20.2 The consumption function

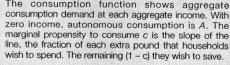

$$C = A + cY$$

The consumption function shows aggregate consumption demand at each aggregate income. With zero income, autonomous consumption is *A*. The marginal propensity to consume *c* is the slope of the line, the fraction of each extra pound that households wish to spend. The remaining $(1 - c)$ they wish to save.

Figure 20.3 The saving function

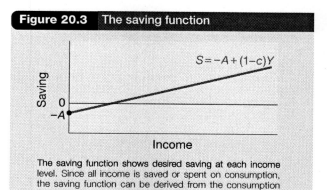

$$S = -A + (1-c)Y$$

The saving function shows desired saving at each income level. Since all income is saved or spent on consumption, the saving function can be derived from the consumption function or vice versa.

Investment demand is firms' desired or planned additions to physical capital (factories and machines) and to inventories.

Investment spending

Income is the key determinant of household consumption or spending plans as described by the consumption function. What about the factors determining the investment decision by firms?

Firms' investment demand depends chiefly on firms' current guesses about how fast the demand for their output will increase. Sometimes output is high and rising, sometimes it is high and falling. Since there is no close connection between the current *level* of income and firms' guesses about how the demand for their output is going to *change*, we make the simple assumption that investment demand is autonomous. Desired investment *I* is constant, independent of current output and income. In Chapter 24 we discuss investment demand in more detail.

[1] *A* is the minimum consumption needed for survival. How do households finance it when their incomes are zero? In the short run they dissave and run down their assets. But they cannot do so for ever. The consumption function may differ in the short run and the long run, an idea we discuss in Chapter 24.

The aggregate demand schedule is a straight line whose position depends on its intercept and its slope. The intercept, the height of the schedule when income is zero, reflects autonomous demand: part of consumption demand and all investment demand. The slope of the schedule is the *MPC*. Changes in income induce movements along a given *AD* schedule.

Autonomous demand is influenced by many things that we study in Chapter 24. It is not fixed forever. But it is independent of income. The *AD* schedule separates out the change in demand directly induced by changes in income. All other sources of changes in aggregate demand are shown as shifts in the *AD* schedule. If firms get more optimistic about future demand and invest more, autonomous demand rises. The new *AD* schedule is parallel to, but higher than, the old *AD* schedule.

20.2 Aggregate demand

Aggregate demand is the amount firms and households plan to spend at each level of income.

In our simple model, aggregate demand is simply households' consumption demand C plus firms' investment demand I.

Figure 20.4 shows the *aggregate demand schedule*. To the previous consumption function it adds a constant amount I for desired investment. Each extra unit of income adds c to consumption demand but nothing to investment demand: aggregate demand rises by c. The *AD* schedule is parallel to the consumption function. The slope of both is the marginal propensity to consume.

| Figure 20.4 | Aggregate demand |

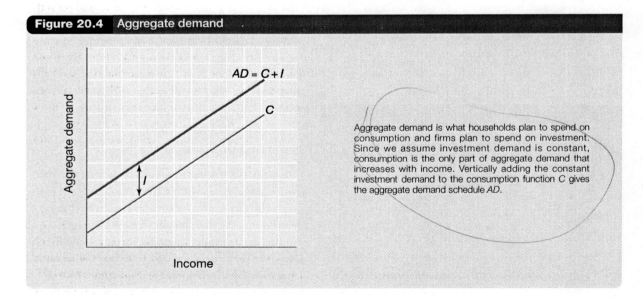

Aggregate demand is what households plan to spend on consumption and firms plan to spend on investment. Since we assume investment demand is constant, consumption is the only part of aggregate demand that increases with income. Vertically adding the constant investment demand to the consumption function C gives the aggregate demand schedule AD.

20.3 Equilibrium output

Wages and prices are *fixed* and output is demand-determined. If aggregate demand falls below potential output, firms cannot sell as much as they would like. There is *involuntary* excess capacity. Workers cannot work as much as they would like. There is *involuntary* unemployment.

To define short-run equilibrium we cannot use the definition used in microeconomics, the output at which both suppliers and demanders are happy with the quantity bought and sold.

We wish to study a situation in which firms and workers would like to supply more goods and more labour. Suppliers are frustrated. At least we can require that demanders are happy.

> When prices and wages are fixed, at short-run equilibrium output aggregate demand or planned spending equals the output actually produced.

Thus, spending plans are not frustrated by a shortage of goods. Nor do firms make more output than they can sell. In short-run equilibrium, actual output equals the output demanded by households as consumption and by firms as investment.

Figure 20.5 shows income on the horizontal axis and planned spending on the vertical axis. It also includes the $45°$ line, along which quantities on the horizontal and vertical axes are equal.

We draw in the AD schedule from Figure 20.4. This crosses the $45°$ line at E. On the $45°$ line, the value of output (and income) on the horizontal axis equals the value of spending on the vertical axis. Since E is the *only* point on the AD schedule also on the $45°$ line, it is the only point at which output and desired spending are equal.

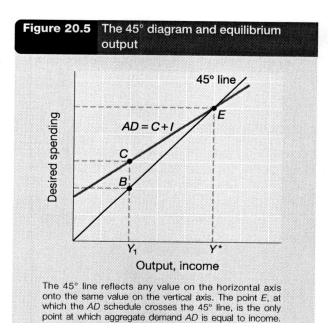

Figure 20.5   The 45° diagram and equilibrium output

The 45° line reflects any value on the horizontal axis onto the same value on the vertical axis. The point E, at which the AD schedule crosses the 45° line, is the only point at which aggregate demand AD is equal to income. Hence E is the equilibrium point at which planned spending equals actual output and actual income.

Hence Figure 20.5 shows equilibrium output at E. Firms produce Y^*. That output is equal to income. At an income Y^* the AD schedule tells us the demand for goods is also Y^*. At E planned spending is exactly equal to the output produced.

At any other output, output is not equal to aggregate demand. Suppose output and income are only Y_1. Aggregate demand exceeds actual output. There is excess demand. Spending plans cannot be realized at this output level.

Figure 20.5 shows that, for all outputs below the equilibrium output Y^*, aggregate demand AD exceeds income and output. The AD schedule lies *above* the $45°$ line along which spending and output are equal. Conversely, at all outputs above the equilibrium output Y^* aggregate demand is less than income and output.

Adjustment towards equilibrium

Suppose in Figure 20.5 the economy begins with an output of Y_1, below equilibrium output Y^*. Aggregate demand AD_1 exceeds output Y_1. If firms have inventories from the past, they can sell more than they have produced by running down stocks for a while. Note that this destocking is *unplanned*: planned changes of stocks are already included in the total investment demand I.

If firms cannot meet aggregate demand by unplanned destocking, they must turn away customers. Either response – unplanned destocking or turning away customers – is a signal to firms to raise output above Y_1. Hence, at *any* output below Y^*, aggregate demand exceeds output and firms get signals to raise output.

Conversely, if output is initially above its equilibrium level, Figure 20.5 shows that output will then exceed aggregate demand. Firms cannot sell all their output, make *unplanned* additions to inventories, and respond by cutting output.

Hence, when output is below its equilibrium level, firms raise output. When output is above its equilibrium level, firms reduce output. At the equilibrium output Y^* firms sell all

| BOX 20-2 | **Firms adjust as demand crashes** |

Demand for goods in the euro zone fell sharply in October 2001, after the terrorist attacks on US cities shattered business and consumer confidence, according to a survey reported by the news agency Reuters. How did firms respond?

The survey of 2500 companies showed that output, new orders, employment and inventories of inputs all hit new lows. Firms stopped buying raw materials and ran down their own stocks of raw materials. New orders, the most easily adjusted item in the survey, fell especially sharply after September 11.

Firms also added to stocks of unsold finished goods. Production fell less quickly than demand. Companies used these devices to avoid expensive and rapid changes in production. However, if lower demand persists, firms have to reduce output in line with lower demand.

their output and make no unplanned changes to their stocks. There is no incentive to change output.

Equilibrium output and employment

In this example, short-run equilibrium output is Y^*. Firms sell all the goods they produce and households and firms buy all the goods they want. But nothing guarantees Y^* is the level of potential output.

The economy can end up at a short-run equilibrium output below potential output, with no forces then present to move output to potential output. At the given level of prices and wages, a lack of aggregate demand will prevent expansion of output above its short-run equilibrium level.

Now you've read this section, why not test your understanding by visiting the Online Learning Centre at www.mcgraw-hill.co.uk/textbooks/begg

20.4 Another approach: planned saving equals planned investment

Equilibrium income equals the demand from investment and consumption. Hence, planned investment equals equilibrium income minus planned consumption. Thus $I = Y - C$. This is not a definition, but holds only when output and income are at the right level to achieve equilibrium output. However, planned saving S is always the part of income Y not devoted to planned consumption C. Thus $S \equiv Y - C$.

Thus $Y - C$ is equal to planned investment but also to planned saving. Since the latter depends on income and output, and since household plans are met only in equilibrium, equilibrium output occurs where planned investment equals planned savings:

$$I = S \tag{4}$$

In modern economies, firms make investment decisions, and the managers of these firms are not the same decision-units as the households making savings and consumption plans. But household plans depend on their income. Since planned saving depends on income but planned investment does not, equation (4) implies that equilibrium income adjusts to make households

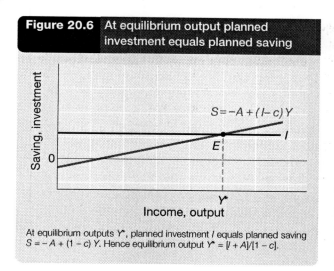

Figure 20.6 At equilibrium output planned investment equals planned saving

At equilibrium outputs Y^*, planned investment I equals planned saving $S = -A + (1 - c)Y$. Hence equilibrium output $Y^* = [I + A]/[1 - c]$.

plan to save as much as firms are planning to invest. Figure 20.6 illustrates.

Planned investment I is autonomous and so a horizontal line. Planned saving is $-A + (1 - c)Y$. It slopes up since the marginal propensity to save is positive. Equilibrium output makes planned saving equal planned investment. Thus $I = -A + (1 - c)Y^*$ Hence equilibrium output Y^* is

$$Y^* = [A + I]/[1 - c] \qquad (5)$$

This better be the same equilibrium output we got by equating actual output to aggregate demand. Of course it is. For then we get $Y^* = C + I = [A + I] + cY^*$ which leads to the same equilibrium output as in equation (5). An example may dispel any doubts.

Suppose investment demand is 10 and the saving function is $S = -10 + 0.1Y$. Hence, equilibrium output Y is 200. At this Y, planned saving is $[-10 + 20] = 10$. Hence 10 is both planned saving and planned investment.

If the saving function is $S = -10 + 0.1Y$, the consumption function must be $C = 10 + 0.9Y$. At an income of 200, consumption demand is 190. Add on 10 for investment demand and aggregate demand is 200. When output and income are 200, aggregate demand is also 200. Again, this proves that equilibrium output is 200.

If income exceeds 200, households want to save more than firms want to invest. But saving is the part of income not consumed. Households are not planning enough consumption, together with firms' investment plans, to purchase all the output produced. Unplanned inventories pile up and firms cut output. Lower output and income reduces planned saving, which depends on income. When output falls back to 200, planned investment again equals planned saving.

Conversely, when output is below its equilibrium level, planned investment exceeds planned saving. Together, planned consumption and planned investment exceed actual output. Firms make unplanned inventory reductions and raise output until it reverts to its equilibrium level of 200.

Planned versus actual

Equilibrium output and income satisfy two equivalent conditions. Aggregate demand must equal income and output. Equivalently, planned investment must equal planned saving.

In the last chapter we showed that *actual* investment is *always* equal to *actual* saving, purely as a consequence of our national income accounting definitions. When the economy is not in equilibrium, planned saving and investment are not equal. However, unplanned investment in stocks, and/or unplanned saving (frustrated consumers), always ensure that actual investment, planned plus unplanned, equals actual saving, planned plus unplanned.

20.5 A fall in aggregate demand

The *slope* of the *AD* schedule depends only on the marginal propensity to consume (*MPC*). For a given *MPC*, the level of autonomous spending $[A + I]$ determines the *height* of the *AD* schedule. Autonomous spending is spending unrelated to income.

Changes in autonomous spending lead to parallel shifts in the *AD* schedule. Investment demand depends chiefly on current guesses by firms about future demand for their output. Beliefs about this future demand can fluctuate significantly, influenced by current pessimism or optimism about the future. Similarly, a fall in consumer confidence reduces autonomous consumption demand.

Suppose firms get pessimistic about future demand for their output. Planned investment falls. If autonomous consumption is unaffected, the aggregate demand schedule *AD* is now lower at each income than before. Figure 20.7 shows this downward shift from *AD* to *AD'*.

Before we go into the details, think what is likely to happen to output. It will fall but how much? When investment demand falls, firms cut output. Households have lower incomes and cut consumption. Firms cut output again, further reducing household incomes. Consumption demand falls further. What brings the process of falling output and income to an end?

Figure 20.7 shows that a given downward shift of the *AD* schedule reduces equilibrium output by a *finite* amount but by an amount larger than the vertical fall in the *AD* schedule. This is because the *AD* schedule has a slope flatter than the 45° line: its slope, the marginal propensity to consume, is always smaller than unity.

Equilibrium moves from *E* to *E'*. Equilibrium output falls *more* than the original cut in investment demand but does not fall all the way to zero.

Table 20.1 explains. Since many students find arithmetic easier than algebra, we illustrate for the particular values [*A* = 10] for autonomous consumption demand and [*c* = 0.9] for the marginal propensity to consume. Thus the particular consumption function is *C* = 10 + 0.9*Y*.

If original investment demand is also 10, the first row of Table 20.1 shows that the original equilibrium output is 200, since consumption demand is then [10 + 180] and investment demand is 10. Thus aggregate demand just equals actual output.

In step 2 investment demand falls to 5. Firms did not expect demand to change and still produced 200. Output exceeds aggregate demand by 5. Firms add this 5 to inventories, then cut output.

Step 3 shows firms making 195, the level of demand in step 2. But when firms cut output, income falls. Step 3 shows consumption demand falls from 190 to 185.5. Since the *MPC* is 0.9, a cut in income by 5 causes a fall in consumption demand by 4.5. The induced fall in consumption demand means that output of 195 still exceeds aggregate demand, which is now 190.5. Again inventories pile up and again firms respond by cutting output.

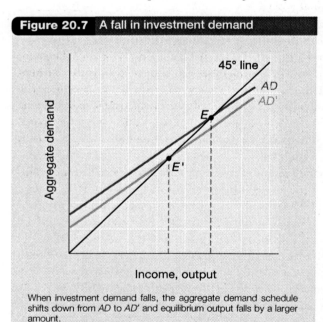

Figure 20.7   A fall in investment demand

When investment demand falls, the aggregate demand schedule shifts down from *AD* to *AD'* and equilibrium output falls by a larger amount.

Table 20.1   Adjustment to a shift in investment demand

	Y	I	C = 10 + 0.9 Y	AD = C + I	Y – AD	Unplanned stocks	Output
Step 1	200	10	190	200	0	Zero	Constant
Step 2	200	5	190	195	5	Rising	Falling
Step 3	195	5	185.5	190.5	4.5	Rising	Falling
Step 4	190.5	5	181.5	186.57	4	Rising	Falling
New equilibrium	150	5	145	150	0	Zero	Constant

At step 4 firms make enough to meet demand at step 3. Output is 190.5 but again this induces a further cut in consumption demand. Output still exceeds aggregate demand. The process keeps going, through many steps, until it reaches the new equilibrium, an output of 150. Output and income have fallen by 50, consumption demand has fallen by 45, and investment demand has fallen by 5. Aggregate demand again equals output.

How long it takes for the economy to reach the new equilibrium depends on how well firms figure out what is going on. If they keep setting output targets to meet the level of demand in the previous period, it takes a long time to adjust. Smart firms may spot that, period after period, they are overproducing and adding to unwanted inventories. They anticipate that demand is still falling and cut back output more quickly than Table 20.1 suggests.

Why does a fall of 5 in investment demand cause a fall of 50 in equilibrium output? Lower investment demand induces a cut in output and income that then induces an *extra* cut in consumption demand. Total demand falls by more than the original fall in investment demand but the process does not spiral out of control. Equilibrium output is 150.

> The multiplier is the ratio of the change in equilibrium output to the change in autonomous spending that caused the change.

In our example, the initial change in autonomous investment demand is 5 and the final change in equilibrium output is 50. The multiplier is 10. That is why, in Figure 20.7, a small downward shift in the AD schedule leads to a much larger fall in equilibrium income and output.

20.6 The multiplier

The multiplier tells us how much output changes after a shift in aggregate demand. The multiplier exceeds 1 because a change in autonomous demand sets off further changes in consumption demand. The size of the multiplier depends on the marginal propensity to consume. The initial effect of a unit fall in investment demand is to cut output and income by a unit. If the MPC is large, this fall in income leads to a large fall in consumption and the multiplier is big. If the MPC is small, a given change in investment demand and output induces small changes in consumption demand and the multiplier is small.

Table 20.2 examines a one-unit *increase* in investment demand. In step 2, firms raise output by 1 unit. Consumption rises by 0.9, the marginal propensity to consume times the one-unit change in income and output. At step 3, firms raise output by 0.9 to meet the increased consumption demand in step 2. In turn, consumption demand is increased by 0.81 (the MPC 0.9 times the 0.9 increase in income) leading in step 4 to a rise in output of 0.81. Consumption rises again and the process continues.

Table 20.2	Calculating the multiplier							
Change in	Step 1	Step 2	Step 3	Step 4	Step 5	*	*	*
I	1	0	0	0	0	*	*	*
Y	0	1	0.9	$(0.9)^2$	$(0.9)^3$	*	*	*
C	0	0.9	$(0.9)^2$	$(0.9)^2$	$(0.9)^3$	*	*	*

To find the multiplier, we add all the increases in output from each step in the table and keep going:

$$\text{Multiplier} = 1 + (0.9) + (0.9)^2 + (0.9)^3 + (0.9)^4 + (0.9)^5 + \ldots$$

The dots at the end mean that we keep adding terms such as $(0.9)^6$ and so on. The right-hand side of this equation is called a geometric series. Each term is (0.9) times the previous term. Fortunately, mathematicians have shown that there is a general formula for the sum of all the terms in such a series.

$$\text{Multiplier} = 1/(1 - 0.9)$$

The formula applies whatever the (constant) value of c the marginal propensity to consume

$$\text{Multiplier} = 1/(1 - c) \tag{6}$$

For the particular value of $c = 0.9$, equation (6) confirms that the multiplier is $1/(0.1) = 10$. Hence a cut in investment demand by 5 causes a fall equilibrium output by 50, as we knew from Table 20.1. Indeed, you might have guessed this from equations (4) and (5). Equilibrium output is simply autonomous demand multiplied by the multiplier!

The marginal propensity to consume tells how much of each extra unit of income is spent on consumption. Thus the MPC is a number between zero and unity. The higher the MPC, the lower is $(1 - c)$. Dividing 1 by a smaller number leads to a larger answer. The general formula for the multiplier in equation (6) confirms that a larger MPC implies a larger multiplier.

The multiplier and the MPS

> The marginal propensity to save is the fraction of each extra unit of income that households wish to save.

Any part of an extra unit of income not spent must be saved. Hence $(1 - c)$ equals MPS, the marginal propensity to save.

Equation (6) says that we can also think of the multiplier as $1/MPS$. The higher the marginal propensity to save, the more of each extra unit of income leaks out of the circular flow into savings and the less goes back round the circular flow to generate further increases in aggregate demand, output and income.

Figure 20.6 confirms that the multiplier exceeds unity. The upward sloping line shows planned saving. Its slope, the marginal propensity to save, is less than unity since most extra income is consumed not saved. Hence the planned saving line has a flat slope. Beginning in equilibrium at E, imagine that the horizontal line, showing investment demand, shifts up by one unit. Since the planned saving line S has a flat slope, a unit increase in planned investment I must now intersect planned saving at a point more than one unit to the right of E. But that is all equation (6) says. The multiplier is $1/MPS$, which exceeds unity.

20.7 The paradox of thrift

The previous section analysed a parallel shift in the aggregate demand schedule caused by a change in autonomous investment demand. We now examine a parallel shift in the AD schedule caused by a change in the autonomous part of planned consumption and savings.

Suppose households increase autonomous consumption demand by 10. There is a parallel upward shift in the consumption function and hence also in the aggregate demand schedule AD. Higher autonomous consumption demand implies an identical fall in autonomous planned saving. There is a parallel downward shift in the saving function.

In equilibrium planned saving always equals planned investment and the latter is unaltered. Hence planned saving cannot change. Equilibrium income must therefore adjust to restore planned saving to the unchanged level of planned investment. Figure 20.8 illustrates.

BOX 20-3   Spending like there's no tomorrow

Nowadays Nigel Lawson advertises diets. He used to be Chancellor of the Exchequer. In the Lawson boom in the late 1980s, heady optimism and easy access to credit made UK consumers spend a lot. Personal savings collapsed as people bought champagne, sports cars and houses. The boom years did not last. As inflation rose, the government raised interest rates to slow down the economy. House prices fell. People's mortgage debt was larger than the value of their houses. To pay off this negative equity, households raised saving sharply in the early 1990s.

By 1997 UK households were borrowing again, as low interest rates fuelled a spending boom and a protracted rise in house prices. Reality TV shows were rivalled only by programmes showing viewers how to do up houses for subsequent letting or sale. The chart below shows that household saving, as a percentage of GDP, has now fallen to the level last seen at the height of the Lawson boom in 1987. By 2004, the Bank of England was citing concerns about rising house prices as a reason to raise UK interest rates.

Clearly, the saving rate can fluctuate a lot. Although in this chapter we assume a constant marginal propensity to save, Chapter 24 discusses more sophisticated theories of consumption and saving.

One final remark. Does it matter whether households borrow in order to finance a foreign holiday or to buy a house for subsequent rental to others? In the former case, no asset is purchased for the future, in the latter case the household acquires an asset that will give rise to future incomes. Simply measuring today's income and today's spending gives a misleading picture of the long-run economic position of the household. We return to this issue in Chapter 23.

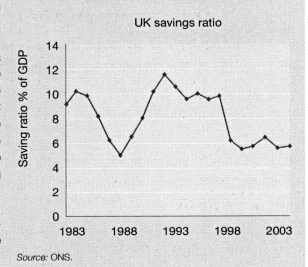

UK savings ratio

Source: ONS.

When a decline in thriftiness, or the desire to save, shifts planned saving from S to S', equilibrium income must rise from Y^* to Y^{**} to maintain the equality of planned saving and planned investment.

The paradox of thrift helps us to understand an old debate about the virtues of saving and spending. Does society benefit from thriftiness and a high level of desired saving at each income level? The answer depends on whether or not the economy is at full employment.

When aggregate demand is low and the economy has spare resources, the paradox of thrift shows that a *reduction* in the desire to save will increase spending and increase the equilibrium income level. Society benefits from higher output and employment. And since investment demand is autonomous, a change in the desire to save has no effect on the desired level of investment.

Suppose, however, that the economy is at potential output. Chapter 25 discusses how this

Figure 20.8   The paradox of thrift

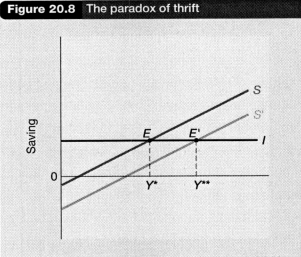

In equilibrium planned saving equals planned investment. A fall in the desire to save induces a rise in equilibrium output to keep planned saving equal to planned investment.

A change in the amount households wish to save of each income leads to a change in equilibrium income, but no change in equilibrium saving, which must still equal planned investment. This is the paradox of thrift.

might happen in the long run once prices and wages have time to adjust. If the economy is at potential output, an *increase* in the desire to save at each income level must increase saving, and reduce consumption, at potential output. However, investment demand *may* increase to restore aggregate demand to its full-employment level. The next few chapters explain why. Hence, in the long run society may benefit from an *increase* in the desire to save. Investment will rise and the economy's capital stock and potential output may grow more quickly.

In this chapter we have focused on the short run before prices and wages have time to adjust. Saving and investment decisions are made by different people. There is no automatic mechanism to translate higher saving into a corresponding rise in investment demand. Since planned saving depends on the level of income, income adjusts to equate planned saving and planned investment.

SUMMARY

- Aggregate demand is planned spending on goods (and services). The *AD* schedule shows aggregate demand at each level of income and output.

- This chapter neglects planned spending by foreigners and by the government, studying consumption demand by households, and investment demand by firms (desired additions to physical capital and to inventories). We treat investment demand as constant.

- Consumption demand is closely though not perfectly related to personal disposable income. Without taxes or transfers, personal disposable income and total income coincide.

- Autonomous consumption is desired consumption at zero income. The marginal propensity to consume (MPC) is the fraction by which planned consumption rises when income rises by a pound. The marginal propensity to save (MPS) is the fraction of an extra pound of income that is saved. Since income is consumed or saved, $MPC + MPS = 1$.

- For given prices and wages, the goods market is in equilibrium when output equals planned spending or aggregate demand. Equivalently, in equilibrium, planned saving equals planned investment. Goods market equilibrium does not mean output equals potential output. It means planned spending equals actual spending and actual output.

- The equilibrium output is demand-determined because we assume that prices and wages are fixed at a level that implies an excess supply of goods and labour. Firms and workers are happy to supply whatever output and employment is demanded.

- When aggregate demand exceeds actual output there is either unplanned disinvestment (inventory reductions) or unplanned saving (frustrated customers). Actual investment always equals actual savings, as a matter of definition. Unplanned inventory reductions or frustrated customers act as a signal to firms to raise output when aggregate demand exceeds actual output. Similarly, unplanned additions to stocks occur when aggregate demand is below output.

- A rise in planned investment increases equilibrium output by a larger amount. The initial increase in income to meet investment demand leads to further increases in consumption demand.

- The multiplier is the ratio of the change in output to the change in autonomous demand that caused it. In the simple model of this chapter, the multiplier is $1/[(1 - MPC)]$ or $1/MPS$. The multiplier exceeds 1 because *MPC* and *MPS* are positive fractions.

● The paradox of thrift shows that a reduced desire to save leads to an increase in output but no change in the equilibrium level of planned savings, which must still equal planned investment. Higher output offsets the reduced desire to save at each output level.

REVIEW QUESTIONS

● Suppose the consumption function is $C = 0.8Y$ and planned investment is 40. (a) Draw a diagram showing the aggregate demand schedule. (b) If actual output is 100, what unplanned actions will occur? (c) What is equilibrium output? (d) Do you get the same answer using planned saving equals planned investment?

● Suppose the MPC is 0.6. Beginning from equilibrium, investment demand rises by 30. (a) How much does equilibrium output increase? (b) How much of that increase is extra consumption demand?

● Planned investment is 100. People decide to save a higher proportion of their income: the consumption function changes from $C = 0.8Y$ to $C = 0.5Y$. (a) What happens to equilibrium income? (b) What happens to the equilibrium proportion of income saved? Explain.

● What part of actual investment is not included in aggregate demand?

● (a) Find equilibrium income when investment demand is 400 and $C = 0.8Y$. (b) Would output be higher or lower if the consumption function were $C = 100 + 0.7Y$?

● **Common fallacies** Why are these statements wrong? (a) If people were prepared to save more, investment would increase and we could get the economy moving again. (b) Lower output leads to lower spending and yet lower output. The economy could spiral downwards forever.

To check your answers to these questions, go to page 641.

Online
LearningCentre
with POWERWEB

To help you grasp the key concepts of this chapter check out the extra resources posted on the Online Learning Centre at www.mcgraw-hill.co.uk/ textbooks/begg. There are quick test questions, economics examples and access to Powerweb articles, all for free!

For even more exercises, recaps and examples to help you study, purchase a copy of the Economics Student Workbook. Simply visit www.mcgraw hill.co.uk/textbooks/begg and follow the links to the Workbook to buy your copy.

chapter 21

Fiscal policy and foreign trade

Learning outcomes

By the end of this chapter, you should understand:

1 how fiscal policy affects aggregate demand

2 short-run equilibrium output in this extended model

3 the balanced budget multiplier

4 automatic stabilizers

5 the structural budget and the inflation-adjusted budget

6 how budget deficits add to national debt

7 the limits to discretionary fiscal policy

8 how foreign trade affects equilibrium output

Fiscal policy is government policy on spending and taxes.

Stabilization policy is government action to keep output close to potential output.

The **budget deficit** is the excess of government spending over government receipts.

The **national debt** is the stock of outstanding government debt.

In most European countries, the governments directly buys about a fifth of national output and spends about the same again on transfer payments. This spending is financed mainly by taxes. What is the macroeconomic impact of government fiscal policy? We show how fiscal policy affects equilibrium output, then study three fiscal issues.

We analyse opportunities and limitations in using fiscal policy to stabilize output. We then examine the significance of the government's budget deficit.

When the government runs a deficit, it spends more than it earns. Deficits worry people. How can the government keep spending more than it receives? We examine the size of the deficit and ask if we should worry.

A government deficit is financed mainly by borrowing from the public by selling bonds, promises to pay specified amounts of interest payments at future dates. This borrowing adds to government debts to the public.[1]

By 2004 UK national debt was £360 billion, about £6100 per person. The third fiscal policy issue we examine is the effect of the national debt.

Most of this chapter is about the government and aggregate demand but we complete our model of income determination by also adding foreign trade. Exports X and imports Z are each nearly 30 per cent of UK GDP. The UK is a very open economy, and the effects of foreign trade are too important to ignore.[2]

---

[1] Government is responsible not merely for its own deficits but also for any losses made by state-owned firms. The public sector net cash requirement (PSNCR) is the government deficit plus net losses of these firms.

[2] In contrast, net property income is 1 per cent of GNP. We continue to treat GNP and GDP as equivalent.

55

21.1 Government and the circular flow

Government spending G on goods and services adds directly to aggregate demand. The government also withdraws money from the circular flow through indirect taxes T_e on expenditure and direct taxes T_d on factor incomes, less transfer benefits B that augment factor incomes. However, transfer payments affect aggregate demand only by affecting other components such as consumption or investment demand.

Table 21.1 shows UK government activity in 2004–05. The main components of G are health, education and defence. Social security payments – state pensions, unemployment benefit and child support – and debt interest payments are the main components of transfer payments.

The main direct taxes are income tax, corporation tax and social security contributions to state schemes for pensions and unemployment benefit. Indirect taxes include VAT, specific duties on tobacco, alcohol and fuel, and the property taxes levied by local government.

Table 21.1   UK public finances 2004–05

Revenue	£bn	Expenditure	£bn
Direct tax		**Goods and services**	
Income tax	128	NHS	81
Corporation tax	35	Education	63
Social security	78	Defence	27
		Law and order	29
Indirect tax		Housing, Environment	17
VAT	73	Transport	
		Industry and agriculture	2
		Transfer payments	
		Social security	138
Interest and dividends	39	Debt interest	25
Excise duties	40	**Other spending**	72
Other receipts	6		
Total revenue	455	**Total spending**	488
Deficit	33		

Source: www.hm-treasury.gov.uk.

21.2 The government and aggregate demand

Since it is a pain to keep distinguishing market prices and basic prices, we assume all taxes are direct taxes. With no indirect taxes, measurements at market prices and at basic prices coincide. For the moment, we still ignore foreign trade.

Aggregate demand AD is consumption demand C, investment demand I, and government demand G for goods and services. Transfer payments affect aggregate demand only by affecting C or I.

$$AD = C + I + G \tag{1}$$

In the short run, government spending G does not vary automatically with output and income. We assume G is fixed, or at least independent of income. Its size reflects how many hospitals the government wants to build and how many teachers it wants to hire. We now have three autonomous components of aggregate demand independent of current income and output: the autonomous consumption demand, investment demand I and government demand G.

The government also levies taxes and pays out transfer benefits. With no indirect taxes, net taxes NT are simply direct taxes T_d minus transfer benefits B. Net taxes reduce personal disposable income – the amount available for spending or saving by households – relative to national income and output. If YD is disposable income, Y national income and output, and NT net taxes,

> **Net taxes** are taxes minus transfers.

$$YD = Y - NT = (1 - t)Y \qquad (2)$$

where for simplicity, we assume that net taxes are proportional to national income. Thus, if t is the *net tax rate*, the total revenue from net taxes is $NT = tY$.

Suppose taxes net of transfer benefits are about 20 per cent of national income. We can think of the (net) tax rate t as 0.2. If national income Y rises by £1, net tax revenue will rise by 20p, so household disposable income will increase only by 80p.

We still assume that households' desired consumption is proportional to their disposable income. For simplicity, suppose autonomous consumption is zero but that, as before, the marginal propensity to consume out of disposable income is 0.9. Households plan to spend 90p of each extra pound of disposable income. The consumption function is now $C = 0.9YD$.

With a net tax rate t, equation (2) says that disposable income YD is only $(1 - t)$ times national income Y. Thus, to relate consumption demand to *national* income, $C = 0.9YD = 0.9(1 - t)Y$.

If national income rises by £1, consumption demand rises by only 0.9 times $(1 - t)$ of a pound. If the net tax rate t is 0.2, consumption demand rises by only £$(0.9 \times 0.8) = £0.72$. Each extra pound of national income increases disposable income by only 80p, out of which households plan to consume 90 per cent and save 10 per cent.

Clearly, spending £0.72 of each extra pound of national income implies a flatter consumption function, when plotted against national income, than spending £0.90 of each extra pounds of national income. The effect of a positive net tax rate t therefore acts like a reduction in the marginal propensity to consume. Figure 21.1 illustrates.

Aggregate demand, and equilibrium output, do not depend on whether the leakage is through saving (as when the MPC is low) or through taxes (as when the MPC multiplied by $(1 - t)$ is low). Either way, the leakage prevents money being recycled as demand for output of firms.

If MPC is the marginal propensity to consume out of *disposable* income, and there is a proportional net tax rate t, then MPC', the marginal propensity to consume out of *national* income, is given by

$$MPC' = MPC \times (1 - t) \qquad (3)$$

We now show how the government affects equilibrium national income and output. We start with an example in which autonomous investment demand is I and the consumption function in terms of disposable income is $C = 0.9YD$.

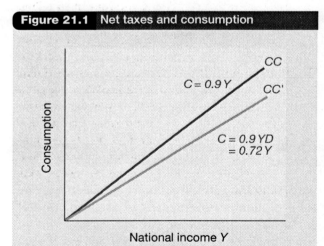

Figure 21.1 Net taxes and consumption

Consumption / National income Y

CC
$C = 0.9Y$
CC'
$C = 0.9YD = 0.72Y$

In the absence of taxation, national income Y and disposable income YD are the same. The consumption function CC' shows how much households wish to consume at each level of national income. With a proportional net tax rate of 0.2, households still consume 90p of each pound of disposable income. Since YD is now only 0.8 Y, households consume only 0.9 × 0.8 = 0.72 of each extra unit of national income. Relating consumption to national income, the effect of net taxes is to rotate the consumption function downwards from CC to CC'.

The effect of net taxes on output

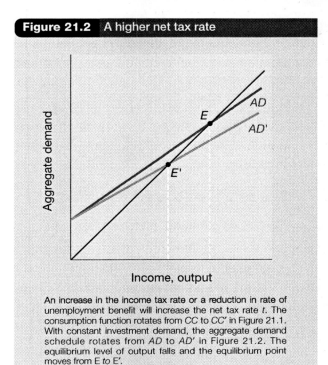

Figure 21.2   A higher net tax rate

An increase in the income tax rate or a reduction in rate of unemployment benefit will increase the net tax rate t. The consumption function rotates from CC to CC′ in Figure 21.1. With constant investment demand, the aggregate demand schedule rotates from AD to AD′ in Figure 21.2. The equilibrium level of output falls and the equilibrium point moves from E to E′.

Suppose initially that government spending is zero. Figure 21.2 illustrates. A rise in the net tax rate from zero to 0.2 makes the consumption function to pivot downward from CC to CC′ in Figure 21.1. We obtain aggregate demand AD by adding the constant investment demand I to the consumption function. Hence, the rise in the net rate that rotates the consumption function from CC to CC′ in Figure 21.1 causes a similar rotation of aggregate demand from AD to AD′ in Figure 21.2. Hence, aggregate demand equals actual output at a lower output level. The aggregate demand schedule now crosses the 45° line at E′ not E. Equilibrium income and output fall.

Raising the net tax rate reduces equilibrium output. When aggregate demand and equilibrium output are below potential output, lower tax rates or higher transfer benefits will raise aggregate demand and equilibrium output.

The effect of government spending on output

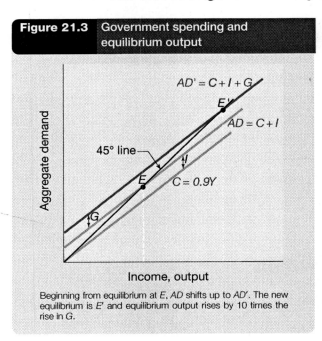

Figure 21.3   Government spending and equilibrium output

Beginning from equilibrium at E, AD shifts up to AD′. The new equilibrium is E′ and equilibrium output rises by 10 times the rise in G.

Now forget taxes and think government spending. Suppose the net tax rate is zero. National income and disposable income coincide. Figure 21.3 shows that higher government spending has an effect similar to that of higher autonomous investment demand studied in Chapter 20. With a marginal propensity to consume of 0.9, the multiplier is again $1/(1 - MPC) = 10$. A rise in government spending G induces a rise in equilibrium output by 10 times that amount. In Figure 21.3 equilibrium moves from E to E′ when the aggregate demand schedule shifts from AD to AD′.

The combined effects of government spending and taxation

Suppose an economy begins with an equilibrium output of 1000 but no government. Assume demand from autonomous consumption and investment is 100. With a marginal propensity to consume out of disposable income of 0.9, a disposable income of 1000 induces consumption demand of 900. Aggegate demand is (900 + 100) = 1000 which is also actual output.

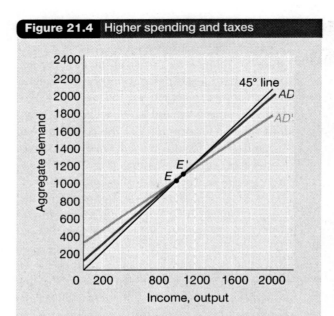

Figure 21.4 Higher spending and taxes

Beginning from equilibrium at E, government spending rises from zero to 200, shifting the AD schedule upwards, and the tax rises from zero to 0.2, making the new schedule AD' flatter. Equilibrium moves from E to E' where AD' intersects the 45° line. Equilibrium output increases from 1000 to 1071.

Now introduce extra autonomous demand of 200 from the government, taking total autonomous demand to 300. Also introduce a net tax rate of 0.2. The marginal propensity to consume out of national income falls from 0.9 to 0.72, and the multiplier becomes $1/(1 - 0.72) = 1/0.28 = 3.57$. Multiplying autonomous demand of 300 by 3.57 yields equilibrium output of 1071, above the original equilibrium output of 1000. Figure 21.4 illustrates.

The balanced budget multiplier

The economy began at an equilibrium output of 1000. With a proportional tax rate of 20 per cent, initial tax revenue was 200, precisely the amount of government spending.

This balanced increase in government spending and taxes did not leave demand and output unaltered. Figure 21.4 shows equilibrium output is larger. The new 200 of government spending raises aggregate demand by 200 and the tax increase cuts disposable income by 200. The MPC out of disposable income is 0.9, so lower disposable income reduces consumption demand by only $0.9 \times 200 = 180$.

The initial effect of the tax and spending package raises aggregate demand by 200 but reduces it by 180. Aggregate demand rises by 20. Output rises, inducing further rises in consumption demand. When the new equilibrium is reached, output has risen a total of 71, from 1000 to 1071. This is the famous balanced budget multiplier.

The multiplier revisited

> The **balanced budget multiplier** says that a rise in government spending plus an equal rise in taxes leads to higher output.

The multiplier relates changes in autonomous demand to changes in equilibrium *national* income and output. The formula in Chapter 20 still applies, but now we use *MPC'*, the marginal propensity to consume out of national rather than out of disposable income.

$$\text{Multiplier} = 1/[1 - MPC'] \qquad (4)$$

With proportional taxes, *MPC'* equals $MPC \times (1 - t)$. For a given marginal propensity to consume out of disposable income, a higher tax rate *t* reduces *MPC'*, raises $(1 - MPC')$, and thus reduces the multiplier. Table 21.2 illustrates.

In Chapter 20, without government the multiplier was simply $1/[1 - MPC]$ or $1/MPS$. With a larger marginal propensity to save, there was a larger leakage from the circular flow between firms and households and the multiplier was correspondingly smaller.

Table 21.2 Values of the multiplier

MPC	t	MPC'	Multiplier
0.9	0	0.90	10.00
0.9	0.2	0.72	3.57
0.7	0	0.70	3.33
0.7	0.2	0.56	2.27
0.7	0.4	0.42	1.72

BOX 21-1   Land of the falling sun

Japan, after three decades of postwar success, screwed up the 1990s. A property crash made banks bankrupt. Instead of admitting this and sorting it out, policy makers ignored the problem. Consumers lost confidence and output fell.

To restore confidence, Japan had big fiscal expansions to boost demand. Japanese consumers and firms decided radical action meant things were worse than previously thought. The autonomous parts of consumption and investment demand fell more than enough to offset the fiscal expansion. Fiscal expansion failed to boost output. In macroeconomics the induced effects can outweigh the direct effect. Only in 2003 did Japanese output growth return to 3% a year.

Japan's macroeconomic misery

	GDP growth (%)	Interest rate (%)	Budget deficit (% of GDP)	Govt. net debt (% of GDP)
1993	0	3	2	5
1994	1	2	2	8
1995	2	1	4	13
1996	5	1	4	16
1997	1	1	3	18
1998	–3	1	5	31
1999	0	0	7	38
2000	2	0	6	44
2001	2	0	6	49
2002	0	0	6	50
2003	3	0	6	50

Source: OECD *Economic Outlook*, June 2004.

Table 21.2 merely extends this insight. Now leakages arise both from saving and from net taxes. When both are large, the multiplier is small. The bottom row of the table has a much smaller multiplier than the top row.

21.3   The government budget

A **budget** is the spending and revenue plans of an individual, a company or a government.

The government budget describes what goods and services the government will buy during the coming year, what transfer payments it will make and how it will pay for them. Most of its spending is financed by taxes. When spending exceeds taxes, there is a budget deficit. When taxes exceed spending there is a budget surplus. Continuing to use G for government spending on goods and services, and NT for net taxes or taxes minus transfer payments,

Government budget deficit = $G - NT$ \hfill (5)

Figure 21.5 shows government purchases G and net taxes tY in relation to national income. We assume G is fixed at 200. With a proportional net tax rate of 0.2, net taxes are $0.2Y$. Taxes are zero when output is zero, 100 when output is 500, 200 when output is 1000. At outputs below 1000, the government budget is in deficit. At an output of 1000 the budget is balanced, and at higher outputs the budget is in surplus. Given G and t, the budget deficit or surplus depends on the level of output and income.

The budget surplus or deficit is determined by three things: the tax rate t, the level of government spending G, and the level of output Y. With a given tax rate, an increase in G will raise output and hence tax revenue. Could the budget deficit be *reduced* by higher spending? We now show that this is impossible.

Investment, savings and the budget

By definition, actual leakages from the circular flow always equal actual injections to the circular flow. Payments cannot vanish into thin air. Our model now has two leakages – saving by

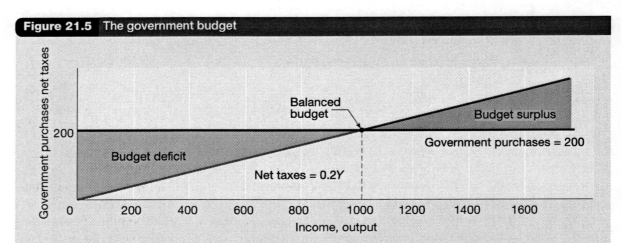

Figure 21.5 The government budget

The budget deficit equals total government spending minus total tax revenue, or government purchases of goods and services minus net taxes. Government purchases are shown as constant, independent of income, while net taxes are proportionate to income. Thus at low levels of income the budget is in deficit; at high income levels, the budget is in surplus.

households and net taxes paid to the government – and two injections – investment spending by firms and government spending on goods and services. Thus *actual* savings plus *actual* net taxes always equal *actual* government spending plus *actual* investment spending.

In the last chapter we saw that, when the economy is not at equilibrium income, actual saving and investment differ from *desired* or *planned* saving and investment. Firms make unplanned changes in inventories and households may be forced to make unplanned savings if demand exceeds the output actually available.

The economy is in equilibrium when all quantities demanded or *desired* are equal to *actual* quantities. In equilibrium, planned saving S plus planned net taxes NT must equal planned government purchases G plus planned investment I. Planned leakages equal planned injections.

$$S + NT = G + I \qquad (6)$$

Without the government, this reduces to the equilibrium condition of Chapter 20: planned saving equals planned investment. Equation (6) implies that in equilibrium desired saving minus desired investment equals the government's desired budget deficit.

$$S - I = G - NT \qquad (7)$$

Equation (7) confirms that a rise in planned government spending G must *raise* the budget deficit. For a given tax rate, a rise in G leads to a parallel upward shift in the aggregate demand schedule. This raises equilibrium income. Provided the tax rate is less than 100 per cent, disposable income must rise. Households increase both desired consumption and desired saving when disposable income rises. Some of the extra disposable income goes in extra desired saving.

Since desired investment I is independent of income, a rise in desired saving raises the left-hand side of equation (7). Hence the right-hand side must rise. Hence, net taxes NT cannot rise as G. Equation (7) promises us that the equilibrium budget deficit rises if government spending increases but the net tax rate is unaltered.

Higher government spending on goods and services increases equilibrium output. With a given tax rate, tax revenue rises but the budget deficit increases (or the budget surplus falls).

We can analyse a tax increase in a similar way. We know from Figure 21.2 that a rise in the tax rate makes the aggregate demand schedule rotate downwards. Equilibrium income must fall. Disposable income falls, both because of lower national income and a higher tax rate. With lower disposable income,

For given government spending *G*, a higher tax rate reduces both equilibrium output and the budget deficit.

desired saving must fall. Hence the left-hand side of equation (7) must fall. Hence the budget deficit is lower.

21.4   Deficits and the fiscal stance

The fiscal stance shows the effect of fiscal policy on demand and output.

Is the budget deficit a good measure of the government's fiscal stance?

Does the size of the deficit show whether fiscal policy is *expansionary*, aiming to raise national income, or *contractionary*, trying to reduce national income?

In itself, the deficit may be a poor measure of the government's fiscal stance. The deficit can change for reasons unconnected with fiscal policy. Even if *G* and *t* are unaltered, a fall in investment demand will reduce output and income. In turn this reduces net tax revenue and raises the budget deficit.

For given levels of government spending and tax rates, the budget has larger deficits in recessions, when income is low, than in booms, when income is high. Suppose aggregate demand suddenly falls. The budget will go into deficit. Someone looking at the deficit might conclude that fiscal policy was expansionary and that there was no need to expand fiscal policy further. That might be wrong. The deficit may exist because of the recession.

The structural budget

The structural budget shows what the budget would be if output were at potential output.

To use the budget deficit as an indicator of the fiscal stance we calculate the *structural or cyclically-adjusted budget*.

Suppose government spending is 200 and the tax rate is 0.2. As in Figure 21.4, the budget is in deficit at any income below 1000 and in surplus at any income above 1000. If, given the other components of aggregate demand, equilibrium output is 800, the actual budget will be in deficit. Net tax revenue will be $0.2 \times 800 = 160$. With government spending at 200, the budget deficit is 40.

Conversely, suppose equilibrium output is 1200. With a tax rate of 0.2, net tax revenue would be 240 but autonomous government spending would still be 200. There would be a budget *surplus* of 40.

Looking at the deficit of 40 when the actual output is 800, we might conclude fiscal policy is too expansionary and the government should tighten fiscal policy to eliminate the deficit. Once we realize that the main cause of the deficit is low income, we are less likely to reach this conclusion. We may also recognize that tightening fiscal policy during a recession is likely to reduce output further.[3]

Inflation-adjusted deficits

A second reason why the actual government deficit may be a poor measure of fiscal stance is the distinction between real and nominal interest rates. Official measures of the deficit treat all nominal interest paid by the government on the national debt as government expenditure.

---

[3] In this chapter we are concerned only with the impact of fiscal policy on aggregate demand. There may be other reasons to worry about a deficit. We examine these in Chapter 27.

During 1975–77, Britain's Labour government had budget deficits of 5.5 per cent of GDP. But the oil price shocks and trade union power meant UK inflation averaged 16 per cent. Since nominal interest rates were 15 per cent, real interest rates were negative. The inflation correction alone – counting real not nominal interest in the budget deficit – reduced the deficit from 5.5 per cent to only 1 per cent during 1975–77. Nowadays inflation is low, so the inflation correction is less important.

One should still correct for the effect of the business cycle on tax revenues. The UK had the Lawson boom in the late 1980s, then the Major slump in the early 1990s, before enjoying steady growth during 1993–2001. The structural budget deficit should exceed the actual deficit in the late 1980s (when the boom boosted tax revenue) and be smaller than the actual deficit in the early 1990s (the slump cut tax rev-

enue and boosted unemployment transfers). Then, after years of steady recovery, the discrepancy between the two should be small by the late 1990s. The table below confirms these predictions.

Recent estimates by the UK Treasury suggest that, after two years, a 1 per cent rise in output (relative to potential) improves the budget by 0.75 per cent of GDP.

Average annual deficit (central and local government)

	88–90	91–94	98–01
Actual deficit (% of GDP)	0.2	5.8	−1.6
Structural deficit (% of GDP)	2.5	4.6	−1.4

Sources: OECD, *Economic Outlook*; D. Begg, 'UK Fiscal Policy since 1970', in R. Dornbusch and R. Layard (eds.), *The Performance of the UK Economy*, Oxford University Press, 1987; HM Treasury, Budget 2001.

It makes more sense to count only the *real* interest rate times the outstanding government debt as an item of expenditure that contributes to the deficit.

The **inflation-adjusted budget** uses real not nominal interest rates to calculate government spending on debt interest.

Suppose inflation is 10 per cent, nominal interest rates are 12 per cent and real interest rates are 2 per cent. From the government's viewpoint, the interest burden is only really 2 per cent on each £1 of debt outstanding. Although nominal interest rates are 12 per cent, inflation will inflate future nominal tax revenue at 10 per cent a year, providing most of the revenue needed to pay the high nominal interest rates. The real cost of borrowing is only 2 per cent.

 **LearningCentre** **Now you've read this section,** why not test your understanding by visiting the Online Learning Centre at www.mcgraw-hill.co.uk/textbooks/begg

21.5 Automatic stabilizers and discretionary fiscal policy

Automatic stabilizers reduce the multiplier and dampen the output response to demand shocks.

Table 21.2 showed that a higher net tax rate *t* reduces the multiplier. Suppose investment demand falls by 100. The larger the multiplier, the larger the fall in equilibrium output. A high net tax rate reduces the multiplier and dampens the output effect of shocks to autonomous aggregate demand. A high net tax rate is a good automatic stabilizer.

Income tax, VAT and unemployment benefit are important automatic stabilizers. At given tax rates and given benefit levels, a fall in income and output raises payments of unemployment benefits and reduces tax revenue. Both effects reduce the multiplier and damp the output response. A given shift of the aggregate demand schedule has a smaller effect on equilibrium income and output. The automatic reduction in net tax revenue acts as a fiscal stimulus. Conversely, in a boom, net tax revenue rises, which helps dampen the boom.

Automatic stabilizers have a great advantage. They are automatic. Nobody has to decide whether there has been a shock to which policy should respond. By reducing the responsiveness of the economy to shocks, automatic stabilizers reduce output fluctuations.

All leakages are automatic stabilizers. A higher saving rate and lower marginal propensity to consume reduce the multiplier. Later in the chapter, we shall see that a high marginal propensity to import also dampens output fluctuations.

Active or discretionary fiscal policy

Discretionary fiscal policy is decisions about tax rates and levels of government spending.

Although automatic fiscal stabilizers are always at work, governments also use *discretionary* fiscal policies to change spending levels or tax rates to stabilize aggregate demand. When other components of aggregate demand are abnormally low, the government can boost demand by cutting taxes, raising spending, or both. When other components of aggregate demand are abnormally high, the government raises taxes or cuts spending.

By now you should be asking two questions. First, why can fiscal policy not stabilize aggregate demand completely? Surely, by maintaining aggregate demand at its full-employment level, the government could eliminate booms and slumps altogether? Second, why are governments

---

BOX 21-3   The limits of fiscal policy

Why can't demand shocks be fully offset by fiscal policy?

1 Time lags It takes time to spot that aggregate demand has changed. It may take six months to get reliable statistics on output. Then it takes time to change fiscal policy. Long-term spending plans on hospitals or defence cannot be changed overnight. And once the policy is changed it takes time to work through the steps of the multiplier process to have its full effect.

2 Uncertainty The government faces two problems. First, it is unsure of key magnitudes such as the multiplier. It only has estimates from past data. Mistaken estimates induce incorrect decisions about the extent of the fiscal change needed. Second, since fiscal policy takes time to work, the government has to forecast the level that demand will reach by the time fiscal policy has its full effects. If investment is low today but about to rise sharply, a fiscal expansion may not be needed. Mistakes in forecasting non-government sources of demand, such as investment, lead to incorrect decisions about the fiscal changes currently required.

3 Induced effects on autonomous demand Our model treats investment demand and the autonomous consumption demand as given. This is only a simplifi-

cation. Changes in fiscal policy may lead to offsetting changes in other components of autonomous demand. If estimates of these induced effects are wrong, fiscal changes have unexpected effects. To study this issue, we extend our model of aggregate demand in Chapter 24.

Why not expand fiscal policy when unemployment is high?

1 The budget deficit When output is low and unemployment high, the budget deficit may be large. Fiscal expansion makes it larger. The government may worry about the size of the deficit itself, an issue we discuss in Section 21.6, or worry that a large deficit will lead to inflation, an issue we explore in Chapter 26.

2 Maybe we are at full employment! Our simple model assumes there are spare resources. Output is demand-determined. Fiscal expansion raises demand and output. But we could be at potential output. People are unemployed, and machines idle, only because they do not wish to supply at the going wages or rentals. If so, there are no spare resources to be mopped up raising aggregate demand. If high unemployment and low output reflect not low demand but low supply, fiscal expansion is pointless. Chapters 25, 26 and 30 discuss the supply side of the economy in more detail.

reluctant to expand fiscal policy and aggregate demand to a level that would completely eliminate unemployment? Box 21.3 provides some of the answers.

21.6 The national debt and the deficit

> The government's debts are called the national debt.

In recent years the UK government had a budget surplus. Historically, this is rare. Most governments have budget deficits. The flow of deficits is what adds to the stock of debt.

The UK government had large deficits in the 1970s. The nominal value of its debt soared from £33 billion in 1971 to £113 billion in 1981. Yet in many of these years the nominal deficit was actually a real surplus once inflation accounting is used. This suggests that the *real* debt must have been falling, not rising. And it was. Moreover, when the economy is growing in *real* terms, real tax revenue is rising, and the government can service a growing real debt without having to increase *tax rates*.

These two arguments – inflation adjustment of the deficit, and the growth of real incomes and the real tax revenue from given tax rates – mean that in many countries debt is not out of control. Although cumulative nominal deficits dramatically raised nominal debt, the ratio of nominal debt to nominal GDP has often *fallen*, as Table 21.3 confirms. The UK debt/GDP ratio in 2004 was half its level 30 years earlier. Fears of a UK debt explosion were misplaced.

Table 21.3 UK national debt, 1973–2004 (net public sector debt as % or GDP)

1973	1979	1985	1991	2001	2004
60	48	46	28	32	33

Sources: OECD, *Economic Outlook*; HM Treasury, Budget 2004.

There are two reasons why concerns about the national debt may be overstated. First, much of it is owed to UK citizens. It is a debt we owe ourselves as a nation. Second, some of the money borrowed by the public sector has been used to finance investment in physical or human capital, which raises *future* output and tax revenue and will help pay off the debt. Prudent businesses sometimes borrow to finance profitable investment. A prudent government may do the same. More investment in rail infrastructure would probably have been good for the UK, even if financed by greater debt.

When should a sensible economist worry about the scale of the public debt? First, *if* the debt becomes large relative to GDP, high tax rates will be needed to meet the debt interest burden. High tax rates may have disincentive effects.

Second, if the government cannot raise tax rates beyond a certain point, a large debt and hence large debt interest payments may cause large deficits that can be financed only by borrowing or printing money. Since borrowing compounds the problem, eventually it is necessary to print money on a huge scale. That is how hyperinflations start. Chapter 26 fills in the details.

By 2004 UK government debt, relative to GDP, was lower than in 1970. However, in some European countries, and also in Japan, it is now large, as Table 21.4 confirms. High debt levels are especially worrying when real interest rates are high.

Table 21.4 Government net debt (% of GDP)

	1981	2002	2005
Belgium	84	100	94
Italy	53	105	106
Netherlands	25	49	59
USA	22	50	50
UK	38	48	42
France	0	63	69
Germany	12	58	67
Japan	19	125	125
Sweden	6	41	51

Source: OECD, *Economic Outlook*.

BOX 21-4   'You've never had it so prudent' . . .

. . . Prime Minister Tony Blair told the Labour Party Conference in 1999. To stop short-sighted politicians boosting the economy too much in the short run and thereby causing long term problems, Chancellor Gordon Brown not only gave the Bank of England independent control of interest rates but also introduced a Code for Fiscal Stability.

The **Code for Fiscal Stability** commits the government to a medium-run objective of financing all current government spending out of current revenues.

Borrowing-financed deficits are allowed only to finance public-sector investment (which should eventually pay for itself by raising future output and hence future tax revenues). A medium-run perspective is needed because the actual deficit fluctuates over the business cycle even if tax rates remain constant. Chancellor Brown's 'golden rule' means that government debt accumulation in the long run (because of borrowing to finance investment) should be accompanied by higher output and tax revenue without requiring any change in tax rates.

Because tax revenues tend to fall when the economy is growing more slowly, there is always some room for dispute about whether the emergence of a tax revenue shortfall can merely be attributed to tem-porary cyclical factors or whether it is likely to persist and therefore require rises in tax rates to put it right again.

Although the Treasury has continued to insist that the UK's long-run budget position is sound, others have begun to disagree. For example, *The Economist* (under the theme *Gordon and Prudence: it's so over, 13/03/2003; 18/04/04*) argued:

But if Mr Brown has helped to banish boom and bust in the economy, he has presided over bust and boom in the public finances. Early in his chancellorship, he made much of his prudence. He sat on spending and put up taxes, notoriously through his £5 billion ($9 billion) 'stealth' raid on pension funds. And once again, the Chancellor was lucky. The dotcom frenzy and stockmarket boom generated a surge in taxes paid by high earners and City firms.

Mr Brown's good fortune tempted him to push his luck. Four years ago, the Chancellor sanctioned an extended spending spree on the public services. Although Mr Brown put up taxes in his post-election budget in 2002, his determination to pump money into public services, especially the National Health Service, has driven the public finances deep into the red. A £15 billion surplus in the fiscal year 2000–01 has turned into a £38 billion deficit (3.4% of GDP) in 2003–04.

This completes our introduction to fiscal policy, aggregate demand and the economy. We now extend our model of income determination to include the sector we have so far neglected – foreign trade with the rest of the world.

21.7   Foreign trade and income determination

We now take account of exports X, goods made at home but sold abroad, and imports Z, goods made abroad but bought domestic residents. Table 21.5 shows UK exports, imports and net exports. Two points should be noted.

Net exports are small relative to GDP. Exports and imports are about equal in size. The UK has fairly balanced trade with the rest of the world.

The trade balance is the value of net exports. If these are positive, the economy has a trade surplus. If imports exceed exports, the economy has a trade deficit.

When a household overspends its income, it dissaves, or is in deficit, and runs down its net assets (selling assets or adding to debt) to meet this deficit. When a country runs a trade deficit with the rest of the world, the country as a whole must sell off some assets to foreigners to pay for this deficit. Chapter 29 explains how this occurs.

Table 21.5 shows that the UK is a very open economy. Exports and imports are each over a quarter of GDP. In the United States, exports and imports are about 12 per cent

Table 21.5	UK foreign trade, 1950–2004 (% of GDP)		
	Exports	Imports	Net exports
1950	23	23	0
1960	20	21	1
1970	22	21	1
1980	27	25	2
2004	25	28	–3

Source: ONS, *Economic Trends*.

of GDP. Foreign trade is much more important for most European countries than for a huge country like the United States, which largely trades with itself.

Net exports $X - Z$ add to our income and expenditure measures of GDP. Hence, the equilibrium condition for the goods market must now be expanded to

$$Y = AD = C + I + G + X - Z \qquad (8)^4$$

What determines desired exports and imports? Export demand depends mainly on what is happening abroad. Foreign income and foreign demand is largely unrelated to domestic output. Hence we treat the demand for exports as autonomous.

Demand for imports rises when domestic income and output rise. Figure 21.6 shows the demand for exports, imports and net exports as domestic income changes. The export demand schedule is horizontal. Export demand is independent of domestic income. Desired imports are zero when income is zero but rises as income rises. The slope of the import demand schedule is the marginal propensity to import.

The **marginal propensity to import (MPZ)** is the fraction of each extra pound of national income that domestic residents wish to spend on extra imports.

The import demand schedule in Figure 21.6 assumes a value of 0.2 for the marginal propensity to import. Each additional pound of national income adds 20p to desired imports. One of the problems facing the UK is that the marginal propensity to import *MPZ* is higher than 0.2. Any increase in national income leads to a large increase in the demand for imports.

At each output, the gap between export demand and import demand is the demand for net exports. At low output, net exports are positive. There is a trade *surplus* with the rest of the world. At high output, there is a trade *deficit* and net exports are negative. By raising import demand while leaving export demand unchanged, higher output worsens the trade balance.

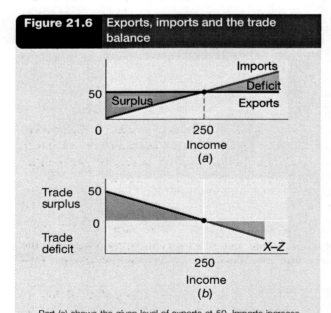

| Figure 21.6 | Exports, imports and the trade balance |

Part (a) shows the given level of exports at 50. Imports increase with the level of income. The diagram assumes a marginal propensity to import, shown by the slope of the import schedule, of 0.2. The trade balance, the difference between planned exports and planned imports, is zero at an income level of 250. Imports and exports both equal 50. At higher levels of income, imports exceed 50 and there is a trade deficit. The net export schedule $X - Z$ in part (b) shows the difference between export and import demand.

Net exports and equilibrium income

Figure 21.7 shows how equilibrium income is determined. We start from the aggregate demand schedule $C + I + G$, described earlier in the chapter, then add net exports NX. At low output, net export demand is positive. Aggregate demand $C + I + G + X - Z$ will then exceed $C + I + G$. As output rises, import demand rises and desired *net* exports fall. At the output of 250, Figure 21.6 tells

---

[4] This also implies $Y + Z = C + I + G + X$. Home output Y plus output Z from abroad equal final demand $C + I + G + X$.

Figure 21.7 Equilibrium income in an open economy

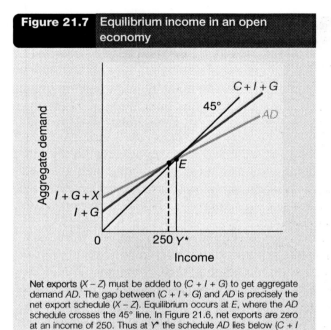

Net exports (X – Z) must be added to (C + I + G) to get aggregate demand AD. The gap between (C + I + G) and AD is precisely the net export schedule (X – Z). Equilibrium occurs at E, where the AD schedule crosses the 45° line. In Figure 21.6, net exports are zero at an income of 250. Thus at Y* the schedule AD lies below (C + I + G).

us that net export demand is zero. Figure 21.7 shows the new aggregate demand schedule AD crossing C + I + G at an output of 250. Beyond this output, net export demand is negative and the aggregate demand schedule is below C + I + G.

At a zero income, Figure 21.7 shows autonomous demand I + G + X. Suppose the marginal propensity to consume out of national income MPC is still 0.72. The C + I + G schedule has a slope of 0.72 but the aggregate demand schedule AD is flatter. Each extra pound of national income adds 72p to consumption demand but also adds 20p to desired imports, since MPZ = 0.2. Thus, each extra pound of national income adds only 52p to aggregate demand for domestic output. The AD schedule has a slope of 0.52.

In Figure 21.7 equilibrium is at E, where aggregate demand equals domestic income and output. Planned spending, actual incomes and domestic output coincide at Y*. Knowing this we can deduce the levels of tax revenue and imports and hence compute both the budget deficit (or surplus) and the trade deficit (or surplus). Neither is automatically zero merely because the economy is at equilibrium output.

The multiplier in an open economy

Each extra pound of national income raises consumption demand *for domestically produced goods* not by MPC', the marginal propensity to consume goods from whatever source, but only by (MPC' – MPZ). The multiplier is lower because there are not only leakages through saving and taxes but also through imports. In an open economy, the multiplier becomes

$$\text{Multiplier} = 1/[1 - (MPC' - MPZ)] \qquad (9)$$

With a value of 0.72 for MPC', the multiplier in the absence of foreign trade would be 3.57. If the marginal propensity to import is 0.2, the multiplier is reduced to 1/[0.48] = 2.08. If the marginal propensity to import was as high as 0.72, equation (9) implies the multiplier would be reduced to 1, which is no multiplier at all.

For small economies, very open to international trade, this leakage through import demand is very important. Small economies that are very open thus face powerful automatic stabilizers.

Higher export demand

A rise in export demand leads to a parallel upward shift in the aggregate demand schedule AD. Equilibrium income must increase. A higher AD schedule crosses the 45° line at a higher level of income. With a higher income, desired imports rise. The analysis of what happens to net exports is very similar to our analysis of the effect of an increase in government spending on the budget deficit.

As a matter of national income accounting, total leakages from the circular flow always equal total injections to the circular flow. And in equilibrium desired spending must coincide with actual income and spending on domestic goods. Hence the amended equilibrium condition for an open economy is

$$S + NT + Z = I + G + X \tag{10}$$

Desired savings plus net taxes plus desired imports equal desired investment plus desired government spending plus desired exports. Higher export demand X raises equilibrium domestic income and output. This raises desired savings, net tax revenue at constant tax rates, and desired imports.[5] Since S, NT and Z all rise when X rises, the rise in desired imports must be smaller than the rise in desired exports. Higher export demand raises the equilibrium level of desired imports but still increases the desired level of net exports. The domestic country's trade balance with the rest of the world improves.

Imports and employment

Do imports steal jobs from the domestic economy? Final demand $C + I + G + X$ is met partly through goods produced abroad, not at home. By reducing imports, we can create extra output and employment at home. This view is correct but also dangerous. It is correct because higher consumer spending on domestic rather than foreign goods *will* increase aggregate demand for domestic goods and so raise domestic output and employment. In Figure 21.7, a lower marginal propensity to import makes the AD schedule steeper and raises equilibrium income and output.

There are many ways to restrict import spending at each level of output. In Chapter 29 we begin the analysis of how the exchange rate affects the demand for imports (and exports). However, imports can also be restricted directly through *import quotas* or indirectly through *tariffs*. We explore these further in Chapter 33.

The view that import restrictions help domestic output and employment is dangerous because it ignores the possibility of retaliation by other countries. By reducing our imports, we cut the exports of others. If they retaliate by doing the same thing, the demand for our exports will fall. In the end, nobody gains employment but world trade disappears. If the whole world is in recession, what is needed is a worldwide expansion of fiscal policies, not a collective, and ultimately futile, attempt to steal employment from other countries.

SUMMARY

- The government buys goods and services, and levies taxes (net of transfer benefits) that reduce disposable income below national income and output.

- Net taxes, if related to income levels, lower the marginal propensity to consume out of national income. Households get only part of each extra pound of national income to use as a disposable income.

- Higher government spending on goods and services raises aggregate demand and equilibrium output. A higher tax rate reduces aggregate demand and equilibrium output.

---

[5] Since tax rates remain constant, higher domestic income raises disposable income, desired consumption, and savings.

● An equal initial increase in government spending and taxes raises aggregate demand and output. This is the balanced budget multiplier.

● The government budget is in deficit (surplus) if spending is larger (smaller) than tax revenue. Higher government spending raises the budget deficit. A higher tax rate reduces it.

● In equilibrium in a closed economy, desired savings and taxes equal desired investment and government spending. An excess of desired savings over desired investment must be offset by an excess of government purchases over net tax revenue.

● The budget deficit is a poor indicator of fiscal stance. Recessions make the budget go into deficit, booms generate a budget surplus. The structural budget calculates whether the budget would be in surplus or deficit if output were at potential output. It is also important to inflation-adjust the deficit.

● Automatic stabilizers reduce fluctuations in GDP by reducing the multiplier. Leakages act as automatic stabilizers.

● The government may also use active or discretionary fiscal policy to try to stabilize output. In practice, active fiscal policy cannot stabilize output perfectly.

● Budget deficits add to the national debt. If the debt is mainly owed to citizens of the country, interest payments are merely a transfer within the economy. However, the national debt may be a burden if the government is unable or unwilling to raise taxes to meet high interest payments on a large national debt.

● Deficits are not necessarily bad. Particularly in a recession, a move to cut the deficit may lead output further away from potential output. But huge deficits can create a vicious circle of extra borrowing, extra interest payments and yet more borrowing.

● In an open economy, exports are a source of demand for domestic goods but imports are a leakage since they are a demand for goods made abroad.

● Exports are determined mainly by conditions abroad and can be viewed as autonomous demand unrelated to domestic income. Imports are assumed to rise with domestic income. The marginal propensity to import (MPZ) tells us the fraction of each extra pound of national income that goes on extra demand for imports.

● Leakages to imports reduce the value of the multiplier to $1/[1 - MPC' + MPZ]$.

● Higher export demand raises domestic output and income. A higher marginal propensity to import reduces domestic output and income.

● The lower the output, the larger the trade surplus, exports minus imports. Higher export demand raises the trade surplus, a higher marginal propensity to import reduces it.

● In equilibrium, desired leakages $S + NT + Z$ must equal desired injections $G + I + X$. Thus any surplus $S - I$ desired by the private sector must be offset by the sum of the government deficit $G - NT$ and the desired trade surplus $(X - Z)$.

REVIEW QUESTIONS

Equilibrium output in a closed economy is 1000, consumption 800 and investment is 80. (a) Deduce G. (b) Investment rises by 50. The marginal propensity to consume out of national income is 0.8. What is the new equilibrium level of C, I, G and Y? (c) Suppose instead that G had risen by 50. What would be the new equilibrium of C, I, G and Y? (d) If potential output is 1200 how much must G rise to make output equal potential output?

The government spends £6 billion on rail track. The income tax rate is 0.25 and the MPC out of disposable income is 0.8. (a) What is the effect on equilibrium income and output? (b) Does the budget deficit rise or fall? Why?

In equilibrium, desired savings equal desired investment. True or false? Explain.

Why does the government raise taxes when it could borrow to cover its spending?

The EU's trade partners have a recession. (a) What happens to the EU's trade balance? (b) What happens to equilibrium EU output? Explain.

Common fallacies Why are these statements wrong? (a) The Chancellor raised taxes and spending by equal amounts. It will be a neutral budget for output. (b) Government policy should balance exports and imports but ensure that the government and private sector spend less than they earn.

To check your answers to these questions, go to page 641.

Online
LearningCentre
with POWERWEB

To help you grasp the key concepts of this chapter check out the extra resources posted on the Online Learning Centre at www.mcgraw-hill.co.uk/textbooks/begg. There are quick test questions, economics examples and access to Powerweb articles, all for free!

For even more exercises, recaps and examples to help you study, purchase a copy of the Economics Student Workbook. Simply visit www.mcgraw hill.co.uk/textbooks/begg and follow the links to the Workbook to buy your copy.

chapter

Money and banking

22

Learning outcomes

By the end of this chapter, you should understand:

1 the medium of exchange as the key attribute of money

2 other functions of money

3 how banks create money

4 the monetary base, the money multiplier, and the money supply

5 different measures of money in the UK

6 how banks compete for deposits and loans

7 motives for holding money

8 how money demand depends on output, prices and interest rates.

Money is any generally accepted means of payment for delivery of goods or settlement of debt. It is the **medium of exchange**.

Money is a symbol of success, a source of crime, and it makes the world go around. Dogs' teeth in the Admiralty Islands, sea shells in parts of Africa, gold in the nineteenth century: all are examples of money. What matters is not the commodity used but the social convention that it is accepted *without question* as a means of payment. We now explain how society uses money to economize on scarce resources used in the transacting process.

22.1 Money and its functions

Although the crucial feature of money is its acceptance as the means of payment or medium of exchange, money has three other functions. It serves as a unit of account, a store of value and a standard of deferred payment.

The medium of exchange

Money, the medium of exchange, is used in half of almost every exchange. Workers exchange labour services for money. People buy or sell goods for money. We accept money not to consume it directly but to use it subsequently to buy things we do wish to consume. Money is the medium through which people exchange goods and services.[1]

A barter economy has no medium of exchange. Goods are swapped for other goods.

To see that society benefits from a medium of exchange, imagine a barter economy, in which the seller and the buyer *each* must want something the other has to offer. Each person is simultaneously a seller and a buyer. To see a film,

[1] For an interesting account of cigarettes as money in prisoner-of-war camps, see R. A. Radford, 'The Economic Organisation of a POW Camp', *Economica*, 1945.

you must swap a good or service that the cinema manager wants. There has to be a *double coincidence of wants.*

Trading is very expensive in a barter economy. People spend a lot of time and effort finding others with whom to make mutually satisfactory swaps. Since time and effort are scarce resources, a barter economy is wasteful. The use of money – any commodity *generally* accepted in payment for goods, services and debts – makes trading simpler and more efficient. By economizing on time and effort spent in trading, society can use these resources to produce extra goods or leisure, making everyone better off.

Other functions of money

The unit of account is the unit in which prices are quoted and accounts kept.

In Britain prices are quoted in pounds sterling, in the United States in dollars. It is convenient to use the same units for the medium of exchange and unit of account. However, there are exceptions. During the German hyperinflation of 1922–23 when prices in marks changed very quickly, German shopkeepers found it more convenient to use dollars as the unit of account. Prices were quoted in dollars but payment was made in marks, the German medium of exchange. Similarly, during 2000–01 many EU shopkeepers quoted prices both in euros and in local currency, even though the euro did not become their medium of exchange until 2002.

Money is a store of value because it can be used to make future purchases.

To be accepted in exchange, money *has* to store value. Nobody will accept money in payment for goods supplied today if the money is worthless when they try to buy goods with it later. But money is not the only, nor necessarily the best, store of value. Houses, stamp collections and interest-bearing bank accounts all serve as stores of value. Since money pays no interest and its real purchasing power is eroded by inflation, there are better ways to store value.

Finally, money is a *standard of deferred payment* or unit of account over time. When you borrow, the amount to be repaid next year is measured in pounds. This is not an essential function of money. UK citizens can get bank loans specifying in dollars the amount to be repaid next year. Thus the key feature of money is its use as a medium of exchange. For this, it must act as a store of value as well. And it is usually, though not invariably, convenient to make money the unit of account and standard of deferred payment as well.

Different kinds of money

In prisoner-of-war camps, cigarettes were money. In the nineteenth century money was mainly gold and silver coins. These are examples of *commodity money*, ordinary goods with industrial uses (gold) and consumption uses (cigarettes) which also serve as a medium of exchange. To use a commodity money, society must either cut back on other uses of that commodity or devote scarce resources to additional production of the commodity. There are cheaper ways for society to make money.

A token money is a means of payment whose value or purchasing power as money greatly exceeds its cost of production or value in uses other than as money.

A £10 note is worth far more as money than as a 7.5×14 cm piece of high-quality paper. Similarly, the monetary value of most coins exceeds what you would get by melting them down and selling off the metal. By collectively agreeing to use token money, society economizes on the scarce resources required to produce a medium of exchange. Since the manufacturing cost is tiny, why doesn't everyone make £10 notes? The survival of token money requires a restriction on the right to supply it. Private production is illegal.[2]

[2] The existence of forgers confirms society is economizing on scarce resources by producing money whose value as a medium of exchange exceeds its production cost.

Society enforces the use of token money by making it *legal tender*. By law, it must be accepted as a means of payment. However, when prices rise very quickly, domestic token money is a poor store of value and people are reluctant to accept it as a medium of exchange. Shops and firms give discounts to people paying in gold or in foreign currency.

In modern economies, token money is supplemented by IOU money. A bank deposit is IOU money. It is a debt of the bank. When you have a bank deposit, the bank owes you money. The bank is obliged to pay when your cheque is presented. Bank deposits are a medium of exchange because they are generally accepted as payment.

> An IOU money is a medium of exchange based on the debt of a private firm or individual.

BOX 22-1   Travellers' tales

The following contrast between a monetary and barter economy is taken from the World Bank, *World Development Report*, 1989.

Life without money

'Some years since, Mademoiselle Zelie, a singer, gave a concert in the Society Islands in exchange for a third part of the receipts. When counted, her share was found to consist of 3 pigs, 23 turkeys, 44 chickens, 5000 cocoa nuts, besides considerable quantities of bananas, lemons and oranges . . . as Mademoiselle could not consume any considerable portion of the receipts herself it became necessary in the meantime to *feed* the pigs and poultry with the fruit.' W. S. Jevons (1898)

Marco Polo discovers paper money

In this city of Kanbula [Beijing] is the mint of the Great Khan, who may truly be said to possess the secret of the alchemists, as he has the art of producing money . . .

He causes the bark to be stripped from mulberry trees . . . made into paper . . . cut into pieces of money of different sizes. The act of counterfeiting is punished as a capital offence. This paper currency is circulated in every part of the Great Khan's domain. All his subjects receive it without hesitation because, wherever their business may call them, they can dispose of it again in the purchase of merchandise they may require. *The Travels of Marco Polo*, Book II

22.2   Modern banking

> Bank reserves are the money available in the bank to meet possible withdrawals by depositors. The reserve ratio is the ratio of reserves to deposits.

When you deposit your coat in the theatre cloakroom, you do not expect the theatre to rent your coat out during the performance. Banks lend out some of the coats in their cloakroom. A theatre would have to get your particular coat back on time, which might be tricky. A bank finds it easier because one piece of money looks just like another.

Unlike other financial institutions, such as pension funds, the key aspect of banks is that some of their liabilities are used as the medium of exchange: cheques allow their deposits to be used as money.

> The money supply is the value of the stock of the medium of exchange in circulation.

At any time, some people are writing cheques on a Barclays account to pay for goods purchased from a shop that banks with Lloyds TSB; others are writing cheques on Lloyds TSB accounts to finance purchases from shops banking with Barclays. The *clearing system* is the process of interbank settlement of the net flows required between banks as a result. Thus the system of clearing cheques represents another way society reduces the costs of making transactions.[3]

---

[3] Society continues to find new ways to save scarce resources in producing and using a medium of exchange. Already many people use credit cards. Some supermarket tills debit customers' bank accounts directly. And shopping by TV and telephone and the internet is growing rapidly.

Liquidity is the cheapness, speed and certainty with which asset values can be converted back into money.

Table 22.1 shows the balance sheet of UK commercial banks in 2004. The banks' assets were mainly loans to firms and households, and purchases of financial securities such as bills and bonds issued by governments and firms. Because many securities are very liquid, banks can lend short term and still get their money back in time if depositors withdraw their money.

In contrast, many loans to firms and households are quite illiquid. The bank cannot easily get its money back in a hurry. Modern banks get by with very few cash reserves in the vault. In Table 22.1 these are so small they are not even recorded separately.

The money in **sight deposits** can be withdraw 'on sight' without prior notice. **Time deposits**, paying higher interest rates, require the depositor to give notice before withdrawing money.

Liabilities of commercial banks include sight and time deposits. Chequing accounts are sight deposits. Time deposits, which include some savings accounts, pay higher interest rates because banks have time to organize the sale of some of their high-interest assets in order to have the cash available to meet withdrawals. Certificates of deposit (CDs) are large 'wholesale' time deposits, a one-off deal with a particular client for a specified period, paying more generous interest rates. The other liabilities of banks are various 'money market instruments', short-term and highly liquid borrowing by banks.

Table 22.1	Balance sheet of UK banks, March 2004			
Assets	£bn	Liabilities	£bn
In foreign currency		*In foreign currency*	
Securities	1230	Sight and time deposits	1322
Loans	1097	Other liabilities	1190
Other assets	177		
In sterling		*In sterling*	
Securities	309	Sight and time deposits	1429
Loans	1600	Other liabilities	555
Other assets	83		
Total	4496	Total	4496

The business of banking

A bank is a business making profits by lending and borrowing. To get money in, the bank offers attractive interest rates to depositors. UK banks increasingly offer interest on sight deposits and offer better interest rates on time deposits.

Banks have to find profitable ways to lend what has been borrowed. Table 22.1 shows how banks lend their money. In sterling, most is lend as advances of overdrafts to households and firms, usually at high interest rates. Some is used to buy securities such as long-term government bonds. Some is more prudently invested in liquid assets. Although these pay a lower interest rate, the bank can get its money back quickly if people withdrawing a lot of money from their sight deposits. And some money is held as cash, the most liquid asset of all.

The bank uses its specialist expertise to acquire a diversified portfolio of investments. Without the existence of the bank, depositors would have neither the time nor the expertise to decide which of these loans or investments to make. UK banks hold reserves that are only 2 per cent of the sight deposits that could be withdrawn at any time. This shows the importance of the other liquid assets in which banks have invested. At very short notice, banks could cash in liquid assets easily and for a predictable amount. The skill in running a bank entails being able to judge how much must be held in liquid assets, including cash, and how much can be lent out in less liquid forms that earn higher interest rates.

A commercial bank borrows money from the public, crediting them with a deposit. The deposit is a liability of the bank. It is money owed to depositors. In turn the bank lends money to firms, households or governments wishing to borrow.

Banks are not the only financial intermediaries. Insurance companies, pension funds and building societies also take in money in order to relend it. The crucial feature of banks is that some of their liabilities are used as a means of payment, and are thus part of the money stock.[4]

> A **financial intermediary** specializes in bringing lenders and borrowers together. **Commercial banks** are financial intermediaries licensed to make loans and issue deposits, including deposits against which cheques can be written.

BOX 22-2 What is a bank?

The traditional image of a bank with long queues of account holders waiting in front of bulletproof glass to pay bills or withdraw cash has long changed. Supermarkets including Tesco and Sainsburys both run banking operations. In addition, numerous insurance companies have opted to develop banking products for their customers and the age of the building society seems at an end with many having demutualized and become fully-fledged banks. At the limit banks have also become virtual, with the likes of Intelligent Finance, Cahoot and First Direct offering telephone or online banking.

However, there are commonalities between the old traditional bank and the new financial service providers. Historically, individuals needed cash in their pocket and high street branches of national banks provided a means of collecting and distributing cash to customers. Supermarkets are equally adept at collecting and distributing cash at the checkout and have sought to develop this service with other financial products. But with the prevalence of debit cards, electronic bill payment and online banking, the collection, storage and distribution of cash becomes virtual, rather than real. Anyone with a bank of computer servers and a shed of telephone staff can operate a basic banking system.

22.3 How banks create money

To simplify the arithmetic, assume banks use a reserve ratio of 10 per cent. Suppose, initially, the non-bank private sector has wealth of £1000 held in cash. This cash is a private sector asset. It is a liability of the government, who issued it, but not a liability of the private banks. The first row of Table 22.2 shows this cash as an asset of the non-bank private sector.

Now people pay this £1000 of cash into the banks by opening bank deposits. Banks have assets of £1000 cash and liabilities of £1000 of deposits, money owed to depositors. If banks were like cloakrooms, that would be the end of the story. Table 22.2 would end in row two.

However, banks do not need all deposits to be fully covered by cash reserves. Suppose banks create £9000 of overdrafts. This is a simultaneous loan of £9000, an asset in banks' balance sheets, and the granting to customers of £9000 of deposits, against which customers can write cheques. The deposits of £9000 are a liability on banks' balance sheets. Now the banks have £10 000 total deposits – the original £1000 when cash was paid in, plus the new £9000 as

---

[4] In fact, building societies now issue cheque books to their depositors. Although official UK statistics do not classify building societies as banks, this example illustrates the practical difficulty in deciding which intermediaries are banks and which of their deposits in practice are accepted as a medium of exchange. Many building societies are now changing their legal status to that of banks.

Table 22.2 Money creation by the banking system

	Banks				Non-bank private sector			
	Assets		Liabilities		Monetary-assets		Liabilities	
Initial	Cash	0	Deposits	0	Cash	1000	Loans from	
	Loans	0					banks	0
Intermediate	Cash	1000	Deposits	1000	Cash	0	Loans from	
					Deposits	1000	banks	0
Final	Cash	1000	Deposits	10 000	Cash	0	Loans from	
	Loans	9000			Deposits	10 000	banks	9000

counterpart to the overdraft – and £10 000 of total assets, comprising £9000 in loans and £1000 cash in the vaults. The reserve ratio is still 10 per cent in row three of Table 22.2.

It does not even matter whether the 10 per cent reserve ratio is imposed by law or is merely profit-maximizing smart behaviour by banks that balance risk and reward. The risk is the possibility of being caught short of cash the reward is the interest rate spread.

> The *interest rate spread* is the excess of the loan interest rate over the deposit interest rate.

How did banks create money? Originally, there was £1000 of cash in circulation. That was the money supply. When paid into bank vaults, it went out of general circulation as the medium of exchange. But the public acquired £1000 of bank deposits against which cheques could be written. The money supply was still £1000. Then banks created overdrafts *not* fully backed by cash reserves. Now the public had £10 000 of deposits against which to write cheques. The money supply rose from £1000 to £10 000. Banks created money.

Financial panics

> A *financial panic* is a self-fulfilling prophecy. Believing a bank will be unable to pay, people rush to get their money out. But this makes the bank go bankrupt.

Everybody knows what the banks are doing. Usually, people do not mind. But if people believe that a bank has lent too much, and will be unable to meet depositors' claims, there will be a *run* on the bank. If the bank cannot repay all depositors, you try to get your money out first while the bank can still pay. Since everyone does the same thing, they ensure that the bank is unable to pay. Some of its loans will be too illiquid to get back in time.

BOX 22-3   A beginner's guide to financial markets

Financial asset A piece of paper entitling the owner to a specified stream of interest payments for a specified period. Firms and governments raise money by selling financial assets. Buyers work out how much to bid for them by calculating the present value of the promised stream of payments. Assets are frequently retraded before the date at which the original issuer is committed to repurchase the piece of paper for a specified price.

Cash Notes and coin, paying zero interest. The most liquid asset.

Bills Short-term financial assets paying no interest directly but with a known date of repurchase by the original borrower at a known price. Consider a three-month Treasury bill. In April the government sells a piece of paper, promising to repurchase it for £100 in July. If people bid £98.5 in April they will make 1.5 per cent in three months by holding the bill to July, when it is worth £100. As July gets nearer, the price at which the bill is retraded climbs towards £100. Buying it from someone else in June for £99.5 and reselling to the government in July for £100 still yields 0.5 per cent in a month, or over 6 per cent a year at

---

BOX 22-3   Continued

compound interest. Treasury bills are easily bought and sold. Their price can only fluctuate over a small range (say, between £98 and £99 in May when they expire in July), so they are highly liquid. People can get their money out easily, cheaply and predictably.

Bonds Longer-term financial assets. Look under government bonds in the *Financial Times*. You will find a bond listed as Treasury 5% 2004. In the year 2004 the government will buy back this bond for £100 (the usual repurchase price). Until then, the bondholder gets interest payments of £5 a year. Bonds are less liquid than bills, not because they are hard to sell, but because the price for which they could be sold, and the cash this will generate, are less certain. To see why, we study the most extreme kind of bond.

Perpetuities Bonds never repurchased by the original issuer, who pays interest forever. Called Consols (consolidated stock) in the UK. Consols 2.5% pay £2.50 a year for ever. Most were issued when interest rates were low. People originally would have bid around £100 for this consol. Suppose interest rates on other assets rise to 10 per cent. Consols are retraded between people at around £25 each so that new pur-

chaser of these old bonds gets about 10 per cent on their financial investment. The person holding a bond makes a capital loss when other interest rates rise and the price of the bonds falls. Moreover, since the price of Consols, once £100, could fall to £25 if interest rates rise a lot, Consol prices are much more volatile than the price of Treasury bills. The longer the remaining life of a bond, the more its current price can move around as existing bondholders try to sell on to new buyers at a rate of return in line with other assets today. Bonds can easily be bought and sold but are not very liquid. You cannot know how much you would get if you had to sell out in six months' time.

Gilt-edged securities Government bonds in the UK. 'Gilt-edged' because the government will not go bust and refuse pay interest.

Company shares (equities) Entitlements to dividends, the part of firms' profits paid out to shareholders rather than retained to buy new machinery and buildings. In good years, dividends are high, in bad years dividends may be zero. Hence a risky asset that is not very liquid. Share prices are volatile. Firms could even go bust, making the shares worthless.

Today, financial panics are rare. A key reason for this, which we discuss in the next chapter, is that the Bank of England will lend to banks in temporary difficulties. Since this is known, it helps prevent a self-fulfilling stampede to withdraw deposits before a bank cannot pay.

22.4   The monetary base and the money multiplier

Cash reserves of commercial banks are a small fraction of total bank deposits. Bank-created deposit money is much the largest part of the money supply in modern economies. You have now mastered the basics, but we now tie up some loose ends. Banks' deposits depend on the cash reserves of the banks. To complete our analysis of how the money supply is determined we need to examine what determines the amount of cash deposited with the banking system.

The *monetary base* or stock of *high-powered money* is the quantity of notes and coin in private circulation plus the quantity held by the banking system.

Through the *central bank*, the Bank of England in the UK, the government controls the issue of token money in a modern economy. Private creation of token money must be outlawed when its value as a medium of exchange exceeds the direct cost of its production.

How much of the monetary base is held by commercial banks as cash reserves? In the previous section, we assumed that the public deposited all its cash with the banks. This was only a simplification. Everyone carries some cash around. We do not write a cheque for a bus fare. It would take too long.

There are other reasons why people hold cash. Some people do not trust banks. They keep their savings under the bed. Remarkably, only three-quarters of British households have chequing accounts. Some people hold cash in order to make illegal or tax-evading transactions in the 'black economy'.

> The money multiplier is the ratio of the money stock to the monetary base.

How is the money supply related to the monetary base, the amount of notes and coin issued by the central bank? The answer to this question is the money multiplier.

$$\text{Money stock} = \text{money multiplier} \times \text{monetary base} \qquad (1)$$

The value of the money multiplier depends on two key ratios: the banks' desired ratio of cash reserves to total deposits, and the non-bank public's desired ratio of cash in circulation to total bank deposits.

Banks' ratio of cash reserves to total deposits determines how much they multiply up any given cash reserves into deposit money. The *lower* the desired cash reserves ratio, the more deposits banks create against given cash reserves and the *larger* the money supply.

Similarly, the *lower* the non-bank public's desired ratio of cash to private sector bank accounts, the *larger* the money supply for any monetary base created by the central bank. Since more of the monetary base is deposited in banks, banks can create more bank deposits.

We give an exact formula for the money multiplier in Box 22.4. UK banks hold cash reserves equal to 1 per cent of their total deposits, and the private sector holds cash in circulation equal to 3 per cent of the value of sight deposits. The formula implies a money multiplier of 27. Each £100 rise in the monetary base increases the money supply by £2700.

At present, it is more important to remember that a fall in either the banks' desired cash reserves ratio or the private sector's desired ratio of cash to bank deposits raises the money multiplier. For a given monetary base, the money supply rises.

What determines the cash reserve ratio desired by banks? The higher the interest rate spread, the more banks wish to lend and the more they risk a low ratio of cash reserves to deposits. Conversely, the more unpredictable withdrawals from deposits are, or the fewer lending opportunities banks have in very liquid loans, the higher cash reserves they have to maintain for any level of deposits.

BOX 22-4   The money multiplier

Suppose banks wish to hold cash reserves R equal to some fraction c_b of deposits D, and that the private sector holds cash in circulation C equal to a fraction c_p of deposits D.

$$R = c_b D \qquad C = c_p D$$

The monetary base, or stock of high-powered money H, is either in circulation or in bank vaults.

$$H = C + R = (c_p + c_b)D$$

Finally, the money supply is circulating currency C plus deposits D.

$$M = C + D = (c_p + 1)D$$

These last two equations give us the money multiplier, the ratio of M to H.

$$M/H = (c_p + 1)/(c_p + c_b) > 1$$

Using the data of Table 22.3, c_p is $[34/(1087-34)] = 0.032$, c_b is $[5/(1087-34)] = 0.005$, and the money multiplier is

$$M/H = (1.032)/(0.037) = 27$$

which of course is simply 1087/39, the ratio of $M4$ to $M0$.

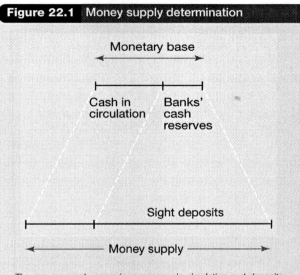

Figure 22.1 Money supply determination

The money supply comprises currency in circulation and deposits at banks. The monetary base, issued by the central bank, is held either as currency in circulation or as banks' cash reserves. Since deposits are a multiple of banks' cash reserves, the money multiplier exceeds 1. The monetary base is 'high-powered' because part of it is multiplied up as the banking system created additional deposits, the major component of the money supply.

The public's desired ratio of cash to deposits partly reflects institutional factors, for example whether firms pay wages by cheque or cash. It also depends on the incentive to hold cash to make untraceable payments to evade taxes. And credit cards reduce the use of cash. Credit cards are a temporary means of payment, a *money-substitute*, not money itself.

A signed credit card slip cannot be used for *further* purchases. Soon, you have to settle your account using money. Nevertheless, since credit cards allow people to carry less cash in their pocket, their increasing use reduces the desired ratio of cash to bank deposits.

Figure 22.1 summarizes our discussion of the monetary base and the money supply. The monetary base, or stock of high-powered money, is held either as cash reserves by the banks or as cash in circulation. Since bank deposits are a multiple of banks' cash reserves, the money multiplier exceeds unity. The money multiplier is larger (*a*) the lower the non-bank public's desired ratio of cash to bank deposits, giving the banks more cash with which to create a multiplied deposit expansion, and (*b*) the lower the banks' desired ratio of cash to deposits, leading them to create more deposits for any given cash reserves.

Now you've read this section, why not test your understanding by visiting the Online Learning Centre at www.mcgraw-hill.co.uk/textbooks/begg

22.5 Measures of money

Money is the medium of exchange available to make transactions. Hence, the money supply is cash in circulation outside banks, plus bank deposits. It sounds simple, but isn't. Two issues arise: which bank deposits, and why only bank deposits?

We can think of a spectrum of liquidity. Cash, by definition, is completely liquid. Sight deposits (chequing accounts) are almost as liquid. Time deposits (savings accounts) used to be less liquid, but now many banks offer automatic transfer between savings and chequing accounts when the latter run low. Savings deposits are almost as liquid as chequing accounts.

UK statistics distinguish *retail* and *wholesale* deposits. Retail deposits are made in high street branches at the advertised rate of interest. Wholesale deposits, big one-off deals between a corporate depositor and a bank at a negotiated interest rate, are also quite liquid.

Everyone used to be clear what a bank was and hence whose deposits counted towards the money supply. Financial deregulation blurred this distinction in the UK and the USA, and is now doing so in continental Europe. Before 1980, UK banks did not lend for house purchase and cheques on building society deposits could not be used at the supermarket checkout. Now 'banks' compete vigorously for mortgages, supermarket chains are in the banking business, and building society cheques are widely accepted as a means of payment. There is no longer a reason to exclude building society deposits from measures of the money supply.

Figure 22.2 UK monetary aggregates (sterling)

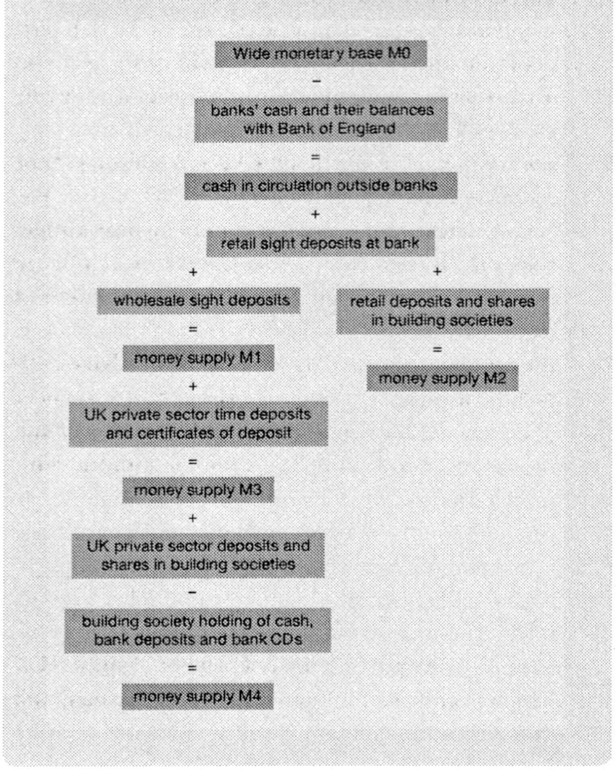

Figure 22.2 shows different monetary aggregates and their relation to one another. M0 is the wide monetary base: cash in circulation outside the banks, cash inside banks, and the banks' own accounts at the Bank of England. M0 is the narrowest measure of money. Wider measures begin from cash in circulation. Adding all sight deposits, we get M1, which used to be considered a good measure of narrow money. Augmenting that by UK private-sector time deposits and CDs gives M3, formerly called sterling M3. That used to be considered the best definition of broad money.

Since there is a spectrum of liquidity, there is no good place to draw a line, everything narrower being money, everything wider not being money. We used to keep track of M0, M1 and M3. This approach was made obsolete by the use of building society deposits as means of payment and by the conversion of many building societies to commercial banks.

To reflect the new reality, monetary statistics now combine banks and building societies, as in Figure 22.2. M2 is cash in circulation plus retail sight deposits at banks and retail deposits and shares in building societies. M4 is the old M3 plus UK private sector deposits and shares in building societies, minus building society holds of cash bank deposits and bank CDs.

Now the government routinely publishes statistics only on M0 and M4. Advances in technology and financial deregulation (which led to greater competition and more financial products on offer) make it easy for customers to substitute between 'broad' and 'narrow' money. Once we leave the monetary base, the first sensible place to stop is M4. Table 22.3 gives actual data for 2004.

Table 22.3 Narrow and broad UK money, March 2004, sterling (£ billion)

	Wide monetary base M0	39
–	Banks' cash and balances at bank	5
=	Cash in circulation	34
+	Banks' retail deposits	610
+	Building society's deposits and shares	146
+	Wholesale deposits	297
=	Money supply M4	1087

Source: Bank of England

22.6 Competition between banks

Financial deregulation, allowing the entry of more and more banks, has made modern banking very competitive. Banks compete with one another both in the interest rates they offer to attract deposits and in the interest rates they charge borrowers for loans.

The interest rate spread between the lending rate and the rate paid on deposits is what covers the cost of providing banking services. When spreads exceed this amount, banks make profits. Profits are a signal for new banks to enter, which competes away spreads. With more competition, interest rates on loans fall and rates paid on deposits rise.

Equilibrium in the banking industry occurs when it is not worth attracting more deposits in order to make more loans. The marginal cost of funds, the deposit interest rate, plus the marginal cost of doing banking business, plus any equilibrium profit margin, just equals the marginal revenue earned on making new bank loans (inclusive of any allowance for possible non-repayment). Under perfect competition, all supernormal profits are competed away by free entry.

Although regulated less than before, banking regulation has not completely disappeared and new banks are carefully licensed. Moreover, there are big scale economies in banking. For both reasons, competition is imperfect and equilibrium profit margins in banking are usually positive. Nevertheless, once we know the exact market structure, we have a good idea of how interest rates on deposits and loans are related. Other things equal, further deregulation of banks will reduce interest rate spreads yet more.

Competition between banks and the influence of regulation affect how much cash it is *optimal* for profit-maximizing banks to suck into the banking system. These two forces also affect the size of cash reserves it is optimal for banks to hold. The key ratios c_p and c_b that determine the size of the money multiplier in Box 22.4 are not fixed constants but the outcome of the competition between banks themselves.

22.7 The demand for money

The quantity of money M4 in the UK was 52 times higher in 2001 than in 1965. Why did UK residents hold so much extra money? We focus on three variables that affect money demand: interest rates, the price level and real income.

Motives for holding money

Money is a stock. It is the quantity of circulating currency and deposits *held* at any given time. Holding money is not the same as *spending* it. We hold money now to spend it later.

Money is the medium of exchange, for which it must also be a store of value. These two functions of money provide the reasons why people wish to hold it. People can hold their wealth in various forms – money, bills, bonds, equities and property. For simplicity, assume that there are only two assets: money, the medium of exchange that pays no interest, and bonds, which we use to stand for all other interest-bearing assets that are not directly a means of payment. As people earn income, they add to their wealth. As they spend, they deplete their wealth. How should people divide their wealth at any instant between money and bonds?

The cost of holding money is the interest given up by holding money rather than bonds.

People hold money only if there is a benefit to offset this cost. What is that benefit?

The transactions motive

The transactions motive for holding money reflects the fact that payments and receipts are *not* synchronized.

Transacting by barter is costly in time and effort. Holding money economizes on these costs. If all transactions were perfectly synchronized, we could be paid at the same instant we did our spending. Except at that instant, we need hold no money at all.

Must we hold money between being paid and making subsequent purchases? We could put our income into interest-earning assets, to be resold later when we need money for purchases. However, every time we buy and sell assets there are brokerage and bank charges. And it takes an eagle eye to keep track of cash flow and judge the precise moment at which money is needed and assets must be sold. If small sums are involved, the extra interest does not compensate for the brokerage fees, the time and the effort. It is easier to hold some money.

How much money we need to hold depends on the value of the transactions we later wish to make and the degree of synchronization of our payments and receipts. Money is a nominal variable, not a real variable. How much £100 buys depends on the price of goods. If all prices double, our receipts and our payments double in nominal terms. To transact as before we need to hold twice as much money.

> The **demand for money** is a demand for *real* money balances.

We need a given amount of real money, nominal money deflated by the price level, to make a given quantity of transactions. When the price level doubles, other things equal, the demand for nominal money balances doubles, leaving the demand for real money balances unaltered. People want money because of its purchasing power in terms of the goods it will buy.

Real GNP is a good proxy for the total real value of transactions. Thus we assume that the transactions motive for holding real money balances rises with real income.

The transactions motive for holding money also depends on the synchronization of payments and receipts. Suppose, instead of shopping throughout the week, households shop only on the day they get paid. Over the week, national income and total transactions are unaltered but people now *hold* less money over the week.[5]

A nation's habits for making payments change only slowly. In our simplified model we assume that the degree of synchronization is constant over time. Thus we focus on real income as *the* measure of the transactions motive for holding *real* money balances.

The precautionary motive

We live in an uncertain world. Uncertainty about the timing of receipts and payments creates a precautionary motive for holding money.

> In an uncertain world, there is a **precautionary motive** to hold money. In advance, we decide to hold money to meet contingencies that we cannot yet foresee.

Suppose you buy a lot of interest-earning bonds and get by with a small amount of money. Walking down the street you see a great bargain in a shop window but have too little money to close the deal. By the time you cash in some bonds, the bargain has gone, snapped up by some with ready money.

How can we measure the benefits from holding money for precautionary reasons? The payoff grows with the volume of transactions we undertake and with the degree of uncertainty. If uncertainty is roughly constant over time, the level of transactions determines the benefit real money held for precautionary reasons. As with the transactions motive, we use real GNP to proxy the level of transactions. Thus, other things equal, the higher real income, the stronger the precautionary motive for holding money.

The transactions and precautionary motives are the main reasons to hold the medium of exchange, and are most relevant to the benefits from holding a narrow measure of money. The wider measure, M4, includes higher-interest-earning deposits. The wider the definition of money, the less important are the transactions and precautionary motives that relate to money as a medium of exchange, and the more we must take account of money as a store of value.

---

[5] By allowing us to pay all at once when the statement arrives monthly, credit cards have this effect.

The asset motive

Forget the need to transact. Think of someone deciding in which assets to hold wealth. At some distant date wealth may be spent. In the short run the aim is a good but safe rate of return.

Some assets, such as company shares, on average pay a high return but are risky. Some years their return is *very* high, in other years it is negative. When share prices fall, shareholders make a capital loss that swamps the dividends they receive. Other assets are less risky but their average rate of return is correspondingly lower.

How should people divide their portfolios between safe and risky assets? You might like to reread Chapter 13. Since people dislike risk, they will not put all their eggs in one basket. As well as holding some risky assets, they will keep some of their wealth in safe assets. The asset motive for holding money is important when we consider why people hold broad measures of money such as M4.

> The asset motive for holding money reflects dislike of risk. People sacrifice a high average rate of return to obtain a portfolio with a lower but safer rate of return.

The demand for money: prices, real income and interest rates

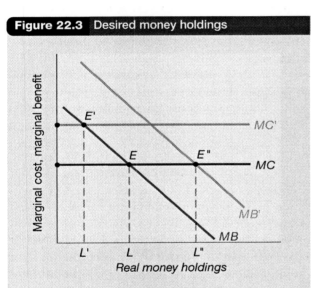

Figure 22.3 Desired money holdings

The horizontal axis shows the purchasing power of money in terms of goods. The *MC* schedule shows the interest sacrificed by putting the last pound into money rather than bonds. The *MB* schedule is drawn for a given real income and shows the marginal benefits of the last pound of money. The marginal benefit falls as money holdings increase. The desired point is *E*, at which marginal cost and marginal benefit are equal. An increase in interest rates, a rise in the opportunity cost schedule from *MC* to *MC'*, reduces desired money holdings from *L* to *L'*. An increase in real income increases the marginal benefit of adding to real balances. The *MB* schedule shifts up to *MB'*. Facing the schedule *MC*, a shift from *MB* to *MB'* increases real money holdings to *L"*.

The transactions, precautionary and asset motives suggest that there are benefits to holding money. But there is also a cost, the interest forgone by not holding high-interest-earning assets instead. People hold money up to the point at which the marginal benefit of holding another pound just equals its marginal cost. Figure 22.3 illustrates how much money people want to hold.

People want money for its purchasing power over goods. The horizontal axis plots real money holdings, nominal money in current pounds divided by the average price of goods and services. The horizontal line *MC* is the marginal cost of holding money, the interest forgone by not holding bonds. *MC* shifts up if interest rates rise.

The *MB* schedule is the marginal benefit of holding money. We draw *MB* for a given real GNP measuring the transactions undertaken. For this level of transactions, it is possible but difficult to get by with a low level of real money holdings. We have to watch purchases and receipts, quick to invest money as it comes in and ready to sell off bonds just before we make a purchase. Nor do we have much precautionary money. We may be frustrated or inconvenienced if, unexpectedly, we want to make a purchase or settle a debt.

With low real money holdings, the marginal benefit of another pound is high. We can put less effort into timing our transfers between money and bonds and we have more money for unforeseen contingencies. For a given real income and level of transactions, the marginal benefit of the last pound of money holdings declines as we hold more real money. With more real money, we have plenty both for precautionary purposes and for transactions purposes. Life is easier. The marginal benefit of yet more money holding is low.

Given our real income and transactions, desired money holdings are at E in Figure 22.2. For any level of real money below L, the marginal benefit of another pound exceeds its marginal cost in interest forgone. We should hold more money. Above L, the marginal cost exceeds the marginal benefit and we should hold less. The optimal level of money holding is L.

To emphasize the effect of prices, real income and interest rates on the quantity of money demanded, we now change each of these variables in turn. If all prices of goods and services double but interest rates and real income are unaltered, neither MC nor MB shifts. The desired point remains E and the desired level of *real* money remains L. Since prices have doubled, people hold twice as much nominal money to preserve their real money balances at L.

If interest rates on bonds rise, the cost of holding money rises. Figure 22.2 shows this upward shift from MC to MC'. The desired point is now E' and the desired real money holding falls from L to L'. Higher interest rates reduce the quantity of real money demanded.[6]

Finally, consider a rise in real income. At each level of real money holdings, the marginal benefit of the last pound is higher than before. With more transactions to undertake and a greater need for precautionary balances, a given quantity of real money does not make life as easy as it did when transactions and real income were lower. The benefit of a bit more money is now greater. Hence we show the MB schedule shifting up to MB' when real income rises.

At the original interest rate and MC schedule, the desired level of money balances is L_0. Thus a rise in real income raises the quantity of real money balances demanded. Table 22.4 summarizes our discussion of the demand for money as a medium of exchange.

So far we have studied the demand for M0, the narrowest measure of money. Wider definitions of money must also recognize the asset motive for holding money. To explain the demand for M4, we interpret MC as the average *extra* return by putting the last pound into risky assets rather than time deposits, which are safe but yield a lower return. For a given wealth, MB is the marginal benefit of time deposits in reducing the risk of the portfolio. If no wealth is invested in time deposits, the portfolio is very risky. A bad year is a disaster. There is a big benefit in having some time deposits. As the quantity of time deposits increases, the danger of a disaster recedes and the marginal benefit of more time deposits falls.

Table 22.4 The demand for money			
Quantity demanded	Effect of rise in		
	Price level	Real income	Interest rate
Nominal money	Rises in proportion	Rises	Falls
Real money	Unaffected	Rises	Falls

A rise in the average *interest differential* between risky assets and time deposits shifts the cost of holding broad money from MC to MC', reducing the quantity broad money demanded. Higher wealth shifts the marginal benefit from MB to MB'. More time deposits are demanded.

Explaining the rise in money holdings from 1965 to 2003

Why were nominal money holdings 60 times higher in 2003 than in 1965? We have identified three explanations: prices, real income and nominal interest rates. Table 22.5 shows how these variables changed over the period.

[6] The cost of holding money is the differential return between bonds and money. If π is the inflation rate and r the nominal interest rate, the real interest rate is $r - \pi$. In financial terms, the real return on money is $-\pi$ the rate at which the purchasing power of money is eroded by inflation. The differential real return between bonds and money is $(r - \pi) - (-\pi)$ $= r$. The *nominal* interest rate is the opportunity cost of holding money.

Although nominal money holdings rose 60-fold, the price level also rose a lot between 1965 and 2003. Table 22.5 shows real money rising near 5-fold over the period. Real GDP was more than twice its initial level. Higher real output and income raise the quantity of real money demanded. As it happens, nominal interest rates hardly changed. But why did real money demand rise much more than real GDP?

A big rise in competition forced banks to pay higher interest rates on *deposits*, thus *reducing* the cost of holding broad money, most of which is now interest-bearing deposits. The cost of holding such a deposit is the small spread between the deposit rate and the interest rate you could earn on bonds. This cost of holding money is now much smaller than the 5 per cent shown in Table 22.5 (which implicitly assumes money earns zero interest). A lower cost of holding money made people hold more real money.

Table 22.5 Holdings of M4, 1965–2003	1965	2003
Index of:		
Nominal M4	100	6074
Real M4	100	476
Real GDP	100	262
Interest rate (%)	6	5

Source: ONS, *Economic Trends*.

SUMMARY

- Money has four functions: a medium of exchange or means of payment, a store of value, a unit of account and a standard of deferred payment. Its use as a medium of exchange distinguishes money from other assets.

- In a barter economy, trading is costly because there must be a double coincidence of wants. Using a medium of exchange reduces the costs of matching buyers and sellers, letting society devote scarce resources to other things. A token money has a higher value as a medium of exchange than in any other use. Because its monetary value greatly exceeds its production cost, token money economizes a lot on the resources needed for transacting.

- Token money is accepted either because people believe it can subsequently be used to make payments or because the government makes it legal tender. The government controls the supply of token money.

- Banks create money by making loans and creating deposits that are not fully backed by cash reserves. These deposits add to the medium of exchange. Deciding how many reserves to hold involves a trade-off between interest earnings and the danger of insolvency.

- Modern banks attract deposits by acting as financial intermediaries. A national system of clearing cheques, a convenient form of payment, attracts funds into sight deposits. Interest-bearing time deposits attract further funds. In turn, banks lend out money as short-term liquid loans, as longer-term less liquid advances, or by purchasing securities.

- Sophisticated financial markets for short-term liquid lending allow modern banks to operate with very low cash reserves relative to deposits. The money supply is currency in circulation plus deposits. Most is the latter.

- The monetary base M0 is currency in circulation plus banks' cash reserves. The money multiplier, the ratio of the money supply to the monetary base, is big. The money multiplier is larger (a) the smaller the desired cash ratio of the banks and (b) the smaller the private sector's desired ratio of cash in circulation to deposits.

- Financial deregulation has allowed building societies into the banking business. M4 is a broad measure of money and includes deposits at both banks and building societies.

- The demand for money is a demand for real money, for its subsequent purchasing power over goods. The demand for narrow money balances the transactions and precautionary benefits of holding another pound with the interest sacrificed by not holding interest-bearing assets instead. The quantity of real money demanded falls as the interest rate rises. Higher real income raises real money demand at each interest rate.

- For wide money such as M4, the asset motive for holding money also matters. When other interest-bearing assets are risky, people diversify by holding some safe money. With no immediate need to transact, this leads to an asset demand for holding interest-bearing bank deposits. This demand is larger the larger the total wealth to be invested and the lower the interest differential between deposits and risky assets.

REVIEW QUESTIONS

(a) A person trades in a car when buying another. Is the used car a medium of exchange? Is this a barter transaction? (b) Could you tell by watching someone buying mints (white discs) with coins (bronze discs) which one is money?

Initially gold coins were used as money but people could melt them down and use the gold for industrial purposes. (a) What must have been the relative value of gold in these two uses? (b) Explain the circumstances in which gold could (i) become a token money and (ii) disappear from monetary circulation completely.

How do commercial banks create money?

Would it make sense to include (a) travellers' cheques, (b) student rail cards, or (c) credit cards in measures of the money supply?

Sight deposits = 30, time deposits = 60, banks' cash reserves = 2, currency in circulaton = 12, building society deposits = 20. Calculate M0 and M4.

Suppose banks raise interest rates on time deposits whenever interest rates on bank loans and other assets rise. Does a rise in the general level of interest rates have a big or small effect on the demand for time deposits?

Common fallacies Why are these statements wrong? (a) Since their liabilities equal their assets, banks cannot create anything. (b) The money supply has risen because of tax evasion. Since cash is untraceable, people are putting less in the banks.

To check your answers to these questions, go to page 642.

400 Part 4 : Macroeconomics

To help you grasp the key concepts of this chapter check out the extra resources posted on the Online Learning Centre at www.mcgraw-hill.co.uk/ textbooks/begg. There are quick test questions, economics examples and access to Powerweb articles, all for free!

For even more exercises, recaps and examples to help you study, purchase a copy of the Economics Student Workbook. Simply visit www.mcgraw hill.co.uk/textbooks/begg and follow the links to the Workbook to buy your copy.

401

chapter 23

Interest rates and monetary transmission

Learning outcomes

By the end of this chapter, you should understand:

1. how a central bank can affect the money supply

2. the central bank's role as lender of last resort

3. money market equilibrium

4. an intermediate target for monetary policy

5. the transmission mechanism of monetary policy

6. how a central bank sets interest rates

7. how interest rates affect consumption and investment demand

> A central bank is banker to the government and to the banks. It also conducts

Today every country of any size has a central bank. Originally private firms in business for profit, central banks came under public control as governments placed more emphasis on monetary policy. Founded in 1694, the Bank of England (www.bankofengland.co.uk) was not nationalized until 1947. The Federal Reserve System, the US central bank, was not set up until 1913.

This chapter examines the role of the central bank and shows how it influences financial markets. The central bank influences the supply of money. Combining this with the demand for money, examined in the previous chapter, we analyse money market equilibrium. The central bank's monopoly on the supply of cash allows it to control equilibrium interest rates. Finally, we discuss how monetary policy decides what interest rates to set.

23.1 The Bank of England

The Bank of England, usually known simply as the Bank, is the UK central bank. It is divided into Issue and Banking Departments. Their balance sheets are shown in Table 23.1.

Banknotes are liabilities of the Bank. To introduce notes into circulation, the Issue Department buys financial securities: bills and bonds issued by the government, commercial firms or local authorities. These are assets of the Issue Department.

The Banking Department is banker to the commercial banks and to the government. Public deposits and bankers' deposits are deposits by government and commercial banks. Reserves and other accounts are deposits by central banks of other countries, by domestic local authorities, and by state-owned firms. Assets are government securities (loans to the government) and advances (loans to banks). Other assets include buildings, equipment and securities issued by private firms.

Table 23.1	Bank of England, balance sheet, April 2004			
Department	**Assets**	**£bn**	**Liabilities**	**£bn**
Issue	Government securities	14.7	Notes in circulation	33.9
	Other securities	19.2		
Banking	Government securities	1.8	Public deposits	0.8
	Advances	7.1	Bankers' deposits	2
	Other assets	8.2	Reserves and other accounts	14.3
	Total assets	51	Total liabilities	51

Source: Bank of England.

Table 23.1 resembles the balance sheet of a commercial bank, with one key difference. *A central bank cannot go bankrupt.* You take £50 to the Bank and cash it in for £50. The Bank gives you £50 in cash. It can always create new cash

23.2 The Bank and the money supply

> The **money supply** is currency in circulation *outside* the banking system, plus deposits of commercial banks and building societies.

The money supply is partly a liability of the Bank (currency in private circulation) and partly a liability of banks (bank deposits). Henceforth we talk of 'banks' without distinguishing banks and building societies.

Chapter 22 introduced the *monetary base*, currency supplied by the Bank both to the banks and to private circulation. The *money multiplier* is the extent to which the money supply is a multiple of the monetary base. The money multiplier is larger (*a*) the smaller the cash reserve ratio of the commercial banks and (*b*) the smaller the private sector's desired ratio of cash to bank deposits.

Hence, the Bank can affect the money supply by altering either the size of the money multiplier or the monetary base. We begin with policies that affect the money multiplier.

Reserve requirements

> A **required reserve ratio** is a minimum ratio of cash reserves to deposits that banks are required to hold.

Banks can hold more than the required cash reserves but not less. If their reserves fall below the required amount, they must immediately borrow cash, usually from the central bank, to restore their required reserve ratio.

Suppose banks have £1 billion in cash and, for commercial purposes, want cash reserves equal to 5 per cent of deposits. Deposits are 20 times cash reserves. Banks create £20 billion of deposits against their £1 billion cash reserves. However, if there is a reserve requirement of 10 per cent, banks only create £10 billion deposits against cash reserves of £1 billion. The money supply falls from £20 billion to £10 billion.

When the central bank imposes a higher reserve requirement than the reserve ratio that prudent banks would anyway have maintained, the effect is fewer bank deposits, a lower money multiplier and a lower money supply for any monetary base. Raising the reserve requirement reduces the money supply.

The discount rate

> The **discount rate** is the interest rate that the Bank charges when banks want to borrow cash.

Suppose banks think the *minimum* safe ratio of cash to deposits is 10 per cent. It does not matter whether this figure is a commercial judgement or a requirement imposed by the Bank. Banks may also hold extra cash. If their cash reserves are 12 per cent of deposits, how far dare they let their cash fall towards the 10 per cent minimum?

Banks balance the interest rate on extra lending against the cost incurred if withdrawals push their cash reserves below the critical 10 per cent. If the central bank lends to banks at market interest rates, there is no penalty in being caught short and having to borrow from the central bank. Banks lend as much as they can and their cash reserves fall to the minimum required.

Suppose the Bank only lends to banks at an interest rate above market interest rates. Now commercial banks will not drive down their reserves to the minimum permitted. They hold extra cash as a cushion, to avoid possibly having to borrow from the central bank at penalty rates.

By setting the discount rate above general interest rates, the Bank can induce banks voluntarily to hold extra cash reserves. Bank deposits are a lower multiple of banks' cash reserves, the money multiplier is reduced, and the money supply is lower for any given level of the monetary base. Variations in the discount rate can change the money supply.

Open market operations

An *open market operation* occurs when the central bank alters the monetary base by buying or selling financial securities in the open market.

Whereas the previous two methods of monetary control alter the money multiplier, open market operations alter the monetary base. Since the money supply is the monetary base multiplied by the money multiplier, they alter the money supply.

The Bank prints £1 million of new banknotes and buys bonds on the open market. There are £1 million fewer bonds in private hands but the monetary base is £1 million higher. Some of the extra cash is held in private circulation but most is deposited with the banks, which then expand deposit lending against their higher cash reserves. Conversely, if the Bank sells £1 million of bonds from its existing holdings, the monetary base falls by £1 million. Banks lose cash reserves, have to reduce deposit lending and the money supply falls.

Open market operations are nowadays the principal channel by which the central bank affects the money supply. Having discussed the central bank's role in monetary control we turn next to its role in financial stability.

BOX 23-1   The repo market

In American movies, people in arrears on their loans have their cars repossessed by the repo man. In the mid 1990s, London finally established a repo market. Frankfurt and Milan had operated repo markets for years. Was the ultra-cautious German Bundesbank involved in dubious car loans?

A gilt repo is a *sale and repurchase agreement*. A bank sells you a bond, simultaneously agreeing to buy it back at a specified price on a particular future date. You have made the bank a short-term loan secured or 'backed' by the long-term bond temporarily in your ownership. Thus repos use the outstanding stock of *long-term* assets as backing for new and secured *short-term* loans.

Reverse repos work the other way. Now you get a short-term loan from the bank by initially selling bonds to the bank, plus an agreement for you to repurchase the bonds at a specified date in the near future at a price agreed now. Reverse repos are effectively secured temporary fixed-term loans by the bank.

Repos and reverse repos are very like other short-term lending and borrowing. They are now used for open market operations. The Bank of England used to conduct open market operations by buying and selling Treasury bills; the Bundesbank made much more use of repo and reverse repo transactions. But they achieved much the same purpose. Now the Bank of England also uses the repo market for open market operations to alter the monetary base.

23.3 Lender of last resort

The lender of last resort lends to banks when financial panic threatens the financial system.

Modern fractional reserve banking lets society produce the medium of exchange with tiny inputs of scarce physical resources. But the efficient production of the medium of exchange yields a system of fractional reserve banking vulnerable to financial panics. Since banks have too few reserves to meet a withdrawal of all their deposits, a hint of big withdrawals may become a self-fulfilling prophecy as people scramble to get their money out before the banks go bust.

To avoid financial panics, people must believe that banks cannot get into trouble. This requires a guarantee that banks can get cash if they really need it. The central bank is the only institution that can manufacture cash in unlimited amounts. The threat of financial panics is greatly diminished if it is known that the central bank will act as lender of last resort.

As lender of last resort, the Bank can maintain confidence in the banking system. A useful side effect is that this eliminates wilds swings in the private sector's desired cash holdings that would otherwise lead to swings in the size of the money multiplier.

Prudential regulation

Last resort lending is useful in helping banks that face a temporary liquidity crisis but whose underlying balance sheet is perfectly sound. Sometimes, however, through poor decisions or bad luck, a bank has made loans that prove worthless. This raises two issues: what to do if a particular bank is in permanent trouble and how to stop this infecting other banks.

A capital adequacy ratio is a required minimum value of bank capital relative to its outstanding loans and investments.

Generally, it is the shareholders of the particular bank who bear the cost of its poor performance. To try to make sure that shareholders have sufficient funds for this purpose, financial regulations require banks to meet capital adequacy ratios.[1] When a bank makes a small loss, this capital reserve supplied by shareholders should be sufficient to meet it. A crisis depletes this capital reserve and thereby reduces the share price of the bank. *Shareholders* suffer but *depositors* are protected since the bank still has adequate funds to meet their liabilities.

If a bank makes larger losses it may go bankrupt. Losses incurred by rogue trader Nick Leeson brought down Barings Bank in the 1990s. Typically, governments then compensate depositors but not shareholders. Barings was actually sold to Dutch Bank ING for a notional amount and deposits were honoured in full. The knowledge that depositors are unlikely to suffer helps prevent unjustified financial panics. The knowledge that shareholders *are* likely to suffer helps keep management on its toes.

When a major bank is in trouble, the central bank may undertake last resort lending to *other* banks to prevent the particular crisis spilling over into a general panic. This may lead to a temporary rise in the money supply. When the crisis is over, a prudent central bank will then undo this effect and restore the money supply to its original level.

23.4 Equilibrium in financial markets

We now combine money supply and money demand to show how equilibrium is determined.

The central bank controls the *nominal* money supply. When we simplify by assuming that the price of goods is fixed, the central bank also controls the *real* money supply. In later

---

[1] Financial regulation is sometimes the responsibility of the central bank, but sometimes the responsibility of a separate financial regulator. In the UK, responsibility was transferred from the Bank of England to the Financial Services Agency in 1997.

> The real money supply L is the nominal money supply M divided by the price level P.

chapters, we allow the price level to change. Changes in nominal money tend to lead to changes in prices. The central bank can still control the real money supply M/P in the short run – it can change M faster than prices P respond – but, in the long run, other forces determine real money M/P. For the moment, we treat the price level as fixed.

Chapter 22 argued that the quantity of real money demanded rises when real income rises but falls when the nominal interest rate rises.

Money market equilibrium

> In money market equilibrium the quantity of real balances demanded and supplied are equal.

Figure 23.1 shows the demand curve LL for real money balances for a given real income. The higher the interest rate and the cost of holding money, the less real money is demanded. With a given price level, the central bank controls the quantity of nominal money and real money. The supply curve is vertical at this quantity of real money L_0. Equilibrium is at E. At the interest rate r_0 the real money people wish to hold just equals the outstanding stock L_0.

Suppose the interest rate is r_1, below the equilibrium level r_0. There is excess demand for money AB in Figure 23.1. How does this excess demand for money bid the interest rate up from r_1 to r_0 to restore equilibrium? The answer is rather subtle. Strictly speaking, there is no market for money. Money is the medium of exchange for payments and receipts in *other* markets. A market for money would exchange pounds for pounds.

The other market relevant to Figure 23.1 is the market for bonds. Since the interest rate is the cost of holding money, people who do not hold money hold bonds. What happens explicitly in the market for bonds determines what is happening in the implicit market for money in Figure 23.1.

Real wealth W is the existing supply of real money L_0 and real bonds B_0. People divide their wealth W between desired real bond holdings B^D and desired real money holdings L^D. Hence

$$L_0 + B_0 = W = L^D + B^D \qquad (1)$$

People cannot plan to divide up wealth they do not have. Equation (1) implies

$$B_0 - B^D = L^D - L_0 \qquad (2)$$

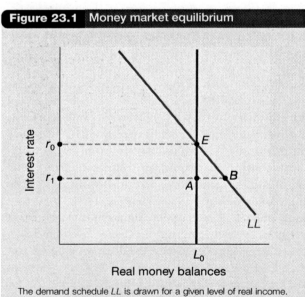

Figure 23.1 Money market equilibrium

The demand schedule LL is drawn for a given level of real income. The higher the opportunity cost of holding money, the lower the real balances demanded. The real money supply schedule is vertical at L_0. The equilibrium point is E and the equilibrium interest rate, r_0. At a lower interest rate r_1 there is excess demand for money AB. There must be a corresponding excess supply of bonds. This reduces bond prices and increases the return on bonds, driving the interest rate up to its equilibrium level at which both markets clear.

An excess demand for money must be exactly matched by an excess supply of bonds. Otherwise people are planning to hold more wealth than they actually possess.

An excess demand for money at the interest rate r_1 in Figure 23.1 bids up the interest rate to its equilibrium level r_0. With excess demand for money, there is an excess supply of bonds. To make people want more bonds, suppliers of bonds offer a higher interest rate.[2] People switch

---

[2] A bond is a promise to pay a given stream of interest payments over a given time period. The bond price is the present value of this stream of payments. The higher the interest rate at which the stream is discounted, the lower the price of a bond. With an excess supply of bonds, bond prices fall, and the interest rate or rate of return on bonds rises.

from money to bonds. The higher interest rate reduces both the excess supply of bonds and the excess demand for money. At the interest rate r_0 money supply equals money demand. Bond supply equals bond demand. Both markets are in equilibrium. People wish to divide their wealth in precisely the ratio of the relative supplies of money and bonds.

From now on, we examine the implicit market for money. However, any statement about the money market is also a statement about the bond market.

BOX 23-2   The big bad bubble

House prices have replaced the weather as Britain's favourite conversational standby, . . . Unlike Britain's temperate and unpredictable climate, however, the nation's housing market is reliably torrid. Another £9.3 billion ($16.7 billion) was borrowed against houses in March, taking the amount of outstanding mortgage debt past £800 billion. House prices were 18.9 per cent higher in April than a year ago. With so much money at stake, every homeowner, house-hunter and buy-to-letter in Britain is an amateur meteorologist, watching for storms on the horizon. It falls to the Bank of England to regulate the weather and distribute the seasons, through its control of the cost of borrowing.

Source: The Economist, 6 May 2004.

Since the late 1990s central bankers across the world have been tasked with controlling inflation within their economies. In the case of the UK interest rate control and inflation management were handed to the Bank of England in 1997. Throughout most of that period UK property values have risen, often with double-digit growth per annum. Some commentators refer to this as an asset price bubble. Property prices are inflating like a bubble and the worry is that at some point the bubble will pop.

The Bank of England is tasked with managing interest rate policy to maintain low growth of prices in general rather than house prices in particular. The Bank therefore argues that it thinks about house prices only to the extent that they have implications for the economy as a whole and therefore for inflation.

Changes in equilibrium

A shift in either money supply or money demand changes equilibrium in the money market (and the bond market). These shifts are examined in Figure 23.2.

A fall in the money supply

Suppose the central bank lowers the money supply. For a fixed price level, lower nominal money reduces the real money supply. Figure 23.2 shows this leftward shift in the supply curve. Real money falls from L_0 to L'. The equilibrium interest rate rises from r_0 to r'. A higher interest rate reduces the demand for real money in line with the lower quantity supplied. Hence a lower real money supply raises the equilibrium interest rate. Conversely, a rise in the real money supply reduces the equilibrium interest rate.

A rise in real income

Figure 23.2 shows real money demand LL for a given real income. A rise in real income increases the marginal benefit of holding money at each interest rate, raising real money demand from LL to LL'. The equilibrium interest rate rises to keep real money demand equal to the unchanged real supply L_0. Conversely, a fall in real income shifts LL to the left and reduces the equilibrium interest rate.

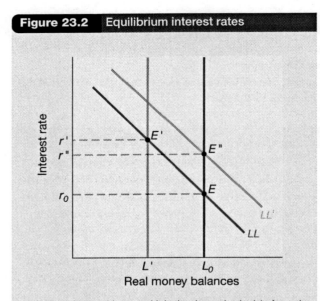

Figure 23.2   Equilibrium interest rates

With a given real income, *LL* is the demand schedule for real money balances. A reduction in the real money supply from L_0 to L' moves the equilibrium interest rates from r_0 to r' to reduce the quantity of money demanded in line with the fall in the quantity supplied. With a given supply of real money L_0 an increase in real income shifts the demand schedule from *LL* to *LL''*. The equilibrium interest rates must increase from r_0 to r''. Higher real income tends to increase the quantity of real money demanded and higher interest rates are required to offer this, maintaining the quantity of real money demanded in line with the unchanged real supply.

More competition in banking

Figure 23.2 also draws money demand *LL* for a given interest rate paid on bank deposits. Holding this rate constant, a rise in bond interest rates *r* raises the cost of holding money and reduces the quantity of money demanded. This is implies the economy moves up a given demand curve *LL*.

However, more competition between banks, reflected in permanently higher interest rates paid on bank deposits, reduces the cost of holding money at each level of *r*. By raising money demand at each interest rate *r*, this shifts the demand for money up from *LL* to *LL'*. For a given money supply, this equilibrium interest rate on bonds is higher.

To sum up, a higher real money supply reduces the equilibrium interest rate, raising real money demand in line with the higher real money supply. Conversely, higher real income, which tends to raise real money demand, must lead to a rise in the equilibrium interest rate, which tends to reduce real money demand. Only then does real money demand remain equal to the unchanged supply. An increase in banking competition has similar effects to a rise in real income.

Now you've read this section, why not test your understanding by visiting the Online Learning Centre at www.mcgraw-hill.co.uk/textbooks/begg.

23.5   Monetary control

The central bank can control the money supply by using open market operations to determine the monetary base, and by using reserve requirements and the discount rate to determine the money multiplier. Easy in theory, but not in practice.

It is hard for the Bank to control the monetary base because it is also lender of last resort. When the banks wish to increase lending and deposits they can *always* get extra cash from the Bank.

Nor is the money multiplier easily manipulated. To affect it, reserve requirements must force banks to hold reserves they would not otherwise have held. This is a tax on banks, stopping them conducting profitable business. Modern banks operating in global markets find ways round these controls. UK banks do business with UK borrowers using financial markets in Frankfurt or New York, and London is disadvantaged as a global financial centre.

The UK has given up required reserve ratios on banks for the purpose of monetary control. Rather, the Bank tries to forecast what ratios of cash to deposits will be chosen by banks and by households, and thus guesses the likely size of the money multiplier.

| BOX 23-3 | The big issue |

Box 21.1 showed Japan's property boom in the late 1980s and crash in the early 1990s. Japanese banks took a big hit. The value of their assets fell drastically. Fears about the health of the banks led to a collapse of both confidence and private spending.

The Bank of Japan tried to get people spending again. Interest rates fell steadily as the Bank printed money. On 3 March 1999 it issued 1800 billion yen (£9 billion), driving short-term interest rates almost to zero.

Zero interest rates failed to boost the Japanese economy because the slump was already so bad that the price level was falling. When inflation is –2 per cent and the nominal interest rate is 0, the real interest rate is +2 per cent. A bigger slump makes prices fall faster, raising the real interest rate yet more. A vicious cycle. Negative inflation is more dangerous than positive inflation.

It is therefore with some relief that during 2003 and 2004 the Japanese economy started to grow again, reducing fears of a deflationary slump. However, the time taken to get the Japanese economy out of intensive care has been worryingly protracted.

Hence precise control of the money supply is difficult. Most central banks no longer try. Instead they set interest rates. The TV news reports decisions by the Bank about interest rates, not decisions about the money supply.

Control through interest rates

Figure 23.3 again shows the market for money. We draw the money demand schedule LL for a given level of real income. If the central bank can control the money supply, then, for a given level of goods prices, it can fix the real money supply at L_0. The equilibrium interest rate is r_0.

Alternatively, the central bank can fix the interest rate at r_0 and supply whatever money is needed to clear the market at this interest rate. In equilibrium, the central bank supplies exactly the quantity of money demanded at the interest rate r_0. The money supply is still L_0.

The central bank can fix the money supply and accept the equilibrium interest rate implied by the money demand equation, or it can fix the interest rate and accept the equilibrium money supply implied by the money demand equation. Central banks now do the latter.

Uncertainty about the exact size of the money multiplier is now unimportant. When the interest rate starts to fall below the level r_0 either because of too little demand for money or too much supply, the Bank reduces the monetary base, through an open market operation, until the interest rate is r_0 again. Conversely, when the interest rate exceeds r_0, the Bank simply increases the monetary base until the interest rate falls to r_0.

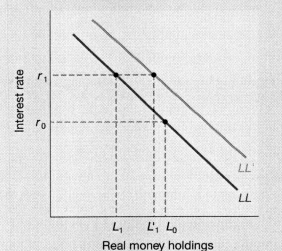

Figure 23.3   Interest rates and monetary control

The money demand schedule LL is drawn for a given level of real income. If the Bank can fix the real money supply at L_0 the equilibrium interest rate will be r_0. Alternatively, if the Bank sets the interest rate r_0 and provides whatever money is demanded, the money supply will again be L_0. To control the money supply by using interest rates, the Bank must know the position of the demand schedule. Fixing an interest rate r_1, the resulting money supply will be L_1 if the demand schedule is LL but will be L'_1 if the demand schedule is LL'.

23.6　Targets and instruments of monetary policy

The **monetary instrument** is the variable over which the central bank makes day-to-day choices.

Setting the interest rate and not the money supply has a second advantage. When money demand is uncertain, fixing the money supply makes the interest rate uncertain, whereas fixing the interest rate makes the money supply uncertain. If the *effects* of monetary policy on the rest of the economy operate mainly via the interest rate, it is better to view monetary policy as the choice of interest rates rather than the money supply.

Two other concepts guide our discussion of monetary policy in later chapters. One is the *ultimate objective* of monetary policy. Possible objectives could include price stability, output stabilization, manipulation of the exchange rate and reducing swings in house prices.

To pursue its ultimate objective, what information does a central bank use at its frequent meetings to decide interest rates? It gets up-to-date forecasts of many variables. Sometimes, it concentrates on one or two key indicators.

An **intermediate target** is a key indicator used to guide interest-rate decisions.

Interest rates are the *instrument* about which policy decisions are made but interest rates are chosen to try to keep the *intermediate target* on track. This shows how interest rates should adjust to the state of the economy. New data on the money supply (largely bank deposits) come out faster than new data on the price level or output. In the heyday of Monetarism, central banks changed interest rates to try to meet medium-run targets for the path of nominal growth. In terms of Figure 23.3 it was as if they were fixing the money supply, not interest rates.

Throughout the world, there have been two key changes in the design of monetary policy in the last decade. First, central banks have been told that their ultimate objectives should concentrate more on price stability and less on other things. Second, money has become less important as an intermediate target. The financial revolution reduced its reliability as a leading indicator of future inflation. When structural changes in the financial sector are causing changes in money demand, it is hard to predict how much money will be held and how much will be spent. Increasingly, central banks use *inflation targets* as the intermediate target to which interest rate policy responds.

23.7　The transmission mechanism

The **transmission mechanism** of monetary policy is the channel through which it affects output and employment.

The central bank sets interest rates, but how do interest rates affect the real economy?

In a closed economy, monetary policy affects consumption and investment demand by affecting real interest rates.[3] The central bank chooses the nominal interest rate. If prices are fixed, this is also the real interest rate. Once we allow prices to vary, monetary policy needs to anticipate what inflation will be. Since the real interest rate is simply the nominal interest rate minus the inflation rate, monetary policy then sets the nominal interest rate to get the desired real interest rate.

Consumption demand revisited

Chapter 20 used a very simple consumption function, an upward-sloping straight line relating

---

[3] In Chapter 29 we show that, in an open economy, there is also a strong relationship between interest rates, the exchange rate and competitiveness. Monetary transmission then includes effects on export and import demand.

410 Part 4 : Macroeconomics

aggregate consumption to the disposable income of households. The slope of this line, the marginal propensity to consume, showed the fraction of each extra pound of disposable income that households wished to spend not save.

The height of the consumption function showed autonomous consumption demand, the part unrelated to personal disposable income. Changes in disposable income moved households *along* the consumption function. Changes in autonomous demand *shifted* the function. How can monetary policy affect autonomous consumption demand?

Household wealth

The **wealth effect** is the shift in the consumption function when household wealth changes.

Suppose real wealth rises because of a stock market boom. Households spend some of their extra wealth on a new car. At each level of disposable income, consumption demand is higher. The entire consumption function shifts up when household wealth increases.

Money and interest rates affect household wealth, and thus consumption and aggregate demand, in two ways. First, since money is a component of household wealth, a higher real money supply adds directly to household wealth. Second, interest rates affect household wealth indirectly. The price of company shares and long-term government bonds is the present value of the expected stream of divided earnings or promised coupon payments. When interest rates fall, future earnings, now discounted at a lower interest rate, are worth more today. Lower interest rates make the price of bonds and corporate shares rise and make households wealthier.[4]

Durables and consumer credit

When spending exceeds disposable income, net wealth falls. People sell off assets or borrow money to finance their dissaving. A lot of borrowing is to finance purchases of *consumer durables*, household capital goods such as televisions, furniture and cars. Splashing out on a new car can cost a whole year's income.

Two aspects of consumer credit or borrowing possibilities affect consumption spending. First, there is the quantity of credit on offer. If banks or retailers make more credit available to customers, people are more likely buy the car or dream kitchen they have always wanted. An increase in the supply of consumer credit shifts the consumption function upwards. People spend more at any level of disposable income. Second, the cost of credit matters. The higher the interest rate, the lower the quantity that households can borrow while still being able to make repayments out of their future disposable incomes.

Money and interest rates thus affect consumer spending by affecting both the quantity of consumer credit and the interest rates charged on it. An increase in the monetary base increases the cash reserves of the banking system and allows it to extend more consumer credit in the form of overdrafts. And by reducing the cost of consumer credit, lower interest rates allow households to take out bigger loans while still being able to meet the interest and repayments.

Those two forces – wealth effects and changes in consumer credit – explain most of the shifts in the consumption function. They are part of the *transmission mechanism* through which monetary policy affects output and employment. Operating through wealth effects or

---

[4] When interest rates are 10 per cent, a bond paying £2.50 for ever is worth £25. New buyers get about 10 per cent a year on their investment. If interest rates fall to 5 per cent, bond prices rise to £50. New buyers still get an annual return in line with interest rates on other assets. A similar argument applies to company shares.

the supply and cost of consumer credit, changes in the money supply and in interest rates, shift the consumption function and the aggregate demand schedule, thus affecting equilibrium income and output.

Two closely-related theories of the consumption function re-interpret these phenomena and make some of their subtleties more explicit.

The permanent income hypothesis

> The permanent income hypothesis says consumption reflects long-run or permanent income.

Developed by Professor Milton Friedman, this hypothesis assumes that people's incomes fluctuate but that people dislike fluctuating consumption. Because of diminishing marginal utility, a few extra bottles of champagne in the good years does not compensate for hunger in the bad years. Rather than allow fluctuations in income to induce fluctuations in consumption, people smooth out fluctuations in consumption. People go without champagne to avoid being hungry.

What determines the consumption people can afford on average? Friedman coined the term *permanent income* to describe people's average income in the long run, and argued that consumption depends not on current disposable income but on permanent income.

Suppose people think current income is unusually high. This temporarily high income makes little difference to their permanent income or the consumption they can afford in the long run. Since permanent income has hardly risen, they hardly increase current consumption. They save most of their temporary extra income and put money aside to see them through the years when income is unusually low. Only if people believe that a rise in today's income will be sustained as higher future incomes will their permanent income rise significantly. Only then will a large rise in current income be matched by a large rise in current consumption.

The life-cycle hypothesis

> The life-cycle hypothesis assumes people make a lifetime consumption plan (including bequests to their children) that is just affordable out of lifetime income (plus any initial wealth inherited).

Developed by Professors Franco Modigliani, Richard Bromberg and Albert Ando, this theory takes a long-run approach like the permanent income hypothesis, but recognizes that changing tastes over a lifetime may undermine complete consumption smoothing.

Each individual household need not plan constant consumption level over its lifetime. There may be years of heavy expenditure (a round-the-world cruise, sending the kids to private school) and other years when spending is a bit less. However, such individual discrepancies tend to cancel out in the aggregate. Like the permanent income hypothesis, the life-cycle hypothesis suggests that it is average long-run income that determines the total demand for consumer spending.

Figure 23.4 shows a household's actual income over its lifetime. Income rises with career seniority until retirement, then drops to the lower level provided by a pension. The household's permanent income is *OD*. Technically, this is the constant annual income with the same present value as the present value of the actual stream of income. If the household consumed exactly its permanent income, it would consume *OD* each year and die penniless. The two shaded areas labelled *A* show when the household would be spending more than its current income and the area *B* shows when the household would be saving.

The household spends its income over its lifetime but area *B* is not the sum of the two areas *A* because of compound interest. In the early years of low income, the household borrows. The area *B* shows how much the household has to save to pay back the initial borrowing *with interest* and accumulate sufficient wealth to see it through the final years when it is again dissaving.

Figure 23.4   Consumption and the life-cycle

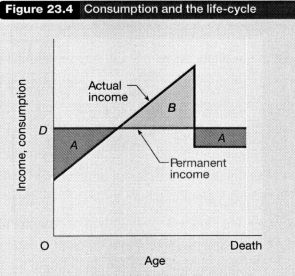

Actual disposable income rises over a household's lifetime until retirement, then falls to the pension level. Permanent income is the constant income level *OD* with the same present value as actual income. Suppose consumption equals permanent income. The two areas *A* show total dissaving and the area *B*, total saving. In the absence of inherited wealth and bequests, *B* must be large enough to repay borrowing with interest and also build up enough wealth to supplement actual income during retirement.

Now let's think about wealth effects and consumer credit again. With more initial wealth, a household can spend more in every year of its lifetime without going broke. We can shift the permanent income line in Figure 23.4 upwards and consumption will rise. Although area *B* is now smaller and the areas *A* are now larger, the household can use its extra wealth to meet this shortfall between the years of saving (the area *B*) and the years of dissaving (the two areas *A*).

Again we conclude that higher wealth leads to more consumption at any current disposable income, but we pick up something we missed earlier. If households believe their *future* income will be higher than previously imagined, this also raises their permanent income. Households can spend more each year and still expect to balance their lifetime budget. They raise *current* consumption as soon as they raise their estimates of future incomes. The present value of future income plays a role very similar to wealth. It is money to be shared out in consumption over the lifetime. Friedman called it 'human wealth', to distinguish it from financial and physical assets. Rises in expected future incomes have wealth effects. They shift up the simple consumption function relating *current* consumption to *current* disposable income.

What about consumer credit? A rise in interest rates reduces the present value of future incomes and makes households worse off. In Figure 23.4, households must enlarge area *B* to meet the extra interest costs of paying back money borrowed in area *A* early in the lifetime. We must shift the permanent income line downwards. A rise in interest rates reduces current consumption not merely by reducing the market value of financial assets, but also by reducing the present value of future *labour* income. By reducing human wealth, it shifts the consumption function downwards.

Finally, what about a rise in the quantity of consumer credit on offer? Figure 23.4 assumes that people spend more than their incomes early in life. Students run up overdrafts knowing

BOX 23-4   Wealth effects

Rising wealth, just like rising income, leads to greater consumption. In the UK rising property prices have enabled home owners to borrow against the equity within their homes, leading to a boom in conservatory building and new car sales. Previously, in the US when share prices tripled during 1992–2000, the richest fifth of Americans raised consumption so much that their saving rate out of disposable income fell from 8.2 per cent to –2.1 per cent. They overspent their income and ate into their assets. The saving rate in the next richest 20 per cent of people fell from 4.7 per cent to –2.1 per cent. There was no fall in the saving rate by the poorest 60 per cent of people, who had few stock market holdings.

This evidence shows wealth effects in action. If share prices fall a lot, the rich will consume less and save more. Lower interest rates can help offset this by raising the present value of future profits, underpinning share prices.

that, as rich economists, they can pay them back later. What if nobody will lend? People without wealth are restricted by their actual incomes, although people with wealth can lend to themselves by running down their wealth. Hence a rise in the availability of consumer credit lets people dissave in the early years. Total consumption rises. More students run up overdrafts and buy cars.

Having discussed how monetary policy affects consumption demand, we conclude our examination of monetary transmission by analysing how interest rates affect investment demand.

Investment demand

In earlier chapters we treated investment demand as autonomous, or independent of current income and output. We now begin to analyse what determines investment demand. Here we focus on interest rates. Other determinants of investment demand are considered in Chapter 31.

Total investment spending is investment in fixed capital and investment in working capital. Fixed capital includes factories, houses, plant and machinery. The share of investment in GDP fluctuates between 10 and 20 per cent.[5] Although the total change in inventories is quite small, this component of total investment is volatile and contributes significantly to changes in the total level of investment.

In a closed economy, aggregate demand is $C + I + G$. Public investment is part of G. We still treat government demand as part of fiscal policy. Thus we assume that G is fixed at a level set by the government. In this section we focus on private investment demand I.

Investment in fixed capital

Firms add to plant and equipment because they foresee profitable opportunities to expand output, or because they can reduce costs by using more capital-intensive production methods. BT needs new equipment because it is developing new products for data transmission. Nissan needs new assembly lines to substitute robots for workers in car production.

The firm weighs the benefits from new capital – the rise in profits – against the cost of investment. The benefit occurs in the future but the costs are incurred when the plant is built or the machine bought. The firm compares the value of extra future profits with the current cost of the investment.

Will the investment yield enough extra profit to pay back *with interest* the loan used to finance the original investment? Equivalently, if the project is funded out of existing profits, will the new investment yield a return at least as great as the return that could been earned by lending the money instead? The higher the interest rate, the larger the return on a new investment must be to match the opportunity cost of the funds tied up.

At any instant there are many investment projects a firm *could* undertake. The firm ranks these projects, from the most profitable to the least profitable. At a high interest rate, only a few projects earn enough to cover the opportunity cost of the funds employed. As the interest rate falls, more and more projects earn a return at least matching the opportunity cost of the funds used to undertake the investment. The firm invests more.

---

[5] These numbers refer to gross investment, the production of new capital goods that contribute to aggregate demand. Since the capital stock is depreciating, or wearing out, some gross investment is needed merely to keep the existing capital stock from falling.

The **investment demand schedule** shows the desired investment at each interest rate.

Figure 23.5 plots the investment demand schedule *II* relating interest rates and investment demand. If the interest rate rises from r_0 to r_1, fewer investment projects cover the opportunity cost of the funds tied up, and desired investment falls from I_0 to I_1.

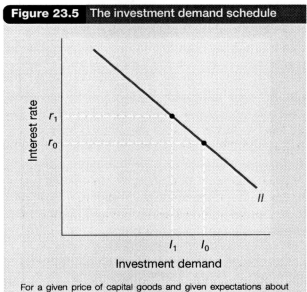

Figure 23.5 The investment demand schedule

For a given price of capital goods and given expectations about the profit stream to which new investments give rise, a higher interest rate reduces the number of projects that can provide a return matching the opportunity cost of the funds used. As interest rates rise from r_0 to r_1, desired investment falls from I_0 to I_1.

The height of the schedule *II* reflects the cost of new capital and the stream of profits to which it gives rise. For a given stream of expected future profits, a higher price of new capital goods reduces the return on the money tied up in investment. Fewer projects match the opportunity cost of any particular interest rate. Since desired investment is then lower at any interest rate, a rise in the cost of new capital goods shifts the investment demand schedule *II* downwards.

Similarly, pessimism about future output demand reduces estimates of the stream of profits earned on possible investment projects. The return on each project falls. At each interest rate, fewer projects match the opportunity cost of the funds. Desired investment falls at any interest rate. Lower expected future demand shifts the investment demand schedule downwards.[6]

The investment demand schedule *II* can be used to analyse both business investment in plant and machinery and residential investment in housing. What about the slope of the schedule? There is a big difference between a machine that wears out in three years and a house or a factory lasting 50 years. The longer the economic life of the capital good, the larger the fraction of its total returns earned in the distant future, and the more the original cost of the goods accumulates at compound interest before the money is repaid.

Hence a change in interest rates has a larger effect the longer the life of the capital good. The investment demand schedule is flatter, and the monetary transmission mechanism more powerful, for long-lived houses and factories than for short-term machinery.[7] A change in interest rates has more effect on long-term projects.

Inventory investment

There are three reasons why firms desire stocks of raw materials, partly finished goods and finished goods awaiting sale. First, the firm may be betting on price changes. Sometimes firms hold

[6] We can make the same points another way. Given the stream of future profits and the interest rate, a firm does all projects for which the present value of operating profits exceeds the initial price of the capital goods. A higher interest rate cuts the present value of profits. Some projects no longer cover the initial cost of capital goods. Higher interest rates reduce desired investment. Similarly, a lower expected future profit stream, or higher purchase price of capital goods, cut the present value of operating profits relative to the initial cost, reducing investment demand.

[7] Equivalently, a 1 per cent rise in the interest rate has a small effect on the present value of earnings over a three-year period but a large effect on the present value of earnings over the next 50 years. Note that this is the same argument as we used in Chapter 22, in saying that a change in interest rates would have little effect on the price (present value of promised payments) of a short-term bond but a large effect on the price of a long-term bond.

large stocks of oil, believing it cheaper to buy now rather than later. Similarly, firms may hold finished goods off the market hoping to get a better price later.

Second, many production processes take time. A ship cannot be built in a month, or even a year. Some stocks are simply the throughput of inputs on their way to becoming outputs.

Third, stocks help smooth costly adjustments in output. If output demand rises suddenly, plant capacity cannot be changed overnight. A firm has to make big overtime payments to meet the upsurge in orders. It is cheaper to carry some stocks, available to meet a sudden rise in demand. Similarly, in a temporary downturn, it is cheaper to maintain output and pile up stocks of unsold goods than to incur expensive redundancy payments to cut the workforce and reduce production.

These are benefits of holding inventories. The cost is that, by retaining unsold goods or buying goods not yet inputs to production, a firm ties up money that could have earned interest. The cost of holding inventories is the interest forgone, plus any storage charges for holding stocks.

Thus the investment demand schedule *II* for fixed capital in Figure 23.4 also applies to increases in working capital, or inventories. Other things equal, a higher interest rate reduces desired stockbuilding, an upward move *along* the investment demand schedule. This is part of the monetary transmission mechanism. But a rise in potential speculative profits, or fall in storage costs for inventories, *shifts* the schedule *II* up and raise inventory investment at any interest rate. Not all changes in investment demand are caused by monetary policy.

BOX 23-5   The credit channel of monetary policy

Recent research emphasizes another aspect of the transmission mechanism through which monetary policy affects consumption and investment, and hence aggregate demand.

The **credit channel** affects the value of collateral for loans, and thus the supply of credit.

A lender usually asks for collateral – assets available for sale if you fail to repay the loan. Collateral is how lenders cope with moral hazard and adverse selection: borrowers who know more about their ability and willingness to repay than lenders know.

Suppose the price of goods falls, raising the real value of nominal assets. People have more collateral to offer lenders, who thus lend more than before at any particular interest rate. The supply of credit rises and aggregate demand for goods increases.

There are really two credit channels, since there are two reasons for changes in the value of collateral. First, changes in goods prices change the real value of nominal assets. Second, and quite distinct, when monetary policy changes the interest rate, this affects the present value of future income from assets and hence the market value of collateral assets themselves.

SUMMARY

● The Bank of England, the UK central bank, is banker to the banks. Because it can print money it can never go bust. It acts as lender of last resort to the banks.

● The Bank conducts the government's monetary policy. It affects the monetary base through open market operations, buying and selling government securities. It can also affect the money multiplier by imposing reserve requirements on the banks, or by setting the discount rate for loans to banks at a penalty level that encourages banks to hold excess reserves.

● There is no explicit market in money. Because people plan to hold the total supply of assets that they own, any excess supply of bonds is matched by an excess demand for money.

Interest rates adjust to clear the market for bonds. In so doing, they clear the money market.

- A rise in the real money supply reduces the equilibrium interest rate. For a given real money supply, a rise in real income raises the equilibrium interest rate.

- In practice, the Bank cannot control the money supply exactly. Imposing artificial regulations drives banking business into unregulated channels. Monetary base control is difficult since the Bank acts as lender of last resort, supplying cash when banks need it.

- Thus the Bank sets the interest rate not money supply. The demand for money at this interest rate determines the quantity of money supplied. Interest rates are the instrument of monetary policy.

- Interest rates take time to affect the economy. Intermediate targets are used as leading indicators when setting the interest rate.

- A higher interest rate reduces household wealth and makes borrowing dearer. Together, these effects reduce autonomous consumption demand and shift the consumption function downwards.

- Consumption demand reflects long-run disposable income and a desire to smooth out short-run fluctuations in consumption. Higher interest rates reduce consumption demand by reducing the present value of expected future labour income.

- Given the cost of new capital goods and expected stream of future profits, a higher interest rate reduces investment demand, a movement down a given investment demand schedule *II*. Higher expected future profits, or cheaper capital goods, shift the *II* schedule upwards.

- These effects of interest rates on consumption and investment demand are the transmission mechanism of monetary policy.

REVIEW QUESTIONS

- The Bank sells £1 million of securities to Mr Jones who banks with Barclays. (a) If Mr Jones pays by cheque, show the effect on the balance sheets of the Bank of England and Barclays Bank. (b) What happens to the money supply? (c) Is the answer the same if Mr Jones pays in cash?

- Now the Bank requires banks to hold 100 per cent cash reserves against deposits. Repeat your answers to question 1. What is the money multiplier?

- What are the desirable properties of a good leading indicator for interest rate decisions?

- People previously without bank overdrafts get credit cards on which they can borrow up to £500. What happens to the consumption function? Why?

Why do higher interest rates reduce investment demand? Be sure to discuss all the different ways in which firms might finance their investment projects.

Why might it take up two years for a change in interest rates fully to affect aggregate demand? What does this imply about decisions to set interest rates?

Common fallacies Why are these statements wrong? (a) By abolishing reserve requirements the Bank gave up any attempt to control the money supply. (b) When real interest rates are negative, people are being paid to hold cash. (c) Consumers are crazy if their spending is up when their disposable income is lower.

To check your answers to these questions, go to page 642.

To help you grasp the key concepts of this chapter check out the extra resources posted on the Online Learning Centre at www.mcgraw-hill.co.uk/textbooks/begg. There are quick test questions, economics examples and access to Powerweb articles, all for free!

For even more exercises, recaps and examples to help you study, purchase a copy of the Economics Student Workbook. Simply visit www.mcgraw hill.co.uk/textbooks/begg and follow the links to the Workbook to buy your copy.

chapter 24

Monetary and fiscal policy

Learning outcomes

By the end of this chapter, you should understand:

1 different forms of monetary policy

2 a monetary target

3 the *IS* and *LM* schedules

4 equilibrium in both the output and money market

5 the effect of a fiscal expansion

6 the effect of a monetary expansion

7 the mix of monetary and fiscal policy

8 how expected future taxes affect current demand

Chapters 20 and 21 introduced a simple model of income determination and studied how fiscal policy affects aggregate demand and equilibrium output. Since Chapter 21, we have studied the demand for money, the supply of money and the determination of interest rates. Interest rates connect the present and the future, affecting spending decisions of both households and firms. We analysed the transmission mechanism by which monetary policy affects aggregate demand.

We now examine the interaction of the markets for goods and for money. Interest rates affect the demand for goods and the level of income and output, but income and output affect the demand for money and the interest rates set by the central bank.

We need to think about both markets at once. In so doing, we explain how equilibrium income and interest rates are simultaneously determined. In this richer model, we then study changes in monetary and fiscal policy. Finally, we discuss how the mix of monetary and fiscal policy affects the composition as well as the level of equilibrium output.

This is the last chapter in which we retain the simplifying assumption that prices are fixed. The interest rate is the key variable connecting the markets for money and output. In the next chapter, we allow prices to change and introduce aggregate supply for the first time.

24.1 Monetary policy rules

To examine the behaviour of the economy under *given* policies, we have to say what we mean by a given policy. The central bank sets the interest rate, passively supplying whatever quantity of money is needed to equate money supply and money demand at this interest rate. At it simplest,

A **monetary policy rule** (MPR) specifies how the central bank adjusts interest rates in response to changes in particular economic variables.

a given monetary policy could mean a given interest rate. However, treating interest rates as fixed ignores the fact that the central bank reacts systematically to changes in economic conditions. Just as we model the behaviour of the private sector, we ought to model the behaviour of the central bank itself.

In the heyday of Monetarism, central banks used to adjust interest rates to stop the money supply deviating from a given target path. For reasons explained at the end of this chapter, most central banks have abandoned this policy, preferring to target the inflation rate itself.

Inflation targeting makes no sense in a model in which we are still assuming that prices are fixed. We introduce inflation targeting in Chapter 25. In this chapter, we assume instead that the central bank pursues a monetary target. Not only is this a good way to introduce many key ideas, it is also useful in understanding how monetary policy was set in the 1980s before inflation targeting became popular.

Following a **monetary target**, the central banks adjusts interest rates to maintain the quantity of money demanded in line with the given target for money supply.

We now combine our analysis of the goods market and money market to examine interest rates and output simultaneously. Chapters 20 and 21 analysed short-run equilibrium output using a diagram with the 45° line and a straight-line aggregate demand line. The height of the aggregate demand line reflected autonomous demand from consumption, investment and government spending; the slope of the line reflected the marginal propensity to spend out of national income.

BOX 24-1 Monetary intelligence

As the Iraq war has shown, good intelligence is a valuable commodity. From where does the Bank of England's Monetary Policy Committee get its briefings, and how does it check these are not being sexed up?

Teams of professional economists and statisticians scrutinize the latest data, and feed them into economic models in order to update predictions. But, as in warfare, this can usefully be supplemented by agents with their ear to the ground. The Bank of England has regional reps who tour the country talking to businesses and civic groups, gathering intelligence about local economic conditions and the latest concerns. This human intelligence is an important supplement to the volumes of statistical data that the MPC must process every month.

Mervyn King, Governor of the Bank, has earned a worldwide reputation for sound judgement and good practice, making monetary policy predictable and effective: 'For much of the postwar period, British macroeconomic policy was too exciting for comfort; we should aim to be boring.'

Choppier waters King's life could get uncomfortably exciting very soon. After an extended period of low interest rates and low inflation, interest rates are starting to rise around the world as global recovery takes hold. And with huge increases in UK house prices during the last few years, it would not take a large increase in interest rates to cause real pain in the housing market.

A political animal There is no denying King's stature among financial policy-makers. The Birmingham native, former economics professor and keen Aston Villa fan, has been a key player in modernizing Britain's once-amateurish economic policy-making since he became chief economist at the Bank in 1991. 'Mervyn King developed the framework under which the bank gave advice to the chancellor,' says Alan Budd, who was chief economic adviser to the British Treasury until 1997. 'When the bank was given independence, it had a system in place.' King still keeps his lines open to Chancellor of the Exchequer Gordon Brown through monthly working breakfasts.

Adapted from 'Inside the Bank of England', *BusinessWeek*, 12 July 2004.

This diagram is not suitable in our extended model. As output changes, interest rates alter, affecting consumption and investment demand. And changes in monetary policy, by changing interest rates at any output level, can shift the aggregate demand schedule. To keep track of all these effects, it is easier to develop a new diagram.

24.2   The *IS–LM* model

The trick is to consider *combinations* of income and interest rates that lead to equilibrium in each of the two markets, output and money, and thus determine the unique combination of income and interest rates yielding equilibrium in both markets at the same time.

The *IS* schedule: goods market equilibrium

> The *IS* schedule shows combinations of income and interest rates at which aggregate demand equals actual output.

The goods market is in equilibrium when aggregate demand equals actual income. Hence, as shorthand, the combinations of interest rates and income compatible with short-run equilibrium in the goods market is called the *IS* schedule.[1]

Figure 24.1 shows the *IS* schedule. It is drawn for a given level of present and future government spending, a given level of present and future taxes, and given present beliefs about future output and income. Holding these constant, lower interest rates increase both investment and consumption demand. At an interest rate r_1, aggregate demand and short-run equilibrium output Y_1 are higher than their level Y_0 when the interest rate is r_0.

Changes in interest rates move the goods market along the *IS* curve. Anything else that affects aggregate demand is shown as a shift in the *IS* schedule.

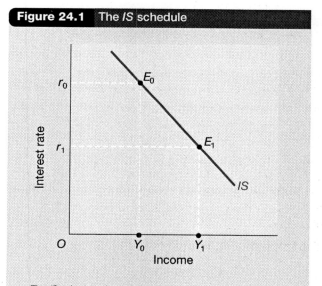

Figure 24.1   The *IS* schedule

The *IS* schedule shows how a change in interest rates affects aggregate demand and short-run equilibrium output. A lower interest rate boosts demand and output. Anything else affecting aggregate demand *shifts* the *IS* schedule.

The slope of the IS schedule

The *IS* schedule slopes down. Lower interest rates boost aggregate demand and output. The *slope* of the *IS* schedule reflects the sensitivity of aggregate demand to interest rates. If demand is sensitive to interest rates, the *IS* schedule is flat. Conversely, if output demand is insensitive to interest rates, the *IS* schedule is steep.

Shifts in the IS schedule

Movements along the *IS* schedule show how interest rates affect aggregate demand and equilibrium

---

[1] The name *IS* schedule derives from the fact that in the simplest model without either a government or a foreign sector, equilibrium income is where planned investment *I* equals planned saving *S*. However, the *IS* schedule – combinations of income and interest rates consistent with equilibrium income – can be constructed for models including the government and foreign sector as well.

output. Other changes in aggregate demand shift the *IS* schedule. For a *given* interest rate, more optimism about future profits raises investment demand. Higher expected future incomes raise consumption demand. Higher government spending adds directly to aggregate demand. Any of these, by raising aggregate demand at a given interest rate, raise equilibrium output at any interest rate, an *upward shift* in the *IS* schedule.

The *LM* schedule: money market equilibrium

The *LM* schedule shows combinations of interest rates and income yielding money market equilibrium when the central bank pursues a given target for the nominal money supply.

Pursuing a monetary target, the central bank endeavours to fix the money supply itself. In Figure 24.2, along the *LM* schedule the demand for money (or liquidity, *L*) equals the given supply of money (*M*). Hence the shorthand *LM*.

The quantity of money demanded rises with output *Y* but falls with the interest rate *r*. In money market equilibrium, money demand equals the given money supply. Hence if output rises from Y_0 to Y_1 – tending to raise the quantity of money demanded – money market equilibrium is restored only if interest rates rise from r_0 to r_1, thereby reducing money demand back to the level of the given money supply. Figure 24.2 shows the upward-sloping schedule *LM* describing money market equilibrium. Higher output and income are accompanied by higher interest rates. When output rises, the interest rate rises to maintain money market equilibrium.

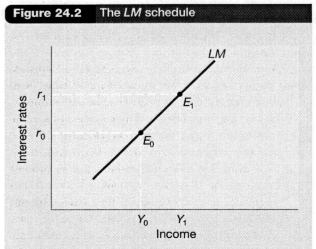

Figure 24.2   The *LM* schedule

The *LM* schedule depicts money market equilibrium and is drawn for a given money supply. Higher income raises the quantity of money demanded. Only if interest rates are higher can the quantity of money demanded continue to equal the unchanged money supply.

The slope of the schedule

The *LM* schedule slopes up. Following a monetary target, higher output induces a higher interest rate to keep money demand in line with money supply. The more sensitive money demand is to income and output, the more the interest rate must change to maintain money market equilibrium, and the steeper the *LM* schedule is. Similarly, if money demand is not responsive to interest rates, it takes a big change in interest rates to offset output effects on money demand and the *LM* schedule is steep. Conversely, the more money demand responds to interest rates and the less it responds to income, the flatter the *LM* schedule is.

Shifts in the LM schedule

Movements along the schedule indicate interest rate changes to implement the *existing* policy as output changes. Shifts in the schedule reflect a *change* in monetary policy.

We draw an *LM* schedule for a *given* nominal money target. A rise in the target money supply means that money demand must also be increased to maintain money market equilibrium. This implies a rightward *shift* in the *LM* schedule. Output is higher, or interest rates lower, raising money demand in line with the rise in real money supply.

Conversely, a lower monetary target shifts the *LM* schedule to the left. Since money demand must also be reduced to preserve money market equilibrium, a higher interest rate is required at each income level. To sum up, moving along the *LM* schedule, higher interest rates need higher income to keep real money demand equal to the fixed supply. A higher (lower) target for money supply shifts the *LM* schedule to the right (left).

24.3   The *IS–LM* model in action

Figure 24.3 shows both the *IS* schedule, depicting combinations of income and interest rates consistent with goods market equilibrium, and the *LM* schedule, depicting combinations of interest rates and income consistent with money market equilibrium when the central bank's monetary policy rule is to pursue a fixed money supply target. Equilibrium in both the money market and the output market is at point *E*, with an interest rate r^* and and income level Y^*.

Fiscal policy: shifting the *IS* schedule

Figure 24.4 shows the effect of a fiscal expansion that shifts the *IS* schedule from IS_0 to IS_1. If monetary policy is unchanged, and still shown by LM_0, equilibrium moves from *E* to E_1. Fiscal expansion leads to higher income but higher interest rates. Higher output tends to increase the quantity of money demanded. Only higher interest rates prevent this from happening.

> A fiscal stimulus to aggregate demand crowds out some private spending. Higher output induces a rise in interest rates that dampen the expansionary effect on demand by reducing some components of private spending.

And, of course, a fiscal contraction has the opposite effects. The *IS* schedule shifts to the left and output falls, tending to reduce money demand. Only lower interest rates restore money demand to the unchanged level of money supply, preserving money market equilibrium. In Figure 24.4, we can view this as the move from E_1 to *E* when the *IS* schedule shifts down from IS_1 to IS_0.

Figure 24.4 makes three other points. First, crowding out is complete – extra government spending *G* leads to an equivalent reduction in consumption and investment (*C + I*), leaving output unaltered – only if the *LM* schedule is vertical. Then, an upward shift in the *IS* schedule raises interest rates but not income.

In practice, the *LM* schedule is never completely vertical, which would occur only if it took an *infinite* rise in interest rates to offset the effect of slightly higher output on money demand. Since the *LM* schedule normally has a positive slope, fiscal expansion raises demand and output despite some induced rise in interest rates.

Second, fiscal policy is not the only autonomous change that is possible in aggregate demand. For example, an increase in export demand would also shift the *IS* schedule to the right, again inducing higher output and higher interest rates. Movements *along* the *IS* schedule show the effect of interest rates. All other shifts in aggregate demand imply *shifts* in the *IS* schedule.

Figure 24.3   Equilibrium in the goods and money markets

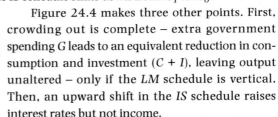

The goods market is in equilibrium at all points on the *IS* schedule. The money market is in equilibrium at all points on the *LM* schedule. Hence only at point *E* are both markets in equilibrium.

Third, Figure 24.4 shows what happens if fiscal expansion is *accompanied* by a looser monetary policy. Fiscal expansion shifts *IS* to the right but monetary expansion – a higher money supply target – shifts *LM* to the right. It is possible to loosen monetary policy just enough to keep

BOX 24-2   A horizontal *LM* schedule

If monetary policy is always adjusted to keep interest rates constant, we may as well view the *LM* schedule as horizontal at the target interest rate. The money supply is passively adjusted to whatever level of money is demanded at that interest rate. Shifts in the *IS* schedule no longer lead to crowding out because the money supply is adjusted to prevent interest rates from changing.

> A horizontal *LM* schedule implies the money supply is adjusted to keep interest rates constant

In Chapter 29 we show that defending a fixed exchange rate may require a constant interest rate and hence a horizontal *LM* schedule. With other exchange rate policies it rarely makes sense to fix interest rates independently of all economic conditions.

Figure 24.4   Fiscal expansion shifts the *IS* schedule

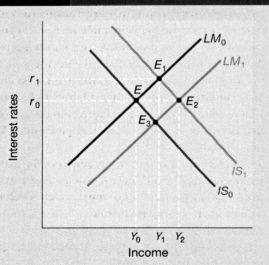

A fiscal expansion shifts the *IS* schedule from IS_0 to IS_1 but leaves the *LM* schedule unaltered at LM_0. Equilibrium moves from E to E_1. Output rises only from Y_0 to Y_1 because the output expansion induces a rise in interest rates from r_0 to r_1 that damps the rise in aggregate demand. By accompanying the fiscal expansion with a monetary expansion from LM_0 to LM_1, policy could make output rise to Y_2. Fiscal expansion makes output rise more if monetary policy is loosened to keep interest rates unaltered.

interest rates at their original level when income expands. Fiscal expansion then leads to a new equilibrium at E_2, with interest rates unchanged at r_0. Hence, the output effect of a fiscal expansion depends on the monetary policy in force. The more the monetary policy prevents a rise in interest rates, the more the fiscal expansion will lead to higher output.

Monetary expansion: shifting the *LM* schedule

Similarly, beginning from E in Figure 24.4, an increase in the target money supply shifts the *LM* schedule from LM_0 to LM_1 : for any income, it requires lower interest rates to help raise money demand in line with the new higher money supply. Lower interest rates also boost income, which also helps raise money demand. Equilibrium moves from E to E_3. Conversely, a reduction in the target money supply shifts the *LM* schedule to the left, leading to higher interest rates but lower output.

Now you've read this section, why not test your understanding by visiting the Online Learning Centre at www.mcgraw-hill.co.uk/textbooks/begg

24.4   Shocks to money demand

In the last three decades, there have been major changes in the structure of the financial sector. Competition between banks has increased dramatically, raising interest rates paid on deposits. Since the opportunity cost of holding money in a bank deposit is only the differential between the deposit interest rate and the higher interest rate available on other financial assets,

Figure 24.5   An unexpected rise in money demand

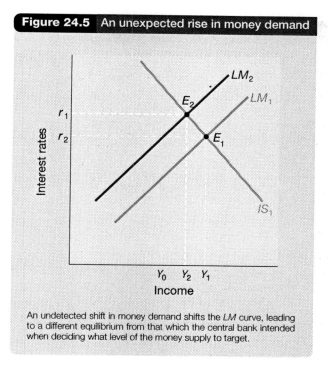

An undetected shift in money demand shifts the *LM* curve, leading to a different equilibrium from that which the central bank intended when deciding what level of the money supply to target.

changes in banking competition change the opportunity cost of holding money *at any market interest rate r*.

We draw an *LM* schedule for a given nominal money target. Greater banking competition raises money demand at every combination of output and interest rates. To keep money demand in line with the unchanged supply, either output must fall or interest rates must rise. The *LM* schedule *shifts* left.

Figure 24.4 showed how changes in money *supply* shift the *LM* schedule under monetary targeting. We have now discovered that changes in money *demand*, other than those caused by changes in output and interest rates, also shift the *LM* schedule under monetary targeting.

In Figure 24.5, LM_1 corresponds to 'low' money demand and LM_2 to 'high' money demand. Suppose money demand increases but the central bank is not yet aware of the change. In choosing what monetary target to set, the central bank is expecting the schedule LM_1 which will place the economy at E_1. In fact, because of the undetected shift in money demand, the actual out-turn is at E_2, not at all what monetary policy intended when it decided what monetary target to set.

In practice, this helps explain why monetary targets were gradually abandoned by many central banks. When money demand was predictable, monetary targets worked fine. As the financial sector has become more sophisticated, more competitive and more volatile, monetary targets were gradually abandoned as the basis for the monetary policy rule.

24.5   The policy mix

Fiscal policy is government decisions about tax rates and spending levels. Changes in fiscal policy shift the *IS* schedule. Changes in monetary policy shift the *LM* schedule.

We now explore consequences of different *IS* and *LM* schedules. Budget deficits can be financed by printing money or by borrowing. In the latter case, there is no short-run connection between monetary and fiscal policy. The government can pursue independent monetary and fiscal policies.

Although both fiscal and monetary policy can alter aggregate demand, the two policies are not interchangeable. They affect aggregate demand through different routes and have different implications for the *composition* of aggregate demand.

Demand management uses monetary and fiscal policy to stabilize output near potential output.

Figure 24.6 shows the mix of monetary and fiscal policy. There are two ways to stabilize income at Y^*. First, there is expansionary or *easy* fiscal policy (high government spending or low tax rates). This leads to a high *IS* schedule, IS_1. To keep income in check with such an expansionary fiscal policy, *tight* monetary policy is needed. With a low money supply target, the schedule LM_1 is far to the left.

Equilibrium at E_1 achieves an output Y^* but also a high interest rate r_1. With high government spending, private demand must be kept in check. The mix of easy fiscal policy and tight

Figure 24.6 The policy mix affects interest rates at any target output

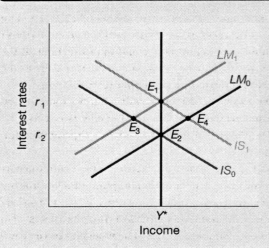

The target income Y can be attained by easy fiscal policy and tight monetary policy. Equilibrium at E_1 the intersection of LM_1 and IS_1, implies high interest rates r_1 and a low share of private sector investment and consumption in GNP. Alternatively, with easy monetary policy and tight fiscal policy, equilibrium at E_2 the intersection of LM_0 and IS_0 still attains the target income but at lower interest rates r_2. The share of private sector investment and consumption in GNP will be higher than at E_1.

BOX 24-3 Monetary *or* fiscal policy?

Box 21.3 noted some reasons why fiscal policy may not be ideal for short-run management of aggregate demand. Some of these reasons – for example, problems in diagnosing where the economy is and forecasting where in might go if policy is left unchanged – apply just as much monetary policy as to fiscal policy. However, two problems are often thought to make fiscal policy less suitable for short-run variation.

First, fiscal policy is difficult to change quickly. Rapid changes in hospital building or in tax rates are more costly than rapid changes in interest rates. Financial markets are used to asset prices changing quickly. Second, it is politically easy to loosen fiscal policy but politically much more difficult to tighten it again later. For this reason, the most important source of short-term movements in fiscal policy is the operation of automatic stabilizers. Since tax rates are not changing, no visible decisions are being made to which voters could object. Yet tax revenue is varying with output.

It used also to be politically difficult to tighten monetary policy. For example, people (voters!) who have borrowed to buy a house get upset when interest rates rise sharply. The main reason that most countries have made their central banks independent of political control in decisions about interest rates is precisely to take the politics out of monetary policy. Nowadays, interest rates can and do change rapidly, in both directions, though usually by very small amounts, as the figure shows.

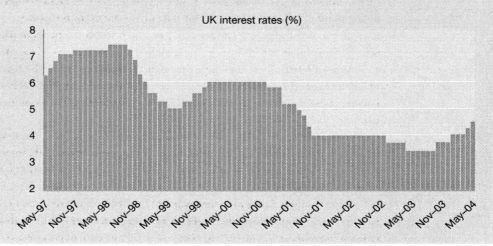

monetary policy implies government spending G is a big share of national income Y^* but private spending $(C + I)$ a small share.

Alternatively, the government can adopt a tight fiscal policy (a low schedule IS_0) and an easy monetary policy (LM_0 far to the right). The target income Y^* is now attained with a lower interest rate r_2 at the equilibrium E_2. With easy monetary policy and tight fiscal policy, the share of private expenditure $(C + I)$ is higher, and the share of government expenditure lower, than at E_1. With lower interest rates, there is less crowding out of private expenditure.

Of course, easy monetary policy *and* easy fiscal policy together are highly expansionary. With the schedules IS_1 and LM_0 the equilibrium in Figure 24.5 is at E_4. Income is well above Y^*. Conversely, with tight monetary policy and tight fiscal policy, and schedules LM_1 and IS_0, equilibrium is at E_3, with income well below Y^*.

What should determine the mix of fiscal and monetary policy? In the long run, the government may care not just about keeping output close to potential output, but about raising potential output. High investment increases the capital stock more quickly, giving workers more equipment with which to work and raising their productivity. Governments interested in long-run growth may choose a tight fiscal policy and an easy monetary policy. Conversely, if governments are politically weak and unable to resist demands for high government spending to pay off various factions, fiscal policy will be loose and a tight monetary policy is needed to keep aggregate demand in line with potential output.

24.6 The effect of future taxes

Chapter 23 argued that consumption demand reflects both *current* disposable income and expected *future* disposable income. Two hundred years ago, the English economist David Ricardo noticed a striking implication. Suppose the path of government purchases G is fixed over time. What path of taxes over time finances this spending?

The government can lend and borrow. In some years, its spending may exceed taxes, in other years taxes must then exceed spending.

Government solvency requires that the present value of the current and future tax revenue equals the present value of current and future spending plus any initial net debts.

For a given planned path of spending, and a suitable planned path of tax revenue, the government cuts taxes this year and pays for it by borrowing. It sells bonds. The tax cut is a fiscal expansion that boosts aggregate demand. Right?

If the tax cut is £1 billion, this is also the value of bonds issued to finance it. The market value of bonds is the present value of future income to bondholders. By assumption, the path of government spending is fixed. Hence, interest payments to bondholders must be financed by higher taxes in the future.

£1 billion is the value of the tax cut, *and* the value of the new bonds, *and* the present value of the extra future taxes. The private sector gets a handout today (a tax cut) offset by a future penalty (higher taxes) of identical present value. The private sector is neither richer nor poorer. Its desired spending should not change. Today's tax cut has no effect on aggregate demand because it is matched by the *prospect* of higher future taxes.

Equivalently, the fall in government saving (larger deficit today) is exactly offset by a rise in private saving: private spending is unaltered and larger disposable incomes (because of the tax cut) go entirely in extra saving (to pay for the future taxes).

Ricardian equivalence says that it does not matter when a government finances a given spending programme. Tax cuts today do not affect private spending if, in present value terms, future taxes rise to match.

Some people getting tax cuts today will die before future taxes arrive. But suppose these people have kids and care about them. After a tax cut today, parents save more to bequeath extra money to their children, or children's children, to pay the higher future taxes. The extra disposable income is saved to raise the bequest for future generations.

Ricardian equivalence does not deny that roadbuilding, financed by higher taxes, affects aggregate demand. Government spending always has real effects. Rather, for a *given* path of real government spending, it may not matter *when* people pay for it. Ricardo himself thought the equivalence hypothesis would not hold in the real world. Economists are still arguing about the extent to which Ricardian equivalence should hold.

Why Ricardian equivalence is too strong

There are three reasons why the tax cuts today *do* stimulate demand a bit even if future taxes are correspondingly higher. First, people without kids get the benefit of tax cuts without paying the full burden of higher future taxes in the distant future. They spend more at once.

Second, by reducing marginal tax rates and distortions, tax cuts may increase potential output and raise income. Expecting higher incomes, people spend more immediately.

Third, solvent governments can borrow at a low interest rate. Ricardian equivalence holds only if we can borrow as easily as the government. If only! Households and firms are riskier than governments. Private people have no residual power to tax or print money when things go wrong. Hence, lenders charge private borrowers a higher rate of interest and may refuse to lend at all.

Now do the sums again. £1 billion is the value of the tax cut, the extra government bonds, and the present value of extra tax payments *discounted at the interest rate faced by the government*. We face a higher interest rate when we try to borrow. *As viewed by us, the present value of our extra future taxes is less than £1 billion because we discount at a higher interest rate.*

The tax cut is a fiscal expansion because in effect the government borrows on the good terms it enjoys, then lends to us at better terms than the capital market. It gives us a loan, tax cuts today, which we repay later in higher taxes. But we are charged the government's low interest rate for our loan. We are better off and spend more. Aggregate demand increases.

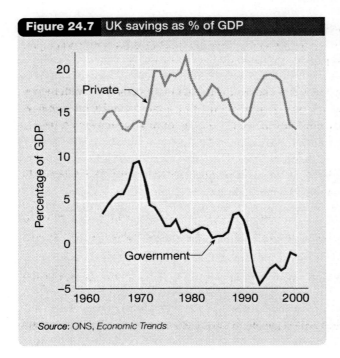

Figure 24.7 UK savings as % of GDP

Source: ONS, *Economic Trends*

Evidence on Ricardian equivalence

Figure 24.7 shows UK evidence on Ricardian equivalence. Does private saving (by firms and households) offset government saving (taxes minus spending)? After financial markets were deregulated in the 1970s, there is *some* negative correlation between private and public saving.

Theory and evidence suggest that complete Ricardian equivalence is too extreme to fit the real world. Tax cuts *do* boost aggregate demand today (though higher future taxes *will* reduce demand at some future date). Ricardian equivalence is not completely right but it is not completely wrong either. Expectations of future conditions affect current behaviour. Private saving rises a bit when public saving falls. The private sector does substitute between present and future, despite obstacles to doing this easily. These obstacles make consumption demand more sensitive to current disposable income than it would be if borrowing was easy and only permanent income mattered.

Current demand by firms and households depends both on current fiscal policy and expected future fiscal policy. Since one does not fully offset the other, for simplicity we can look at current fiscal policy in isolation. We need to remember only that some of its quantitative effects will be smaller if people expect fiscal policy to have to be reversed at some future date.

24.7 Demand management revisited

In the last five chapters we have studied how aggregate demand determines output and employment. Fiscal and monetary policy can manage aggregate demand, aiming to keep the economy close to its full-employment level. In periods of recession, when aggregate demand is insufficient, monetary and fiscal expansion can boost demand, output and employment.

Thus far, we have treated the price level as given. If the price level can change, boosting demand may lead not to higher output but to higher prices. In the next chapter, we begin the study of prices and inflation. In so doing, we introduce aggregate supply, and hence the balance between aggregate supply and aggregate demand.

However, you have now completed the first stage of macroeconomics, learning how to analyse the demand side of the economy. Even after mastering the analysis of supply, adjustment and price behaviour, the demand analysis of the last few chapters remains a key part of the story, especially in the short run.

SUMMARY

● A given fiscal policy means a given path of government spending and tax rates. A given monetary policy must specify the implicit monetary policy rule by which interest rates are set. In this chapter, we assume that is to achieve a given money supply target.

● The IS schedule shows combinations of interest rates and output compatible with short-run equilibrium output in the goods market. Lower interest rates boost demand and output. Other causes of shifts in demand are shown as shifts in the IS schedule.

● The LM schedule shows combinations of interest rates and output compatible with money market equilibrium when the central bank pursues a money supply target. Higher output is associated with higher interest rates to maintain the equality of money supply and money demand.

● The intersection of IS and LM schedules shows simultaneous equilibrium in both goods and money markets, jointly determining output and interest rates.

● With a given monetary policy, a fiscal expansion increases output, money demand and interest rates, thus crowding out or partially displacing private consumption and investment demand.

● For a given fiscal policy, a monetary expansion leads to lower interest rates and higher output.

● The mix of monetary and fiscal policy affects the equilibrium interest rate as well as the level of output.

- ⬤ Ricardian equivalence says that for a given present value of government spending, the private sector does not care *when* this is financed by taxes, since the total present value of taxes is the same. A tax cut today has no effect on aggregate demand since people anticipate higher future taxes to finance the extra debt interest.

- ⬤ Ricardian equivalence is only true under extreme assumptions and not generally true in practice. Hence tax cuts today do have some effect today. This effect is damped by the knowledge that, unless government spending is also cut, future taxes will have to rise.

- ⬤ Demand management helps stabilize output. Fiscal policy may be difficult to adjust quickly, and may be difficult politically to reverse later: much of its impact on aggregate demand thus arises through automatic stabilizers with an unchanged fiscal policy.

REVIEW QUESTIONS

⬤ Why do people usually save a 'once-off income tax rebate'?

⬤ For each of these shocks, say whether it shifts the *IS* schedule, *LM* schedule and in which direction: (a) an expected future fiscal expansion; (b) a higher money supply target; (c) a rise in money demand caused by higher interest rates being paid by banks on bank deposits.

⬤ A small country that has adopted the euro must accept the single interest rate set for the whole of Euroland. Draw the *LM* schedule relating the interest rate to that country's national output. Why would this schedule ever shift?

⬤ Suppose the European Central Bank has a monetary policy rule that relates Euroland's interest rate to total output in Euroland. If the small Euroland country's output is perfectly correlated with the output of all Euroland, draw the *LM* schedule (a) for Euroland, (b) for the small member country.

⬤ **Common fallacies** Why are these following statements wrong? (a) If tax rates never change, fiscal policy cannot stabilize output. (b) Higher government spending makes interest rates rise, which could cut aggregate demand by more than the rise in government spending. (c) Future policy cannot affect present behaviour.

To check your answers to these questions, go to page 642.

To help you grasp the key concepts of this chapter check out the extra resources posted on the Online Learning Centre at www.mcgraw-hill.co.uk/textbooks/begg. There are quick test questions, economics examples and access to Powerweb articles, all for free!

For even more exercises, recaps and examples to help you study, purchase a copy of the Economics Student Workbook. Simply visit www.mcgraw hill.co.uk/textbooks/begg and follow the links to the Workbook to buy your copy.

chapter 25

Aggregate supply, prices and adjustment to shocks

Learning outcomes

By the end of this chapter, you should understand:

1. inflation targets for monetary policy

2. the *ii* schedule

3. the macroeconomic demand schedule *MDS*

4. aggregate supply in the classical model

5. the equilibrium inflation rate

6. complete crowding out in the classical model

7. why wage adjustment may be slow

8. short-run aggregate supply

9. temporary and permanent supply shocks

10. how monetary policy reacts to demand and supply shocks

11. flexible inflation targets

Keynesian models suggest that higher aggregate demand always raises output. However, with only finite resources, the economy cannot expand output indefinitely. We now introduce aggregate supply – firms' willingness and ability to produce – and show how demand and supply together determine output. Aggregate demand reflects the interaction of the markets for goods and money. Aggregate supply reflects the interaction of the markets for goods and labour.

Introducing supply means that we abandon the simplifying assumption that output is determined by demand alone. With both supply and demand, we can also explain what determines prices. We no longer need to assume that prices are given. And since inflation is simply the growth of prices from period to period, a model of prices is also a model of inflation. This allows us to represent monetary policy as inflation targeting, the policy rule actually followed by most central banks today.

To get started, we swap the Keynesian extreme, with fixed wages and prices, for the opposite extreme, full wage and price flexibility.

In the classical model, the economy is *always* at full capacity. Any deviation of output from full capacity causes instant price and wage changes to restore

The **classical model** of macroeconomics assumes wages and prices are completely flexible.

output to potential output. In the classical model, monetary and fiscal policy affect prices but not output, which is always at potential output.

In the short run, until prices and wages adjust, the Keynesian model is relevant. In the long run, once all prices and wages have adjusted, the classical model is relevant. We study how the economy evolves from the Keynesian short run to the classical long run.

25.1 Inflation and aggregate demand

Inflation is the growth rate of the price of aggregate output.

With an **inflation target**, the central bank adjusts interest rates to try to keep inflation close to the target inflation rate.

If a central bank behaves predictably, its behaviour should be modelled. Chapter 24 explained why the growing instability of money demand led central banks to abandon monetary targeting. Nowadays, most central banks pursue an inflation target. Target inflation π^* varies from country to country but is usually around 2 per cent a year. Why not a target of zero inflation? Policy makers are keen to avoid *deflation* (negative inflation) which can become a black hole. Even if the nominal interest rate r is reduced to zero, the real interest rate i, which is simply $(r - \pi)$, can be large if inflation π is large but negative.

In turn, high real interest rates cause further contraction and make inflation more negative still, making real interest rates even higher. If nominal interest rates have already been reduced to zero, monetary policy can do nothing further to combat shrinking aggregate demand. To avoid this black hole, setting a positive inflation target leaves a margin of error. If inflation today is 2 per cent and an unforeseen shock reduces inflation by 1 per cent, there is still time for the central bank to act to boost the economy before it gets too close to a deflationary spiral.

Figure 25.1 shows how monetary policy works when interest rates are set in pursuit of an inflation target. When inflation is high, the central bank ensures that real interest rates are high, which reduces aggregate demand, putting downward pressure on inflation.

With a vertical *ii* schedule, inflation would be completely stabilized at its target rate π^*. If inflation started to rise, real interest rates would be raised by whatever was necessary to restore inflation to its target level. Conversely, if inflation started to fall, real interest rates would be reduced to whatever level it took immediately to restore inflation to target.

Such a monetary policy would be very aggressive. By the end of this chapter, you will understand why some of its side effects would be undesirable. The *ii* schedule shown in Figure 25.1 shows more moderate intervention. When inflation is too high, the central bank raises real interest rates a bit; when inflation is too low, real interest rates are reduced a bit.

Although the central bank is interested in the real interest rate, which affects aggregate demand, the central bank does not directly control the price of output or the inflation rate. Hence, to achieve the *ii* schedule shown in Figure 25.1, the

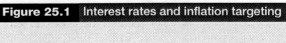

Figure 25.1   Interest rates and inflation targeting

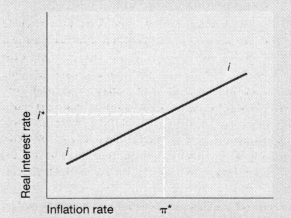

When inflation is above (below) the target π^*, real interest rates are set higher (lower) than normal. Along the schedule *ii*, a given monetary policy is being pursued. If the inflation target is π^*, the corresponding real interest rate will be i^*.

Under inflation targeting, the *ii* schedule shows that at higher inflation rates the central bank will wish to have higher real interest rates.

The central bank sets the **nominal interest rate** r not the **real interest rate** i.

central bank first forecasts inflation, then sets a nominal interest rate r to achieve the real interest rate $i\,(= r - \pi)$ that it desires.

One important implication of Figure 25.1 is that a rise in inflation must lead to a *larger* rise in the nominal interest rate, for only then will the real interest rate be higher when inflation is higher.[1] Merely raising nominal interest rates in line with inflation would mean a constant real interest rate.

We regard a given *ii* schedule as a given monetary policy. Moving along the schedule, the central bank is adjusting interest rates to inflation according to the policy rule already adopted.

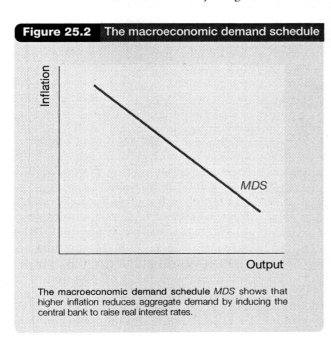

Figure 25.2   The macroeconomic demand schedule

The macroeconomic demand schedule *MDS* shows that higher inflation reduces aggregate demand by inducing the central bank to raise real interest rates.

The macroeconomic demand schedule *MDS* shows how higher inflation induces lower output because a central bank raises interest rates.

Changes in monetary policy are shown by *shifts* in the schedule. A looser monetary policy means a downward shift in the *ii* schedule, a lower interest rate at each possible inflation rate. A tighter monetary policy shifts the *ii* schedule upwards, a higher interest rate at each possible inflation rate.

If π^* is the inflation target, then the chosen height of the *ii* schedule determines the corresponding real interest rate i^* when the inflation target is being met. A tighter monetary policy (higher *ii* schedule) thus implies either accepting a higher real interest rate i^* at the given inflation target π^*, or a lower inflation target π^* at the same real interest rate i^*.

Figure 25.2 shows the level of aggregate demand for output when interest rates obey the *ii* schedule implied by inflation targeting. Movements *along* the macroeconomic demand schedule *MDS* show how inflation makes the central bank alter real interest rates and thus aggregate demand.[2] The *MDS* schedule is flat when (*a*) interest rate decisions react a lot to inflation and (*b*) interest rates have a big effect on aggregate demand. The *MDS* is steep when (*a*) interest rate decisions do not respond much to inflation and (*b*) changes in interest rates have a small effect on aggregate demand.

Shifts in the *MDS* reflect all other shifts in aggregate demand *not* caused by the effect of inflation on interest rate decisions. Thus, *MDS* shifts up if fiscal policy eases, net exports rise or monetary policy eases (a lower *ii* schedule).

The macroeconomic demand schedule relates aggregate demand, output, and inflation. Next we turn to aggregate supply.

---

[1] Across countries, higher inflation is often matched by equally higher nominal interest rates, leaving real interest rates roughly constant. This reflects the relative constancy of i^* in the long run. For short-run data for a single country, nominal interest rates vary more than inflation, reflecting the central bank behaviour embodied in Figure 25.1. Recognizing that interest rates must rise sharply when inflation increases has been a key breakthrough of monetary policy design in the last two decades.

[2] A similar *MDS* schedule exists if the central bank pursues a money supply target instead. For a given path of nominal money M, higher inflation, by raising prices more, reduces the real money supply M/P by more. With lower real money supply, interest rates rise to reduce real money demand and maintain money market equilibrium. Higher real interest rates reduce aggregate demand, just as in Figure 25.2. Under a monetary target, interest rates rise because inflation has reduced the real money supply. Under inflation targeting, interest rates rise in direct response to inflation itself and then the real money supply is then reduced to make this an equilibrium. Either way, higher inflation induces higher real interest rates and lower aggregate demand.

25.2 Aggregate supply

The **aggregate supply schedule** shows the *output* that firms wish to supply at each inflation rate.

At **potential output** all inputs are fully employed. It is long-run equilibrium output.

Money illusion exists if people confuse nominal and real variables.

In the classical model, the **aggregate supply schedule** is vertical at potential output. Equilibrium output is independent of inflation.

When prices and wages are completely flexible, output is always at potential output.

Potential output depends on the level of technology, the quantities of available inputs (labour, capital, land, energy) in long-run equilibrium, and the efficiency with which resources and technology are exploited. In the long run, investment in physical and human capital raises inputs of labour and capital, technical progress improves technology, and supply-side policies reduce distortions and raise efficiency. In the short run, we treat potential output as given.

With flexible wages and prices, how does a rise in inflation (and correspondingly faster growth of nominal wages) affect the incentive of firms to supply goods and services?

Thinking in real terms, firms compare the real wage (the nominal wage W divided by the price level P) with the real benefit of labour, the extra output it makes. Similarly, workers compare real take-home pay (its purchasing power over goods and services) with the disutility of sacrificing more leisure in order to work longer. If wages and prices both double, real wages are unaffected. Neither firms nor workers should change their behaviour. Aggregate supply is unaffected by pure inflation since everything nominal rises by the same proportion, as shown in Figure 25.3.

Figure 25.3 The vertical *AS* schedule

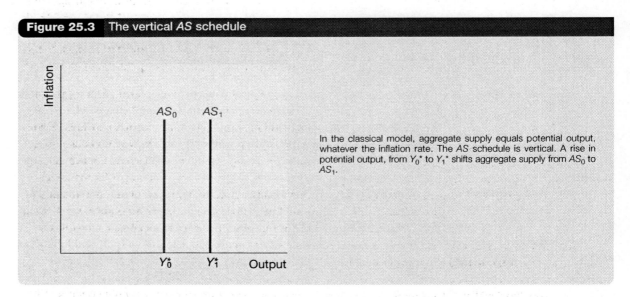

In the classical model, aggregate supply equals potential output, whatever the inflation rate. The *AS* schedule is vertical. A rise in potential output, from Y_0^* to Y_1^* shifts aggregate supply from AS_0 to AS_1.

Wage and price flexibility ensures all nominal variables rise together. Without money illusion, people see through nominal changes: real variables are unaltered. In the classical model, real things determine real things and nominal things determine other nominal things. Better technology, more capital or greater labour supply raise potential output, shifting the vertical supply curve from AS_0 to AS_1 in Figure 25.3. However, for any given level of potential output, lower inflation does *not* reduce the real output that firms wish to supply.

25.3   Equilibrium inflation

For the classical model, Figure 25.4 shows the macroeconomic demand schedule MDS_0 and the vertical aggregate supply schedule AS_0. Output is at potential output and inflation is $\pi_0{}^*$. At point A there is equilibrium in all markets: for output, money and labour.

Figure 25.4   Equilibrium inflation

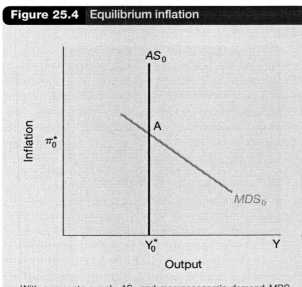

With aggregate supply AS_0 and macroeconomic demand MDS_0, inflation is π_0^* and output is Y_0^*.

The labour market is in equilibrium anywhere on the AS_0 schedule, since the economy is at potential output and full employment. A is also on the macroeconomic demand schedule along which interest rates are adjusted in line with monetary policy and the aggregate demand for goods equals the actual output of goods.

The equilibrium inflation rate $\pi_0{}^*$ reflects the positions of the AS and MDS schedules. Potential output $Y_0{}^*$ reflects technology, efficiency and available input supplies. The macroeconomic demand schedule depends on the IS schedule, showing how interest rates affect aggregate demand, and on the ii schedule of Figure 25.1, showing how interest rates respond to deviations of inflation from its target level.

To ensure that equilibrium inflation $\pi_0{}^*$ coincides with the inflation target π^* the central bank chooses the correct height of the ii schedule in Figure 25.1, thereby ensuring the MDS schedule has the correct height to make equilibrium inflation $\pi_0{}^*$

BOX 25-1   Anchors away!

When prices can change, monetary policy must anchor all nominal variables.

> A nominal anchor determines the *level* of other nominal variables. Market forces determine real variables.

Suppose the interest rate r is simply constant. In the classical model, output is Y^*. Y^* and r determine money demand M/P. Nominal money M is passively supplied to get the right level of real money M/P. If the market imagines prices P will be larger, the Bank supplies more nominal money M to maintain equilibrium M/P. Since prices are completely flexible, *any* price level can be the equilibrium price level! The economy has no nominal anchor, no starting point.

A target for nominal money M is one nominal anchor. Money demand determines M/P but, with M now known, the market knows where to set P. An

inflation target is an alternative nominal anchor. Given *last* period's price level, now known and unalterable, an inflation target for the price increase between last period and this period is also a target for the current price level P. With money demand M/P and the price level P now known, money market equilibrium determines M. Later we show a nominal exchange rate can also act as a nominal anchor.

Price level or inflation rate?

Since last period's price level is now known, statements about today's inflation π are equivalent to statements about today's price level P. All the diagrams in this chapter could be drawn with P rather than π on the vertical axis. We prefer to show inflation for two reasons. First, it fits more easily with inflation targeting, the actual policy of modern central banks. Second, it has a clearer link to the Phillips curve in the following chapter.

coincide with the target inflation rate π^*. If π_0^* is too low, the central bank loosens monetary policy, shifting the ii schedule down and the MDS schedule up. If π_0^* exceeds the inflation target, a tighter monetary policy shifts the ii schedule up and the MDS schedule down.

A supply shock

Monetary policy accommodates a permanent supply change by altering the real interest rate (shift in the ii schedule) to induce a similar change in aggregate demand.

Supply shocks may be beneficial, such as technical progress, or may be adverse, such as higher real oil prices or loss of capacity after an earthquake. Suppose potential output rises. In Figure 25.5 the AS schedule shifts to the right, from AS_0 to AS_1. For a *given* MDS schedule, equilibrium inflation falls to π^*_2 with a equilibrium at D.

However, the central bank still wants a long-run equilibrium inflation rate π^*_0. Hence, in response to the supply shock, the central bank loosens monetary policy, shifting the ii schedule downwards and the MDS schedule upwards.

Lower real interest rates boost aggregate demand in line with higher potential output Y_1^*. The new equilibrium is at C not D. With unchanged inflation, the lower real interest rate also implies a lower nominal interest rate.

Lower interest rates raise the demand for money. To restore money market equilibrium, the central bank must then supply more money. Conversely, if high oil prices permanently reduce aggregate supply, shifts AS_1 to AS_0. Beginning at point C, the central bank must then tighten monetary policy, so that higher real interest rates reduce aggregate demand in line with the lower aggregate supply.

Figure 25.5   A supply shock

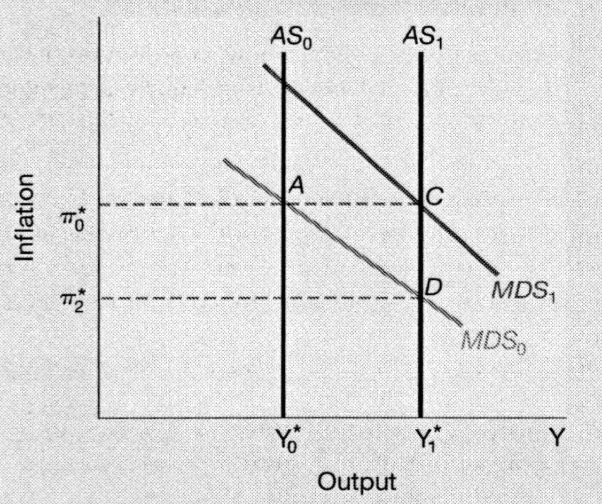

With aggregate supply AS_0 and macroeconomic demand MDS_0, inflation is π_0^* and output is Y_0^*. A rise in supply shifts aggregate supply from AS_0 to AS_1. The central bank accommodates this extra supply, reducing i^* in order to shift demand to MDS, thus maintaining equilibrium inflation at π^*_0. Equilibrium then shifts from A to C.

A demand shock

Suppose aggregate demand shifts up because of easier fiscal policy or greater private sector optimism about future incomes and profits. Beginning from equilibrium at A in Figure 25.6, but keeping supply fixed at AS_0, a demand shift from MDS_0 to MDS_1 leads to a new equilibrium at B.

The central bank can continue to hit its inflation target π_0^* only by tightening monetary policy to offset the demand shock. In full equilibrium, with unchanged supply AS_0, aggregate demand must not change. By raising real interest rates, the central bank can reduce aggregate demand again. The central bank thus tightens monetary policy (upward shift in ii schedule) until the demand shock is fully offset and MDS_1 has shifted down to MDS_0 again. Equilibrium remains at A and the inflation target π_0^* is still achieved.

In the classical model with a vertical AS schedule, a rise in government spending crowds out an equal amount of private spending. Aggregate demand remains equal to potential output.

The original rise in demand could have come from the private or the public sector. If it was higher private demand, the higher real interest rate simply reduces private demand back to its original level. If it was higher government spending, the central bank raises interest rates until private spending falls by as much as government spending increased.

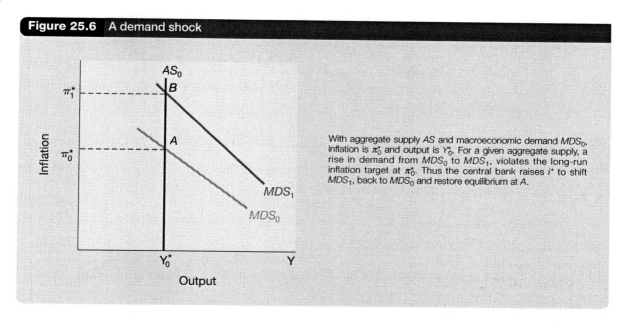

Figure 25.6 A demand shock

With aggregate supply *AS* and macroeconomic demand MDS_0, inflation is π_0^* and output is Y_0^*. For a given aggregate supply, a rise in demand from MDS_0 to MDS_1, violates the long-run inflation target at π_0^*. Thus the central bank raises i^* to shift MDS_1, back to MDS_0 and restore equilibrium at *A*.

Note the distinction between partial crowding out in the Keynesian model and complete crowding out in the classical model. In the Keynesian model, output was demand-determined in the short run. Higher *output* induced the central bank to raise interest rates, which partly offset the expansionary effect of higher government spending.

In the classical model, aggregate supply is the binding constraint. Output does not change. When higher government expenditure raises aggregate demand, higher interest rates must reduce consumption and investment to leave aggregate demand unaltered.

We may draw a second conclusion from Figure 25.6. Suppose monetary policy changes because the inflation target in raised from π_0^* to π_1^*.

With a higher target inflation rate, the central bank no longer needs such high real interest rates at any particular level of inflation. Real interest rates fall and the macroeconomic demand schedule shifts up from MDS_0 to MDS_1. With an unchanged *AS* schedule, equilibrium moves from *A* to *B*.

In the new equilibrium, inflation is higher but real output is unaltered. Since it is a full equilibrium, all real variables are then constant. One of these variables is the real money stock M/P.

Since prices grow at the rate π_1^*, the nominal money supply must also grow at this rate.

> In the classical model, faster nominal money growth is accompanied by higher inflation but leaves real output constant at potential output.

The idea that nominal money growth is associated with inflation, but not growth of output or employment, is the central tenet of *Monetarists*. Figure 25.6 shows this is correct in the classical model with full wage and price flexibility and no money illusion.

How long does this all take?

The classical model studies the economy once all variables have fully adjusted. Instead of thinking of adjustment as instant, we can view the classical model as applying to a long enough time for slower adjustment to be completed. This means not just wage and price adjustment, but time for the central bank to work out what is going on and amend monetary policy if necessary, and time for these interest rate changes to have their full effect on private behaviour. Suppose the economy faces a fall in aggregate demand. What happens next?

The classical model

With aggregate supply unaffected, a fall in aggregate demand leads to lower inflation, to which the central bank immediately responds by easing monetary policy, reducing the real interest rate, boosting private sector demand and thus restoring aggregate demand to the unchanged level of potential output.[3]

The Keynesian model

Before wage and price adjustment is possible, there is no change in inflation to which the central bank can respond. The initial effect of lower aggregate demand is a simply a fall in output. The rest of this chapter studies the adjustment process by which the economy gradually makes the transition from the Keynesian short run to the classical long run. To do so, we introduce the short-run aggregate supply curve.

 **Now you've read this section,** why not test your understanding by visiting the Online Learning Centre at www.mcgraw-hill.co.uk/textbooks/begg

25.4   The labour market and wage behaviour

Downward shocks cause recessions lasting years not weeks. Why don't changes in prices restore potential output faster? Firms relate prices to costs. Wages are the largest part of costs. Sluggish wage adjustment to departures from full employment is main cause of slow adjustment of prices.

For both firms and workers, a job is often a long-term commitment. For the firm, it is costly to hire and fire workers. Firing entails a redundancy payment and the loss of the expertise the worker had built up on the job. Hiring entails advertising, interviewing and training a new worker in the special features of that firm. Firms are reluctant to hire and fire workers just because of short-term fluctuations in demand.

For the worker, looking for a new job costs time and effort and throws away experience, seniority, and the high wages justified by the high productivity that comes from having mastered a particular job in a particular firm. Like firms, workers care about long-term arrangements. Firms and workers reach an understanding about pay and conditions *in the medium term*, including how to handle fluctuations in the firm's output in the short run.

A firm and its workers have explicit contracts, or implicit agreements, specifying working conditions. These include normal hours, overtime requirements, regular wages and pay schedules for overtime work. The firm then sets the number of hours, within the limits of these conditions, depending on how much output it wishes to make in that week.

When demand falls, the firm initially reduces hours of work. Overtime ends and factories close early. If demand does not recover, or declines further, firms start firing workers. Conversely,

---

[3] A similar analysis applies under monetary targeting. Suppose this is 2 per cent annual growth in nominal money. Long run inflation will also be 2 per cent. A fall in aggregate demand bids down wage and price growth *below what they would have been*. With inflation below 2 per cent but an unchanged nominal money growth of 2 per cent, the real money supply expands. This causes a fall in real interest rates and boosts aggregate demand back to potential output. Thereafter, money and prices both grow at 2 per cent. The real money supply is permanently higher and real interest rates permanently lower.

BOX 25-2   Altogether now . . . A global boom at last appears to be under way . . .

Fed up with economic doom-mongers? In the third quarter of 2003, the world economy grew at its fastest pace for two decades. Much of this was due to the impressive lift-off in America, whose GDP grew at an annual rate of 7.2 per cent. But by no means all of it: the recent recovery has been truly global, with most economies picking up speed.

Japan finally pulled out of a decade of deflation,

recording its seventh consecutive quarter of positive ouput growth. The euro area grew by 1.6 per cent. But the stunning growth came from emerging economies. China's GDP rose at an annual rate of 18 per cent in the third quarter, seasonally adjusted; Singapore's grew by 17 per cent, and Taiwan's by 24 per cent

Adapted from *The Economist*, 20 November 2003.

in a boom a firm makes its existing workforce work overtime. Then it seeks temporary workers to supplement the existing labour force. Only when the firm is sure that higher sales will be sustained does it hire extra permanent workers.

Wage adjustment

Wages are not set in a daily auction in which the equilibrium wage clears the market for labour. Firms and workers both gain from long-term understandings. This mutual commitment partly insulates a firm and its workforce from temporary conditions in the labour market.

Nor can a firm and its workforce spend every day haggling. Bargaining is costly, using up valuable time that could be used to produce output. Bargaining costs mean wages change only at discrete intervals. Immediate wage adjustment to shocks is ruled out. At best, firms must wait until the next scheduled date for a revision in the wage structure. In practice, complete wage adjustment is unlikely to take place even then. Chapter 10 discussed other reasons why involuntary unemployment is not instantly eliminated by wage adjustment.

Recap

In the short run (the first few months), changes in labour input are largely changes in hours. In the medium run (up to two years), as changes in labour demand persist, the firm begins to alter its permanent workforce. In the long run (perhaps four to six years), adjustment is complete.

In the short run, trends in wages are largely given. The firm has some flexibility over earnings, as distinct from negotiated wage rates, because fluctuations in overtime and short time affect average hourly earnings. But this flexibility is limited. In the medium run, the firm begins to adjust the path of wages. In the long run, the process is complete and the economy is back at potential output.

We now use this analysis to think about the market for output. By distinguishing supply in the short run and the long run, our model of output reflects *both* supply and demand, even in the short run. Nevertheless, its short run behaviour is like the simple Keynesian case in which output is demand determined. Its long-run behaviour is fully classical.

25.5   Short-run aggregate supply

In Figure 25.7 the economy is at potential output at A. In the short run, the firm inherits a given rate of nominal wage growth (not shown in the figure). Previous wage negotiations anticipated remaining in long-run equilibrium at A with inflation π_0. By keeping up with inflation,

The **short-run supply curve** *SAS* shows how desired output varies with inflation, for a given inherited growth of nominal wages.

nominal wage growth expected to maintain the correct real wage for labour market equilibrium.

If inflation exceeds the expected inflation rate π_0, this helps firms by raising their output prices. The real wage is lower than expected. If this had been foreseen when wages were negotiated, the inherited nominal wage would have been higher – but it was not foreseen. Firms take advantage of their good luck by supplying a lot more output. They can afford to pay overtime to ensure that the workforce co-operates, and may also take on temporary extra staff.

Conversely, if inflation is below π_0, the real wage is now higher than anticipated when the nominal wage was agreed. Since labour is now costly, firms cut back output a lot. They move from A to B in Figure 25.7. Firms move along the supply schedule *SAS* in the short run.

If demand and output remain low, the growth rate of negotiated nominal wages gradually falls. With lower wage growth, firms do not need to raise output prices so quickly. The short-run aggregate supply schedule shifts down from *SAS* to *SAS₁* in Figure 25.7. Lower inflation moves the economy down its macroeconomic demand schedule, increasing the demand for goods. If full employment and potential output are still not restored, negotiated wage growth falls again, leading to a short-run aggregate supply schedule such as *SAS₂*.

These short-run aggregate supply schedules give a realistic picture of adjustment to demand shocks. Because the short-run aggregate supply schedule is flat, a shift in aggregate demand leads mainly to changes in output, not prices, in the short run. This is the Keynesian feature. But deviations from full employment gradually change wage growth and short-run aggregate supply. The economy gradually works its way back to potential output. That is the classical feature. We now describe adjustment in more detail.

Figure 25.7 Short-run aggregate supply

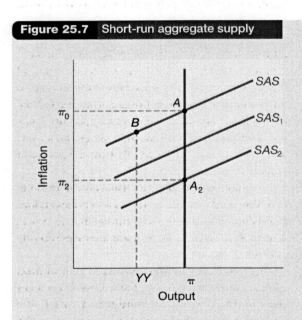

Firms raise prices when wage costs rise. Each short-run aggregate supply schedule reflects a different rate of inherited nominal wage growth. For any given rate, higher inflation moves firms up a given short-run supply schedule. A persisting boom or slump gradually bids nominal wage growth up or down, shifting short-run aggregate supply schedules. When these shift enough to restore to the rate at which *MDS* and *AS* intersect, potential output is restored.

25.6 The adjustment process

We now combine the macroeconomic demand schedule with the short-run aggregate supply schedule to show how demand or supply shocks set up an adjustment process. In combining the *MDS* and *SAS* schedules, we assume that the goods market clears, even in the short run. Short-run aggregate supply gradually changes over time as wage growth adjusts to the rate that restores full employment and potential output, placing firms eventually on their long-run aggregate supply schedule.

Output is no longer demand-determined when aggregate demand lies below the level of potential output. In the short run, firms are also on their short-run supply schedules producing what they wish, *given the inherited nominal wages*.

However, sluggish wage adjustment prevents immediate restoration of full employment. When aggregate demand for goods falls, firms reduce output and employment. Since wages do not fall at once, there is involuntary unemployment. *Employment* is demand-determined in the short run.

Figure 25.8 shows a downward shift in the macroeconomic demand schedule from *MDS* to *MDS'* because monetary policy is tightened (a higher *ii* schedule in Figure 25.1). In the long run, aggregate demand must return to potential output and the economy will end up at E_3. Hence, the tighter monetary policy can be viewed as a cut in the target inflation rate from π^* to π_3^*.

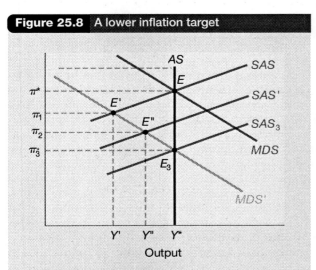

Figure 25.8   A lower inflation target

Beginning at *E*, a lower inflation target shifts *MDS* to *MDS'*. Given inherited wage growth, the new equilibrium is at *E'*. Output falls from Y^* to Y', and actual inflation is only π_1. Since wages have risen faster than prices despite the fall in output, unemployment rises. In the next wage settlement, nominal wage growth slows, and the short-run supply schedule becomes *SAS'*. Equilibrium is now at *E''*, and output recovers to Y''. Once wage growth slows enough to make SAS_3 the supply curve, long-run equilibrium is re-established at E_3.

When monetary policy is first tightened, interest rates are initially raised since actual inflation at *E* is now above target. Macroeconomic demand shifts down to *MDS'*. In the classical model there is an instant adjustment of prices and wages to keep the economy at full employment and potential output. Equilibrium inflation immediately falls to π_3^* and the new equilibrium is at E_3. Output remains at potential output Y^*.

These classical results are valid only in the long run. When adjustment of wages and prices is slow, the economy faces the short-run aggregate supply schedule *SAS*, reflecting the nominal wages recently agreed.

In the short run, the downward shift in *MDS* causes a move from *E* to *E'*. Since firms cannot cut costs much, they reduce output to Y'. At *E'* the goods market clears at the intersection of the demand schedule *MDS'* and the supply schedule *SAS*. Inflation has fallen a little because of lower demand but output has fallen a lot. With lower inflation than the expectation built into nominal wage agreements, *real wages have risen*, despite the fall in output. Once firms can adjust employment, some workers are fired and unemployment rises.

In the medium run, this starts to reduce wage growth. With inherited wages lower than they would have been, firms move on to a lower short-run aggregate supply schedule *SAS'*. The goods market now clears at *E''*. Output and employment recover a bit, but some unemployment persists. Since inflation has fallen, the central bank is less worried about the amount by which inflation exceeds its new target, and cuts real interest rates, moving the economy down *MDS'* to *E''*.

In the long run, adjustment is complete. Wage growth and inflation fall to π_3^*. The short-run aggregate supply schedule is SAS_3 in Figure 25.8. The economy is in full equilibrium at the E_3, on *AS*, *SAS*, and *MDS'*. Output is Y^* and the labour market is back at full employment.

The real world lies between the extreme simplifications of the simple Keynesian model and classical models. In practice, prices and wages are neither fully flexible nor fully fixed. A tougher inflation target has real effects in the short run, since output and employment are reduced. But after wages and prices adjust fully, output and employment return to normal. Inflation is permanently lower thereafter.

| BOX 25-3 | Output gaps 1980–2004 |

The output gap (Y–Y*) is the percentage deviation of actual output Y from potential output Y*. Each year the Paris-based Organization for Economic Cooperation and Development (OECD) estimates potential output for all its member countries. The charts below show estimates for the UK, Germany and Finland. Positive output gaps are booms, negative gaps indicate slumps.

The diagram shows the UK slump in the early 1980s, as the Thatcher government cut back demand to reduce inflation; the Lawson boom of the mid-1980s that led to renewed inflation; the Major recession in the early 1990s as policy was tightened to cut inflation again; and recovery after 1993. It confirms the switch to inflation targeting after 1992 has generally led to a more stable macroeconomy.

Germany also had a slump in the early 1980s as it fought inflation from the second oil shock. In 1990, German unification gave a massive fiscal expansion as investment in East Germany drained the West German budget. High interest rates were needed to reduce

inflation, so demand then fell sharply. We also show Finland, whose exports rose after the opening of trade with Russia, but then collapsed as the former Soviet Union imploded. Since the mid–1990s, Finland has made a strong recovery, helped by hi-tech firms like Nokia.

25.7 Sluggish adjustment to shocks

| Figure 25.9 | A permanent supply increase |

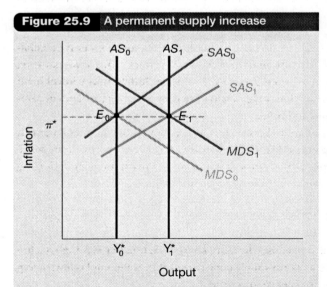

A permanent rise in supply shifts AS_0 and SAS_0 to AS_1. By permanently reducing interest rates, the central bank shifts MDS_0 to MDS_1, meeting its inflation target π^* in the new equilibrium at E_1. If the central bank acts quickly, no further shifts in SAS_1 are required.

A permanent supply shock

Suppose a change in attitudes towards women working leads to an increase in labour supply. Potential output rises. In the long run, aggregate demand must rise in line with aggregate supply. Lower real interest rates allow higher aggregate demand at the unchanged inflation target π^*. Provided monetary policy is loosened, the rightward shift in MDS can match the rightward shift in aggregate supply. By accommodating the extra supply with looser monetary policy, the inflation rate remains π^* and the economy moves directly to the new long-run equilibrium, from E_0 to E_1 in Figure 25.9.

Because of lags in diagnosing the shock, and in the response of consumption and investment demand to lower interest rates, Figure 25.9 exaggerates the ease of adjustment to a permanent supply shock. In practice, output may not jump all the way to the new level of potential output.

If the macroeconomic demand schedule does not fully and immediately shift to MDS_1, output is below Y^*_1. This reduces inflation and the central bank responds with lower interest rates. Over time, the macroeconomic demand schedule will drift to the right until it reaches MDS_1 in Figure 25.9.

A temporary supply shock

A temporary supply shock leaves potential output unaffected in the long run. With the vertical AS schedule unaltered, the short-run supply curve must shift. Although the SAS schedule is *mainly* influenced by inherited nominal wages, it is *also* affected by other input prices. Suppose a temporary oil price rise makes firms charge higher prices at any output level. Figure 25.10 shows a shift upwards in short-run supply, from SAS to SAS'. The new short-run equilibrium is at E'. Inflation rises but output and employment fall because the central bank raises real interest rates in response to higher inflation.

If the central bank maintains its inflation target π^*, lower output and employment at E' gradually reduce inflation and nominal wage growth, shifting SAS' gradually back to SAS. The economy slowly moves down the MDS schedule back to the original equilibrium at E.

A different outcome is possible. When the higher oil prices shifts SAS to SAS', it is possible to *avoid* the period of low output as the economy moves along MDS from E' back to E. A *change* in monetary policy can *shift MDS* up enough to pass through E''. Output can quickly return to potential output but only because the inflation target[4] has been loosened from π^* to $\pi^{*\prime\prime}$. The new long-run new equilibrium is then at E''.

A central bank caring a lot about output stability may accommodate short-run supply shocks, even if this means higher inflation. A central bank caring more about its inflation target than about output stability will not accommodate temporary supply shocks.

It matters a lot whether the supply shock is temporary or permanent. If potential output is *permanently* affected, aggregate demand *must* eventually rise to match. Once a supply side shock is diagnosed as permanent, it should be accommodated.

A **permanent supply shock** changes potential output. A **temporary supply shock** shifts the short-run aggregate supply schedule but leaves potential output unaltered.

Monetary policy accommodates a temporary supply shock when monetary policy is altered to help stabilize output. The consequence, however, is higher inflation.

Figure 25.10   A temporary supply shock

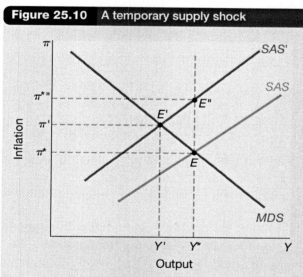

Higher oil prices force firms to raise prices. In the short-run, SAS shifts up to SAS', and equilibrium shifts from E to E'. Higher inflation reduces aggregate demand since the central bank raises real interest rates. Once the temporary supply shock disappears, SAS' gradually falls back to SAS, and eventual equilibrium is restored at E.

Demand shocks

Figure 25.11 explores demand shocks *not* caused by monetary policy. If demand is high, facing MDS' the economy moves along its short-run supply curve to point A. If demand is low, facing MDS'' the economy moves along the SAS curve to point B.

[4] Looser monetary policy shifts the *ii* schedule to the right in Figure 25.1. However, once long-run equilibrium is restored i^* must be unaltered: since aggregate supply is eventually unaltered, aggregate demand cannot eventually change. The only way for the central bank to loosen monetary policy without changing i^* is to accept a higher inflation target π^*.

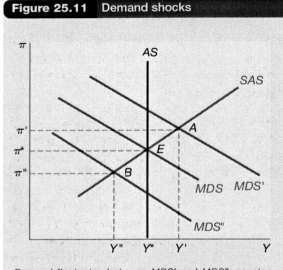

Figure 25.11 Demand shocks

Demand fluctuates between *MDS′* and *MDS″*, causing fluctuations in output and inflation. If the central bank can react quickly, it can offset demand shocks by changing *i** to shift demand back to *MDS*. Stabilizing inflation at π^* has the effect of stabilizing output at *Y**.

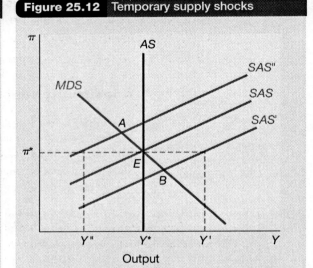

Figure 25.12 Temporary supply shocks

Output

Short-run supply fluctuates between *SAS′* and *SAS″*. If interest rates are set to stabilize inflation at π^*, output fluctuates between *Y′* and *Y″*. Monetary policy cannot stabilize both output and inflation in response to supply shocks. It makes sense to set interest rates to allow some inflation fluctuations in order to reduce output a bit. For the Taylor rule implied by *MDS* the economy fluctuates between points *A* and *B*. A flatter *MDS* schedule would imply smaller inflation fluctuations but larger fluctuations in output.

Suppose the central bank diagnoses that an expansionary demand shock has occurred. It can tighten monetary policy and shift *MDS′* back down to *MDS* again. Similarly, it can loosen monetary policy in response to low aggregate demand *MDS″*, restoring *MDS* again. The economy remains at *E*. Both inflation *and* output are stabilized.

It is easy for the central bank to tell where inflation is relative to its target rate. It is harder to estimate the level of potential output, which can change over time. This is part of the modern case for using inflation targeting as the intermediate target of monetary policy. When all shocks are demand shocks, it works perfectly.

> When all shocks are demand shocks, stabilizing inflation also stabilizes output, even in a Keynesian model.

Suppose instead, that all shocks are supply shocks. Figure 25.12 shows the long-run supply curve *AS*, vertical at potential output *Y**, and a set of short-run supply curves whose average level is *SAS* but which fluctuate between *SAS′* and *SAS″*

On average, output is *Y** and inflation is π^*. If interest rates are varied very aggressively to stabilize inflation in the face of supply shocks, the *MDS* schedule is effectively horizontal at π^*. Inflation is stabilized, but output fluctuates between *Y′* and *Y″* when supply fluctuates between *SAS′* and *SAS″*. Unlike the case of demand shocks, it is no longer possible to stabilize output *and* inflation.

Similarly, it is possible to stabilize output completely but only at the cost of allowing big fluctuations in inflation. The *MDS* schedule is then vertical at potential output. A rise in short-run supply to *SAS′* induces a big rise in interest rates to reduce aggregate demand to *Y** again. With high supply but low demand, inflation is temporarily low (relative to inherited wage growth) and firms wish to supply only *Y**. When supply shrinks temporarily to *SAS″*, firms supply output *Y** only if inflation is high (relative to inherited wage growth), which needs a low interest rate to boost demand.

25.8 Tradeoffs in monetary objectives

Facing supply shocks, Figure 25.12 implies that it is a bad idea either to stabilize inflation completely at π^* (which induces big fluctuations in output) or to stabilize output at Y^* (which induces big fluctuations in inflation). The macroeconomic demand schedule MDS in Figure 25.12 is a particular compromise in the way interest rates are set.[5]

Any MDS schedule through point E achieves the targets π^* and Y^* on average. The particular schedule MDS in Figure 25.12 makes the economy fluctuate between A (when supply is SAS″) and B (when supply is SAS′). This achieves acceptable fluctuations in both output and inflation. A steeper MDS schedule, still through A, induces lower output fluctuations but larger inflation fluctuations. A flatter schedule has the opposite effect. The steepness of the schedule reflects the relative weight the central bank places on stabilizing inflation and output.

This tradeoff does not arise for demand shocks. Figure 25.11 showed that, by fully offsetting demand shocks, the central bank stabilizes both output and prices. In reality, the central bank faces both supply and demand shocks, and cannot always diagnose which is which. It must choose a monetary rule that gives reasonable answers under both kinds of shocks.

Flexible inflation targeting commits a central bank to hit inflation targets in the medium run but gives it some discretion about *how quickly* to hit its inflation target.

There is no conflict between output stability and inflation stability when shocks are demand shocks. It makes sense to try to hit the target as quickly as possible. Similarly, a permanent supply shock requires a permanent change in demand, which there is little reason to postpone. However, facing a *temporary supply shock*, Figure 25.12 shows that it makes sense temporarily to allow inflation to deviate from its target in order to mitigate the shock to output.

The *ii* schedule in Figure 25.1 reflects the average behaviour of the central bank under flexible inflation targeting. Deviations of inflation from target are not all immediately eliminated, but they are eventually eliminated by the policy of raising (lowering) real interest rates whenever inflation is too high (low). Temporary deviations of inflation from target are the price to be paid for ensuring that output fluctuations are not too large.

The key to successful flexible inflation targeting is that any deviation of inflation from target should be *temporary*. Credible central banks persist with high interest rates until inflation is restored to its target rate. And when credible central banks reduce interest to boost demand, nobody fears that the inflation target has been increased, and there is no reason for nominal wage bargains to fear a permanent rise in inflation.

In contrast, weak central banks that lack credibility may cause panic by easing monetary policy today. People worry that they will not be tough enough later to reverse this demand expansion. Foreseeing sustained expansion, inflation gets going. This insight places credibility centre stage, where it belongs. Chapter 26 examines the economics of credibility and its effect on inflation.

---

[5] And this finally explains why in Figure 25.1 the central bank does not simply choose a vertical *ii* schedule at the target inflation rate. When adjustment is sluggish and supply shocks occur, this would imply big swings in output.

SUMMARY

- The classical model of macroeconomics assumes full flexibility of wages and prices and no money illusion.

- The *ii* schedule shows, under a policy of inflation targeting, how the central bank achieves high interest rates when inflation is high and low interest rates when inflation is low. Central banks set nominal not real interest rates, and hence must first forecast inflation in order to calculate what nominal interest rate they wish to set.

- The *ii* schedule shifts to the left, a higher real interest rate at each inflation rate, when monetary policy is tightened, and to the right, a lower real interest rate at each inflation rate, when monetary policy is loosened.

- The macroeconomic demand schedule shows how higher inflation reduces aggregate demand by inducing monetary policy to raise real interest rates.

- The classical model always has full employment. The aggregate supply schedule is vertical at potential output. Equilibrium inflation is at the intersection of the aggregate supply schedule and the macroeconomic demand schedule. The markets for goods, money and labour are all in equilibrium. Monetary policy is set to make the equilibrium inflation rate coincide with the inflation target.

- In the classical model, fiscal expansion cannot increase output. To continue to hit its inflation target, the central bank must raise real interest rates to restore aggregate demand to the level of potential output. Higher government spending crowds out an equal amount of private spending, leaving demand and output unaltered.

- Changing the target inflation rate leads to an equivalent change in the growth of wages and nominal money in the classical model, but not to a change in output.

- In practice, wages adjust slowly to shocks since job arrangements are long term. Wage adjustment is sluggish not merely because wage bargaining is infrequent, but because workers prefer their long-term employers to smooth wages.

- Prices mainly reflect labour costs. The short-run aggregate supply schedule shows firms' desired output, given the inherited growth of nominal wages. Output is temporarily responsive to inflation, since nominal wages are already determined. As wage adjustment occurs, the short-run supply schedule shifts.

- The Keynesian model is a good guide to short-term behaviour but the classical model describes behaviour in the long run.

- Permanent supply shocks alter potential output. Temporary supply shocks merely alter the short-run supply curve for a while.

- If its effects were instant, monetary policy could completely offset demand shocks, stabilizing both inflation and output. Temporary supply shocks force a trade-off between output stability and inflation stability. The output effect of permanent supply shocks cannot be escaped indefinitely.

446 Part 4 : Macroeconomics

● Flexible inflation targeting implies the central bank need not immediately hit its inflation target, allowing some scope for temporary action to cushion output fluctuations.

REVIEW QUESTIONS

● (a) Define the macroeconomic demand schedule. (b) How does a fiscal expansion affect the schedule under a flexible inflation target? (c) How would the central bank have to change monetary policy to hit its given inflation target in the long run?

● Suppose opportunities for investing in high tech applications boost aggregate demand in the short run, but aggregate supply in the long run. Using *AS* and *MDS* schedules, show why output might rise *without* much inflation.

● How do the following affect the short-run supply schedule, and hence output and inflation in the short run: (a) a higher tax rate; (b) higher labour productivity?

● An economy has the choice of having half its workers make annual wage agreements every January, and the other half make annual wage agreements every July, or instead forcing everyone to make their annual agreement on 1 July. Which system is likely to induce greater wage flexibility (a) during a period of a few months (b) during a period of several years?

● OPEC raises the price of oil for a year but then a new supply of oil from Russia bids oil prices back down again. Contrast the evolution of the economy if monetary follows (a) a fixed interest rate, (b) flexible inflation targeting, (c) a nominal money target.

● **Common fallacies** Why are these statements wrong? (a) Fiscal expansion can increase output for ever. (b) Higher inflation always reduces output.

To check your answers to these questions, go to page 642.

Online LearningCentre with POWERWEB

To help you grasp the key concepts of this chapter check out the extra resources posted on the Online Learning Centre at www.mcgraw-hill.co.uk/textbooks/begg. There are quick test questions, economics examples and access to Powerweb articles, all for free!

For even more exercises, recaps and examples to help you study, purchase a copy of the Economics Student Workbook. Simply visit www.mcgraw hill.co.uk/textbooks/begg and follow the links to the Workbook to buy your copy.

chapter 26

Inflation, expectations and credibility

Learning outcomes

By the end of this chapter, you should understand:

1. the quantity theory of money

2. how nominal interest rates reflect inflation

3. seigniorage, the inflation tax and why hyperinflations occur

4. when budget deficits cause money growth

5. the Phillips curve

6. the costs of inflation

7. central bank independence and inflation control

8. how the Monetary Policy Committee sets UK interest rates

On its election in 1997 the Labour government made the Bank of England independent, with a mandate to achieve low inflation.

> Inflation is a rise in the price level. Pure inflation means that prices of goods and inputs rise at the same rate.

Sustained inflation is a recent phenomenon. Before 1950, prices rose in some years but fell in other years. The UK price level was no higher in 1950 than in 1920. Figure 26.1 shows that the UK price level fell sharply in some interwar years when inflation was negative. The postwar price level has never fallen. Since 1950 the price level has risen 20-fold, more than its rise over the previous three centuries. This story applies in most advanced economies.

The effects of inflation depend on what causes it. We start with the causes of inflation, then examine its effects, which partly depend on whether inflation was anticipated or took people by surprise. We contrast costs that inflation imposes on individuals and costs it imposes on society as a whole. We conclude by considering what the government can do about inflation.

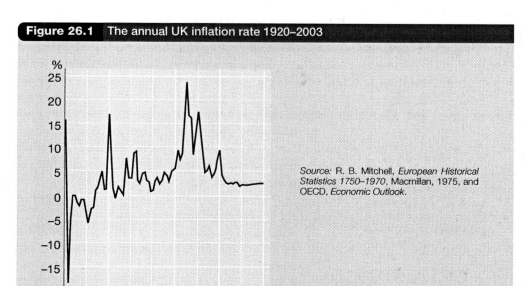

Figure 26.1 The annual UK inflation rate 1920–2003

Source: R. B. Mitchell, *European Historical Statistics 1750–1970*, Macmillan, 1975, and OECD, *Economic Outlook*.

26.1 Money and inflation

There is a link between nominal money and prices, and thus between nominal money growth and inflation.

> The real money supply M/P is the nominal money supply M divided by the price level P.

People demand money because of its purchasing power over goods. They demand *real* money. When real income is Y and the interest rate is r, the symbol $L(Y, r)$ shows the stock of real money demanded. This rises with real income Y, since the benefit of holding money increases. It falls with the interest rate r, since the cost of holding money is higher.

$$M/P = L(Y, r) \tag{1}$$

BOX 26-1 The quantity theory of money: MV = PY

The velocity of circulation V is nominal income PY divided by nominal money M. If prices adjust to keep real output at potential output Y^*, assumed constant, M and P must move together, *provided velocity V stays constant*. Velocity is the speed at which the stock of money is passed round the economy as people transact. If everyone holds money for less time and passes it on more quickly, the economy can need less money relative to nominal income. How do we assess whether velocity is constant, as the simple quantity theory requires?

The quantity theory equation implies $M/P = Y/V$. Think of the left-hand side as real money supply, the right-hand side as real money demand, which rises with real income and falls with velocity. But money demand rises with real income and falls with nominal interest rates. Hence velocity is just the effect of interest rates on money demand. Higher nominal interest rates reduce real money demand. People *hold* less money relative to income. Velocity rises.

While inflation and nominal interest rates are rising, velocity is rising. But if inflation and nominal interest rates settle down at a particular level, velocity is then constant. Thereafter, the simple quantity theory once more applies.

This assumes prices are fully flexible. In the short run, if inflation is sluggish, changes in nominal money, unmatched by changes in inflation, thus change the real money supply. The quantity theory of money will fail in the short run, until full adjustment occurs.

In money market equilibrium, real money supply and demand are equal. Flexible interest rates maintain continuous money market equilibrium. Equation (1) always holds.

If nominal wages and prices adjust slowly in the short run, higher nominal money supply M leads initially to a higher the real money stock M/P since prices P have not yet adjusted. The excess supply of real money bids down interest rates. This boosts the demand for goods. Gradually this bids up goods prices. In the labour market, nominal wages start to rise.

> The quantity theory of money says that changes in nominal money lead to equivalent changes in the price level (and money wages) but have no effect on output and employment.

After complete adjustment of wages and prices, a once-off rise in nominal money leads to an equivalent once-off rise in wages and prices. Output, employment, interest rates and real money revert to their original levels. Equation (1) states this argument succinctly. After adjustment is complete, the demand for real balances is unchanged. Hence the price level changes in proportion to the original change in the nominal money supply.

The growth of nominal money is also related to inflation, the growth of prices. The theory is over 500 years old and may date from Confucius. The quantity theory is espoused by Monetarists, who argue that *most* changes in prices reflect changes in the nominal money supply. However, the theory must be interpreted with care.

Money, prices and causation

Suppose the demand for real money is constant over time. For money market equilibrium, the real money supply M/P is then constant. If monetary policy fixes nominal money M, this determines prices P to get the required level of M/P implied by money demand.

Conversely, monetary policy may choose a target path for the price level P (and hence of course for inflation, which depends only on comparing prices this period with prices last period). Changes in this path then *cause* changes in the nominal money supply to achieve the required real money supply. Equation (1) says prices and money are correlated but is agnostic on which causes which. That depends on the form of monetary policy pursued. With an intermediate target for nominal money, the causation flows from money to prices. With a target for prices or inflation, the causation flows the other way.

Whichever direction of causation, inflation is eventually a monetary phenomenon. Sustained inflation is possible only if the central bank keeps printing nominal money. If nominal money was held constant, continuing inflation would eventually so erode the real money stock that equilibrium real interest rates would become very high, thereby dampening inflation itself. Take away the oxygen of nominal money growth and the inflationary fire must go out.

Is real money demand constant?

The quantity theory of money presumes that real money demand is constant. But is it? Table 26.1 shows nominal money, prices, real money and real income in three countries over a long period. Even in the long run, the simple quantity theory is not correct. Nominal money rose 10 times as much as prices in Japan but only twice as much in France. The three countries had different real income growth, affecting real money demand. Real money supply changes thus had to differ. Prices and nominal money changed by *different* amounts.

Table 26.1 Nominal money and prices, 2003 (1962 = 100)			
	Japan	France	UK
Real income	1329	313	259
Nominal money	4641	1589	7743
Prices	447	777	1318
Real money	1038	205	588

Source: IMF, *International Financial Statistics*.

In the UK, financial deregulation and competition between banks offered depositors attractive interest rates on bank deposits (a big part of the money supply). The demand for real money rose a lot in the UK because of banking deregulation. Another reason for cross-country differences was differences in inflation. These affect real money demand by affecting nominal interest rates. We study this effect in the next section.

To sum up, even after adjustment is complete, changes in real income and interest rates can alter real money demand. However, *if* real income and interest rates were unaltered, changes in nominal money would eventually be accompanied by equivalent changes in nominal wages and prices.

Inflation

So far we have studied levels. Now think about rates of change. Equation (1) implies that the growth in real money demand equals the growth in the real money supply, the excess of nominal money growth over the growth in prices. Hence

$$\text{Inflation rate} = [\text{nominal money growth}] - [\text{real money demand growth}] \qquad (2)$$

Since real income and interest rates *usually* change only a few percentage points a year, real money demand usually changes slowly.[1] The essential insight of the quantity theory of money is that real variables usually change slowly.

Large changes in one nominal variable (money) are accompanied by large changes in other nominal variables (prices, nominal wages) to keep real money (and real wages) at their equilibrium values. This is a useful first look at inflation, but we have simplified too much.

26.2   Inflation and interest rates

The **Fisher hypothesis** says higher inflation leads to similarly higher nominal interest rates.

Table 26.2 shows interest and inflation rates for selected countries. Countries with high inflation have high interest rates. An extra percentage point of inflation is accompanied by a nominal interest rate also about one percentage point higher, a proposition first suggested by Professor Irving Fisher.

$$\text{Real interest rate} = [\text{nominal interest rate}] - [\text{inflation rate}] \qquad (3)$$

The Fisher hypothesis says that *real* interest rates do not change much. If they did, there would be large excess supply or demand for loans. Higher inflation is largely offset by higher nominal interest rates to stop the real interest rate changing much. Table 26.2 shows this is a good rule of thumb in reality.[2]

Higher inflation is associated with faster nominal money growth and higher nominal interest rates. The latter reduce the demand for real money, requiring

Table 26.2 Inflation and interest rates 2001 (% per annum)		
	Inflation	Interest rate
Turkey	62	57
Russia	20	25
Venezuela	12	15
Hungary	8	11
Chile	4	3
Switzerland	1	2
Japan	–1	0

Source: *The Economist.*

[1] An exception is the hyperinflation example of the next section.

[2] Chapter 25 argued that this is likely to be a long-run relationship. In the short run, higher inflation must induce a larger rise in nominal interest rates if real interest rates are to push inflation back towards its target.

money and prices to grow at *different* rates until the real money supply adjusts to the change in real money demand. To show how this works, we study a spectacular example, the German hyperinflation of the 1920s.

Hyperinflation is a period of very high inflation.

Hyperinflation

Bolivian inflation reached 11 000 per cent in 1985 and Ukraine's inflation topped 10 000 per cent in 1993. The most famous example is Germany in 1922–23.

Germany lost the First World War. The German government had a big deficit, financed by printing money. Table 26.3 shows what happened. The government had to buy faster printing presses. In the later stages of the hyperinflation, they took in old notes, stamped on another zero, and reissued them as larger-denomination notes in the morning.

Table 26.3	The German hyperinflation, 122–23 (January 1922 = 1)			
	Money	**Prices**	**Real money**	**Inflation, % monthly**
Jan 1922	1	1	1.00	5
Jan 1923	16	75	0.21	189
Jul 1923	354	2 021	0.18	386
Sept 1923	227 777	645 946	0.35	2 532
Oct 1923	20 201 256	191 891 890	0.11	29 720

Source: Data adapted from C.L. Holtfrerich, *Die Deutsche Inflation 1914–23*, Walter de Gruyter, 1980.

Prices rose 75-fold in 1922, much more in 1923. By October 1923 it took 192 million Reichsmarks to buy a drink that had cost 1 Reichsmark in January 1922. People carried money in wheelbarrows to go shopping. According to the old joke, thieves stole the barrows but left the near-worthless money behind.

If inflation is π and the nominal interest rate is r, the real interest rate is $(r-\pi)$ but the real return on non-interest-bearing cash is $-\pi$, which shows how quickly the real value of cash is being eroded by inflation. The extra real return on holding interest-bearing assets rather than cash is $(r-\pi) - (-\pi) = r$. The *nominal* interest rate measures the *real* cost of holding cash. Nominal interest rates rise with inflation. In the German hyperinflation the cost of holding cash became enormous.

The **flight from cash** is the collapse in the demand for real cash when high inflation and high nominal interest rates make it very expensive to hold cash.

Table 26.3 shows that by October 1923 real money holdings were only 11 per cent of their level in January 1922. How did people get by with such small holdings of real cash?

People, paid twice a day, shopped in their lunch hour before the real value of their cash depreciated too much. Any cash not immediately spent was quickly deposited in a bank where it could earn interest. People spent a lot of time at the bank.

What lessons can we draw? First, *rising* inflation and *rising* interest rates significantly reduce the demand for *real* cash. Hyperinflations are a rare example in which a real quantity (real cash) changes quickly and by a lot. Second, and as a result, money and prices can get quite out of line when inflation and nominal interest rates are rising. Table 26.3 shows that prices rose by six times as much as nominal money between January 1922 and July 1923, reducing the real money supply by 82 per cent, in line with the fall in real money demand.

26.3   Inflation, money and deficits

Persistent inflation must be accompanied by continuing money growth. Governments sometimes print money to finance a large budget deficit. Hence, budget deficits may explain why governments have to print money rapidly. If so, tight *fiscal* policy is needed to fight inflation and make low inflation targets credible.

The level of GDP affects how much tax revenue the government gets at given tax rates. If government debt is low relative to GDP, the government can finance deficits by borrowing. It has enough tax revenue with which to pay interest and repay the debt. For governments with low debt, there may be no relation between their budget deficit and how much money they print. Sometimes they print money, sometimes they issue bonds. We do not expect a close relation between deficits and money creation in a country like the UK.

Nevertheless, many years of deficits may make government debt large relative to GDP. As lenders get scared, the government can no longer finance deficits by more borrowing. It must either tighten fiscal policy, to shrink the deficit, or print money to finance the continuing deficit.

To ensure that the European Central Bank does not face fiscal pressure to print too much money and thus create inflation, members of the eurozone are supposed to obey the Stability and Growth Pact, which restricts their budget deficits to less than 3 per cent of GDP, except in severe recession. Similarly, the UK's Code for Fiscal Stability commits the UK government not to keep running big deficits that steadily raise government debt relative to GDP.

Deficits, money growth and real revenue

A hyperinflation is a situation in which fiscal policy is out of control. A government with a persistently high deficit, financed by borrowing, now has so much debt that nobody will lend it any more. Instead, it prints money to finance its deficit.

How much real revenue can the government get by printing banknotes? The government has a monopoly on cash. As a token money, its production cost is tiny relative to its value as money. The government prints money for nothing, then uses it to pay nurses and build roads.

Seigniorage is real revenue acquired by the government through its ability to print money.

Real money demand M/P rises with real income. Long-run growth of real income allows the government some scope to raise M without adding to P. This is seigniorage. A second potential source of real revenue is the inflation tax.

The *inflation tax* is the effect of inflation in raising real revenue by reducing the real value of the government's nominal debt.

Suppose real income and output are constant but that a weak government cannot shrink its budget deficit and now has debt so large that nobody will lend to it. It prints money to cover the budget deficit. If ΔM is the amount of new cash created, this finances an amount of real spending $(\Delta M)/P$, which is the same as $(\Delta M/M) \times (M/P)$, the growth rate of cash multiplied by the real demand for cash. The rise in nominal money must feed into prices sooner or later. Suppose the rate of nominal money growth $(\Delta M/M)$ equals the inflation rate π. Thus

real revenue from inflation = $[\pi] \times [M/P]$

Inflation helps the government by reducing the real value of the non-interest-bearing part of the government debt, namely cash. Think of inflation as the tax rate and real cash as the tax base for the inflation tax.

Now for the part that may be new to you. If money growth and inflation rise, does the government get more *real* revenue from the inflation tax? Higher inflation raises nominal interest rates and hence reduces the real demand for cash.

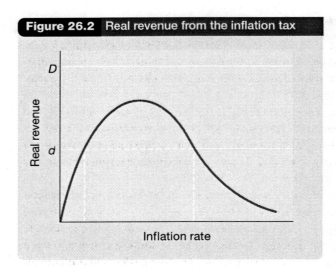

Figure 26.2   Real revenue from the inflation tax

Figure 26.3 shows the answer. At low inflation, real cash demand is high, but the multiple of inflation and real cash demand is small. Similarly, at high inflation, although inflation tax rate is high, the tax base – real cash demand – is now tiny because nominal interest rates are so high. The multiple of inflation and real cash is again low. Real revenue raised through the inflation tax cannot be increased indefinitely. After a certain point, faster money growth and higher inflation shrink the tax base more than they raise the tax rate.

The figure has two implications. First, if the government needs to cover a particular *real* deficit *d* by printing money, there may be two rates of money growth and inflation that do the job. Either is a long-run equilibrium in which inflation is constant.

Second, if for political reasons the government has a real deficit as large as *D*, printing money cannot do the job. The economy explodes into hyperinflation. At high inflation, real cash demand is already low. Raising inflation further causes such a large percentage fall in the tiny demand for real cash that inflation tax revenue falls, the government prints even more cash, and the problem gets even worse.

That is how hyperinflation starts. The only solution is to cut the size of the deficit. Often the government does this by defaulting on its debt, which slashes the burden of interest payments.

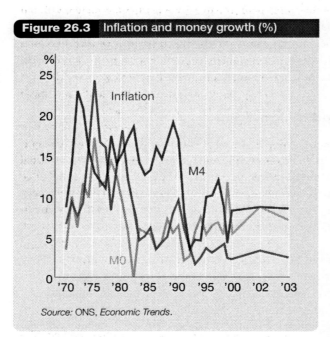

Figure 26.3   Inflation and money growth (%)

Source: ONS, Economic Trends.

UK money growth and inflation

The UK has never had a hyperinflation. Figure 26.3 shows UK data comparing inflation with the annual growth rate of M0 and M4 since 1970.

Even if there is a long-run relation between money growth and inflation, there need be no strong short-run relationship. Changes in interest rates and in real income lead to changes in real money demand that complicate the relationship between money growth and inflation in the short run.

Having examined the causes of inflation, we now examine its consequences.

26.4   Inflation, unemployment and output

One of the most famous relationships in postwar macroeconomics is the Phillips curve.

The Phillips curve shows a higher inflation rate is accompanied by a lower unemployment rate. It suggests we can *trade off* more inflation for less unemployment, or vice versa.

The Phillips curve

In 1958 Professor Phillips of the London School of Economics found a strong statistical relationship between annual inflation and annual unemployment in the UK. Similar relationships were found in other countries. The Phillips curve is shown in Figure 26.4.

The Phillips curve seemed a useful compass for choosing macroeconomic policy. By its choice of fiscal and monetary policy, the government set aggregate demand and hence unemployment. The Phillips curve showed how much inflation then ensued. Higher aggregate demand bid up wages and prices, causing higher inflation but lower unemployment.

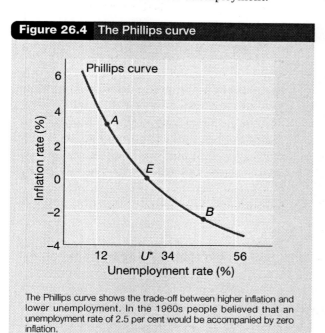

Figure 26.4   The Phillips curve

The Phillips curve shows the trade-off between higher inflation and lower unemployment. In the 1960s people believed that an unemployment rate of 2.5 per cent would be accompanied by zero inflation.

The Phillips curve in Figure 26.4 shows the trade-off that people believed they faced in the 1960s. In those days UK unemployment was rarely over 2 per cent of the labour force. People believed that if they reduced aggregate demand until unemployment rose to 2.5 per cent, inflation would fall to zero.

Since then there have been years when *both* inflation and unemployment were over 10 per cent. Something happened to the Phillips curve. The next two chapters explain why the simple Phillips curve of Figure 26.4 ceased to fit the facts.

Equilibrium unemployment is not zero, for reasons that we explore in Chapter 27. Suppose equilibrium employment and potential output are fixed in the long run but there is sluggish wage and price adjustment. Chapter 25 discussed the vertical long-run aggregate supply curve, and sloping short-run supply curve, relating output and the price level. These ideas are easily translated from inflation and output to inflation and unemployment.

The vertical long-run Phillips curve

The natural rate of unemployment and natural level of output are their values in long-run equilibrium.

In long-run equilibrium, the economy is at both potential output and equilibrium unemployment. Sometimes these are referred to as the natural level of output and natural rate of unemployment. Both are determined by real things, not nominal things. They depend on the supply of inputs, the level of technology, the level of tax rates and so on. They do not depend on inflation, provided all prices P and nominal wages W are rising together. Equilibrium unemployment depends on the real wage W/P, as we discuss in Chapter 27.

Just as long-run aggregate supply is vertical at potential output – output is unaffected by inflation – so the long-run Phillips curve is vertical at equilibrium unemployment. Equilibrium unemployment is independent of inflation. Plotting inflation and unemployment, Figure 26.5 shows the long-run Phillips curve vertical at equilibrium unemployment U^*.

In long-run equilibrium, inflation is constant. People correctly anticipate inflation and adjust the growth of nominal wages to keep real wages constant, at the real wage required for long-run equilibrium. Similarly, nominal interest rates are sufficiently high to offset inflation

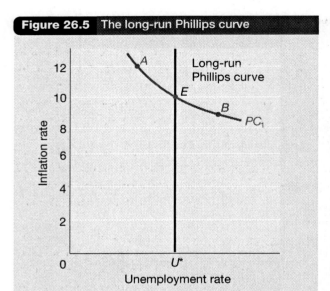

Figure 26.5 The long-run Phillips curve

Since people care about real variables not nominal variables, when full adjustment has been completed people will arrange for all nominal variables to keep up with inflation. The vertical long-run Phillips curve shows that eventually the economy gets back to the natural rate of unemployment U^*, whatever the long-run inflation rate. There is no long-run trade-off between inflation and unemployment. The short-run Phillips curve PC_1 shows short-run adjustment as before. The height of the short-run Phillips curve depends on the rate of inflation and nominal money growth in long-run equilibrium, as shown by the position of point E on the long-run Phillips curve.

and maintain real interest rates at their equilibrium level. Everyone adjusts to inflation because it can be completely foreseen.

Suppose inflation is 10 per cent a year. This is consistent with many forms of monetary policy. We can think of monetary policy as having either as a target of 10 per cent annual money growth, or an inflation target of 10 per cent a year. In Figure 26.5 long-run equilibrium is at E. Inflation is 10 per cent, as everybody expects. Nominal money grows at 10 per cent a year. Unemployment is at its natural rate.

The short-run Phillips curve

Beginning from E, suppose something raises aggregate demand. Unemployment falls, inflation rises and the economy is at A. Then the central bank raises interest rates to achieve its targets (in whichever form), and the economy slowly moves back down the short-run Phillips curve PC_1 from A to E again. Since interest rates take time to affect aggregate demand, this may take one or two years.

Conversely, beginning from E, a downward demand shock takes the economy to B in the short run. The central bank alters interest rates to bring the economy steadily back from B to E.

The **short-run Phillips curve** shows that, in the short run, higher unemployment is associated with lower inflation. The height of the short-run Phillips curve reflects expected inflation. In long-run equilibrium at E, expectations are fulfilled.

The short-run Phillips curve corresponds to the short-run supply curve for output. Given inherited wages, higher prices make firms supply more output and demand more workers. For any level of last period's prices, higher prices today imply higher inflation today. In Chapter 25 the height of the short-run aggregate supply curve depended on inherited growth rate of nominal wages. Similarly, the height of short-run Phillips curve reflects inherited nominal wage growth.

When workers and firms expect high inflation, they agree a large rise in nominal wages. If inflation turns out as expected, real wages are as forecast and the nominal wage growth was justified. If inflation is higher than expected, real wages are lower than planned. Firms supply more output and demand more labour. High inflation (relative to expectations) goes with lower unemployment. The short-run Phillips curve slopes down. Its height reflects the inflation expectations embodied in the inherited wage agreement.

This explains why most economies had high inflation at each unemployment rate in the 1970s and 1980s: the short-run Phillips curve had shifted upwards. Governments were printing money at a faster rate than before. The long-run equilibrium inflation rate was high and expected to be so.

The point E lay further up the long-run Phillips curve in Figure 26.5. The short-run Phillips curve through this point was much higher than the short-run Phillips curve in the data originally studied by Professor Phillips. The 1970s and 1980s were a period of high inflation. The original Phillips curve data had been for a period of much lower inflation.

We draw two conclusions. First, it was wrong to interpret the original Phillips curve as a *permanent* trade-off between inflation and unemployment. It was the temporary trade-off, corresponding to a particular short-run aggregate supply schedule, while the economy adjusted to a demand shock.

Second, the speed with which the economy moves back along the Phillips curve depends on two things: the degree of flexibility of nominal wages, and hence prices, and the extent to which monetary policy adjusts interest rates to restore demand more quickly. Complete wage flexibility would restore the vertical Phillips curve and the vertical aggregate supply curve. Rapid adjustment of interest rates would offset the demand shock, restoring output, unemployment and inflation to their long-run equilibrium levels.

Extreme monetarists believe that wage flexibility is very high. In the extreme version, it is only the fact that workers make annual wage settlements that prevents the economy always being in long-run equilibrium. Changes in aggregate demand unforeseen when nominal wages were set mean that wages and prices are temporarily at the wrong level. But such mistakes are rectified as soon as wages are renegotiated.

If wage and price adjustment are more sluggish than this, full employment is not immediately restored. However, we know from the previous chapter that monetary policy can completely compensate for a demand shock once it has been diagnosed. Nor is there any conflict between stabilizing inflation and stabilizing output or employment. Such conflicts arise only in response to supply shocks.

We have made considerable progress in understanding the Phillips curve but there is more still to study. First, we need to analyse changes in long-run inflation expectations, which shift the short-run Phillips curve. Second, we need to examine supply shocks. Temporary supply shocks also shift the short-run Phillips curve. Permanent supply shocks alter equilibrium unemployment and shift the long-run Phillips curve.

Figure 26.6 Expectations and credibility

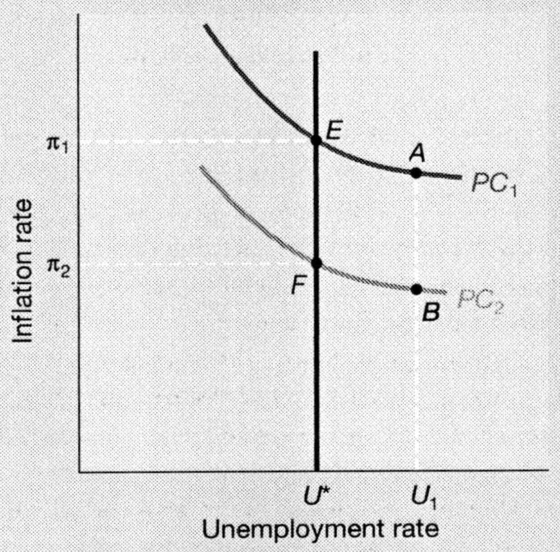

Beginning at E, the target inflation rate is cut from π_1 to π_2. Having expected inflation π_1, nominal wage growth has been too high. Firms cut back output and employment and the economy moves to A. If the new policy is credible, the next wage settlement reflects lower inflation expectations, the short-run Phillips curve shifts to PC_2 and the economy moves from A to B. Thereafter, it slowly adjusts along PC_2 to F.

However, if people doubt that the new tough policy will be sustained, nominal wages may keep growing at π_1. The short-run Phillips curve remains PC_1. Unemployment stays high, and inflation refuses to fall.

Expectations and credibility

Figure 26.6 puts this apparatus to work to discuss what happens when a new government is elected with a commitment to reduce inflation. The economy begins in long-run equilibrium at E facing the short-run Phillips curve PC_1. Nominal money, prices and money wages are all rising at the rate π_1.

The government wants to reduce inflation to π_2 to reach point F. The day the government is elected it announces a cut in the inflation target from π_1 to π_2. Overnight, firms inherit nominal wage increases that had anticipated the old inflation rate π_1. They have little scope to reduce inflation. If inflation does fall, real wages are now too high. Firms reduce output and employment. Inflation falls a little and unemployment rises. The economy moves along the short-run Phillips curve PC_1 to A.

What happens next? In the good scenario, workers believe the tighter monetary policy will last. The next wage bargain is based on inflation expectations π_2. The short-run Phillips curve shifts down to PC_2 and the economy moves from A to B. Inflation falls quickly. The economy then moves slowly along PC_2 from B to F.

Now for the bad scenario. When the economy first reaches A, workers do not believe that the tough new monetary policy will last. They think π_1 will remain the inflation rate in the long run. Thinking inflation will remain high, workers do not reduce nominal wage growth. They believe PC_1 not PC_2 will be relevant.

> A self-fulfilling prophecy is an expectation that creates the incentive to make it come true.

Suppose workers are wrong. Although nominal wages grow at π_1, the tough policy lasts and actual inflation is below π_1. Real wages rise and unemployment gets worse without much fall in inflation. The worse the slump becomes, the more likely the government is to give in, easing monetary policy to boost aggregate demand again. A belief that the government's nerve will crack can become a self-fulfilling prophecy. The economy stays on PC_1 and the attempt to reduce inflation fails. Gradually the economy moves back along PC_1 to equilibrium at E.

This explains why governments go to such lengths to commit to tight monetary policy. The sooner people accept that long-run inflation will be low, the sooner nominal wage growth will slow. Making central banks independent is an institutional reform design to increase the credibility of monetary policy by insulating it from short-term political expediency.

Supply shocks

> A permanent supply shock affects equilbrium unemployment and potential output. A temporary supply shock leaves these long-run values unaffected, but shifts the short-run Phillips curve and the short-run aggregate supply schedule for output.

In the long-run, the Phillips curve is vertical at equilibrium unemployment U^*. But U^* is not constant. Chapter 27 documents the rise and fall of U^* since the 1960s. In terms of Figure 26.6, a rise in equilibrium unemployment shifts the vertical long-run Phillips curve to the right. Changes in equilibrium unemployment reflect permanent supply shocks.

The short-run Phillips curve can shift for two reasons. Inherited nominal wage growth changes if inflation expectations change, as analysed in Figure 26.6. Alternatively, a change in firms' desired supply of output and demand for workers, for a given rate of inherited nominal wage growth, shifts the short-run Phillips curve. Examples include a change in oil prices, in regulations or in tax rates.

Figure 26.7 shows an adverse temporary supply shock. The short-run Phillips curve shifts up, from PC_1 to PC_2. If monetary policy accommodates the shock, the target inflation rate rises from π_1 to π_2. The economy moves from E to F with no change in output or unemployment, but at the cost of higher inflation. Eventually, the shock wears off, since it is temporary, and the economy reverts to E, with another accommodating change in monetary policy.

Alternatively, monetary policy may *not* fully accommodate the supply shock. In Chapter 25, Figure 25.9 showed that this would mean higher inflation *and* lower output. Now, the analogue is higher inflation *and* higher unemployment.

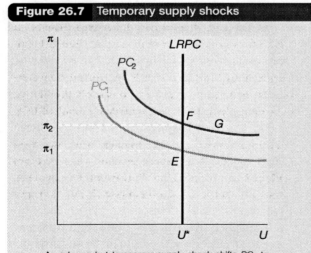

Figure 26.7 Temporary supply shocks

An adverse but temporary supply shock shifts PC_1 to PC_2, without affecting $LRPC$. Beginning from E monetary policy can accommodate the shock, moving to F. If interest rates are raised to prevent inflation rising as high as π_2, the fall in demand raises unemployment. At G the economy experiences stagflation, both high inflation and high unemployment.

> **Stagflation** is high inflation and high unemployment, caused by an adverse supply shock.

To prevent inflation shifting up by as much as the vertical shift up in the short-run Phillips curve, monetary policy makes sure that aggregate demand falls a bit. Hence inflation rises a bit and unemployment rises a bit. The economy moves from E to G in Figure 26.7. Output stagnates despite higher inflation.

Again, the credibility of policy is crucial. If workers think the government, afraid of high unemployment, will accommodate any shock, large wage rises buy temporarily higher real wages until prices adjust fully. And in the long run, monetary policy is loosened to maintain aggregate demand at full employment, so there is little danger of extra unemployment.

Once a government proves that it will not accommodate shocks, nominal wage growth slows. Workers then fear that higher wages will reduce demand and price workers out of a job.

Forty years of inflation and unemployment

The original Phillips curve seemed to offer a permanent trade-off between inflation and unemployment. It also suggested both inflation *and* unemployment could be low.

At that time, governments were committed to full employment even in the short run. Any shock tending to raise inflation – including temporary supply shocks – was accommodated by a higher money supply to prevent a fall in aggregate demand. Money growth and inflation steadily rose. After the mid-1970s, government policy changed in most countries. The emphasis is now on keeping inflation low. Inflation fell after the early 1980s.

What about unemployment? We now understand that the Phillips curve is vertical in the long run at equilibrium unemployment. The rise and fall of equilibrium unemployment explained much of the rise and fall in actual unemployment. It was not the whole story.

The short-run Phillips curve is the *temporary* trade-off between inflation and unemployment while the economy adjusts to a demand shock and works its way back to long-run equilibrium. The height of the short-run Phillips curve mainly reflects anticipated inflation.

At the start of the 1980s, inflation was high because it had been high in the past. Anti-inflation policies were just beginning to bite. When tight money was first introduced, aggregate demand fell and the economy moved to the right along the short-run Phillips curve. In addition to high equilibrium unemployment, many countries had a short-run Keynesian slump. Unemployment exceeded its equilibrium level.

In the 1990s, many European economies reduced inflation to low levels to show they were fit candidates for monetary union. The UK also adopted tight policies to get inflation down. First, it joined the Exchange Rate Mechanism and, when that failed, it made the Bank of England independent of political control.

Once inflation expectations had been brought down, super-tight policies were unnecessary. British unemployment fell a lot after 1993. In part, it was a recovery from the Keynesian recession of 1990–92. In part, supply-side policies reduced equilibrium unemployment. Thereafter, the UK enjoyed an unprecedented period of low inflation and fairly stable output growth. The Bank of England gets much of the credit.

Now you've read this section, why not test your understanding by visiting the Online Learning Centre at www.mcgraw-hill.co.uk/textbooks/begg

---

26.5 The costs of inflation

People dislike inflation, but why is it so bad? Some reasons commonly given are spurious.

Inflation illusion?

People have inflation illusion if they confuse nominal and real changes. People's welfare depends on real variables, not nominal variables.

It is wrong to say that inflation is bad because it makes goods more expensive. If *all* nominal variables rise at the same rate, people have larger nominal incomes and can buy the same physical quantity of goods as before. If people realize that prices have risen but forget that nominal incomes have also risen, they have inflation illusion. It is real incomes that tell us how many goods people can afford to buy.

A second mistake is more subtle. Suppose there is a sharp rise in the real price of oil. Oil-importing countries are worse off. Domestic consumption per person has to fall. It can fall in one of two ways.

If workers do not ask for 'cost-of-living' wage increases to cover the higher cost of oil-related products, real wages fall. Nominal wages buy fewer goods. Suppose too that domestic firms absorb higher oil-related fuel costs and do not pass on these costs in higher prices. There is no rise in domestic prices or nominal wages. The domestic economy has adjusted to the adverse supply shock without inflation. People are worse off.

Suppose instead that people try to maintain their old standard of living. Workers claim cost-of-living rises to restore their real wages and firms protect their profit margins by raising prices in line with higher wage and fuel costs. There is a lot of domestic inflation, which the government accommodates by printing extra money. Eventually the economy settles down in its new long-run equilibrium position.

People must still be worse off. The rise in the real oil price has not disappeared. It still takes more domestic exports, made possible by lower domestic consumption, to pay for the more expensive oil imports. In the new long-run equilibrium, workers find that their wages do not quite keep up with higher prices, and firms find that higher prices do not quite keep up with higher costs. The market has brought about the required fall in real domestic spending, letting resources go into exports to pay for the more expensive oil imports.

People notice (a) rising prices and (b) lower real incomes but draw the wrong conclusion. It is not the inflation that has made them worse off but the rise in oil prices. Inflation is a symptom of the initial refusal to accept the new reality.

We now turn to better arguments about the cost of inflation. Our discussion has two themes. First, was the inflation fully expected in advance? Or were people surprised? Second, do our institutions, including regulations and the tax system, let people adjust fully to inflation once they expect it? The costs of inflation depend on the answer to these two questions.

Complete adaptation and full anticipation

Imagine an economy with annual inflation of 10 per cent for ever. Everybody anticipates it. Nominal wages growth and nominal interest rates incorporate it. Real wages and real interest rates are unaffected. The economy is at full employment. Government policy is also fully adjusted. Nominal taxes are changed every year to keep real tax revenue constant. Nominal government spending rises at 10 per cent a year to keep real government spending constant. Share prices rise with inflation to maintain the real value of company shares. The tax treatment of interest earnings and capital gains is adjusted to reflect inflation. Pensions and other transfer payments are raised every year, in line with expected inflation.

This economy has no inflation illusion. Everyone has adjusted to it. This explains the long-run vertical Phillips curve in the previous section. But is complete adjustment possible?

Nominal interest rates usually rise with inflation to preserve the real rate of interest. But the nominal interest rate is the opportunity cost of holding cash. When inflation is higher, people hold less real cash.

Shoe-leather costs of inflation are the extra time and effort in transacting when we economize on holding real money.

Society uses money to economize on the time and effort involved in undertaking transactions. High nominal interest rates make people economize on real money. Using more resources to transact, we have fewer resources for production and consumption of goods and services.

When prices rise, price labels have to be changed. Menus are reprinted to show the higher price of meals.

Menu costs of inflation are the physical resources needed for adjustments to keep real things constant when inflation occurs.

The faster the rate of price change, the more often menus must be reprinted if real prices are to remain constant. Among the menu costs of inflation is the effort of doing mental arithmetic. If inflation is zero, it is easy to see that a beer costs the same as it did three months ago. When inflation is 25 per cent a year, it takes more effort to compare the real price of beer today with that of three months ago. People without inflation illusion try to think in real terms but the mental arithmetic involves time and effort.

How big are menu costs? In supermarkets it is easy to change price tags. The cost of changing parking meters, pay telephones and slot machines is larger. In countries with high inflation, pay phones usually take tokens whose price is easily changed without having physically to alter the machines.

Even when inflation is perfectly anticipated and the economy has fully adjusted to inflation, we cannot avoid shoe-leather costs and menu costs. These costs are big when inflation is high but may not be too big when inflation is moderate. However, if we cannot adjust to expected inflation, the costs are then larger.

Fully anticipated inflation when institutions don't adapt

Assume inflation is fully anticipated but institutions prevent people fully adjusting to expected inflation. Inflation now has extra costs.

Taxes

Tax rates may not be fully inflation-adjusted. One problem is fiscal drag.

Fiscal drag is the rise in real tax revenue when inflation raises nominal incomes, pushing people into higher tax brackets in a progressive income tax system.

Suppose income below £4000 is untaxed but you pay income tax at 25 per cent on all income over £4000. Initially, you earn £5000 and pay income tax of £250. After ten years of inflation, all wages and prices double but tax brackets and tax rates remain as before. You now earn £10 000. Paying tax at 25 per cent on the £6000 by which your nominal income exceeds £4000, you pay nominal tax of £1500. Wages and prices only doubled but your nominal tax payment rose from £250 to £1500. Fiscal drag raised the real tax burden. The government gained from inflation. You lost.

For an inflation-neutral tax system, nominal tax brackets must rise with inflation. The real tax exemption is constant if the nominal limit increases from £4000 to £8000. Everything is then inflation-adjusted. You would pay £500 in tax, double what you paid before.

Percentage taxes on value, such as VAT, automatically raise nominal tax revenue in line with the price level. However, *specific* duties, such as £5 a bottle on whisky, must be raised as the price level rises. In the UK there is no *automatic* formula for raising such duties. Each year the government decides.

Taxing capital

Income tax on interest income is also affected by inflation. Suppose there is no inflation. Nominal and real interest rates are both 4 per cent. With a 40 per cent tax rate, the after-tax real return on lending is 2.6 per cent. Now suppose inflation is 11 per cent and nominal interest rates are 15 per cent to keep a pre-tax real interest rate of 4 per cent. Suppose lenders must pay income tax on nominal interest income. The after-tax nominal interest rate is 9 per cent (0.6 × 15). Subtracting 11 per cent inflation, the after-tax *real* interest rate is −2 per cent. This compares with +2.6 per cent when inflation was zero.

When inflation was 11 per cent, nominal interest rates were 15 per cent. Eleven per cent of this was not real income, merely a payment to keep up with inflation. Only 4 per cent was the real interest rate providing real income. But income tax applied to all 15 per cent. Higher inflation reduced the real return on lending because the tax system was not properly inflation-adjusted. The government gained more real tax revenue. You lost.

Capital gains tax is another example. Suppose people pay tax of 40 per cent of any capital gain made when asset prices rise. When inflation is zero, only real gains are taxed. When inflation is 10 per cent, nominal asset prices rise merely to preserve their real value. People pay capital gains tax even though they are not making real capital gains.

Inflation accounting uses fully inflation-adjusted definitions of costs, income and profit.

Institutional imperfections help explain why inflation has real effects even inflation is fully anticipated. These effects can be large. Usually, the government is the winner.

Unexpected inflation

Previously, we assumed that inflation was fully anticipated. What if inflation is a surprise?

Redistribution

When prices rise unexpectedly, people with nominal assets lose and people with nominal liabilities gain. Nominal contracts to buy and sell, or lend and borrow, can reflect expected inflation, but cannot reflect surprise inflation.

Expecting inflation of 10 per cent, you lend £100 for a year at 12 per cent, expecting a real interest rate of 2 per cent. Unexpectedly, inflation is 20 per cent. The real interest rate on your loan is [12–20] = −8 per cent. You lose by lending. Conversely, borrowers gain 8 per cent. Their nominal income rises 20 per cent with inflation but they repay at 12 per cent interest.

For every borrower, there is a lender. One person's gain is another person's loss. In the aggregate they cancel out. But unexpected inflation redistributes real income and wealth, in this case from lenders to borrowers. This may lead to economic dislocation. Some people may have to declare bankruptcy, which then affects other people. We also have to make a value judgement about whether we like the redistribution that is taking place.

One redistribution is between the government and the private sector. *Unexpected* inflation reduces the real value of all outstanding nominal government debt. It is as if the government had taxed us in order to repay this debt.[3]

---

[3] Why stress unexpected inflation? Because expected inflation is already built into the terms on which bonds were originally issued. Expected inflation affects nominal interest rates.

The old and the young

In practice, many savers are the old. Having paid off their mortgages and built up savings during their working life, they put their wealth into nominal bonds to provide income during retirement. These people lose out from surprise inflation.

Nominal debtors are the young and, mainly, those entering middle age with a large mortgage. They gain when surprise inflation raises house prices and nominal incomes without a matching rise in the nominal sum they owe the bank or building society.

Surprise inflation redistributes from the old to the young. We may judge this redistribution undesirable. With technical progress and productivity growth, each generation is richer than the one before. Redistribution from the old to the young raises intergenerational inequality.

Uncertain inflation

Uncertainty about future inflation has two costs. First, it makes planning more complex, raising the real resources society uses to make plans and do business. Second, people dislike risk. Chapter 13 explained why. The extra benefits of the champagne years are poor compensation for the years of starvation. People would rather average out these extremes and live comfortably all the time. The psychic costs of worrying about how to cope with the bad years may also be important.

When people make nominal contracts, uncertainty about inflation means uncertainty about the eventual real value of the nominal bargains currently made. This is a true cost of inflation. If a lower average level of inflation also reduces uncertainty about inflation, this may be a reason to aim for low inflation. The institutions that commit the government to low inflation may also reduce the scope for uncertainty about inflation. If so, lower average inflation has a real benefit because it is also more certain.

26.6 Defeating inflation

In the long run, inflation will be low if money growth is low. This may require fiscal policy to remain fairly tight so that deficits are low. However, to get to this position from an initial position of high inflation, it may be necessary to get through an intermediate period of high unemployment.

Could this transition be made more quickly and less painfully? The more credible the new policy, the faster the adjustment of expectations and behaviour.

Incomes policy

Incomes policy is the direct control of wages and other incomes.

A freeze on wage increases certainly brings inflation down quickly. Historically, it has not been able to keep inflation down. Why were past incomes policies unsuccessful?

Once governments intervene in the labour market, they often cannot resist pursuing other aims at the same time. For example, they try to compress relative wages across different skills in the name of fairness. Such policies alter real wages for particular skills, causing excess supply in some skills and excess demand in others. Market forces eventually break the policy.

At best incomes policy is a temporary adjustment device. In the long run, low nominal money growth is essential if low inflation is to be maintained. Some incomes policies failed

BOX 26-2	**Central bank independence**

Central bankers are cautious entities unlikely to favour rapid money growth and inflation. So why do these occur? Either because the government cares so much about unemployment that it never tackles inflation, or because it is politically weak and ends up with a budget deficit which it finances, at least to some extent, by printing money. Essentially, inflation arises when governments overrule cautious bankers. Proposals for central bank independence mean *independence from the government*. In the long run, output is at potential output, so eventually independ-

ent central banks should lead to lower inflation without a permanent fall in output. Central bank independence is a pre-commitment by government to keep money tight and inflation low.

The two figures below, shows that both predictions of the theory work out in practice – countries with more independent central banks have lower average inflation, but not lower real output growth in the long run.

Source: A. Alesina and L. Summers, 'Central bank independence and macroeconomic performance: some comparative evidence', *Journal of Money, Credit and Banking*, May 1993.

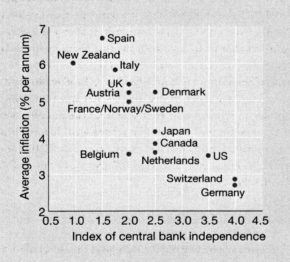

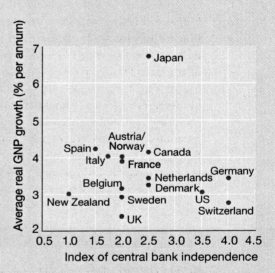

because governments introduced a wage freeze but kept printing money, a guarantee that excess demand for workers would eventually break the policy.

Long-term incomes policies are also hard to administer because equilibrium real wages for particular skills change over time. Freezing the existing wage structure gradually sets up powerful market forces of excess supply and excess demand.

Institutional reform

This approach takes a long-run view. It is concerned not with the temporary costs of first getting inflation down, but with how to *keep* inflation down. Box 27.2 provides evidence that central bank independence is a useful pre-commitment to tight monetary policy and low inflation. Institutional pre-commitment is all the rage, as the following examples show.

The Maastricht Treaty

Signed in 1991, the treaty set out conditions both for entering the eurozone and after admission to it. The first requirement was to avoid loose fiscal policy: a ceiling of 3 per cent on budget deficits relative to GDP. High-debt countries were also supposed to initiate actions to bring their debt/GDP levels below 60 per cent. Moreover, euro entrants first had to succeed in disinflating to low levels, measured both directly by changes in price indexes and indirectly by nominal interest rates (the Irving Fisher effect again!).

Not only did EU governments have to sign up for tight policy in the 1990s and beyond, euro hopefuls had to undertake institutional reform, making their national central banks formally independent. The Maastricht Treaty also made the new European Central Bank independent of government, with a mandate to pursue price stability.

UK policy 1992–97

Despite losing the peg to the Deutschmark after leaving the ERM in 1992, subsequent UK inflation was remarkably low. During 1992–97, UK monetary policy worked as follows. The Chancellor announced the inflation target for the coming years. Each month Treasury and Bank officials tried to agree on a recommendation about interest rates to meet this medium-run objective while looking after the short-term needs of the real economy. At the monthly meeting of Chancellor and Governor, the arguments were considered *then the Chancellor alone decided*.

Previous Chancellors always 'took the Bank's views into account'. What was new? Since the minutes of the Governor–Chancellor meeting were published a few weeks later, any objections by the Bank were highly publicized. Moreover, and separate from the monthly meetings, the Bank was given responsibility to produce a quarterly *Inflation Report*, openly published and *completely free from Treasury control*. The Report quickly became very influential, because of its clear analysis, and a model for other central banks.

UK policy since 1997

In May 1997, the new Chancellor, Gordon Brown, gave the Bank of England 'operational independence' to set interest rates. The Bank aims to achieve an inflation target set by the Chancellor. In an emergency (a very adverse supply shock), the government can temporarily raise the target rather than force the Bank to initiate a drastic recession merely to hit the inflation target quickly. Nevertheless, any change in the target is politically hard except in truly exceptional circumstances. Operational independence is a commitment to policies favouring low inflation.

26.7   The Monetary Policy Committee

Headline inflation was actual inflation, the growth in the retail price index RPI. Underlying inflation was the growth of RPIX, which is the retail price index omitting the effect of mortgage interest rates on the cost of living.

Since 1997 UK interest rates have been set by the Bank of England's Monetary Policy Committee (MPC), which meets monthly to set interest rates to try to hit the inflation target laid down by the Chancellor. Initially, the target was 2.5 per cent annual inflation, plus or minus 1 per cent. The target applied to underlying inflation not headline inflation.

Why omit mortgage interest from the price level on which monetary policy should focus? Suppose inflation is too high. To reduce aggregate demand, interest rates are raised. But higher interest rates *raise* the retail price index RPI by raising the cost of living for homeowners. Asking monetary policy to focus on the growth of RPIX simplifies interest rate decisions. Moreover, when temporary changes in interest rates are required to get the economy back on track, it may also be more sensible to target the underlying rate of inflation.

Different countries construct price indexes in slightly different ways from one another. EU countries have each adopted a common procedure for calculating their Consumer Price Index (CPI), making cross-country comparisons of inflation more meaningful. In December 2003, the UK Chancellor instructed the Bank of England to switch from using RPIX to using the CPI as the basis for inflation targeting.

For statistical reasons, the CPI tends to grow less rapidly than RPIX. At the time of the crossover, UK inflation was 2.9 per cent measured by the growth rate of RPIX but only 1.3 per cent measured by the growth rate of the CPI. Hence, Gordon Brown also changed the target inflation rate from 2.5 per cent growth in RPI to 2 per cent growth in the Consumer Price Index.

The quarterly *Inflation Report* includes the famous fan chart for CPI inflation. Figure 27.3 shows the fan chart in April 2004. The darker the projected line, the more likely the outcome. Figure 27.3 shows that in April 2004 the Bank was expecting UK inflation to average around 1.8 per cent in 2005, but that by the end of 2006 the range of possible outcomes had widened to between 1.4 per cent and 3.2 per cent.

> A fan chart not only shows the most likely future outcome but also indicates the probability of different outcomes.

Why was the MPC given a target for inflation, not nominal money? How does it work? And how easy has it been for the MPC to decide where to set interest rates?

Figure 26.8   Inflation projection made in April 2004

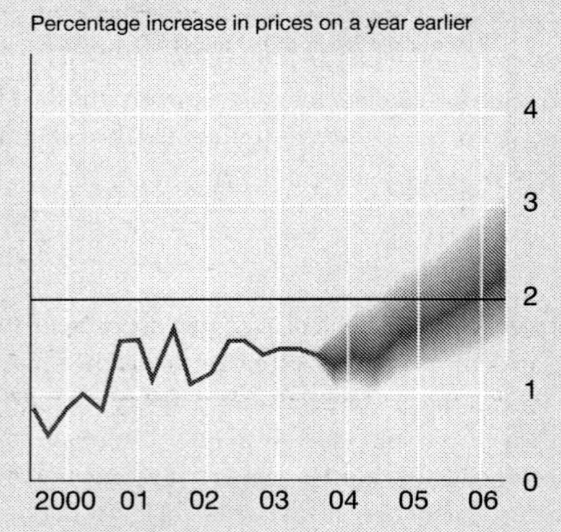

Percentage increase in prices on a year earlier

Source: Bank of England.

Inflation targets

Without a nominal anchor, nothing ties down the price level or any other nominal variable. Market forces determine real variables such as money M divided by prices P. Setting interest rates can influence M/P but not separately determine M and P. An intermediate target – an announced path for a nominal variable – is required. For example, if we know M and can work out money demand M/P, we can deduce the price level P.

Nominal money is a logically possible nominal anchor, and is attractive as an intermediate target because new data on money come out faster than data on prices or output. However, monetary targets fell out of favour because large and unpredictable changes in real money demand made it hard to know where to set the nominal money target. When it is hard to predict M/P, it is difficult to know where to set M in order to get the desired path of P.

As explained in previous chapters, most modern central banks implicitly follow a flexible inflation target.

Back to the future

Delays in data availability mean that the MPC has to forecast where the economy is today. Moreover, the interest rate medicine takes up to two years to have its full effect on private behaviour.

466   Part 4 : Macroeconomics

Hence the MPC has to *forecast* the path of prices at least two years into the future merely to know where to set interest rates *today*.

On occasion, the MPC may raise interest rates even though current inflation is under control. This means that, in the absence of any change in interest rates, the MPC is forecasting that inflation will be too high. It then has to act quickly to keep inflation on track.

So far so good

Most people give the MPC high marks for their performance so far. It was prepared to change interest rates even when this was unpopular, and inflation has remained close to its target level. Since inflation expectations are low, nominal interest rates are low as well.

Figure 26.8 shows the history of UK interest rates since 1974. Although the Bank's operational independence to set interest rates was granted in 1997, Figure 26.8 shows that the decisive break was in 1992 when sterling left the Exchange Rate Mechanism and changed nominal anchors from a pegged exchange rate to an inflation target. The MPC has built on the earlier success during 1992–97.

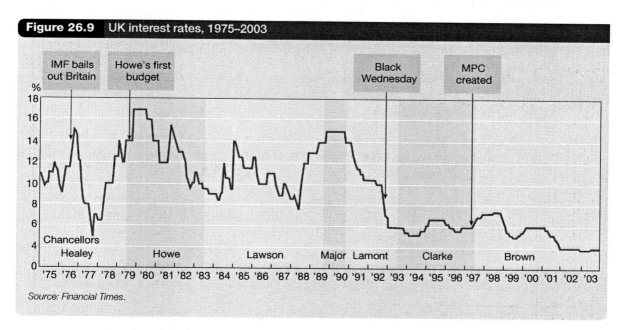

Figure 26.9 UK interest rates, 1975–2003

Source: Financial Times.

SUMMARY

- The quantity theory of money says changes in prices are caused by equivalent changes in the nominal money supply. In practice, prices cannot adjust at once to changes in nominal money, so interest rates or income alter, changing real money demand. Nevertheless, in the long run changes in prices are usually associated with changes in nominal money.

- The Fisher hypothesis is that 1 per cent rise in inflation leads to a similar rise in nominal interest rates so real interest rates change little in the long run. Since the nominal interest rate is the cost of holding money, higher inflation reduces real money demand. The *flight from cash* during hyperinflation is a vivid example.

- For a solvent government, there need be no close relation between the budget deficit and nominal money growth. In the long run, persistent borrowing to finance large deficits may leave the government so indebted that further borrowing is impossible. It must resort to printing money or take fiscal action to cut the deficit.

- The long-run Phillips curve is vertical at equilibrium unemployment. If people foresee inflation and can completely adjust to it, inflation has no real effects.

- The short-run Phillips curve is a temporary trade-off between unemployment and inflation in response to demand shocks. Supply shocks shift the Phillips curve. The height of the short-run Phillips curve also depends on underlying money growth and expected inflation. The Phillips curve shifts down if people believe inflation will be lower in the future.

- Temporary supply shocks also shift the short-run Phillips curve. Stagflation is high inflation plus high unemployment.

- Some so-called costs of inflation reflect inflation illusion or a failure to see inflation as the consequence of a shock that would have reduced real incomes in any case. The true costs of inflation depend on whether it was anticipated and on the extent to which the economy's institutions allow complete inflation-adjustment.

- Shoe-leather costs and menu costs are unavoidable costs of inflation and are larger the larger the inflation rate. Failure fully to inflation-adjust the tax system may also impose costs, even if inflation is anticipated.

- Unexpected inflation redistributes income and wealth from those who have contracted to receive nominal payments (lenders and workers) to those who have contracted to pay them (firms and borrowers).

- Uncertainty about future inflation rates imposes costs on people who dislike risk. Uncertainty may be greater when inflation is already high.

- Incomes policy may accelerate a fall in inflation expectations, allowing disinflation without a large recession. But it is unlikely to succeed in the long run. Only low money growth can deliver low inflation in the long run.

- Operational independence of central banks is designed to remove the temptation faced by politicians to print too much money.

REVIEW QUESTIONS

Your real annual income is constant, and initially is £10 000. You borrow £200 000 for 10 years to buy a house, paying interest annually, repaying the £200 000 in a final payment at the end. List your annual incomings and outgoings in the first and ninth years if inflation is 0 and the nominal interest rate is 2 per cent a year. Repeat the exercise if annual inflation is 100 per cent and the nominal interest rate 102 per cent. Are the two situations the same in real terms?

468 Part 4 : Macroeconomics

Does this explain why voters mind about high inflation even when nominal interest rates rise in line with inflation?

(a) Explain the following data. (b) Is inflation always a monetary phenomenon?

2001	Money growth %	Inflation %
Euro area	3	2
Japan	12	– 3
UK	6	2
Australia	15	3
USA	8	2

Source: The Economist.

Looking at data on inflation and unemployment over ten years, could you tell the difference between supply shocks and demand shocks?

Name three groups that lose out during inflation. Does it matter whether this inflation was anticipated?

Common fallacies Why are these statements wrong? (a) Getting inflation down is the only way to cure high unemployment. (b) Inflation stops people saving. (c) Inflation stops people investing.

To check your answers to these questions, go to pages 642–43.

Online **Learning Centre** with POWERWEB

To help you grasp the key concepts of this chapter check out the extra resources posted on the Online Learning Centre at www.mcgraw-hill.co.uk/textbooks/begg. There are quick test questions, economics examples and access to Powerweb articles, all for free!

For even more exercises, recaps and examples to help you study, purchase a copy of the Economics Student Workbook. Simply visit www.mcgraw hill.co.uk/textbooks/begg and follow the links to the Workbook to buy your copy.

Unemployment

Learning outcomes

By the end of this chapter, you should understand:

1 classical, frictional and structural unemployment

2 voluntary and involuntary unemployment

3 determinants of unemployment

4 how supply-side policies reduce equilibrium unemployment

5 private and social costs of unemployment

6 hysteresis

In the early 1930s, over a quarter of the UK labour force was unemployed. Society threw away output by failing to put people to work. For the next 40 years, macroeconomic policy tried to manage aggregate demand to avoid a rerun of the 1930s. Figure 26.1 shows that the policy succeeded.

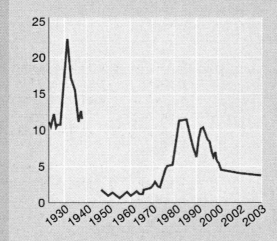

Figure 27.1   UK unemployment (%)

Sources: B. R. Mitchell, *Abstracts of British Historical Statistics* and B. R. Mitchell and H. G. Jones, *Second Abstract of British Historical Statistics,* Cambridge University Press; ONS, Economic Trends.

In the 1970s, high inflation emerged for reasons discussed in the previous chapter. Governments eventually tightened monetary and fiscal policy to get inflation under control. The mix of tighter demand policies and adverse supply shocks led to a big rise in unemployment in the 1980s.

470 Part 4 : Macroeconomics

After the economy adjusted, deficient demand was no longer the cause of high unemployment. Equilibrium unemployment remained high because of adverse changes in supply. Better supply-side policies since 1990 have reduced unemployment to levels not seen since the early 1970s.

Table 27.1 shows that the fight against unemployment was even harder to win in other countries. Why did high unemployment persist so long, especially in continental Europe? What can governments do about unemployment? This chapter aims to answer these questions.

Table 27.1 Unemployment 1972–2004 (%)

	1972	1982	1992	2004
UK	4	11	10	5
Ireland	8	14	15	5
Italy	6	8	9	9
France	3	10	10	10
EU	3	9	9	9
USA	5	10	8	5

Source: OECD, *Economic Outlook*.

27.1   The labour market

The labour force is people with a job or registered as looking for work. The participation rate is the fraction of the population of working age who are in the labour force. The unemployment rate is the fraction of the labour force without a job but registered as looking for work.

Not everyone wants a job. The people who do are called the labour force.

Some people looking for work do not register as unemployed. They do not appear in official statistics for the registered labour force or the registered unemployed. Yet from an economic viewpoint, such people *are* in the labour force and *are* unemployed. For the moment, our data on the labour force or the unemployed refer only to those registered.

Figure 27.1 shows that UK unemployment was high in the interwar years, especially in the 1930s. By comparison, the postwar unemployment rate was tiny until the late 1970s. In the 1980s it started to get back to pre-war levels but then fell steadily after 1990.

Stocks and flows

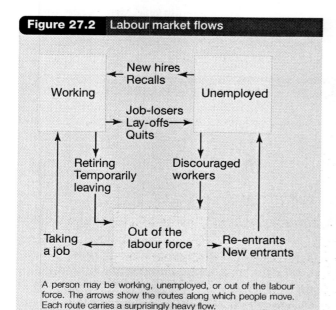

Figure 27.2 Labour market flows

A person may be working, unemployed, or out of the labour force. The arrows show the routes along which people move. Each route carries a surprisingly heavy flow.

Unemployment is a stock concept measured at a point in time. Like a pool of water, its level rises when inflows (the newly unemployed) exceed outflows (people getting new jobs or quitting the labour force altogether). Figure 27.2 illustrates this important idea.

There are three ways for workers to become unemployed: some people are sacked or made redundant (job-losers); some are temporarily laid off but expect eventually to be rehired by the same company; and some voluntarily quit their existing jobs. But the inflow to unemployment also comes from people not previously in the labour force: school-leavers (new entrants) and people who, having left the labour force, are now returning to look for a job (re-entrants).

People leave the unemployment pool in opposite directions. Some get jobs. Others give up looking for jobs and leave the labour force completely.

Discouraged workers, pessimistic about finding a job, leave the labour force.

Some of this latter group may simply have reached the retirement age at which they receive a pension, but many are discouraged workers.

Table 27.2 shows that the pool of unemployment is not stagnant. The stock of unemployed is 800 000. Over 2.4 million people a year flow into and out of unemployment.

When unemployment is high, people have to spend longer in the pool before they find a way out. Table 27.3 gives data on the duration of unemployment. Unemployment is no longer a temporary stopover on the way to better things. A higher unemployment rate usually also means that people are spending longer in the pool of unemployment before escaping.

Table 27.2 UK unemployment (millions) 2004	
Inflow to unemployment	2.4
Outflow from unemployment	2.5
Stock of unemployed	0.8

Source: ONS, Labour Market Trends.

Table 27.3 Percentage of unemployed by duration, 2004					
	3 months	3–6 months	6–12 months	12–24 months	24+ months
Male	43	22	19	12	5
Female	50	22	17	8	4

Source: Labour Market Trends.

The composition of unemployment

Table 27.4 gives a recent breakdown of unemployment by sex and age. Young workers find it harder to get a job. Unlike established workers with accumulated skills and job experience, young workers have to be trained from scratch. Youth unemployment exceeds the national average. The unemployment rate is lower for women than for men. In part this may reflect the fact that employment in the declining industries had traditionally been predominantly male. Men are worse hit by redundancies in steelworks and shipyards.

Table 27.4 Unemployment rates, 2004 (% of relevant group)		
Age	Men	Women
<25	14	11
25–59	5	4

Source: ONS, Labour Market Trends.

27.2   Analysing unemployment

We now develop a theoretical framework in which to analyse unemployment. We can classify unemployment by the source of the problem or by the nature of behaviour in the labour market.

Types of unemployment

Economists used to classify unemployment by source: frictional, structural, demand-deficient or classical.

Frictional unemployment is the irreducible minimum unemployment in a dynamic society.

It includes people whose handicaps make them hard to employ. More importantly, it includes people spending short spells in unemployment as they hop between jobs in a dynamic economy.

Structural unemployment reflects the time taken to acquire human capital. A skilled welder may have worked for 25 years in shipbuilding but is made

Structural unemployment arises from the mismatch of skills and job opportunities as the pattern of demand and supply changes.

Demand-deficient unemployment occurs when output is below full capacity.

Classical unemployment describes the unemployment created when the wage is deliberately maintained above the level at which the labour supply and labour demand schedules intersect.

redundant at 50 when the industry contracts in the face of foreign competition. That worker may have to retrain in a new skill which is more in demand in today's economy. But firms may be reluctant to take on and train older workers. Such workers become the victims of structural unemployment.

Until wages and prices have adjusted to their new long-run equilibrium level, a fall in aggregate demand reduces output and employment. Some workers want to work at the going real wage rate but cannot find jobs. Only when demand has returned to its long-run level is demand-deficient unemployment eliminated.

Since the classical model assumes that flexible wages and prices maintain the economy at full employment, classical economists had difficulty explaining high unemployment in the 1930s. They concluded that the wage was prevented from adjusting to its equilibrium level. Classical unemployment can be caused either by the exercise of trade union power or by minimum wage legislation that enforces a wage in excess of the equilibrium wage rate.

The modern analysis of unemployment takes the same types of unemployment but classifies them differently to highlight the behavioural implications and consequences for government policy. Modern analysis stresses the difference between *voluntary* and *involuntary* unemployment.

Equilibrium unemployment

Figure 27.3 shows the labour market. The labour demand schedule *LD* slopes down. Firms demand more workers at a lower real wage. The schedule *LF* shows how many people are in the labour force. A higher real wage increases the number of people wishing to work. However, the schedule is pretty steep. Many people are in the labour force whatever the real wage.

The schedule *AJ* shows how many people accept job offers at each real wage. The schedule is to the left of the *LF* schedule: only people in the labour force can accept a job. How far *AJ* lies to the left of *LF* depends on several things. Some people are inevitably between jobs at any instant. Also, a particular real wage may tempt some people into the labour force even though they will accept a job only if they find an offer with a rather higher real wage than average.

We draw these schedules for a given level of jobseekers allowance (formerly called unemployment benefit). When wages are high, job seekers grab available jobs. The two upward sloping schedules are close together. When wages are low (relative to unemployment benefit),

---

BOX 27-1   The lump-of-labour fallacy

Those without an economics training often think there is a simple solution for reducing unemployment. Shorten the working week, so that the same amount of total work is shared between more workers, leaving fewer people unemployed. What's wrong with this argument?

It presumes the demand for labour (hours × people) is fixed, whatever the cost of hiring workers or their benefit in goods produced and revenue earned. In practice, both would be affected by the proposal.

You go to work for 7 hours a day but probably have an hour of dead time (coffee breaks, tidying your desk, being nice to colleagues, talking about sport, sneaking out to the shops). This is a fixed cost, say an hour of time. There are probably economies of scale to shift length. Shortening the shift length adds to the cost of labour, making firms less competitive and reducing their demand for labour. Moreover, if you only work 20 hours a week instead of 37, you have less money to spend. If everyone spends less, firms sell less and need fewer, not more, workers.

Few economists think compulsory reductions in the length of the work week is a promising solution to the problem of high unemployment.

potential workers are more selective in accepting job offers. People invest in searching for a good job. The two schedules are further apart.

Labour market equilibrium is at E in Figure 27.3. Equilibrium employment is N^*. The distance EF is equilibrium unemployment.

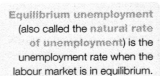

> **Equilibrium unemployment** (also called the **natural rate of unemployment**) is the unemployment rate when the labour market is in equilibrium.

This unemployment is entirely *voluntary*. At the equilibrium real wage w^*, N_1 people want to be in the labour force but only N^* accept job offers. The remainder do not want to work at the equilibrium real wage.

Equilibrium unemployment includes frictional and structural unemployment. Suppose a skilled welder earned £500 a week before being made redundant. The issue is not why workers became redundant (the decline of the steel industry), but why these workers will not take a lower wage as a dishwasher to get a job. Their old skills are obsolete. Until new skills are learned, dishwashing may be their only skill valued by the labour market. People not prepared to work at the going wage rate for their skills, but wanting to be in the labour force, are voluntarily unemployed.

> A worker is **voluntarily unemployed** if, at the given level of wages, she wishes to be in the labour force but does not yet wish to accept a job.

What about classical unemployment, for example if unions keep wages above their equilibrium level? This is shown in Figure 27.3 as a wage w_2 above w^*. Total unemployment is AC. As individuals, AB workers want jobs at the wage w_2 but cannot find them. Firms wish to be at point A. As individuals, the workers AB are involuntarily unemployed.

> An **involuntarily unemployed** worker would accept a job offer at the going wage rate.

However, through their unions, workers collectively opt for the wage w_2 above the equilibrium wage, thus reducing employment. For workers as a whole, the extra unemployment is voluntary. We include classical unemployment in equilibrium unemployment. If unions maintain the wage w_2, the economy stays at A, and AC is equilibrium unemployment.

Figure 27.3 Equilibrium unemployment

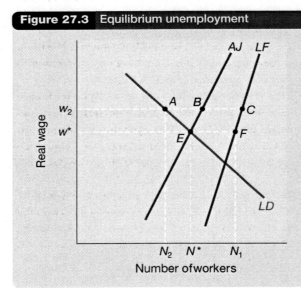

The schedules LD, LF, and AJ show, respectively, labour demand, the size of the labour force, and the number of workers willing to accept job offers at any real wage. AJ lies to the left of LF both because some labour force members are between jobs and because optimists are hanging on for an even better job offer. When the labour market clears at E, EF is the natural rate of unemployment, the people in the labour force not prepared to take job offers at the equilibrium wage w^*. If union power succeeds in maintaining the wage w_2 in the long run, the labour market will be at A, and the natural rate of unemployment AC now shows the amount of unemployment chosen by the labour force collectively by enforcing the wage w_2.

Figure 27.4 illustrates how Keynesian or de-mand-deficient unemployment may arise. Initially, labour demand is LD, and the labour market is in equilibrium at E with equilibrium unemployment EF. Then labour demand shifts down to LD'. Before wages or prices adjust, the real wage is still w^*. At this wage, workers want to be at E but firms want to be at A. The distance AE is demand-deficient unemployment, involuntary unemployment caused by sluggish adjustment of wages and prices. EF remains voluntary unemployment.

If labour demand remains LD', eventually real wages fall to w^{**} to restore equilibrium at G. However, by reducing interest rates, monetary policy can shift labour demand up to LD again and restore equilibrium at E. At A output and employment are low. Involuntary unemployment also reduces wage growth and inflation. The central bank cuts interest rates and start boosting aggregate demand for output, which shifts LD' up.[1]

Thus, we can divide total unemployment into two parts. The equilibrium or natural rate is the equilibrium unemployment determined by normal labour market turnover, structural mismatch, union power and incentives in the labour market. Keynesian unemployment, also called demand-deficient or cyclical unemployment, is involuntary unemployment in disequilibrium, caused by low aggregate demand and sluggish wage adjustment.

This division helps us think clearly about the policies needed to tackle unemployment. Keynesian unemployment reflects spare capacity and wasted output. By boosting labour demand, policy can mop up this spare capacity and increase output and employment. Wage adjustment could logically accomplish the same outcome, but may take several years to do so. The more sluggish market forces are, the more it makes sense for policy to intervene. Most forms of monetary policy have the consequence that interest rates will adjust to such a situation and help offset the original demand shock. The automatic fiscal stabilizers also act in this direction.

In marked contrast, when the economy is already in long-run equilibrium, further demand expansion is pointless. Even though unemployment is not zero, there is no spare capacity. At points E or G in Figure 27.4, all remaining unemployment is voluntary.

It is true that, beginning from G, shifting labour demand up from LD' to LD achieves a small reduction in equilibrium unemployment. The distance EF is smaller than GH because the AJ and LF schedules are not parallel to one another. However the main effect of raising demand is to bid up wages, not to increase output or employment.

Hence, when the economy begins with only voluntary unemployment, reductions in unemployment and increases in output are mainly accomplished not by demand policies but by supply-side policies. These policies either *shift* the supply schedules AJ and LF or they reduce distortions that prevented the economy getting to points like E or G.

The next section presents some evidence on the relative magnitude of unemployment responses to demand and supply, and then analyses these supply-side policies in more detail.

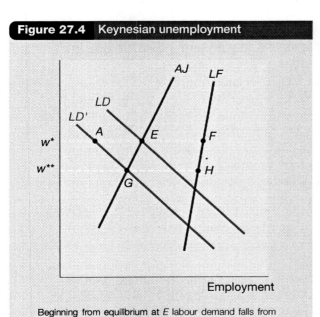

Figure 27.4   Keynesian unemployment

Beginning from equilibrium at E labour demand falls from LD to LD'. Before price and wage adjustment occurs, the economy moves to A. EF is still voluntary unemployment, but now AE is involuntary employment, since workers want to be at E at a real wage w^*. If labour demand remains LD', eventually real wages fall to w^{**} to restore equilibrium at G. By reducing interest rates, monetary policy can shift labour demand up to LD and restore equilibrium at E. Eliminating spare capacity AE allows higher output and employment.

[1] Suppose instead that the central bank has a nominal money target. Involuntary unemployment bids down wages and prices, raising the real money supply. This induces an *automatic* fall in interest rates to increase money demand in line with the higher money supply. Under monetary targeting the pace of the interest rate cuts reflects how quickly wages and prices adjust to unemployment and raise the real money supply. Under other monetary policies, the pace of interest rate cuts is an explicit policy choice.

27.3   Explaining changes in unemployment

Empirical research aims to decompose causes of unemployment into those that changed equilibrium and those that caused demand-deficient unemployment. Estimates by Professors Stephen Nickell, Richard Layard and Richard Jackman of the London School of Economics are given in Table 27.5, which averages UK unemployment rates during seven periods, from 1956–59 through to 1991–95. Averaging reduces the influence of short-run fluctuations. The top row shows the sustained rise in unemployment after the late 1960s and its steady fall after 1990.

Table 27.5 UK unemployment 1956–95							
Unemployment (%)	56–59	60–68	69–73	74–80	81–87	88–90	91–95
Actual rate (%)	2.2	2.6	3.4	5.2	11.1	7.3	9.3
Estimated natural rate (%)	2.2	2.5	3.6	7.3	8.7	8.7	8.9

Sources: R. Layard, S. Nickell and R. Jackman, *Unemployment*, Oxford University Press, 1991; S. Nickell, 'Inflation and the UK Labour Market' in T. Jenkinson, *Readings in Macroeconomics*, Oxford University Press, 1996.

The second row confirms that much of this pattern reflected the rise and fall of equilibrium unemployment, which quadrupled between the 1950s and the 1980s. Indeed, until the start of the 1980s, almost *all* the rise in unemployment reflected a deterioration of supply-side factors.

Equilibrium unemployment fell in the 1990s and continued to fall during 1996–2004 after the end of the period studied by Nickell, Layard, and Jackman. How do we know the equilibrium unemployment kept falling? Because UK unemployment fell all the way to 4 per cent by 2002 *without causing a rise in inflation*. If actual unemployment had fallen below the level of equilibrium unemployment, excess demand for workers would have started to bid up wages, causing a rise in inflation.

Demand and unemployment

Table 27.5 shows that up to 1980 actual unemployment was close to its equilibrium rate – hardly surprising, since demand management policies aimed to keep output close to potential output. Although the rise in unemployment up to 1980 was due to supply-side factors, since 1980 the story is rather different.

Table 27.5 shows that, whenever actual unemployment rose to 10 per cent or more, much of the unemployment was Keynesian, due to deficient demand. For example, during 1981–87, of the actual unemployment rate of 11.1 per cent, only 8.7 per cent was equilibrium unemployment: the rest was due to insufficient demand. In the recession during 1990–92, when unemployment rates again reached double digits, the UK again had significant Keynesian unemployment.

However, in both episodes Keynesian unemployment did not last forever. The late 1980s (and late 1990s) were periods in which output was at, or above, potential. Taking a 40-year view, most of the story is the rise and fall of equilibrium unemployment.

Supply-side economics is the use of microeconomic incentives to alter the level of full employment, the level of potential output and equilibrium unemployment.

Supply-side factors

Keynesians believe that the economy can deviate from full employment for quite a long time, certainly for several years. Monetarists believe that the classical full-employment model is relevant much more quickly. Everyone agrees that in the long run the performance is changed only by affecting the level of full employment and the corresponding level of potential output.

We now discuss four reasons why equilibrium unemployment rose and then fell during 1970–2003.

Mismatch occurs if the skills that firms demand differ from the skills the labour force possesses.

First, increasing skill mismatch raised equilibrium unemployment after 1970. Recent research emphasizes that the labour market is not very good at processing workers as they step out of one job and hope to step into another. The larger the mismatch is, the harder the task is to perform, and the more likely it is that people get stuck in unemployment.

When firms no longer want the skills possessed by the existing workforce, the labour demand curve *LD* shifts leftwards. In Figures 27.3 and 27.4 at lower equilibrium real wage, voluntary unemployment (the gap between *AJ* and *LF*) is larger. A rise in mismatch explained some of the rise in unemployment in the 1970s and 1980s.

Conversely, in the 1990s government policy has stressed reconnecting the unemployed with the labour market, rather than leaving them to languish in long-term unemployment. By offering the unemployed advice on how to get back into work quickly, government policy stopped people being stigmatized as unemployable. This raised the demand for their labour, reducing equilibrium unemployment. At a higher real wage, *AJ* and *LF* are closer together.

A second potential explanation of a rise in equilibrium unemployment is a rise in the generosity of unemployment benefit relative to wages in work.

BOX 27-2   Did the tax carrot work?

Evidence from the past

A lower marginal tax rate makes people substitute work for leisure. But tax cuts also make workers better off. This income effect makes them want to consume more leisure and hence work less. The combined effect on hours of work is small for those already in work. Of more importance is the decision about whether to work at all. Chapter 10 showed that higher take-home pay, for example because of tax cuts, makes more people join the labour force by reducing the significance of the fixed costs of working (commuting, babysitters, giving up social security).

The UK evidence shows that tax cuts have a tiny effect on labour supply by men and single women. But for married women, higher take-home pay encourages labour force participation.

The Thatcher programme

In the 1980s the Thatcher government began a major programme of tax cuts and tax reforms. The real value of personal allowances – how much you can earn before paying income tax – rose by 25 per cent. The basic rate of income tax fell from 33 to 25 per cent and for top income-earners from 83 to 40 per cent. Many politicians anticipated a surge in labour supply. Most economists were pessimistic because of the evidence from the past.

The effect of the Thatcher programme is assessed by C. V. Brown, 'The 1988 Tax Cuts, Work Incentives and Revenue', *Fiscal Studies*, 1988. Brown finds that the big rise in tax allowances led to less than 0.5 per cent extra hours of labour supply. The cut in the basic rate of income tax had no detectable effect at all. The massive cut in the marginal tax rate of top earners had a small effect in stimulating extra hours of work by the rich. The evidence from the past stood up well to a big change of tax policy.

Implications for New Labour

Gordon Brown has quietly been raising taxes to help the poor and provide better funding for public services. Neither theory nor past evidence suggests that this will have a large and adverse incentive effect. The government's problem with tax increases is not economic but political (see Box 16.3).

The **replacement rate** is the level of benefits relative to wages in work.

A higher replacement rate may entice more people into the labour force, shifting *LF* to the right. More significantly, it shifts *AJ* to the left. People spend longer in unemployment searching for the right job. For both reasons, equilibrium unemployment increases.

Most empirical research concludes that higher benefits caused some of the increase in equilibrium unemployment, though less than is sometimes supposed. In practice, UK unemployment benefit (now jobseekers allowance) did not rise enough to explain the rise in unemployment.

However, benefits policy probably does explain some of the fall in equilibrium unemployment after 1992. First, as in other countries such as the Netherlands, the UK redefined many of its long-term unemployed as sick. People on sickness benefit are no longer measured as unemployed. This improves statistical unemployment, though of course in economic terms it is entirely cosmetic.

Second, New Labour's employment policy viewed getting the unemployed back into work as the best form of social policy. People get out of the house, reacquire the work habit, meet other people and rebuild their confidence. Accordingly, New Labour has focused both on *Welfare to Work* and *Making Work Pay*. These two programmes are described in Box 10.2.

Trade union power is measured by the ability of unions to coordinate lower job acceptances, thereby increasing wages but reducing employment.

A third source of changes in equilibrium unemployment has been changes in trade union power. Rises in union power, especially in the 1970s, had a big effect on equilibrium unemployment. Powerful unions made labour scarce and forced up its price. By shifting the *AJ* curve to the left, unions forced up real wages but increased equilibrium unemployment. Conversely, the fall in union power has shifted the *AJ* schedule right, reducing equilibrium unemployment.

Union power increased in the 1970s partly because sympathetic governments passed legislation enhancing worker protection, and partly because many nationalized industries were sheltered state monopolies from which unions could extract potential profits as extra wages for their members.

Union power declined after the 1980s partly because a less sympathetic government reduced the legal protection of unions, partly because privatization removed the Treasury as last-resort funder of union wage claims, and partly because globalization increased competition in general.

The final important source of changes in equilibrium unemployment was changes in the size of the tax wedge between the cost of labour to the firm and the take-home pay of the worker. A key theme of supply-side economists is the benefits that stem from reducing the marginal tax rate.

The **marginal tax rate** is the fraction of each extra pound of income that the government takes in tax. This creates a **tax wedge** between the price the purchaser pays and the price the seller receives.

We discussed tax rates and work incentives in detail in Chapter 10. A cut in marginal tax rates, and a consequent increase in the take-home pay derived from the last hour's work, make people substitute work for leisure. Against this *substitution effect* must be set an *income effect*. If people pay less in taxes, they have to do less work to reach any given target living standard. Thus, theoretical economics cannot prove that tax cuts raise desired labour supply. Most empirical studies confirm that, at best, tax cuts lead to only a small rise in labour supply. Further details are in Chapter 10. Figure 27.5 shows how tax rates affect equilibrium unemployment.

Suppose the marginal tax rate equals the vertical distance *AB*. Equilibrium employment is then N_1. The tax drives a wedge between the gross-of-tax wages paid by firms and the net-of-tax wages received by workers. Firms wish to hire N_1 workers at the gross wage w_1. Subtracting the income tax rate *AB*, N_1 workers want to take job offers at the after-tax wage w_3. Thus N_1 is

BOX 27-3   A manifesto to raise employment

Rich economies are recovering from another slow-down and unemployment is on the rise once again. . . . But the aim this time is not just to reduce unemployment but to raise employment.

Eh? What's the difference? Plenty, in fact. To be counted as unemployed, people usually have to be part of the labour force: they must be available to work and actively looking for a job. But there are many other people of working age – housewives, students, lone parents, disabled people and early retirees – who neither have work nor seek it. These are termed the 'economically inactive'. Policies to cut unemployment aim to lower it as a share of the labour force. Policies to raise employment aim to raise the proportion of the whole working-age population with jobs, not just by getting the unemployed into work but also by mobilizing the economically inactive.

Source: The Economist, 18th September 2003.

The OECD has a number of polices for mobilizing the economically inactive. (1) make work pay for the low-skilled through the provision of work-related top up benefits. (2) Reduce companies' costs of hiring low-skill workers, by reducing red tape and payroll taxes such as employer contributions to national insurance schemes. (3) Help with family commitments, such as child care. Finally (4) restrict the availability of out-of-work benefits, increasing the incentive to find work.

A problem with these polices is that they focus on the low-skilled. In the UK many high-skilled workers, such as teachers, have become economically inactive by taking up generous early retirement packages. A more holistic approach to keeping workers within the labour force may be required.

Figure 27.5   A cut in marginal income tax rates

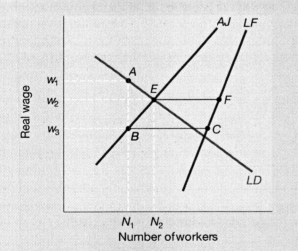

An income tax makes the net-of-tax wage received by households lower than the gross wage paid by firms. *AB* measures the amount each worker pays in income tax, and equilibrium employment is N_1, the quantity that households wish to supply at the after-tax wage w_3 and that firms demand at the gross wage w_1. At the after-tax wage w_3 the natural rate of unemployment is *BC*. If income tax were abolished, equilibrium would be at *E*. Employment would rise from N_1 to N_2 and the natural rate of unemployment would fall from *BC* to *EF*. Relative to the fixed level of unemployment benefit, the rise in take-home pay from w_3 to w_2 reduces voluntary unemployment.

equilibrium employment, where quantities supplied and demanded are equal. The horizontal distance *BC* shows equilibrium unemployment, the number of workers in the labour force not wishing to work at the going rate of take-home pay.

Suppose taxes are abolished. The gross wage and the take-home pay now coincide and the new labour market equilibrium is at *E*. Two things happen. First, equilibrium employment rises. Second, although more people join the labour force because take-home pay has risen from w_3 to w_2, equilibrium unemployment falls from *BC* to *EF*. A rise in take-home pay relative to unemployment benefit reduces voluntary unemployment. If lower tax rates reduce equilibrium unemployment, higher tax rates increase equilibrium unemployment.

Another possible supply-side policy is to cut unemployment benefit. For a given labour force schedule *LF*, fewer people now wish to be unemployed at any real wage. The schedule *AJ*, showing acceptances of job offers, shifts to the right. This raises equilibrium employment (and hence potential output) and reduces equilibrium unemployment.

What about changes in the national insurance contributions paid both by firms and by workers? These are mandatory contributions to state schemes that provide unemployment and health insurance. They act like an income tax, driving a wedge *AB* between the total cost to a firm of hiring another worker and the net take-home pay of a worker. Figure 27.5 implies that a fall in these contributions will raise equilibrium employment and cut equilibrium unemployment.

Supply-side policies can reduce equilibrium unemployment. Where this involves being tough on those already relatively disadvantaged, there is a conflict between efficiency and fairness, and only through the political process can society express its view.

Now you've read this section, why not test your understanding by visiting the Online Learning Centre at www.mcgraw-hill.co.uk/textbooks/begg

27.4 Cyclical fluctuations in unemployment

We discuss business cycles in Chapter 31. Cycles may reflect fluctuations in demand or fluctuations in supply. Since supply usually changes slowly, most of the sharp movements in the short run are caused by changes in demand.

There is a cyclical relationship between demand, output, employment and unemployment. On average, boosting aggregate demand by 1 per cent will not raise employment by 1 per cent or reduce unemployment by one percentage point, even if the economy begins with spare resources. Table 27.6 shows two periods of demand growth and two periods of rapid demand decline. In practice, booms lead initially to a sharp increase in shift lengths and hours worked; slumps lead to the abolition of overtime, the introduction of short time, and a marked decline in hours worked.

Table 27.6 Output, employment and unemployment

Cumulative change in	79ii–81ii	86ii–88ii	90ii–91ii	92iv–98ii
Real GDP (%)	−7.8	+9.1	−3.4	+16.8
Employment (%)	−6.3	+2.5	−2.9	+ 6.8
Employed (million)	−1.7	+0.5	−0.7	+ 1.5
Unemployed (million)	+1.4	−0.9	+0.6	− 1.2

Source: ONS, *Economic Trends*.

The table confirms that changes in demand and output lead to smaller changes in employment. For example, when output grew 28 per cent between the second quarter of 1992 and the fourth quarter of 2002 employment rose by only 3 per cent. Nor do changes in employment lead to corresponding changes in unemployment. The last two rows of the table show that rapid expansion or contraction of employment leads to significantly smaller changes in unemployment.

One reason is the 'discouraged worker effect'. When unemployment is high and rising, some people who would like to work grow pessimistic and stop looking for work. No longer registered as looking for work, they are not recorded in the labour force or the unemployed. Conversely, in a boom, people who had previously given up looking for work rejoin the labour force since there is now a good chance of finding a suitable job. Hence in booms and slumps recorded employment data change by more than recorded unemployment data.

27.5 The cost of unemployment

The private cost of unemployment

It is important to distinguish between voluntary and involuntary unemployment. When individuals are voluntarily unemployed, they reveal that they do better by being unemployed than by immediately taking a job offer that they face at the going wage rate. The private cost of unemployment (the wage forgone by not working) is less than the private benefits of being unemployed. What are these benefits?

The first is transfer payments from government. Workers who have contributed to the national insurance scheme get jobseekers allowance for the first 12 months after becoming unemployed. Thereafter they get income support, the ultimate backstop in the British welfare state.

There are other benefits of being unemployed. First, there is the value of leisure. By refusing a job, some people reveal that the extra leisure is worth more to them than the extra disposable income if they·took a job. Second, some people expect to get a better job by being choosier about accepting job offers. These future benefits must be set against the current cost, a lower disposable income by being out of work.

When people are involuntarily unemployed, the cost changes. Involuntary unemployment means that people would like to work at the going wage but cannot find a job because there is excess labour supply at the existing wage rate. These people are worse off by being unemployed.

The distinction between voluntary and involuntary unemployment matters because it may affect our value judgement about how much attention to pay to unemployment. When unemployment is involuntary, people are suffering more and the case for helping them is stronger.

The social cost of unemployment

Again we distinguish between voluntary and involuntary unemployment. When unemployment is voluntary, individuals prefer to be unemployed. Does this unemployment also benefit society?

An individual receives transfer payments during unemployment but these transfers give no corresponding benefit to society as a whole. They may ease the collective conscience about poverty and income inequality, but they are not payments for the supply of any goods or services that other members of society may consume. Since the private benefit exceeds the social benefit, too many people may be voluntarily unemployed.

This does not mean that society should go to the opposite extreme and eliminate voluntary unemployment completely. First, society is perfectly entitled to adopt the value judgement that it will maintain a reasonable living standard for the unemployed, whatever the cost in resource misallocation. Second, the efficient level of voluntary unemployment is well above zero.

In a changing economy, it is important to match up the right people to the right jobs. Getting this match right lets society make more output. Freezing the existing pattern of employment in a changing economy leads to a mismatch of people and jobs. The flow through the pool of unemployment allows people to be reallocated to more suitable jobs, raising potential output in the long run.

Two points from our earlier discussion are also relevant here. First, even when unemployment is high, flows both in and out of the pool are large relative to the pool itself. Second, people who do not get out of the pool quickly are in danger of stagnating when unemployment

BOX 27-4　Hysteresis and high unemployment in Europe

Supply and demand curves are supposed to be independent of one another. The labour supply curve or job acceptances schedule *AJ* shows the people willing to work at each real wage whatever the position of the labour demand curve *LD*, and vice versa. But this may be wrong.

In the diagram, the initial equilibrium is at *E*. Something then shifts labour demand down from *LD* to *LD'*. Suppose this causes a permanent fall in labour supply. *JA* shifts to *JA'*. When labour demand reverts to *LD*, the new equilibrium is at *F*, not *E*. The short-run history of the economy has affected its long-run equilibrium.

> An economy experiences hysteresis when its long-run equilibrium depends on the path it follows in the short run.

Hysteresis may explain high and persistent unemployment in Europe. Here are some channels through which it might work.

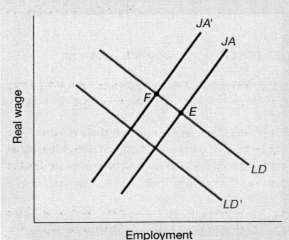

Employment

The insider–outsider distinction

Outsiders are unemployed without jobs. Only insiders with jobs participate in wage bargaining. At the original equilibrium *E*, the numerous insiders in work ensure that real wages are low enough to preserve their own jobs. When a recession occurs, *LD* shifts to *LD'*. Some insiders get fired and become outsiders. Eventually, as explained in Chapter 25, market forces restore labour

demand to *LD*. But now there are fewer insiders than originally. They exploit their scarcity by securing higher wages for themselves, rather than encouraging firms to rehire. The economy is trapped in the high-wage, low-employment equilibrium at *F* instead of the low-wage, high-employment equilibrium at *E*. Thereafter, only long-run supply-side measures aimed at breaking down insider power can gradually break the economy out of this low-employment equilibrium.

Discouraged workers

Again, the economy begins at *E*. It has a skilled and energetic labour force. A temporary recession leads to unemployment. If the recession is protracted, we see the emergence of long-term unemployed and a culture in which people stop looking for jobs. Again, when demand picks up, labour supply has been permanently reduced and equilibrium reverts to *F*, not *E*. Only long-term supply-side measures to restore the work culture will succeed.

Search and mismatch

When employment is high at *E*, firms are trying to find scarce workers, and potential workers are searching hard for a job. A recession makes firms advertise fewer vacancies, and workers realize it is a waste of time searching for jobs. When demand picks up again, both firms and workers are accustomed to low levels of search. New jobs are not created.

The capital stock

At *E* the economy has a lot of capital. Labour productivity is high and firms want lots of workers. During a temporary recession, firms scrap old machines. When demand picks up again, firms have permanently lower capital. The demand for labour, which depends on the marginal product of labour, never rises to its original level. Again, the economy returns to *F* not *E*.

Policy implications of hysteresis

Hysteresis means that a temporary fall in demand induces permanently lower employment and output,

BOX 27-4   Continued

and higher equilibrium unemployment. There are two policy implications. First, once the problem has emerged, it is dangerous to try to break out of it simply by expanding aggregate demand. Before long-run supply can respond, you get major inflation. Supply-side policies, needed to rebuild aggregate supply, take a long time to work.

Second, because the problem is so hard to cure once it occurs, it is vital not to let demand fall in the first place. The payoff to demand management is higher than in an economy with a unique long-run equilibrium, where all that is at stake is how quickly the economy reverts to its original point.

is high: the fraction of the unemployed who have been unemployed for over a year is higher in the 1990s than at the end of the 1970s when unemployment was much lower.

Involuntary or Keynesian unemployment has an even higher social cost. Since the economy is producing below capacity, it is literally throwing away output that could have been made by putting these people to work. Moreover, since Keynesian unemployment is involuntary, it may entail more human and psychological suffering than voluntary unemployment. Although hard to quantify, it is also part of the social cost of unemployment.

SUMMARY

- People are either employed, unemployed or out of the labour force. The level of unemployment rises when inflows to the pool of the unemployed exceed outflows. Inflows and outflows are large relative to the level of unemployment.

- As unemployment has risen, the average duration of unemployment has increased.

- Women face lower unemployment rates than men. The unemployment rates for older workers, and especially for young workers, are well above the national average.

- Unemployment can be classified as frictional, structural, classical or demand-deficient. In modern terminology, the first three types are voluntary unemployment and the last is involuntary unemployment. The natural rate of unemployment is the equilibrium level of voluntary unemployment.

- In the long run, sustained rises in unemployment must reflect increases in the natural rate of unemployment. During temporary recessions, Keynesian unemployment is also important.

- Supply-side economics aims to increase equilibrium employment and potential output, and to reduce the natural rate of unemployment, by operating on incentives at a microeconomic level. Supply-side policies include reducing mismatch, reducing union power, tax cuts, reductions in unemployment benefit, retraining and relocation grants, and investment subsidies.

- A 1 per cent increase in output is likely to lead to a much smaller reduction in Keynesian unemployment. Some of the extra output will be met by longer hours. And as unemployment falls, some people, effectively in the labour force but not registered, look for work again.

● Hysteresis means that short-run changes can move the economy to a different long-run equilibrium. It may explain why European recessions have raised the natural rate of unemployment substantially.

● People voluntarily unemployed reveal that the private benefits from unemployment exceed the private cost in wages forgone. Society derives no output from transfer payments to support the unemployed. However, society would not benefit by driving unemployment to zero. Some social gains in higher productivity are derived from improved matching of people and jobs that temporary unemployment allows.

● Keynesian unemployment is involuntary and hurts private individuals who would prefer to be employed. Socially it represents wasted output. Society may also care about the human misery inflicted by involuntary unemployment.

● Most European countries took two decades to reverse the high unemployment of the 1980s.

REVIEW QUESTIONS

● What is the discouraged-worker effect? Suggest two reasons why it occurs.

● 'The average duration of an individual's unemployment rises in a slump. Hence the problem is a higher inflow to the pool of unemployment, not a lower outflow.' Do you agree?

● Why is teenage unemployment so high?

● 'The microchip caused a permanent rise in the level of unemployment.' Did it? What about all previous technical advances?

● How is high unemployment be explained by (a) a Keynesian, (b) a classical economist?

● Explain why boosting demand sometimes fails to reduce unemployment.

● **Common fallacies** Why are these statements wrong? (a) Unemployment is always a bad thing. (b) So long as there is unemployment, there is pressure on wages to fall. (c) Unemployment arises only because greedy workers are pricing themselves out of a job.

To check your answers to these questions, go to page 643.

To check your answers to these questions, go to page 643.

To help you grasp the key concepts of this chapter check out the extra resources posted on the Online Learning Centre at www.mcgraw-hill.co.uk/ textbooks/begg. There are quick test questions, economics examples and access to Powerweb articles, all for free!

For even more exercises, recaps and examples to help you study, purchase a copy of the Economics Student Workbook. Simply visit www.mcgraw hill.co.uk/textbooks/begg and follow the links to the Workbook to buy your copy.

Economic growth

chapter 30

Learning outcomes

By the end of this chapter, you should understand:

1 growth in potential output

2 Malthus's forecast of eventual starvation

3 how technical progress and capital accumulation made the forecast wrong

4 the neoclassical model of economic growth

5 the convergence hypothesis

6 the growth performance of rich and poor countries

7 whether policy can affect growth

8 whether growth must stop to save the environment

During 1870–2002 UK real GDP grew 10-fold and real income per person 5-fold. On average, we are richer than our grandparents but less rich than our grandchildren will be. Table 30.1 shows that these long-term trends were even more dramatic elsewhere. During 1870–2002, real GDP in Japan rose 100-fold and real income per person 27-fold.

Table 30.1 prompts three questions. What is long-run economic growth? What causes it? And can economic policies affect it? We mainly focus on industrial countries. Chapter 36 examines growth, or the lack of it, in poor countries.

Economists were always fascinated by the theory of economic growth. In 1798 Thomas Malthus's *First Essay on Population* predicted that output growth would be far outstripped by population growth, causing starvation and an end to population growth, the origin of the notion of economics as 'the dismal science'. Some countries are still stuck in a Malthusian trap, others broke through to sustained growth and prosperity. We examine how they did it.

Table 30.1 Real GDP and per capita real GDP, 1870–2002

| | Real GDP | | Per capital real GDP | |
	Ratio of 2002 to 1870	Annual growth	Ratio of 2002 to 1870 (%)	Annual growth (%)
Japan	100	3.7	27	2.7
USA	66	3.4	10	1.8
Australia	45	3.1	4	1.2
Sweden	33	2.8	14	2.2
France	15	2.2	10	1.9
UK	10	1.9	5	1.3

Source: Angus Maddison, 'Phases of Capitalist Development', in R. C. O. Matthews (ed.), *Economic Growth and Resources*, vol. 2, Macmillan, 1979; updated from IMF, *International Financial Statistics*.

As Table 30.1 shows, an extra 0.5 per cent on the annual growth rate makes a vast difference to potential output after a few decades. By the end of the 1960s, economists had worked out a theory of economic growth. It yielded many insights but had one central failing. It predicted that government policy made no difference to the long-run growth rate.

In the mid-1980s, a simple insight spawned a new approach, in which long-run growth is affected by private behaviour and government policy. We briefly explain this new approach to economic growth.

Finally, we consider whether growth is good. Might it be better to grow more slowly? Can the costs of growth outweigh its benefits?

30.1   Economic growth

The growth rate of a variable is its percentage rise per annum. To define economic growth we must specify both the variable to measure and the period over which to measure it. Table 30.1 uses real GDP. We get similar results using real GNP or national income.

GDP and GNP measure the total output and total income of an economy. Even so, they are very incomplete measures of *economic* output and income. Moreover, it is hard to account for the introduction of new products. Nor does more GDP guarantee more happiness.

Economic growth is the rate of change of real income or real output.

GDP and economic output

GDP measures the net output or value added in an economy by measuring goods and services bought with money. It omits output not bought and sold and therefore unmeasured. Two big omissions are leisure and externalities such as pollution and congestion.

In most industrial countries, average hours of work have fallen at least ten hours a week since 1900. In choosing to work fewer hours, people reveal that the extra leisure is worth at least as much as the extra goods they could have bought by working longer. When people decide to swap washing machines for extra leisure, recorded GDP falls. GDP understates the true economic output of the economy. Conversely, the output of pollution reduces the net economic welfare that the economy is producing and ideally should be subtracted from GDP.

Including leisure in GDP would have raised recorded GDP in both 1870 and 2000. Since the value of leisure probably rose less quickly than measured output, which rose 10-fold in the UK and 100-fold in Japan, a more comprehensive output measure might show a slower growth rate. Conversely, pollution and congestion have increased rapidly. Allowing for them would also reduce true growth rates below the measured growth rates in Table 30.1.

New products

In 1870 people had no TV, cars or computers. Statisticians do their best to compare the value of real GDP in different years but new products make it hard to compare across time. We can estimate how much people's real income rises when a new product does an old task more cheaply. The calculation is harder when the new product allows a new activity not previously possible. In previous chapters, we argued that a small amount of inflation probably reflects real prices increases justified by better quality or completely new products.

GDP and happiness

Even with an accurate and comprehensive measure of GDP, two problems remain. First, do we care about total GDP or GDP per capita? This depends on the question we wish to ask. Total GDP shows the size of an economy. However, if we care about the happiness of a typical individual in an economy, it is better to look at GDP per capita. Table 30.1 tells us that, although real GDP grew more quickly in Australia than in France or Sweden during 1870–2000, in part this reflected rapid population growth, largely through immigration. Sweden and France had faster growth in GDP per person over the period. Even so, real GDP per person is an imperfect indicator of the happiness of a typical citizen. When income is shared equally between citizens, a country's per capita real GDP tells us what every person gets. But some countries have very unequal income distributions. A few people earn a lot, and a lot of people earn only a little. Such countries may have fairly high per capita real income but many citizens still in poverty.

Finally, even when GDP is adjusted to measure leisure, pollution and so on, higher per capita GDP need not lead to greater happiness. Material goods are not everything. But they help. Movements in which people return to 'the simple life' have not had much success. Most of the poorer countries are trying to increase their GDP as quickly as possible.

A recent phenomenon?

Table 30.1 makes a final point. Even an annual growth rate of only 1.3 per cent in per capita GDP led to a 5-fold rise in UK per capita real GDP between 1870 and 2000. In 1870, UK per capita income was about £1900 in 2000 prices. If its annual growth rate had always been 1.3 per cent, per capita real income would have been £370 in 1750, £75 in 1630 and £16 in 1510. This is implausible. Hence, it is only in the last 250 years that per capita real income has risen steadily.

In the long run, output fluctuations around potential output are swamped by the growth of potential output itself. If potential output rises 2 per cent a year, it will increase 7-fold in less than a century. To explain growth we must think about changes in potential output.

30.2 Growth: an overview

The production function shows the maximum output obtainable from specified quantities of inputs, given the existing technical knowledge.

For simplicity, we assume that the economy is always at potential output. The production function tells us that higher potential output can be traced to more inputs of land, labour, capital and raw materials, or to technical advances that let given inputs make more output.

In the long run, population growth may be affected by per capita output, which affects the number of children people decide to have, and the health care and nutrition people then get. Nevertheless, we simplify by assuming that the rate of population growth is independent of economic factors. Thus we assume that anything that raises output also raises per capita output.

Capital

Productive capital is the stock of machinery, buildings and inventories with which other inputs combine to make output. For a given labour input, more capital raises output. However, capital depreciates over time. Some new investment is needed just to stop the existing capital stock from shrinking. And with a growing labour force, even more investment is needed if capital per worker is to be maintained. With yet faster investment, capital per worker rises over time, increasing the output each worker can produce. Higher capital per worker is a key means of raising output per worker and per capita income.

Labour

Employment can rise for two reasons. There may be population growth or a larger fraction of a given population may have jobs. Labour input also depends on hours worked per person. For a given number of workers, more hours worked raises effective labour input, raising output.

Weekly hours worked have fallen a lot since 1870. The rise in per capita real output in Table 30.1 does not reflect longer hours. Since 1945, labour input has risen mainly because more women have joined the labour force.

Human capital

Human capital is the skill and knowledge embodied in the minds and hands of workers. Education, training and experience allow workers to make more output. For example, much of Germany's physical capital was devastated during the Second World War but the human capital of its labour force survived. Given these skills, Germany recovered rapidly after 1945. Without this human capital, there would have been no postwar German economic miracle.

Land

Land is especially important in an agricultural economy. If each worker has more land, agricultural output is higher. Land is less important in highly industrialized economies. Hong Kong and Singapore have grown rapidly despite overcrowding and a scarcity of land. Even so, more land would help.

Increases in the supply of land are pretty unimportant to growth. In theory land is the input whose total supply to the economy is fixed. In practice the distinction between land and capital is blurred. By applying more fertilizer per acre, the effective quantity of farming land can be increased. With investment in drainage or irrigation, marshes and deserts can be made productive.

Raw materials

Given the quantity of other inputs, more input of raw materials allows more output. When raw materials are scarce and expensive, workers take time and care not to waste them. With more plentiful raw materials, workers work more quickly.

Depletable resources can be used only once. **Renewable resources** can used again if not over-exploited.

When a barrel of oil has been extracted from the ground and used to fuel a machine, the world has one less barrel of oil reserves. If the world has a finite stock of oil reserves, it will eventually run out of oil, though perhaps not for centuries.

In contrast, timber and fish, if harvested in moderation, are replaced by nature and can be used as production inputs forever. However, if over-harvested they become extinct. With only a few whales left, whales find it hard to find mates with which to breed. The stock of whales falls.

Factor contributions and scale economies

The marginal product of a factor is extra output when that input rises by a unit but all other inputs are held constant. Microeconomics tells us that marginal products eventually decline as the input increases. With two workers already on each machine, another worker does little to raise output.

Economies of scale

Instead of increasing an input in isolation, suppose all inputs are doubled together. If output exactly doubles, there are *constant returns to scale*; if output more (less) than doubles, there are *increasing (decreasing) returns to scale*.

Scale economies reinforce growth. Any rise in inputs gets an extra bonus in higher output. There may be engineering reasons for scale economies. Simple mathematics shows that it takes less than twice the steel input to build an oil tanker of twice the capacity. On the other hand, many developing countries regret their resources tied up in huge steel mills that are now inefficient. Bigger is not always better. In practice, economists often assume constant returns to scale.

Having discussed the different production inputs, we turn now to the role of technical knowledge.

30.3 Technical knowledge

Technical advances in productivity come through **invention**, the discovery of new knowledge, and **innovation**, the incorporation of new knowledge into actual production techniques.

At any given time, a society has a stock of technical knowledge about ways in which goods can be produced. Some of this knowledge is written down in books and blueprints but much is reflected in working practices learned by hard experience.

Inventions

Major inventions can lead to spectacular increases in technical knowledge. The wheel, the steam engine and the modern computer are examples. Technical progress in agriculture has also been dramatic. Industrial societies began only when productivity improvements in agriculture freed some of the workforce to produce industrial goods without leaving people short of food. Before then, everyone had to work the land merely to get enough food to survive. The replacement of animal power by machines, the development of fertilizer, drainage and irrigation, and new hybrid seeds, all played a large part in improving agricultural production and enabling economic growth.

Embodiment of knowledge in capital

To introduce new ideas to actual production, innovation often requires investment in new machines. Without investment, bullocks cannot be transformed into tractors even once the know-how for building tractors is available. Major new inventions thus lead to waves of investment and innovation as the ideas are put into practice. The mid-nineteenth century was the age of the train, and the mid-twentieth century the age of the car. We are now in the age of the microchip.

Learning by doing

Human capital can matter as much as physical capital. With practice, workers get better at doing a particular job. The most famous example is known as the Horndal effect, after a Swedish steelworks built during 1835–36 and kept in the same condition for the next 15 years. With no change in the plant or the size of the labour force, output per worker-hour nevertheless rose by 2 per cent a year. Eventually, however, as skills become mastered, further productivity increases are harder to attain.

BOX 30-1 The road to riches

For centuries, per capital income growth was tiny. Most people were close to starvation. Now we take growth for granted. After 1750 industrialization changed everything. Capital and knowledge, accumulated by one generation, were inherited and augmented by the next generation.

Why 1750? Partly because mathematical and scientific ideas reached a critical mass, allowing an explosion of practical spinoffs. Yet many pioneers of the Industrial Revolution were common-sense artisans with little scientific training. Conversely, the ancient Greece of Pythagoras and Archimedes achieved scientific learning but not economic prosperity.

By the start of the 15th century, China understood hydraulic engineering, artificial fertilizers and veterinary medicine. It had blast furnaces in 200BC, 1500 years before Europe. It had paper 1000 years before Europe, and inventing printing 400 years before Gutenberg. Yet by 1600 China had been overtaken by Western Europe and by 1800 had been left far behind.

Economic historians continue to debate the root causes of progress but three ingredients seem crucial: values, politics and economic institutions. Growth entails a willingness to embrace change. China's rulers liked social order, stability and isolation from foreign ideas, fine attitudes when progress was slow and domestic but a disaster when the world experienced a profusion of new technologies and applications.

Powerful Chinese rulers could enforce bans and block change in their huge empire. Even when individual European rulers tried to do the same, competition between small European states undermined this sovereignty and offered opportunities for growth and change. Economic competition helped separate markets from political control. Rights of merchants led to laws of contracts, patent, company law and property. Competition between forms of institution allowed more effective solutions to emerge and evolve. Arbitrary intervention by heads of state was reduced. Opportunities for business, trade, invention and innovation flourished.

The making of Western Europe

Date	Per capita income (1990 prices)	Inventions
1000	400	Watermills
1100	430	Padded horse collar
1200	480	Windmills
1300	510	Compass
1400	600	Blast furnace
1500	660	Gutenberg printing press
1600	780	Telescope
1700	880	Pendulum clock, canals
1800	1280	Steam engine, spinning and weaving machines, cast iron, electric battery
1900	3400	Telegraph, telephone, electric light, wireless
2000	17400	Steel, cars, planes, computers, nuclear energy

Source: The Economist, 31 December 1999.

Research and development

What determines the amount of invention and innovation? Some new ideas are the product of intellectual curiosity or frustration ('There must be a better way to do this!'). But like most activities, the output of new ideas depends to a large extent on the resources devoted to looking for them, which in turn depend on the cost of tying up resources in this way and the prospective benefits from success. Some research activities take place in university departments, usually funded at least in part by the government, but a lot of research is privately funded through the money firms devote to research and development (R&D).

The outcome of research is risky. Research workers never know whether or not they will find anything useful. Research is like a risky investment project. The funds are committed before the benefits (if any) start to accrue but there is one important difference. Suppose you spend a lot of money developing a better mousetrap. When you succeed, everyone copies your new mousetrap: the price is bid down, and you never recoup your initial investment. In such a world, there would be little incentive to undertake R&D.

If the invention becomes widely available, society gets the benefit but the original developer does not: there is an *externality*. Private and social gains do not coincide and the price mechanism does not provide the correct incentives. Society tries to get round this *market failure* in two ways. First, it grants *patents* to private inventors and innovators, legal monopolies for a fixed period of time that allow successful research projects to repay investments in R&D by temporarily charging higher prices than the cost of production alone. Second, the government subsidizes a good deal of basic research in universities, in its own laboratories and in private industry.

30.4 Growth and accumulation

In this section we explore the links between output growth, factor accumulation and technical progress. We organize our discussion around a simple production function

$$Y = A \times f(K, L) \tag{1}$$

Variable inputs capital K and labour L combine to produce a given output $f(K, L)$. The function f tells us how much we get out of particular amounts of inputs K and L. This function f never changes. We capture technical progress separately through A, which measures the extent of technical knowledge at any date. As technical progress takes place, we get more output from given inputs, a rise in A. For simplicity we assume that land is fixed.

Malthus, land and population

Writing in 1798 and living in a largely agricultural society, Malthus worried about the fixed supply of land. As a growing population worked a fixed supply of land, the marginal product of labour would fall. Agricultural output would grow less quickly than population. The per capita food supply would fall until starvation reduced population to the level that could be fed from the given supply of agricultural land.

In terms of equation (1), starving people consume all their income. Without savings, society cannot invest in capital, so K is zero. The production function then has diminishing returns to labour: adding more workers drives down productivity.

Some poor countries today face this *Malthusian trap*. Agricultural productivity is so low that everyone must work the land to produce food. As population grows and agricultural output fails to keep pace, famine sets in and people die. If better fertilizers or irrigation improve agricultural output, population quickly expands as nutrition improves, and people are driven back to starvation levels again.

Yet Malthus's prediction was not correct for all countries. Today's rich countries broke out of the Malthusian trap. How did they do it? First, they raised agricultural productivity (without an immediate population increase) so that some workers could be switched to industrial production. The capital goods then produced included better ploughs, machinery to pump water and drain fields, and transport to distribute food more effectively. As capital was applied in agriculture, output per worker rose further, releasing more workers to industry while maintaining enough food production to feed the growing population.

Second, the rapid technical progress in agricultural production led to large and persistent productivity increases, reinforcing the effect of moving to more capital-intensive agricultural production. In terms of equation (1), rises in A and in K let output grow faster than labour, causing a *rise* in living standards.

Thus, even the existence of a factor in fixed supply need not make sustained growth impossible. If capital can be accumulated, more and more capital can be substituted for fixed land, allowing output to grow at least as rapidly as population. Similarly, continuing technical progress allows continuing output growth even if one factor is not increasing.

The price mechanism provides the correct incentives for these processes to occur. With a given supply of land, higher agricultural production raises the price of land and the rental paid for land. This gives an incentive to switch to less land-intensive production methods (heavy fertilizer usage, battery chickens) and an incentive to focus on technical progress that lets the economy get by with less land. A similar argument applies to any natural resource in finite supply.

Capital accumulation

Postwar theories of economic growth date back to work in the 1940s by Roy Harrod in England and Evsey Domar in the United States. In the late 1950s Bob Solow of MIT assembled the nuts and bolts of the neoclassical growth theory, the basis of empirical work ever since.[1]

The theory is *neoclassical* because it does not ask how actual output gets to potential output. Over a long enough period, the only question of interest is what is happening to potential output itself. Neoclassical growth theory simply assumes that actual and potential output are equal.

Along the **steady-state path**, output, capital and labour grow at the same rate. Hence output per worker and capital per worker are constant.

In a growing economy, **capital-widening** extends the existing capital per worker to new extra workers. **Capital-deepening** raises capital per worker for all workers.

In this long run, labour and capital grow. Usually, equilibrium means that things are not changing. Now we apply equilibrium not to levels but to growth rates and ratios. The steady state is the long-run equilibrium in growth theory.

Assume that labour grows at a constant rate n. To keep things simple, we also assume a constant fraction s of income is saved; the rest is consumed. Aggregate capital formation (public and private) is the part of output not consumed (by both public and private sectors). Investment first widens and then perhaps deepens capital.

To keep capital per person constant, we need more investment per person the faster population growth n (extra workers for whom capital must be

---

[1] Solow won a Nobel Prize for his work on long-run growth. He is also famous for his one-liners. Since, in short-run analysis, he is an unrepentant Keynesian, many of his famous barbs are aimed at those who believe that prices clear markets quickly: 'Will the olive, unassisted, always settle half way up the martini?'

provided) and the more capital per person k that has to be provided. Figure 30.1 plots the line nk along which capital per person is constant.

Adding more capital per worker k increases output per worker y, but with diminishing returns: hence the curve y in Figure 30.1. Since a constant amount of output is saved, sy shows the saving per person. Since saving and investment are equal, it also shows investment per person.

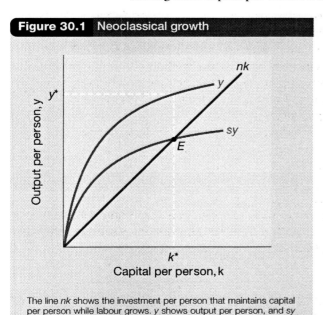

Figure 30.1   Neoclassical growth

The line nk shows the investment per person that maintains capital per person while labour grows. y shows output per person, and sy is both saving and investment per person. At the steady state E, investment is just sufficient to keep capital per person constant at k^*. Per capita output is then y^*. Output and capital grow with population.

In the steady state, capital per person is constant. Hence investment per person sy must equal nk, the investment per person needed to keep k constant by making capital grow as fast as labour. k^* is the steady-state capital per person and y^* the steady-state output per person. Capital, output and labour all grow at the same rate n along this steady-state path.

Figure 30.1 also shows what happens away from the steady state. If capital per worker is low, the economy is left of the steady state. Per capita saving and investment sy exceed nk, the per capital investment required to keep capital in line with growing labour. So capital per person rises. Conversely, to the right of the steady state, sy lies below nk and capital per person falls. Figure 30.1 says that, from whatever level of capital the economy begins, it gradually converges to the (unique) steady state.

A higher saving rate

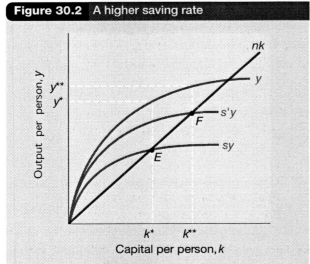

Figure 30.2   A higher saving rate

The original steady state is at E. An increase in the fraction of income saved, from s to s', leads to a steady state at F. This raises capital and output per worker, but eventually has no effect on the growth rate. Since y^{**} is constant, output and labour still grow at rate n.

Suppose people permanently increase the fraction of income saved, from s to s'. We get more saving, more investment and hence a faster rate of output growth. Oh no we don't! Figure 30.2 explains why not.

There is no change in the production function relating output to inputs. At the original savings rate s, the steady state is at E. At the higher savings rate, $s'y$ shows savings and investment per person. At F it equals nk, the per capita investment needed to stop k rising or falling. Thus F is the new steady state.

F has more capital per worker than E. Productivity and output per worker are higher. That is the permanent effect of a higher saving rate. It affects levels, not growth rates. In *any* steady state, L, K and Y all grow at the same rate n, and that rate is determined 'outside the model': it is the rate of growth of labour and population. We return to this issue shortly.

In Figure 30.2, the higher saving rate raises output and capital per worker. To make the transition from E to F, there must be a temporary period in which capital grows faster than labour; only then can capital per worker rise as required. A higher saving rate, if successfully translated into higher investment to keep the economy at full employment, causes faster output growth for a while but not for ever. Once capital per worker rises sufficiently, higher rates of saving and investment go entirely in capital widening, now more demanding than before. Further capital deepening, the basis of productivity growth, cannot continue without bound.

 **Now you've read this section,** why not test your understanding by visiting the Online Learning Centre at www.mcgraw-hill.co.uk/textbooks/begg

30.5 Growth through technical progress

We have made a lot of progress but still have some problems. First, the theory does not fit *all* the facts. So far, the theory says output, labour and capital all grow at rate n. Although capital and

BOX 30-2 Aborted take offs on the growth runway

We assumed people save a constant fraction s of their income. Even poor people earning only y save sy and consume $(1-s)y$. But if y is low enough, $(1-s)y$ is too low to stop starvation. So they consume all their income and save none. Below a critical income level y_0, saving is zero. What does the Solow diagram look like now? Suppose k_0 is the capital per person that just generates the critical income y_0. Higher capital generates savings as in previous diagrams and nk is still the gross investment needed to maintain a given capital–labour ratio in the face of growing population. There are now three steady states!

If capital begins above k_1 the economy converges to the steady state at E. Between k_1 and k_2 saving and investment exceed the amount needed for capital widening: capital-deepening also occurs and the economy grows. Above k_2, saving and investment are insufficient to maintain the capital–labour ratio and the economy shrinks. Either way it ends at E. This is the case analysed in Figures 30.1 and 30.2. Suppose, next, the economy begins at exactly k_1. Saving and investment just maintain the capital–labour ratio. So this is a steady state but an unstable one. A little above k_1 the economy begins converging on E. And below k_1 there is insufficient saving and investment to provide for the growing population. Capital per person shrinks

and keeps shrinking till the economy reaches $k = 0$.

In this model, countries beginning with capital below k_1 are stuck in a poverty trap. They cannot break out. All output is consumed to prevent starvation. There is never a surplus to begin accumulation and growth. This model can also explain why convergence seems to occur within the OECD (countries already above k_1) but why simultaneously many countries are stuck in poverty. Modern growth in the last two centuries began when some key events first generated the surplus to allow saving and accumulation to begin.

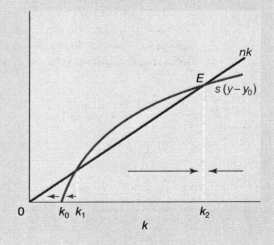

output do grow at similar rates, in practice both grow more rapidly than labour. That is why we are better off than our great grandparents.

The answer may lie in technical progress, which we ignored in trying to explain output growth entirely through growth in factor supplies (population growth and the accumulation of capital). It turns out that *labour-augmenting technical progress* would do the trick.

Population growth might eventually double the number of workers. Imagine instead that the number of workers is constant but that new knowledge allows the same workers to do the work of twice as many as before, as if the population had grown.

> **Labour-augmenting technical progress** increases the effective labour supply.

Suppose this progress occurs at rate t. Effective labour input grows at rate $(t + n)$ because of technical progress and population growth. Now go back to Figure 30.1 and simply put $(t + n)k$ instead of nk. To make this valid, we have to measure capital and output not per worker but per worker-equivalent. Worker-equivalents are created by population growth or technical progress. Otherwise the diagram is identical.

E remains the steady state. Output per worker-equivalent and capital per worker-equivalent are constant. Since worker-equivalents grow at rate $t + n$, so must capital and output. Since actual workers increase at rate n, output and capital per actual worker each increase at rate t. Now our growth theory fits all the facts. Living standards grow over time at rate t.

It is uncomfortable that the two key growth rates, n and t, are determined outside the model. For that reason, for the next 30 years the main use of this growth theory was in growth accounting: showing how to decompose actual output behaviour into the parts explained by changes in various inputs and the part residually explained by technical progress. We next examine the results of accounting for growth.

30.6 Growth in the OECD

The Organization for Economic Cooperation and Development is a club of the world's richest countries, from industrial giants like the United States and Japan to smaller economies like New Zealand, Ireland and Turkey. Table 30.2 shows the growth of OECD countries since 1950.

Productivity growth slowed sharply after 1973 in all OECD countries. Several explanations were put forward. Some stressed the rise in trade union power, enjoying greater legal protection in the 1970s. If this explanation is correct, the supply-side reforms of the late 1980s should have led to high productivity growth in the 1990s. There is little evidence of this.

1973 was also the year of the first OPEC oil price shock, when real oil prices quadrupled. This had two effects. First, it diverted R&D to long-term efforts to find alternative energy-saving technologies. These efforts may take decades to pay off and raise actual productivity. Second, higher energy prices made much of the capital stock economically obsolete overnight.

Table 30.2 Average annual growth in real output per person employed (%)

	OECD	Japan	Germany	Italy	France	Sweden	UK	USA
1950–73	3.6	8.0	5.6	5.8	4.5	3.4	3.6	2.2
1973–79	1.4	2.9	3.1	2.9	3.0	1.5	1.6	0
1979–90	1.5	3.0	1.6	1.9	2.6	1.7	2.1	0.7
1990–99	1.3	0.9	3.4	1.3	1.4	1.9	1.5	1.3
2000–04	1.7	1.3	1.2	1.1	1.5	2.1	1.8	2.2

Sources: S. Dowrick and D. Nguyen, 'OECD Comparative Economic Growth 1950–85', *American Economic Review*, 1989; OECD, *Economic Outlook*.

Energy-guzzling factories were closed. The world lost part of its capital stock, which reduced output per head. In practice, scrapping took a long time, and was given renewed impetus by another sharp rise in oil prices in 1980–81. That is why its effects were drawn out over such a long period.

Having discussed differences in growth across periods, we now examine differences across countries. The one sheds light on the other. The fact that OECD countries move together across sub-periods shows that many aspects of growth are outside a country's own control. Technical progress diffuses across countries quite quickly, wherever it originates. Countries are increasingly dependent on the same global economy.

Even so, growth rates differ markedly across countries. Can growth theory explain why? First, it suggests that, if countries have access to the same technology, differences in output growth should reflect differences in labour force growth. Table 30.1 provides some degree of corroborating evidence: differences in per capita output growth are less marked than differences in output growth.

Second, we need to know how long it takes to get to the steady state, a question to which Figures 30.1 and 30.2 provide no direct answer. Is output growth over two or three decades an adjustment *towards* the steady state, or can we assume that an economy has reached it within that time?

The convergence hypothesis

Figure 30.1 has a unique steady state at E and whatever the level of capital per worker with which an economy begins, the figure implies that it will eventually converge to E. Poor countries with a low inheritance of capital grow extra rapidly until they reach the steady-state growth rate of output and capital; rich countries with a very high inheritance of capital grow at below-average rates until capital per worker falls back to its steady-state level k^*.

When capital per worker is low, it does not take much investment to equip new workers with capital (capital-widening), so the rest of investment can go on raising capital per worker (capital-deepening). When capital per worker is already high, it takes a lot of saving and investment just to maintain capital-widening, let alone to deepen capital. This is one reason for the convergence hypothesis.

> The convergence hypothesis asserts that poor countries grow more quickly than average but rich countries grow more slowly than average.

This explanation for convergence relies purely on the effect of capital accumulation. A second explanation for convergence or 'catch-up' operates through a different channel. Technical progress no longer falls out of the sky at a fixed rate. Suppose instead we have to invest real resources (universities, research labs, R&D) in trying to make technical improvements. It is rich countries that have the human and physical capital to undertake these activities, and it is in rich countries that technical progress is made. However, once discovered, new ideas are soon disseminated to other countries.

Since poorer countries do not have to use their own resources to make technical breakthroughs, they can devote their scarce investment resources to other uses, such as building machines. By slipstreaming the richer countries, they can temporarily grow faster.

> The part of output growth not explained by the growth of measured inputs is known as the Solow residual.

Using a standard production function and data on the growth of capital and labour inputs, we can try to see how much of output growth is explained in each country by the growth of its factor inputs.

Solow naturally attributed it to technical progress. The residual is quite large and varies quite a lot across countries.

BOX 30-3 Standards of living and the convergence hypothesis

The table below shows World Bank estimates of per capita income in 1997 and of its annual real growth during 1980–97. Three points stand out. First, the east Asian economies – China, Korea, Hong Kong, Thailand, Singapore – grew very quickly. Even India is now growing steadily. Second, convergence cannot be a powerful force in the world or the very poorest countries would be growing very rapidly. In reality, poor countries stay poor and sometimes even decline in absolute terms. Third, within the rich OECD countries, convergence is much more reliable. The richest OECD countries tend to grow less quickly than the poorer OECD countries. These conclusions apply not just in the particular data shown below – they are widely replicated in all empirical studies.

Why did the East Asian 'tigers' grow so quickly in the postwar period? What was their secret? Professor Alwyn Young of MIT has shown that there is little mystery about their rapid growth, even though they did sustain dramatic rates. These economies managed rapid growth in measured inputs – labour (via increases in participation rates), capital (via high saving and investment rates) and human capital (via substantial expenditure on education). Once we allow for the rapid growth of these inputs, Young showed that the growth of output in the tigers was not very different from what standard estimates, based on OECD and Latin American countries, would have led us to expect. (See: A. Young: 'The tyranny of numbers: Confronting the statistics realities of the East Asian growth experience', *Quarterly Journal of Economics*, 1995.)

Per capita GNP (000s of 1997 US $) and annual % growth 1980–97

	97 level $ 000	1980–97 growth (%)		97 level $ 000	1980–97 growth (%)
Poor and middle income			OECD		
Mozambique	0.1	−1.2	Portugal	10.5	2.9
Bangladesh	0.3	2.3	Spain	14.5	2.0
Nigeria	0.3	−1.2	Ireland	18.3	4.2
China	0.8	11.0	Italy	20.1	1.4
Indonesia	1.1	5.5	UK	20.7	2.0
Philippines	1.2	1.1	France	26.5	2.0
Turkey	3.1	1.7	USA	28.7	1.7
Korea	10.5	7.8	Switzerland	44.3	1.6

Source: World Bank, *World Development Report*.

Table 30.3 sheds some light on this issue. Professor Nick Crafts of the London School of Economics took the Solow residuals and tried to see how many of them could be explained by catch-up. The lower a country's per capita GDP relative to the United States (the assumed technical leader), the larger the potential for catch-up should be. Table 30.3 shows catch-up in each sub-period and the 'residual', i.e. that part of growth unexplained by inputs or catch-up.

The table makes several interesting points. First, on average there is a role for catch-up: countries with below-average productivity enjoy on average a faster rate of technical progress as they make use of ideas already in operation in richer countries.

Second, some countries are more able to make use of catch-up opportunities than others. Once we allow for 'average catch-up', big differences remain across countries (the residuals in the table). These may reflect the social and political framework in which the economy must operate. Change usually helps the majority but has very adverse effects on a few people whose skills are made obsolete or whose power is suddenly removed. The large number of winners should club together to buy off the few big losers, allowing change to proceed.

Table 30.3   Catch-up (CU) and residual growth (RG) (% per year)

	1950–60		1960–73		1979–88	
	CU	RG	CU	RG	CU	RG
Austria	2.8	1.0	1.3	0.0	0.5	20.9
Belgium	2.1	20.7	1.1	0.3	0.4	0.8
Denmark	1.9	21.4	1.1	0.1	0.6	20.9
France	2.1	0.2	1.0	0.6	0.3	1.1
Germany	2.9	2.0	1.0	20.3	0.3	1.1
Italy	2.4	0.2	1.2	0.8	0.4	0.1
Netherlands	1.9	20.2	0.8	20.3	0.2	0.6
Norway	1.8	21.3	0.9	20.9	0.4	0.0
Sweden	1.3	0.1	0.8	0.3	0.3	20.3
Switzerland	1.1	0.1	0.7	21.0	0.5	20.6
UK	1.6	20.8	0.8	20.6	0.5	0.8
USA	0.0	0.7	0.0	0.1	0.0	0.3
Japan	4.0	0.4	2.2	2.2	0.9	0.0

Source: N. Crafts, 'Reversing Relative Decline', *Oxford Review of Economic Policy*, 1991.

Note: CU is effect of normal catch-up, RG the residual growth unexplained by input growth or normal catch-up.

Some societies are much better than others organizing the deals that allow catch-up to be achieved more rapidly.

An example: evaluating Thatcherism

Mrs Thatcher was elected in 1979 to breathe new efficiency and dynamism into the British economy, a long-run task properly evaluated by growth accounting. A rise in the long-run path of potential output needs the supply of more inputs or greater productivity from those inputs.

Although tax cuts aimed to raise labour supply, in fact they had little effect. Higher take-home pay provides an incentive to work longer but an equally powerful incentive for richer people to want more leisure. Nor were the 1980s a decade of high investment in the UK. Investment rates were lower than during 1950–70.

The success of Thatcherism hinged on getting higher output from given inputs. This is what the Solow residual measures. Table 30.3 shows that during 1950–70 the UK had negative residuals: allowing for input growth and 'normal catch-up', UK output grew less quickly than the norm. In contrast, the final column of Table 30.3 shows that during 1979–88 the residual increased substantially: the UK did better than the norm.

Supporters of Thatcherism take this as evidence of success. But was it a once-off improvement in output levels or the start of permanently faster growth? It will take a few more decades of data to adjudicate.

30.7   Endogenous growth

Endogenous growth implies the steady-state growth rate is affected by economic behaviour and economic policy.

Solow's theory made economic growth depend on population growth and technical progress. Both proceed at given rates. The subsequent literature on catch-up makes technical progress respond to economic and political factors. But it would be nice to have a stronger link between economic behaviour and the rate of economic growth. We want to make growth *endogenous*, or determined within our theory.

The original insight is due to Professor Paul Romer of Chicago University. Saving, investment and capital accumulation lie at the heart of growth. In Solow's theory, applying more and more capital to a given path for population runs into the diminishing marginal product of capital. It cannot be the source of permanent growth in productivity.

We know there must be diminishing returns to capital alone at the level of individual firms, otherwise one firm would get more and more capital, become steadily more productive, and gradually take over the entire world! Because diminishing returns to capital hold at the level of the firm, economists had assumed they held also at the level of the economy.

Romer's insight was the possibility (likelihood?) that there are significant externalities to capital. Higher capital in one firm increases productivity in *other* firms. When British Telecom invests in better equipment, other firms can do things previously impossible. The insight also applies to human capital. Training by one firm has beneficial externalities for others.

Thus the production function of each individual firm exhibits diminishing returns to its own capital input, but also depends on the capital of other firms. No firm, acting in isolation, would wish to raise its capital without limit. But when all firms expand together the economy as a whole may face constant returns to aggregate capital.

Consider the following simple example of the aggregate economy. Per capital output y is proportional to capital per person k. To isolate the role of accumulation, suppose there is no technical progress. Thus $y = Ak$ where A is constant. Given a constant saving rate s and population growth at rate n, is there a steady state in which capital per person grows at rate g? If so, investment for capital-deepening is gk and investment for capital-widening, to keep up with population growth, is nk. Hence in per capita terms

Gross investment $= (g + n)k = sy = sAk =$ gross saving

Hence $gk = (sA - n)k$ and the steady-state growth rate g is

$$g = (sA - n) \tag{2}$$

Why does this confirm the possibility of *endogenous* growth? Because it depends on parameters that could be influenced by private behaviour or public policy. In the Solow model, without technical progress, steady-state growth is always n, whatever the savings rate s or the level of productivity A. Equation (2) says that any policy that succeeded in raising the saving rate s would *permanently* increase the *growth rate g*. Similarly, any policy achieving a once-off rise in the *level* of A, for example greater workplace efficiency, would permanently increase the growth rate of k. Since $y = Ak$, this means permanently faster output growth.

Not only can government policy affect growth in this framework, government intervention may increase efficiency. In the simple Romer model outlined above, there are externalities in capital accumulation: individual firms neglect the fact that, in raising their own capital, they also increase the productivity of *other* firms' capital. Government subsidies to investment might offset this externality.

Since Romer's original work, there has been huge interest in endogenous growth. Sustaining small additions to annual growth rates eventually makes a big difference to living standards. As a result of this research we now have many potential channels of endogenous growth. For example, instead of assuming the rate of technical progress is given, we can model the industry that undertakes R&D to produce technical progress. Constant returns in this industry will generate endogenous growth. In fact, constant returns to aggregate production of any *accumulatible* factor (knowledge, capital, etc.) will suffice.

Note, too, that endogenous growth models explain why growth rates in different countries might permanently be different. This might explain why convergence does not take place

BOX 30-4   Arabia's field of dreams

Thirty years ago there was nothing in Dubai but a creek, a sheikh's palace and a dodgy reputation as the smuggling capital of the Arabian Gulf.

Source: The Economist, 27 May 2004.

With only 6 per cent of GDP from oil and gas, Dubai has been spending its revenues wisely. A new palm-shaped island off Jumeirah beach will quadruple Dubai's coastline to 125 miles. Along with the building of 270 hotels and 30 shopping malls, Dubai has an international airport capable of processing 60 million passengers a year. Its own airline, Emirates, has bucked industry trends and turned in a profit in all but one of the last twenty years and recently placed orders topping $19 billion for new aircraft, including 45 Airbus A380s, super-jumbo double-decker aircraft. Finally, with world's largest man-made port at Jebel Ali, Dubai is the centre of regional cargo trade.

The Dubai economy is growing, its population is growing and it is attracting investment away from its Middle-East neighbours. With different government policy, Dubai's long-term future might have looked very different.

---

and why some countries remain poor indefinitely. Different countries have different growth rates g.

While endogenous growth theory is an exciting development, it also has its critics. Most criticisms boil down to a key point. Whatever the relevant accumulatible factor, why should there be *exactly* constant returns in the aggregate? With diminishing returns, we are back in the Solow model where long-run growth is exogenous. With increasing returns, the economy would settle not on steady growth but on ever more rapid expansion of output and capital. We know this is not occurring. So for endogenous growth only constant returns to accumulation will do. Some people think this seems just too good to be true.

30.8 The costs of growth

Can the benefits of economic growth be outweighed by its costs? Pollution, congestion and a hectic life-style are a high a price to pay for a more cars, washing machines and video games.

Since GNP is an imperfect measure of the true economic value of the goods and services produced by the economy, there is no presumption we should want to maximize the growth of measured GNP. We discussed issues such as pollution in Chapter 15. Without government intervention, a free market economy produces too much pollution. But complete elimination of pollution is also wasteful. Society should undertake activities accompanied by pollution up to the point at which the net marginal benefit of the goods produced equals the marginal pollution cost imposed on society. Government intervention, through pollution taxes or regulation of environmental standards, can move the economy towards an efficient allocation of resources in which marginal social costs and benefits are equalized.

The full implementation of such a policy would (optimally) reduce the growth of measured GNP below the rate when there is no restriction on activities such as pollution and congestion. And this is the most sensible way in which to approach the problem. It tackles the issue directly. In contrast, the 'zero-growth' solution is a blunt instrument.

The zero-growth approach fails to distinguish between measured outputs accompanied by social costs and measured outputs without additional social costs. It does not provide the correct incentives. The principle of targeting, a key insight of the welfare economics discussed in Part 3, suggests that it is more

The zero-growth proposal argues that, because higher measured GNP imposes environmental costs, it is best to aim for zero growth of measured GNP.

efficient to tackle a problem directly than to adopt an indirect approach that distorts other aspects of production or consumption. Thus, when there is too much pollution, congestion, environmental damage or stress, the best solution is to provide incentives that directly reduce these phenomena. Restricting growth in measured output is a crude alternative, distinctly second best.

Some problems might evaporate if economists and statisticians could measure true GNP more accurately, including the 'quality of life' activities (clean air, environmental beauty, etc.) that yield consumption benefits but at present are omitted from measured GNP. Voters and commentators assess government performance against measurable statistics. A better measure of GNP might remove perceived conflicts between measured output and the quality of life.

This is also a good way to address 'sustainable growth'. At present, Mediterranean beauty spots become concrete jungles of hotels and bars; once the environment is spoiled, upmarket tourists move on somewhere else. An economist's advice, however, is not to abandon being a tourist destination, but to keep track of environmental depreciation and only engage in activities that show a clear return after proper costing of environmental and other damage. Embodying these costings in actual charges also provides the market incentive to look after the environment.

No matter how complete the framework, the assessment of the desirable growth rate will always be a normative question hinging on the value judgements of the assessor. Switching resources from consumption, however defined, to investment will nearly always reduce the welfare of people today but allow greater welfare for people tomorrow. The priority attached to satisfying wants of people at different points in time is always a value judgement.

SUMMARY

- Economic growth is the percentage annual increase in real GNP or per capita real GNP in the long run. It is an imperfect measure of the rate of increase of economic well-being.

- Measured GNP omits the value of leisure and of untraded goods and demerits that have an impact on the quality of life. Differences in income distribution make per capita real GNP a shaky basis for comparisons of the welfare of the typical individual in different countries.

- Significant rates of growth of per capita GNP occurred only in the last two centuries in the advanced economies. In other countries persistent growth is even more recent.

- Potential output can be increased either by increasing the inputs of land, labour, capital and raw materials, or by increasing the output obtained from given input quantities. Technical advances are an important source of productivity gains.

- An apparently fixed supply of a production input, such as a particular raw material, need not make growth impossible in the long run. As the input becomes scarce, its price rises. This makes producers substitute other inputs, increases incentives to discover new supplies and encourages inventions that economize on the use of that resource.

- The simplest theory of growth has a steady state in which capital, output and labour all grow at the same rate. Whatever its initial level of capital, the economy converges on this steady-state path. This theory can explain output growth but not productivity growth.

- Labour-augmenting technical progress allows permanent growth of labour productivity and enables the simple growth theory to fit many of the facts.

- There is a tendency of economies to converge, both because capital-deepening is easier when capital per worker is low and because of catch-up in technology. Implementing technical change may depend on how well society is organized to buy off (or defeat) the losers.

- Thatcherism did induce an identifiable rise in the UK productivity growth, even after controlling for factor accumulation and catch-up opportunities. It is difficult to be sure whether Thatcherism changed the growth rate for ever.

- Theories of endogenous growth are built on constant returns to accumulation. If aggregate investment does not encounter diminishing returns to capital, choices about saving and investment can affect the long-run growth rate of productivity. An externality on a giant scale provides a powerful rationale for government intervention to encourage education, training and physical capital formation.

- Nevertheless, endogenous growth rests on the presence of constant returns to accumulation. Nobody has yet explained why this should hold.

REVIEW QUESTIONS

- What is the distinction between total output and per capita output? Which grows more rapidly? Why? Always?

- 'Britain produces too many scientists, too few engineers.' What kind of evidence might help you decide if this is true? Will a free market lead people to choose the career that most benefits society?

- Name two economic demerits. Suggest feasible ways in which they might be measured. Should they be included in GNP? Could they be?

- 'If the convergence hypothesis is correct, the poor African countries should have grown long ago!' Is this correct? Do newer approaches to economic growth help explain why some countries remain so poor?

- 'Because we know Malthus got it wrong we are relaxed about the fact that some minerals are in finite supply.' Is there a connection? Explain.

- **Common fallacies** Why are these statements wrong? (a) Since the earth's resources are limited, growth cannot continue for ever. (b) If we saved more, we would definitely grow faster.

To check your answers to these questions, go to page 643.

To help you grasp the key concepts of this chapter check out the extra resources posted on the Online Learning Centre at www.mcgraw-hill.co.uk/ textbooks/begg. There are quick test questions, economics examples and access to Powerweb articles, all for free!

For even more exercises, recaps and examples to help you study, purchase a copy of the Economics Student Workbook. Simply visit www.mcgraw hill.co.uk/textbooks/begg and follow the links to the Workbook to buy your copy.

chapter 31

Business cycles

Learning outcomes

By the end of this chapter, you should be able to:

1 distinguish trend growth and economic cycles around this path

2 discuss why business cycles occur

3 analyse why output gaps may fluctuate

4 discuss whether potential output also fluctuates

5 assess whether national business cycles are now more correlated

6 apply these principles to UK business cycles

After a deep recession in 1990–92, the UK left the Exchange Rate Machanism, cut interest rates and let the pound depreciate. Prime Minister John Major delayed the next general election until May 1997, in the hope that recovery would increase the 'feel-good factor' and allow a Conservative victory. It did not.

The incoming Labour government then made the Bank of England independent, to try to take some of the politics out of economic policy making. The Chancellor, Gordon Brown, also emphasized fiscal prudence to keep inflation expectations in check. Yet as the 2001 election approached, Labour came under pressure to spend more money to improve public services. Transforming public services became the principal domestic policy of the Labour government after 2001.

In the absence of further tax increases, economists feared that the economy might overheat, or that the Bank would have to raise interest rates to high levels to prevent this. The pound remained high in anticipation of high future interest rates. When the dot.com bubble burst in 2001 and world recession was further reinforced by the terrorist attacks of September 11 in the US, in retrospect the UK fiscal expansion looked a blessing. Coupled with rapid interest rate reductions by the Bank of England, it shielded the UK from the slowdown being felt elsewhere.

These episodes illustrate many of the issues that we examine in this chapter. First, is there a business cycle? Output fluctuates a lot in the short run but a cycle does not mean merely temporary departures from trend: it also requires a degree of regularity. Can we see it in the data? Can monetary and fiscal policy insulate economies from business cycles?

We also explore the international dimension. Can a single country display cycles that are out of phase with those in its trading partners? What does this have to do with the Chancellor's test for when the UK might be ready to adopt the euro? Is globalization making business cycles more correlated across countries? If they are, might this explain why a single monetary policy could become increasingly appropriate?

31.1 Trend and cycle: statistics or economics?

The **trend path of output** is the smooth path of long-run output once its short-term fluctuations are averaged out.

The **business cycle** is the short-term fluctuation of total output around its trend path.

In practice, aggregate output and productivity do not grow smoothly. In some years they grow very rapidly but in other years they actually fall.

Actual output fluctuates around this hypothetical trend path.

Figure 31.1 shows a stylized picture of the business cycle. The black curve is the steady growth in trend output over time. Actual output follows the coloured curve. Point *A* represents a *slump*, the bottom of a business cycle. At *B* the economy has entered the *recovery* phase of the cycle. As recovery proceeds, output climbs above its trend path, reaching point *C*, which we call a *boom*. Then the economy enters a *recession* in which output is growing less quickly than trend output and is possibly even falling. Point *E* shows a *slump*, after which recovery begins and the cycle starts again.

Figure 31.2 shows the annual percentage growth of real GDP and of real output per employed worker in the UK during the period 1975–2003. Output and productivity grew most rapidly in 1986–88 and least rapidly in 1975, 1980–81 and 1990–92. The figure makes three basic points. First, the growth of output and productivity fluctuates in the short run. Second, although cycles are not perfectly regular, there is evidence of a pattern of slump, recovery, boom and recession, with a complete cycle lasting around five or six years. Third, output and output per person are closely correlated in the short run. The rest of the chapter seeks to explain these facts.

Figure 31.1 The business cycle

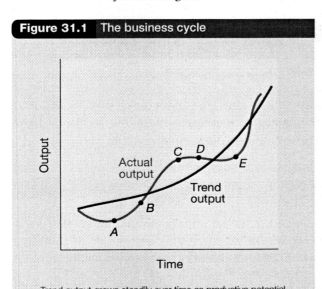

Trend output grows steadily over time as productive potential increases. Actual output fluctuates around this trend. Point *A* slows a slump, the trough of a cycle. At *B* recovery has begun and it continues until the peak of the cycle is reached at *C*. At *C* there is a boom. Then a period of recession follows until the next slump is reached at *E*. It takes roughly five years to move from one point in the cycle to an equivalent point in the next cycle, for example from *A* to *E*.

Any series of points may be decomposed statistically into an average trend and fluctuations around that trend. We initially assume that potential output grows smoothly. Later we consider whether potential output itself can fluctuate significantly in the short run.

Thus, we start by assuming that business cycles reflect fluctuations in the output gap. The data in Figure 31.2 show that cycles are too regular to be a coincidence. What causes business cycles?

The **output gap** is the deviation of actual output from potential output.

Since we associate potential output with aggregate supply in the long run, it seems natural to think first about aggregate demand shocks as the source of cyclical deviations of actual output from potential output. We know what shifts demand: changes in export demand, in the desire to save, in expected future profits and incomes, and in monetary and fiscal policy.

We could argue that demand shocks just happen to be cyclical, generating cycles in output gaps and actual output. However, that is not an *explanation* of the business cycle: it does not tell us why demand shocks have this cyclical pattern. One version of this approach does at least claim to be a theory.

Suppose voters, having short memories, are heavily influenced by how the economy is doing immediately prior to the election. Knowing this, the government uses monetary

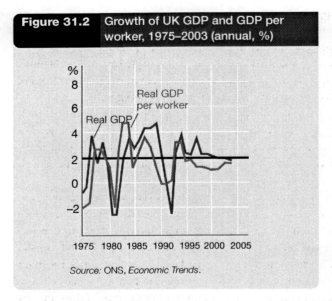

Figure 31.2 Growth of UK GDP and GDP per worker, 1975–2003 (annual, %)

Source: ONS, *Economic Trends.*

A **political business cycle** arises if politicians manipulate the economy for electoral advantage.

and fiscal policy to manipulate aggregate demand. Policy is tight just after a government is elected, creating a slump and spare capacity. As the next election date approaches, expansionary policy can then create unsustainably rapid growth by mopping up the spare capacity again. Voters misinterpret this as permanently faster growth of potential output and gratefully re-elect the government.

This theory provides a reason for fluctuations and also suggests why business cycles tend to last about five years – that is often the period between successive elections. The theory probably contains a grain of truth. On the other hand, it supposes that voters are pretty naive and do not see what the government is up to. Voters are not always so short-sighted. In 1997 the Major government lost the election despite fast output growth. Voters thought Labour could do even better.

Recent institutional changes to improve the credibility of policy – central bank independence and rules emphasizing fiscal prudence – act in the direction of reducing the scope for political business cycles in the future. Having discussed political causes of cycles, we now concentrate on economic causes.

31.2 Theories of the business cycle

Fluctuations in export demand might cause cycles. One country's exports are another country's imports and these imports will fluctuate only if foreign income fluctuates. International trade helps explain how cycles get transmitted from one country to another but we require a theory of domestic business cycle to initiate the process.

Sluggish adjustment is necessary but not sufficient to generate cycles caused by demand shocks. It is necessary because rapid adjustment would quickly eliminate output gaps and restore output to potential output. It is not sufficient because sluggishness only explains why the return to potential output takes time. An oil tanker moves sluggishly but it does not oscillate its way into port. Cycles require a mechanism by which deviations in one direction then set up forces that cause output to overshoot potential output on its return.

Having ruled out the government, a theory of a domestic cycle must be based on consumption or investment spending. Investment spending is the most likely candidate, since investment spending is more likely to take time to assess and adjust. Firms do not rush into major and irreversible investment projects, nor are new factories built overnight.

The multiplier–accelerator model of the business cycle

The multiplier–accelerator model distinguishes the consequences and the causes of a change in investment spending. The consequence is straightforward. In the simplest Keynesian model, higher investment leads to a larger rise in income and output in the short run. Higher investment not only adds directly to aggregate demand but, by increasing incomes, it adds indirectly to consumption demand. Chapters 21 and 22 examined the multiplier effect on output.

What about the cause of a change in investment spending? Firms invest when their existing capital stock is smaller than the capital stock they would like to hold. When firms are holding the optimal capital stock, the marginal cost of another unit of capital just equals its marginal benefit, the present-value of future operating profits to which it is expected to give rise over its lifetime. This present value can be increased either by a fall in the interest rate at which the stream of expected future profits is discounted or by an increase in the future profits expected.

Thus far we have focused on the role of changing interest rates in changes in investment demand. However, although nominal interest rates change a lot, real interest rates change a lot less. The simplest way to calculate the present value of a new capital good is to assess the likely stream of *real* operating profits (by valuing future profits at *constant prices*) and then discount them at the *real* interest rate.

In practice, changes in interest rates may *not* be the most important source of changes in investment spending. Almost certainly, changes in expectations about future profits are more important. The dot.com bubble collapsed not because of high real interest rates but because people realized they had been too optimistic about the future profits to be made.

The accelerator model of investment assumes that firms guess future output and profits by extrapolating past output growth. Constant output growth leads to a constant level of investment. It takes *accelerating* output growth to *raise* desired investment.

More generally, if real interest rates and real wages change slowly, the main source of short-term changes in beliefs about future profits is beliefs about future levels of sales and output. Other things equal, higher expected future output raises expected future profits and raises demand for investment in new capacity. This is the insight of the accelerator model of investment.

The accelerator is only a simplification. A complete model of investment would examine changes in expected future profits and changes in (real) interest rates. Even so, many empirical studies confirm that the accelerator is a useful simplification.

How firms respond to changes in output depends on two things: first, the extent to which firms believe that current output growth will be sustained in the future; second, the cost of quickly adjusting investment plans, capital installation and the production techniques thus embodied. The more costly it is to adjust *quickly*, the more firms spread investment over a longer period.

This simple multiplier–accelerator model can lead to a business cycle. In Table 31.1 we make two specific assumptions, although the argument holds much more generally. First, we assume that the value of the multiplier is 2. An extra unit of investment raises income and output by 2 units. Second, we assume that current investment responds to the growth in output *last* period. If last period's income grew by 2 units, we assume that firms raise current investment by 1 unit.

In period 1, the economy is in equilibrium with output $Y_1 = 100$. Since output is constant, last period's output change was zero. Investment $I_1 = 10$, which we can think of as the investment needed to offset depreciation and keep the capital stock intact.

Suppose in period 2 that some component of aggregate demand rises by 20 units. Output increases from 100 to 120. Since we have assumed that a growth of 2 units in the previous period's output leads to a unit increase in current investment,

Table 31.1	The multiplier–accelerator model of he business cycle		
Period	Change in last period's output $(Y_{t-1} - Y_{t-2})$	Investment I_t	Output Y_t
$t = 1$	0	10	100
$t = 2$	0	10	120
$t = 3$	20	20	140
$t = 4$	20	20	140
$t = 5$	0	10	120
$t = 6$	–20	0	100
$t = 7$	–20	0	100
$t = 8$	0	10	120
$t = 9$	20	20	140

the table shows that in period 3 there is a 10-unit increase in investment in response to the 20-unit output increase during the previous period. Since the assumed value of the multiplier is 2, the 10-unit *increase* in investment in period 3 leads to a further increase of 20 units in output, which increases from 120 to 140.

In period 4 investment remains at 20 since the output growth in the previous period was 20. Thus output in period 4 remains at 140. But in period 5 investment reverts to its original level of 10, since there was no output growth in the previous period. This fall of 10 units in investment leads to a multiplied fall of 20 units in output in period 5. In turn this induces a further fall of 10 units of investment in period 6 and a further fall of 20 units in output.

Since the rate of output change is not accelerating, investment in period 7 remains at the level of period 6. Output is stabilized at 100 in period 7. With no output change in the previous period, investment in period 8 returns to 10 units again and the multiplier implies that output rises to 120. In period 9 the 20 unit increase in output in the previous period increases investment from 10 to 20 units and the cycle begins all over again.

The multiplier–accelerator model explains business cycles by the dynamic interaction of consumption and investment demand. The insight of the model is that it takes *accelerating* output growth to increase investment. Once output growth stabilizes, so does investment. In the following period, investment must *fall*, since output growth has been reduced. The economy moves into a period of recession but once the rate of output fall stops accelerating investment starts to pick up again.

This simple model is not the definitive model of a business cycle. If output keeps cycling, surely firms stop extrapolating past output growth to form assessments of future profits? Firms, like economists, recognize that there is a business cycle. The less investment decisions respond to the most recent change in past output, the less pronounced the cycle will be.

Ceilings and floors

The multiplier–accelerator model can generate cycles even without any physical limits on the extent of fluctuations. Cycles are even more likely when we recognize the limits imposed by supply and demand. Aggregate supply provides a *ceiling* in practice. Although it is possible temporarily to meet high aggregate demand by working overtime and running down stocks of finished goods, output cannot expand indefinitely.

This tends to slow down growth as the economy reaches a boom. Having overstretched itself, the economy has to bounce back off the ceiling and begin a downturn. Conversely, there is a *floor* below which aggregate demand cannot fall. Gross investment (including replacement investment) cannot be negative unless, for the economy as a whole, machines are unbolted and shipped abroad for sale to foreigners. Falling investment is an important component of a downswing but investment cannot fall indefinitely, whatever our model of investment behaviour.

Fluctuations in stockbuilding

Having examined investment in fixed capital, we now look at inventory investment in working capital. Firms hold stocks of goods despite the cost, namely the interest payments on the funds tied up in producing the goods for which no revenue from sales has yet been received. What is the corresponding benefit of holding stocks? If output could be instantly and costlessly varied it would always be possible to meet sales and demand by varying current production. Holding stocks makes sense because it is expensive to adjust production *quickly*. Output expansion may involve heavy overtime payments and costs of recruiting new workers. Cutting output may

involve expensive redundancy payments. Holding stocks allows firms to meet short-term fluctuations in demand without incurring the expense of short-run fluctuations in output.

How do firms respond to a fall in aggregate demand? Since rapid output adjustment is
expensive, in the short run firms undertake the adjustments that can be made more cheaply.
They reduce hours of overtime and possibly even move on to short-time working. If demand
has fallen substantially, this still leaves firms producing a larger output than they can sell. Firms
build up stocks of unsold finished output.

If aggregate demand remains low, firms gradually reduce their workforce, partly through
natural wastage and partly because it becomes cheaper to sack some workers than to meet the
interest payments on ever larger volumes of stocks. Once aggregate demand recovers again,
firms are still holding all the extra stocks built up during recession. Only by increasing output
more slowly than the increase in aggregate demand can firms eventually sell off these stocks and
get back to their long-run equilibrium position.

Costs of employment adjustment explain both the pattern of inventories over the business
cycle and the pattern of labour productivity in Figure 31.2. Output per worker rises in a boom
and falls in a slump. In other words, output adjusts more quickly than employment. This is what
we expect, given the costs of adjusting employment rapidly.

A fall in demand is met initially by cutting hours and increasing stocks. With a shorter
working week, output per worker falls. Only as the recession intensifies do firms undertake the
costlier process of sacking workers and restoring hours to their normal level. Conversely, a
boom is the time when output and overtime are high and productivity per worker peaks.

Competitiveness

Chapter 29 identified another potential mechanism that could generate cycles. An economy on
a fixed exchange rate experiences a downward domestic demand shock. Interest rates, fixed at
world levels to peg the exchange rate, cannot be used to restore aggregate demand.

Recession eventually bids down wages and prices, raising competitiveness and restoring
internal balance by raising the demand for net exports. However this is not external balance,
since net exports are now positive. With a current account surplus, the country gets richer and
additional wealth gradually boosts consumption demand. The economy now has a boom,
which bids up prices and reduces competitiveness. Long-run equilibrium is restored when the
current account falls back to zero.

This is a proper story about cycles. Output gaps induce changes in the price level that
restore internal balance only by destroying external balance. This sets off a movement in the
opposite direction that gradually reverses all these effects. Adjustment entails necessary over-
shooting of the final equilibrium.

31.3 Real business cycles

So far our analysis of business cycles focuses on demand shocks and cyclical movements in output gaps. This is compatible with our earlier analysis of sluggish wage adjustment in the short
run. This view of cycles is consistent with a model that is Keynesian in the short run but classical or Monetarist in the long run.

Not all economists share our assessment of how the economy works. In particular, there is
an influential school, known as the New Classical economists, whose intellectual leader is the
Nobel laureate Robert Lucas of the University of Chicago. Although we discuss competing

---

BOX 31-1   The real-wage puzzle

In a recession, firms employ fewer workers. A competitive firm would pay workers the real value of their marginal product. Given a diminishing marginal product of labour, cutting back on workers should raise labour's marginal product. Fewer workers have the same capital as before to work with. So real wages should rise in a slump. But they don't. They fall. This is the *real-wage puzzle* over the business cycle.

Real business cycle theorists suggest that a temporarily adverse shock may make it advisable to engage in some intertemporal labour substitution. When times are tough, you do not sacrifice much by taking time off; lifetime earnings can be rebuilt when conditions are easier. So recessions, caused by temporarily low productivity, make firms offer temporarily low wages and households temporarily reduce their labour supply. We get low employment *and* low wages.

The Keynesian response is that recessions and unusually high unemployment reflect more than an intertemporarily optimal decision to catch up on sleep and leisure until wages improve. During a recession, utilization of capital capacity is severely cut back. There may be fewer workers but with machines also idle the effective input of capital falls. If the latter is sufficiently large, labour's marginal product will fall even though there are fewer workers than before. Temporarily, there is even less capital.

---

views of macroeconomics more fully in the next chapter, one implication of the New Classical view should be discussed immediately.

A key assumption of the New Classical school is that all markets clear almost instantaneously. Effectively, output is almost always at its full-employment level.[1]

Proponents of the theory argue that macroeconomics should base theories of firms and households in a microeconomic analysis of choice between the present and the future. For example, this approach would view each household as making a plan to supply labour and demand goods both now and in the future in such a way that lifetime spending was financed out of lifetime income plus any initial assets. Such plans would then be aggregated to get total consumption spending and total labour supply. An equivalently complex story would apply to firms and investment.

> **Real business cycle theories** explain cycles as fluctuations in potential output itself.

One implication of this approach is that it is no longer helpful to distinguish between supply and demand. If labour supply and consumption demand are part of the same household decision, things that induce the household to change its consumption demand also induce it to change its labour supply.

For this reason, real business cycle theorists simply discuss what happens to actual output, which reflects both supply and demand and, by assumption, equates the two at potential output. In this view, the economy is then bombarded with shocks (e.g. breakthroughs in technology, changes in government policy) which alter these complicated plans and give rise to equilibrium behaviour that looks like a business cycle.

Why is this approach called the *real* business cycle approach? In the classical model, nominal money only affects other nominal variables. Output and employment depend only on real variables. Since real business cycle theorists believe in the classical model, they take it for granted that the source of business cycles must be in real shocks. Fancy dynamics can then explain why shocks last and have convoluted effects.

---

[1] For an accessible introduction to these issues, see the lively exchange between Charles Plosser and Greg Mankiw in the *Journal of Economic Perspectives*, Summer 1989.

Intertemporal substitution: a key to persistence

Real business cycle theories need to combine rapid market adjustment to equilibrium with sluggish behaviour of aggregate output over the business cycle. Intertemporal substitution means making trade-offs over time, postponing or bringing forward actions in the sophisticated long-run plans of households and firms. This behaviour can cause effects to persist and look like part of a business cycle.

Suppose the productivity genie visits while we are all asleep. When we wake up, our productivity has doubled. But only for a year. We know that by next year our productivity will have returned to normal. We face a temporary productivity shock, a blip in our technology. What should we do?

We are definitely wealthier after the genie's visit. We are pleased it happened. We could simply behave as before, working just as hard and investing just as much. In that case, our extra productivity would make extra output this year but it is output that we would blow entirely on consumption this year. We would get little extra utility out of the hundredth bottle of champagne and we would be making no provision for the future. There must be a better way.

We could put in a temporary spurt of extra work while we are superproductive but in itself that would only exacerbate the problem: even more champagne today, still nothing extra for tomorrow. In fact, because leisure is a luxury and because we are better off than before, we may feel like taking it easy and doing less work.

We need a way of transferring some of our windfall benefit into future consumption. The solution is investment. A sharp rise in the share of output going to investment will provide more capital for the future, thereby allowing higher future consumption even after our productivity bonus has evaporated. Once we get to the future, being then richer than we would have been without the genie, we may in consequence work less hard than we would have done, since leisure is a luxury.

The point of this example is to show that even a temporary shock can have effects that persist well into the future. Persistence occurs both through investment (in human as well as physical capital) and through intertemporal labour substitution – deciding when in one's life to put in the effort.

Real business cycle theories still need to be worked out fully. Apart from optimism about the speed of adjustment, they have been criticized on two grounds. First, they are usually theories of persistence not cycles. Shocks have long-drawn-out effects but these are rarely cyclical. To 'explain' business cycles, so far real business cycle theorists have had to assume a cyclical pattern to the shocks themselves. The theory is therefore incomplete.

Second, and related, since the most widely researched example involves shocks to technology, a cyclical pattern of shocks implies that in some years technical knowledge actually diminishes: we forget how to do things. Not just once, but regularly every few years. This may be a bit hard to swallow.

However, this can be given a more plausible interpretation. In the dot.com bubble of the late 1990s, investors made extravagant projections about future productivity growth and associated profits from the new technologies. By 2000 evidence was accumulating that previous estimates, necessarily guesses in a new situation, were too optimistic. In 2001 investment collapsed, particularly in the United States where dot.com optimism had been greatest.

Thus, the adverse shock was not a fall in existing technology – which is indeed implausible – but in estimates about future technology, which affects current behaviour since firms, households and governments all make long-term plans.

BOX 31-2   Synchronized swimming

Unlike previous recessions in recent decades, in 2001 the world's leading economies all stagnated together. The OECD's *Economic Outlook* (December 2001) identified three reasons for greater synchronization of national cycles.

First, some large shocks in the past were country specific, such as German unification. In 2001 everybody was coping with the end of the dot.com bubble and the collapse of confidence in the aftermath of the terrorist attacks in the US.

Second, national cycles have anyway been getting smaller. This has several causes: a trend away from volatile manufacturing towards less volatile services; better inventory management made possible by information technology; less volatile consumption as financial liberalization allows consumers to borrow more easily in bad times; and better monetary policy now that central banks are independent of political control.

Third, interdependence is greater. For decades, international trade has grown faster than output, increasing interdependence. Trade liberalization has reinforced this. Financial integration has also led to smaller interest rate disparities.

The impact of a more synchronized global cycle is that regional policymakers may have to react to events that began elsewhere. US recession quickly spilled over into Europe, Latin America and Asia.

Policy implications

Research on real business cycles still has much to accomplish but it does have a vital message for macroeconomic policy. If the theory is right, it destroys the case for trying to stabilize output over the business cycle. Fluctuations in output are fluctuations in an *equilibrium* output that efficiently reconciles people's desires.

For example, in the parable of the genie, the induced effects on investment, labour supply, output and consumption implement people's preferred way to take advantage of the beneficial opportunity. Trying to prevent these ripples is misguided policy.

Although important, this caveat undermines the case for stabilization policy only if we buy totally the assumptions of complete and instant market-clearing and the absence of any externalities. For most economists these assumptions are too extreme to reflect the real world, which continues to exhibit Keynesian features in the short run. Valid reasons for stabilization policy then remain.

Even so, real business cycle theories force us all to acknowledge that there is no reason why potential output should grow as smoothly as trend output. The latter is a statistical artefact whose construction, averaging, forces it to be smooth.

Our discussion of supply-side economics in Chapters 27 and 30 suggested that there are forces that can change full employment and potential output, both in the short run and in the long run. The most sophisticated theory of the business cycle might involve short-term Keynesian fluctuations in aggregate demand around a path of potential output which itself was fluctuating. Nevertheless, the Keynesian component is likely to be important in the short run.

 **Now you've read this section,** why not test your understanding by visiting the Online Learning Centre at www.mcgraw-hill.co.uk/textbooks/begg

---

31.4   An international business cycle?

National politicians want all the credit when output is high but produce a cast-iron alibi when the economy turns sour. They say domestic difficulties were caused by a world recession. How

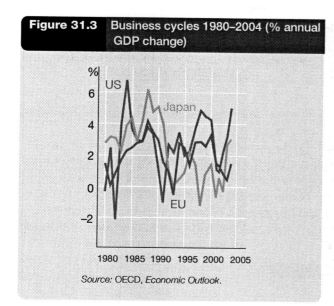

Figure 31.3 Business cycles 1980–2004 (% annual GDP change)

Source: OECD, *Economic Outlook*.

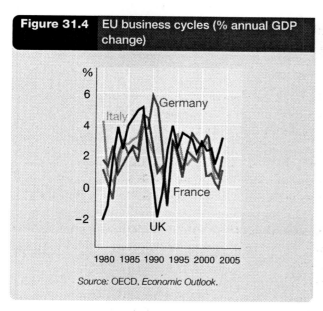

Figure 31.4 EU business cycles (% annual GDP change)

Source: OECD, *Economic Outlook*.

good is their alibi?

Figure 31.3 plots data during 1980–2004 for the three major players in the world economy: the US, Japan and the EU. Although output fluctuations are by no means identical, they have some similarities. The 1982–83 period was one of recession, followed by rapid recovery; 1987–89 was a boom, from which there was a large crash in 1991–92. Japan alone failed to recover in the late 1990s. However, in 2001–03 the US, Japan and Germany (the EU's leading economy) were all in simultaneous recession.

Figure 31.4 shows business cycles in the four largest countries of the EU. It confirms that countries of the EU move more closely with one another than with Japan or the USA, and suggests European integration may also be increasing over time. We discuss European integration in Chapter 35.

These patterns warn us how interdependent the leading countries have become in the modern world. Economies are becoming more open. In product markets, protectionist policies are being removed, through global institutions like the World Trade Organization and through regional integration as in the creation of a Single European Market.

Improvements in transport and telecommunications also favour greater integration of product markets. When R&D costs are large, producers need a global market if they are to recover their overheads. Product market integration provides an international transmission mechanism through exports and imports. Increasingly, we have a global financial market. Closer financial integration increases the likelihood that different countries pursue similar monetary policies.

The business cycle is transmitted from one country to another not just through private sector decisions about imports and exports (and induced effects on labour supply, investment and consumption) but also, sometimes, through induced changes in the economic policy of other governments.

31.5 UK recovery after 1992

The 1980s saw financial reform in most countries. Deregulation of credit and greater competition in its supply were particularly marked in the US and the UK. The recession of the early 1990s was the first world recession since the financial revolution. Did it make any difference? Imagine you had been a consumer in the boom of 1986–88. Life looked rosy and for the first time in modern history financial institutions were competing vigorously to lend you money. So of course you borrowed. The boom surely wouldn't end just yet, would it? Table 31.2 shows the collapse of the saving rate. There was a consequent rise in UK household debt.

Perhaps if you had known more about business cycles, you would have been a bit more realistic. In any case, when the crash came, you got badly hurt. Around the world, interest rates rose as governments tried to stop economies overheating at the end of the 1980s. The interest cost of your huge debt soared.

Worse still, the collateral you had offered when you borrowed – your house or your portfolio on the stock market – was suddenly much less valuable. Higher interest rates induce lower asset prices by reducing the present value of the future income that the assets provide. In the UK, Japan and the United States, the three countries where consumer debt had risen most in the 1980s, asset prices had fallen 25 per cent by 1992.

Table 31.2 shows how consumers responded. Having acquired too much debt in the 1980s, they tried to put things right at the start of the 1990s. They saved a larger fraction of their incomes in order to try to repay some of the debt and bring it back to manageable proportions.

This can be a slow process. When debt is nearly as large as income, and only a small fraction of income is saved, debt cannot be paid off very quickly. The continuing 'debt overhang' explains why the feel-good factor was slow to return after 1992. It helps explain why consumer spending recovered only slowly and why the Major government lost the 1997 election.

Paradoxically, the success of the Major government in defeating inflation after 1992 (see Chapter 28) paved the way for reductions in nominal interest rates and a recovery in the housing market. Table 31.2 shows that by 1999 the saving rate had collapsed again as consumers went on another spending spree.

Table 31.2	UK household saving (% of disposable income)				
1981	1988	1992	1996	2002	2003
12	6	12	9	5	6

Source: ONS, Economic Trends.

31.6 The odyssey after 2001

The 21st century got off to a bad start. The dot.com bubble burst, the events of September 11 severely dented confidence and fears that Al Qaeda might destabilize oil giant Saudi Arabia induced a dramatic rise in oil prices.

2001 was a bleak year. Growth forecasts were steadily cut back and central banks responded with aggressive interest rate reductions to try to prevent demand falling too much.

Table 31.3 shows that during 2001 interest rates were reduced by 4.5 percentage points in the US where the fall in aggregate demand was greatest, by 2 percentage points in the UK, and by 1.5 percentage points in the euro zone. Since Japanese interest rates were almost zero at the start of 2001, there was no scope to cut them further.

Japan illustrates the danger of getting into a vicious cycle of deflation. Falling

Table 31.3	Interest rate cuts in 2001 (percentage points)
US	4.5
Canada	3.0
UK	2.0
Australia	1.75
euro area	1.5
New Zealand	1.25
Japan	0.25

Source: OECD Economic Outlook.

prices induce consumers to postpone consumption, nominal debts rise in real value and real interest rates are uncomfortably high. Even once nominal interest rates have been cut to zero, negative inflation makes real interest rates positive.

One reason why other countries' policy makers continue to try to dampen their business cycles is to avoid falling into a black hole as Japan has done. Since Japan's difficulties were initially prompted by allowing a boom to go on too long, wise policy has to prevent the excesses of booms in order to prevent the subsequent difficulties of severe slumps.

By 2003, the powerful stimulus from monetary and fiscal expansion had restored output growth to normal levels, in marked contrast to the euro zone, where the European Central Bank had been slow to cut interest rates and where fiscal rules placing ceilings on budget deficits had limited the degree to which fiscal policy could come to the rescue.

SUMMARY

- The trend path of output is the long-run path after short-run fluctuations are ironed out. The business cycle describes fluctuations in output around this trend. Cycles last about five years but are not perfectly regular.

- A political business cycle arises from government manipulation of the economy to make things look good just before an election.

- Persistence requires either sluggish adjustment or intertemporal substitution. Persistence is necessary but not sufficient for cycles.

- The multiplier–accelerator model assumes investment depends on expected future profits, which reflect past output growth. The model delivers a cycle but assumes that firms are stupid: their expectations neglect the cycle implied by their own behaviour.

- Full capacity and the impossibility of negative gross investment provide ceilings and floors that limit the extent to which output can fluctuate.

- Fluctuations in stockbuilding are important in the business cycle. The need to restore stocks to original levels explains why output continues to differ from demand even during the recovery phase.

- Real business cycles are cycles in potential output itself. In such circumstances, it is not desirable for policy to dampen cycles.

- Some swings in potential output do occur but many short-run fluctuations probably reflect Keynesian departures from potential output. Aggregate demand and aggregate supply both contribute to the business cycle.

- Increasing integration of world financial and product markets has made most countries heavily dependent on the wider world. Business cycles in the rich countries are closely correlated.

- In 2001 central banks cut interest rates to prevent recession from spiralling. Japan's difficulty escaping from the deflation trap suggests that dampening business cycles remains an important aim for other countries.

REVIEW QUESTIONS

'If firms could forecast future output and profits accurately, there could not be a business cycle.' Is this true?

Heavily dependent on output of oil and fishing, Norway's business cycle goes the other way from that in other European countries. Why?

Why might voters care more about the direction in which the economy is heading than about the absolute level of its position at election time?

Would it help the world economy if all the largest countries elected governments on the same day? Why, or why not?

What is real about a business cycle?

Common fallacies Why are these statements wrong? (a) Closer integration of national economies will abolish business cycles. (b) The more we expect cycles, the more we get them. (c) Because output and labour productivity are closely correlated, fluctuations in productivity are the main cause of business cycles.

To check your answers to these questions, go to pages 643–44.